OECD Digital Economy Outlook 2017

OECD
BETTER POLICIES FOR BETTER LIVES

This document, as well as any data and map included herein, are without prejudice to the status of or sovereignty over any territory, to the delimitation of international frontiers and boundaries and to the name of any territory, city or area.

Please cite this publication as:
OECD (2017), *OECD Digital Economy Outlook 2017*, OECD Publishing, Paris.
http://dx.doi.org/10.1787/9789264276284-en

ISBN 978-92-64-27626-0 (print)
ISBN 978-92-64-27628-4 (PDF)
ISBN 978-92-64-27629-1 (ePub)

The statistical data for Israel are supplied by and under the responsibility of the relevant Israeli authorities. The use of such data by the OECD is without prejudice to the status of the Golan Heights, East Jerusalem and Israeli settlements in the West Bank under the terms of international law.

Photo credits: Maro Haas.

Corrigenda to OECD publications may be found on line at: *www.oecd.org/publishing/corrigenda*.

Foreword

The biennial OECD Digital Economy Outlook *examines and documents evolutions and emerging opportunities and challenges in the digital economy. It highlights how OECD countries and partner economies are taking advantage of information and communication technologies (ICTs) and the Internet to meet their public policy objectives. Through comparative evidence, it informs policy makers of regulatory practices and policy options to help maximise the potential of the digital economy as a driver for innovation and inclusive growth. This second edition of the* OECD Digital Economy Outlook *provides a holistic overview of converging trends, policy developments and data on both the supply and demand sides of the digital economy, and illustrates how the digital transformation is affecting economies and societies.*

The OECD Digital Economy Outlook 2017 *has been prepared by the OECD Secretariat under the guidance of the OECD Committee on Digital Economy Policy (CDEP), chaired by Wonki Min (Korea). It has benefited from the input of delegates to the Committee and its Working Parties on Communications Infrastructure Services Policy (CISP), on Measurement and Analysis of the Digital Economy (MADE), and on Security and Privacy in the Digital Economy (SPDE). A large part of its content builds on the responses by OECD countries and partner economies to the 2016* OECD Digital Economy Outlook Policy Questionnaire.

The OECD Digital Economy Outlook 2017 *was prepared by the Division on Digital Economy Policy in the OECD Directorate for Science, Technology and Innovation. It was produced under the direction/co-ordination of David Gierten, with assistance by Cristina Serra Vallejo. Authors include, by alphabetical order, Laurent Bernat, Frederic Bourassa, Anne Carblanc, Lauren Crean, Michael Donohue, Marie-Lou Dupont, David Gierten, Gaël Hernandez, Bong Soo Keum, Elif Koksal-Oudot, Molly Lesher, Pierre Montagnier, Sam Paltridge, Karine Perset, Lorrayne Porciuncula, Giorgio Presidente, Christian Reimsbach-Kounatze, Elettra Ronchi, Carthage Smith, Cristina Serra Vallejo, Vincenzo Spiezia, Jan Tscheke, Verena Weber, Jeremy West and Yuki Yokoromi. External authors for chapter 7 are Primavera De Filippi, Cyrus Hodes and Nicolas Miailhe. Editorial work was undertaken by Jennifer Allain, Janine Treves, Angela Gosmann and by the OECD Public Affairs and Communications Directorate. Sarah Ferguson and María Castaño provided assistance with formatting.*

Finally, the data and assistance provided by Airbnb, Akamai, General Motors, Neftcraft, and Teligen, a division of Strategy Analytics Ltc., are gratefully acknowledged, as is the assistance of other colleagues in the OECD who have provided data for the analysis.

The OECD Digital Economy Outlook 2017 *has been declassified by the OECD Committee on Digital Economy Policy (CDEP) on 27 July 2017 by written procedure and prepared for publication by the OECD Secretariat.*

Table of contents

Part II
Trends

Tables

Figures

Executive summary

Governments are waking up to the opportunities and challenges brought by digital transformation

With its potential to galvanise economies, digital transformation is now high on the global agenda. OECD countries have set their objectives at the 2016 Cancún Ministerial on the Digital Economy. To maximise the benefits of digital transformation for innovation, growth and social prosperity, they are focusing efforts on the policy implications of the digital transformation, improving measurement, and developing an integrated policy framework for a whole-of-government approach. Despite good progress in the implementation of national digital strategies (NDSs) across the OECD co-ordination remains a major challenge. Only few countries have charged a high-level official or body dedicated to digital affairs with the co-ordination of their NDS.

Despite the ongoing effects of the crisis, information technology services continue to grow and spur a positive outlook

Since the global economic crisis, value added in the information and communication technology (ICT) sector as a whole has decreased in the OECD in line with total value added. Within the ICT sector, however, value added in telecommunication services and in computer and electronics manufacturing has decreased while it has increased in information technology (IT) services and remained constant in software publishing. These contrasting trends, which are being reflected in OECD ICT employment, are expected to continue in the coming years as the share of venture capital investment in ICTs – an indicator of business expectations – is back to its 2000 peak. The ICT sector remains a key driver of innovation, accounting for the largest share of OECD business expenditure on research and development and for over one-third of total patent applications worldwide.

Developing apace, communication infrastructures and services are upgrading for a new surge of data

Growth in communication markets is driven by demand and, in many countries, by adapted regulatory frameworks that spur competition, innovation and investment. Telecommunication investments as a share of revenue have increased and operators further deploy fibre optics into their networks. For both fixed and mobile broadband, average prices have fallen and subscriptions increased, while mobile data usage grows exponentially in some countries. Convergence in telecommunication and broadcasting drives mergers and acquisitions and triggers revisions of regulatory frameworks and institutions. Broadband speeds of 1 Gigabit per second (Gbps) are no longer outliers and the first 10 Gbps commercial offers are being deployed in view of a new surge of data such as from connected and autonomous vehicles.

ICT usage keeps growing but remains unequally distributed across countries and among firms and individuals

Average ICT usage among individuals is at a new high but still unequally distributed across countries and social groups, in particular for more sophisticated mobile Internet usage such as online purchases or banking. Elderly and less educated are lagging most. Governments are focusing on vocational training, primary or secondary education, and target public expenditures on devices and connectivity in schools. Meanwhile, users are concerned about online security and privacy, both of which are key barriers for Internet usage, including amid the highly educated. Among firms, small and medium-sized enterprises (SMEs) are lagging behind in basic and more advanced ICT usage. Usage of cloud computing and big data analysis is growing fast, albeit from a small base. Robots are increasingly used in production, but concentrated in a few countries so far.

Digital innovation and new business models are driving transformation, including of jobs and trade

Data-driven innovation, new business models, and digital applications are changing the workings of science, governments, cities, and sectors like health and agriculture. Policies to support digital innovation tend to focus on innovation networks, access to finance, and data (re-)use, but pay less attention to investment in ICTs, knowledge-based capital and data analytics. The effects of the digital transformation manifest in job destruction and creation in different sectors, the emergence of new forms of work, and a reshaping trade landscape, in particular for services. In response, many governments are reviewing labour laws and trade agreements.

Effective use of ICTs in life and for work requires more specialist and generic skills in ICTs complemented by better foundational skills

Effective use of ICTs in life and for work requires adequate skills. "IT staff" ranks second among the top ten jobs that employers have difficulties filling, notably in services, although shortages of ICT specialist skills seem limited to only a few countries, at least in Europe. Meanwhile, generic ICT skills are insufficient among many workers using ICTs every day, as are ICT foundational skills, such as problem solving and communication, which are increasingly necessary to adapt to changing jobs. A few countries are implementing programmes to match current ICT training priorities with expected skills needs, but only few have adopted a comprehensive ICT skills strategy to date.

Concerns about digital security and privacy restrain ICT adoption and business opportunities

With growing intensity of ICT use, businesses and individuals face greater digital security and privacy risks. SMEs in particular need to introduce or improve digital security risk management practices. Many countries respond with national digital security strategies, but few have a national privacy strategy so far. Meanwhile, privacy risks add to consumers' concerns about online fraud, redress mechanisms, and online product quality, which limit trust and might slow business-to-consumer e-commerce growth. Most consumer protection policies still focus on trust in e-commerce generally and are only beginning to grapple with new issues emerging in peer platform markets.

The promises of artificial intelligence are accompanied by important policy and ethical questions

Artificial intelligence (AI) is going mainstream, enabling machines to perform human-like cognitive functions. Enhanced by machine learning, big data and cloud computing, algorithms can identify increasingly complex patterns in large data sets and already outperform humans in some cognitive functions. While promising gains in efficiency and productivity, AI may amplify existing policy challenges and raise new policy and ethical questions, for example in relation to its potential effects on the future of work and skills development or its implications for oversight and transparency, responsibility, liability, as well as safety and security.

The potential of blockchain hinges on grappling with technical hurdles and policy challenges

Blockchain enables transactions without any trusted party. Bitcoin, for example, a virtual currency based on blockchain, operates independently of any central bank or any other financial institution. Beyond bitcoin, blockchain applications create opportunities in many areas, including in the financial and public sectors, education, and the Internet of Things, by reducing transaction costs, facilitating accountability, and enabling guaranteed execution through smart contracts. Much of this potential still hinges on grappling with technical hurdles and policy challenges such as how to enforce law in the absence of any intermediary or how and to whom to impute legal liability for torts caused by blockchain-based systems.

List of acronyms, abbreviations and units of measure

AGI	Artificial general intelligence
AI	Artificial intelligence
ANI	Artificial narrow intelligence
APEC	Asia-Pacific Economic Cooperation
APNIC	Asia Pacific Network Information Center
ARCEP	Autorité de régulation des communications électroniques et des postes
ASI	Artificial super intelligence
ATP	Agriculture technology provider
B2B	Business to business
B2C	Business to consumer
BDA	Big data analytics
BERD	Business expenditure on research and development
BEREC	Body of European Regulators for Electronic Communications
BRIICS	Brazil, Russian Federation, India, Indonesia, China and South Africa
CAIP	Canada Accelerator and Incubator Program
CBPR	Cross-border Privacy Rules
CIGI	Centre for International Governance Innovation
CIS	Communication and information search
CISO	Chief information security officer
CNIL	Commission nationale de l'informatique et des libertés (France)
CNMC	Comisión Nacional de los Mercados y la Competencia (Spain)
CRC	Comisión de Regulación de Comunicaciones (Colombia)
CRM	Customer relationship management
CRTC	Canadian Radio-television and Telecommunications Commission
CSIRT	Computer Security Incident Response Team
CSN	Consumer Sentinel Network (United States)
DARPA	Defense Advanced Research Projects Agency
DDI	Data-driven innovation
DDoS	Distributed denial of service
DEO	*OECD Digital Economy Outlook*
DESI	Digital Economy and Society Index (European Union)
DoS	Denial of service

DSL	Digital subscriber line
EDI	Electronic data interchange
EEA	European Economic Area
EHR	Electronic health record
EPO	European Patent Office
ERP	Enterprise resource planning
EU	European Union
EUIPO	European Union Intellectual Property Office
FCC	Federal Communications Commission (United States)
FIRST	Forum of Incident Response and Security Team
FTA	Free-trade agreement
FTC	Federal Trade Commission (United States)
GATS	General Agreement on Trade in Services
GATT	General Agreement on Tariffs and Trade
GB	Gigabyte
GBP	British pound
Gbps	Gigabits per second
GDP	Gross domestic product
GDPR	General Data Protection Regulation (European Union)
GM	General Motors
GPS	Global Positioning System
IAPP	International Association of Privacy Professionals
ICPEN	International Consumer Protection and Enforcement Network
ICT	Information and communication technology
IMR	International mobile roaming
IoT	Internet of Things
IP	Internet protocol
IP5	Five Intellectual Property [offices]
IPv6	Internet Protocol version 6
ISP	Internet service provider
IT	Information technology
JPO	Japan Patent Office
kb	Kilobit
kB	Kilobyte
KBC	Knowledge-based capital
kbps	Kilobits per second
KIPO	Korean Intellectual Property Office
km	Kilometre
KRW	Korean wong

LAN	Local area network
LINX	London Internet Exchange
LPWA	Low-power, wide-area
LTE	Long-term Evolution
LTE-M	Long-term Evolution for Machines
M&A	Merger and acquisition
M2M	Machine to machine
MB	Megabyte
Mbps	Megabits per second
MHz	Megahertz
MNO	Mobile network operator
MOU	Memorandum of understanding
MVNO	Mobile virtual network operator
NAICS	North American Industry Classification System
NCSA	National Cyber Security Alliance (United States)
NDS	National digital strategy
NIS	New Israeli shequel
OAIC	Office of the Australian Information Commissioner
OBD	On-Board diagnostics
OGD	Open government data
OPS	Office productivity software
OTT	Over the top
P2P	Peer to peer
PB	Petabyte
PET	Privacy-enhancing technology
PGP	Pretty Good Privacy
PIAAC	Programme for the International Assessment of Adult Competencies
PPP	Public-private partnership
PSI	Public sector information
PSTRE	Problem solving in technology-rich environments
R&D	Research and development
RCD	Registered Community Designs (European Union)
RFID	Radio frequency identification
RLAH	Roam like at home
SCM	Supply-chain management
SIPO	State Intellectual Property Office of the People's Republic of China
SME	Small and medium-sized enterprise
SSL	Secure socket layer
STEM	Science, technology, engineering and mathematics

STRI	Services Trade Restrictiveness Index
TiVA	Trade in value-added
Tor	The Onion Router
TSM	Telecoms Single Market
USD	United States dollar
USPTO	United States Patent and Trademark Office
USTR	United States Trade Representative
VAT	Value-added tax
VC	Venture capital
VoD	Video on demand
VoIP	Voice over Internet Protocol
VoLTE	Voice over Long-term Evolution
WTO	World Trade Organization

PART I

Policies

Chapter 1

Going digital

The digital transformation is high on the global agenda and OECD countries are working towards making the transformation work for the economy and society. This chapter provides an introduction to the digital transformation, with a discussion of how it affects multiple policy areas, a presentation of key policy and measurement building blocks that can be considered for developing an integrated policy framework, and an analysis of the current state of national digital strategies that are being implemented across the OECD.

The statistical data for Israel are supplied by and under the responsibility of the relevant Israeli authorities. The use of such data by the OECD is without prejudice to the status of the Golan Heights, East Jerusalem and Israeli settlements in the West Bank under the terms of international law.

The digital transformation is high on the global agenda

From the 2016 G7, OECD and G20 ministerial events to the 2017 G20 Ministerial, the digital transformation has now firmly taken root on the global agenda. There is broad recognition at the highest level of government in many countries and among global leaders that digitalisation is transforming our lives. There is an equally widespread sense of the urgency to marshal the digital transformation to achieve more inclusive and sustainable prosperity.

The OECD Cancún Ministerial on the Digital Economy held in June 2016 was a milestone in this process, with ministers from 43 countries concurring that digitalisation can hold the key to a brighter future, and calling for a whole-of-government approach to unlocking its benefits for growth and well-being, and kick-starting a new policy-making era as the best path to enabling the digital transformation to benefit all, in all countries.

This first chapter sets the scene for the *OECD Digital Economy Outlook 2017*. It brings forward the main messages from the Cancún Ministerial, describes the new wave of digital technologies that drive the ongoing transformation of economies and societies, and identifies avenues to understand how the digital transformation manifests itself and affects policies. It further explores key policy and measurement building blocks for the digital transformation, and examines the state of current digital national strategies against this background.

The 2016 Cancún Ministerial on the Digital Economy has set the OECD agenda for the digital transformation

The Cancún Ministerial provided a forum to discuss how to harness the economic and social benefits of the digital economy in countries of various levels of development. Several countries from Latin America and the Caribbean, from Africa and Asia joined OECD countries at the event. All recognised that the digital transformation that has been underway for a few decades is stretching to the whole economy and society in many countries, with digital infrastructures nearly fully deployed in the OECD zone, Internet access grown from 4% to 40% of the world's population in just 20 years, and emerging and developing economies are increasingly using digital technologies in areas from e-commerce to agriculture and banking.

Overall, ministers agreed that unlocking the benefits of the ongoing digital transformation requires addressing the challenges created by this transformation, in particular for jobs, skills and trust. They also stressed the urgency for governments to be proactive and to adopt a policy-making approach whereby all stakeholders are invited to the table to develop and implement a clear way forward to shape the digital transformation, one which builds on a fully integrated policy approach. Throughout the event, participants highlighted the need to fill the data deficit and better measure the breadth, pace and consequences of the digital transformation and the effectiveness of related policy actions.

Box 1.1. The main messages from the Cancún Ministerial

It is urgent to develop a strategic vision and fully integrated policy approach to digitalisation to better understand how it is transforming our lives, how we can unlock its benefits and how we can help those in danger of being left behind. In doing so, we should consider the following:

- Internet openness drives social, economic and cultural development.
- Stimulating digital innovation across the economy is essential.
- There are many opportunities to improve networks and services through convergence of different communication technologies.
- It is critical to ensure we have the appropriate frameworks to enable tomorrow's Internet of Things.
- Consumer trust is a key element of boosting growth of the digital economy.
- Managing digital security and privacy risk is needed for economic and social prosperity.
- All stakeholders have a role to play in facilitating new markets and new jobs in the digital age.
- Greater use of digital technologies increases demand for new skills.

Source: OECD (2016a), "Meeting the policy challenges of tomorrow's digital economy", *www.oecd.org/internet/ministerial*.

Finally, the 43 countries that endorsed the Ministerial Declaration (see Annex 1.A2) committed to work with the OECD and all stakeholders to:

- help preserve the fundamental openness of the Internet while concomitantly meeting certain public policy objectives, such as the protection of privacy, security, intellectual property and children on line, as well as the reinforcement of trust in the Internet
- identify, develop and activate the mix of skills needed to enable inclusive participation in an increasingly digitalised economy; and analyse new work arrangements enabled by digital technologies and their implications for job quality and labour relations
- develop privacy and data protection strategies at the highest level of government that incorporate a whole-of-society perspective while providing the flexibility needed to take advantage of digital technologies for the benefit of all; and support the development of international arrangements that promote effective privacy and data protection across jurisdictions, including through interoperability among frameworks
- assess the effects of digital transformation on society and on all parts of the global economy to identify expected benefits and challenges, and to examine how national strategies and policies can address these transformations and take advantage of innovation to help bridge digital divides
- strengthen the collection of internationally comparable statistics on the adoption and use of broadband infrastructures and digital services together with the use of digital technologies by firms and individuals across the economy and society; and contribute to developing new metrics for the digital economy, such as on trust, skills and global data flows.

Many of these ambitions were reaffirmed at the 2017 OECD Ministerial Council Meeting, where countries specifically recognised the need to promote and protect the global free flow of information; the importance of global, market-relevant technical standards; the need to enhance the international dialogue on privacy and digital security, intellectual property rights and consumer protection; as well as high-speed broadband connectivity (OECD, 2017a).

The digital transformation of the economy and society

From the outset, two technological pillars, digitisation and interconnection, have been driving the digital transformation, complemented by a growing ecosystem of inter-related technologies. Digitisation is the conversion of an analogue signal conveying information (e.g. sound, image, printed text) to binary bits. Although still costly to digitise or collect, information can be represented in a universal manner, and it can be stored as data. Digital data can be used – processed, stored, filtered, tracked, identified, duplicated and transmitted – infinitely by digital devices without degradation, at very high speeds and at negligible marginal cost. The Internet has led to growing interconnections that allow this to occur globally. In contrast, processing and disseminating analogue information is slow and the variety of formats (e.g. paper, film reel, magnetic tapes, etc.) severely limits links, combinations and replication. In short, digitisation reduces physical constraints to information sharing and exploitation (see, for example, OECD [2015a]).

An ecosystem of digital technologies drives the ongoing transformation of economies and societies

Digitisation and interconnection have been empowered by exponentially growing computing power, with the number of transistors per square inch in an integrated circuit having doubled every 18 to 24 months, or a 100-fold improvement in a decade, for nearly 50 years (Moore's Law). This growth is well illustrated by the mainstreaming of the smartphone since 2007 and is further accelerated by computing delivered via the cloud as a service. Combined with constant mobile connectivity, a wide range of new products, applications and services has emerged over the past decade, forming a growing ecosystem of technologies and applications, which, through increasing use by individuals, firms and governments, is driving the digital transformation (OECD, 2016b). Key components of this ecosystem are:

- The Internet of Things (IoT), which comprises devices and objects whose state can be altered via the Internet, with or without the active involvement of individuals (OECD, 2015a). It includes objects and sensors that gather data and exchange these with one another and with humans. The networked sensors in the IoT serve to monitor the health, location and activities of people and animals and the state of production processes, the efficiency of city services and the natural environment, among other applications (OECD, 2016c). The number of connected devices in and around people's homes in OECD countries is expected to increase from 1 billion in 2016 to 14 billion by 2022 (OECD, 2015a). These devices are a key source of data that are feeding big data analytics.
- Big data analytics, which is a set of techniques and tools used to process and interpret large volumes of data that are generated by the increasing digitisation of content, the greater monitoring of human activities and the spread of the IoT (OECD, 2015a). It can be used to infer relationships, establish dependencies, and perform predictions of outcomes and behaviours. Firms, governments and individuals are increasingly able to access unprecedented volumes of data that help inform real-time decision making by combining a wide range of information from different sources. Big data analytics also enable machine learning, a driver of AI.

- AI can be understood as machines performing human-like cognitive functions. Its rapid diffusion is driven by recent strides in machine learning, an AI discipline that automatically identifies patterns in complex data sets. AI is making devices and systems smart and empowers new kinds of software and robots that increasingly act as self-governing agents, operating much more independently from the decisions of their human creators and operators than machines have previously done. AI is expected to help solve complex questions, generate productivity gains, improve the efficiency of decision making and save costs.
- Blockchain is a decentralised and disintermediated technology that facilitates economic transactions and peer-to-peer interactions. In addition to supporting information exchange, it enables protocols for value exchange, legal contracts and similar applications. Permissionless blockchains such as Bitcoin function as a tamper-proof distributed database and act as an open, shared and trusted public ledger that cannot be tampered with and can be inspected by everyone. The combination of transparent transactions, strict rules and constant oversight that characterise a blockchain-based network provides the conditions for its users to trust the transactions conducted on it, without the need for any trusted authority or intermediary operator.

Many other technologies underpin the current digital transformation, including cloud computing, open-source software like Hadoop, robotics, grid and neural computing, virtual reality, etc. Some of these have applications in almost all sectors of the economy and can be considered true "general-purpose" technologies. Others have more narrow applications in specific sectors. Together they are combinatorial and form an ecosystem of technologies that underpin a wide-ranging and rapid digital transformation of the economy and society, and increasingly of governments, in many areas, and which is leading to shifts in markets and economic behaviour that are fundamentally different from the analogue era to which we are used.

Identifying avenues to understand how the digital transformation affects policies

Underpinned by digitisation, interconnection and the growing ecosystem of digital technologies, digitalisation is transforming our economies and societies by changing the ways people interact, businesses function and innovate, and governments design and implement policies. Ongoing work by the OECD to help understand how the digital transformation affects policies proposes a preliminary set of "vectors of digital transformation" to identify core properties and cross-cutting effects of this transformation as it manifests itself across society, economic sectors and policy areas (Box 1.2).

Each of these suggested vectors can have policy implications in more than one, and often in several, areas. For example, the effects of scale without physical mass may challenge policies that target "big" or "small" firms by measures of mass, such as the number of employees, and more generally provoke a debate about what qualifies as being *de minimis* and exempt from certain policies (e.g. duties, taxes, social costs), or "small" and thereby qualified for certain benefits or subsidies. Digital businesses that attain large scale, notably platforms that benefit from network externalities and economies of scope, can lead to market concentration and winner-take-most dynamics at least for a period of time. Digital firms' ability to asymmetrically acquire and analyse data, including across an ecosystem of products, may raise policy questions from traditional concerns over privacy to appropriate competition policy for entities whose central role in data acquisition and analysis may present a barrier to entry for other firms. Finally, while platforms concentrate markets on line, they also foster decentralisation of activity at the edge of networks, e.g. in the "gig economy", which can complicate the enforcement of rules designed for large entities rather than for microenterprises or the self-employed, and can raise issues of working conditions and social protection. Finally, digital businesses often scale fast, outpacing policy making and legal or regulatory review, and benefit from possibilities for regulatory arbitrage.

Box 1.2. **Vectors of digital transformation**

Digital products, interactions and markets have distinctive characteristics that underlie ongoing economic and social change. These often transformative characteristics can support, or challenge, policies. Ongoing work by the OECD has identified some of the most prominent characteristics in a proposed set of eight "vectors of digital transformation", listed below under three headings: 1) scale, scope and speed; 2) ownership, assets and economic value; and 3) relationships, markets and ecosystems. These "vectors" are suggested to improve the understanding of the digital transformation and related policy implications.

1. Scale, scope and speed

Scale with little mass: While digital products and services have diverse economic characteristics (e.g. networks, semiconductors, smartphones, computing), core digital elements – software, data and standards – stand out. Fixed costs contrast with low, close to zero, marginal costs. Combined with the global reach of the Internet, this allows firms and platforms to scale very quickly, often with few employees, tangible assets or a geographic footprint.

Panoramic scope: The digitisation of functions allows for unprecedented complexity in products (the smartphone) and services (a huge catalogue of offerings). Standards enable components and products from different sources to work together, furthering economies of scale and scope, from combining, processing and integrating digital resources at a global level.

Temporal dynamics: It is often observed that digital technology accelerates communications, commerce, the diffusion of information and innovation, and changes in economic and social practices. However, the implications are far more complex: digital acceleration takes place against legacy time frames, slow institutional processes, entrenched behaviours and limited human attention. Technology also enables the manipulation of time, facilitating the preservation of the past and making it readily probed, indexed, repurposed, resold and remembered.

2. Ownership, assets and economic value

"Soft" capital: The growing importance of intangible sources of value, especially software and data, has been widely recognised. Physical goods – jet engines, tractors, specialised equipment – can generate and return data so that it becomes a service – or a hybrid of good and service. This is coupled with the emergence of platforms that allow firms and individuals to rent out or share their real capital easily.

Value mobility: As a result of their intangible, machine-encoded nature, software and data can be stored or exploited anywhere, decoupling value from specific geographic locations.

3. Relationships, markets and ecosystems

Intelligence at the edges: The "end-to-end" principle of the Internet has moved the intelligence of the network from the centre to the periphery. Armed with computers and smartphones, users can design and construct their own networks through mailing lists, hyperlinks and social networks, creating distinct communities. But they must typically take on responsibilities that used to reside in the centre (e.g. privacy and security).

Platforms and ecosystems: Digital technology enables expanded interactions and behaviour among individuals, communities, businesses and governments. This has propelled the development not only of direct relationships, but of digitally empowered multi-sided markets, commonly known as platforms. Some of the largest platforms are linked with varying degrees of integration, interoperability, data sharing and openness, essentially serving as proprietary ecosystems.

Loss of place: Value mobility and the global reach of the Internet enable value creation, transaction and interaction regardless of location and borders.

The effects of "soft" capital, including the hybridisation of goods and services, can have implications for policies directed at encouraging investment, such as tax incentives, accounting rules for (accelerated) depreciation and subsidies for foreign direct investment, as well as measures of investment, which in many cases were designed for tangible, physical capital residing in the jurisdiction, not for intangibles or investment that become part of a service that may be purchased from abroad. This further challenges trade policy that relies on a distinction between trade in goods (e.g. a computer) and services ("software as a service", or the cloud), while increasingly data flows allow a good to be offered as a complement to a service package. More generally, the intangible nature of bits and their ability to be stored in any location that depends less on a physical as opposed to a logical determination, creates opportunities for policy arbitrage across jurisdictions and challenges policies that rely on the geographic location of the digital activity where value creation occurs. This includes, for example, corporate and labour taxation, trade and its dependence on rules of origin, antitrust enforcement based on well-defined markets, labour regulations formulated around employees and employers in a particular place, and education policy and its focus on teachers or students in a particular school or district. Lastly, value mobility and the global reach of the Internet enable value creation, transaction and interaction regardless of location and borders, which may challenge traditional principles of territoriality, geographically based communities and sovereignty.

Key policy and measurement building blocks for the digital transformation

The digital transformation is progressively challenging every aspect of the economy and society, requiring many different policy areas to be considered simultaneously in an integrated approach and forcing governments to reach across traditional policy silos and across different levels of government to develop a whole-of-government vision and strategy. As identified in a 2017 report for the OECD Council at ministerial level, key actions to be taken for developing an integrated policy framework are to ensure that the foundations for the digital transformation are in place and that policies across all areas enable the digital transformation for the economy and society (OECD, 2017b).

This section provides indicators that are being developed under the OECD-wide project "Going Digital: Making the Transformation Work for Growth and Well-being". These indicators can help to assess where a country stands in relation to the foundations of the digital economy and its capability to seize the benefits of the digital transformation. These indicators will evolve as new insights are gained from ongoing work on measurement, economic analysis and policy evaluation. Additional indicators to assess policy coherence and strategy development will be developed in the context of the Going Digital project.

Building the foundations for the digital transformation

Framework conditions

The digital transformation does not occur in isolation; it is shaped by, and contributes to shaping, the broader economy and society as a whole. Framework policies play an important role in ensuring that the conditions exist for the digital transformation to flourish. Open trade and investment regimes create new avenues for rapidly upgrading technologies and skills, and increasing specialisation. Efficient, open financial markets help to allocate financial resources to firms investing in the digital transformation, while competitive product markets foster consumer welfare, allow new firms to challenge incumbents, efficient firms to grow and inefficient ones to exit. Well-functioning labour markets can support the inevitable structural change. More broadly, sound macroeconomic policies help reduce uncertainty and create an enabling environment for the digital economy to grow.

Figure 1.1 shows some selected indicators of framework conditions: the strength of barriers to entrepreneurship, trade and investment and the restrictiveness of regulations on telecommunications, professional services, retail trade and international trade. By way of illustration, the figure compares the above indicators in one of the best-performing countries (Australia) with the OECD average. All indicators in Australia are in line with or below the OECD average, suggesting that framework conditions in Australia are more favourable to the creation of innovative start-ups, new business models and new services enabled by digital technologies.

Figure 1.1. **Framework conditions for the digital transformation**

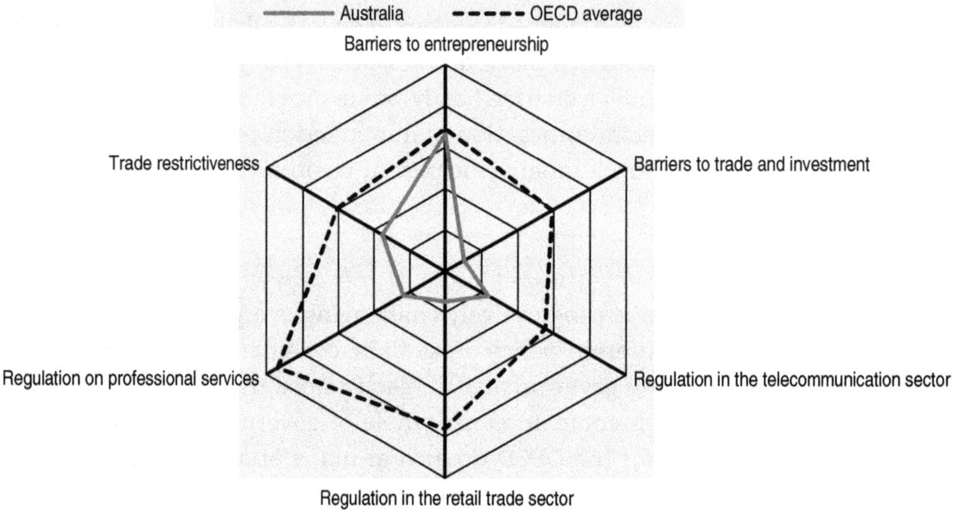

Note: All indicators have been standardised and range between 0 and 1.
Sources: Author's calculations based on OECD, *Product Market Regulation Database*, *www.oecd.org/economy/pmr* and OECD, *Services Trade Restrictiveness Index Regulatory Database*, *www.oecd.org/tad/services-trade/services-trade-restrictiveness-index.htm* (accessed March 2017).

StatLink http://dx.doi.org/10.1787/888933584355

Accessible digital infrastructures and services

Digital infrastructures, including efficient, reliable and widely accessible broadband communication networks and services, data, software, and hardware, are the foundations on which the digital economy is based. It is essential that governments promote investment in digital infrastructures and competition in the provision of high-speed networks and services, ensuring that key complementary enablers are in place, e.g. fibre optic backhaul, sufficient spectrum and increasing uptake of Internet Protocol version 6 (IPv6) Internet addresses. Individuals, businesses (including small and medium-sized enterprises [SMEs]) and governments need reliable and widespread access to digital networks and services to benefit from digital opportunities.

Figure 1.2 shows some selected indicators of access to and quality of digital infrastructures and telecommunication services: the number of fixed and mobile subscriptions per 100 inhabitants, their average connection speed, some selected price measures for fixed and mobile broadband, as well as the number of machine-to-machine SIM cards, which is a proxy for the IoT. By way of illustration, the figure compares the above indicators in one of the best-performing countries (Norway) with the OECD average. Norway performs better than the OECD average on all the indicators, except for the price of the fixed broadband basket (20 Gigabytes [GB]), which is more expensive in real terms (based on purchasing power parity). Higher fixed broadband prices may reflect higher average speeds, but may also slow down the development of new digital services delivered through fixed broadband.

Figure 1.2. **Access to digital infrastructures**

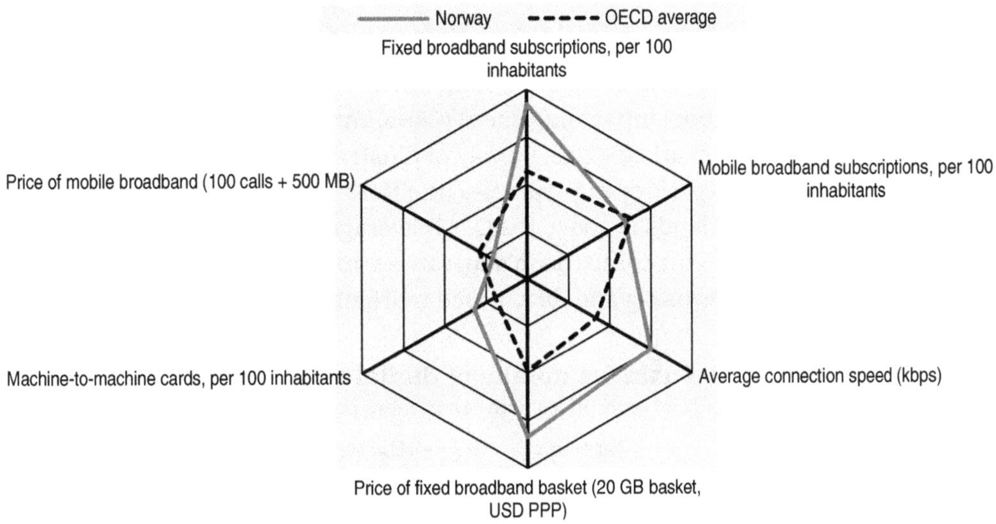

Notes: All indicators have been standardised and range between 0 and 1. GB = Gigabyte; kbps = kilobits per second; PPP = purchasing power parity.

Sources: Author's calculations based on OECD, "Broadband database", *OECD Telecommunications and Internet Statistics* (database), *www.oecd.org/sti/broadband/oecdbroadbandportal.htm* (accessed July 2017), Akamai, *www.akamai.com* (accessed July 2017) and Teligen/Strategy Analytics, *https://www.strategyanalytics.com/access-services/networks/tariffs---mobile-and-fixed#.WaP9_Xr57ql* (accessed July 2017).

StatLink http://dx.doi.org/10.1787/888933584374

Making the digital transformation work for the economy and society

This building block focuses on policies that help enable the effective use of digital technologies by workers, firms and governments; policies that foster innovation and help address challenges in specific sectors of the economy; and policies that promote the use of digital technologies to improve the functioning of governments and public service delivery. It also includes policies to foster trust in and acceptance of digital technologies, and policies that can help all individuals, including citizens, workers, consumers and society adjust to the digital transformation, including by ensuring that all people have the skills they need to adapt to and excel in an increasingly digital world. It also includes policies that use digital tools to enhance well-being, including by providing more equitable access to public services, such as healthcare.

Effective use

Access to digital networks provides the technical foundation for the digital transformation of the economy and society, but does not by itself necessarily ensure effective use. Other factors also need to be addressed, notably skills. Effective use of digital technologies requires a wide range of skills, including information and communication technology (ICT) specialist skills, generic ICT skills and complementary skills such as information processing, self-direction, problem solving and communication. Effective use also requires firms to take into account in their decision-making and operational processes the specific risks related to the use of digital technologies, particularly with respect to digital security (e.g. theft of trade secrets, disruption of operations, reputational damages, financial losses, etc.) and privacy protection. It is also crucial that governments encourage organisational change, including investments in data and other knowledge-based capital, to realise the full potential of the digital transformation. A lack of firm dynamics, which can lead to the co-existence of poorly performing firms with very low levels of ICT use and star performers, is another important contributor to effective use.

Figure 1.3 shows the proportion of firms using common digital technologies or engaged in selected online activities: big data, cloud computing, social media, supply-chain management, customer relationship management (CRM), enterprise resource planning (ERP), radio frequency identification and e-sales. By way of illustration, the figure compares these indicators in one of the best-performing countries (the Netherlands) with the OECD average. Digital uptake in the Netherlands is above the OECD average for all usages, particularly big data, CRM and social media. This comparison suggests a stronger orientation of Dutch firms towards social network advertising and data-based marketing.

Figure 1.3. **Business uptake of digital technologies**

As a percentage of enterprises with ten or more persons employed

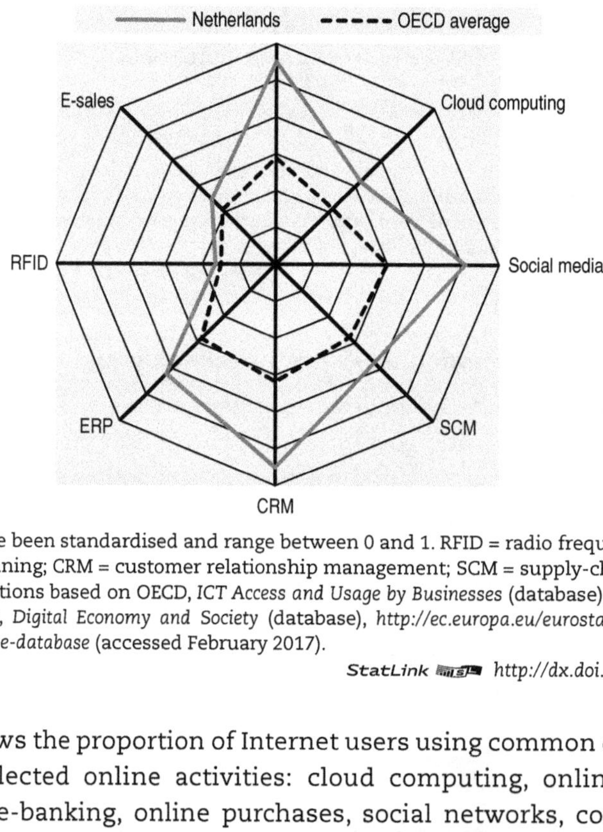

Notes: All indicators have been standardised and range between 0 and 1. RFID = radio frequency identification; ERP = enterprise resource planning; CRM = customer relationship management; SCM = supply-chain management.
Sources: Author's calculations based on OECD, *ICT Access and Usage by Businesses* (database), *http://oe.cd/bus* (accessed July 2017) and Eurostat, *Digital Economy and Society* (database), *http://ec.europa.eu/eurostat/web/digital-economy-and-society/data/comprehensive-database* (accessed February 2017).

StatLink *http://dx.doi.org/10.1787/888933584393*

Figure 1.4 shows the proportion of Internet users using common digital technologies or engaged in selected online activities: cloud computing, online courses, health-related searches, e-banking, online purchases, social networks, content creation and e-government. By way of illustration, the figure compares these indicators in one of the best-performing countries (Belgium) with the OECD average. In Belgium, social networks, cloud computing, e-banking and online courses are more diffused among individuals than the OECD average while fewer people create content on line or search for health-related information on line.

Figure 1.4. **Use of digital technologies by Internet users**

As a percentage of Internet users aged 16-74

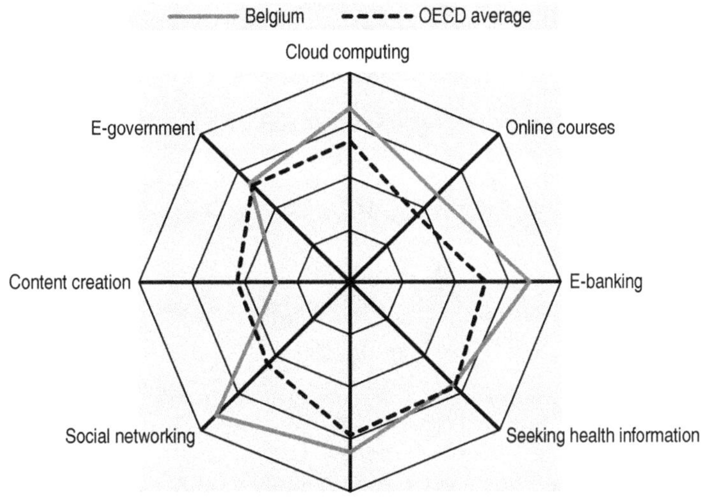

Note: All indicators have been standardised and range between 0 and 1.

Sources: Author's calculations based on OECD, *ICT Access and Usage by Households and Individuals* (database), *http://oe.cd/hhind* (accessed July 2017) and Eurostat, *Digital Economy and Society* (database), *http://ec.europa.eu/eurostat/web/digital-economy-and-society/data/comprehensive-database* (accessed February 2017).

StatLink http://dx.doi.org/10.1787/888933584412

Figure 1.5 compares selected indicators of digital skills, tertiary education and training in one of the best-performing countries (Finland) with the OECD average. While graduation rates and the demand for ICT specialists are in line with the OECD average, the proportion of individuals with high ICT skills and firms offering ICT training are significantly higher in Finland. This suggests that Finland has invested and continues to invest in the skills necessary to foster productivity and growth in the digital economy.

Innovation and effects of digital technologies in specific sectors

Digital technologies can help foster economic growth, including through positive "spillover effects" within and across sectors. Technologies, smart applications – including data analytics – and other innovations in the digital economy can also improve services and help address policy challenges in a wide range of areas, including education, finance, insurance, health, transportation, energy, agriculture and fisheries, both between and within countries. Digital technologies contribute not only to innovation in goods and services, but also to innovation in processes, business models and organisational arrangements.

Figure 1.6 compares several indicators of ICT-related innovation and ICT specialisation in one of the best-performing countries (Sweden) with the OECD average. While Sweden is close to the OECD average in terms of its share of ICT trademarks and ICT research and development (R&D) expenditures, the ICT shares of total value added and employment as well as the proportion of ICT specialists are significantly higher. The comparison highlights Sweden's strong specialisation in the production of ICT products relative to other OECD countries.

Figure 1.5. **Digital skills, tertiary education and training**

As a percentage of all graduates, 16-74 year-old individuals or enterprises with ten or more persons employed

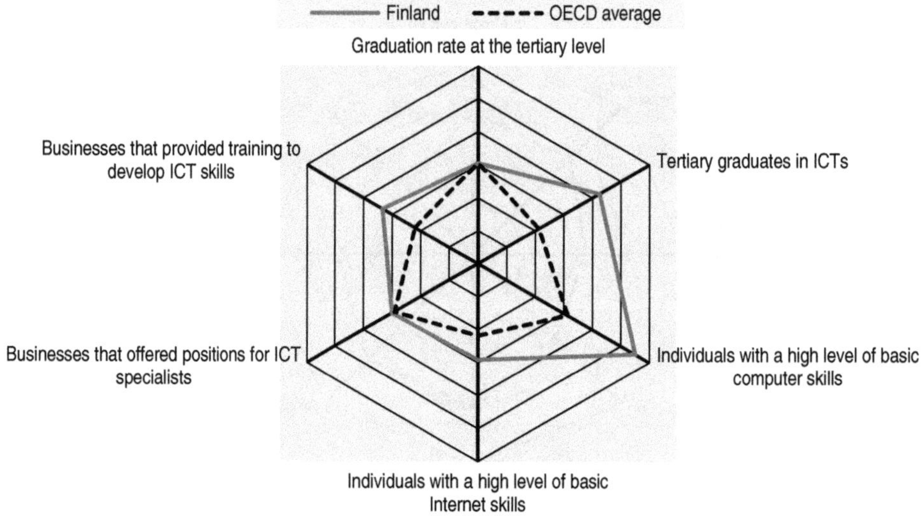

Notes: All indicators have been standardised and range between 0 and 1. ICT = information and communication technology.

Sources: Author's calculations based on OECD, *Education Database*, *www.oecd.org/education/database.htm* (accessed July 2017) and Eurostat, *Digital Economy and Society* (database), *http://ec.europa.eu/eurostat/web/digital-economy-and-society/data/comprehensive-database* (accessed June 2017).

StatLink *http://dx.doi.org/10.1787/888933584431*

Figure 1.6. **ICT-related innovations**

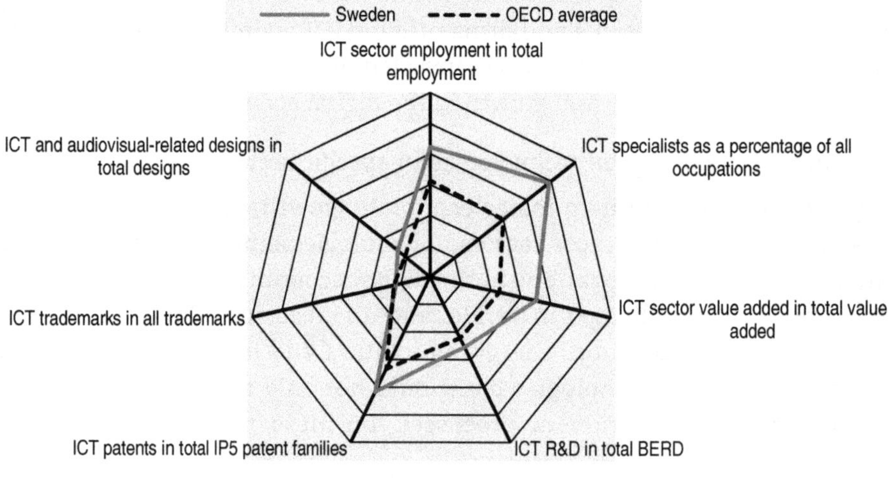

Notes: All indicators have been standardised and range between 0 and 1. The Five Intellectual Property (IP5) offices comprises the European Patent Office (EPO), the Japan Patent Office (JPO); the Korean Intellectual Property Office (KIPO), the State Intellectual Property Office of the People's Republic of China (SIPO) and the United States Patent and Trademark Office (USPTO). BERD = business expenditure on research and development.

Sources: Author's calculations based on OECD, *STAN: OECD Structural Analysis Statistics* (database), ISIC Rev.4, *http://oe.cd/stan* (accessed July 2017); Australian, Canadian and European labour force surveys and the *United States Current Population Survey* (accessed July 2017); OECD, "STAN R&D: Research and development expenditure in industry - ISIC Rev. 4", *STAN: OECD Structural Analysis Statistics* (database), *http://dx.doi.org/10.1787/stan-data-en* (accessed June 2017); and OECD, *STI Micro-data Lab: Intellectual Property* (database), *http://oe.cd/ipstats* (accessed July 2017).

StatLink *http://dx.doi.org/10.1787/888933584450*

Trust and acceptance

Trust is fundamental to the functioning of the digital economy; without it, individuals, firms and governments won't use digital technologies, and an important source of potential growth and social progress will be left unexploited. Greater co-operation in developing comprehensive and coherent national strategies for digital security and privacy across the economy and society, with a focus on issues such as personal data protection, resilience of critical infrastructures (e.g. water, energy, finance), incentives (e.g. cyber insurance, public procurement), public health and safety, SMEs, and related skills development, are essential. At the same time, it is important to continue to effectively protect consumers engaged in e-commerce and other online activities for the digital economy to flourish.

Figure 1.7 compares selected indicators of digital security and trust in one of the best-performing countries (Luxembourg) with the OECD average. Awareness of digital security risks in Luxembourg seems higher than for the OECD average, reflecting a higher frequency of security incidents. Behaviours and technologies to protect users against these risks are also more diffused. Yet, the proportion of business with no formal policies to manage ICT privacy risks and of individuals having disclosure of personal information on the Internet is higher than the average.

Figure 1.7. **Digital security and trust**

As a percentage of 16-74 year-old individuals or enterprises with ten or more persons employed

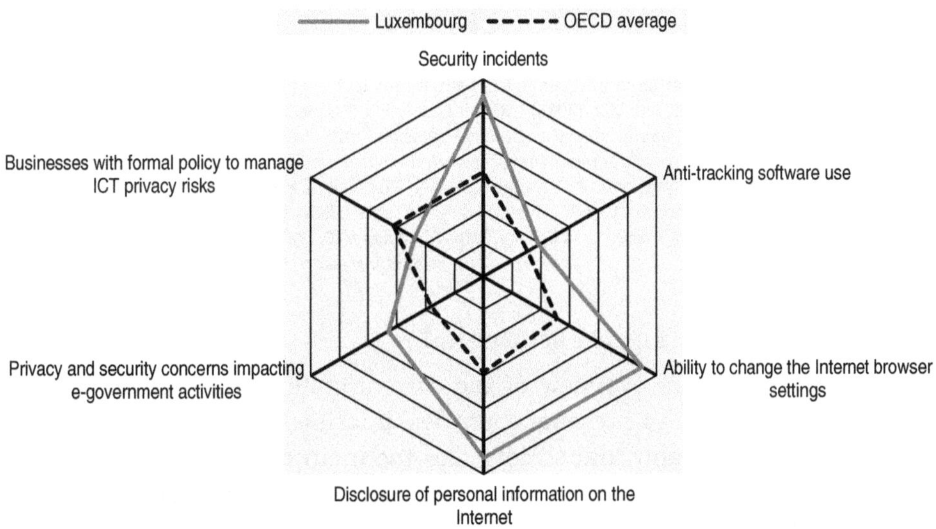

Notes: All indicators have been standardised and range between 0 and 1. ICT = information and communication technology.

Sources: Author's calculations based on OECD, *ICT Access and Usage by Households and Individuals* (database), *http://oe.cd/hhind*, OECD, *ICT Access and Usage by Businesses* (database) *http://oe.cd/bus* (both accessed July 2017) and Eurostat, *Digital Economy and Society* (database), *http://ec.europa.eu/eurostat/web/digital-economy-and-society/data/comprehensive-database* (accessed February 2017).

StatLink http://dx.doi.org/10.1787/888933584469

Societal adjustment to the digital transformation

The economy and society are being deeply affected from the digital transformation. On the one hand, automation may reduce employment in some occupations while job platforms may increase non-standard jobs, i.e. short-term, part-time or low-paid jobs, and widen the gender wage gap. On the other hand, e-services, particularly e-health, may help society to address the challenges of the aging population and increasing social expenditures.

Figure 1.8 compares some selected indicators of societal aspects in one of the best-performing countries (Denmark) with the OECD average. The share of temporary employment, low-paid jobs and the gender wage gap are significantly smaller in Denmark than the OECD average. The proportion of elderly individuals, who may benefit the most from e-health, is higher. Also, positive perceptions about the impact of science and technology on society are more widespread in the public opinion.

Figure 1.8. **Digitalisation and society**

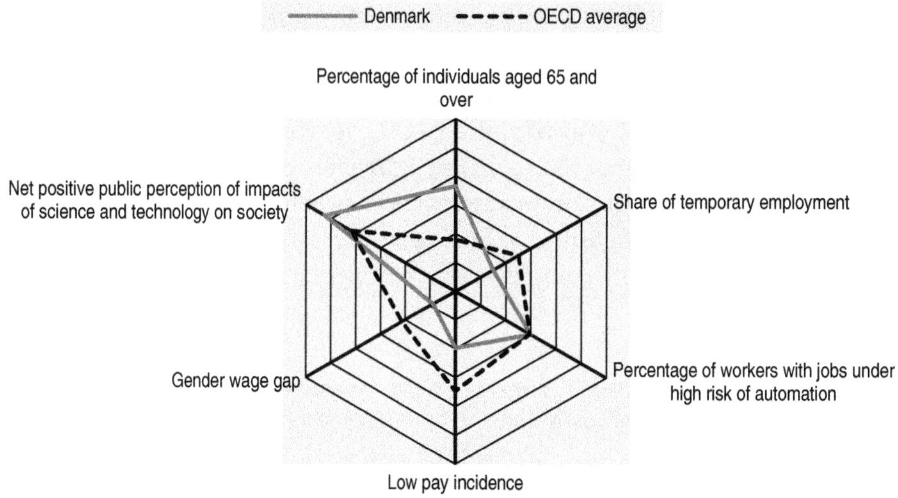

Note: All indicators have been standardised and range between 0 and 1.

Sources: Author's calculations based on UN (2015), *World Population Prospects: The 2015 Revision*, *www.un.org/en/development/desa/publications/world-population-prospects-2015-revision.html*; OECD, *Employment and Labour Market Statistics* (database), *www.oecd-ilibrary.org/employment/data/oecd-employment-and-labour-market-statistics_lfs-data-en* (accessed March 2017); Arntz, M., T. Gregory and U. Zierahn (2016), "The risk of automation for jobs in OECD countries: A comparative analysis", *http://dx.doi.org/10.1787/5jlz9h56dvq7-en* and OECD (2015b), *OECD Science, Technology and Industry Scoreboard 2015: Innovation for Growth and Society*, *http://dx.doi.org/10.1787/sti_scoreboard-2015-en*.

StatLink *http://dx.doi.org/10.1787/888933584488*

The current state of national digital strategies

This section provides an overview of the current state of NDSs in OECD countries and partner economies. It also presents countries' priorities among policy objectives for developing the digital economy and society, and the main challenges that governments perceive while working towards these objectives. Key findings include that: NDSs have become the norm across OECD countries and policy objectives to develop the digital economy and society, largely pursued by NDSs, are a high priority; many governments are monitoring the implementation of their NDS and are on track in most measured areas; and, despite some commonalities, current approaches to govern national digital strategies (NDSs) significantly differ across countries.

National digital strategies have become the norm across the OECD

Of the 32 OECD countries and the 6 partner economies that answered the *OECD Digital Economy Outlook* Policy Questionnaire in 2016, all of them indicated that they have an NDS, agenda or programme, except for the United States, which takes a decentralised, market-driven approach to its digital strategy.[1] Almost two-thirds of NDSs are stand-alone strategies, while the remaining ones are a component of a broader national strategy, e.g. a national innovation strategy, and in many cases the NDS interacts with other strategies, such as for innovation. Most European OECD countries have aligned their NDS with the Digital Agenda for Europe, the European Digital Single Market Strategy, the Europe 2020 Strategy, the European Union eGovernment Action Plan, or a combination thereof (Box 1.3). More than two-thirds of all countries had an NDS prior to the current one. Almost all of the countries with a first NDS have built on or replaced previous policies or strategies with their NDS. Currently, on average, NDSs have a time frame for implementation of seven years and are about halfway to being implemented, either with a budget directly associated with the NDS (two-thirds) or more indirectly via budgets of ministries and agencies involved in implementation (the remaining third).

Box 1.3. **The EU Digital Single Market**

One of the European Commission's ten political priorities is the completion of the Digital Single Market through a strategy that aims to open up digital opportunities for people and business and enhance Europe's position as a world leader in the digital economy. Today, the European Digital Market is made up of 54% of US-based online services, 42% of national online services and only 4% of European Union (EU) cross-border online services.

A Digital Single Market would ensure the free movement of persons, services and capital, individuals and businesses to seamlessly access and exercise online activities under conditions of fair competition, and a high level of consumer and personal data protection, irrespective of their nationality or place of residence. The Digital Single Market can create opportunities for new start-ups and allow existing companies to better seize the advantage of a market of over 500 million people. Completing a Digital Single Market could contribute EUR 415 billion a year to Europe's economy, create jobs and transform public services.

The Digital Single Market Strategy was adopted on 6 May 2015 and includes 16 specific initiatives delivered by the Commission in January 2017. Legislative proposals are now being discussed by the co-legislator, the European Parliament and the Council.

The Digital Single Market Strategy is built on three pillars:

1. **Access**: better access for consumers and businesses to digital goods and services across Europe.
2. **Environment**: creating the right conditions and a level playing field for digital networks and innovative services to flourish.
3. **Economy and society**: maximising the growth potential of the digital economy.

The evolution of EU member states' performance in digital developments is tracked by the Digital Economy and Society Index (DESI), which is a composite index that summarises relevant indicators on Europe's digital performance and tracks the evolution of EU member states in digital competitiveness. Member states' progress is monitored in the context of the Digital Single Market strategy.

Source: EC (2017), "Digital Single Market", *https://ec.europa.eu/digital-single-market/en/digital-single-market* (accessed 2 May 2017).

Policy objectives pursued by national digital strategies are high priority

Policy objectives for the development of the digital economy and society and which are largely pursued by NDSs are a high priority across all countries. Table 1.1 shows a priority ranking of 15 policy objectives, based on responses from 35 countries. Overall, 68% of the objectives were considered to be a high priority, 15% medium-high, 14% medium, and only 3% low or medium-low priorities. On the one hand, this might imply that most of these objectives are high priorities for governments; on the other, it could indicate a lack of prioritisation among these objectives in many countries. Strengthening e-government services and further developing telecommunication infrastructure rank the highest for 2017. When considering expected priorities over the next three to five years, strengthening security moves up two positions and further developing telecommunication infrastructure drops by three (Table 1.1, second column). Table 1.1 also provides the number of countries that mention the listed objectives as part of their NDS (third column) as well as additional objectives that are not covered in the priority ranking but are frequently mentioned as objectives of NDSs (bottom of the table).

Table 1.1. **Priority ranking of policy objectives for digital developments**

Policy objectives	Priority in 2017	Next 3-5 years	National digital strategy objectives
	Ranking	Expected change	Number of countries
Strengthening e-government services	1	Same	21
Further developing telecommunication infrastructure	2	↓3	22
Promoting ICT-related skills and competences	3	Same	16
Strengthening security	4	↑2	18
Enhancing access to data, including PSI and OGD	5	↑1	6
Encouraging the adoption of ICTs by businesses and small and medium-sized enterprises in particular	6	↓1	3
Encouraging ICT adoption in specific sectors, e.g. healthcare, education	7	↑1	3
Strengthening privacy	8	Same	5
Strengthening digital identities	9	Same	2
Promoting the ICT sector, including its internationalisation	10	Same	2
Promoting e-commerce across the economy	11	↓1	5
Tackling global challenges, e.g. Internet governance, climate change	12	↑1	1
Strengthening consumer protection	13	↓1	0
Advancing e-inclusion, e.g. of elderly and disadvantaged groups	14	↑1	4
Preserving Internet openness	15	Same	4
Additional objectives of national digital strategies			
Fostering science, innovation and entrepreneurship			16
Ensuring access to the Internet, services and information			12
Developing digital content and culture			10
Increasing the use of digital technologies			10
Developing a sound regulatory approach for digital environments			3

Notes: Both the current ranking and the expected changes over the next three to five years should be considered with caution, given a weak differentiation among the indicated priorities. ICT = information and communication technology; PSI = public sector information; OGD = open government data.

Achieving these objectives can be a goal in itself; however, several countries consider their achievement to contribute to reaching higher level objectives, such as gross domestic product (GDP) growth (Brazil, Denmark, Germany, Israel, Japan, Mexico, Slovenia, Sweden), jobs (Denmark, Germany, Latvia), productivity (Finland, the Russian Federation, Switzerland), competitiveness (Estonia, Latvia, the Netherlands, the Russian Federation), quality of life and well-being (Estonia, Lithuania, the Netherlands, the Russian Federation, Turkey), democracy and transparency (Sweden, Switzerland), inclusiveness and inclusion (the People's Republic of China, Israel, Norway, Slovenia, Sweden), or combating climate change and fostering sustainable development (Sweden, Switzerland).

Challenges in working towards these objectives

Governments face several challenges working towards the policy objectives listed in Table 1.1. For 2017, among the 10 main challenges identified by 31 countries, the three most prominent are: 1) a lack of awareness, implementation and enforcement; 2) insufficient skills, training and education; and 3) co-ordination, including multi-stakeholder, multi-lateral and multi-level governance co-ordination (see Table 1.A1.1 in Annex 1.A1). This aggregate view hides more detailed information, which reveals that the top three challenges are quite different for each policy objective (see Table 1.A1.2 in Annex 1.A1). Looking three to five years ahead, the expected top 3 challenges are the same as for 2017, but notable changes occur in the order of the 10 main challenges that countries expect and in the expected challenges per policy objective.

Approaches to governing national digital strategies vary across countries

Current approaches to governing NDSs vary across countries. Information from 35 countries provides an overview of the responsibilities allocated for the development, co-ordination, implementation, and monitoring of NDSs (Table 1.2). The lead on strategy development is often taken by a ministry or body that is not dedicated to digital affairs, while only a minority of countries so far is charging a ministry or body that is dedicated to digital affairs. Almost all countries engage multiple private stakeholders and public bodies to contribute input to developing their NDS. Strikingly, only few countries (Austria, Luxembourg, Mexico, the Slovak Republic) have a single high-level government official, e.g. in the Prime Minister's Office, Presidency or Chancellery, or a ministry or body dedicated to digital affairs to co-ordinate their NDS. However, effective co-ordination is essential for developing and implementing a whole-of-government approach with an NDS. The implementation of the NDS is the responsibility of several ministries, bodies or institutions in the majority of countries, and in some, multiple stakeholders are involved in implementing it. Bodies responsible for monitoring the implementation of the NDS tend to be the same as those who lead the development and the co-ordination of the NDS.

Table 1.2. **National digital strategy governance**

Number of countries that have allocated respective responsibilities

	Lead the development	Contribute input	Co-ordinate	Implement	Monitor
Government, e.g. Prime Minister, Presidency, Chancellery, Ministerial Council	4	0	5	1	6
Digital affairs ministry or body or ministerial position	8	1	10	3	8
Ministry or body not dedicated to digital affairs	15	2	13	1	11
Several ministries, bodies or institutions	6	14	5	26	7
Multiple public and private stakeholders	1	17	0	3	0

Many governments are monitoring the implementation of their national digital strategy

Many governments have set up measurable targets within a specific time frame to monitor the implementation of their NDS, and most are making good progress towards reaching their targets. Table 1.3 presents the main categories of the targets that 24 OECD countries and 5 partner economies have set up. On average, monitoring started in 2013, and the time frame for reaching determined targets are between six and eight years. The greatest number of targets was set up for measuring progress in broadband infrastructure development and performance, and the fewest for ICT skills and other skills development (Table 1.3). Some countries monitor the implementation of their NDS via a supranational index, such as the European Union's Digital Economy and Society Index (DESI), and others have built their own aggregate digitalisation index, such as Germany and Mexico.

Table 1.3. **National digital strategy targets and progress in implementation**

Target category[1]		Percentage of targets reached as of 2016	Target year
1	Broadband infrastructure development and performance	66%	2020
2	Public sector services and performance	78%	2020
3	Internet and services uptake	56%	2020
4	Use of digital technologies	62%	2018
5	E-commerce (firms, individuals) and digital business processes	52%	2020
6	ICT skills and other skills development	65%	2019

1. Ordered by the number of targets set up per category.
Notes: This table is based on information from 31 countries on 173 monitored target values. National and supranational aggregate indices are not taken into account in the table. In addition to the target categories listed in this table, several governments have set up targets on ICT sector development, digital content promotion, and privacy and personal data protection; however, the number of targets and corresponding data are insufficient to constitute meaningful averages for these categories.

Progress, as measured by 2016, shows that in each target category, on average, more than 50% of the targets had been reached. This corresponds to an average annual progress for all targets combined of slightly over 100%. Areas in which governments are least on track towards reaching their targets include Internet and services uptake and e-commerce. Specific measures that countries put in place to implement their NDS are discussed in Chapter 2.

Note

1. The United States approaches digital economy policy through a portfolio strategy: it has a collection of policies, regulations and laws that are associated with specific issues and/or sectors that together support the evolution and enhancement of the digital economy. Elements include, in no particular order, policies relating to telecommunication and the Internet, digital privacy, cybersecurity, big data, smart information technology (IT) delivery, open data, IT R&D, educational technology, online education, and environmental information systems. The portfolio strategy is evidenced at both the national (federal) and subnational (state and local) levels. It can be described in a variety of ways; key dimensions include: 1) digital access and participation – broadband, wireless and other telecommunication plus support for inclusive access; 2) openness – open access to government data, open access to results of federally funded research, and the free flow of information and commerce; 3) trustworthiness – cybersecurity, reliability and resilience, privacy, protection of civil liberties in the online and big data environments, protection of intellectual property rights. The United States nurtures the continued development and improvement of the technologies that underlie the digital economy and that contribute to advancing the above dimensions.

References

Arntz, M., T. Gregory and U. Zierahn (2016), "The risk of automation for jobs in OECD countries: A comparative analysis", *OECD Social, Employment and Migration Working Papers*, No. 189, OECD Publishing, Paris, *http://dx.doi.org/10.1787/5jlz9h56dvq7-en*.

EC (European Commission) (2017), "Digital Single Market", webpage, *https://ec.europa.eu/digital-single-market/en/digital-single-market* (accessed 2 May 2017).

OECD (Organisation for Economic Co-operation and Development) (2017a), "Making globalisation work: Better lives for all", *2017 Ministerial Council Statement*, OECD, Paris, *www.oecd.org/mcm/documents/C-MIN-2017-9-Final-EN.pdf*.

OECD (2017b), "Going Digital: Making the Transformation Work for Growth and Well-Being", MCM 2017 Document, *www.oecd.org/mcm/documents/C-MIN-2017-4%20EN.pdf*.

OECD (2016a), "Meeting the policy challenges of tomorrow's digital economy", webpage, *www.oecd.org/internet/ministerial*.

OECD (2016b), *OECD Science, Technology and Innovation Outlook 2016*, OECD Publishing, Paris, *http://dx.doi.org/10.1787/sti_in_outlook-2016-en*.

OECD (2016c), "The Internet of Things: Seizing the benefits and addressing the challenges", *OECD Digital Economy Papers*, No. 252, OECD Publishing, Paris, *http://dx.doi.org/10.1787/5jlwvzz8td0n-en*.

OECD (2015a), *Data-Driven Innovation: Big Data for Growth and Well-being*, OECD Publishing, Paris, *http://dx.doi.org/10.1787/9789264229358-en*.

OECD (2015b), *OECD Science, Technology and Industry Scoreboard 2015: Innovation for Growth and Society*, OECD Publishing, Paris, *http://dx.doi.org/10.1787/sti_scoreboard-2015-en*.

UN (United Nations) (2015), *World Population Prospects: The 2015 Revision*, United Nations, New York, *www.un.org/en/development/desa/publications/world-population-prospects-2015-revision.html*.

ANNEX 1.A1

Challenges to achieving policy objectives for digital developments

Table 1.A1.1. **Main challenges to achieving policy objectives for digital developments**

More prominent ↑	Main challenges in 2017		Main challenges over the next three to five years	Less prominent ↓
	Awareness, implementation, enforcement	1	Awareness, implementation, enforcement	
	Skills, training, education	2	Co-ordination, including multi-stakeholder, multi-lateral and multi-level governance co-ordination	
	Co-ordination, including multi-stakeholder, multi-lateral and multi-level governance co-ordination	3	Skills, training, education	
	Policy design and measures	4	Public investment or funding	
	Laws or regulation	5	Technical, including standards and interoperability	
	Technical, including standards and interoperability	6	Trust, including privacy, security, consumer protection	
	ICT adoption, business digitalisation, innovation	7	Laws and regulation	
	Public investment or funding	8	Policy design and measures	
	Private investment or access to finance	9	ICT adoption, business digitalisation, innovation	
	Trust, including privacy, security, consumer protection	10	Private investment or access to finance	

Note: This table presents a ranking of the most frequently mentioned challenges to achieve the policy objectives listed in Table 1.1. The ranking is based on information from 31 countries with 344 observations for 2017 and 286 observations for the next three to five years.

Table 1.A1.2. **Top three challenges per policy objective**

Policy objectives	In 2017			Next 3-5 years		
	Top 3 challenges			Top 3 challenges		
Strengthening e-government services	5	3	8	1	2	6
Further developing telecommunication infrastructure	9	1	8	10	4	1
Promoting ICT-related skills and competences	2	1	3	3	1	10
Strengthening security	1	4	2	1	4	5
Enhancing access to data, including PSI and OGD	4	6	5	1	5	7
Encouraging the adoption of ICTs by businesses and small and medium-sized enterprises in particular	2	9	7	9	1	3
Encouraging ICT adoption in specific sectors, e.g. healthcare, education	1	4	3	1	3	5
Strengthening privacy	5	1	4	1	7	6
Strengthening digital identities	1	5	8	1	5	2
Promoting the ICT sector, including its internationalisation	x[1]	2	7	8	7	3
Tackling global challenges, e.g. Internet governance, climate change	1	3	4	2	1	10
Promoting e-commerce across the economy	4	7	2	6	3	9
Strengthening consumer protection	5	1	3	1	2	7
Advancing e-inclusion, e.g. of elderly and disadvantaged groups	2	1	3	1	3	4
Preserving Internet openness	5	4	6	x[1]	9	10

1. Refers to "Incentives", a challenge that is not among the ten main challenges listed in Table 1.A1.1.

Notes: This table presents the three most frequently mentioned challenges for each digital economy policy objective, based on the ranking of the main challenges for 2017 and for the next three to five years presented in Table 1.A1.1. ICT = information and communication technology; PSI = public sector information; OGD = open government data.

ANNEX 1.A2

Ministerial Declaration on the Digital Economy: Innovation, Growth and Social Prosperity ("Cancún Declaration")

WE, the Ministers and representatives of Argentina, Australia, Austria, Belgium, Canada, Chile, Colombia, Costa Rica, the Czech Republic, Denmark, Ecuador, Egypt, Estonia, Finland, France, Germany, Greece, Hungary, Iceland, Indonesia, Ireland, Israel, Italy, Japan, Korea, Latvia, Lithuania, Luxembourg, Mexico, the Netherlands, New Zealand, Norway, Poland, Portugal, the Slovak Republic, Slovenia, Spain, Sweden, Switzerland, Turkey, the United Kingdom, the United States, and the European Union, assembled in Cancún, Mexico, on 22-23 June 2016;

COMMITTED to the rule of law and respect for human rights, to advancing freedom and democracy, and to increasing economic, civic and social opportunities for all;

RECOGNISE that the world economy is becoming ever more digital; that growing use of and investment in digital technologies and knowledge-based capital is profoundly transforming our societies;

RECOGNISE that the digital economy is a powerful catalyst for innovation, growth and social prosperity; that our shared vision is to promote a more sustainable and inclusive growth focused on well-being and equality of opportunities, where people are empowered with education, skills and values, and enjoy trust and confidence;

RECOGNISE that advancing our vision relies on the participation of all countries and on collective action to seize the opportunities and tackle the evolving challenges of the digital economy;

RECOGNISE in this regard, that we need to adopt holistic and whole-of-society approaches that encompass coherent evidence-based policies to stimulate investment in higher speed broadband connectivity, reduce barriers to use of digital technologies, foster research, innovation and new business opportunities, strengthen trust, promote job quality and address skill needs;

RECOGNISE that the 1998 Ministerial Conference on Electronic Commerce in Ottawa and 2008 Ministerial on the Future of the Internet Economy in Seoul helped pave the way for the digital economy to flourish through a successful combination of policies developed in close collaboration with experts from business and industry, trade-unions, civil society and the Internet technical community through their advisory committees; and that we need to continue working closely together and with all stakeholders;

RECOGNISE that the OECD Recommendations of the Council on Principles for Internet Policy Making, Consumer Protection in E-commerce, Digital Security Risk Management for Economic and Social Prosperity, Cryptography Policy and Protection of Privacy and Transborder Flows of Personal Data, which all stem from multi-stakeholder cooperation, provide a robust foundation for guiding the development of coherent policies for an increasingly digitalised economy;

FURTHER RECOGNISE in this regard, the important contribution of the Internet Governance Principles of the NETmundial Multistakeholder Statement;

UNDERLINE the critical need for continued multi-stakeholder, consensus-driven approaches to developing global technical standards that enable interoperability and a secure, stable, global, open, and accessible Internet; and the equally critical ongoing need for open, transparent and inclusive processes in global multi-stakeholder Internet governance;

FURTHER UNDERLINE that our initiatives to support the digital economy also help attain the United Nations 2030 Agenda for Sustainable Development and the outcomes of the World Summit on the Information Society and its ten year review; and that we need to promote gender equality and be inclusive of vulnerable or disadvantaged groups;

DECLARE that we will:

1. **Support the free flow of information** to catalyse innovation and creativity, support research and knowledge sharing, enhance trade and e-commerce, enable the development of new businesses and services, and increase people's welfare through policies, grounded in respect for human rights and the rule of law, that reinforce the Internet's openness, in particular its distributed and interconnected nature, while respecting applicable frameworks for privacy and data protection, and strengthening digital security;
2. **Stimulate digital innovation and creativity** to spur growth and address global social issues through coordinated policies that promote investment in digital technologies and knowledge-based capital, encourage availability and use of data, including open public sector data, foster entrepreneurship and the development of small and medium enterprises, and support the continued transformation of all economic sectors, including public services;
3. **Increase broadband connectivity and harness the potential of interconnected and converged infrastructures and digital services** to bridge digital divides and foster innovation by adopting technologically neutral frameworks that foster investment in broadband networks, protect consumers, promote competition and enable opportunities for all;
4. **Embrace the opportunities arising from emerging technologies and applications** such as the Internet of Things, cloud computing, digital transformation of manufacturing and data analytics, while addressing their economic and social effects, and assessing the appropriateness of policy and regulatory frameworks, and of global standards;
5. **Promote digital security risk management and the protection of privacy at the highest level of leadership** to strengthen trust, and develop to this effect collaborative strategies that recognise these issues as critical for economic and social prosperity, support implementation of coherent digital security and privacy risk management practices, with particular attention to the freedom of expression and the needs of small and medium enterprises and individuals, foster research and innovation and promote a general policy of accountability and transparency;

6. **Stimulate and help reduce impediments to e-commerce within and across borders** for the benefit of consumers and businesses by adopting policies and regulatory frameworks that strengthen consumer trust and product safety, promote competition and support consumer-driven innovation, and enable co-operation among consumer protection and other relevant authorities within and among countries;
7. **Take advantage of the opportunities arising from online platforms** that enable innovative forms of production, consumption, collaboration and sharing through interactions among and between individuals and organisations, while assessing their social and economic benefits and challenges as well as the appropriateness of related policy and regulatory frameworks;
8. **Spur the employment opportunities created by the digital economy** by reducing barriers to investment in and adoption of digital technologies in all economic sectors, promoting an attractive and agile business environment, in particular for new digital entrants, adapting labour policies and programmes to foster job quality and social protection, in particular in new work arrangements facilitated by digital technologies, and by continuing to address job displacement and mitigate the related social cost especially for vulnerable groups;
9. **Strive for all people to have the skills needed to participate in the digital economy and society** through policies that improve the capacity of educational and training systems to identify and respond to the demand for general and specialist digital skills; that facilitate up- and re-skilling through lifelong learning and on-the-job training; and that promote digital literacy as well as inclusive and effective use of ICTs in education and training;

FURTHER DECLARE that we will deliver on our objectives in a timely manner in close co-operation with all stakeholders, and that, with the support of the OECD, we will share experiences and work collaboratively to:

- help preserve the fundamental openness of the Internet while concomitantly meeting certain public policy objectives, such as the protection of privacy, security, intellectual property and children online, as well as the reinforcement of trust in the Internet;
- identify, develop and activate the mix of skills needed to enable inclusive participation in an increasingly digitalised economy; and analyse new work arrangements enabled by digital technologies and their implications for job quality and labour relations;
- develop privacy and data protection strategies at the highest level of government that incorporate a whole-of-society perspective while providing the flexibility needed to take advantage of digital technologies for the benefit of all; and support the development of international arrangements that promote effective privacy and data protection across jurisdictions, including through interoperability among frameworks;
- assess the effects of digital transformation on society and on all parts of the global economy to identify expected benefits and challenges, and to examine how national strategies and policies can address these transformations and take advantage of innovation to help bridge digital divides;
- strengthen the collection of internationally comparable statistics on the adoption and use of broadband infrastructures and digital services together with the use of digital technologies by firms and individuals across the economy and society; and contribute to developing new metrics for the digital economy, such as on trust, skills and global data flows;

INVITE the OECD to further develop its work related to the digital economy, and in this regard, to build on its work in other areas, including the OECD Skills Strategy and the update of the OECD Jobs Strategy;

CALL ON the OECD to continue to provide us with strong evidence and the innovative analysis needed to develop sound policies to achieve our objectives and contribute to a flourishing digital economy.

OECD Digital Economy Outlook 2017

Chapter 2

Policy and regulation

This chapter discusses government policy and regulation in four main areas: access and connectivity, usage and skills, digital innovation, and digital risk and trust. For each of these areas, it provides an overview of policy trends, identifies the most common policy measures and instruments, and discusses good practices as well as challenges to be addressed.

The statistical data for Israel are supplied by and under the responsibility of the relevant Israeli authorities. The use of such data by the OECD is without prejudice to the status of the Golan Heights, East Jerusalem and Israeli settlements in the West Bank under the terms of international law.

Introduction

This chapter discusses policy and regulation in the areas of access and connectivity; information and communication technology (ICT) usage and skills; innovation, applications and transformation; and digital risk and trust. Although these areas may seem rather distinct, policy issues for each of them are increasingly inter-related and need to be considered from an overarching perspective. Such a perspective is being developed by most OECD countries in their national digital strategy (NDS). As underlined in Chapter 1, which discusses those strategies, fully seizing the benefits of the digital economy requires a whole-of-government approach that proactively addresses the broad range of policy issues and their relationships across policy areas.

For example, the Internet of Things (IoT) may soon be a commonplace of daily life, with many billions of interconnected objects around the world. "Smart" devices, equipment, machines and infrastructure are creating opportunities for automation and for interaction in real time. IoT applications and services, enhanced by data analytics, are expected to help to reinvigorate industry, meet some of the needs of increasingly elderly populations, function as core elements of smart cities, and support the achievement of United Nations' Sustainable Development Goals.

But to unleash the potential economic and social benefits that are associated with the IoT – and digital technologies more generally – an enabling, comprehensive policy framework is needed. That framework would include interdependent policies for building the necessary infrastructure and fostering interoperability (Chapter 3 discusses trends in this area); developing the necessary skills for effective use by individuals, firms and governments (Chapter 4); promoting innovation, applications and transformation (Chapter 5); and finally, building trust (Chapter 6) in digital technologies, including the IoT.

Governments continue to align digital economy priorities directly with certain socio-economic objectives, such as improving care for the sick and elderly, making more career opportunities available to girls and women, providing better educations to poor children and those who live in remote areas, and promoting growth and employment. Leading priorities in this context include furthering access to high-speed broadband networks and overhauling laws to improve the speed and coverage of communication services. Many countries have also focused on providing training and spurring innovation in the ICT sector, as well as on encouraging ICT usage through e-government services, training programmes and subsidies. At the same time, countries continue to address the challenges and risks arising from the digital transformation by introducing national digital security strategies, while privacy protection continues to be prominent on governments' agendas.

It has also become clearer than ever that the digital transformation can be disruptive, and that well-considered policies are needed not only to allow the disruption to occur, but to encourage it so that its benefits can be realised fully and without unnecessary delays. Thus, countries have launched initiatives aimed at helping start-ups or young small and medium-sized enterprises (SMEs) through accelerators or incubators, and have promoted digital applications and services with a variety of policy measures. However, measures are also needed to cushion the blow when the digital transformation displaces workers and to protect consumers in the new commercial settings that are evolving. Consequently, policies in support of vocational training and higher education in ICT are common, may involve partnerships with the private sector, and sometimes aim to assist specific groups, such as the unemployed. Furthermore, the digital transformation of jobs has triggered reviews of labour laws and sector-specific employment rules. Meanwhile, as the e-commerce marketplace evolves, so do policy responses to protect consumers and ensure trust. For example, policy makers have begun to grapple with the challenge of applying consumer protection frameworks to peer platform and other online platform markets. They have also taken steps to address consumer protection-related impediments to cross-border e-commerce.

In sum, the digital transformation is an opportunity to be welcomed, but it also brings certain challenges that need to be managed. Generally speaking, the digital transformation is changing the world faster than many rules and regulations have evolved. Governments can benefit from mechanisms to periodically review their regulatory frameworks and, where appropriate, update them to ensure that they are well suited to the increasingly digitalised world.

Much of the information in this chapter is drawn from responses to the 2016 *OECD Digital Economy Outlook* (DEO) Policy Questionnaire. All OECD countries, as well as seven partner economies, submitted responses to at least one of the eight sections of the questionnaire.

Access and connectivity

The digital economy relies on efficient access to and effective use of communication infrastructures and services. In June 2016, discussions at the OECD Cancún Ministerial on the Digital Economy underlined policy makers' determination to improve high-speed communication infrastructures and services in ways that boost competitiveness and enable greater participation in the opportunities they create. A key challenge in this respect was assessing policies and regulation in light of convergence between formerly distinct sectors, such as telecommunication and broadcasting, and the need for different parts of government to work more closely together to meet challenges and seize opportunities posed by changes in communication markets.

This section is based on responses from all OECD countries and Colombia to the telecommunication section of the 2016 *OECD DEO* Policy Questionnaire. It reviews recent changes in communication policies, communication laws and regulatory frameworks, then discusses developments in convergence and the associated developments in market structures. It further examines changing responsibilities of communication regulators affected by convergence of the telecommunication and broadcasting sectors, and looks at interconnection between networks and the significant developments in international mobile roaming (IMR).

The key findings on access and connectivity are that convergence in the telecommunication and broadcasting markets is driving changes in regulatory approaches, including a move to more converged regulators and governments undertaking convergence reviews to reform regulation. There is a trend of adapting regulation, especially in fixed telecommunication markets, and towards infrastructure-sharing mechanisms and ensuring competition. The market has been found to largely self-regulate peering and transit agreements between Internet service providers (ISPs). In IMR, regulation is emerging to ensure competition exists through "roam like at home" (RLAH) offers, while at the same time some technological innovations are emerging as substitutes to regular international roaming services. In terms of developing the ICT sector itself, governments devote the largest focus on encouraging innovation in SMEs and start-ups, followed by supporting businesses to invest and export as ways to further their impact. The most commonly used policies are governmental funding projects or training programmes aimed at giving businesses the tools they need to innovate, followed by incubators and accelerators, which are hybrids combining both a monetary aspect along with a training component and are primarily directed at SMEs and start-ups.

Several OECD countries have adapted regulation and promoted infrastructure-sharing mechanisms

Over the past two years, communication policy makers and regulators have been active in furthering access to high-speed broadband networks and adapting regulatory frameworks. The following provides a brief overview of communication reviews as well as changes in policies and regulatory frameworks across OECD countries, the results of which are expected to be positive in spurring competition, innovation and investment in communication markets.

Several OECD countries are currently reviewing their regulatory frameworks, public policies and telecommunication laws. Overall, a trend towards streamlining regulation, mainly in the fixed telecommunication market, can be observed. Switzerland, for example, launched a public consultation on a partial revision of its telecommunication law, particularly to: 1) strengthen the consumer's position in the communication market and to better protect youth; 2) limit international roaming prices; 3) render the use of spectrum more flexible; 4) reduce administrative burdens for telecommunication operators; and 5) improve network access conditions for the different market players. Based on the consultation, the Swiss Federal Council tasked the Federal Department of the Environment, Transport, Energy and Communications to prepare a draft version of the Telecommunications Act by September 2017. Denmark has initiated a comprehensive review of public policy on electronic communication with stakeholder workshops and bilateral meetings. The review is planned to be concluded in 2017. The United Kingdom is carrying out a major review of the so-called General Conditions, i.e. the rules that all telecommunication companies have to meet in order to operate in the United Kingdom, with the aim to make conditions clearer, reduce the cost of compliance and lift regulation where rules are determined to be no longer necessary. In December 2016, the Swedish regulator, the Post and Telecom Authority, passed legislation to deregulate the fixed telephony market, putting in place a 12-month transitory period to fully enact the decision.

In September 2016, the European Union (EU) published its proposal to overhaul its telecommunication law, the European Electronic Communications Code (EC, 2016a), with the main objectives of increasing speed and coverage in the European Union. The new proposal foresees adjustments in areas such as next-generation access; spectrum licensing; and a co-ordinated approach in the European Union towards spectrum management, regulatory obligations for electronic communications services, including over-the-top (OTT) services, as well as must-carry and electronic programming guides. It further plans to increase the powers of the Body of European Regulators for Electronic Communications (BEREC). A further notable proposal in the directive is to amend numbering provisions in the machine-to-machine market. The proposal allows "national regulators to assign numbers to undertakings other than providers of electronic communications networks and services", a reform that has been highlighted in several OECD reports as one which could improve competition (OECD, 2012b; 2015b).

To further spur competition in communication markets and reduce costs, many countries are increasingly working on infrastructure-sharing provisions. For example, EU member states must transpose the European Union Broadband Cost Reduction Directive (2014/61/EU) into national law (European Parliament and European Council, 2014). The directive addresses infrastructure sharing, information sharing, and co-ordination of civil works between communication operators and utility operators to facilitate the roll-out of high-speed broadband networks. It enables ISPs to get access to the passive infrastructure of any other network provider. In this respect, Finland, Hungary, Ireland, Spain and Sweden, for example, have already enacted national legislation. The Czech Republic, Latvia and Slovenia are currently in the process of transposing the directive into national law. In Spain, practices such as passive infrastructure sharing have been one of the key factors in the increasing deployment of fibre to the premises and residences of business and consumers.

In mobile markets, OECD countries continue to open their 700 Megahertz (MHz) spectrum band, much valued by network operators for its propagation characteristics in providing improved services. In November 2015, France conducted an auction for the allocation of the 700 MHz band simultaneously on six lots of 5 MHz for an amount of 2.8 billion euros. Chile opened the band for commercial Long-term Evolution (LTE, a standard for high-speed mobile communications) services in May 2016. The three operators that won the spectrum license are obliged to cover 1 281 localities as well as 13 highways on a length of 850 kilometres. In 2017, Australia auctioned an additional 30 MHz of 700 MHz spectrum that was left unsold in a 2013 round. Finland undertook auction for the 700 MHz band in November 2016. The auction was a simultaneous multi-round auction whereby all spectrum blocks were auctioned at the same time. It was carried out over the Internet.[1] A total of six frequency pairs of 5 MHz each were auctioned and no more than two frequency pairs of 5 MHz were allocated to any individual organisation. Mexico licensed the 700 MHz band in the context of the creation of a 4G mobile wholesale access network, the *Red Compartida*. This network will be capable of being continually upgraded to the latest mobile technology releases, including 5G, once they are commercially available. Altán Redes won the auction, with a bid to cover 92.2% of the Mexican population by 2024. The company signed a public-private partnership (PPP) with Promtel formally initiating work towards establishing the wholesale broadband network, which will start operating in March 2018 with a minimum coverage of 30% of the country's population. The United Kingdom plans to make the 700 MHz spectrum band available for use across the entire country by 2022 at the latest, and the European Union plans to make the 700 MHz band available for wireless broadband by 2020.

Convergence contributes to revisions of regulatory frameworks and institutions

New players are offering audiovisual content delivery, spurring convergence in the telecommunication and broadcasting sectors

New services have blurred the contours of the telecommunication and broadcasting sectors, which were previously distinct. In turn, this has tested existing (legacy) regulatory and policy settings and encouraged a reconsideration of these frameworks. The emergence of OTT video service providers and the popularisation of triple- or quadruple-play service bundles, for example, have made decisions on issues such as must-carry/must-offer obligations and copyright and retransmission harder to allocate between formerly distinct regulatory realms.

There is an increasing diversity of distribution channels for audiovisual content in OECD countries. Most countries now have offers from public and commercial television broadcasters that include the option to watch broadcast content via the Internet, both in real time (linear online streaming) and in an on-demand, non-linear fashion (e.g. catch-up television). Offers vary in nature. While some provide real-time streaming only for subscribers, many offer linear streaming to the general public over the Internet (although these are often geo-restricted to the country or region of origin for copyright-related reasons). On-demand broadcast content is usually available for a limited time only and some providers require users to have a subscription for access.

Non-traditional players are also offering audiovisual content, especially through on-demand Internet platforms. However, as most OECD countries either do not regulate these services at all or regulate them very lightly,[2] most regulators have not systematically collected data on these services and rely mostly on data from private sources. Intellectual property is another evolving factor for audiovisual content. Historically, content developers have tried to segment these rights to different delivery platforms or performance windows. Acquisition of content by platforms (via recent or planned mergers or through deeper distribution agreements) may result in more innovative and flexible modes for consumers to enjoy content.

In Europe, as part of the Digital Single Market Strategy (EC, 2015), the European Commission adopted an amendment to the European Audio-visual and Media Services Directive in May 2016 and in September 2016 submitted a legislative proposal for a European Electronic Communications Code. That proposal would revise the five European directives[3] and two European Commission regulations and make them one single instrument. The revised European Audio-visual and Media Services Directive sets a new approach to online platforms (including those without editorial responsibility for content, such as video-sharing platforms) by prohibiting hate speech, protecting minors, promoting European works across all content platforms and proposing rules for more responsible video-sharing platforms (EC, 2016a). It further proposes subjecting OTTs to regulation only if they use numbering or are connected to the public switched telephone network, congruent with BEREC's taxonomy (BEREC, 2015). Regulators in EU member states would also be able to request information from OTTs.

Currently, most OECD countries have very few regulations concerning audiovisual content provision by OTTs (which do not provide a licensed or authorised audiovisual service). Definitions of video-on-demand (VoD) services within legal frameworks in the OECD usually encompass services provided to consumers via a licensed broadcasting undertaking. In Canada, for example, VoD licensees are required to adhere to various programming codes that also apply to broadcasters and there are provisions preventing vertically integrated broadcasters from making television programming available on an exclusive or otherwise preferential basis. In Europe, consistent with the current European Audio-visual and Media Services Directive,[4] notification from VoD providers can also be required, as in Hungary and the United Kingdom, which maintain national directories of all notified VoD service offerings.[5,6]

Convergence in the telecommunication and broadcasting sectors is a driver for mergers and acquisitions

This convergence between previously distinct parts of the communication industry is the main driver for mergers and acquisitions (M&As) in OECD countries. Between 2014 and 2016, mergers or acquisitions between cable network operators and mobile network operators (MNOs) featured prominently among the transactions with a market value of around USD 500 million or above (Annex 2.A1). However, as the case of Spain indicates, the trend towards convergence makes it harder for policy makers and regulators to assess outcomes (Box 2.1). Operators such as Vodafone purchased a number of fixed network operators while operators such as BT and Liberty Global purchased MNOs. In most cases the firms aim to offer a bundle of services, to benefit from the complimentary nature of the networks and to compete more effectively against rivals.

Box 2.1. **Mergers and market developments in Spain**

Between 2014 and 2016, there were several mergers at the core of the digital economy in Spain. The largest were between Vodafone and ONO, which was approved in July 2014, as well as between Orange and Jazztel, in May 2015. In the first case, Vodafone, the second-largest mobile operator, acquired ONO, the third-largest fixed network operator with its own cable network in most parts of Spain and a mobile virtual network operator (MVNO). In the second case, Orange, the third-largest mobile network operator and third-largest fixed network operator, acquired Jazztel, the fourth-largest fixed network operator. While both Orange and Jazztel primarily used unbundled local loops from Telefónica, they had also started significant investments in their own fibre networks. Jazztell also had an MVNO. This merger was approved by the European Commission with remedies that included:

- a bitstream wholesale offer to a competitor, using Orange's unbundled local loops access to Telefónica's fixed copper network, with cost-oriented prices, for a period of 4 + 4 years
- the sale to a competitor of a fibre network in five Spanish cities, which covered nearly 800 000 homes or commercial units
- ensuring that the competitor has wholesale mobile access in attractive commercial conditions (including 4G), for a period of 4+4 years.

Subsequently, in 2016, a merger was announced between MásMóvil, which has the fibre assets divested by Orange and Jazztel, and Yoigo, the fourth-largest mobile network operator, which was approved by the Spanish Competition Authority (Comisión Nacional de los Mercados y la Competencia [CNMC]) without imposing any commitment on the merging parties. Additionally, in 2015 Telefónica acquired DTS, the main satellite pay TV operator in Spain. As a result of this acquisition, Telefónica increased its already high market share in pay TV, as its premium content is the key to selling bundles in Spain. The agreement to an increased concentration of ownership was subject to several commitments to promote competition, such as the provision of a premium channel offer.

In October 2016, AT&T announced its intention to buy Time Warner for USD 85 billion. If approved by authorities, this will be one of the biggest upcoming M&As. Cable networks continue to merge with regional operators in countries such as Germany and the United States, while MNOs competing in the same market merged in Germany, Ireland and Italy. Meanwhile, in 2016, MNO mergers did not proceed in Denmark and the United Kingdom, where new entrants did not emerge from remedy negotiations.

Regulatory authorities have applied remedies or required conditions on many of these mergers. Sometimes approvals were subject to a divestment of part of the newly merged entity, such as in Belgium for the Liberty Global and Base case. In other cases, such as the one in Canada involving Shaw Communications, the fact that Shaw did not previously own a mobile network meant that authorities assessed there was no need to oppose the transaction. It was also noted that approval would not result in any change in spectrum concentration and accordingly no remedies were applied to this transaction.

In approving MNO mergers, authorities impose a number of conditions, including the divestment of spectrum or facilities (e.g. towers) to open possibilities for new MNOs or an undertaking from the merged player to offer wholesale access to mobile virtual network operators (MVNOs) and so forth. In OECD countries, remedies applied in more recent mergers appear to be more pro-competitive in terms of their goals than the remedies applied in earlier cases. This may indicate that remedies applied in earlier cases did not meet initial expectations in terms of emergence of MVNOs in merged markets, or of developments in prices and investment.

In the area of fixed networks, regulatory authorities also applied a number of conditions before approving mergers. In Portugal, authorities required divestment of network operators. In the United States, as a condition of approving the AT&T and DirecTV merger, the new entity was required by the Federal Communications Commission (FCC) to deploy fibre to the premises network facilities to 12.5 million mass market locations within four years of the merger's closing date.

Following a merger or acquisition approval, OECD countries take a number of different approaches to assessing or monitoring market developments. When specific conditions are imposed, the merged entity will generally have to report on fulfilling those remedies. While not all authorities conduct specific post-merger reviews, they are common in a number of countries. For example, Austria's Federal Competition Authority and the Austrian Regulatory Authority for Broadcasting and Telecommunications published two reports assessing the effects of the merger between Hutchison 3G Austria and Orange Austria that took place in 2012.

One question that arises in a post-merger case or in general monitoring of market developments is whether regulatory authorities have the information they need to assess outcomes. Assessing compliance with a precise remedy may be less challenging than assessing general outcomes such as effects on prices and investment, even though proponents of mergers often hold out more effective competition and incentives for investment as a reason for requesting approval. A further consideration for assessments is the increasing use of shared network facilities between MNOs and its potential influence on investment, particularly when this is combined with MNO mergers.

Several countries are undertaking convergence reviews to reform regulatory frameworks in light of the changing market

As communication services continue to evolve and the use of OTT services grows, a number of governments have been carrying out convergence reviews to evaluate whether different services should be brought under the same framework. In some cases, specific units have been created to ensure that policy makers have the necessary information to take informed decisions. In Australia, the government created a Bureau of Communications Research, a unit of the Department of Communications responsible for assessing new convergence trends in the communication sector. In October 2016, the bureau released a report analysing recent communication trends in that country, such as the increased demand for faster Internet services, the disruption of traditional broadcasting business models by increased demand for OTT services and local content costs, and a growth in content produced in Australia due to new entrants and platforms. The Australian Competition and Consumer Commission also announced a study on the communications market in Australia, which will examine network capacity, access to dark (unused) fibre and OTT services development. The results will be issued in 2017.

In Spain, the competition authority (Comisión Nacional de los Mercados y la Competencia [CNMC]) released a report in 2015 on the use of OTT services, which found that the main exceptions were more frequent use of messaging applications on mobile connexions (76% use in mobile against 43% in fixed) and for downloading of audiovisual content (38% of those using fixed connexions and 21% using mobile) (CNMC, 2015). Similarly, the Danish Agency for Culture published a Media Development Report in 2015 with data and analysis on the use of media on different platforms over time in that country (Danish Agency for Culture and Palaces, 2015). In 2015, New Zealand commenced the implementation of a cross-government work programme on convergence. The programme entailed an exercise to increase the understanding of issues such as content standards, taxation and the development of creative industries (MBIE and MCH, 2015). As a result of the exercise, certain programmes were designed, some of which are part of New Zealand's Business Growth Agenda (MBIE, 2015). In the United Kingdom, Ofcom is conducting a Digital Convergence Review, which led to an interim report in February 2016 that set out the focus of the United Kingdom's future convergence strategy and defined the process of deregulation in some cases (Ofcom, 2016).

In some countries, proposals for upcoming work on the issues around convergence are set out in the work programmes of relevant agencies. For example, the Canadian Radio-television and Telecommunications Commission's (CRTC) strategic plan for 2016-19 revolves around the main pillars of connecting Canada with accessible, innovative and quality communication services, creating more local content and protecting users (CRTC, 2016). Korea is undergoing a similar process through the development of its Communications Commission's overall plan for 2017-19.

Some countries have created converged regulators who have responsibility for both the telecommunication and broadcasting sectors

To encourage a more coherent regulatory approach, an increasing number of countries have reformed their communication authorities and adopted a converged structure that integrates both the telecommunication and audiovisual sectors.

Some of the benefits of establishing a converged regulator have included:

- a one-stop shop for the industry and consumers
- better enforcement and coherence among the different regulatory areas (e.g. audiovisual services, networks, communication services)
- the ability to examine the full value chain from networks to content, undertake comprehensive competition analysis, identify possible leverage of market power in neighbouring markets (bundling issues) and evaluate concerns from content standards to exclusive dealing, whereby upstream providers foreclose competing companies downstream
- cost savings, with the caveat that actual savings are dependent on the resulting structure and functioning of a converged regulator.

Most recently, in 2013, Mexico, Slovenia and Spain reformed their communication regulatory authorities to introduce a converged structure. These countries add to the list of those that had already adopted some features of a converged structure, such as Australia, Austria, Canada, Estonia, Finland, Hungary, Italy, Korea, Switzerland, the United Kingdom and the United States. The so-called "converged regulators", which vary substantially in their structure and capacity, now total 13 among OECD countries (see Annex 2.A2).

Interconnection rates and approaches to Internet traffic exchange remain areas of interest

Termination rates have declined in recent years, with some exceptions

Interconnection rates such as mobile termination rates and fixed termination rates apply to telecommunication operators providing telephony service. In OECD countries, mobile termination rates for all mobile operators (MNOs and MVNOs) generally apply. In the case of fixed operators, mobile termination rates can apply to all of them, as in Finland, Germany and Spain, or only to operators holding significant market power, as in Belgium, Denmark and Ireland.

The interconnection rates and the methodology used to update termination rates are dependent on the regulatory authority. In the United States, interstate and intrastate intercarrier charges for exchanged traffic can vary by carrier, although most rates were capped in 2011 and many terminating rates either have been or are being transitioned to bill-and-keep. In Europe, some countries use a market analysis and national consultation to elaborate a proposal for changes in the termination rates. For EU member states, such proposals must be submitted to the European Commission. In Colombia, interconnection rates are negotiated by operators in their contracts but need prior approval of an initial reference offer by the regulator (Comisión de Regulación de Comunicaciones [CRC]).

Outside the OECD area, international termination rates continue to be a concern in countries where the government establishes a cartel and applies a uniform surcharge on incoming telephone calls (OECD, 2014a). International termination rates have also drawn attention among OECD countries, with some concerned that the rates do not reflect a cost-oriented approach. In the European Union, since 1 January 2016, some regulators have begun to allow mobile operators to treat the international termination rate differently from the national termination one. Subsequently, prices change frequently (e.g. almost on a monthly basis), leading to tensions between European mobile operators and their counterparts. As Swiss operators, for example, are no longer offered the "European tariff", this has been said to have undermined relations between MNOs.

Outside of Europe these developments have drawn the attention of the Office of the United States Trade Representative (USTR). According to the USTR, several operators within the European Union are charging higher rates for the termination of international traffic originating from outside that area than they are for traffic that originates within member states. This creates a two-tiered approach for termination, which the USTR says does not appear to reflect incremental costs for termination of such traffic.

The questions raised by the USTR were familiar ones between OECD countries in the days when the international accounting rate system was used between operators in different countries, most of which had monopolies. This system was largely superseded once telecommunication markets were liberalised and competition was able to drive rates closer to cost. Nonetheless, as regulators around the world recognise, every network operator potentially has a degree of monopoly power in terminating traffic to their own customers and, as such, the same vigilance applied to domestic rates should also apply to international rates.

Peering and transit between Internet service providers is largely self-regulated by the market

The interconnection of ISPs and the terms in which traffic is exchanged among them is an area largely self-regulated by market players. Recent market developments, in particular peering and transit disputes between market players, such as the Netflix-Comcast cases in the United States, have led to the debates becoming a matter of public record. In 2015, the regulatory agency in the Netherlands analysed seven prominent international disputes and concluded that in all cases except one some form of actual restrictive interconnection behaviour caused the dispute to arise, though it did not generally find actions it would describe as "anticompetitive" (ACM, 2015). It further noted that consumer harm would only arise in a situation where there was not enough interconnection capacity between the parties involved, something it had not identified in the Netherlands. The Autorité de régulation des communications électroniques et des postes (ARCEP), the communication regulatory agency of France, has also begun an administrative inquiry to clarify technical and financial conditions of interconnection between ISPs and content providers as well as between operators.

Communication regulators do not generally collect information on IP interconnection agreements because they are not subject to direct regulation. In most countries, the operator's decision on whether and how to connect is driven by competitive market forces rather than by government regulation. However, national regulators have, by law, the authority to request such information in most cases. Some countries have specific requirements to send interconnection agreements to the relevant ministry or regulator, as in the Czech Republic and Korea. In March 2012, ARCEP decided to collect information on technical and pricing conditions for interconnection and data routing. The analysis of these interconnection data collected regularly for the period 2012-2016 was published for the first time in the report of 30 May 2017 on the state of the Internet in France (ARCEP, 2017).

Recent developments related to M&A have highlighted the importance given by regulators to interconnection. In the Charter Communications acquisition of Time Warner Cable and Bright House Network in the United States, the FCC imposed an obligation on the resulting operator to make interconnection available on a non-discriminatory, settlement-free basis to companies that meet basic criteria, something other commercial players say is consistent with both companies' previous practices. Other conditions include addressing data caps, usage-based pricing for residential broadband, residential broadband build-out and more. In the same case, the Justice Department also examined whether the merger would allow the resulting company to become an unavoidable gatekeeper for Internet-based services, including online video distribution, that rely on a broadband connection to reach consumers.

International mobile roaming is evolving, influenced by innovation, competition and regulation

Technological innovations are emerging as partial substitutes to regular international mobile roaming services, but competition is driving the greatest change

The IMR market continues to be transformed in OECD countries. Key factors driving this trend include technological change, commercial responses to increased demand and regulation (where competition has been determined to be insufficient). Furthermore, there is an ever-increasing range of technologies that allow consumers to bypass traditional IMR if they are willing to accept a degree of imperfect substitution. These technological paths, in one way or another, substitute the services of a home country provider, such as the complete substitution of an operator-specific SIM by one from an intermediary, such as Apple (Bourassa et al., 2016).

Over time, some of the technological alternatives to the use of conventional IMR services are overcoming aspects of imperfect substitution. An example is the Interphone sticker, which was introduced in September 2016. It enables the use of virtual SIMs from operators in participating countries, but critically enables the retention of a home country mobile number for incoming calls.[7] That being said, while the rates in such an approach may be far lower than regular roaming, they tend to be much higher than obtaining a local SIM. On the other hand, if a user is willing to forego his or her mobile number and rely on data-only services, the emerging options are more propitious. Users of the Apple SIM on an iPad, for example, can select and pay local rates from two or more operators when visiting countries such as Japan and the United States without the need to insert a local SIM from the country. At the end of the day, however, all substitutes for SIMs from either the origin or the destination country rely on competitive markets. In other words, SIMs need to be unlocked for foreign use and there need to be participating operators in the visited country (i.e. without direct access to local rates, charges are higher than local rates via intermediaries).

The most widely used technological substitution for regular IMR services is Wi-Fi. In the past, while this option enabled access to data services and use of OTT telephony, it still had limitations in terms of the use of a regular mobile number. This is also changing; in March 2016, AT&T began to allow customers to use Wi-Fi when calling from abroad. These calls do not incur IMR charges, but rather the charges associated with the customers' regular service plans. Offers called RLAH, appearing in an increasing number of countries, go a step farther. RLAH offers have become increasingly commonplace in countries such as France, Israel, Mexico, the United Kingdom and the United States and became mandatory within European Economic Area (EEA) countries from 15 June 2017, though they are conspicuously absent in many countries (see Annex 2.A3).

Regulation is emerging to ensure competition in international mobile roaming and affordable prices to the end user

The other substantial developments in IMR have been in the area of regulation. In Mexico, for example, the emergence of RLAH offers coincided with new market entry enabled by the lifting of foreign investment barriers. A further notable feature of the Mexican market, though believed to be nascent in its potential use, has been the introduction of MVNOs and the ability of those players to directly negotiate their own direct international roaming agreements. In many countries MVNOs do not have this ability and action to overcome such barriers could provide an additional option for countries that find that insufficient competition is developing in the IMR market.

The highest profile regulatory changes have undoubtedly been those in the European Union. In November 2015, the European Parliament and Council reached agreement on the Telecoms Single Market (TSM) (Regulation EU 2015/2120; European Parliament and European Council [2015]), which set out a timetable for further reductions in intra-EU retail roaming caps in April 2016 (to EUR 0.05 per minute for outgoing calls, EUR 0.02 per SMS and EUR 0.05 per megabyte of data). It also required RLAH to be subject to fair use criteria (to ensure that only periodic roaming would have to be covered) and sustainability criteria (to allow, in exceptional cases, a derogation from RLAH if roaming costs were not covered). The European Union approved a Fair Use Policy in December 2016, which details regulations to ensure the effective application of RLAH offers and to make certain that the most competitive domestic offers remain competitive (EC, 2016b). In January 2017, the European Union agreed upon a set of wholesale roaming rules defining the rates which EU operators can charge one another for use of their respective networks abroad, a final step to ensure the introduction of RLAH for periodic roaming by 15 June 2017 (EC, 2016c).

The TSM regulation followed three years after the previous roaming regulation (Roaming III), which came into force on 1 July 2012. In summary, that regulation had extended anti-bill shock and transparency mechanisms (including the EUR 50 data cap) to EU roamers travelling beyond the European Union's borders and introduced retail caps for data for the first time, as in other countries like Canada. In Canada, the CRTC's 2013 Wireless Code placed an automatic cap on international data roaming charges at USD 76 within a single billing cycle unless the customer explicitly agreed to pay additional charges. The TSM also established a mechanism for introducing structural solutions to decouple regulated mobile roaming services from domestic services, which were set out in European Union implementing acts following a consultation of BEREC and also provided for BEREC guidelines on wholesale access.

The European Union's regulatory initiatives in the IMR market have provided a benchmark for many countries and have shown the role that regional bodies can play in significantly reducing prices and creating competition in IMR services. Israel, for example, used the European Union prices for bilateral agreements with Poland and the Russian Federation. Regional regulatory bodies are also active in this area, though they generally do not have the powers available to the European Union.

In the future, bilateral agreements should lead to price reductions and provide a paradigm for other countries to follow suit where there is insufficient competition (Bourassa et al., 2016). Some of these bilateral agreements have been undertaken between countries with free-trade agreements (FTAs) and could provide a framework to follow for other regions with FTAs. They could also help alleviate some concerns that bilateral or regional agreements may have to be opened up to third parties as part of most-favoured-nation obligations. Australia and Singapore updated and signed their FTA in October 2016.[8] A key element of this agreement deals with IMR between the two countries. Notably, the agreement provides that either country, if it sees fit, may regulate wholesale rates and make these rates available to mobile operators from the other country. That being said, both countries subsequently had spectrum auctions that will lead to the introduction of a fourth MNO in each of their respective markets. Moreover, the same company (TPG) won the auctions to provide the new MNO in both countries. As such, the new entrant, looking to attract customers, is well placed to differentiate its services by offering improved roaming between these markets. If it does so, the tools available via the FTA may not be required. On the other hand, if competition does not address the high IMR rates between the two countries, authorities now have a regulatory mechanism to address this issue.

ICT sector development support is focused on training programmes and measures to spur innovation

The most commonly used policies are government-funded innovation measures and training programmes

All countries surveyed for this edition of the DEO have policies to support the growth of the ICT sector. Most target innovation, investment or exports. Thirty-five of the 38 countries[9] that responded to the ICT sector development section of the 2016 *OECD DEO* Policy Questionnaire reported having at least one policy that specifically supports innovation, compared to 24 with measures directed at expanding firm exports, 22 with policies that promote ICT sector investment and 15 with policies related to other ICT sector development (Figure 2.1). Comparatively, innovation policies seem to hold greater importance, as countries had 95 distinct policies to promote innovation in the ICT sector, as opposed to investment and exports, which had 54 and 48 policies, respectively.[10]

This support is delivered through a variety of conduits, including tax incentives, loans, research and development (R&D) subsidies, export subsidies, block grants, and educational training programmes. Of all the policies reported by countries in the survey, 35% targeted SMEs and start-ups, while 22% were focused on companies in the ICT sector, 17% were open to all companies and the remaining 26% had other firm requirements.

Figure 2.1. **Policies to support ICT sector growth**

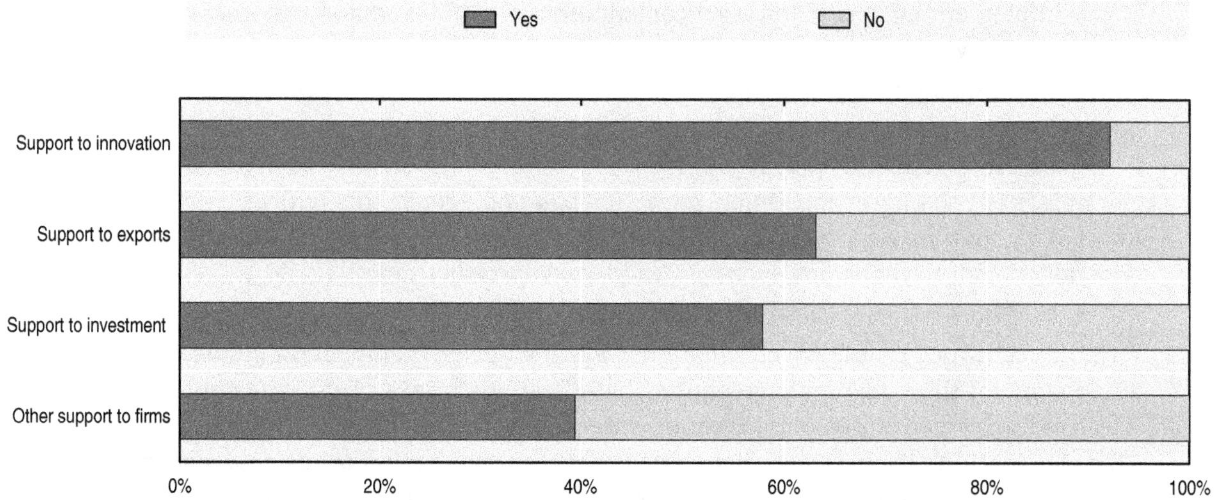

Note: The total number of respondents for this question is 38. See note 9 at the end of the chapter for the list of countries.

StatLink http://dx.doi.org/10.1787/888933584507

The most prevalent governmental policy measure to strengthen the ICT sector is funding, which may include subsidies for companies to undertake further investment in infrastructure or R&D, or to encourage exports (Figure 2.2). Governmental funding programmes support ICT sector growth in 95% (36 out of 38) of the surveyed countries. As an example, Austria's ICT of the Future programme provides financial support to companies that explore new ICT research topics and possible associated applications, and to encourage development based on these topics.[11] Mexico and Turkey also offer subsidies to specific industries to encourage exports. Another form of governmental funding is through a venture capital (VC) fund, as is seen in the Czech Republic and Estonia.[12]

Government-sponsored training programmes are also commonly seen as a way to develop expertise in ICT and thereby to promote innovation. These projects may be aimed at developing knowledge, sharing experiences and creating best practices, or providing expertise on a subject so that local firms can better compete in the market. For instance, the United Kingdom offers education materials on social media sales to businesses to improve their social commerce skills, while the Switzerland Global Enterprise and Spain's Tech Center both advise companies on export promotion. The People's Republic of China (hereafter "China"), Colombia and Finland are other countries which have implemented training programmes directed to the development of the ICT sector. Seventeen countries in the survey had some form of training programme, making it the second most common ICT policy after funding. Additionally, 14 countries offer a mixed policy approach, which often includes a training component in conjunction with other types mentioned above, like grants, subsidies, loans or tax exemptions.

Figure 2.2. **Policy initiatives to support ICT sector growth**

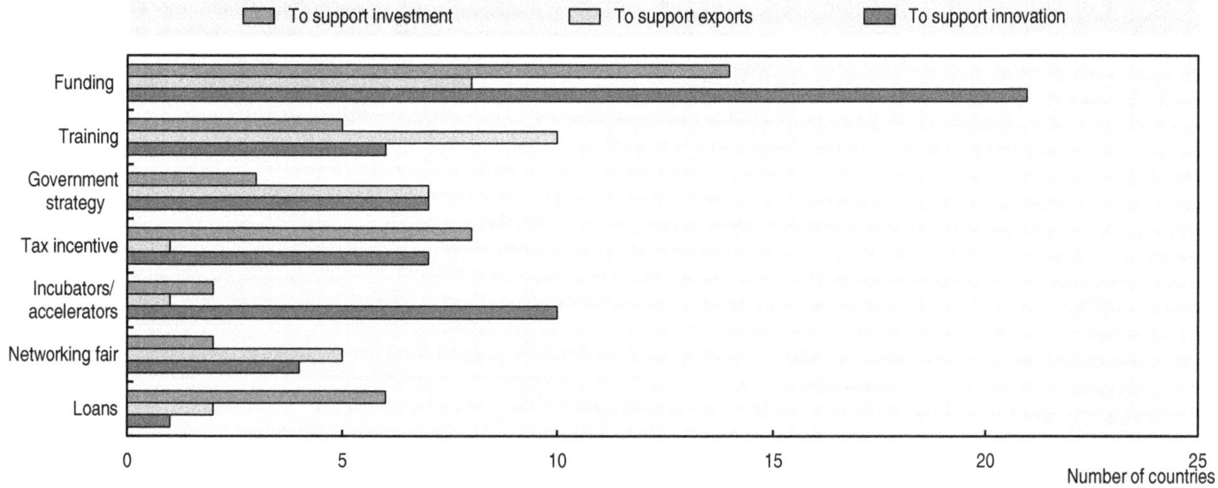

StatLink http://dx.doi.org/10.1787/888933584526

Incubators and accelerators are popular tools to promote innovation in ICT start-ups and small and medium-sized enterprises

Several governments, in an effort to promote innovation, have launched initiatives aimed at helping start-ups or young SMEs through accelerators or incubators. Fifteen of the 38 respondent countries have such initiatives, making it the third most common ICT policy. While both accelerators and incubators share the same aim – to help starting businesses grow – their methods differ. Both types of institutions rely on a network of entrepreneurs to promote synergies and learning from other members, as well as some sort of mentorship, but accelerators also provide intensive education along with seed funding for the selected businesses in exchange for taking ownership of a share of the business. Given this initial investment, the competition is fierce for a spot in an accelerator's portfolio, and the intensive period of education and mentorship usually culminates in a "Demo Day" after a few months (Hathaway, 2016). Among the governments that have taken this approach, for instance, the United Kingdom has set up the HutZero programme, which is an early-stage accelerator focused on cybersecurity. The programme offers an intensive period of business education and mentorship.[13] Another example is Luxembourg's Fit4Start programme, which accepts start-ups to make up a cohort two times per year with the winning start-ups having access to EUR 50 000 in funding in addition to "lean start-up" training and coaching to prepare the cohort for a final pitch at the end of four months.[14] Brazil, France and Israel have similar programmes for start-ups and early-stage SMEs.

Other governments have adopted the approach of hosting an incubator in their country. An incubator usually charges its members a fee for access to shared office space, educational services and mentorship opportunities. The duration of the membership, from one to five years, is often longer than with an accelerator and the selection process is much less competitive (Table 2.1). In Denmark, the Danish Agency for Science, Technology and Innovation, together with the Ministry of Higher Education and Science, has launched the Innovation Incubator Scheme to help encourage start-ups early in their business development.[15] Hungary, Latvia and Portugal have similar projects. Some governments, like Israel[16] and Singapore, have recognised the value of these organisations for start-ups and have offered support. The Singaporean government's Incubator Development Programme provides grant support of up to 70% of costs to enhance the capabilities of incubators and venture accelerators to assist and grow innovative start-ups in the country. However, the "business models" of these government-sponsored initiatives differ from their private sector counterparts. For instance, a government's seed investment often does not result in partial ownership in the company once it has "graduated", nor do chosen companies usually have to pay membership fees to partake in the incubator scheme.

Table 2.1. **Main characteristics of incubators and accelerators**

	Incubators	Accelerators
Duration	One to five years	Three to six months
Cohorts	No	Yes
Business model	Rent; non-profit	Investment; can also be non-profit
Selection	Non-competitive	Competitive, cyclical
Venture stage	From early to late	Early
Education	*Ad hoc*, human resources, legal	Seminars
Mentorship	Minimal, tactical	Intense, by self and others
Venture location	On-site	On-site

Source: Hathaway, I. (2016), "What start-up accelerators really do", *https://hbr.org/2016/03/what-startup-accelerators-really-do*.

Canada encourages both accelerators and incubators through the Canada Accelerator and Incubator Program (CAIP). In 2013-15, CAIP provided approximately USD 80 million over five years to outstanding business accelerators and business incubators. The funds are non-repayable. The Industrial Research Assistance Program collects data annually and will evaluate CAIP's outcome after its completion in 2019-20. Other governments, such as Lithuania and Norway, have programmes where the government acts as a guarantor for start-up companies or SMEs to facilitate access to finance in their early development stages. For example, the Czech Republic, France, Italy, Latvia and Mexico offer governmental loans, some of which have preferential grace periods and interest rates, to companies.

Tax incentives are another tool used by policy makers from 15 of the countries surveyed. Brazil, for instance, offers tax breaks to investors who have bought debt issued by telecommunication operators to finance broadband infrastructure projects, as well as to the operators themselves who have investment projects to expand or modernise telecommunication networks. Other countries allow companies to depreciate the value of goods above the normal rate of depreciation; in Italy, for example, companies can depreciate new capital goods at a rate of 140% and high-tech purchases such as nanotechnologies, big data and smart materials up to a rate of 250%. Costa Rica, Lithuania, Sweden and Turkey also offer various forms of tax exemptions. Finally, many governments establish high-level strategies as a way to support ICT development at a broader scale, for instance in digital or innovation strategies.

Usage and skills

This section provides information on policies and regulation for increasing ICT usage by individuals, firms and governments, as well as for enhancing ICT skills. The discussion is based on responses from 38 countries.[17] There is strong evidence that the use of ICTs drives innovation, which can enhance productivity and competitiveness (OECD, 2016a). ICTs help reduce transaction costs and enhance the scope of communication with the different stakeholders of an organisation. That enables, for instance, faster creation and diffusion of ideas and knowledge, both within and between organisations, which can translate into benefits such as enhanced collaboration during R&D activities. The use of ICTs can also enable greater product differentiation, enhance customer relationships and improve supply-chain management. All of that can ultimately lead to an increase in productivity and higher market shares (OECD, 2016a).

ICT-related skills are another key enabler of digital innovation. This is confirmed by business innovation surveys showing that firms using internal or external skills related to ICTs and data are more likely to innovate.[18] In most countries for which data are available, around 60% of the innovative firms employ software developers and around 40% employ mathematicians, statisticians and database managers (compared to around 30% and 20% respectively for non-innovative firms) (OECD, 2016a).

ICT usage is being promoted through e-government, training programmes and subsidies

Most of the potential value brought by digitalisation lies in the adoption and use of ICTs. For companies, ICTs connect businesses to digitally managed global value chains and offer a platform for selling to customers worldwide. This allows firms to scale up quickly and in some cases to compete on a national or even a global scale. In areas where there are obstacles to accessing knowledge, such as some rural areas, the Internet is an important source of information supporting business innovation and knowledge accumulation. ICT applications, ranging from basic accounting or inventory applications for smaller companies to more complex services such as customer relationship management software or enterprise resource planning systems for larger ones, render business processes more efficient. Overall, the Internet and ICTs drive firm productivity and reduce barriers to market entry.

Several studies have analysed the link between ICT adoption, firm performance and the contribution to economic growth and have been able to demonstrate the positive effects of greater ICT adoption on firms' productivity, performance and the economy as a whole (e.g. Gaggle and Wright, 2014; Grazzi and Jung, 2016; Haller and Siedschlag, 2011). Grazzi and Jung (2016) were also able to demonstrate that firms that adopt broadband are more likely to innovate.

Policies to promote ICT use by individuals and firms include, for example, financial support to households and individuals for purchasing ICT goods or services, support to firms for ICT investment and expenditures, and the promotion of e-government services.

Of the 38 countries that responded to the ICT usage section of the questionnaire, almost all had at least one policy in place to increase the use of ICT tools in the public administration and governmental services, reflecting governments' priority to become more digital. Thirty-five governments reported having policies to encourage the use of ICTs in businesses, along with 33 that had policies directed at increasing usage among individuals (Figure 2.3). However, when analysing the actual policies themselves, the priority for governments seemed to be increasing the use of ICTs within their own administrations rather than encouraging businesses and individuals to use ICTs. This is exemplified by the total number of policies reported for each target group: over 390 policies were reported to improve ICT use within governmental bodies, in contrast to 104 for individuals and households, and just over 120 directed to businesses. One point that must be acknowledged is that many of the policies reported as encouraging usage among businesses were actually focused on aiding innovative ICT companies (which was discussed above), rather than encouraging all types of companies to adopt the use of ICTs in their work processes. Therefore, since such policies have already been explored, they are omitted from the analysis here, leaving only those policies directly related to increasing ICT usage by businesses more generally. As said above, given the volume of policies in support of ICT usage in the public administration, governments seem to place less priority on encouraging households and businesses to incorporate ICT technology more systematically. Alternatively, it is possible that governments are seeking to achieve higher uptake of ICTs by households and businesses through more general business, framework and investment policies.

Figure 2.3. **Policies to support ICT usage**

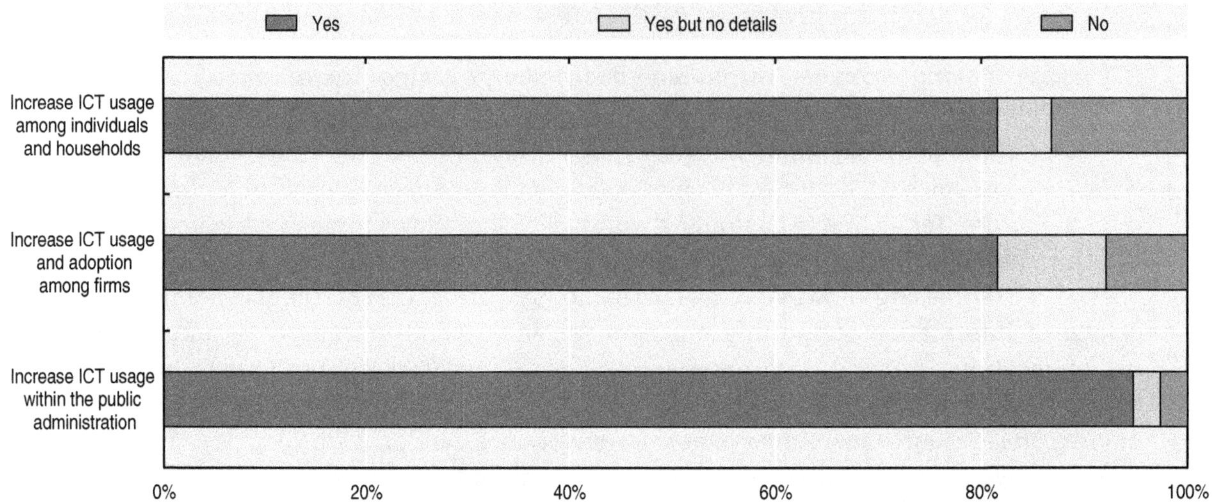

Notes: The "Yes but no details" category is shown separately from the "Yes" category simply to reflect that the fact that some countries indicated that they have such a policy, but they did not provide any supporting or verifiable details. The total number of respondents for this question is 38. See note 17 at the end of the chapter for the list of countries. ICT = information and communication technology.

StatLink http://dx.doi.org/10.1787/888933584545

The key findings for this section are that governments are focusing on becoming digital by incorporating ICT tools internally as well as offering services online for individuals and businesses. Online handling of governmental administrative requests is the most common e-service offered and includes tax declarations, updating personal information and the civil registry, and consular services. Many governments also have policies to share public sector information (PSI) through open data portals. Policies aimed directly at increasing the usage of ICT tools by individuals and firms are secondary to improving ICT usage in the public administration; however, among those offered, training and subsidies are most commonly used for both individuals and businesses.

Governments are offering their services online and focusing on becoming more efficient through the use of ICT tools

Policies to promote the adoption of ICTs by public administrations can be split broadly into three categories: the first involves creating or promoting e-government services for individuals; the second involves creating or promoting e-government services for firms; and the third is focused on improving the internal functioning of governments themselves and making them more transparent through the public availability of information. Each of these categories is given roughly equal priority in terms of the number of policies (Figure 2.4).

Figure 2.4. **Policies to promote ICT adoption by public administrations**

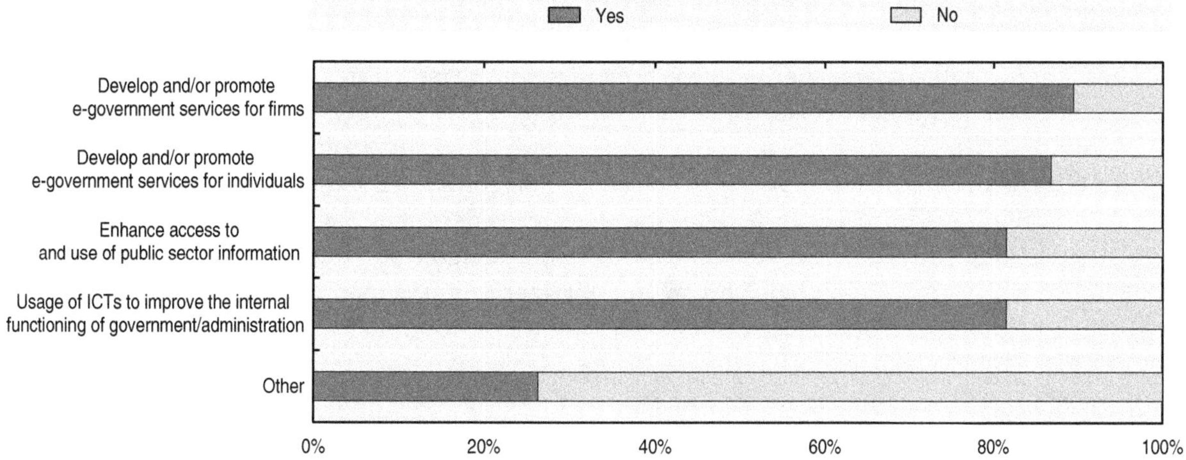

Notes: The total number of respondents for this question is 38. See note 17 at the end of the chapter for the list of countries. ICT = information and communication technology.

StatLink http://dx.doi.org/10.1787/888933584564

Policies to develop or promote e-government services for individuals and households are aimed overall at bringing governmental services for citizens online. This includes allowing citizens to pay their taxes, submit various forms and update their personal information online. Eighty-seven per cent of the countries surveyed have a policy of this type. By way of example, Colombia has several initiatives to migrate paper-based forms online; these include having a digital registry to track and update civil registration, medical records, and electronic documentation of education and military service. Colombia has also made some consular services available online, including for the issuance and renewal of passports. Switzerland has implemented an electronic voting system for voters abroad, and a few cantons have recently begun to offer this option for Swiss residents. Austria, Israel, Korea and Portugal are other examples of countries which offer various e-services for citizens. Along the same line of making governmental services more efficient by going digital, many governments have converted to solely digital media to communicate with citizens. Norway has adopted a "digital-by-default" approach, forcing citizens to actively choose to receive paper mail in lieu of receiving communication digitally via a secure digital mailbox. Austria and Lithuania have similar programmes for digital communication.

Given that many of these e-services include the transfer of personal data, some countries (slightly less than a quarter of those surveyed) have developed e-ID and e-authentication services to make these online services more secure. Policies specifically related to digital security and privacy are discussed in more detail later in this chapter, as well as in OECD (2016a). Therefore, the policies represented here may not be fully representative of all the security initiatives that countries have put in place.

Over half of the countries that responded to the survey have created a website to communicate relevant information related to the e-services provided by the government. Information dissemination and awareness of available e-tools is integral to stimulate further use of e-government services among citizens. It is also important that the site be easily navigable and that users can find related information on services. Several countries have "one-stop" websites, and some, such as Korea and Slovenia, even offer their websites in multiple languages to be accessible to foreigners living in the country.

Similar policies are directed towards firms. For instance, web portals for a "one-stop" point for e-government information and online submission of forms are also offered for businesses. Given that they often reduce the governmental administration burden both for firms and governments, it is no surprise that these services are also available to businesses. Online submission of forms, including online tax services, is by far the most common policy directed towards businesses, with 31 of the 38 countries having such a policy. Many countries allow all paperwork to be completed electronically for official registration as a legal entity (Latvia, the Russian Federation, Spain and Switzerland). Other examples of e-forms specifically for firms include e-invoicing for government suppliers (Belgium, Colombia, Norway and Switzerland); online licensing systems (the Czech Republic and Singapore); and online tax declaration, including value-added tax (VAT) and customs declaration (Israel, Korea, Mexico and Switzerland, among others). One-third of the countries surveyed have "one-stop" portals directed towards business users which contain more specialised information related to the establishment and registration of a legal business entity and provide links to access the required online forms. Austria, Denmark, Finland, Portugal and Spain are among the countries that offer such online business portals.

Unique to e-services for businesses is the large number of governmental processes directed towards a single online platform for public procurement. Such portals integrate all of a government's buying and selling across governmental entities in one place. By making all government procurement specifications available via the Internet, companies have equal access to information, making the public procurement system more transparent. Japan's "Government Electronic Procurement System" provides a good example of the various digital procedures incorporated within the e-public procurement process, including the public notice of specification, bid, open bill, conclusion of contract, performance evaluation on contract and payment. Just under half of the countries surveyed have such public procurement processes online, including many EU countries, Costa Rica, Korea, Singapore, Switzerland and Turkey.

Approximately one-third of governments are also reviewing the e-services available to firms in an effort to make internal processing of business administration more efficient and to reduce the regulatory burden where possible. This often entails sharing information among governmental offices more seamlessly, offering integrated services for business, and allowing firms to comment and file complaints with governmental services as a feedback loop to drive further improvements. Slovenia has established a Single Business Point, which aims to reduce the number and volume of data required of firms for reporting purposes and is in the process of a review to further reduce administrative burdens and simplify regulatory procedures. Canada has a number of initiatives to make internal processing more efficient for businesses. The Canada Revenue Agency is establishing a standard identifier for businesses to be recognised across the government. It is also implementing several service transformation initiatives such as single sign-on, real-time status updates and e-payments. In addition, to facilitate digital transformation, Innovation, Science and Economic Development Canada (ISED) is implementing a department-wide strategy to deliver innovative, integrated client-centric digital services to improve the ways in which businesses can access government services. Through this initiative, ISED aims to work closely with the Federal, Provincial, Territorial and Municipal partners to better engage clients. Brazil, the Netherlands and Singapore are additional examples of countries that are reforming their internal processes.

Open data portals and legislation for access to public sector information aim to improve transparency

The theme of governments "going digital" is central to policies aimed at improving internal governmental functioning, with over 80% of respondents reporting at least one policy to support the digitalisation of governmental functions. While related to the digitalisation efforts highlighted in the paragraphs above, these policies are more focused on bringing governmental documents and registries online, keeping them up to date and easy to find and access, and promoting zero paper policies through digital communication. Some examples of such processes include the Czech Republic's electronic legislative library, which enables tracking of legislative documents, monitoring of comments and the secure storage of all versions. China and Costa Rica have implemented zero paper policies, while Canada, Japan and Poland have put in place electronic documentation management for the exchange, update and version control of electronic documents, as well as the disposal of obsolete documents within the public administration.

Sharing information between ministries is also a common theme. Approximately 60% of governments have policies to increase internal information sharing and collaboration, which includes ensuring interoperability between governmental platforms. By way of example, Colombia's Interoperability Framework is an effort to help the state function as a single institution, and establishes a common interoperable platform for the seamless exchange of information. The Information Management Framework in Norway defines the data responsibilities of each agency, and is establishing a common framework to integrate the data from various agencies to create a common data directory. Finland, Israel, Luxembourg and the Russian Federation have similar policies in place.

Thirty-one of the 38 governments surveyed reported having at least one policy in place to increase public access to governmental information. These open data programmes have a dual aim: the first is to promote transparency and accountability within the government by making information available to the public. Chile offers an example of an open data initiative with such an aim, as it allows access to the public sector budget through its "Open Budget" platform. Brazil publishes all governmental expenditures online on its Transparency Portal. Both of these programmes are a step towards transparent governments. The second aim of open data initiatives is to promote access to and effective reuse of data, so that the data may be used for research or innovation towards the benefit of society. The objectives of the open data campaigns in Canada and Israel are indeed to increase public access to information to encourage innovation in the public sector and the society more broadly. However, that is not to say that open data initiatives cannot accomplish both aims; they can simultaneously encourage the effective reuse of data and increase the transparency of the public administration.

About 58% of the governments surveyed have legislation establishing public access to information and defining parameters on which information is publicly shared. The EU Directive on the reuse of PSI provides a common legal framework for public access to government-held data (EC, 2017a). The directive aims to promote transparency and competition in the market and focuses on the economic benefits of the reuse of information. EU member states were obliged to transpose the directive into national law by 2015, which all EU respondents to the survey had done at the time of writing. Brazil, Costa Rica, Japan and Mexico also have such legislation defining the PSI to which the public should have access.

Training programmes and subsidies are the most common types of policy to encourage the use of ICTs by individuals and households

A number of different policy configurations, both financial and non-financial, encourage individuals and households to use ICTs in their daily lives, with non-financial programmes being slightly more prevalent. Training in the use of ICTs is the most common non-financial policy, with over half of the countries reporting a policy of this type. Of these, 44% have policies that target specific disadvantaged groups who may lack basic ICT skills due to the digital divide resulting from income disparity, disability or age. Norway and Singapore have digital literacy programmes for seniors, while China targets rural communities, and Brazil and Israel target low-income households and individuals. Canada and Latvia both have training programmes to give jobseekers the skills needed in the current market; Latvia has allocated over EUR 100 million to training programmes under its NDS, to be disbursed from 2014 to 2020. Among the countries that responded to the questionnaire, Hungary, Latvia and Poland reported the highest budgets for training programmes. The "Enable IT" programme in Singapore aims to train persons with a disability to use assistive technology to better meet the demands of their daily lives, both personally and professionally. Several countries have programmes to "train the teachers" as a more effective way of disseminating ICT skills; China, Estonia and Poland have adopted this approach.

In addition to training programmes, governments also frequently conduct communication campaigns to promote digital technologies, e-services and ICT tools. These campaigns are generally directed towards a broad audience, with only around one-quarter being targeted to a specific group. Most of the campaigns, which are largely sponsored by governments in European countries, have the goal of promoting the safe use of the Internet. Finally, a smaller proportion of countries have projects to build telecommunication infrastructure to increase broadband access to previously underserved areas. Hungary, Lithuania, Luxembourg, Poland and Slovenia have projects of this sort, often incorporated within their respective NDSs. As these countries are all members of the European Union, these initiatives are likely related to meeting the European Union's broadband targets of enabling access to all households at a speed of at least 30 Megabits per second (Mbps), and to half of all households at 100 Mbps by 2020 (EC, 2015). Costa Rica and Turkey both have similar initiatives, although these have more varied aims, like establishing public Wi-Fi access points or mobile telecommunication infrastructure.

Over two-thirds of policies that use financial incentives to support usage are specifically directed at disadvantaged groups who historically have had less access to ICT equipment or training, such as senior citizens, people in rural and remote areas without access to the Internet, or people from disadvantaged, low-income areas. Roughly 70% of financial-based policies come in the form of a grant or stipend to either purchase ICT equipment or services, like establishing broadband and paying for the service, or to be used towards classes in ICT skills. Israel offers a subsidy for low-income households to purchase personal computers as well as a three-year warranty on ICT equipment and optional ICT training. Other countries offering similar programmes are Austria, Canada, China, Colombia, Costa Rica, Hungary and Singapore. One-fifth also offer a tax incentive for an ICT purchase, as in Brazil, which grants an exemption on the purchase of smartphones, or in Denmark and Poland, which offer tax advantages for the installation of a broadband connection.

Policies supporting ICT usage in firms overlap with policies to develop the ICT sector overall

Encouraging the use of ICT tools in businesses can be done through both financial and non-financial means. Financial-based schemes are slightly more common, with 24 countries reporting 55 distinct financial policies, compared to 20 countries answering that they have 50 non-financial initiatives. Of the policies based on financial schemes, monetary support for the purchase of ICT equipment or towards ICT development is the most common, with 16 countries out of 24 using this method. Spain and Turkey both have programmes to encourage SMEs to adopt cloud computing solutions, while Singapore's iSPRINT Programme enables SMEs to use smart technology as a way to boost productivity and growth. Other countries such as Belgium, Estonia, Hungary and Poland support investment in R&D infrastructure and the integration of ICT and e-business tools for the optimisation of business operation and management. France, Japan and Mexico have similar policies.

Roughly a quarter of the respondents reported having a tax incentive for ICT purchases or for R&D. However, other OECD work shows that 29 of the 35 OECD countries have an R&D tax credit (OECD and EC, 2017: 4). For example, Canada offers a tax incentive to any Canadian business conducting R&D and Japan offers various tax incentives for companies to increase investment in digitalisation and in facilities designed to increase productivity. Meanwhile, Singapore's productivity and tax credit allows eligible businesses to deduct up to 400% on expenditures incurred on prescribed activities that promote innovation and productivity, and China offers a VAT exemption and income tax reductions for SMEs.

Policies that are not directly financial are more concerned with increasing the use of ICTs by business by offering targeted training. Training accounts for over half of the individual policies reported by countries, with 10 of the 20 countries having at least one such training programme. The training itself is mostly focused on the digitalisation of business services, e-commerce or on the effective use of digital media. Germany's "Trusted Cloud" training programme helps SMEs gain an understanding of cloud computing and its possible applications within their business. Australia and Switzerland offer training courses and information related to effective digital business management: Australia's "Digital business kits" offer tailored tips for operating online, as well as case studies and support to businesses. Meanwhile Switzerland provides information on information technology (IT) infrastructure, IT security, and e-commerce and advises SMEs on the potential steps to make businesses more digital on its digital.swiss and SME portals.

The policies listed here, both for financial and non-financial initiatives, strongly overlap with policies directed at the overall development of the ICT sector. This is perhaps unsurprising, as increasing firms' use of ICT and incentivising them to purchase ICT goods and conduct R&D is linked to increasing ICT sector development overall. However, only policies aimed at increasing ICT use in firms were used for this discussion; others related to supporting the overall development of ICT businesses through innovation and support of ICT industries, start-ups and SMEs were not included in the analysis as they have already been discussed. For a more detailed description of the policies to encourage overall ICT sector development, please see the end of the section on "Access and connectivity".

ICT skills development policies frequently target vocational training and primary or secondary education, but some countries adopt more comprehensive strategies

Digitalisation is bringing many opportunities, but it is also bringing new challenges and policy makers need to understand how digitalisation can help boost productivity and create new jobs. Digitalisation is often viewed as a source of new job growth, both in the

ICT sector and more broadly due to its role as a catalyst for business innovation across all other sectors of the economy. It is also important, however, to acknowledge and address the net impact on employment and skills. It is clear that digitalisation is driving a significant reorganisation of businesses around the world, and that this is affecting labour demand as well as, ultimately, employment. The net effects of digitalisation on jobs are complex and still poorly understood. What is known, though, is that when any significant new technology emerges, workers and users need new skills to be able to capture the potential productivity gains.

ICT skills have become an important requirement for employment across the economy, but a significant portion of the population still lacks the basic skills necessary to function in this new environment (OECD, 2012a). Data from the OECD Programme for the International Assessment of Adult Competencies (PIAAC) show that the demographic factors most commonly associated with a lack of core skills and no computer experience are people aged 55-65, people with less than an upper-secondary level of education and people in semi-skilled occupations. This lack of ICT skills in the adult population is of particular concern for policy makers because the groups with the lowest ICT skills tend to be among the demographic groups at the highest risk of losing their jobs in the current technological transformation of the workforce. Labour market disruptions will affect some workers more than others, and often those that will be the most affected will be those with the lowest levels of ICT skills and those who are the least prepared to update their skills.

Furthermore, a scarcity of ICT specialist skills may hinder adoption of ICTs. For instance, surveys point to the shortage of skilled data specialists as one of the biggest impediments to the use of data analytics in business. In the United States, since 1999, occupations for those with advanced ICT skills have been among those with the fastest growth in relative wages, suggesting (combined with other evidence) a possible shortage of such skills (OECD, 2017).

Policies for improving ICT skills typically include ICT literacy objectives in state/federal curricula, vocational training and higher education programmes in ICT, transition funds, paid educational leave, and support to firms for providing ICT training to workers (Figure 2.5).[19]

More specifically, all 38 countries that responded to the skills section of the survey have at least one type of ICT education and training policy in place. The most common type of policy, implemented in more than 80% of the countries, involves support for vocational training and higher education in ICT, which includes, for example, undergraduate degree programmes, courses that may or may not lead to a technical certification, and private initiatives or PPPs to educate ICT specialists. Almost three-quarters of countries allocate funds to set ICT literacy objectives in state/federal curricula and over 70% buy ICT goods and services for students, e.g. personal computers and broadband connections in schools. Close to 60% of countries support ICT training for workers through programmes such as courses for the unemployed or for people who simply want to update their skills. Note that, while the programmes and policies described here are mostly implemented by governments, this is not intended to suggest that they bear all the responsibility for promoting ICT skills. Employers can, and do, invest in developing employees' ICT skills as well. In addition, some governments provide support or incentives to firms for providing ICT training to employees.

Figure 2.5. **Policies to improve ICT skills**

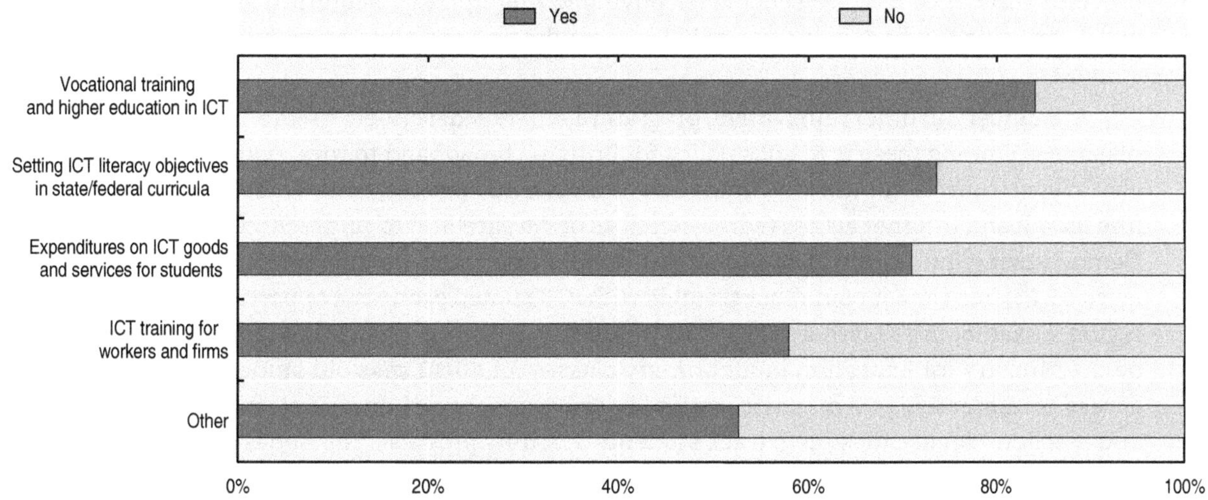

Notes: The total number of respondents for this question is 38. See note 17 at the end of the chapter for the list of countries. ICT = information and communication technology.

StatLink http://dx.doi.org/10.1787/888933584583

The key findings for this section are that policies supporting vocational training and higher education in ICT are common, sometimes involve PPPs, and occasionally aim to help specific groups such as the unemployed, women, and the elderly. Some countries have adopted more comprehensive strategies for ICT skills development that target all segments of society and all levels of specialisation. In schools, most public spending on ICT is for computer hardware and Internet connections. Furthermore, ICT literacy objectives in school curricula are moving beyond proficiency in word processing, spreadsheets and coding to include goals like teaching students how to use ICTs safely and responsibly. Several countries have implemented forward-looking programmes that match present ICT training priorities with expected future skills needs in various industrial sectors.

Computing devices and Internet connections dominate public expenditures on ICT goods and services for schools

Questionnaire results indicate that the two most common types of government ICT expenditure policies involve financial support for either ICT equipment or Internet connections for public schools. Each of these types of policies has been implemented in about half of the respondent countries. A quarter of the countries also mentioned having policies for buying or developing digital learning materials, such as e-textbooks.

Several countries have implemented policies designed to help poor and/or disabled students to gain or improve access to ICTs. For example, Chile's Digital Empowerment of Persons with Disabilities policy aims to improve access, participation, retention and learning for students with a disability or disease through the use of ICT. The programme delivers technologies and digital resources, including teaching training for the efficient use of those resources. Its purpose is to improve their pedagogical practices to give students a more inclusive and sustainable education. Costa Rica's "Tecno@prender" programme is aimed partially at educational institutions in zones that have shown lower economic development. It supports curriculum development and the promotion of a meaningful learning process for students by providing ICT infrastructure and equipment as well as connectivity in educational institutions. Estonia has a needs-based support system for students who cannot afford digital devices or who have specialised digital device needs due to a disability. Israel provides assistance to 2 400 schools for buying ICT equipment, acquiring Internet access and supporting teachers in the use of ICTs, depending on the socio-economic level of their students.

A number of other innovative programmes were described in the questionnaire responses. Among these is Brazil's policy for bringing broadband to rural public schools: to obtain spectrum for commercial operation of mobile 4G services, companies must provide free broadband Internet access (wired, wireless or via satellite) to rural schools. Colombia's Democratizing Innovation in the Americas programme connects vulnerable young people (aged 15-25) from low-income backgrounds with ICT-related economic opportunities in their region. Luxembourg's MathemaTIC is an interactive learning application (app) introduced by the Ministry for Education in all primary classes for 10-12 year-old students. They can access MathemaTIC 24/7 on any connected device, at school, home or elsewhere. Parents and teachers can use the app to track students' learning progress. The app is also available in several languages. Mexico's Digital Inclusion programme is notable for its breadth as well as the fact that it aims to prepare students for the 21st century by focusing more on creating information than consuming it. The programme provides connectivity and digital devices; training to promote teachers' ICT skills and their ability to apply them in pedagogic activities; digital educational resources that will be curated and evaluated to ensure their quality and impact; initiatives that promote creativity and research for solving today's social problems through ICT; and ongoing monitoring and evaluation that will allow the programme managers to find ways to improve it. About 2 million students and teachers are expected to benefit from this policy. Finally, through policies such as E-school bag, Slovenia has developed 30 interactive e-textbooks covering mathematics, sciences, languages, history, etc.

Some policies for developing students' ICT skills are being implemented at very substantial scales. China, for instance, has a long-term policy that aims to give all primary and secondary schools full network coverage, including fixed broadband and Wi-Fi. So far, 87% of Chinese schools are fully covered. Poland aims to create a network connecting all of its approximately 30 000 schools via broadband Internet access by 2018. Turkey's FATIH project will invest about USD 1.3 billion to equip all schools with broadband Internet connections and smartboards and to distribute tablets to 8 million students.

ICT literacy objectives in school curricula are expanding beyond proficiency in productivity software and coding

With respect to ICT literacy in state and national school curricula, objectives have branched out beyond teaching competency in coding and the use of productivity software such as word processing and spreadsheets. Several countries have recognised the need to provide students with the means to use ICTs safely and responsibly, as well. For example, Japan not only encourages its schools to familiarise pupils with computers and information and communications networks and to teach basic operation skills, but to provide instruction on information ethics and how to use information devices appropriately. Similarly, Portugal's Seguranet Project promotes safe Internet and mobile device usage in the educational community. In addition to basic computer and programming skills and the use of software, Latvia's school curriculum includes digital security.

Other countries' ICT curricula include such topics as teaching students how to critically assess what they see online and encouraging them to take advantage of e-government resources. Singapore's Media and Digital Literacy programmes, for example, aim to nurture discerning citizens who have the ability to evaluate media content effectively and to use, create and share content safely and responsibly. The Digital Poland programme, meanwhile, aims to enhance students' ability to use the Internet and specifically includes the use of e-public services.

Of course, countries also continue to support educational opportunities for coding and general digital skills development, as well. Canada's CanCode programme is an example of such efforts. CanCode will invest approximately USD 40 million over two years, starting in 2017-18, to support initiatives providing educational opportunities for coding and digital skills development to Canadian youth from kindergarten through high school.[20]

Policies in support of vocational training and higher education in ICT are common, may involve partnerships with the private sector, and sometimes aim to assist specific groups, such as the unemployed, women and the elderly

A large majority of respondents have policies in place to support vocational training and higher education in ICT. Frequently, but not always, these involve programmes that lead to a university degree or a vocational certification. They are also often funded entirely by the public sector.

However, several countries have formed partnerships with corporations, professional associations and other groups to fund and design programmes that produce trained personnel with ICT skills that match available jobs. Estonia's Ministry of Education and Research, for example, co-operates with private sector partners and universities to support the IT Academy initiative. It promotes the further development of IT higher education through scholarships, summer schools, in-service training and IT curricula development, among other things. The United Kingdom has begun to offer digital degree apprenticeships, which are the product of a government-backed collaboration between employers and higher education institutions. These apprenticeships help employers to tailor graduate-level candidates to their business needs through on-the-job and academic training, while young people are given opportunities to study for an honours degree while they work.

Many policies are aimed at helping specific groups of people rather than students in general. Most common among these are programmes designed specifically for training unemployed people to begin new careers in ICT-related fields. The Czech Republic's Ministry of Labour and Social Affairs, for example, has a nearly USD 100 million strategy to increase digital literacy and e-skills development among job seekers, including displaced workers. Turkey offers hundreds of vocational training courses to the unemployed to help prepare them for ICT-related occupations. The Netherlands has a programme called Make IT Work that is for highly educated but unemployed people who are looking for a new career in ICT. It retrains them for jobs such as software engineering, business analysis, ICT project management and ICT consulting. Israel's Welfare and Social Services Ministry offers training and job placement in ICT specifically for disadvantaged populations. An innovative feature of that programme is that it includes grants to employers who give jobs to trainees. All of these programmes should help to soften some of the job displacement effects that are part of the digitalisation process.

The unemployed are not the only group that policy makers are aiming to assist with ICT training, though. In Australia, where only one in four IT graduates are women, the National Innovation and Science Agenda supports the improvement of gender equity and diversity in

STEM (science, technology, engineering and mathematics) fields, including ICT, by increasing opportunities for women. Among the initiatives is a new grant programme designed to foster interest in STEM among women and girls. Luxembourg supports a programme with similar objectives called Rails Girls, an idea that began in Finland but is now a global, non-profit volunteer community. It promotes women-only coding classes such as app programming. Another group, the elderly, is the focus of an Austrian policy that supports a training course leading to a further qualification for ICT teachers and trainers who work with older citizens. In addition, a Colombian Ministry of Information and Communications Technology's initiative called Apps.co has so far trained more than 65 000 budding entrepreneurs to develop their ideas into sustainable digital businesses.

A number of countries have implemented forward-looking programmes that strive to match current ICT training priorities with expected skills needs in various industrial sectors

In Belgium, for example, the Employment Agency of Wallonia carries out prospective studies on the expected impact of the digital transformation on occupations and skills in a wide variety of fields. The resulting catalogue of emerging and future jobs is then used to select training courses to be reinforced. Finland's Ministry of Transport and Communications carried out such a study in 2016 specifically to find out what types of skills are needed by companies with respect to data use and intelligent robotics and automation. Spain's Ministry of Energy, Tourism and the Digital Agenda has developed a white paper for the design of university degrees taking into account the differences in supply and demand of profiles related to the digital economy. To sum up, it is an effort for an early alignment between industry and the educational system within the digital economy. Meanwhile, the Latvian Ministry of Economics has made medium- and long-term forecasts every year since 2008 that enable the higher education system to better match the supply of IT specialists to the labour market's demand for them.

Some countries have adopted a comprehensive strategy for ICT skills development targeting all segments of the population and all levels of specialisation, from general basic skills to research-level training in emerging technologies

For example, the recently launched Portugal INCoDE.2030 initiative on digital skills involves several measures organised around five priority lines of action – inclusion, education, qualification, specialisation and research – that respond to three challenges – citizenship, employment and knowledge. The initiative is a co-operative effort between government, business and other stakeholders. It includes measures designed to improve digital inclusion and literacy, the physical and cognitive access of the whole population to digital services, ICT programmes at all education levels, teacher training, analytic skills for a data-driven economy and society, production and diffusion of information, privacy and security, training for high value-added jobs, lifelong ICT learning, R&D for the production of new knowledge and advanced forms of ICT applications (including: big data, the IoT, and blockchain; information and intelligent systems involving artificial intelligence (AI) and human-centred computing; and computing and communication foundations involving quantum computing and other areas). The initiative has a co-ordination structure across all government sectors and involves tailored partnerships that pull together primary and secondary schools, higher education, vocational schools and universities, research organisations, businesses, civil society, and public administration agencies.

Innovation, applications and transformation

Two major trends are making digital technologies transformational for industrial production. One is the decline in their cost, which enables wider diffusion, including to SMEs. The other is the growing integration of three key digital technologies: big data analytics, cloud computing and the IoT. This combination of technologies is enabling new types of applications such as 3-D printing, autonomous machines and systems, and human-machine integration. These are the applications that are likely to drive the greatest industrial innovation, and thus productivity, effects in the future (OECD, 2017). The questionnaire explored these trends, the extent to which countries are capitalising on them, and how, with questions on topics such as what is being done to further encourage diffusion (see the previous section on usage and skills), promote interoperability and boost data analytics capabilities.

This section is based on responses to the innovation, applications and transformation section of the *OECD DEO* Policy Questionnaire by 35 countries.[21] The responses related to this section were particularly extensive and led to a multitude of key findings. First, with regard to policies for improving conditions for digital innovation, most of them involve support for innovation networks or better access to financing. It is surprising that more of these policies do not target young firms, as research shows that they play a central role in innovation, growth and job creation.[22] Moreover, few countries reported policies that are designed to boost investment specifically in ICTs or knowledge-based capital (KBC). The policies of that nature that were reported varied and included training to help IT and digital content businesses access foreign investment, general financial support to SMEs that introduce e-business solutions, and removing a cap on foreign ownership in the communication sector. Furthermore, given the promise of data-driven innovation (DDI), the level of attention and resources being devoted to policies for creating data analytics capacity is surprisingly low. Relatively few countries have policies that are specifically about data analytics, and some of them are comparatively small steps. The amount of spending is nowhere near what is being spent on other types of digital economy policies. Another key finding is that new and proposed regulations for markets where digital technologies are raising new challenges for competition show that policy makers are focusing on peer/online platform markets. Some of the measures they are implementing increase government control over digital technologies, whereas others grant them greater freedom.

With respect to applications, countries' policies for fostering digital content creation and diffusion do not follow a distinct pattern. They include measures such as digitising cultural resources and making them available online, allowing newspapers to share their information on an independent digital platform, and building an online knowledge library that provides unlimited access to scientific periodicals and e-books. Another key finding is that a small number of countries have addressed the need for interoperable standards for the IoT, but most have not. On the other hand, policies for facilitating data (re)use across organisations and sectors are popular and take many forms. The impetus behind these policies usually involves a desire to encourage innovation, to improve public services and efficiency within government agencies, or to promote open government. Meanwhile, e-health policy measures range from small steps to ambitious undertakings and tend to involve research funding, health data platforms or telemedicine.

Countries have undertaken, or are contemplating undertaking, a wide variety of reforms and reviews of their regulatory frameworks in light of the digital transformation, many of which concern labour laws or sector-specific employment rules. These include statutory reforms to formally recognise or define new work status categories and employment arrangements; the deregulation of certain sectors to remove barriers to the development of new services; and public, multi-stakeholder dialogues on the future of work. Few countries have yet gone so far as to enact entirely revised labour laws in light of the new forms of work enabled by digital technologies, but several have added new provisions and regulations to recognise developments such as teleworking and informal work contracts.

Finally, demonstrating that digitalisation is also transforming trade agreements, nearly half of the countries surveyed have included provisions related to trade in a digital world in their bilateral or regional trade agreements. These provisions tend to concern online privacy, cross-border data transfers, consumer protection for online transactions, restrictions on certain types of Internet content, and restrictions on the imposition of customs duties on trade in digital products.

Improving the conditions for digital innovation is a key policy objective

The following discussion addresses policies and regulatory measures for stimulating or addressing digital innovation in business models and markets. It includes a discussion of regulations for product and service markets in which digital technologies are raising challenges for competition.

Twenty-nine of the 35 countries that responded to the digital innovation section of the questionnaire have, or plan to have, at least one type of policy for stimulating digital innovation, technologies and business models, and/or addressing related effects. The most common type of policy, implemented in 21 of the countries, aims to improve conditions for digital innovation, such as by encouraging ICT diffusion, supporting innovation networks or expanding access to finance. Sixteen countries reported having policies that enhance incentives to invest in ICTs and/or KBC.[23] Thirteen countries have policies that stimulate the creation of data analytics capacity, for example by investing in technologies and training. Twelve countries facilitate organisational change within and among firms, such as by encouraging teleworking and teleconferencing. Finally, seven countries have revised their competition rules for data-driven markets. Figure 2.6 provides a visual representation of this distribution of policies.

Figure 2.6. **Policies to support innovation**

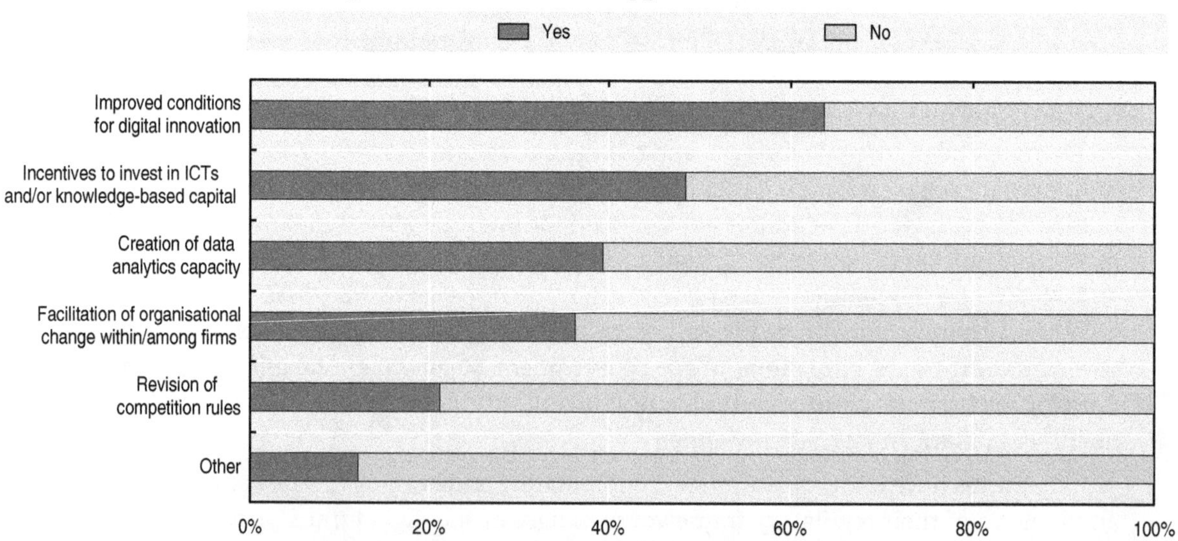

Note: ICT = information and communication technology.

StatLink http://dx.doi.org/10.1787/888933584602

Many digital innovation policies involve support for innovation networks and better access to financing

Most of the policies for improving the conditions for digital innovation described by the respondents involve creating better access to financing or supporting innovation networks. With respect to financing, Brazil's Ministry of Science, Technology, Innovation and Communications has a noteworthy programme called Project Inova Empresa. It provides businesses and R&D institutes with lines of credit and other financial support to promote innovation, including digital innovation. Initiated in 2013, Inova Empresa has a budget of up to USD 11 billion and has helped approximately 400 businesses and 140 R&D institutes in the ICT sector alone.

Germany has taken a multi-pronged approach to financing digital innovation. The Federal Ministry for Economic Affairs and Energy, sometimes in co-operation with the European Investment Fund, has developed a suite of five funds[24] that provide different kinds of financing to innovative companies at various stages of development. For example, one fund provides equity to business angels for financing innovative companies in their early phases, while another is designed specifically to finance fast-growing but underfunded companies. Another fund teams up with investors from the private sector to provide VC to innovative start-ups and young technology companies, while another provides VC to innovative technology companies in the seed phase. Some of those funds have existed for more than ten years while others started in 2016. Altogether, they have a budget of approximately USD 4 billion.

Regarding innovation networks, Denmark's Ministry of Higher Education and Science and the Danish Agency for Science, Technology and Innovation have helped to build 22 such networks. These networks offer companies access to the latest research and innovation trends within their respective fields of expertise. The networks also help companies to find collaboration partners on small- or large-scale research and innovation projects by connecting private companies, researchers, the public sector, technological service providers and other partners, both in Denmark and abroad. Each network receives a main grant of approximately USD 2 million from the agency for science, technology and innovation, but they also attract funding from other public and private sources. In all, 7 522 companies have participated in these networks and 5 348 of them have fewer than 50 employees.

In 2017, Switzerland's Commission for Technology and Innovation will promote R&D projects concerning ICT with a minimum of USD 30 million. More than 40% of all start-ups coached by the commission will come from the ICT sector. Additionally, the Commission for Technology and Innovation has set up several theme-based national innovation networks that work on issues such as additive manufacturing, Industry 4.0, the digital economy, and interactive and imaging technologies. These networks will receive an annual payment from the government that ranges from approximately USD 200 000 to USD 400 000.

One programme that does not fit into either the funding or innovation network categories is a partnership between the UK Treasury and the Bank of England. Its purpose is to broaden access to payment systems for non-bank payment institutions. The objective is to allow FinTech payment firms to access payment systems directly. Currently, these firms must access payment systems via a bank (indirect access), which comes at a cost. Direct access is expected to boost competition starting in 2018, when the arrangement will go live.[25]

Finally, the questionnaire results show that 5 of the 18 countries that mentioned having at least one policy for improving digital innovation conditions specifically aimed their policy (or policies) at SMEs, while another 5 aimed their policy at start-ups. One might have expected a sharper focus on start-ups, or at least on young firms generally. As mentioned earlier, OECD research has shown that more than half of SMEs are older businesses, but it is young SMEs (less than five years old) that play a central role in enhancing innovation, growth and job creation (OECD, 2014b).

Another topic that received little attention in the questionnaire responses was efforts to build a regulatory environment in which businesses can thrive and fail. By reducing the cost and administrative burden of starting up a new company, governments can increase incentives to innovate. This includes implementing bankruptcy regulations that reduce the costs of failure and ease the legal procedures for restarting a business, which would better recognise the fact that innovation is risky and occurs through "trial and error" (Adalet McGowan and Andrews, 2015). Figure 5.5 in Chapter 5 provides a comparative view of the level of administrative burdens that start-ups face in various countries.

Inadequate or outdated regulation may also limit the returns that firms can achieve from their investments in digital technologies, as it can hold them back from entering new markets or developing new products or business models. For example, recent OECD work finds that product market regulation, employment protection legislation and ICT regulation have significant effects on the uptake of ICT hardware (DeStefano, De Backer and Moussiegt, 2017).

Few countries reported policies that boost investment specifically in ICTs or knowledge-based capital for the purpose of fostering innovation

While questionnaire results mentioned earlier show substantial policy activity with respect to stimulating both ICT usage by firms and ICT sector development generally, only 3 of the 35 countries that responded to the digital innovation section of the questionnaire mentioned a policy tailored specifically to increase investment in ICTs or KBC for the purpose of increasing innovation. Those policies were varied and included Colombia's training programme to help IT and digital content businesses access foreign investment, Lithuania's general financial support to SMEs that introduces e-business solutions for optimising business processes, and Mexico's telecommunication sector reform that removed a cap on foreign ownership.

These results seem to indicate some limitations concerning the questionnaire, though, as they do not necessarily conform to findings in other studies. For example, the OECD has published lengthy reports on KBC and the many policies that countries use to stimulate investment in it (OECD, 2013a; 2015d). In the case of ICT-specific investment promotion instruments, one reason for their scarcity in the questionnaire responses may be that government measures overall have shifted from investment support to supporting R&D and innovation expenses, although they are increasingly counted as investment. Another reason may be that ICTs are considered to be a self-evident component embedded in any kind of investment and might therefore not be categorised separately or limited only to ICTs.

Ten countries listed at least one policy that may augment ICT or KBC investment, but those policies are more general measures, such as tax credits for all types of R&D or grants for investments in companies that are considered to be innovative.

The attention and resources devoted to policies for creating data analytics capacity is surprisingly low

As explained in Chapter 5, DDI holds great potential to create economic benefits and has already begun to deliver on its promise in many sectors. Overall, however, policy makers seem to be paying relatively little attention to their countries' data analytics capacities.

That is not to say that nothing is being done. Some respondents mentioned formidable programmes. These include efforts such as setting up big data research centres and designing postgraduate degree programmes. One country, Colombia, has a national Big Data Strategy for its public sector, entailing a contract with the Massachusetts Institute of Technology that will result in a general architecture and pilot projects to showcase the use and benefits that big data analytics can bring to the public sector.

But in all, only eight countries described policies that were specifically about data analytics, and many of those were comparatively small steps, such as holding big data contests and conducting assessment studies. There was nothing in this area that approached the billions of dollars that are being spent on the other types of digital economy policies mentioned earlier.

New and proposed regulations for markets where digital technologies are changing market dynamics suggest that policy makers are focusing on online platform markets

Reflecting the potentially disruptive impact that online platforms such as Uber and AirBnb are having on existing industries, respondents mentioned the road transportation and accommodation sectors more than any others when asked to describe new or contemplated regulations for markets in which digital technologies are raising competition challenges. (Among the 18 respondents that reported such regulations, 8 listed transportation measures and 5 listed accommodation measures.)

The responses that provided information about the specific nature of the regulations, however, were split almost evenly between those that described measures to increase government control over digital technologies (7) and those that described granting greater freedom to or otherwise assisting digital technologies (9). In a few cases the measures contained both types of elements.

At first glance, the split may appear to indicate a difference of opinion among the surveyed countries about whether competition from disruptive digital technologies is to be welcomed or feared. The nature of the restrictive measures that are mentioned in the questionnaire responses, though, mainly reveals concerns for consumers and tax collection rather than worries about protecting incumbent firms. France's recent Law for a Digital Republic, for example, imposed new rules for online platform operators, but they are largely aimed at protecting consumers' personal data.[26] Meanwhile, in the other category, new or proposed regulations reflect a desire to promote digital technologies. For example, Finland's new Transport Code, adopted in May 2017, deregulates market access in the transport sector, including in the taxi market. The objective is to enable digitalisation of the whole transport sector primarily by removing regulatory obstacles to digitalisation and innovation, by being technology-neutral, and by introducing new rules on access to essential information of transport services through open APIs. In the second phase of the reform, Finland is considering applying the MyData model[27] to further promote the adoption of the Mobility as a Service[28] concept.

Digital applications and services are promoted by a variety of policy measures

All 35 countries that responded to this section of the questionnaire have or plan to have in place at least one policy or regulatory measure to enhance digital applications and services. The most common type of policy, implemented in almost 80% of the countries, facilitates data (re)use across organisations and sectors, e.g. by promoting open formats (Figure 2.7).

Figure 2.7. **Policies to promote digital applications and services**

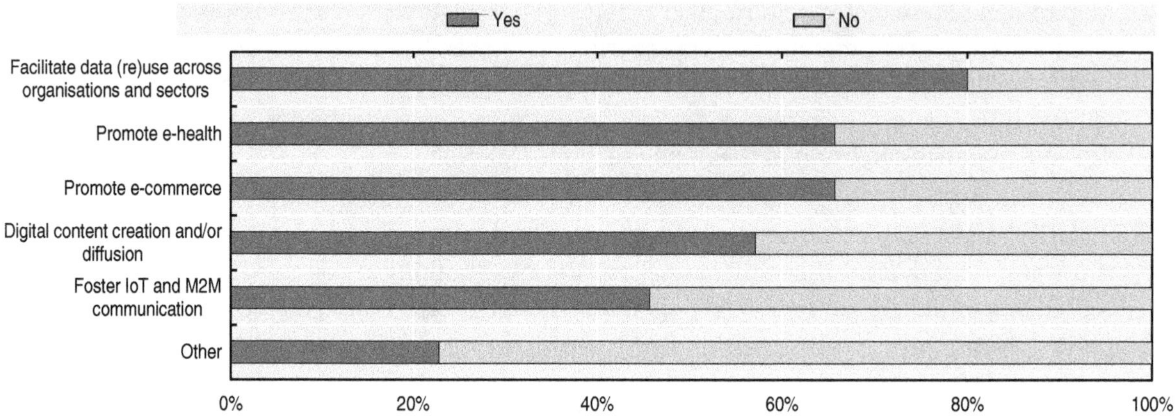

Note: IoT = Internet of Things; M2M = machine to machine.

StatLink http://dx.doi.org/10.1787/888933584621

Countries' policies for fostering digital content creation and diffusion do not follow a distinct pattern

Countries' responses about digital content creation and diffusion reveal widely varying policies rather than a consistent pattern. The most frequently mentioned policy measure, digitising cultural resources and making them available online, showed up in only five countries' responses. Some of the other notable policies include:

- Belgium's "Infotelligence", which allows francophone daily newspaper publishers to share the collection, processing, use and presentation of their information on an independent digital platform. Using big data and AI, it will allow publishers to better understand the behaviour and needs of their readers and to customise the supply of information. Consequently, the platform will offer readers better organised, more relevant content. An express aim of the project is to lead the sector away from international online giants such as Google, Apple, Facebook and Instagram.
- Colombia's Apps.co initiative, mentioned earlier, helps to transform ideas for applications (apps) into sustainable businesses – including games, apps for the disabled and apps for the government. So far it has funded 84 projects at a cost of approximately USD 3.5 million.
- Israel's "Campus" is an open, edX-based, national online education platform for high school students, underprivileged populations and government employees. It is projected to benefit between 100 000 and 200 000 people in 2017, rising to 1.5 million in 2019.
- Portugal has a somewhat different education-related programme called B-on (Biblioteca do Conhecimento Online), which is an online knowledge library that provides unlimited and permanent access for research and higher education institutions to full texts of scientific periodicals and e-books through nationally negotiated contracts.

A small number of countries have addressed the need for interoperable Internet of Things standards, but most have not

Only Germany, Japan, the Netherlands and Spain mentioned having efforts underway to promote the development and application of interoperable standards for the IoT.

This is an area where more policy makers could make important strides: recent surveys of potential cloud users have highlighted a lack of standards – specifically open standards – as one of the biggest barriers to their use of advanced ICTs such as the IoT (OECD, 2016a: 33). As an example, an executive survey by the World Economic Forum (WEF, 2015) indicates that lack of interoperability ranks behind security concerns, but before uncertain return on investments, among the top three barriers to IoT adoption. Fear of potential vendor lock-in is often the culprit, as users know they can become extremely vulnerable to price increases if they cannot practicably migrate to another vendor.

Policies for facilitating data (re)use across organisations and sectors are popular and take many forms

Policies for encouraging and facilitating data use and reuse across organisations are common among the respondents, with 28 of the 35 countries indicating that such policies are in place. Motivations generally revolve around a desire to encourage innovation in both the private and public sectors, improve public services, improve efficiency within government agencies, and promote open government.

About two-thirds of the data use and reuse policies focus on making government data available (or more available) in open formats. One popular measure is to create a national open data portal where the public can access a wide variety of open datasets. Alternatively, Chile holds an annual public hackathon, in which participants compete to develop the best applications using open public datasets. Since 2012, Portugal has had a National Digital Interoperability Regulation, which specifies a series of open formats and essentially states that the government must always provide information in open formats rather than in proprietary ones. Slovenia's Act on Access to Public Sector Information similarly promotes open formats, as does Spain's National Interoperability Framework, which includes a set of technical standards that cover all aspects of the digitalisation of public services. The Japanese government has taken many steps to improve the use of data (see Box 2.2 for details on some of them).

Other measures adopted by several countries, including Canada, Estonia, Israel, Latvia, Luxembourg and Spain, are based on the "once-only principle". That principle holds that public agencies are allowed to collect data only if they are not already in another public sector database. In other words, if a company or an individual has already submitted data to the public sector, then that company or individual should not have to submit it again, but rather the public sector itself should cross-use data. That clearly motivates government agencies to adopt common formats and share data across organisational boundaries, though it may also raise data protection concerns.

One measure unlike any others mentioned in the survey has been implemented in the United Kingdom, where a working group consisting of industry experts from the banking, data, consumer and business communities developed an open banking standard in 2016. The standard offers guidance on how banking data should be created, shared and used by its owners and those who access it, so as to help people transact, save, borrow, lend and invest their money. The underlying idea was that enabling the sharing of data that banks have historically held will improve people's banking experience. When securely shared or published openly using open application programming interfaces, the data can be used to build useful applications and resources to help people find what they need. For example, customers can look for a mortgage more easily, banks can find customers whose needs match up well with a new product, and businesses can share data with their accountants. That, in turn, will improve competition, and efficiency and stimulate innovation in the banking sector.[29]

E-health policy measures range from small steps to ambitious undertakings and tend to involve research funding, health data platforms or telemedicine

One example of funded research is the German Federal Ministry of Education and Research's R&D programme for medical technology, which aims to stimulate patient-centred innovation, support high-potential SMEs and promote digitalisation in healthcare generally. Ministries in several other countries, such as Norway and the United Kingdom, have issued papers about how the health and care system could use technology, including e-health, to improve outcomes for patients and citizens.

Box 2.2. **Facilitating the use of public and private sector data in Japan**

Having recognised that information technology is not only a key to achieving strong economic growth but also an important tool for transforming Japanese society and creating a safe, secure and comfortable life for citizens, the Japanese government established the Declaration to Be the World's Most Advanced IT Nation in June 2013 to serve as its information technology (IT) strategy. Since then, all parts of the Japanese government have been co-operating to promote measures based on the IT Declaration, including breaking down barriers between ministries so as to achieve cross-cutting co-ordination. Furthermore, the Basic Act on the Advancement of Utilizing Public and Private Sector Data was promulgated in December 2016 to develop the environment for using public and private sector data.

The initiatives undertaken over the last three years have now started to bear fruit and some of the major ones involve data use. One initiative was to create user-oriented administrative services by reforming administrative information systems. The government promoted radical business process re-engineering through IT use, breaking down barriers between administrative areas with the aim of creating ways to facilitate linkages between the information systems of central and local governments and business operators. Through these efforts, the government wanted to ensure that public services are run efficiently and are convenient for users. The consolidation of administrative information systems and their migration to the cloud is reducing operating costs. The savings are being invested in efforts to enhance the value added by e-government.

An example is the government's effort to set up new information systems for the Social Security and Tax Number System. By consolidating the central government's administrative information systems and transferring them to the cloud, Japan has saved money that it is now using to cover part of the cost of further system development and upgrades (including security measures). In fact, 908 central administrative information systems are forecast to be eliminated by fiscal year 2018 (FY2018) – a reduction of approximately 63% compared to FY2012 (when there were 1 450 systems). In addition, 316 systems are due to be migrated to the cloud-based common government platform by FY2021. As a result, operating costs are expected to decline by nearly USD 900 million annually across all systems, subject to cost reductions, by FY2021. That is a savings of approximately 28% versus FY2013.

Another measure adopted in connection with the goal of reforming administrative information systems was setting up an infrastructure for multilayer interoperability, consisting of projects for creating a common vocabulary and Japanese characters. The former facilitates data exchange and use through the establishment of common notation, meanings and data structures for names, addresses and other vocabulary. The latter enables formal and simplified ideographic variants of personal and company names to be recorded and used appropriately in administrative information systems. The government expects that this infrastructure will enable administrative information systems to be linked across organisational and operational boundaries, facilitating smoother provision of public services.

Box 2.2. Facilitating the use of public and private sector data in Japan *(cont.)*

A second type of initiative was to promote safe, secure data circulation. The idea was to improve the quality of life for Japanese citizens by means such as identifying and resolving challenges affecting a super-aging society with a low birth rate and creating new services based on data use. Japan has implemented many measures to achieve that goal, including encouraging open data initiatives by central and local governments and administrative agencies. The measures include initiatives such as establishing a government data catalogue website with around 16 000 datasets and formulating the Government of Japan Standard Terms of Use (Version 2.0), approved by the Inter-Ministry Council of Chief Information Officers on 24 December 2015. To support the open data initiatives of local governments, the central government has formulated and distributed the Local Government Open Data Promotion Guidelines. In addition, it is raising awareness and offering personnel-based support through open data evangelists. These are experts with deep knowledge about open data, appointed and dispatched to local governments by the National Strategy Office of ICT, Cabinet Secretariat. Their role is to popularise and promote awareness of open data among local governments and support open data initiatives.

Source: Headquarters for the Promotion of an Advanced Information and Telecommunications Network Society (IT Strategic Headquarters) (2016), "Declaration to Be the World's Most Advanced IT Nation", *http://japan.kantei.go.jp/policy/it/index_e.html* (accessed 9 May 2017).

Seven countries mentioned having policy measures to create platforms, standardise health records, and link healthcare procedures and services to the people who received them, the health professionals who provided them and the facilities where they were performed. Some of these systems, such as Brazil's Unified Health System National Card (which operates through an electronic registry), have existed for years. Others, like Costa Rica's Single Digital Health Record system, a platform to be used by primary healthcare centres of the Costa Rican Social Security Fund, are currently under development.

Finally, China, Colombia and Germany noted that they have telemedicine policies in place. The main purpose of these programmes is to extend healthcare to more places in a cost-effective manner. One telemedicine centre in China, for instance, is connected to more than 700 two-way satellite sites and more than 60 remote vehicle satellite mobile terminals that cover more than 1 300 locations across the country, facilitating remote diagnosis and treatment. Germany currently has more than 200 regional telemedicine projects underway.[30]

Overall, countries' policy measures on e-health range from rather modest to immense. On the more modest end of the spectrum are projects such as building web-based medical appointment and cancellation systems. Towards the other end are efforts such as Germany's R&D funding programme for medical technology, mentioned earlier, which has a ten-year budget of well over USD 500 million. China's effort to develop big data for health and medical applications, meanwhile, involves building 100 regional clinical medicine data centres to give urban and rural residents standardised electronic health records and fully functional health cards. In 2016, the national population and health science data-sharing platform released data sets that included biomedical, basic medical, clinical, public health, Chinese medicine, pharmacy, population and reproductive health information. The total data volume was 49.1 terabytes, equivalent to about 20 billion single-spaced typewritten pages of data.

Digital transformations of jobs and trade have triggered reviews of legal or regulatory frameworks and the inclusion of digital aspects in trade agreements

The following discussion covers policies and regulatory measures that address the digital transformation of jobs and/or trade, including reviews of regulatory frameworks, active labour market policies, and bilateral and regional trade agreements that include provisions related to trade in a digital world. It also covers new labour laws, regulation and social partners' agreements related to new forms of work enabled by digital technologies. For additional information, see OECD (2014c; 2015c; 2016b).

Twenty-eight of the 35 countries that responded to the digital transformation section of the questionnaire have at least one type of policy that addresses the digital transformation of production, jobs or trade. Among those countries, 13 indicated that they are reviewing or have already reformed relevant regulatory frameworks, such as general labour laws or sector-specific rules.

Countries have undertaken, or are contemplating undertaking, a wide variety of reforms and reviews of their regulatory frameworks in light of the digital transformation, many of which concern labour laws or sector-specific employment rules

Measures related to the digital transformation of jobs fall into two broad categories: those that have already been implemented and those that are about considering the possibility of regulatory reforms. In the former group are efforts that include:

- statutorily defining telework (Slovenia) and regulating the relationship between companies and teleworkers (Colombia)
- conducting *ex ante* and *ex post* reviews of the administrative burdens imposed by regulations, with digitalisation being an increasingly important factor (Switzerland)
- digitalisation and deregulation of transport and enabling the Mobility as a Service concept with data-related rules (Finland) and FinTech (Switzerland) sectors to remove barriers to the development of new services
- a comprehensive reform of labour law in light of the rapid development and progress of technologies (Lithuania; see the next subsection for more details on the new law).

The measures that involve ongoing considerations of regulatory reform in light of digital transformation include:

- possible changes to on-call time regulations for workers in the ICT sector (Estonia)
- deliberations on labour market regulations that are being challenged by the online platform economy (Norway)
- the design of a digital test concept for evaluating the suitability of all current regulations for meeting the challenges brought by digitalisation (Switzerland)
- a public, multi-stakeholder dialogue process on the future of work (Germany).

Germany's dialogue process is a major effort. Entitled Work 4.0, it is part of a comprehensive review of labour market and social policies. In 2015, the Federal Ministry of Labour and Social Affairs initiated the process by publishing a green paper for discussion.[31] The paper outlined the main trends, important areas for action and key social issues concerning the world of work in the future. It also contained a set of fundamental questions that initiated a broad dialogue about how society will work in the future. The questions were addressed with the help of experts from the fields of research and operational practice, social partners and associations, including trade unions helmed by the German Trade Union Federation. The Federal Ministry of Labour and Social Affairs published a white paper detailing policy proposals in late 2016.[32]

Norway's deliberations on labour market reforms are also extensive. A committee is assessing the opportunities and challenges that arise from the sharing economy. Its work emphasises the potential for the more efficient use of resources. The committee is also focused on identifying regulations that are being challenged by the sharing economy, including labour market regulations. Its mandate includes:

- evaluating whether regulations should be adjusted to achieve a greater degree of symmetry between the sharing economy and traditional activities, and evaluating whether there are regulations from which certain players should be exempted
- assessing the potential effects of the sharing economy on labour, including employees and contractors; in this regard, the committee will also consider the consequences of more people being able to be self-employed and the need for changes in the rules that apply to this group
- examining regulations in individual markets where sharing economy actors are especially prominent, and considering whether it is necessary to change the regulations as a result of new technology or new business models.

Few countries have enacted entirely revised labour laws in light of the new forms of work enabled by digital technologies, but several have added new provisions and regulations to recognise developments such as teleworking and informal work contracts

Seventeen of the 35 countries that responded to this section of the questionnaire listed new labour laws, regulations or social partners' agreements related to new forms of work enabled by digital technologies that they have developed or are currently developing. Among the specific new measures implemented or under discussion in those countries, new types of workers' status and contracts were mentioned the most frequently.

For example, Austria's Ministry of Labour, Social Affairs and Consumer Protection is currently observing and discussing trends on workers' status so that it can be in a position to implement informed, appropriate measures to address the transformation of work and ensure employee protection. The ministry has its eye on phenomena such as crowd working, recruitment via Internet platforms and comparable new forms of work. It is particularly concerned about the risk that these phenomena could cause job insecurity and replace regular forms of work. Depending on the relevance of these concerns in the future, the ministry may have to develop instruments to maintain proper working and remuneration conditions. Linked to this example, Austria's Industry 4.0 platform[33] includes both social partners. Affiliates of the Austrian Trade Union Federation (Österreichischer Gewerkschaftsbund [ÖGB]) are taking part in the general discussions and various working groups.

In the Czech Republic, an amendment to the Labour Code is currently working its way through the legislative process. The amendment will change, among other things, provisions that concern work performed outside the employer's site, such as telework. The new approach is that whenever electronic communications networks are used for off-site work: 1) the employer must provide the hardware and software necessary for the performance of the work, except when the employee performs the work using his/her own equipment, and to ensure, particularly in terms of software, data protection in case of their transfer; and 2) the employee must act so as to protect the data and information related to the performance of the work.

Similarly, Lithuania has just completed a full revision of its Labour Code, which now includes principles regarding the protection of employees' personal data and the privacy of their personal lives. The code now provides that the exercise of the right of ownership to the

ICTs used in the workplace must not infringe the inviolability of employees' communications. Lithuania's new Labour Code also introduced several new types of employment contracts: for apprenticeships, project work, workplace sharing and multiple-employer contracts.

Colombia is one of several countries that have set certain mandatory terms for contracts involving telework. Among the key issues that telecommuting contracts must specify are:

- the technology and required environment, and how to perform the work in terms of time and if possible space
- the days and times that the teleworker will carry out his or her activities for the purpose of defining liability in case of an accident and preventing ignorance of the legal maximum working week
- the responsibilities regarding custody of work items and the method of delivery by the teleworker when finalising the telework
- the security measures that the teleworker must know and comply with.

The international legal framework for trade in a digital world

International trading relationships are governed by bilateral, regional, and multilateral trade and investment agreements, which play an essential complementary role to domestic structural reforms. Multilateral action is of particular importance in promoting the mutual interests of countries in terms of trade liberalisation, locking-in domestic reform and building confidence between firms and the societies in which they operate.

Trade-related aspects of the digital transformation are covered under multilateral agreements and plurilateral agreements forged at the World Trade Organization (WTO). WTO agreements are technologically neutral, so disciplines pertaining to trade in goods under the General Agreement on Tariffs and Trade (GATT), or trade in services under the General Agreement on Trade in Services (GATS), apply equally in the online and offline worlds. Hence a wide range of WTO agreements are considered relevant to trade in a digital world, including the Agreement on Trade-Related Aspects of Intellectual Property Rights, the Agreement on Technical Barriers to Trade, the Information Technology Agreement and its recently concluded expansion, and the Trade Facilitation Agreement. Yet with rapid changes in technology, there is a discussion among WTO members about whether there is a need to update or clarify existing rules and commitments.

Already in 1998, in recognition of the growth of e-commerce and the opportunities it presented for trade, WTO members agreed to establish a work programme to examine trade-related issues concerning e-commerce (WTO, 1998). They also agreed not to impose customs duties on electronic transmissions. While the agreement not to impose customs duties on electronic transmissions has been extended at every WTO Ministerial since the initial agreement, the work programme has varied over the years.

As the digital transformation has progressively deepened, countries have also begun to include issues specifically related to trade in a digital world in bilateral and regional trade agreements. In addition to specifying that general provisions of the agreement also apply in the online world, some bilateral and regional trade agreements include specific chapters on digital services, e-commerce and telecommunication. While agreements vary, these chapters sometimes include:

- measures that prohibit the imposition of customs duties
- measures aimed at non-discriminatory treatment of digital products

- measures that promote paperless trading
- measures that prevent the imposition of localisation requirements for computing facilities
- measures protecting the movement of cross-border data flows
- measures regarding privacy online
- measures on data protection
- measures ensuring enforceable consumer protection for online transactions
- restrictions on certain types of Internet content (e.g. routing traffic to domestically owned firms, blocking particular sites)
- measures to restrict the imposition of mandatory requirements to transfer or provide access to a software's source code
- measures concerning unsolicited commercial electronic messages (i.e. to advocate for the effective regulation of unsolicited spam and telemarketing)
- measures promoting strong and balanced copyright protection and enforcement.

In this respect, current and future negotiations of bilateral and regional trade agreements, which increasingly touch upon some of the emerging and complicated trade issues, as well as discussions within the WTO context, will most likely pave the way to further developing the trade-related aspects of the digital transformation.

Nearly half of the countries surveyed have included trade-related aspects of the digital transformation in their bilateral or regional trade agreements

Eighteen of the 35 countries that responded to the digital transformation section of the questionnaire indicated that issues related to trade in a digital world have been included in their bilateral or regional trade agreements. Within such agreements, five of the topics in the list above appeared with roughly equal frequency: 1) privacy on line; 2) cross-border data flows; 3) consumer protection for online transactions; 4) restrictions on certain types of Internet content; and 5) prohibitions on the imposition of customs duties.

Chile provided an extensive response and has provisions of nearly all the types mentioned above within its trade agreements. See Box 2.3 for more information on those provisions, most of which were mentioned by other respondents, as well.

Box 2.3. **Trade-related aspects of the digital transformation in trade agreements: The case of Chile**

Being aware that the digital transformation, catalysed by the Internet, is creating powerful opportunities for increasing participation in international trade, especially in sectors that have traditionally been considered non-tradable, Chile has incorporated trade-related aspects of the digital transformation in its trade negotiations. With respect to free-trade agreements (FTAs), this has involved negotiating telecommunication and electronic commerce chapters that facilitate trade conducted electronically by ensuring that it takes place efficiently and with appropriate consumer protections:

- **Measures regarding privacy online.** Many of the FTAs negotiated by Chile include provisions that recognise the economic and social benefits of protecting users' personal information and the contribution that this makes to enhancing consumer confidence, especially in electronic commerce. Chile has adopted provisions in its FTAs that mandate the adoption of laws or regulations for the protection of personal information. Another set of provisions allows taking measures that are deemed necessary to ensure the security and confidentiality of messages and to protect end users' personal data. See, for instance, the Trans-Pacific Partnership's Article 14.7: Online Consumer Protection, and the Pacific Alliance's Article 13.8: Protection of Personal Information.

Box 2.3. **Trade-related aspects of the digital transformation in trade agreements: The case of Chile** *(cont.)*

- **Measures regarding cross-border data flows.** In accordance with the technical architecture of modern electronic communications networks, and having regard for the end-to-end principle, Chile's practice in this area has been to allow, as a general rule, the cross-border transfer of information by electronic means when this activity is necessary for conducting business. However, nothing prevents a party from taking measures that are necessary to ensure the security and confidentiality of messages and to protect end users' personal data, provided that those measures are not applied in a manner that would constitute a means of arbitrary or unjustifiable discrimination or a disguised restriction on trade.
- **Measures concerning consumer protection for online transactions.** As a way to increase consumer confidence, Chile has recognised the importance of adopting and maintaining transparent and effective measures to protect consumers from fraudulent and deceptive commercial activities, including provisions mandating, adopting or maintaining consumer protection laws to proscribe fraudulent and deceptive commercial activities that cause harm or potential harm to consumers engaged in online commercial activities. Certain FTAs also include provisions that aim to enhance co-operation between national consumer protection agencies or other relevant bodies on activities related to cross-border electronic commerce in order to enhance consumer welfare.
- **Restrictions on certain types of Internet content.** Chile does not include this kind of restriction, as it would be against consumers' choice to access and use services and applications available on the Internet.
- **Measures that restrict the imposition of customs duties on electronic transmissions.** Chile has a standing practice of not imposing customs duties on electronic transmissions, including electronically transmitted content. Chile seeks to ensure non-discriminatory treatment of digital products (computer programmes, text, videos, images, sound recordings or other products that are digitally encoded and that can be transmitted electronically) that are transmitted electronically, which includes guaranteeing that these products will not face discriminatory measures based on the nationality or territory where they are produced.

Digital risk and trust

As highlighted in Chapter 6, individuals (including consumers) and businesses have several means at their disposal to enhance the level of trust in the digital economy, ranging from transparent online reviews for consumers to risk management practices in organisations. However, evidence presented in Chapter 6 also shows that there are still several challenges to be addressed. This section discusses the role of public policies in addressing these challenges, with a focus on digital security, privacy and consumer protection. It discusses current policy trends, including the development of national strategies related to digital security and privacy. The digital security policy measures discussed include measures to build capacity, international co-operation, and measures to promote digital security risk management, information sharing and exchange, and the digital security industry. The discussion of privacy-related policies includes, for example, policy measures to promote awareness raising and education, technical measures for privacy protection, and international co-operation.

The key findings for this section are, first, that nearly all countries surveyed have now introduced national digital security strategies. The most frequently mentioned measures in these strategies aim to build capacity through education and skills and to strengthen digital security through international co-operation. Some steps are also being taken to promote SMEs' digital security risk awareness and to foster good practice. Second, countries are implementing more measures to address greater challenges to privacy. These measures include promoting privacy awareness, developing skills, and empowerment. Fostering privacy as a business priority and supporting related innovation also feature prominently among privacy-related government policies. Legal interoperability across borders is seen as one of the biggest international challenges, particularly by non-European countries. However, while most governments engage in international collaboration, a substantial number still lag in co-ordinating their own domestic privacy policies. Finally, consumer protection policies are evolving along with e-commerce markets.

Nearly all countries surveyed reported having introduced national digital security strategies

National digital security strategies are essential to establish the trust needed for economic and social activities to fully benefit from digital innovation. In 2016, 29 of the 33 countries that responded[34] to the digital security risk section of the 2016 *OECD DEO* Policy Questionnaire indicated they had introduced national digital security strategies (Figure 2.8) and the other 4 were in the process of developing one. National strategies are developed by a variety of government agencies and organisations, ranging from the Cybersecurity Agency in France and Singapore to the Ministry of Defence in Denmark and the Ministry of the Interior in Iceland. Although most countries had involved non-governmental stakeholders in the development of their national strategy, only 56% reported having carried out a broad public consultation on the strategy. Nearly half of the surveyed countries are planning to revise their strategy in 2017-18.

Figure 2.8. **Number of countries introducing national digital security strategies**

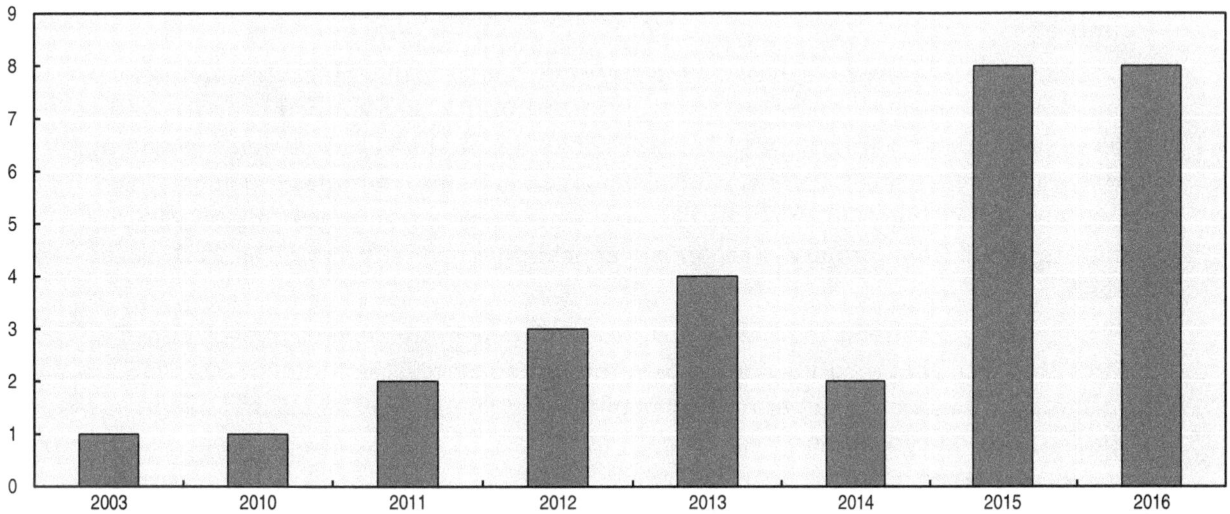

StatLink http://dx.doi.org/10.1787/888933584640

Figure 2.9 shows several types of measures to strengthen digital security that were frequently mentioned by countries. Most prominent are measures that aim to build capacity through education and skills, including steps to promote digital security risk awareness in SMEs, and international co-operation.

Figure 2.9. **Policy measures to strengthen digital security**

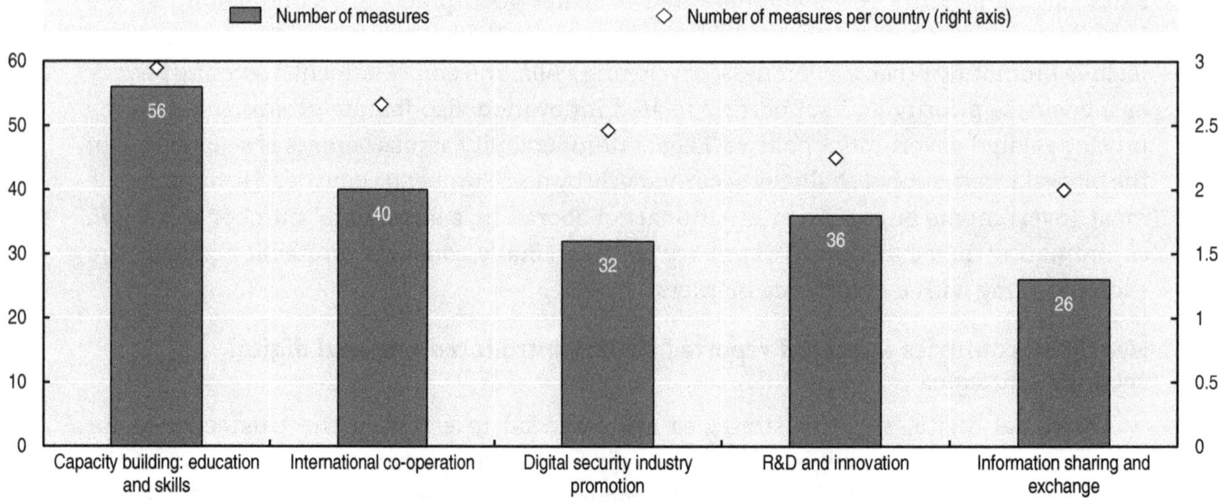

Note: This figure is based on a total of 190 policy measures to strengthen digital security reported by 19 countries.

StatLink http://dx.doi.org/10.1787/888933584659

Capacity building focusses on education and skills development

Demand for cybersecurity specialists has increased significantly in recent years but supply has remained low. Increasing the current pool of skilled digital security and risk management professionals is a policy objective for 31 of the 33 countries that responded to this section of the questionnaire. According to Burning Glass, in the United States, online job postings for digital security professionals took approximately 14% longer to fill than the average for all IT jobs. Digital security talent shortages are reported by all countries.

Among the main barriers to attracting more individuals to digital security professions, countries mentioned low awareness of career opportunities, which is compounded by the limited statistics on job offerings and absence of a standard higher education curriculum. Today, digital security is part of specialised postgraduate programmes, certifications or professional trainings, whereas what is needed is a system in which digital security skills are honed from primary to secondary education, university as well as work-based training.

Countries are introducing a wide range of policy measures and initiatives aimed at addressing the digital security skills gap. In the United States, the National Initiative for Cybersecurity Education is a partnership between government, academia and the private sector focused on cybersecurity education, training and workforce development. In 2017 Luxembourg created the Cyber Security Competence Centre, based on a PPP with the objective of delivering cybersecurity services and training. In the United Kingdom, the National Cyber Security Centre established in 2016 aims to work with industry, government and academia to support the next generation of researchers, students and innovation. In France, the National Digital Security Agency has recently launched a number of training and professional certification initiatives (e.g. CyberEdu, SecNumedu) in collaboration with universities and the private sector. Korea's MSIP/KISA provides scholarships for digital security college students, including budget support for universities.

Steps are being taken to promote digital security risk awareness and to foster good practice in small and medium-sized enterprises

When asked about the three most pressing digital security challenges affecting economic and social activities, most countries responding to the survey mentioned cyberattacks against small firms or cyberattacks that disrupted or prevented economic and social activities and cybercrime/cyberespionage that involved the theft of digital intellectual property and assets.

SMEs, and early-stage start-ups in particular, are critical to economic growth; they drive competition and innovation, and contribute to job creation. They also face distinct challenges in managing digital security and privacy risk. A digital security incident that can result in a loss of consumer trust, damage to reputation or a drop in revenue may be more damaging for an SME than for a larger company because they are more likely to find it difficult to weather a temporary loss of customers or revenue. As well, SMEs may not have the resources or expertise to effectively assess and manage risk. On the positive side, SMEs that are aware of the risk and can demonstrate they have robust digital security and privacy practices may have a competitive advantage when seeking partnership opportunities with larger organisations.

Promoting digital security risk awareness by SMEs was a specific objective of 82% of countries. However, only 46% of countries who responded have developed specific incentives (rewards and/or sanctions) for business to promote digital security risk management. Japan and Korea provide tax incentives for companies that invest in digital security products.

The United Kingdom also requires that "only companies that have a valid Cyber Essentials certification can supply central government with any services that require the processing of personal data". The Cyber Essentials scheme identifies some fundamental technical security controls that an organisation needs to have in place to help defend against Internet-borne threats.

Lithuania can apply "economic sanctions" against companies that do not meet legal obligations regarding digital security.

Countries use a wide range of other policy measures and actions to promote digital security risk management as a business priority. These include:

- toolkits and good practice guidelines
- training courses for entrepreneurs and employees
- guidance on effective de-identification/anonymisation/pseudonymisation practices
- updating and maintaining privacy-enhancing measures (such as encryption)
- audit controls
- risk assessments (privacy impact assessments and threat risk assessments)
- up-to-date and revised information-sharing agreements.

Nineteen out of 33 countries reported that there was interest in digital risk insurance (cyberinsurance) as a market-based approach to manage business risk. Insurance coverage for digital security risk is viewed by these countries as a means for companies and individuals to transfer a portion of their financial exposure to insurance markets. Insurance companies can also potentially contribute to the management of digital security risk by promoting awareness, encouraging measurement and providing incentives for good practice. Those same countries generally have considered measures to encourage businesses to adopt digital security risk insurance. The digital security risk insurance market is still developing, however, and countries that did respond reported that they were just looking at how policy in this area could be applied. Canada, for example, reported that it is in the early stages of assessing this issue as part of its cyber review.

These opinions are reflected countries' responses when they were asked to rank, in order of relevance, eight main obstacles to the adoption of risk insurance in their countries (Table 2.2).

Table 2.2. **Obstacles to the adoption of risk insurance**

Obstacle	Mean rank
Lack of actuarial models	3
Insurance premiums are too expensive	3
Management does not see the value of this type of insurance	3
Coverage is inadequate	4
Current insurance policies are considered sufficient	4
Digital security risk does not warrant insurance	4
There is no market for digital security insurance products	5
There is no supply of digital security insurance products	6

The top two obstacles for most countries were:

1. Lack of actuarial models: More comprehensive data on the frequency and impact of digital security incidents (and the related claims payments) is needed for the development of actuarial models and to provide more confidence in the underwriting of insurance coverage for digital security risk.
2. Cost of insurance premiums: The premiums for digital security insurance per million in coverage has been estimated to be three times more expensive (for the same amount of coverage) than general liability coverage and six times more expensive than property coverage.

International co-operation enables progress on information sharing and at the technical level

Facilitating international co-operation on cross-border digital security issues is a priority for all responding countries. Countries mentioned a large number of initiatives aimed at improving international collaboration particularly to promote greater information sharing and exchange on digital security incidents.

The European Directive on Security of Networks and Information Systems (NIS Directive) adopted in 2016 represents a very significant step in this direction. The directive requires EU member states to increase their preparedness by establishing a Computer Security Incident Response Team (CSIRT) and a competent national authority in charge of digital security, and to improve strategic co-operation and exchange of information with each other. Additionally it requires EU member states to adopt appropriate measures to promote of a culture of digital security risk management. Member states are also asked to "ensure that the competent authorities have the necessary powers and means to assess the compliance of operators of essential services with their obligations", which includes an obligation to notify incidents having a significant impact on the continuity of the essential services they provide.[35]

The NIS Directive's aim is to create a collaboration framework, within which member states and the European Commission can share early warnings on risks and incidents. Co-operation is facilitated by the creation of a single point of contact in each country; the establishment of a "Co-operation Group" with representatives of the member states, the European Commission and the European Network and Information Security Agency; and by the creation of a CSIRT Network. EU members have until May 2018 to adopt appropriate laws and regulations to comply with the directive; some countries such as France[36] and Germany[37] have already adopted legislative and regulatory measures in this area.

In accordance with its International Strategy for Cyberspace, the policy priorities of the United States are to promote innovative open markets; enhance security, reliability and resilience of global networks; and extend law enforcement collaboration. There are many venues and forums in which the United States promotes information sharing. A key area of focus is information sharing between CSIRTs with national responsibility. Accordingly, the US government works closely with foreign authorities, as well as through international and regional organisations focused on cybersecurity information sharing. Similarly, Australia partners with international law enforcement, intelligence agencies and other computer emergency response teams. The country is planning to appoint a Cybersecurity Ambassador who will identify opportunities for practical international co-operation and ensure Australia has a co-ordinated, consistent and influential voice on international cybersecurity issues.

Canada's Computer Emergency Response Team (CERT) works with the international CERT community in an effort to address and co-ordinate responses to serious cybersecurity incidents. In Colombia, the "National Digital Security Police of Colombia, through the Police Cyber Center, is part of international agreements and alliances in order to report incidents." Latvia has a memorandum of understanding (MOU) in place for co-operation in cybersecurity with Estonia and Lithuania. Separate MOUs cover agreements with Azerbaijan and Kazakhstan and Georgia. Spain highlighted the role of the international Forum of Incident Response and Security Teams (FIRST)[38] in co-ordinating incident reporting. France is actively promoting its approach for the protection of critical infrastructure to other countries. It will also be part of formal collaborations in Europe as a result of the implementation of the NIS Directive including the "European network of CSIRTs". France is also participating in CERT-level co-operation groups (TF CSIRTs, FIRST, NatCSIRT, AfricaCERT), bringing together CSIRTs around the world. Finally, 24 OECD countries, 13 partner economies, 8 international organisations and 11 companies have joined the Global Forum for Cyber Expertise launched in 2015 in the context of the Global Conference on Cyber Space. The objective of the Global Forum for Cyber Expertise is to exchange best practices and expertise on cyber capacity building. The aim is to identify successful policies, practices and ideas and multiply these on a global level.

Countries are implementing a growing range of measures to address increasing challenges to privacy

The diffusion of the new digital technologies such as the IoT, big data and algorithmic decision making through AI (see Chapter 7) are raising questions as to the potential impacts on individual privacy and data protection. For the large majority of governments responding to the 2016 questionnaire (25 out of 34 countries),[39] these technologies pose significant challenges in the application of existing regulation. Some governments have highlighted that these new technologies raise new societal and ethical challenges that need to be better understood and may need to be addressed through the development of new data governance framework and policies. For example, the French data protection authority (Commission nationale de l'informatique et des libertés [CNIL]) has established a working group on innovation and digital technology that is undertaking a reflection on these issues (see below). Effective anonymisation or de-identification of personal data in the context of open (government) data also rank high among the identified technological challenges, which many governments aim to address through innovation-enhancing policy measures.

Many countries (15 out of 34) also highlight the international dimension of privacy as a policy issue of growing importance, given the increasing reliance on cross-border data flows. In this context, global interoperability, by way of co-ordination and harmonisation of privacy frameworks, remains a challenge to be addressed. This is true not only at the international level (between national privacy regimes), but also at the national level (between regional privacy laws) in some countries.[40]

In contrast, the adoption of the new EU data protection framework, comprising the General Data Protection Regulation (GDPR) (Regulation (EU) 2016/679), which will apply from 25 May 2018, and the so-called Police Directive (Directive (EU) 2016/680), ensures a harmonised set of data protection rules within the European Union and also provides for an expanded set of transfer tools aimed at facilitating international data flows (see EC [2017b]). The significance of the GDPR goes beyond EU member states as it will affect, for instance, international businesses active in the European Union as far as they are offering goods and services or monitoring the behaviour of EU citizens (OECD, 2016g). Legal interoperability therefore remains crucial, as highlighted in Part 6 of the OECD (2013b) *Recommendation of the Council concerning Guidelines Governing the Protection of Privacy and Transborder Flows of Personal Data* (hereafter "OECD Privacy Guidelines") on international co-operation and interoperability, which states that: "Member countries should encourage and support the development of international arrangements that promote interoperability among privacy frameworks that give practical effect to these Guidelines."

In most countries, the use of big data by governments emerges as a major legal challenge for privacy protection. Of the 32 countries responding to the question on privacy challenges, 18 have highlighted that the reuse of personal data across government agencies constituted a policy challenge for privacy protection. Among them, around half indicated that the collection of personal data for (national) security interest was one of the biggest policy challenges, in particular in cases where personal data was collected from the private sector. In 2016, Brazil adopted Decree No. 8.789, which regulates the sharing of databases containing personal information held by governmental bodies. The decree allows government processing of personal data, and more specifically the gathering of personal data for national security reasons, including access of personal data through legal interception, which has raised concerns especially when OTT services are involved. A different approach has been adopted in the European Union. As part of the new EU data protection legal framework, the Police Directive aims at protecting the right to the protection of personal data with regard to the processing of personal data by competent authorities for the purposes of the prevention, investigation, detection or prosecution of criminal offences or the execution of criminal penalties. This new directive, which needs to be transposed into national law in all EU member states by 6 May 2018, contributes to harmonising data protection rules in the area of law enforcement and thus provides the basis for the free flow of personal data. In that regard, the use of big data technologies in the field of law enforcement by EU member states must comply with the requirements of the directive.

Responses to the 2016 *OECD DEO* Policy Questionnaire reveal that governments have adopted a wide range of policy measures to address the privacy challenges highlighted above (and in Chapter 6). Among these policy measures, promoting privacy awareness ranks by far the highest (Figure 2.10). Of the 424 policy measures on privacy that responding countries reported having, one-quarter (105) were adopted to raise privacy awareness and education (in government, business and individuals). Another quarter were adopted to empower individuals either through easy and clear redress possibilities or through mechanisms to enhance individuals' control over their personal data (in both cases, 97 measures in total). Other policy measures that ranked high on governments' agendas included measures to foster privacy as a business priority and to support privacy-related innovation and the adoption of technical measures (136), followed by the promotion of international co-operation and the co-ordination and harmonisation of privacy legislation across government agencies (49). The following sections discuss the most frequently adopted policy measures in more detail.

Figure 2.10. **Policy measures to promote privacy**

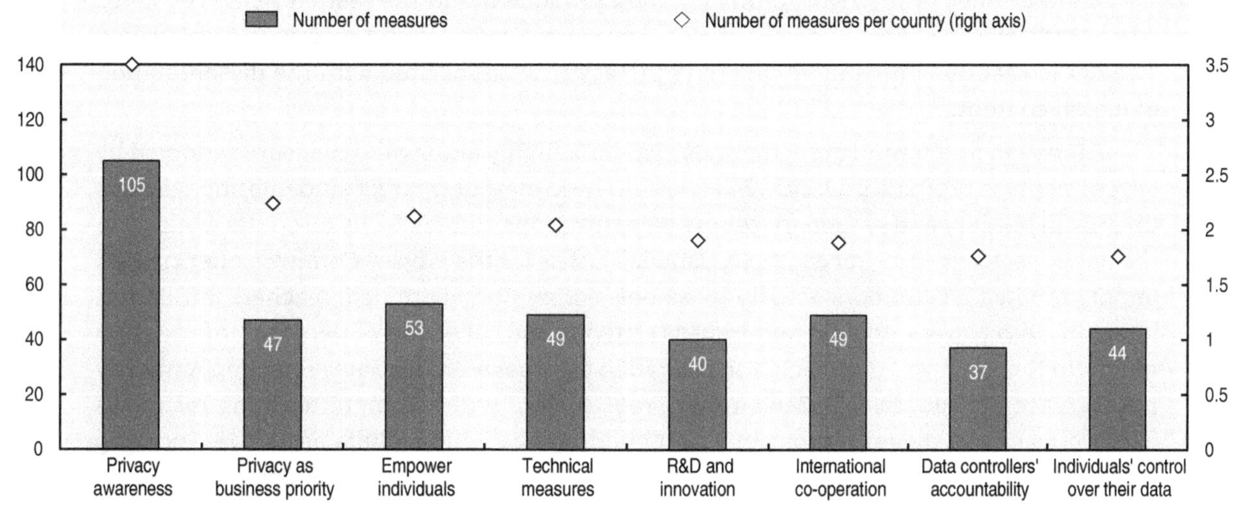

Note: This figure is based on a total of 424 policy measures to promote privacy reported by 30 countries.

StatLink http://dx.doi.org/10.1787/888933584678

Awareness, skills and empowerment are the most frequent policy levers used by governments to promote privacy protection

To better protect privacy, it is necessary to be both aware and well informed about all potential privacy risks. Policy makers and privacy enforcers recognise raising the level of awareness, skills and empowerment as a key lever to better address privacy risks (OECD, 2016g). In fact, enhancing privacy awareness and education is the most frequently adopted policy measure, in particular by privacy-enforcement agencies. Most agencies do so by providing guides and good practices, including offline or online publications; online publications are usually available through dedicated websites. Some agencies provide templates to help organisations develop privacy notices or privacy management plans such as in the case of the Office of the Australian Information Commissioner (OAIC). The OAIC developed a specific privacy management plan template for public sector agencies.[41] The EU GDPR requires data protection supervisory authorities to carry out awareness-raising activities addressed to data controllers and processors, as well as to individuals, in particular in the educational context.

Many government agencies are reaching out to the public through events such as conferences, consultations and workshops. While some of these events aim to provide the public with basic knowledge and a better understanding of privacy (see, for example, regular roadshows and talks organised by Singapore's Personal Data Protection Commission [PDPC] to educate the public on the importance of protecting their personal data), others are dedicated to more specific and advanced privacy issues. Examples of the latter include public workshops organised by the US Federal Trade Commission (FTC) to examine the privacy and security implications of emerging technologies, including smart TVs, drones and ransomware, and to discuss what impact those changes will have on the marketplace, or a series of public debates on the ethical questions raised by algorithmic decision making initiated in January 2017 by the CNIL in accordance with its new mission of looking at the ethical and societal issues raised by digital technologies. Several agencies are also using media, including in some cases serious games, to raise awareness about privacy issues. The Israeli Law Information and Technology Authority, for instance, initiated a comprehensive plan for media appearances in television, radio, newspapers and on the Internet with regards to the importance of the right to privacy, data protection and the related risks. The CNIL, as another example, has organised a web campaign based around a serious game called "Fred et le chat démoniaque" to illustrate privacy risks associated with the dissemination of digital content.

Education and training programmes also rank highly among the measures adopted by governments to promote privacy. While most of these measures target students and teachers (mainly in primary and secondary education institutions), others focus on adults working in the public sector. In 2015, for example, Canada's Office for the Privacy Commissioner created and distributed a classroom activity to schools across Canada to help teachers familiarise students with privacy policies and issues related to the collection of personal information online. In Norway, the Center for ICT in Education together with the Data Protection Authority put in place an initiative, DuBestemmer (YouDecide), to disseminate teaching resources about privacy and digital responsibility for children and young adults aged 9-18. Focusing on government officials, the Japanese Ministry of Internal Affairs and Communications developed a course about the implications of privacy within the government. There are also some notable education programmes aimed at the private sector, such as the "Start with Security" initiative by the FTC (2015), which highlights the key data security principles for businesses of all sizes and in all sectors.

In terms of mechanisms for enhancing empowerment, most governments have measures to simplify privacy complaint procedures, such as introducing digital services,[42] and in some cases emphasising the introduction and/or simplification of compensation claim procedures.[43] A recent development is the implementation of mechanisms to enhance individuals' access to their own personal data, such as the provision on the "right of data portability" included in the EU GDPR. Other countries have also implemented or are considering implementing similar rights. For example, the Blue Button initiative of the US Department of Health and Human Services allows patients to download their health records quickly and securely. The Israeli Law Information and Technology Authority, as another, published draft guidelines for public consultation according to which service providers must transfer consumers' electronic transcripts of phone conversations or chats upon their request. All these mechanisms are in line with the Individual Participation Principle of the OECD Privacy Guidelines: In the world of big data, data portability seems the only reasonable means to provide data "in a form that is readily intelligible to [the individual]". This is because data portability enables the individual to apply data analytics and related services to his or her own personal data to gain the knowledge needed to "challenge data relating to him". However, questions on how best to implement data portability remain unanswered.

Fostering privacy as a business priority and supporting related innovation rank high among government policies

While regulatory developments are ongoing, there is increasing understanding that regulation is only one element in strengthening privacy protection. A recent development, for example, is the promotion of privacy as a business opportunity. Governments have adopted different types of approaches to achieve this objective. A large majority of governments rely on awareness-raising campaigns as discussed above. The Finnish Ministry of Transport and Communications, for instance, organises the Digital Business Forum on Data Protection two to three times a year with the goal not only to help companies prepare for GDPR implementation, but also to see data protection as a business opportunity. Similarly, the Israeli Law Information and Technology Authority has highlighted in its Vademecum for Business[44] ten best practices that can improve not only a firm's corporate social responsibility image, but also business performance, essentially by increasing consumers' trust.

Many governments are also implementing certification schemes to increase business' incentives to implement effective privacy-enhancing processes. In Korea, for instance, the Korea Communications Commission incentivises businesses to obtain the Privacy Certification by reducing fines or postponing sanctions when a certified business faces a privacy violation investigation due to a personal data breach. Similarly, in the United Kingdom, the Information Commissioner's Office is currently planning a privacy seals programme that could act as a "stamp of approval" demonstrating good privacy practice and high data protection compliance standards. In some other cases, governments are promoting privacy as a business priority by emphasising the link between digital security and privacy protection. For instance, this is the case in Mexico, where the Federal Institute for Access to Public Information and Data Protection provides a table of functional equivalence between digital security standards and in collaboration with the Spanish National Cybersecurity Institute has developed a strategic plan to help organisations improve their digital security when processing personal data. Last but not least, the EU GDPR creates the possibility to implement certification schemes that will help data controllers to demonstrate compliance and individuals to assess the level of data protection afforded by products and services. These certification schemes might be used both to demonstrate compliance with the new rules for processing operations at the EU level and to provide adequate safeguards for international data transfers.

R&D is being increasingly promoted by governments to address privacy issues arising from emerging technologies such as the IoT. Governments are also promoting R&D in privacy-enhancing technologies (PETs), including anonymisation and cryptography technologies and techniques, as well as their adoption across organisations. While it is true that most countries have policy measures that aim directly or indirectly at the promotion of (academic) research (the "R" of R&D), policy measures promoting the development of business-relevant technologies and applications (the "D" of R&D) as well as new business models remain rather rare. Very few countries have established funding schemes to directly support privacy-related R&D and innovation. But there are positive exceptions: France's Investments Programme for the Future (Programme d'investissements d'avenir) supports the development of PETs. In October 2015, a call for projects was launched within the programme to mobilise up to

EUR 10 million for innovative companies in three areas: 1) the anonymisation of personal data; 2) the protection of privacy in the context of the IoT; and 3) innovative privacy architectures, such as distributed architectures. The objective of this call for projects is to encourage good practices in PETs and to support companies in developing commercial solutions. Another example is SPRING Singapore, an agency under the Ministry of Trade and Industry that developed a funding scheme (the Capability Development Grant) to promote the adoption privacy-enhancing processes in SMEs. Up to 70% of the project cost of an SME for enhancing its privacy measures are covered by the grant.

While most governments engage in international collaboration, many still lag in co-ordinating their own domestic privacy policies

International co-operation remains and will continue to be an important policy area for privacy protection as the volume of cross-border data flows increases. Governments ranked the potential incompatibilities of legal regimes as a key rationale in favour of international co-operation, above the lack of resources to address international privacy issues and existing restrictions on international data sharing, including the current practices of law enforcement and intelligence agencies to collect or exchange personal data internationally. Of the 34 countries responding to this section of the questionnaire, 26 could name at least one initiative through which they co-operate internationally. Participation in the Global Privacy Enforcement Network was most frequently cited as a key arrangement for privacy co-operation, beside the Article 29 Working Party (in the case of EU member states) and the Asia-Pacific Economic Cooperation (APEC) Cross-border Privacy Enforcement Arrangement (in the case of APEC countries). Furthermore, the APEC Cross-border Privacy Rules System (CBPRs) (APEC, n.d.), a third-party certification mechanism of an organisation's privacy protection policies and practices, which is based on the OECD Privacy Guidelines, is growing steadily. As of June 2017, Canada, Japan, Mexico and the United States had joined the CBPRs. Korea had applied and the Philippines, Singapore and Chinese Taipei were considering participation. In Japan, the CBPRs is considered a requirement for cross-border personal information transfer. APEC and the EU are discussing ways to promote interoperability between binding corporate rules under the EU Directive and APEC/CBPRs regarding both the applicable standards and the application process under each system. In addition, for the European Union and the United States, an important development has been the establishment of the EU-US Privacy Shield Framework, which ensures the free flow of data from controllers/processors in the European Union to Privacy Shield-certified US companies while guaranteeing a high level of data protection.[45] Also worth mentioning are the new provisions on international co-operation for the protection of personal data in the EU GDPR that are focused on facilitating effective enforcement co-operation, providing international mutual assistance, and promoting discussion and the exchange of best practices with third-country authorities.

Privacy policy making and regulation involves multiple government agencies, including but not limited to privacy-enforcement agencies and ministries in charge of justice or legal affairs and the digital economy. But it also involves government agencies in charge of specific sectors such as healthcare, finance and transportation, to name just a few. This means that privacy policy making and regulation requires ongoing mechanisms or processes to ensure co-ordination and coherence of policy and regulatory developments and implementation. However, while most governments engage in international collaboration, in particular through their privacy-enforcement agencies, domestic co-ordination of national privacy policy and regulatory development remains poor in a number of countries. According to the responses to the 2016 *OECD DEO* Policy Questionnaire, a third of all responding countries do not have an ongoing mechanism or process in place to ensure co-ordination and coherence of their privacy policies and regulations at the national level, and where countries report having such mechanisms in place, the extent to which these are effective remains uncertain.

In many countries privacy policy co-ordination is achieved at different levels during policy development. This can involve cross-governmental working groups, national consultation procedures and PPPs. In other countries, a dedicated co-ordination body exists – in some cases attached to highest level of government (e.g. the Prime Minister's Office) – to ensure co-ordination and coherence of policies and regulations across government agencies. This is the case in Israel, for example, where a central unit in the Prime Minister's Office is evaluating the efficiency of Israeli regulations, including privacy regulations. In some countries, the introduction of a co-ordination mechanism was established in the context of the development and/or implementation of their national digital economy strategy (see Chapter 1). In the process of the 2015 launch of Digital Roadmap Austria, for instance, a co-ordination team was formed and more than 100 experts from all federal ministries as well as a number of local authorities and associations, social partners, unions and employers' associations, and other organisations were involved. Subsequently, hundreds of citizens took part in an online consultation process. The resulting consultation paper was the basis for the present Roadmap. In other cases, the negotiation of the GDPR has been a driver to establish or enhance domestic co-ordination mechanisms in a number of EU member states. In Belgium, for instance, processes have been put in place to co-ordinate between the different public authorities, as well as to engage with the private sector during the negotiation of the GDPR. To what extent these co-ordination processes and mechanisms are still used and effective to ensure the continuous co-ordination and coherence of privacy policy and regulation remains to be seen. At the EU level, the new data protection legal framework provides for mechanisms to ensure co-ordination across member states. The consistency mechanism foreseen in the GDPR will help to ensure consistent application of the rules, in particular when a supervisory authority intends to adopt measures that may affect a significant number of individuals in different member states. Dispute resolution mechanisms and new ways of exchanging relevant information between authorities will also support co-ordination at the EU level.

The development of national privacy strategies promises to enhance a whole-of-government approach to privacy

Legislation continues to be the primary response to addressing personal data protection. Rather than being directed at all stakeholders, these laws typically impose obligations on organisations subject to the law and require them to grant individuals specific rights. As highlighted in the previous sections, there are a wide range of complementary measures such as education and awareness raising, which are often left to privacy-enforcement authorities or civil society bodies. While protection by the law is essential, privacy in an increasingly data-driven economy would thus benefit from a multifaceted strategy, reflecting a whole-of-society vision supported at the highest levels of government, as called for in the OECD Privacy Guidelines (Part 5) and more generally in Chapter 1 of the current report, in the section entitled "The current state of national digital strategies".

The OECD Privacy Guidelines recommend that governments "develop national privacy strategies that reflect a co-ordinated approach across governmental bodies". Along the model of "digital security strategies", such multifaceted privacy strategies would help create the conditions for privacy protection to become a differentiator in the marketplace while providing the flexibility needed to capitalise on emerging technologies. They could also encourage R&D and innovation with respect to privacy by design approaches and help focus efforts by privacy-enforcement authorities and other actors. Co-ordinated privacy strategies at the national level would help foster co-operation among all stakeholders and lessen uncertainty in data flows.

While many countries have adopted national digital security strategies, very few have adopted equivalent privacy policy strategies, despite the need to introduce, or improve existing, co-ordination mechanisms as highlighted above. According to the responses to the 2016 *OECD DEO* Policy Questionnaire, more than half of the countries (18 out of 34) clearly indicated that they did **not** have a national privacy strategy. For most countries, including those that report having a national privacy strategy, the concept is either misunderstood or remains unclear.

As the e-commerce marketplace evolves, so do policy responses to protect consumers and ensure trust

Policy makers have implemented a number of initiatives to protect and empower digital consumers and address some of the impediments to trust described in Chapter 6. The recent revisions to the *OECD Recommendation on Consumer Protection in E-commerce* provide a robust foundation to guide policy initiatives for a global online marketplace. More specifically, the Recommendation addresses challenges relating to information disclosure, misleading and unfair commercial practices, confirmation and payment, fraud and identity theft, product safety issues, and dispute resolution and redress. Its provisions have been adapted to cover digital content, privacy and security, consumer reviews and ratings, new payment mechanisms, and the use of mobile devices to conclude transactions. In addition, the Recommendation updated a number of provisions, including the ones related to the essential role of consumer protection authorities. It highlights the need to enhance such authorities to protect consumers online, and exchange information and co-operate in cross-border matters (OECD, 2016c).

Policy makers are beginning to grapple with the challenge of applying consumer protection frameworks to online platform markets

Online platform markets have steered debates in many OECD countries over how to regulate economic activity. In this area, regulators must balance competing considerations: appropriate regulatory measures can protect consumers but unnecessary or excessive regulation can impact the disruptive innovation associated with these platforms, thus reducing the benefits for consumers. When access to an online platform is a service in itself, the OECD *Recommendation of the Council on Consumer Protection in E-commerce* highlights that consumer laws should apply. Less obvious is whether and how responsibilities can be imposed on platforms for users' actions (OECD, 2016c). In June 2016, the European Commission issued its "European agenda for the collaborative economy", which is part of the Single Market Strategy. It provides non-binding guidance on how existing EU law should apply to the collaborative economy, including peer-to-peer markets, and clarifies key issues facing market operators and public authorities, such as consumer protection, market access requirements, liability if a problem arises, labour law and tax (EC, 2016d). In 2017, the Commission concluded a review of EU consumer protection laws, suggesting that enhanced transparency of online platforms could be one area for possible change (EC, 2017c).

A number of countries have recently looked into issues related to the development of online platform markets, along with appropriate policy responses, by conducting studies or organising events. In 2015, the US FTC held a public workshop entitled the "Sharing" Economy: Issues Facing Platforms, Participants, and Regulators" to examine competition, consumer protection and economic issues arising from the activity of the online platform markets. A staff report drawing on the workshop's discussions and more than 2 000 public comments examines regulatory approaches to protect consumers and the public. One observation made by participants was that regulatory issues in these platforms may diverge from those posed by traditional suppliers. Moreover, online platforms are innovating at a rapid pace, which will likely require adjusting regulation as these platforms develop, thus requiring flexibility in regulatory approaches and avoidance of pre-emptive regulation (FTC, 2016).

In 2015, the Competition Bureau of Canada undertook a comprehensive study of the taxi industry in light of the rapid expansion and proliferation of ride-sharing services such as Uber. The aim of the study was to explore how existing regulations for taxi and limousine services could be adapted to govern ride-sharing services. The bureau concluded that regulators should both ensure that new regulations on ride-sharing services were no broader than necessary to achieve policy goals while also relaxing existing regulations on traditional taxis, with the aim of creating a level playing field. That way, consumers can benefit from lower prices, reduced waiting times and higher quality service. Ultimately, competition can ensure that consumers have the broadest range of products and services at the best possible prices (Competition Bureau of Canada, 2015).

Self-regulation initiatives such as codes of conduct, accountability measures and enforcement mechanisms interface with other policy initiatives and existing consumer laws. Sharing Economy UK in partnership with Oxford University and SAID business school recently developed the TrustSeal, the first trust mark for the sharing economy. It sets out minimum standards for businesses to ensure certain standards of business conduct. Trust mechanisms such as reviews and endorsements have sometimes been associated with a form of self-regulation, although it is difficult to assess the extent to which such mechanisms protect consumers.

Mechanisms for cross-border enforcement co-operation should be strengthened to protect consumers in e-commerce

The issue of cross-border barriers to e-commerce growth is discussed in Chapter 6. These barriers are affecting consumer trust in e-commerce as consumers may find it difficult to understand which rules apply to their transactions and what rights and responsibilities apply in case of a problem. The 2016 OECD *Recommendation of the Council on Consumer Protection in E-commerce* (OECD, 2016c) encourages countries to improve the ability of their consumer protection enforcement authorities to co-operate and co-ordinate with each other with a view to provide for effective consumer protection enforcement co-operation in the context of global e-commerce. One example at national level is the US SAFE WEB Act, passed in 2006 and reauthorised in 2012, which gives the FTC enhanced abilities to combat cross-border fraud, including through enhanced information sharing and investigative assistance powers that allow the FTC to co-operate with foreign counterparts. At the international level, the Econsumer.gov website, a project of more than 35 countries under the umbrella of the International Consumer Protection and Enforcement Network, helps consumer protection and law enforcement authorities gather and share cross-border consumer complaints that can be used to investigate and take action against international scams.

Within the context of its Digital Single Market Strategy, the European Commission is looking at different measures to reduce barriers to cross-border e-commerce, notably by removing key differences between domestic and global e-commerce marketplaces. In May 2016, the Commission put forward a proposal for the reform of the Consumer Protection Co-operation, with the aim of equipping EU enforcement authorities with the powers they need to better co-operate in cross-border investigations. It also made a proposal for a regulation on geo-blocking, a form of discrimination based on the place of residence. To improve and facilitate dispute resolution in cross-border online disputes, in 2013 the European Union adopted its Directive on Consumer Alternative Dispute Resolution and its Regulation on Online Dispute Resolution, which were followed in 2016 by an Online Dispute Resolution platform. This platform, available in 23 languages, assists consumers in finding access to bodies that offer online dispute resolution.

Some countries have engaged in bilateral agreements that facilitate cross-border co-operation on e-commerce issues. For instance, the Korea Consumer Agency has signed MOUs with the National Consumer Affairs Center of Japan, the Better Business Bureau and the Office of the Consumer Protection Board of Thailand, which sets out procedures for cross-border dispute resolution.

The complexities of global e-commerce supply chains highlight the need for greater co-operation to detect and deter the sale of unsafe products to consumers

The 2016 OECD *Recommendation of the Council on Consumer Protection in E-commerce* recognises that consumer product safety issues have become more challenging as global e-commerce supply chains become more complex. It calls for online businesses to not offer, advertise or market unsafe goods or services. It also encourages businesses to co-operate with the competent authorities when a good or a service on offer is identified as presenting a risk to the health or safety of consumers (OECD, 2016c).

In recent years, a number of market surveillance activities and enforcement actions have been undertaken by consumer product safety authorities in order to detect and deter unsafe products made available through e-commerce. This includes having in place organisations dedicated to e-commerce market surveillance, such as the "Control of e-commerce of Food, Feed, Cosmetics, Commodities and Tobacco" in Germany or the Electronic Commerce Surveillance Centre in France, and developing specific guidelines and strategies on market surveillance (OECD, 2016e). The 2016 National Market Surveillance Programme in Turkey includes market surveillance activities and procedures for detecting unsafe products (Turkish Government, 2016).

Co-operation between market surveillance and custom authorities as well as international co-operation between authorities is essential considering the important cross-border element of product safety issues. In the European Union, the RAPEX-China system enables information sharing on unsafe products between the EC and Chinese authorities. The Cooperative Engagement Framework between Canada, Mexico and the United States provides a framework for sustained and increased co-operation on consumer product safety in North America. Online sweeps, such as the OECD online product safety sweep conducted in 2015 in 25 jurisdictions, are also seen as an effective way of enhancing international co-operation (OECD, 2016e).

Notes

1. *https://www.viestintavirasto.fi/en/spectrum/radiospectrumuse/spectrumauction.html.*
2. Examples of such light regulation include requiring companies that are providing services to notify the regulator and imposing minimum content standards (i.e. protection of minors, illegal content and advertising rules).)
3. These are the Framework Directive (2002/21/EC), the Authorisation Directive (2002/20/EC), the Access Directive (2002/19/EC), the Universal Service Directive (2002/22/EC) and the Directive on Privacy and Electronic Communications (2002/58/EC).
4. Not amended, therefore still not encompassing platforms without editorial responsibility.
5. For a full list of notified on-demand services in the United Kingdom see: *http://stakeholders.ofcom.org.uk/binaries/broadcast/on-demand/List_of_Regulated_Video_On_Demand_Services.pdf.*
6. For the directory of regulated VoD in Hungary see: *http://mediatanacs.hu/dokumentum/163976/lekerheto_audiovizualis_mediaszolgaltatasok.pdf.*
7. *http://interfone.com.*
8. *http://dfat.gov.au/trade/agreements/safta/pages/singapore-australia-fta.aspx#news.*
9. Australia, Austria, Belgium, Brazil, Canada, Chile, China, Colombia, Costa Rica, the Czech Republic, Denmark, Estonia, Finland, France, Germany, Hungary, Ireland, Israel, Italy, Japan, Korea, Latvia, Lithuania, Luxembourg, Mexico, the Netherlands, New Zealand, Norway, Poland, Portugal, the Russian Federation, Singapore, Slovenia, Spain, Sweden, Switzerland, Turkey and the United Kingdom.
10. Note that this portion of the questionnaire covers innovation policies only for the ICT sector. A much wider review of innovation policies is available in OECD (2016f).
11. To find out more about Austria's ICT of the Future programme, see: *https://www.ffg.at/en/ictofthefuture.*
12. Further information on Estonia's Venture Capital Fund can be found at: *www.kredex.ee/en/venture-capital-4.*
13. See *www.hutzero.co.uk* for further details.
14. For more information, see: *www.gouvernement.lu/5380127/27-fit4start?context=3422869* (in French only).
15. For more information, see: *http://ufm.dk/en/research-and-innovation/cooperation-between-research-and-innovation/commercialisation-and-entrepreneurship/the-innovation-incubator-scheme/the-innovation-incubator-scheme#cookieoptin.*
16. More of Israel's schemes directed towards promoting innovative start-ups can be found at: *http://innovation-israel-en.mag.calltext.co.il/?article=4.*
17. The following countries responded to the sections of the survey on usage and on skills: Australia, Austria, Belgium, Brazil, Canada, Chile, China, Colombia, Costa Rica, the Czech Republic, Denmark, Estonia, Finland, France, Germany, Hungary, Ireland, Israel, Italy, Japan, Korea, Latvia, Lithuania, Luxembourg, Mexico, the Netherlands, New Zealand, Norway, Poland, Portugal, the Russian Federation, Singapore, Slovenia, Spain, Sweden, Switzerland, Turkey and the United Kingdom.
18. Estimates are based on the voluntary, *ad hoc* module in the EU Community Innovation Survey 2010 on the skills available in enterprises and on methods to stimulate new ideas and creativity. The indicator corresponds to the percentage of firms in the relevant innovation category responding affirmatively to the question: "During the three years 2008 to 2010, did your enterprise employ individuals in-house with the following skills, or obtain these skills from external sources?" Innovative enterprises had innovation activities during 2008-10, relating to the introduction of new products, processes, and organisational or marketing methods. This includes enterprises with ongoing and abandoned activities for product and process innovation. The question on innovation-relevant skills also applies to non-innovative enterprises. Estimates are based on firms with "core" NACE Rev. 2 economic activities (B, C, D, E, G46, H, J58, J61, J62, J63, K and M71).
19. A compilation of such policies, based on EU member states' best practices, has been developed by the European Commission with the support of Member States' experts from member states. See: *https://ec.europa.eu/digital-single-market/en/news/shared-concept-national-digital-skills-strategies.*
20. For more information on the CanCode programme, see *https://www.canada.ca/en/innovation-science-economic-development/programs/science-technology-partnerships/cancode.html.*

21. Australia, Austria, Belgium, Brazil, Canada, Chile, China, Colombia, Costa Rica, the Czech Republic, Denmark, Estonia, Finland, France, Germany, Hungary, Ireland, Israel, Japan, Korea, Latvia, Lithuania, Luxembourg, Mexico, the Netherlands, Norway, Poland, Portugal, the Russian Federation, Slovenia, Spain, Sweden, Switzerland, Turkey and the United Kingdom.
22. One area where there are plenty of policies targeting young firms is ICT sector development, as mentioned in the first section of this chapter. Among 38 respondents, 26 countries had policies aimed at both start-ups and SMEs, while 18 had policies specifically aimed at start-ups alone.
23. Again, other OECD work shows that 29 of the 35 OECD countries have an R&D tax credit (OECD and EC, 2017: 4).
24. For more information on these funds, see: *www.eif.org/what_we_do/resources/erp/index.htm?lang=-en*, *www.eif.org/what_we_do/equity/eaf/Germany.htm*, *www.eif.org/what_we_do/equity/news/2016/eif-bmwi-new-instrument-venture-capital-germany.htm* and *http://high-tech-gruenderfonds.de/en/#title*.
25. For more information, see: *www.bankofengland.co.uk/publications/Pages/speeches/2016/914.aspx* and *https://services.parliament.uk/bills/2016-17/digitaleconomy.html*.
26. This may not be an altogether representative data set, however, because disruptors such as Uber and Tesla, Inc. have faced many regulations – though not always new ones – that were designed to protect incumbents (OECD, 2015a).
27. For more information on this initiative, see: *https://www.lvm.fi/documents/20181/859937/MyData-nordic-model/2e9b4eb0-68d7-463b-9460-821493449a63?version=1.0*.
28. See: *https://www.lvm.fi/mobility-as-a-service*.
29. For more information on this initiative, see: *https://www.paymentsforum.uk/sites/default/files/documents/Background%20Document%20No.%201%20-%20Introducing%20the%20Open%20Banking%20Standard%202016.pdf*.
30. An overview may be found at: *https://telemedizinportal.gematik.de*.
31. An English language version of the paper is available at: *www.bmas.de/EN/Services/Publications/arbeiten-4-0-greenpaper-work-4-0.html*.
32. An English version was published in March and is available at: *www.bmas.de/EN/Services/Publications/a883-white-paper.html*.
33. See *http://plattformindustrie40.at* for more information.
34. Australia, Austria, Belgium, Canada, Chile, Colombia, Costa Rica, Denmark, Finland, France, Iceland, Italy, Japan, Korea, Latvia, Lithuania, Luxembourg, Mexico, the Netherlands, New Zealand, Norway, Poland, Portugal, the Russian Federation, Singapore, the Slovak Republic, Slovenia, Spain, Sweden, Switzerland, Turkey, the United Kingdom and the United States.
35. Articles 14 and 15 of the Directive (EU) 2016/1148 of the European Parliament and of the Council of 6 July 2016 concerning measures for a high common level of security of network and information systems across the European Union: *http://eur-lex.europa.eu/legal-content/EN/TXT/?uri=uriserv:OJ.L_.2016.194.01.0001.01.ENG&toc=OJ:L:2016:194:TOC*.
36. *https://www.ssi.gouv.fr/en/cybersecurity-in-france/ciip-in-france*.
37. *http://ehoganlovells.com/cv/53b6c1e3cb33dedddd11ffd68c0022e08d10c4e4*.
38. *https://www.first.org/about*.
39. Australia, Austria, Belgium, Brazil, Canada, Chile, Colombia, Costa Rica, Denmark, Estonia, Finland, France, Hungary, Iceland, Israel, Italy, Japan, Korea, Lithuania, Luxembourg, Mexico, the Netherlands, New Zealand, Norway, Poland, the Russian Federation, Singapore, the Slovak Republic, Slovenia, Spain, Switzerland, Turkey, the United Kingdom and the United States.
40. Canadian businesses, for example, are required to comply with privacy laws at both the federal and provincial/territorial level.
41. The privacy management plan template developed by the OAIC is dedicated to public sector agencies.
42. See, for example, *https://privacy.org.nz/your-rights/complaint-form* in the case of New Zealand.
43. In 2015, Korea allowed individuals to provide claims for damages: up to three times of the amount of the punitive damage and up to KRW 3 million in the case of statutory damages.
44. See: *http://194.242.234.211/documents/10160/2416443/Privacy%3A+working+with+business-vademecum.pdf*.
45. It is estimated that the Privacy Shield underpins over USD 290 billion in digitally deliverable services trade across the Atlantic each year.

References

ACM (Authority for Consumers and Markets) (2015), "IP interconnection in the Netherlands: A regulatory assessment", Authority for Consumers and Markets, The Hague, *www.acm.nl/nl/publicaties/publicatie/14769/Onderzoek-IP-interconnectie-in-Nederland* (accessed 9 May 2017).

Adalet McGowan, M. and D. Andrews (2015), "Skill mismatch and public policy in OECD countries", *OECD Economics Department Working Papers*, No. 1 210, OECD Publishing, Paris, *http://dx.doi.org/10.1787/5js1pzw9lnwk-en*.

APEC (Asia-Pacific Economic Cooperation) (n.d.), "Cross-border Privacy Rules System", webpage, *www.cbprs.org/* (accessed 29 August 2017).

ARCEP (Autorité de régulation des communications électroniques et des postes) (2017) "State of Internet in France 2017", Autorité de régulation des communications électroniques et des postes, Paris, *https://www.arcep.fr/uploads/tx_gspublication/State-Of-Internet-in-France-2017_may2017.pdf* (accessed 27 July 2017).

BEREC (Body of European Regulators for Electronic Communications) (2015), "Draft report on OTT services", *BoR*, Vol. 15/142, Body of European Regulators for Electronic Communications, Riga, *http://berec.europa.eu/eng/document_register/subject_matter/berec/public_consultations/5431-draft-berec-report-on-ott-services* (accessed 9 May 2017).

Bourassa, F. et al. (2016), "Developments in international mobile roaming", *OECD Digital Economy Papers*, No. 249, OECD Publishing, Paris, *http://dx.doi.org/10.1787/5jm01sq78vmx-en*.

CNMC (Comisión Nacional de los Mercados y la Competencia) (2015), "Caracterización del uso de algunos servicios over the top en España (Comunicaciones electrónicas y servicios audiovisuales)" [Characterisation of the use of some over-the-top services in Spain (Electronic communications and audiovisual services)], *Documento de Trabajo*, No. 4, Comisión Nacional de los Mercados y la Competencia, Barcelona, Spain, *https://www.cnmc.es/node/356182*.

Competition Bureau of Canada (2015), "Modernizing regulation in the Canadian taxi industry", Competition Bureau of Canada, 26 November, *www.competitionbureau.gc.ca/eic/site/cb-bc.nsf/eng/04007.html* (accessed 9 May 2017).

CRTC (Canadian Radio-television and Telecommunications Commission) (2016), "Examination of differential pricing practices related to Internet data plans", *Telecom Notice of Consultation*, CRTC 2016-192, Canadian Radio-television and Telecommunications Commission, Ottawa, Ontario, *www.crtc.gc.ca/eng/archive/2016/2016-192.htm* (accessed 9 May 2017).

Danish Agency for Culture and Palaces (2015), *Media Development in Denmark 2015*, Ministry for Culture, Copenhagen, *http://english.slks.dk/publications/media-development-in-denmark-2015* (accessed 9 May 2017).

DeStefano, T., K. de Backer and L. Moussiegt (2017), "Determinants of digital technology use by companies", *OECD Science, Technology and Industry Policy Papers*, No. 40, OECD Publishing, Paris, *http://dx.doi.org/10.1787/a9b53784-en*.

EC (European Commission) (2017a), "European legislation on reuse of public sector information", European Commission, Brussels, *https://ec.europa.eu/digital-single-market/en/european-legislation-reuse-public-sector-information* (accessed 4 April 2017).

EC (2017b), "Communication from the Commission to the European Parliament and the Council on exchanging and protecting personal data in a globalised world", COM(2017)7 final, European Commission, Brussels, *https://ec.europa.eu/newsroom/document.cfm?doc_id=41157*.

EC (2017c), "Results of the Fitness Check of consumer and marketing law and of the evaluation of the Consumer Rights Directive", European Commission, Brussels, *http://ec.europa.eu/newsroom/just/item-detail.cfm?item_id=59332* (accessed 16 June 2017).

EC (2016a), "Proposal for a Directive of the European Parliament and of the Council amending Directive 2010/13/EU [Audiovisual Media Services Directive (AVMSD)]", COM(2016)287 (final), European Commission, Brussels, *http://eur-lex.europa.eu/legal-content/EN/TXT/?qid=1464618463840&uri=COM:2016:287:FIN* (accessed 6 July 2017).

EC (2016b), "Roaming implementing regulation", Act, 15 December, European Commission, Brussels, *https://ec.europa.eu/digital-single-market/en/news/roaming-implementing-regulation* (accessed 9 May 2017).

EC (2016c), "Roaming", webpage, *https://ec.europa.eu/digital-single-market/en/roaming* (accessed 9 May 2017).

EC (2016d), "Communication from the Commission to the European Parliament, the Council, the European Economic and Social Committee and the Committee of the Regions: A comprehensive approach to stimulating cross-border e-commerce for Europe's citizens and businesses", COM(2016) 320final, European Commission, Brussels, *www.cdep.ro/afaceri_europene/CE/2016/COM_2016_320_EN_ACTE_f.pdf.*

EC (2015), "A Digital Single Market Strategy for Europe", COM(2015)192 (final), European Commission, Brussels, *http://eur-lex.europa.eu/legal-content/EN/TXT/?qid=1447773803386&uri=CELEX%3A52015DC0192* (accessed 9 May 2017).

European Parliament and European Council (2015), "Regulation (EU) 2015/2120 of the European Parliament and of the Council of 25 November 2015 on Laying Down Measures Concerning Open Internet Access and Amending Directive 2002/22/EC on Universal Service and Users' Rights Relating to Electronic Communications Networks and Services and Regulation (EU) No. 521/2012 on Roaming on Public Mobile Communication Networks Within the Union", *Official Journal of the European Union*, 26 November, L 310/1, *http://eur-lex.europa.eu/legal-content/EN/ALL/?uri=CELEX%3A32015R2120.*

European Parliament and European Council (2014), "Directive 2014/61/EU of the European Parliament and of the Council of 15 May 2014 on Measures to Reduce the Cost of Deploying High-Speed Electronic Communications Networks", *Official Journal of the European Union*, 23 May, L 155/1, *http://eur-lex.europa.eu/eli/dir/2014/61/oj* (accessed 9 May 2017).

FTC (Federal Trade Commission) (2016), "The 'sharing' economy: Issues facing platforms, participants & regulators", FTC Staff Report, Federal Trade Commission, Washington, DC, November, *www.ftc.gov/system/files/documents/reports/sharing-economy-issues-facing-platforms-participants-regulators-federal-trade-commission-staff/p151200_ftc_staff_report_on_the_sharing_economy.pdf.*

FTC (2015), "Start with security: A guide for business", Federal Trade Commission, Washington, DC, *https://www.ftc.gov/tips-advice/business-center/guidance/start-security-guide-business.*

Gaggle, P. and G. Wright (2014), "A short-run view of what computers do: Evidence from a UK tax incentive", *Discussion Paper Series*, No. 752, July, University of Essex, Colchester, United Kingdom.

Grazzi, M. and J. Jung (2016), "ICT, innovation and productivity: Evidence from Latin American firms", in: *Firms' Innovation and Productivity in Latin America and the Caribbean: The Engine of Economic Development*, Palgrave, New York.

Haller, S.A. and I. Siedschlag (2011), "Determinants of ICT adoption: Evidence from firm-level data", *Applied Economics*, Vol. 43/26, pp. 3 775-3 788, *http://dx.doi.org/10.1080/00036841003724411.*

Hathaway, I. (2016), "What start-up accelerators really do", *Harvard Business Review*, 1 March, *https://hbr.org/2016/03/what-startup-accelerators-really-do* (accessed 15 March 2016).

Headquarters for the Promotion of an Advanced Information and Telecommunications Network Society (IT Strategic Headquarters) (2016), "Declaration to Be the World's Most Advanced IT Nation", Government of Japan, *http://japan.kantei.go.jp/policy/it/index_e.html* (accessed 9 May 2017).

MBIE (2015), "Business Growth Agenda", Ministry of Business, Innovation and Employment, Wellington, New Zealand, *www.mbie.govt.nz/info-services/business/business-growth-agenda* (accessed 9 May 2017).

MBIE (Ministry of Business, Innovation and Employment) and MCH (Ministry for Culture and Heritage) (2015), "Exploring digital convergence: Issues for policy and legislation", Ministry of Business, Innovation and Employment and Ministry for Culture and Heritage, Wellington, New Zealand, *http://convergencediscussion.nz* (accessed 9 May 2017).

OECD (Organisation for Economic Co-operation and Development) (2017), "Benefits and challenges of digitalising production", in *The Next Production Revolution: Implications for Governments and Business*, OECD Publishing, Paris, *http://dx.doi.org/10.1787/9789264271036-en.*

OECD (2016a), "Stimulating digital innovation for growth and inclusiveness: The role of policies for the successful diffusion of ICT", *OECD Digital Economy Papers*, No. 256, OECD Publishing, Paris, *http://dx.doi.org/10.1787/5jlwqvhg3l31-en.*

OECD (2016b), "Be flexible! Background brief on how workplace flexibility can help European employees to balance work and family", OECD, Paris, *www.oecd.org/els/family/Be-Flexible-Backgrounder-Workplace-Flexibility.pdf.*

OECD (2016c), *Recommendation of the Council on Consumer Protection in E-commerce*, OECD, Paris, *https://www.oecd.org/sti/consumer/ECommerce-Recommendation-2016.pdf.*

OECD (2016d), "Protecting consumers in peer platform markets: Exploring the issues", *OECD Digital Economy Papers*, No. 253, OECD Publishing, Paris, *http://dx.doi.org/10.1787/5jlwvz39m1zw-en.*

OECD (2016e), "Online product safety: Trends and challenges", *OECD Digital Economy Papers*, No. 261, OECD Publishing, Paris, *http://dx.doi.org/10.1787/5jlnb5q93jlt-en*.

OECD (2016f), *OECD Science, Technology and Innovation Outlook 2016*, OECD Publishing, Paris, *http://dx.doi.org/10.1787/sti_in_outlook-2016-en*.

OECD (2016g), "Managing digital security and privacy risk", *OECD Digital Economy Papers*, No. 254, OECD Publishing, Paris, *http://dx.doi.org/10.1787/5jlwt49ccklt-en*.

OECD (2015a), "Hearing on disruptive innovation," OECD, Paris, *https://www.oecd.org/officialdocuments/publicdisplaydocumentpdf/?cote=DAF/COMP(2015)3&docLanguage=En*.

OECD (2015b), *OECD Digital Economy Outlook 2015*, OECD Publishing, Paris, *http://dx.doi.org/10.1787/9789264232440-en*.

OECD (2015c), "Non-standard work, job polarisation and inequality", Chapter 4 in: *In It Together: Why Less Inequality Benefits All*, OECD Publishing, Paris, *http://dx.doi.org/10.1787/9789264235120-7-en*.

OECD (2015d), "Enquiries into intellectual property's economic impact", OECD, Paris, *www.oecd.org/sti/ieconomy/KBC2-IP.Final.pdf*.

OECD (2014a), "International traffic termination", *OECD Digital Economy Papers*, No. 238, OECD Publishing, Paris, *http://dx.doi.org/10.1787/5jz2m5mnlvkc-en*.

OECD (2014b), "Young SMEs, growth and job creation", *Policy Brief*, OECD, Paris, *www.oecd.org/sti/young-SME-growth-and-job-creation.pdf*.

OECD (2014c), "Non-regular employment, job security and the labour market divide", Chapter 4 in: *OECD Employment Outlook 2014*, OECD Publishing, Paris, *http://dx.doi.org/10.1787/empl_outlook-2014-en*.

OECD (2013a), *Supporting Investment in Knowledge Capital, Growth and Innovation*, OECD Publishing, Paris, *http://dx.doi.org/10.1787/9789264193307-en*.

OECD (2013b), *Recommendation of the Council concerning Guidelines Governing the Protection of Privacy and Transborder Flows of Personal Data*, OECD, Paris, *www.oecd.org/internet/ieconomy/privacy-guidelines.htm*.

OECD (2012a), "ICT skills and employment: New competences and jobs for a greener and smarter economy", *OECD Digital Economy Papers*, No. 198, OECD Publishing, Paris, *http://dx.doi.org/10.1787/5k994f3prlr5-en*.

OECD (2012b), "Machine-to-machine communications: Connecting billions of devices", *OECD Digital Economy Papers*, No. 192, OECD Publishing, Paris, *http://dx.doi.org/10.1787/5k9gsh2gp043-en*.

OECD and EC (European Commission) (2017), "OECD Review of National R&D Tax Incentives and estimates of R&D tax subsidy rates, 2016", TAX4INNO Project 674888, OECD, Paris, *www.oecd.org/sti/RDTaxIncentives-DesignSubsidyRates.pdf*.

Ofcom (2016), "Making communications work for everyone: Initial conclusions from the Strategic Review of Digital Communications", Office of Communications, London, *https://www.ofcom.org.uk/phones-telecoms-and-internet/information-for-industry/policy/digital-comms-review/conclusions-strategic-review-digital-Communications* (accessed 9 May 2017).

Turkish Government (2016), "National Market Surveillance Programme for 2016", *http://ec.europa.eu/DocsRoom/documents/15742?locale=fr* (accessed 9 May 2017).

WEF (World Economic Forum) (2015), "Industrial Internet of Things: Unleashing the potential of connected products and services", WEF Industry Agenda, World Economic Forum, Geneva, January, *http://www3.weforum.org/docs/WEFUSA_IndustrialInternet_Report2015.pdf*.

WTO (World Trade Organization) (1998), "Work programme on electronic commerce", WT/L/274, World Trade Organization, Geneva, *https://docsonline.wto.org/dol2fe/Pages/FormerScriptedSearch/directdoc.aspx?DDFDocuments/t/WT/L/274.DOC* (accessed 16 March 2017).

ANNEX 2.A1

Selected communication mergers, circa USD 500 million or above, 2014-16

Country	Transaction
Australia	Between 2014 and 2016, TPG Telecom and Vocus Communications both acquired multiple networks to become the second and fourth-largest Internet service providers by subscriptions.
Belgium	In 2016, Telenet, Liberty Global Belgian's subsidiary, merged with the mobile network operator base.
Canada	In 2016, Shaw Communications, a cable operator, acquired the mobile network operator (MNO) Wind. In 2015, an incumbent MNO, Rogers, acquired a new MNO entrant, Mobilicity. In 2014, Bell Canada acquired the related entity Bell Aliant.
Denmark	In 2016, Syd Energi and Nyfors merged – both provide fibre infrastructures.
France	In 2014, Numericable, cable operator, purchased MNO SFR.
Germany	In 2014, the two MNOs Telefónica and E-Plus merged. Mergers between cable companies included Tele Columbus and Primacom in 2015, United Internet and Versatel in 2014 as well as the MNO Vodafone with Kabel Deutschland also in 2014.
Greece	In 2014, Vodafone Greece acquired HOL, a major, alternative fixed network operator.
Ireland	The two MNOs, H3GI and Telefónica (O2), merged in 2014.
Italy	The two MNOs "3 Italia" and Wind Telecomunicazioni (VimpelCom) merged in 2016.
Netherlands	In 2014 there was a merger between two cable network operators – Liberty Global's UPC – Ziggo. In 2016, Vodafone and Ziggo subsequently merged.
Portugal	In 2014, ZON TV Cabo Portugal, was acquired by NOS Comunicações. In the same year MEO-Serviços de Comunicações e Multimédia, was acquired by PT Comunicações. PT Comunicações then changed its name to MEO-Serviços de Comunicações e Multimédia. Cabovisão and ONITELECOM were acquired by Grupo Apaxin 2015. In June 2015, Altice completed the acquisition of 100% of the share capital of PT Portugal, SGPS, owners of MEO-Serviços de Comunicações e Multimédia; consequently, the European Commission required Altice to divest from ONI and Cabovisão. In January 2016, Altice announced the completion of the sale of ONI and Cabovisão to the Apax France investment fund.
Spain	The MNO Vodafone and ONO, a cable operator, merged in 2014, as did the MNO Orange with the fixed network Jazztel in 2015. Additionally, in 2015 Telefónica acquired DTS, the main satellite pay TV operator in Spain.
United Kingdom	BT, a fixed network provider, acquired Everything Everywhere (EE), an MNO.
United States	In 2016, Charter/Time Warner Cable/Bright House was a merger of three cable providers and in the same year Altice and Cablevision a merger of a US and international cable provider. Also in 2016, Verizon Communications, Inc. acquired the licenses and assets of XO Communications, a competitive voice and broadband provider operating throughout the United States. In addition, Radiate Holdings, a private equity entity, acquired two cable/broadband entities whose strategy is to overbuild existing cable providers in several states. In 2015, Altice had merged with Suddenlink, a cable provider. In the same year, the Federal Communications Commission (FCC) approved the sale of Verizon wireline assets in California, Florida and Texas to Frontier. In 2015, the FCC also approved the acquisition of DirectTV, a satellite TV provider, by AT&T. In 2014, two fixed providers, Level 3 and tw telecom merged. In the same year, Frontier purchased AT&T's fixed-line subsidiary in Connecticut.

ANNEX 2.A2

Converged regulators

Country	Converged national regulatory authorities	Telecommunications	Broadcasting carriage regulation	Broadcasting spectrum allocation	Broadcasting content regulation
Australia	Yes	Australian Communications and Media Authority (ACMA)	ACMA	ACMA	ACMA
Austria	No	Telekom-Kontrol-Kommission (TKK), supported by RTR-GmbH	KommAustria (supported by RTR-GmbH)	KommAustria (supported by RTR-GmbH)	KommAustria (supported by RTR-GmbH)
Belgium	No	Belgian Institute for Postal Services and Telecommunications (BIPT)	Vlaams Commissariaat voor de Media (VCM); Conseil supérieur de l'audiovisuel (CSA); Government of the German Community	BIPT; VCM; CSA; Government of the German Community	VCM; CSA; Government of the German Community
Canada	Yes	Canadian Radio-television and Telecommunications Commission (CRTC)	CRTC	Innovation, Science and Economic Development Canada	CRTC
Chile	No	Subsecretaría de Telecomunicaciones (Subtel)	Subtel	Subtel	Consejo Nacional de Televisión (CNTV)
Colombia	No	Comisión de Regulación de Comunicaciones (CRC)	Autoridad Nacional de Televisión (ANTV)	ANTV; Agencia Nacional del Espectro (ANE)	ANTV
Czech Republic	No	Czech Telecommunications Office (CTU)	CTU	CTU; Council for Radio and Television Broadcasting	Council for Radio and Television Broadcasting
Denmark	No	Danish Business Authority (DBA)	Danish Energy Agency (DEA)	DEA	Ministry of Culture and the Radio and Television Board
Estonia	Yes	Estonia Technical Regulatory Authority (ETRA)	ETRA	ETRA	ETRA; Estonian Broadcasting Council (RHN)
Finland	Yes	Finnish Communications Regulatory Authority (FICORA)	FICORA; Ministry of Transport and Communications	FICORA	FICORA; Ministry of Transport and Communications
France	No	Autorité de régulation des communications électroniques et des postes (ARCEP)	ARCEP	Conseil supérieur de l'audiovisuel (CSA)	CSA and Direction générale des médias et des industries culturelles (DGMIC)
Germany	No	Bundesnetzagentur (BNetzA)	BNetzA, Association of Regulatory Authorities for Broadcasting (ALM), Commission on Concentration in the Media (KEK)	BNetzA	ALM
Greece	No	Hellenic Telecommunications and Post Commission (EETT)	Ministry of Press and Mass Media and Greek National Council for Radio and Television (NCRTV)	EETT	NCRTV
Hungary	Yes	National Media and Infocommunications Authority (NMHH)	NMHH	NMHH	NMHH

Country	Converged national regulatory authorities	Telecommunications	Broadcasting carriage regulation	Broadcasting spectrum allocation	Broadcasting content regulation
Iceland	No	Post and Telecom Administration (PTA)	PTA; Media Commission (Fjölmiðlanefnd)	PTA	Media Commission (Fjölmiðlanefnd)
Ireland	No	Commission for Communications Regulation (ComReg)	ComReg, Broadcasting Authority of Ireland (BAI)	ComReg	BAI
Israel	No	Ministry of Communications (MOC)	MOC	MOC	MOC and the Second Authority for Television and Radio
Italy	Yes	Autoritá per le garanzie nelle comunicazioni (AGCOM)	AGCOM	Ministry of Economic Development (MISE)	AGCOM
Japan	No	Ministry of Internal Affairs and Communications (MIC)	MIC	MIC	MIC
Korea	Yes	Ministry of Science and ICT(MSIT); Korea Communications Commission (KCC)	KCC	MSIT, KCC	KCC
Latvia	No	Public Utilities Commission (PUC)	National Electronic Mass Media Council (NEPLP)	Electronic Communication Office(ESD)	NEPLP
Luxembourg	No	Institut luxembourgeois de régulation (ILR)	Autorité luxembourgeoise indépendante de l'audiovisuel (ALIA)	ILR	ALIA
Mexico	Yes	Instituto Federal de Telecomunicaciones (IFT)	IFT	IFT	IFT
Netherlands	No	Autoriteit Consument & Markt (ACM)	Dutch Media Authority (CvdM)	ACM	CvdM
New Zealand	No	Commerce Commission of New Zealand (ComCom)	Ministry of Economic Development	Ministry of Economic Development	NZ On Air; Broadcasting Standards Authority (BSA)
Norway	No	Norwegian Communications Authority (Nkom)	Ministry of Culture and Church Affairs; Norwegian Media Authority; Nkom	Nkom	Norwegian Media Authority
Poland	No	Prezes Urzędu Komunikacji Elektronicznej (UKE)	National Broadcasting Council (KRRiT)	UKE; KRRiT	KRRiT
Portugal	No	Autoridade Nacional de Comunicações (ANACOM)	Entidade Reguladora para a Comunicação Social (ERC)	ANACOM	ERC; Instituto da Comunicação Social (ICS)
Slovak Republic	No	Telecommunications Regulatory Authority of the Slovak Republic (TUSR)	Council for Broadcasting and Retransmission (RVR)	TUSR; RVR	RVR
Slovenia	Yes	Agency for Communications Networks and Services of the Republic of Slovenia (AKOS)	AKOS	AKOS	AKOS
Spain	Yes	Comisión Nacional de Mercados y de la Competencia (CNMC)	CNMC	Ministry of Industry, Energy and Tourism (MINETUR)	CNMC and regional audiovisual authorities
Sweden	No	Swedish Post and Telecom Authority (PTS)	Swedish Broadcasting Authority	PTS	Swedish Broadcasting Authority
Switzerland	Yes	Federal Communications Commission (ComCom); Office fédéral de la communication (OFCOM)	Federal Council; Federal Department of Environment, Transport, Energy and Communications (DETEC); OFCOM	OFCOM	DETEC; OFCOM; Autorité indépendante d'examen des plaintes en matière de radio-télévision (AIEP)
Turkey	No	Information and Communication Technologies Authority (ICTA)	Radio and Television Supreme Council (RTUK)	Telecommunications Authority; RTUK	RTUK
United Kingdom	Yes	Office of Communications (Ofcom)	Ofcom; Department for Culture, Media and Sport	Ofcom	Ofcom
United States	Yes	Federal Communications Commission (FCC)	FCC; local government for cable television franchises	FCC	FCC; Federal Trade Commission (FTC); Department of Justice

ANNEX 2.A3

2016 Roam like at home offers

Home country	Roaming in:	Operators	Note
Austria	EEA countries, Switzerland	A1	For Switzerland, up to 300 MB/month
Belgium	EU countries and Norway	Proximus	Up to 240 MB/month
	EU countries, People's Republic of China, Egypt, Switzerland, Turkey, United States	Orange	Up to 1 GB/year
	EEA countries	BASE	Up to 600 MB/month
Canada	United States	WIND Mobile	Up to 1 GB/month
	United States	Videotron	Up to 5 GB/month for up to 90 days/year
Colombia	Canada and United States	Uff!Mobile	Up to 2 GB/month
Czech Republic	EU countries	T-Mobile	Up to 300 MB/month
	EU countries, Norway, Switzerland	02	Up to 300 MB/month
	EEA countries, Switzerland	Vodafone	Up to 100 MB/day
Denmark	EEA countries, Switzerland	TDC	Up to 30 days/year, 2 GB/month
	EEA countries, Switzerland	Telenor	Up to 30 days/year, 10 GB/month
	EEA countries, Switzerland	Telia	Up to 30 days/year, 10 GB/month
	EEA countries; Hong Kong, China; Switzerland; Singapore; United States	Hi 3G	Up to 30 days/year, 10 GB/month (excluding Sweden)
Estonia	EEA countries, Switzerland	Telia	Up to 300 MB/month
Finland	EU countries	Sonera	Up to 600 MB/month (excluding Denmark, Estonia, Latvia, Lithuania, Norway, Sweden)
	EU countries	Elisa	Up to 500 MB/month
France	EEA countries, Switzerland, Canada, United States	Orange	
	EEA countries, United States	SFR	
	EEA countries, Australia, Canada, Israel, United States	Iliad Free	Up to 35 days/year
	EEA countries and Switzerland	Bouygues	Up to 35 days/year
Germany	EEA countries, Australia, Canada, New Zealand, Switzerland, United States	T-Mobile	
	EEA countries	02	Up to 1 GB/month
	EU countries	Vodafone	
Greece	EEA countries	Cosmote	
	EU countries	Vodafone	
	EU countries	Wind	Up to 500 MB/month
Hungary	EU countries	Telenor	
	EU countries	Vodafone	
Ireland	32 European destinations	Vodafone	
	EEA countries	Meteor	
Israel	23 countries	Golan Telecom	NIS 49 (USD 13) one-time handling fee required
Italy	EEA countries, Switzerland, United States	TIM	Up to 28 days/year
	EEA countries, Albania, Switzerland, Turkey, United States	Vodafone	Up to 100 MB/day
Japan	United States	Softbank	Users need an iPhone 6 or newer/iPad Air2 or newer

Home country	Roaming in:	Operators	Note
Latvia	Estonia, Lithuania	Tele2	
	EEA countries	Bite	
Lithuania	Denmark, Estonia, Finland, Latvia, Norway, Sweden	Omnitel	
	EEA countries	Bite	
Luxembourg	EU countries	Join	
	EEA countries, Switzerland	POST	Up to 1 GB/month
	EEA countries, Switzerland	Tango	Up to 20 GB/year
	EEA countries	Orange	Up to 2 GB/month
Mexico	Canada and United States	AT&T Mexico	Limited to Internet access using Facebook/ Messenger, Twitter and WhatsApp
	North America, Central America and Pacific Alliance countries	TelCel	Voice, SMS, data, WhatsApp
Netherlands	EU countries	KPN	Up to 60 days/year
	EEA countries, Australia, Japan, New Zealand, Switzerland, Turkey	Vodafone	
	EEA countries, Switzerland	T-Mobile	
Norway	EEA countries	Telenor	
	EEA countries	Telia	45 days/90 days
Poland	EU countries	Orange	Up to 100 MB/month
	EU countries	Play	Up to 500 MB/month
	EEA countries	Plus	
	Albania, Austria, Czech Republic, Croatia, Germany, Greece, Hungary, Macedonia, Montenegro, Netherlands, Romania, Slovak Republic	T-Mobile	Up to 1 GB/month
Portugal	EEA countries, United States	MEO	Up to 200 MB in 15 days/year
	EU countries	Vodafone	
	EU countries	NOS	Up to 100 MB/month, 15 days/year
Slovak Republic	EU countries	Telekom	Up to 500 MB/month
	EU countries	02	
Slovenia	EEA countries, Former Yugoslav Republic of Macedonia, Serbia		
Spain	EU countries, United States	Vodafone	
	EEA countries	Orange	Up to 100 MB/month
Sweden	Nordic and Baltic countries	Telia	
	EEA countries	Telenor	Up to 1 Mbps outside Scandinavia
	Denmark	Hi 3G	
Switzerland	European Union and Western Europe/rest of the world (with some exceptions)	Swisscom	Up to 24 GB/year in EU/western European countries, up to 1 GB/year in the rest of the world
	EEA countries, Canada, United States	Sunrise	Up to 2 GB/month
	EU countries/rest of the world (more than 170 countries)	Salt	Up to 1 GB/month in EU countries, and another 1 GB/month in the rest of the world
United Kingdom	EEA countries	EE	Up to 500 MB/month
	EEA countries	02	
	EEA countries, Albania, Bosnia, Switzerland, Turkey	Vodafone	Up to 4 GB/month
	EEA countries; Australia; Hong Kong, China; Indonesia; Israel; Macau; New Zealand; Sri Lanka; Switzerland; United States	3G-UK	
United States	Mexico	AT&T	
	Argentina, Bolivia, Brazil, Canada, Chile, Colombia, Costa Rica, Dominican Republic, Ecuador, El Salvador, Guatemala, Honduras, Mexico, Nicaragua, Panama, Paraguay, Peru, Uruguay, Venezuela	Sprint	Up to 1 GB
	Over 140 countries	T-Mobile (US)	For Canada and Mexico, unlimited data usage without a speed cap. For the rest of the world, speed capped at 128 kbps.

Notes: From 15 June 2017, Operators of EEA member countries listed in this table (other than Finland and Lithuania) are complying with Regulation (EU) No 531/2012, as amended by Regulation (EU) 2015/2120, and no longer levy any surcharge on roaming service customers in EEA member countries. EEA = European Economic Area; GB = Gigabyte; MB = Megabyte; kbps = kilobits per second.

PART II

Trends

Chapter 3

Access and connectivity

Information and communication technologies (ICTs) are the backbone of the digital economy and society. This chapter examines recent trends and structural features of the ICT sector, telecommunication markets, and broadband infrastructures and services. It focuses on the one hand on recent trends in ICT sector value added and employment, growth of ICT manufacturing and services, trade in ICT goods and services, and ICTs' role for innovation, and on the other hand on investment and revenues in communication markets, fixed and mobile broadband subscriptions, and core aspects in the development of the Internet of Things. Policy and regulation related to access and connectivity are discussed in Chapter 2.

The statistical data for Israel are supplied by and under the responsibility of the relevant Israeli authorities. The use of such data by the OECD is without prejudice to the status of the Golan Heights, East Jerusalem and Israeli settlements in the West Bank under the terms of international law.

Introduction

Information and communication technologies (ICTs) are the backbone of the digital economy and society. This chapter reviews trends and recent developments in core sectors, including ICT supplying sectors and communication services, which provide the foundations for access to and connectivity within digital environments. It focuses on the ICT sector, communication markets, broadband networks and the Internet of Things (IoT).

The ICT sector is a key driver of innovation, accounting for the largest share (23%) of business expenditure on research and development (BERD) in the OECD. About 37% of all patent applications are in ICT technologies. In 2015, the ICT sector accounted for 4.5% of total value added in OECD countries, largely concentrated in services (80%). At the end of 2016, over 70% of the United States' venture capital (VC) investments went to the ICT industry.

Employment in the ICT sector has proved resilient to the 2007 crisis and has been growing since 2013. This trend is mainly driven by sustained job creation in information technology (IT) services and software. These trends are expected to continue in the coming years, as the share of VC investment in ICTs is back to the peak it reached in 2000.

Communication networks are critical for the development of digital economies. They underpin the broader use of ICTs for economic and social development and assist in achieving policy goals. In recent years, communication infrastructures and services have continued to develop apace, driven by increasing demand, tremendous innovation and growing competitiveness. More than ever, OECD countries welcome these developments, recognising their potential to strengthen and sustain their economies and to improve social welfare.

In terms of infrastructure, communication operators have deployed fibre optics further into their networks to support the evolving "last mile" technologies that are designed to make copper, wireless and coaxial cable able to deliver higher speeds or, in the case of some, taken fibre all the way to the premises of their customers. While the devices people use in their daily lives are increasingly wireless, whether over cellular mobile services or Wi-Fi connectivity, this is only possible if fixed networks are available with sufficient capacity to meet the growing demands for data that are generated in digital economies.

Backbone facilities have for many years been made up almost entirely of fibre networks. The lines used to connect to these backbones provide the backhaul necessary to connect wireless towers or end users directly. For fixed network access this is necessary to support the increasing capacity being offered to users. The first 10 Gigabits per second (Gbps) commercial broadband offers have started to be deployed and, while still few in number, point to the future. Not so long ago offers from 100 Megabits per second (Mbps) to 1 Gbps were the outliers but today they are increasingly commonplace in OECD countries.

Fixed-line gigabit services will require major investment in backhaul networks to meet demand and, for the same reason, so will wireless networks. Many believe commercial 5G services will be brought into play around 2020 with an increasing number of trials already underway. Just as each previous generation of mobile technology needed higher capacity backhaul networks, so too will 5G. Moreover, the cells for 5G are expected to be smaller than for previous generations requiring many more locations. Some will be the traditional towers with a greater array of transmitters, to make more efficient use of available spectrum, but others will be located on urban infrastructures, from lampposts to street signs and rooftops.

The development of gigabit fixed and 5G wireless networks will necessitate ever-closer attention, as more infrastructures will need to be deployed and the use of IoT devices and machine to machine (M2M) keeps growing, for example for autonomous vehicles, which are likely to spur large increases in the amount of data they generate. Some of the demands of these services will be well met by technologies such as Long-term Evolution for Machines (LTE-M),[1] with the first such networks now being deployed.

Key findings for the ICT sector are that since the global economic crisis, value added in the ICT sector as a whole has decreased in the OECD in line with total value added. Within the ICT sector, however, value added in telecommunication services and in computer and electronics manufacturing has decreased while it has increased in IT services and remained constant in software publishing. These contrasting trends, which are being reflected in OECD ICT employment, are expected to continue in the coming years as the share of venture capital investment in ICTs – an indicator of business expectations - is back to its 2000 peak. The ICT sector remains a key driver of innovation, accounting for the largest share of OECD BERD and for over one third of total patent applications worldwide.

Key findings for infrastructures, services and the IoT are that demand and innovation are driving positive developments in communication infrastructures and services. Fixed broadband subscriptions continue to increase, while average prices for both fixed and mobile broadband access are decreasing, and mobile broadband subscriptions are at a new high, with mobile data usage growing exponentially in some countries and Wi-Fi helping to offload some of the traffic. The IoT continues to evolve with M2M subscriptions on the rise and different wireless options promising improved connectivity.

Trends in the ICT sector

Growth in the ICT sector is increasingly driven by software production and services, with the latter accounting for more than 80% of total ICT value added. Slower growth in the ICT sector seems due to the sluggish performance of the semiconductor industry, which was previously a key branch of the industry. However, despite an overall decline in value, the share of ICT goods and services in total trade continues to increase. Production and export of ICT goods and services are increasingly concentrated in a few OECD countries, with six of them accounting for about 80% of world exports of ICT goods. The ICT sector remains a key driver of innovation, with over 30% of all patent applications in the OECD being related to ICT.

The ICT sector has not fully recovered from the crisis, but computer and data-related services drive a positive outlook

Recent trends in value added and employment

Since the global economic crisis, value added in the OECD ICT sector has remained constant, in line with the total value added (Figure 3.1). Several factors are at play and there are undoubtedly shifts between the sectors that make up this category. Between 2008 and 2015, value added in telecommunication services (-10%) and computer and electronics manufacturing (-7%) decreased as a result of a combination of factors, including increased use of production in OECD partner economies and the value added being recorded in different areas. While demand for devices and services are increasing, this is to some extent offset by global and local competition reducing prices. In addition, once recorded in telecommunication services, value added faces increased competition due to the greater use of software defined services. On the other hand, value added increased by 16% in IT services and by 12% in software.

Figure 3.1. **Growth in the value added of the ICT sector and its sub-sectors in the OECD area**

USD current prices (2008 = 100)

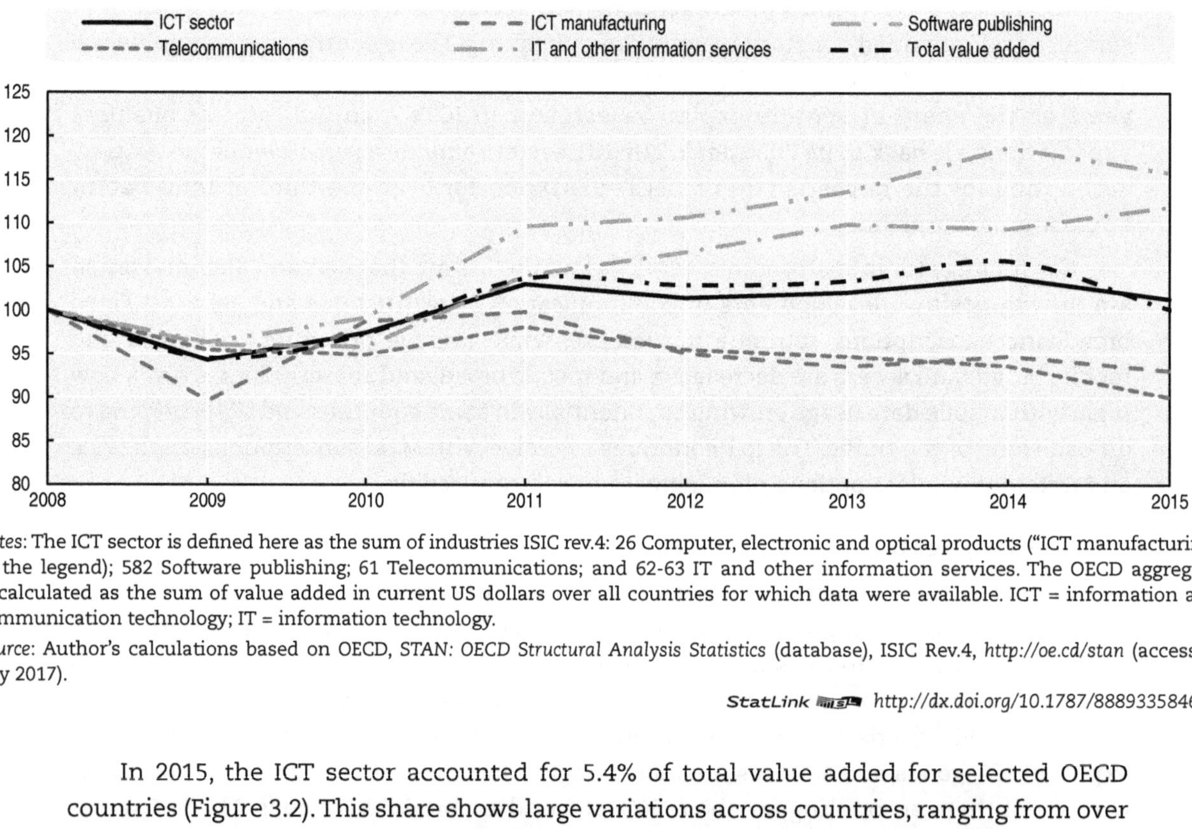

Notes: The ICT sector is defined here as the sum of industries ISIC rev.4: 26 Computer, electronic and optical products ("ICT manufacturing" in the legend); 582 Software publishing; 61 Telecommunications; and 62-63 IT and other information services. The OECD aggregate is calculated as the sum of value added in current US dollars over all countries for which data were available. ICT = information and communication technology; IT = information technology.

Source: Author's calculations based on OECD, *STAN: OECD Structural Analysis Statistics* (database), ISIC Rev.4, *http://oe.cd/stan* (accessed July 2017).

StatLink *http://dx.doi.org/10.1787/888933584697*

In 2015, the ICT sector accounted for 5.4% of total value added for selected OECD countries (Figure 3.2). This share shows large variations across countries, ranging from over 10% of total value added in Korea to less than 3% in Mexico and Turkey. Sweden has the second-largest share (over 7%), followed by Finland (close to 7%).

In the majority of OECD countries, the value added tends to concentrate in ICT services, which accounts for three-quarters of total ICT sector value added (4% of total value added), reflecting a broader trend of specialisation in services rather than manufacturing. Within ICT services, IT and other information services industries are prominent in most OECD countries. Exceptions are Greece, Luxembourg and Mexico, where the value added is concentrated in the telecommunications industries.

Figure 3.2. **Value added of the ICT sector and sub-sectors, 2015**

As a percentage of total value added at current prices

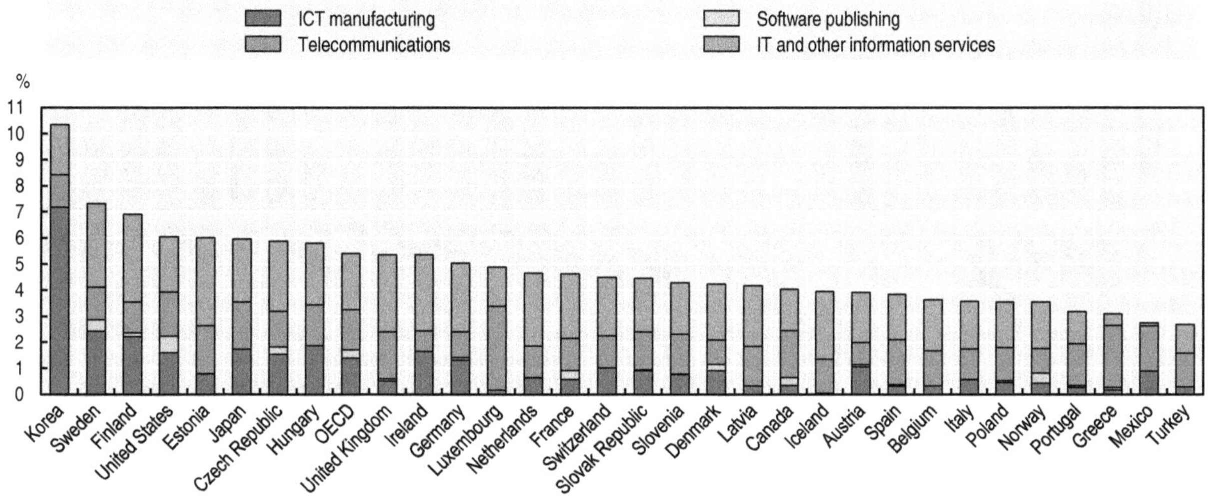

Notes: The ICT sector is defined here as the sum of industries ISIC rev.4: 26 Computer, electronic and optical products ("ICT manufacturing" in the legend); 582 Software publishing; 61 Telecommunications; and 62-63 IT and other information services. Data for Germany, Latvia, Poland, Portugal, Spain and Switzerland are for 2014. Data for Canada and Korea are for 2013. Data on software publishing were not available for Hungary, Iceland, Ireland, Japan, Korea, Luxembourg and Turkey; therefore their share could be underestimated. 2015 data on software publishing are estimates based on weights from 2014. In Switzerland, data for category 26 Computer, electronic and optical products were estimated to correct the effect of the watches industry; therefore the ICT sector share is not fully comparable with the rest of countries as it was calculated according to the OECD definition of the ICT sector. Data for Japan and the United States were partially estimated based on official data by industry. The OECD aggregate is calculated as the sum of value added in current US dollars over all countries for which data were available. IT = information technology; ICT = information and communication technology.

Source: Author's calculations based on OECD, *STAN: OECD Structural Analysis Statistics* (database), ISIC Rev.4, *http://oe.cd/stan* (accessed July 2017).

StatLink http://dx.doi.org/10.1787/888933584716

Figure 3.3 shows the evolution in the years following the crisis of the share of ICT goods and services in total value added by country. The picture is somewhat mixed. In certain countries, notably Finland, Ireland, Japan and Luxembourg, this share decreased between 2008 and 2015. In others, however, the share increased – notably in Estonia, Iceland, Latvia, Norway and Sweden.

From 2008 to 2015, employment in the ICT sector proved resilient and it has grown faster than total employment (Figure 3.4). This is mainly caused by the continued growth in the number of people employed in specific sub-sectors, such as the IT and other information services industries and the software publishing industries. On the other hand, the two sub-sectors that have not shown any signs of recovery following the crisis in terms of employment are the ICT manufacturing and the telecommunication industries, which continue to decrease.

Figure 3.3. **Evolution of the share of value added of the ICT sector**

As a percentage of total value added at current prices

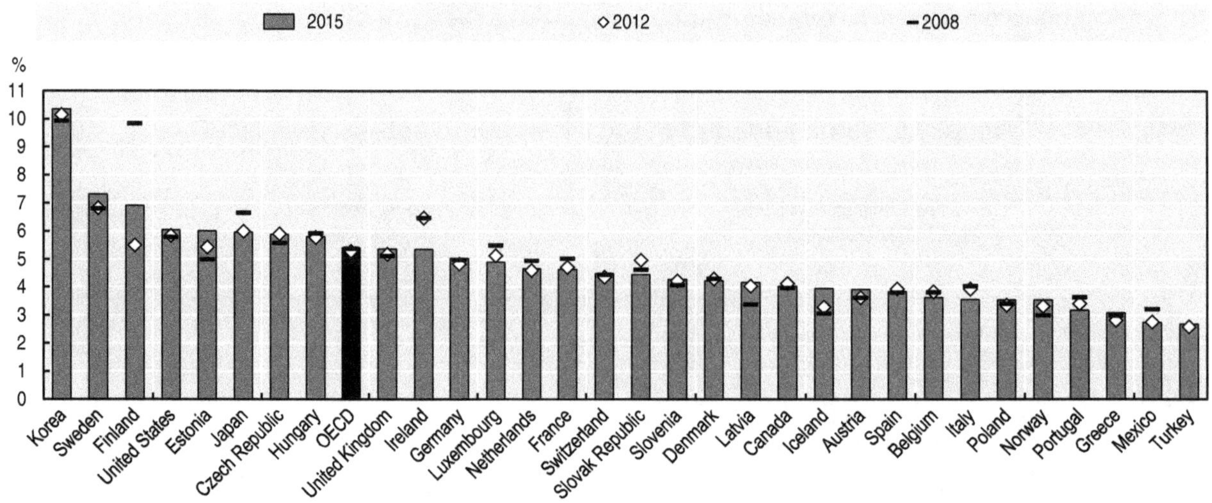

Notes: The ICT sector is defined here as the sum of industries ISIC rev.4: 26 Computer, electronic and optical products; 582 Software publishing; 61 Telecommunications; and 62-63 IT and other information services. Data for Germany, Latvia, Poland, Portugal, Spain and Switzerland are for 2014. Data for Canada and Korea are for 2013. The OECD aggregate is calculated as the sum of value added in current US dollars over all countries for which data were available.

Source: Author's calculations based on OECD, STAN: *OECD Structural Analysis Statistics* (database), ISIC Rev.4, *http://oe.cd/stan* (accessed July 2017).

StatLink *http://dx.doi.org/10.1787/888933584735*

Figure 3.4. **Growth of employment in the ICT sector and its sub-sectors in the OECD area**

Number of persons employed (2008 = 100)

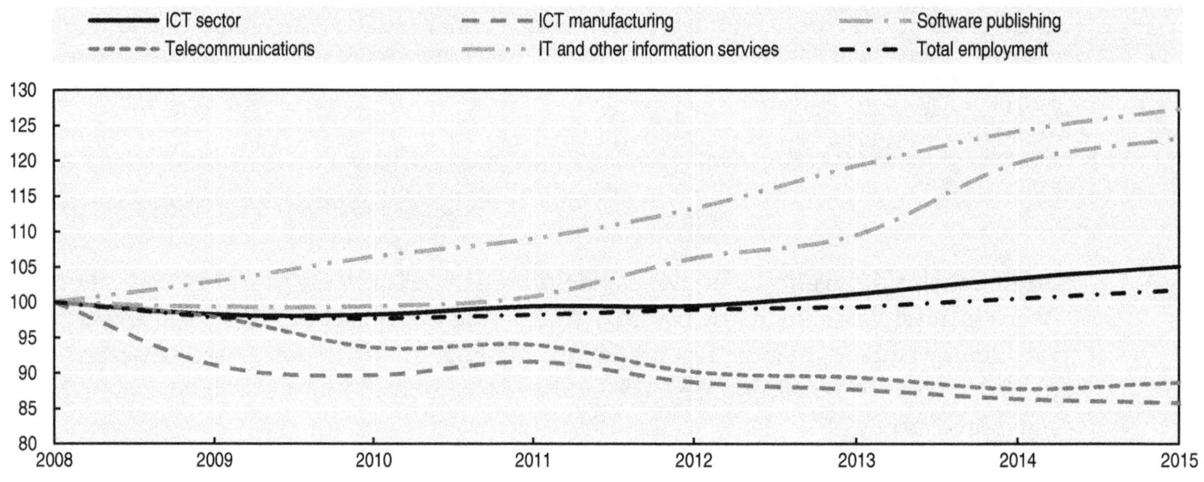

Notes: The ICT sector is defined here as the sum of industries ISIC rev.4: 26 Computer, electronic and optical products ("ICT manufacturing" in the legend); 582 Software publishing; 61 Telecommunications; and 62-63 IT and other information services. The OECD aggregate is calculated as the sum of persons employed over all countries for which data were available. IT = information technology; ICT = information and communication technology.

Sources: Author's calculations based on OECD, STAN: *OECD Structural Analysis Statistics* (database), ISIC Rev.4, *http://oe.cd/stan* (accessed July 2017) and OECD, *SDBS Structural Business Statistics (ISIC Rev. 4)*, *http://dx.doi.org/10.1787/sdbs-data-en* (accessed July 2017).

StatLink *http://dx.doi.org/10.1787/888933584754*

In 2015, the ICT sector accounted for 3% of total employment for selected OECD countries. Estonia, Korea and Luxembourg had the largest shares of ICT employment in total employment, at 4% and over. The smallest shares were in Greece, Lithuania, Mexico and Portugal (less than 2% of total employment). ICT services (software publishing, together with the telecommunications industry and IT and other information services), accounted for almost 80% of ICT employment on average (Figure 3.5).

Figure 3.5. **Employment in the ICT sector and sub-sectors, 2015**

As a percentage of total employment

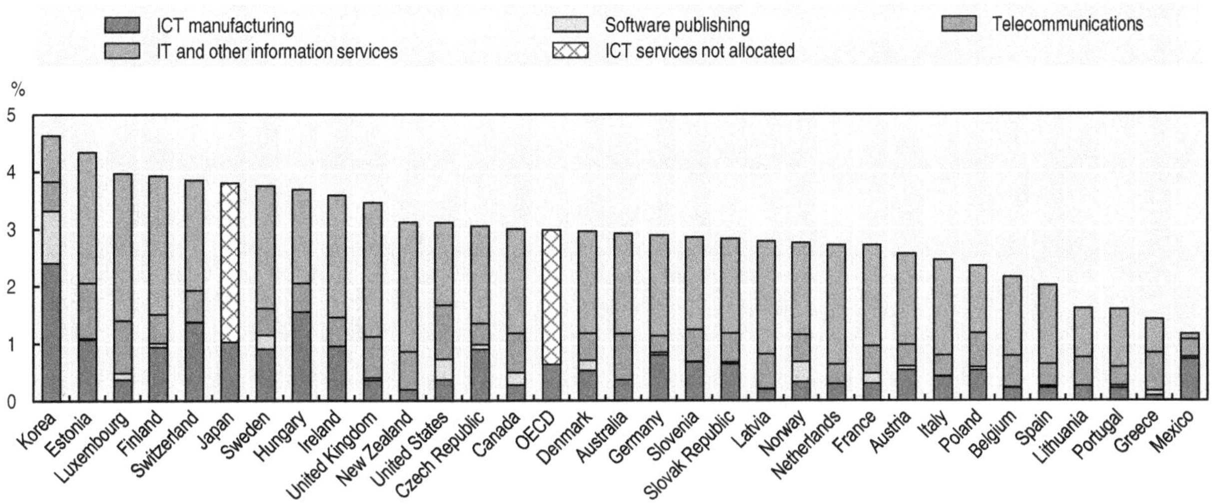

Notes: The ICT sector is defined here as the sum of industries ISIC rev.4: 26 Computer, electronic and optical products ("ICT manufacturing" in the legend); 582 Software publishing; 61 Telecommunications; and 62-63 IT and other information services. Data for Germany, France, Latvia, Lithuania, Portugal, Spain Sweden and Switzerland are 2014. 2015 data on software publishing are estimates based on weights from 2014. The OECD aggregate is calculated as the sum of persons employed over all countries for which data were available. IT = information technology; ICT = information and communication technology.

Sources: Author's calculations based on OECD, STAN: *OECD Structural Analysis Statistics* (database), ISIC Rev.4, *http://oe.cd/stan* (accessed July 2017) and OECD, *SDBS Structural Business Statistics (ISIC Rev. 4)*, *http://dx.doi.org/10.1787/sdbs-data-en* (accessed July 2017).

StatLink *http://dx.doi.org/10.1787/888933584773*

Figure 3.6 shows changes in the share of ICT in total employment in the years following the crisis. In most countries, with the exception of Finland, Germany, Japan and Mexico, the ICT sector's share of total employment has held steady or increased since 2008.

A significant part of ICT value added and employment in OECD countries is accounted for by foreign affiliates (i.e. local firms owned or controlled by a foreign company). In 2015, the share of ICT value added produced by foreign affiliates was above 75% in Estonia and Hungary, 62% in Poland and above 50% in Austria and the Czech Republic. ICT employment matches these figures, although the employment shares tend to be lower (except in Estonia and Finland) due to higher productivity of foreign affiliates relative to domestic firms (Figure 3.7).

Outlook for the ICT sector

Statistics on value added and employment are only available until 2015. However, some short-term indicators can provide an outlook for the ICT sector in more recent times. In 2016, production in the ICT sector had not yet fully recovered from the global economic crises that occurred in 2007 and 2009. Output growth in ICT manufacturing industries was sluggish from late 2010 onwards in most countries, especially for those hit more severely by the crisis. The same trend can be observed in ICT services, although the effects of the crisis were milder (OECD, 2015).

Figure 3.6. **Evolution of the share of ICT in total employment**

As percentage of total employment

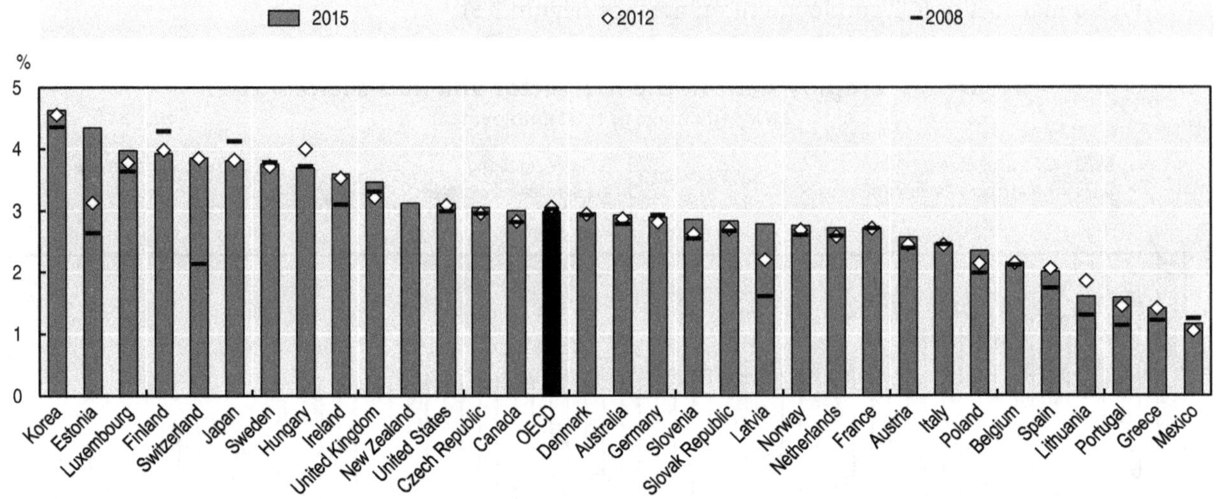

Notes: The ICT sector is defined here as the sum of industries ISIC rev.4: 26 Computer, electronic and optical products; 582 Software publishing; 61 Telecommunications; and 62-63 IT and other information services. Data for Germany, France, Latvia, Lithuania, Portugal, Spain Sweden and Switzerland are 2014. The OECD aggregate is calculated as the sum of persons employed over all countries for which data were available.

Sources: Author's calculations based on OECD, STAN: *OECD Structural Analysis Statistics* (database), ISIC Rev.4, *http://oe.cd/stan* (accessed July 2017) and OECD, *SDBS Structural Business Statistics (ISIC Rev. 4)*, *http://dx.doi.org/10.1787/sdbs-data-en* (accessed July 2017).

StatLink http://dx.doi.org/10.1787/888933584792

Figure 3.7. **Value added and employment in the ICT sector accounted for by foreign affiliates, 2015**

As a proportion of total value added and total employment

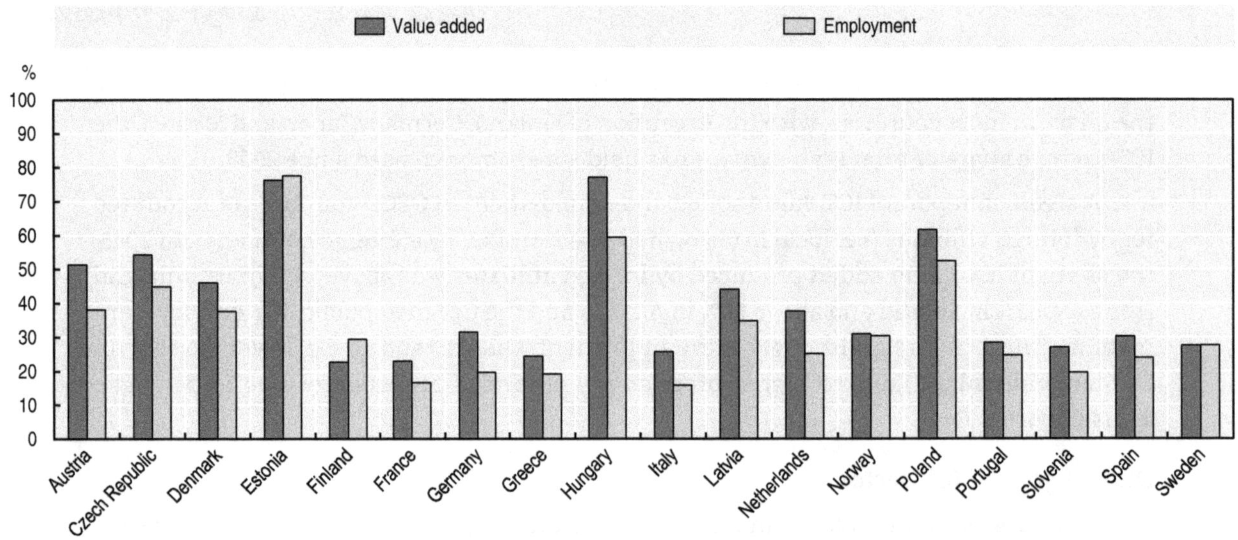

Notes: The ICT sector here is a proxy for the sum of industries ISIC rev.4 26 Computer, electronic and optical products; 61 Telecommunications; and 62-63 IT and other information services. Data refer to 2015 or latest available year.

Sources: Author's calculations based on OECD, STAN: *OECD Structural Analysis Statistics* (database), ISIC Rev.4, *http://oe.cd/stan* (accessed July 2017) and OECD, *Activity of Multinational Enterprises Database*, *www.oecd.org/fr/sti/ind/amne.htm* (both accessed July 2017).

StatLink http://dx.doi.org/10.1787/888933584811

Over 2015-16, output growth in manufacturing slowed down in most economies (Figure 3.8), with a few noteworthy exceptions:

- The People's Republic of China (hereafter "China") continued to grow at a sustained rate of 10% annually.
- Growth in the United States has remained relatively stable, around 5% per year.
- In the European Union (EU), ICT manufacturing output grew significantly (15%) in 2015 but growth seems to has come to a halt more recently.
- Growth in Korea has has largely been positive since late 2015 while Japan has witnessed mainly negative growth rates over that period.
- Output growth was negative in Chinese Taipei from June 2015 to June 2016 but started to increase afterwards, reaching 10% by the end of 2016.

Figure 3.8. **Growth of the ICT manufacturing industries**

Industrial production indices, year-on-year percentage change, three-month moving average

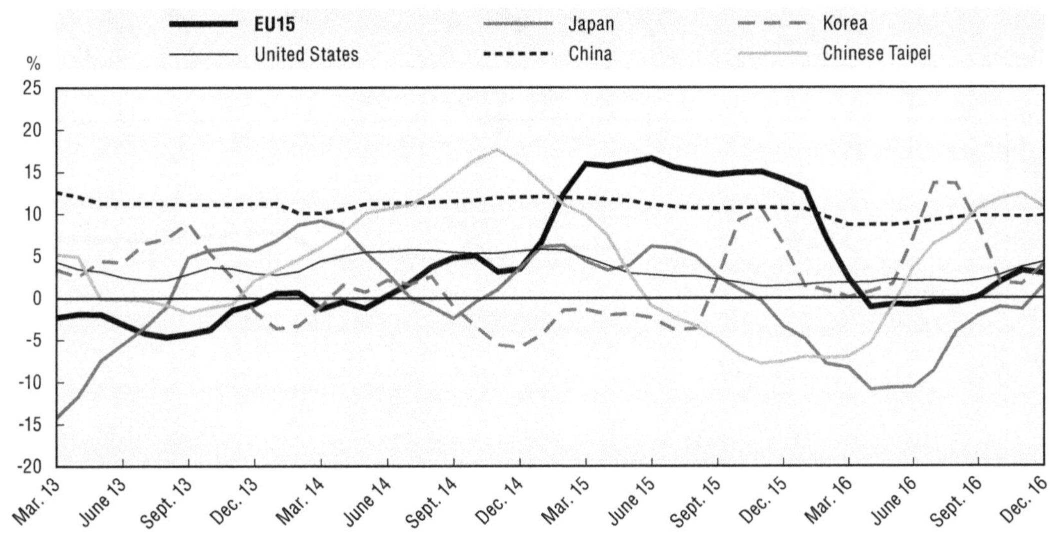

Notes: Data are seasonally adjusted. ICT manufacturing is defined here as manufacture of computer, electronic and optical products (ISIC rev. 4, 26). China = the People's Republic of China.

Sources: Author's calculatons based on industrial production indices from national statistical offices (for details, see note 2 at the end of the chapter) and Eurostat, *Short-term Business Statistics* (database), *http://ec.europa.eu/eurostat/web/short-term-business-statistics/data/database* (accessed March 2017).

StatLink http://dx.doi.org/10.1787/888933584830

Figure 3.9 shows trends in ICT services over 2013-16. Turnover in telecommunication industries (panel A) has remained stable in most economies, except China where it has been growing at a spectacular rate since 2014, reaching over 60% in 2016.

Trends in IT and other information services industries (panels B and C) are more positive. Overall, turnover[3] in computer and other related services industries increased in 2016, ranging between 7% in the EU15 and about 2% in Japan. Turnover growth was also positive in data-processing industries in 2016. The United States and the EU15 have shown increasing growth rates since mid-2014, up to 10% in the third quarter of 2016, slowing down afterwards. Korea registered the highest growth rate (15%) in 2016, after a dip in 2015.

Figure 3.9. **Growth of the ICT services industries**

Turnover, year-on-year percentage change, three-month moving averages

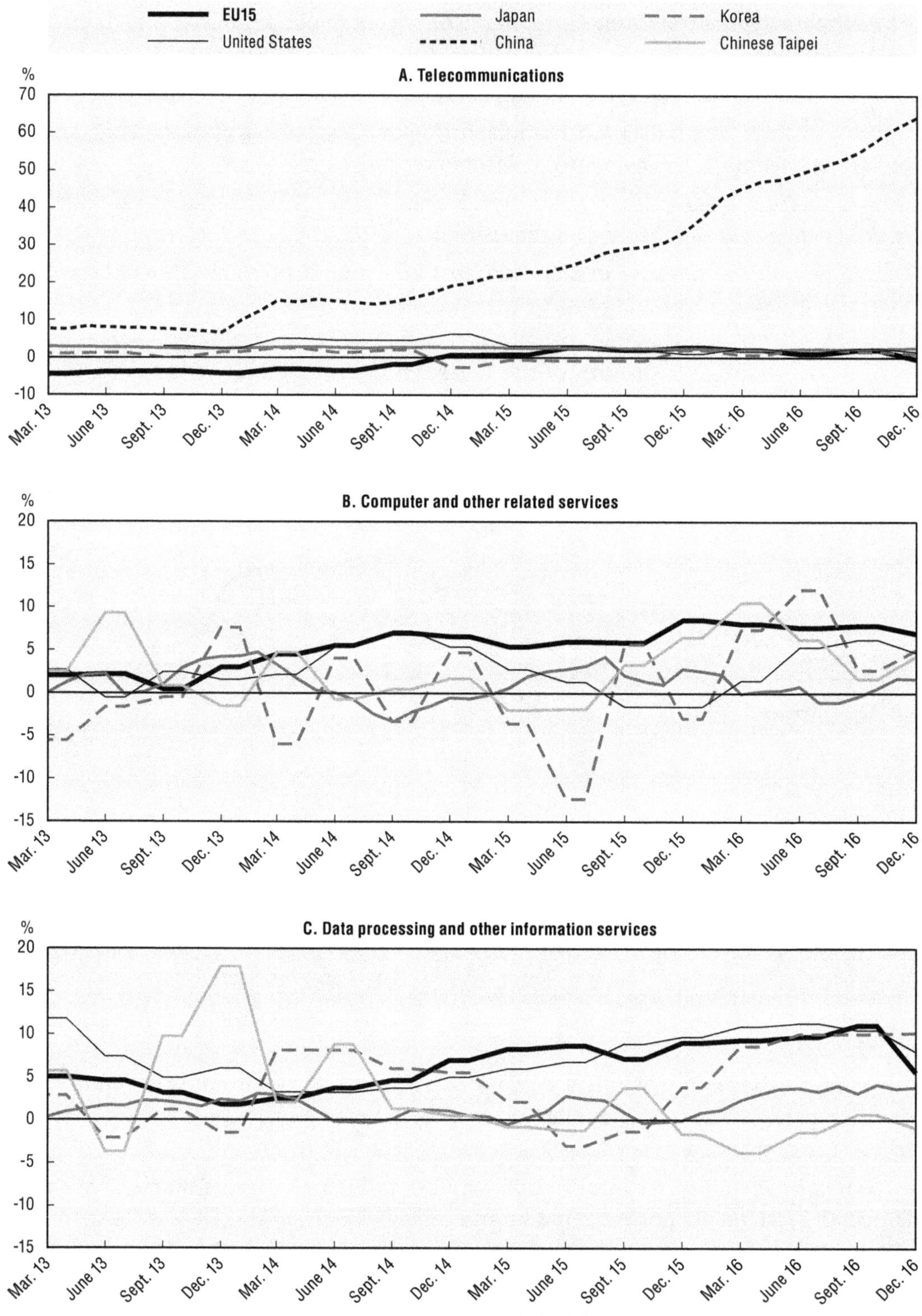

Notes: If available, data are seasonally adjusted. China = the People's Republic of China.

Sources: Author calculations based on quarterly indices of services, revenues and monthly tertiary services indices from national statistical offices (for details, see note 4 at the end of the chapter) and the index of turnover from Eurostat, *Short-term Business Statistics* database, *http://ec.europa.eu/eurostat/web/short-term-business-statistics/data/database* (accessed March 2017).

StatLink http://dx.doi.org/10.1787/888933584849

Semiconductor production remains a leading indicator for the ICT sector. Semiconductors are fundamental for growth and innovation in the digital economy – e.g. mobile technologies, IoT, smart technologies (sensors, visual recognition, etc.). Industry sales have been growing very modestly in the past two years, only 1.1% in 2016, and are not expected to regain major traction in the near future (Figure 3.10). The main reasons seem to be declining average sales prices for semiconductors coupled with high research and development (R&D) and investment costs for the increasingly complex fabrication of semiconductors (KPMG, 2016). The Asia-Pacific region and Japan account for 71% of total annual sales. This is also where growth remains the highest: semiconductor sales in China and Japan grew by 9.2% and 3.8% respectively.

Figure 3.10. **Worldwide semiconductor market by region**

Annual sales, USD billion, current prices and year-on-year growth

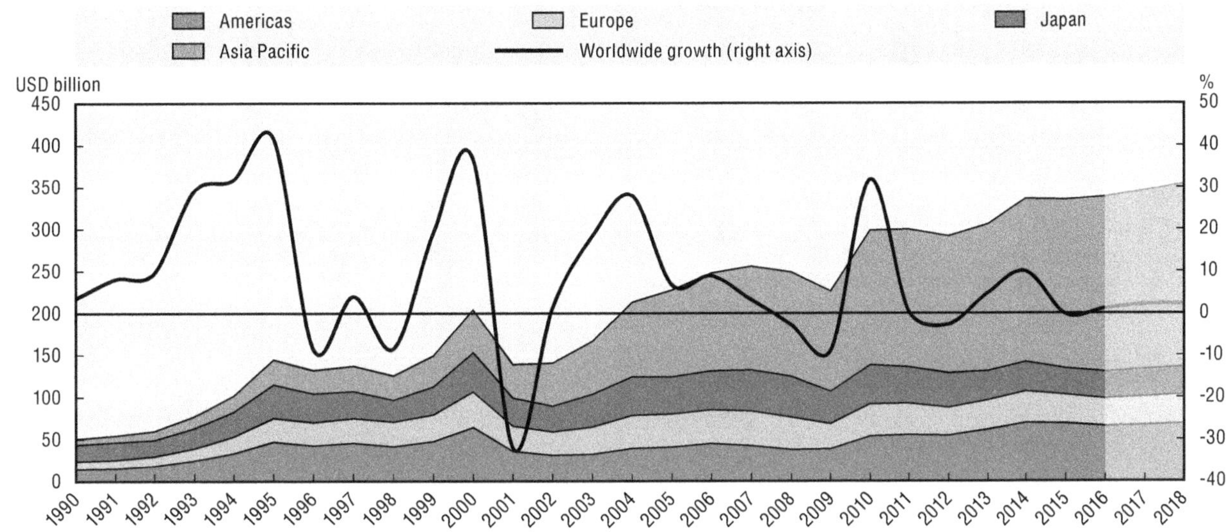

Note: Data for 2017 and 2018 are forecasts.

Source: Author's calculations based on World Semiconductor Trade Statistics (WSTS), *https://www.wsts.org/* (accessed February 2017).

StatLink *http://dx.doi.org/10.1787/888933584868*

VC investment, a market indicator of upcoming business opportunities, shows a global slowdown. In 2016, global VC investment was about USD 101 billion, a 23% decrease over the previous year. While VC investment in Asia and North America continued to fall in the last quarter of 2016, Europe saw an increase in funding (PwC, 2017).

In the United States, despite the overall slowdown, the ICT industries remain a key area of focus for VC investment, accounting for 71% of total VC investment in Q4 2016 (Figure 3.11). This share has remained stable since 2014, and is back to the level before the dot.com bubble.

The share of ICT goods and services in total trade continues to increase despite an overall decline in value terms

This section presents developments in gross trade patterns of ICT goods and services over time. These sectors are core building blocks of the digital economy and gross trade patterns help illustrate how international demand for and transactions of ICT goods and services have evolved. Chapter 5 includes a description of how the digital transformation is reshaping the broader trade landscape, particularly for services, and includes an analysis of trade in ICT goods and services in value-added terms, as well as data on trade restrictions on services in certain ICT services.

Figure 3.11. **Trends in venture capital investments in the United States**

USD billion and year-on-year growth, 4Q moving average

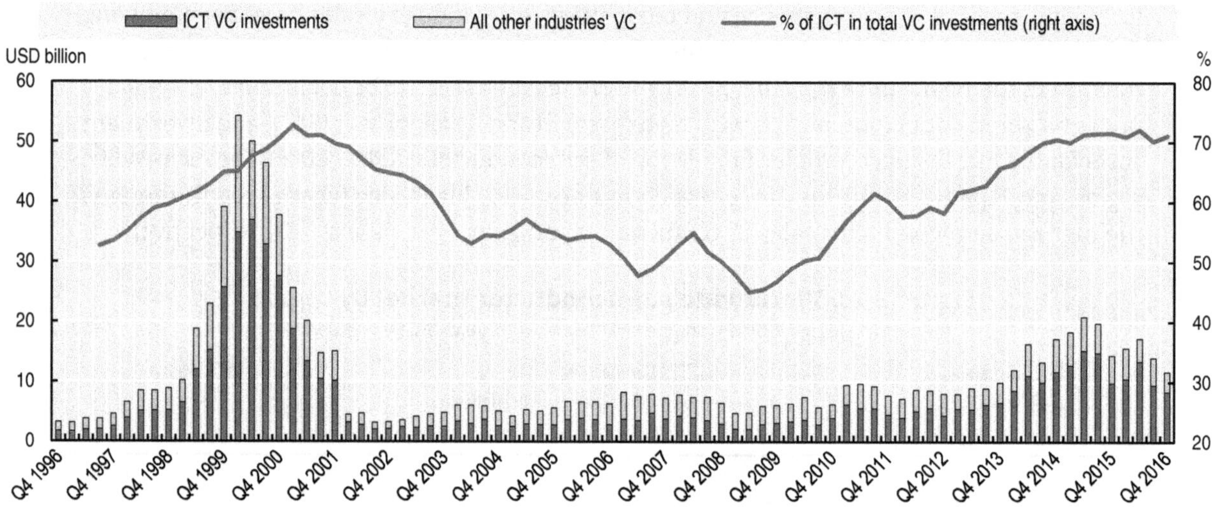

Notes: The aggregate venture capital (VC) investment in ICT is defined here as the sum of computer hardware and services, electronics, Internet, mobile and telecommunications, and software. The share of ICT of the total is expressed as a 4Q moving average. VC = venture capital; ICT = information and communication technology.

Source: Author's calculations based on PwC/National Venture Capital Association, MoneyTree Report, which draws on Thomson Reuters data, *https://www.pwc.com/us/en/technology/moneytree.html* (accessed February 2017).

StatLink *http://dx.doi.org/10.1787/888933584887*

Trade in ICT goods

Over 2008-15, the value of world trade in ICT goods increased by 12%, exports from China increased by 49%, while OECD exports decreased by 13% (Figure 3.12). Over the same period, imports of ICT goods in value terms from China increased by 60% while OECD imports remained stable (1%).

Figure 3.12. **Trade in ICT goods**

Indices 2008 = 100, USD at current prices

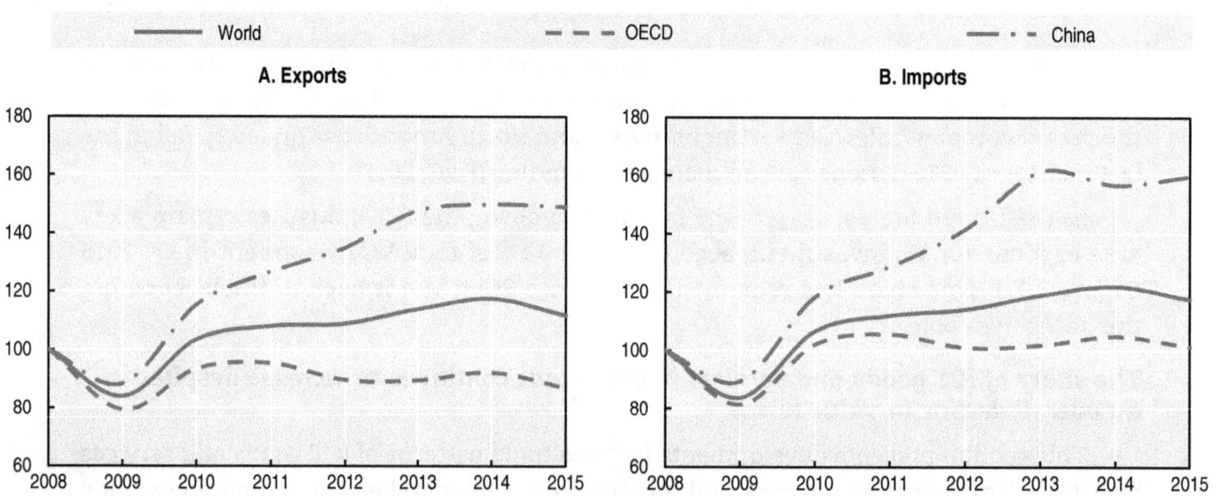

Notes: ICT goods defined according to the definition included in the *OECD Guide to Measuring the Information Society 2011* (OECD, 2011). Global exports and imports are calculated by summing all reported trade (imports and exports) from all declaring countries in the Bilateral Trade database. World exports exclude re-imports for China and re-exports for Hong Kong, China. World imports exclude re-imports for China. China's trade is adjusted for re-imports.

Source: OECD, "STAN bilateral trade database by industry and end-use category, ISIC Rev. 4 (Edition 2016)", *STAN: OECD Structural Analysis Statistics* (database), *http://dx.doi.org/10.1787/d670358a-en* (accessed March 2017).

StatLink *http://dx.doi.org/10.1787/888933584906*

In 2015, the value of world exports of ICT goods decreased by 3.4%, down to USD 1.9 trillion[5] while the share of ICT goods in total goods exports increased by 11%. However, the decrease was smaller for ICT goods than for total trade in goods. As a result, the share of ICT in total trade in goods increased (Figure 3.13). Imports of ICT goods followed the same pattern. In 2015, the share of ICT goods in total imports worldwide increased (from 11.8% to 13.1%) but the value of global imports of ICT goods declined by 3.3% to just over USD 2.1 trillion.[6]

Figure 3.13. **ICT goods trade compared to overall trade**

As a percentage of total merchandise exports and imports

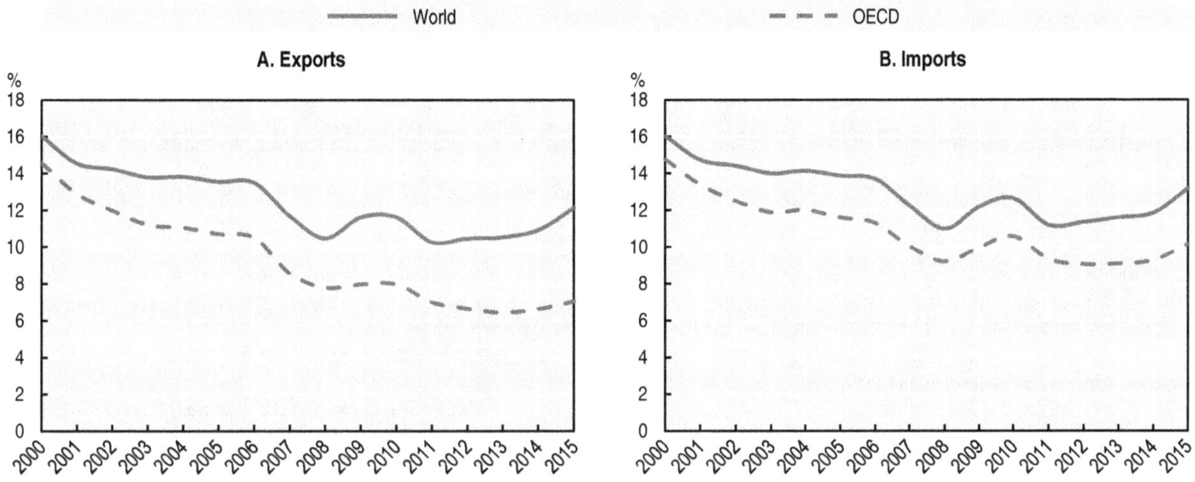

Notes: ICT goods defined according to the definition included in the *OECD Guide to Measuring the Information Society 2011* (OECD, 2011). Global exports and imports are calculated by summing all reported trade (imports and exports) from all declaring countries in the BTDIxE database. Based on trade values in gross terms, i.e. no adjustment made for re-imports and re-exports.

Source: OECD, "STAN bilateral trade database by industry and end-use category, ISIC Rev. 4 (Edition 2016)", STAN: *OECD Structural Analysis Statistics* (database), *http://dx.doi.org/10.1787/d670358a-en* (accessed March 2017).

StatLink *http://dx.doi.org/10.1787/888933584925*

Exports of ICT goods are increasingly concentrated in a few economies. In 2016, the top ten exporters, which include six OECD countries, accounted for 85% of world exports of ICT goods, up from 70% in 2001 (Figure 3.14). Partly due to offshoring of production, Japan's share in world exports of ICT goods decreased from 10% in 2001 to 4% in 2016, while China's share grew from 6% to 32%, with a tenfold increase in current US dollars. Korea is the only OECD country whose share continues to grow (5.5% in 2001, 6.8% in 2007 and 7.6% in 2016).

The trend towards a re-composition of exports from computers and peripherals to communication equipment continued (Figure 3.15). In 2015, the share of ICT exports in communications equipment has reached the share of computers and peripherals exports (26%), while electronic components exports continue to account for the largest share of ICT exports (33%).

Trade in ICT services

Over 2010-16, the value of OECD export of ICT services increased by 40%, just below the growth of world trade of ICT services but faster than total trade in services (Figure 3.16). In 2016, world exports of ICT services increased by 5%, from USD 470 billion to up to USD 493 billion. As a result, the share of global exports of ICT services in total services increased by 2 percentage points, reaching over 10% in 2016.

Figure 3.14. **Top ten world exporters of ICT goods**

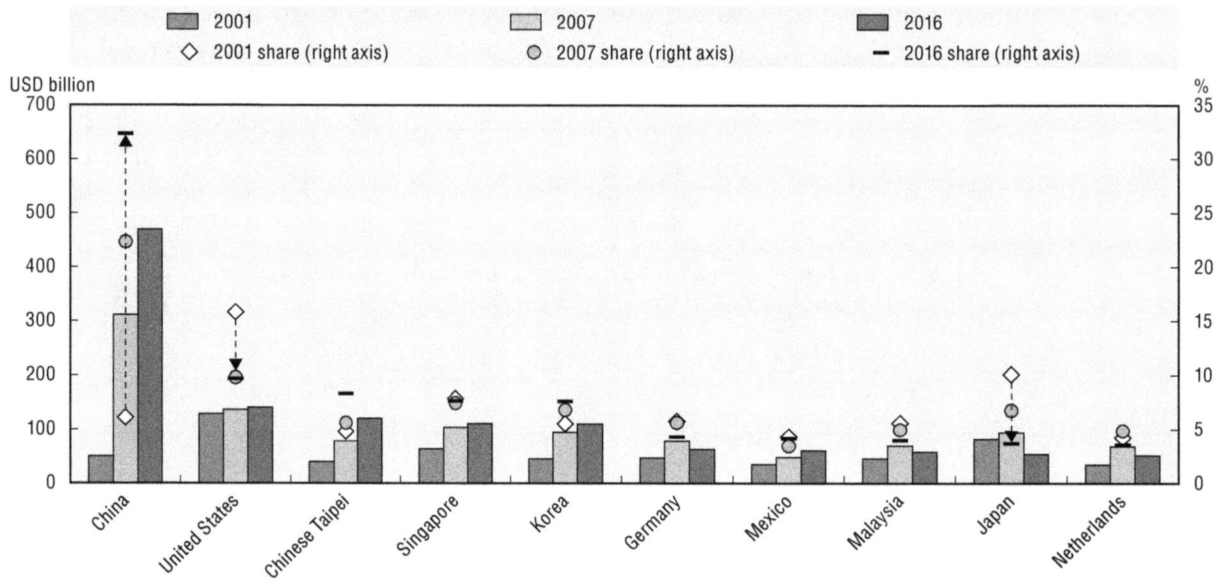

Notes: World is estimated adding up all declaring economies which reported ICT exports in all three years; world excludes re-imports for the People's Republic of China ("China" in the figure) and re-exports for Hong Kong, China. China's ICT exports are adjusted for re-imports. 2016 data for China and the Netherlands are estimates based on reported values in 2015.

Source: OECD, "STAN Bilateral trade database by industry and end-use category, ISIC Rev. 4", *STAN: OECD Structural Analysis Statistics* (database), *http://oe.cd/btd* (accessed July 2017).

StatLink *http://dx.doi.org/10.1787/888933584944*

Figure 3.15. **World exports of ICT goods by ICT product category**

USD billion and as a percentage of total ICT goods exports

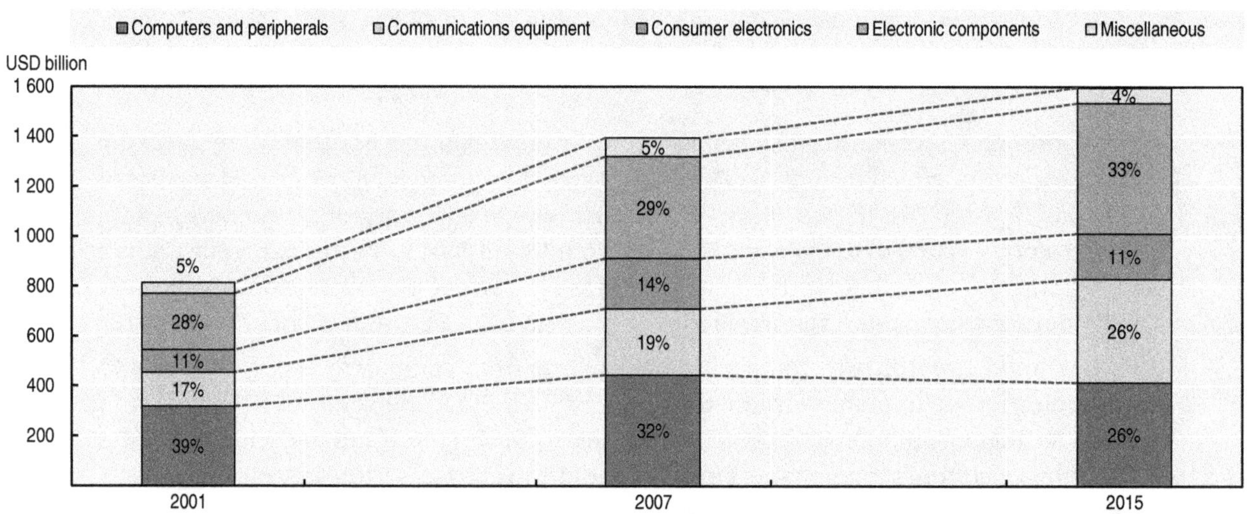

Notes: World total is estimated based on the 103 BTDIxE declaring economies which reported ICT exports in all three years; world total excludes re-imports for China and re-exports for Hong Kong, China. China's ICT exports are adjusted for re-imports.

Source: OECD, "STAN bilateral trade database by industry and end-use category, ISIC Rev. 4 (Edition 2016)", *STAN: OECD Structural Analysis Statistics* (database), *http://dx.doi.org/10.1787/d670358a-en* (accessed March 2017).

StatLink *http://dx.doi.org/10.1787/888933584963*

Figure 3.16. **Exports of ICT services**

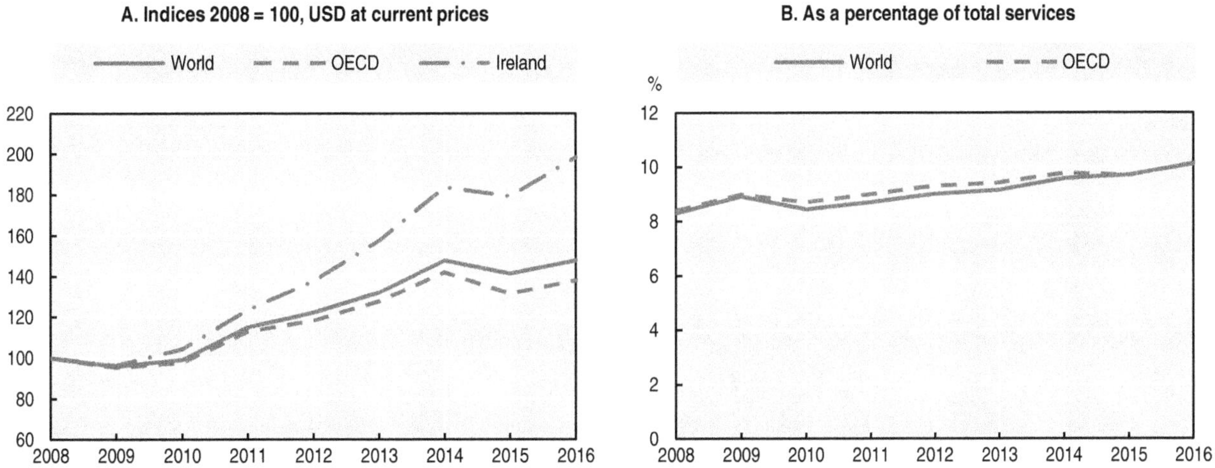

Note: ICT services are defined here as telecommunications, computer and information services.

Source: UNCTAD, "Services (BPM6): Exports and imports by service-category, shares and growth, annual, 2005-2016", *http://unctadstat.unctad.org/wds/TableViewer/tableView.aspx?ReportId=87017* (accessed June 2017).

StatLink http://dx.doi.org/10.1787/888933584982

As for trade in ICT goods, a few economies account for a significant share in global exports of ICT services (Figures 3.17 and 3.18). Ireland, which benefits from the presence of a high concentration of transnational corporations relative to the size of its domestic market, continues to be the leading exporter of ICT services (over 14% of global services), followed by India (11%) and the Netherlands and the United States (both with 8%). China is also among the top ten exporters of ICT services, along with France, Germany, Sweden, Switzerland and the United Kingdom. Together, these ten countries account for two-thirds of total exports of global services.

Figure 3.17. **OECD and major exporters of ICT services**

As a percentage of total world exports

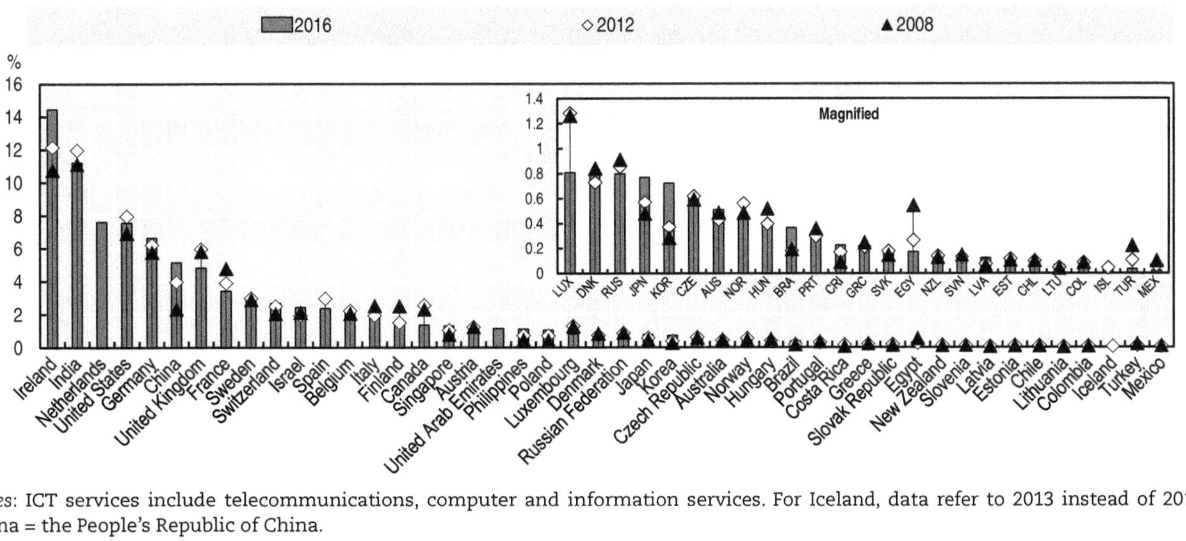

Notes: ICT services include telecommunications, computer and information services. For Iceland, data refer to 2013 instead of 2012. China = the People's Republic of China.

Source: UNCTAD, "Services (BPM6): Exports and imports by service-category, shares and growth, annual, 2005-2016", *http://unctadstat.unctad.org/wds/TableViewer/tableView.aspx?ReportId=87017* (accessed June 2017).

StatLink http://dx.doi.org/10.1787/888933585001

Figure 3.18. **Top ten world exporters of ICT services**

USD billion and percentage shares

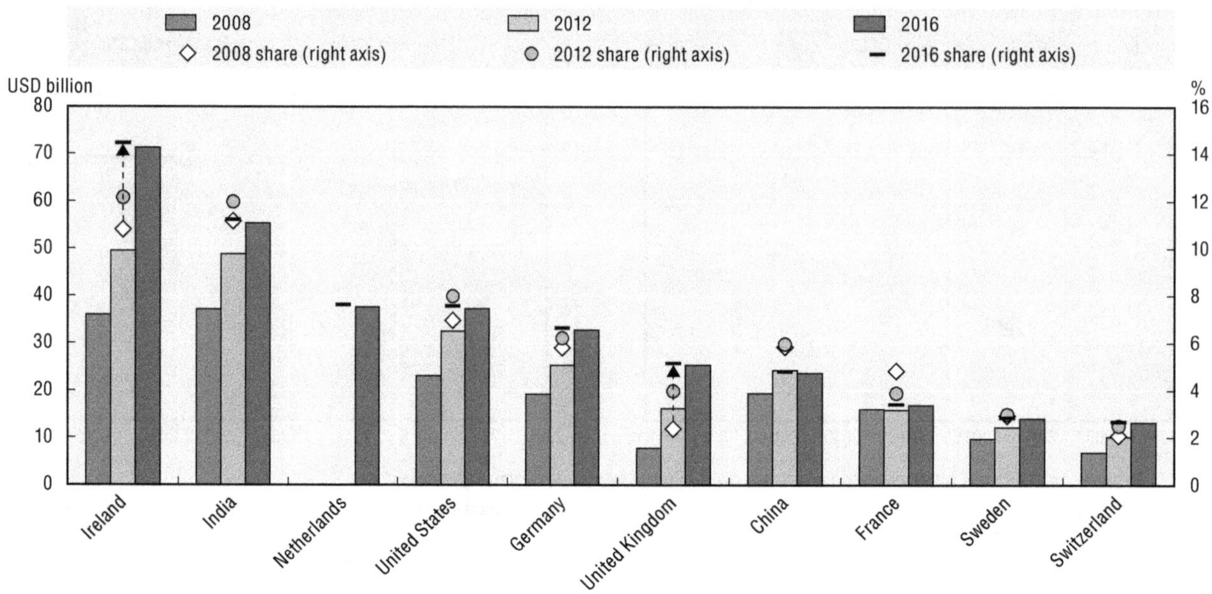

Notes: ICT services are defined here as telecommunications, computer and information services. China = the People's Republic of China.

Source: UNCTAD, "Services (BPM6): Exports and imports by service-category, shares and growth, annual, 2005-2016", *http://unctadstat.unctad.org/wds/TableViewer/tableView.aspx?ReportId=87017* (accessed June 2017).

StatLink *http://dx.doi.org/10.1787/888933585020*

ICTs play a key role in today's innovation activities

Enterprises in the ICT sector are leading across all types of innovation activities, while innovators are often intensive users of ICTs. In most OECD countries, the ICT sector accounts for the largest share of BERD, representing about 24% of total BERD and 0.4% of the gross domestic product (GDP). In 2015, ICT BERD relative to GDP was highest in Chinese Taipei (1.77%), Korea (1.73%), Israel (1.61) and Finland (1.04), followed by the United States, Sweden and Japan (about 0.6%), (Figure 3.19).

Figure 3.20 shows detailed information on the breakdown of the business R&D expenditure in the ICT sector and provides information on the weight of the ICT sector BERD in total BERD. In 2014-15, Chinese Taipei and Korea devoted 71% and 49% of their total BERD to ICT manufacturing. Despite the drop in Nokia's activities, Finland continues to spend over 41% of its total BERD on ICT manufacturing, which is the same as Singapore, followed by Japan, Sweden and the United States, which all spent above 15% of total BERD.

IT and other information services represent more than 50% of total ICT business R&D expenditure in a majority of countries. The highest shares of R&D expenditure on software publishing in total ICT BERD were observed in the United States and Norway, accounting for 33% and 23% respectively. Telecommunication services account for a lower share of ICT BERD in most countries, except for Australia, Portugal and the United Kingdom, where it represents about 25% of total ICT BERD.

Figure 3.19. **ICT and total business expenditure on R&D intensities, 2015**

As a percentage of GDP

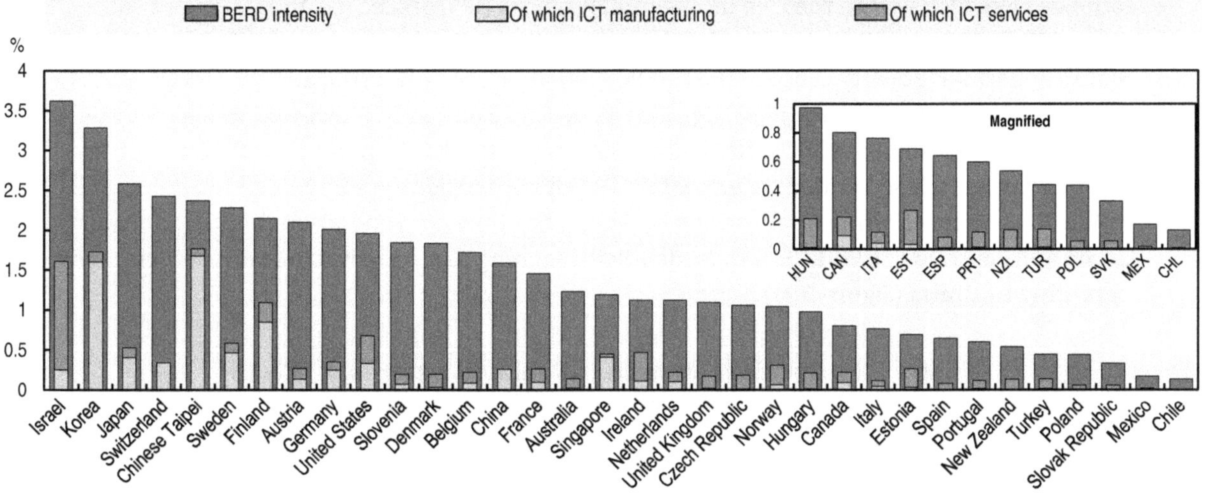

Notes: The ICT sector is defined as the sum of "ICT manufacturing" and "ICT services", which comprises "ICT trade industries", "Software publishing", "Telecommunications" and "IT and other information services", defined according to the OECD ICT sector definition based on ISIC Rev.4. When detailed data were not available, divisions 26, 58 and 63 were used as a proxy for ICT manufacturing, Software publishing industries and Data processing, hosting and related activities; web portals respectively. For Canada, Denmark, Finland, Hungary, Israel, Italy, the Netherlands, Poland, Portugal, Romania, Slovenia, the United Kingdom and the United States, data refer to 2014. For Austria, Belgium, France, Ireland, New Zealand, Singapore and Sweden, data refer to 2013. For Australia, data refer to 2011. GDP = gross domestic product; BERD = business expenditure on research and development; ICT = information and communication technology; China = the People's Republic of China.

Sources: OECD, "Research and Development Statistics: Business enterprise R-D expenditure by industry - ISIC Rev. 4", *OECD Science, Technology and R&D Statistics* (database), *http://oe.cd/sti/rds*; OECD, "Main Science and Technology Indicators", *OECD Science, Technology and R&D Statistics* (database), *http://dx.doi.org/10.1787/data-00182-en* (accessed July 2017).

StatLink *http://dx.doi.org/10.1787/888933585039*

Figure 3.20. **BERD in the ICT sector, 2015**

As a percentage of GDP and of total BERD

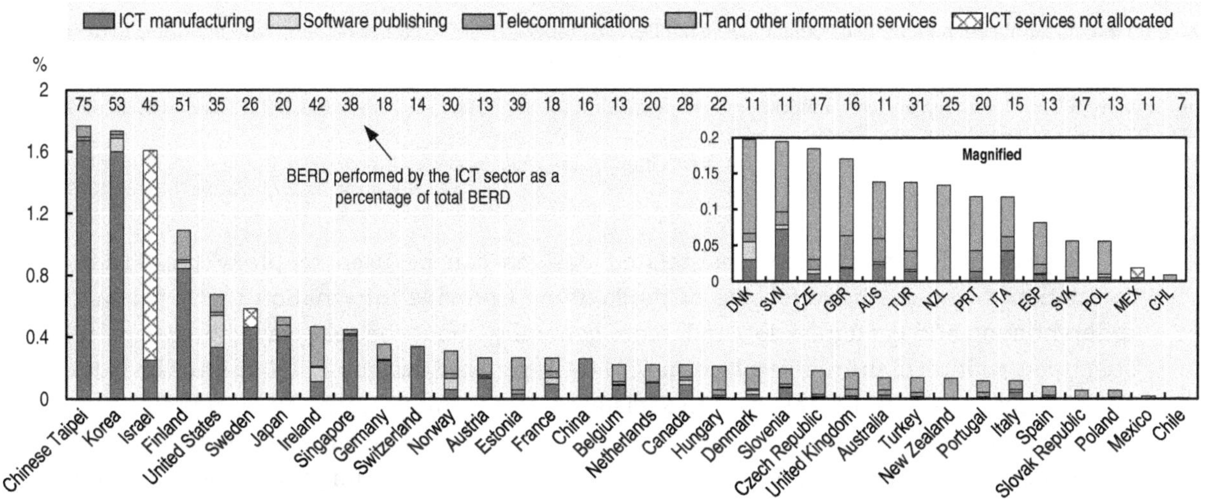

Notes: For Canada, Denmark, Finland, Hungary, Israel, Italy, the Netherlands, Poland, Portugal, Romania, Slovenia, the United Kingdom and the United States, data refer to 2014. For Austria, Belgium, France, Ireland, Singapore and Sweden, data refer to 2013. For Australia, data refer to 2011. "ICT services not allocated" refers to ICT services industries within ISIC rev.4 58-63 that cannot be separated. BERD = business expenditure on research and development; GDP = gross domestic product; ICT = information and communication technology; IT = information technology; China = the People's Republic of China.

Source: OECD, "STAN R&D: Research and development expenditure in industry - ISIC Rev. 4", *STAN: OECD Structural Analysis Statistics* (database), *http://oe.cd/anberd* (accessed February 2017).

StatLink *http://dx.doi.org/10.1787/888933585058*

While R&D provides one measure of innovation input, patents, registered designs and trademarks capture elements of innovation output. In 2012-15, more than 0.9 million patent families were filed within the Five Intellectual Property (IP5) offices (i.e. the European Patent Office [EPO], the Japan Patent Office [JPO], the Korean Intellectual Property Office [KIPO], the State Intellectual Property Office of the People's Republic of China [SIPO] and the United States Patent and Trademark Office [USPTO]). Patent applications in ICT technologies accounted for almost 37% of total applications, against 35% over the 2002-05 period. In OECD countries, ICT-related patents accounted for almost 34% of all applications, a slight decrease compared to the 2002-05 level, while applications by Brazil, the Russian Federation, India, Indonesia, China and South Africa (BRIICS) almost doubled, reaching 58%, largely as a result of increased patenting by China (Figure 3.21).

Figure 3.21. **Specialisation in ICT-related patents, 2012-15**

Patents in ICT as a percentage of total IP5 patent families

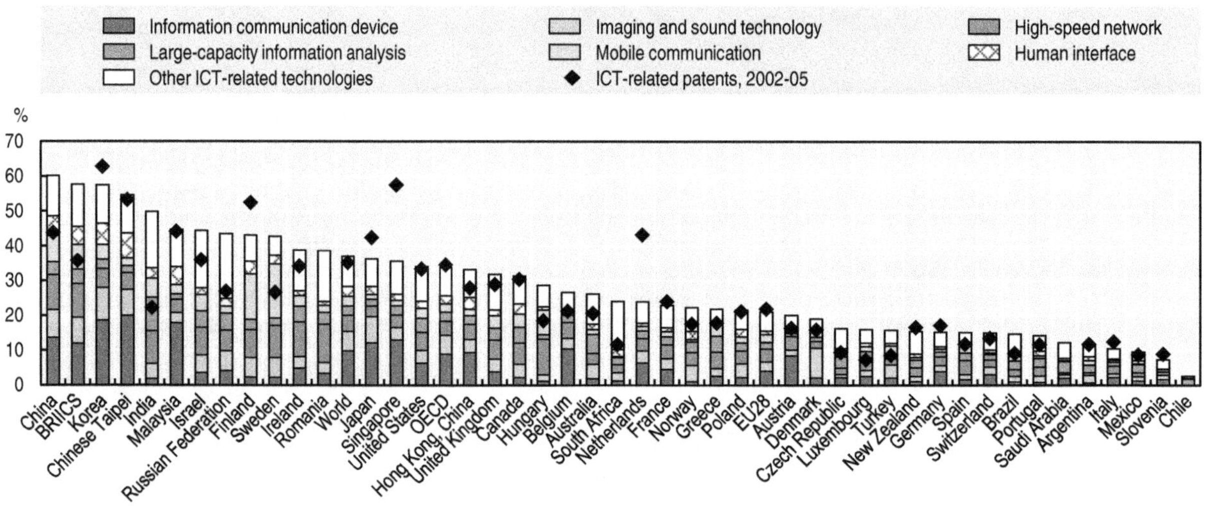

Notes: Data refer to families of patents filed within the Five Intellectual Property (IP5) offices, by first filing date, according to the inventor's residence using fractional counts. Patents in ICT are identified following a new experimental classification based on their International Patent Classification (IPC) codes. Only economies with more than 150 patent families in 2012-15 are included. Data from 2014 and 2015 are incomplete. ICT = information and communication technology. BRIICS = Brazil, Russian Federation, India, Indonesia, China and South Africa. China = the People's Republic of China.

Source: OECD, *STI Micro-data Lab: Intellectual Property* (database), *http://oe.cd/ipstats* (accessed June 2017).

StatLink *http://dx.doi.org/10.1787/888933585077*

Registered ICT and audiovisual-related designs can be used to proxy innovation in relation to the aesthetic feature of products and provide information about product differentiation and customisation and, more generally, about the role played by design to shape competition in the marketplace. In 2011-14, registered designs in ICT and audiovisual devices accounted for 9.6% of European Registered Community Designs (RCD), representing a 2 percentage point increase over 2006-09. Across all economies, about 60% of registered ICT and audiovisual-related designs refer to data-processing and recording equipment, followed by communication and audiovisual devices (Figure 3.22).

The United States and Korea are the most active economies in ICT and audiovisual-related RCD (both gaining shares with respect to 2006-09), followed by Germany and

Japan (both losing shares), with the other large European economies tailing behind. China more than doubled its share but remains a minor player with regard to designs registered in Europe. The United States scores high in data-processing equipment and Korea in communication equipment, while France and Japan lead in the design of audiovisual devices.

Korea shows the strongest specialisation in ICT and audiovisual-related designs, which represent almost 65% of Korean total RCD. Other economies specialising in this field are Canada, Japan, Chinese Taipei and the United States.

Figure 3.22. **Top 20 applicants' share in ICT and audiovisual-related designs, 2006-09 and 2011-14**

As a percentage of total ICT and audiovisual-related European Registered Community Designs

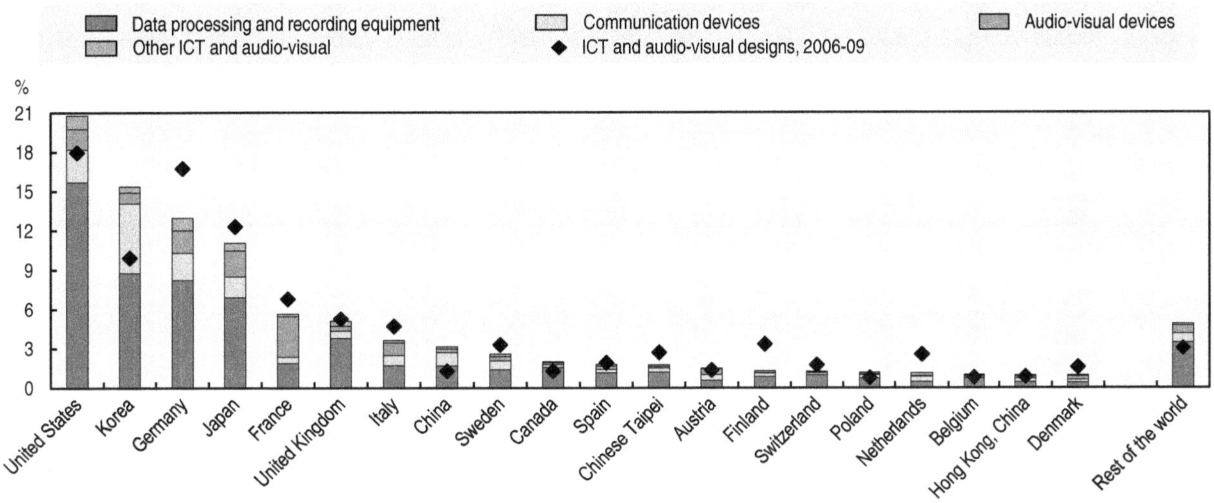

Notes: Total ICT and audiovisual designs correspond to designs in classes 14, 16 and 18. Data processing and recording equipment correspond to the Locarno subclasses 14-01, 14-02 and 14-04; communication devices correspond to the subclass 14-03; audiovisual devices correspond to the class 16. ICT = information and communication technology. China = the People's Republic of China.

Source: OECD, *STI Micro-data Lab: Intellectual Property* (database), *http://oe.cd/ipstats* (accessed February 2017).

StatLink http://dx.doi.org/10.1787/888933585096

The distribution of trademarks offers a distinctive perspective on the competitive position of economies concerning ICT products. Indeed, national trademark shares do not align with R&D, patents or export shares. The United States appears to be the largest overall player, accounting for 76% of total ICT-related trademark applications at the United States Patent and Trademark Office (USPTO) and more than 12% at the European Union Intellectual Property Office (EUIPO) (Figure 3.23). ICT-related trademarks on the European market are conversely led by applicants in Germany, followed by the United States, the United Kingdom, Spain, France and Italy. In the last five years, a number of large trademark players, such as Japan and the United States, lost shares in EU branding to the benefit of China, Korea and smaller EU countries, while Germany and Spain were able to hold their positions.

Figure 3.23. **ICT-related trademarks, top 20 applicants, 2006-09 and 2011-14**

As a percentage of total ICT-related trademark applications at EUIPO and USPTO

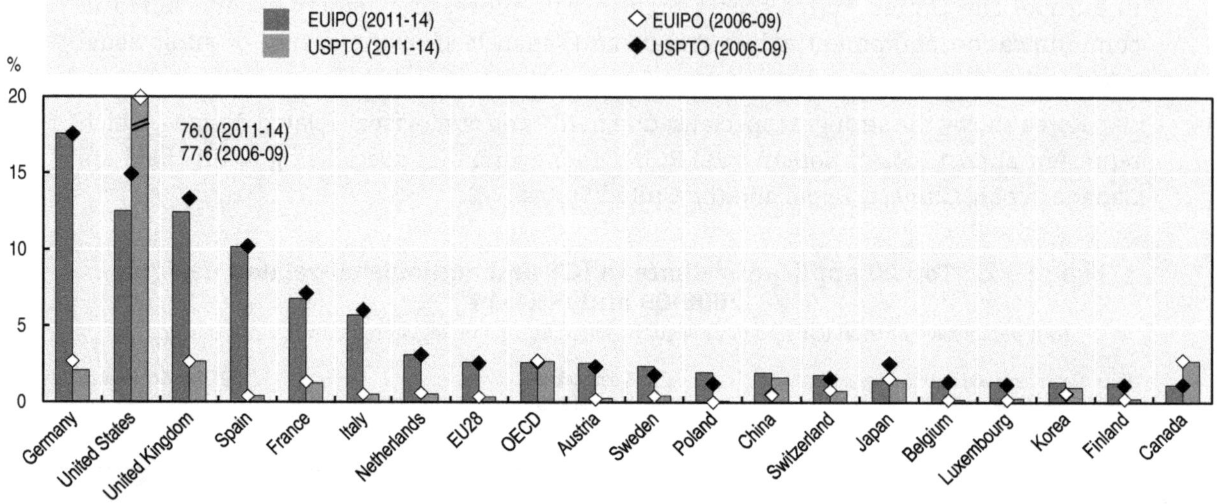

Note: ICT = information and communication technology; EUIPO = European Union Intellectual Property Office; USPTO = United States Patent and Trademark Office; China = the People's Republic of China.

Source: Author's calculations based on OECD, *STI Micro-data Lab: Intellectual Property* (database), *http://oe.cd/ipstats* (accessed November 2016).

StatLink *http://dx.doi.org/10.1787/888933585115*

Communication markets

Communication networks are critical for the development of Digital Economies. They underpin the broader use of all ICTs for economic and social development as well as in assisting to achieve the many goals set by policy makers. Indicators on network dimensions and development, as well as the take-up of services over these infrastructures, are at the forefront of any assessment of the ability of a country to seize the potential benefits of ICTs.

While the number of telecommunication subscriptions continues to grow, industry revenue fell slightly over the period 2013-15. This may be explained by the evolving market players and the changing nature of subscriptions as well as increased competition. Network operators continue to provide the access paths and connections, but new players such as over-the-top (OTT) providers are increasingly offering applications, which may influence reported sector revenue. In addition, mobile, fixed broadband and M2M subscriptions are increasing, while traditional fixed lines are decreasing. However, these subscriptions are offered at different price points; for example M2M subscriptions are often at a lower price than traditional mobile services (i.e. lower average revenue per subscription unit), which may contribute to current revenue trends relative to ongoing subscription growth.

Trends in the number of subscriptions and industry revenue appear to decouple

The long-term relationship between increased communication subscriptions and growth in industry revenue, which was consistent for more than a century, appears to have somewhat decoupled in recent years. After reaching peaks in 2008 and 2011, total industry revenues has been flat or declined over 2011-15. Between 2013 and 2015, telecommunication revenue decreased by 6%, from USD 1.312 trillion to USD 1.235 trillion (Figure 3.24). Notwithstanding the decrease in industry revenue, the number of subscriptions to telecommunication services continued its extraordinary growth as witnessed already over the past two decades.

Figure 3.24. **Trends in telecommunication revenue and investment**

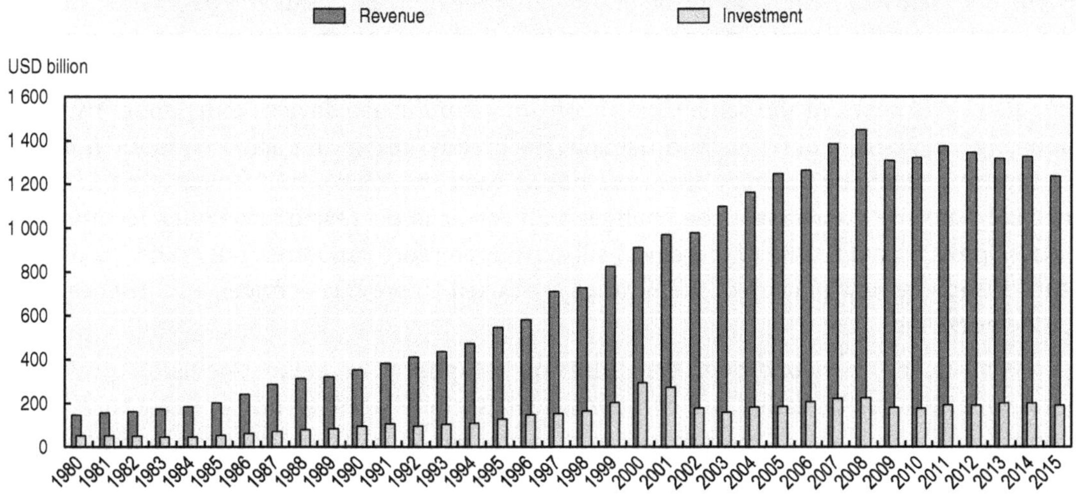

Source: OECD, "Telecommunications database", OECD Telecommunications and Internet Statistics (database), *http://dx.doi.org/10.1787/data-00170-en* (accessed July 2017).

StatLink *http://dx.doi.org/10.1787/888933585134*

By 2015, there were more than 2.3 billion telecommunication access paths in OECD countries (Figure 3.25). This was up more than 150 million access paths from 2013 for an overall increase of 7%. The access paths that continue to grow are fixed and mobile broadband subscriptions, as well as subscriptions for M2M communication services. In contrast, the number of fixed lines with traditional telephony subscriptions continued its longer term decline. This raises the question of why there is a divergence between subscription growth and overall telecommunication revenue.

Figure 3.25. **Trends in access paths**

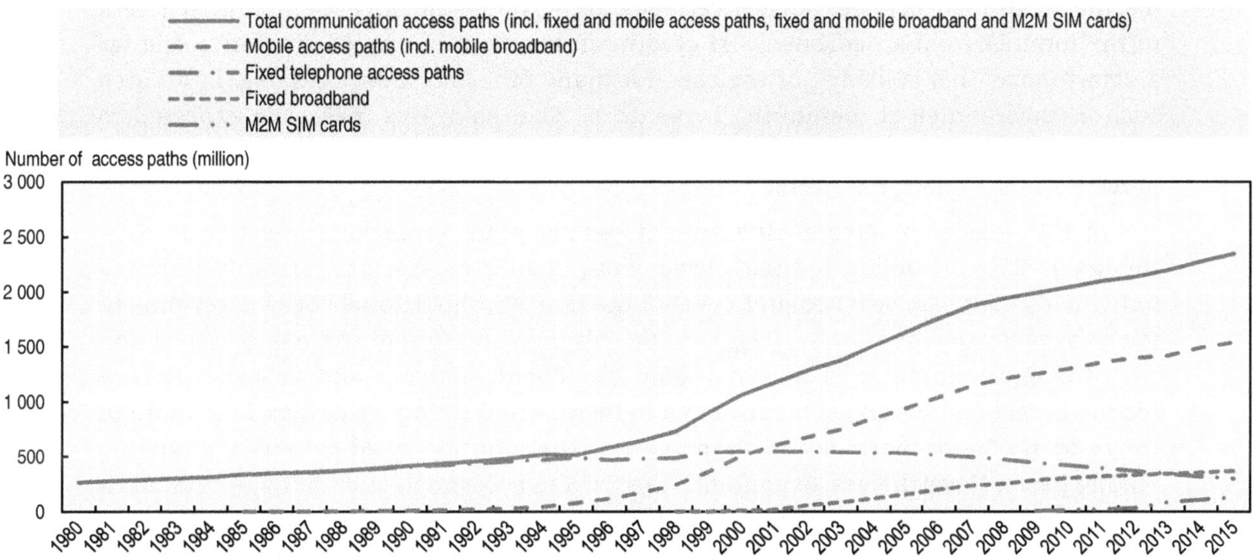

Note: M2M = machine to machine.

Source: OECD, "Telecommunications database", *OECD Telecommunications and Internet Statistics* (database), *http://dx.doi.org/10.1787/data-00170-en* (accessed June 2017).

StatLink *http://dx.doi.org/10.1787/888933585153*

Changes to telecommunication earnings and expenses are due to a number of factors. Some are relatively neutral in terms of incoming receipts and outgoing payments. Others reflect a longer term decoupling of the historically close relationship between service revenue growth and that for access paths. A decrease in termination charges results in lower revenues, but also lower costs. At the same time, if consumers purchase devices independently from subscription plans, that revenue remains in the broader sector but is not counted in terms of service revenue by network operators nor as costs, which overall results in a relatively neutral outcome. Conversely, the changes that result in decreasing revenues recorded by access providers at a time of increased subscriptions more fundamentally reflect a partial substitution by new players of the entities that used to provide services and devices over those networks.

Historically, network operators offering telephony or cable television provided what might today be called the complete ecosystem of access and services. Now, they continue to provide the access paths and garner revenue from connections and usage but do not necessarily provide the applications. Sometimes these services are provided by entities that some call OTT providers. The income for OTT services, such as Voice over Internet Protocol (VoIP) or video on demand, is not wholly captured in statistics on telecommunication revenue unless provided by network access operators. In other words, the overall revenue that may be attributed to the sector with increased access is not necessarily declining, but could be shifting or expanding in new directions given the large increase in OTT services.

A further factor explaining why telecommunication revenues are not proceeding at the same pace as the growth of access subscriptions is the changing nature of subscriptions. Between 2013 and 2015, the number of traditional fixed telecommunication lines decreased by 12.5%. Over the same period, mobile subscriptions increased by 8.5%, fixed broadband by 7.9% and M2M by 50.5%. The pricing of some of these services is, however, often substantially different from traditional approaches or the greater use of bundles (i.e. the inclusion of services once priced separately). While the price for unlimited access to the Internet from a dedicated SIM card in an automobile may be similar to one for a smartphone, this is likely not the case for many other M2M services (e.g. in an area such as environmental monitoring by sensors). That said, this market is expected to grow substantially in the coming years, providing tremendous opportunities for wireless networks in the enterprise sector.

In 2015, telecommunication investment was higher in proportion to revenue at 15.7% though at USD 194 billion some 3% lower than in 2013 in absolute terms. In terms of individual countries, New Zealand devoted the largest proportional share of revenue to telecommunication investment (Figure 3.26). This high investment share is in association with the development of a national fixed broadband network and an expansion of mobile broadband coverage. It continues to be reflected in higher demand for "fibre to the residence" subscriptions and an increase in the country's fixed penetration ranking among peers. Nevertheless, expanding rural coverage for mobile broadband remains a priority in New Zealand. Meanwhile countries such as Korea, Latvia and Japan, which have the highest penetration of fibre in fixed networks and well-developed mobile broadband coverage, are devoting a lower relative proportion of revenue to investment. In those countries the next increase to overall investment is likely to be the result of forthcoming 5G mobile networks.

Figure 3.26. **Investment in telecommunications as a percentage of revenue**

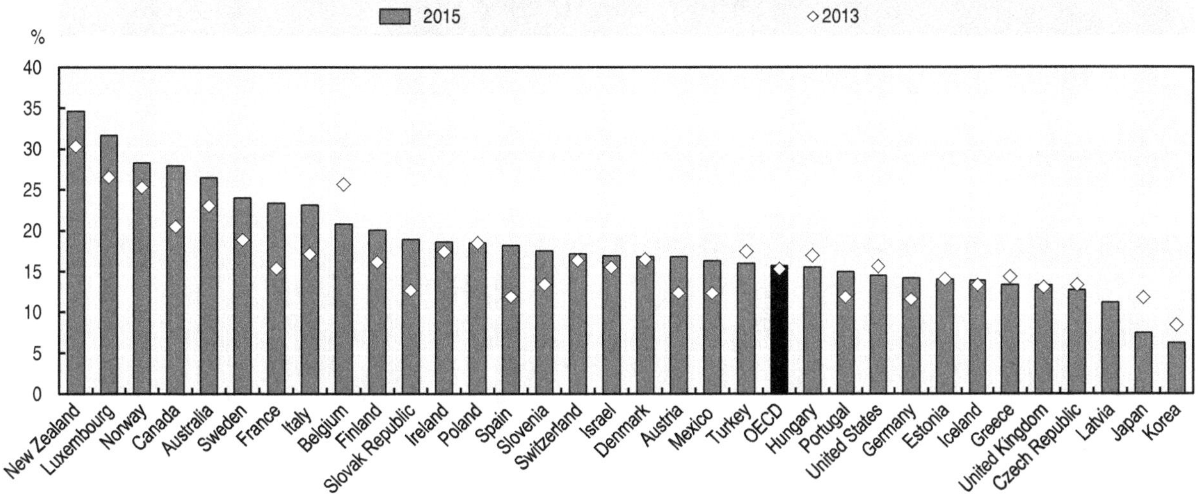

Source: OECD, "Telecommunications database", *OECD Telecommunications and Internet Statistics* (database), *http://dx.doi.org/10.1787/data-00170-en* (accessed July 2017).

StatLink http://dx.doi.org/10.1787/888933585172

Broadband networks

Fixed and mobile broadband subscriptions have continued to increase in the OECD, reflecting their ongoing complementarity. Substitution certainly occurs, such as when mobile telephones are used instead of fixed telephones for voice services, but the most intensive use of wireless devices, such as smartphones, is over Wi-Fi supplied by fixed networks. Prices in both fixed and mobile broadband have decreased, with mobile plans increasingly being priced based on data usage rather than telephony, mirroring the rapid increase in the demand for mobile data in the market. In terms of fixed broadband technology, digital subscriber line (DSL) still represents the largest category, though it is gradually being replaced by fibre as network operators invest in faster networks. Given the increased importance of mobile broadband, this edition of the *OECD Digital Economy Outlook* measures for the first time the actual usage of mobile data volume and finds a steep increase in the use of mobile data per mobile broadband subscription across the OECD.

Fixed broadband subscriptions continue to increase across the OECD

The number of fixed broadband subscriptions continues to increase across the OECD. Data for fixed-line broadband show that subscriptions in OECD countries reached 387 million as of December 2016, up from 372 million a year earlier and leading to an average penetration rate of 30.1%. Switzerland, Denmark, the Netherlands and France topped the list with 50.1%, 42.4%, 41.9% and 41.4% respectively (Figure 3.27).

For many countries growth is slower than in previous years, reflecting their higher penetration rates. Turkey and Mexico defied this trend adding 9.3% and 9.2% respectively between December 2015 and December 2016, but generally the countries growing at the highest rates have penetration rates below the OECD average. Notable increases were experienced in Portugal (7.6%), Australia (7.5%) and Greece (5.5%) (Figure 3.28).

Overall, the data indicate that the market continues to view fixed and mobile broadband technologies as complimentary. That being said, in five countries the number of fixed broadband subscriptions declined between December 2015 and December 2016. These were Estonia, Switzerland, Luxembourg, Finland and Poland.

Figure 3.27. **Fixed broadband subscriptions per 100 inhabitants, by technology, December 2016**

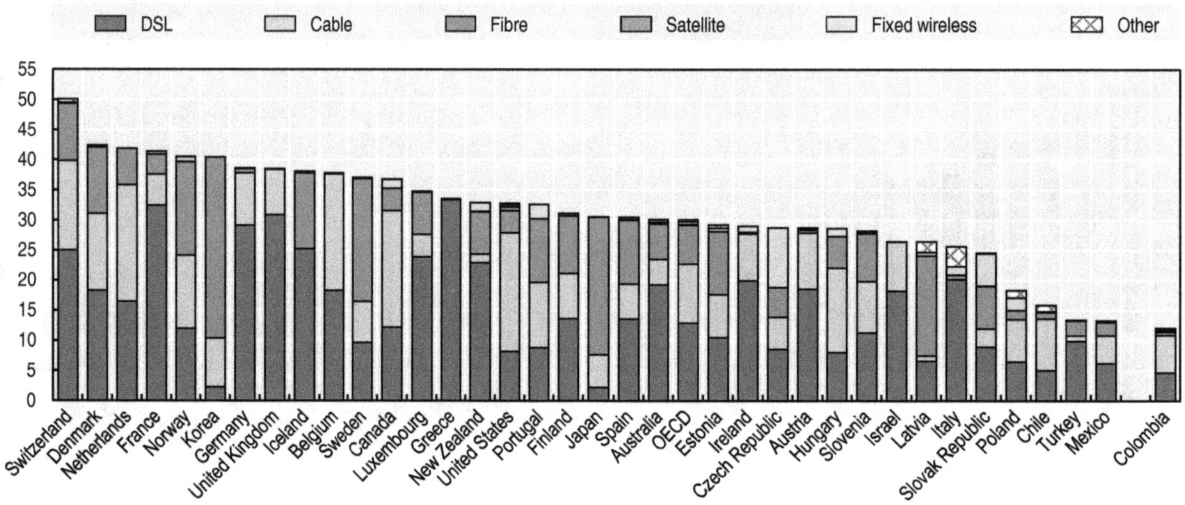

Note: DSL = digital subscriber line.

Source: OECD, "Broadband database", *OECD Telecommunications and Internet Statistics* (database), *www.oecd.org/sti/broadband/oecdbroadband portal.htm* (accessed July 2017).

StatLink http://dx.doi.org/10.1787/888933585191

Figure 3.28. **Fixed broadband subscriptions per 100 inhabitants, percentage increase, December 2015-December 2016**

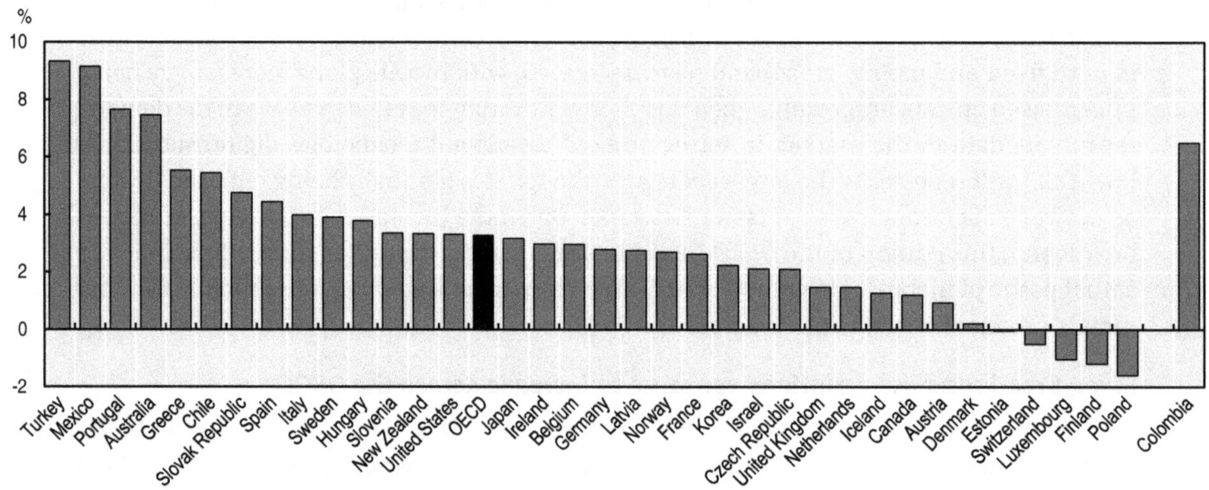

Source: OECD, "Broadband database", *OECD Telecommunications and Internet Statistics* (database), *www.oecd.org/sti/broadband/oecdbroadband portal.htm* (accessed July 2017)

StatLink http://dx.doi.org/10.1787/888933585210

Wi-Fi access is undoubtedly the technology that best illustrates the complimentary nature of fixed and wireless networks. OpenSignal, a tool that uses crowdsourced data provided by smartphone users on a voluntary basis, illustrates this phenomenon well. In August 2016, OpenSignal reported the amount of time their users were connected to Wi-Fi. Across OECD countries this ranged from 40% in Turkey to 70% in the Netherlands. This likely reflects the Netherlands' high penetration of fixed broadband networks – among the highest in the OECD – together with a high population density and as a result a greater proximity to Wi-Fi coverage. As OpenSignal points out, however, these figures are the amount of time connected to Wi-Fi and not the amount of data downloaded. Nonetheless, all available indicators show that users download the bulk of smartphone traffic when connected to Wi-Fi networks. This can be over 80% in some OECD countries and even higher in countries with lower Internet access penetration. In India, for example, users of Wi-Fi provided by Google in partnership with RailTel, a telecommunication operator with fibre along railway tracks, download 15 times more data on their smartphones than on days where they only rely on cellular networks (Rajan, 2016). Key factors include the availability of reliable power and fibre backhaul at Indian railway stations as well as the fact that this service is offered free to users. In other words, Indian users regard the uncharged access in the same way users in OECD countries regard access to Wi-Fi as being at a lower cost than cellular networks.

In a sense, all wireless technologies are essentially extensions of fixed networks. Wi-Fi extends fixed networks over a short range and cellular networks over a much larger area while both allow nomadic and mobile usage. Which one is viewed as substituting for the other is only moot in the sense that a user will take decisions on types of subscriptions (e.g. higher or lower amounts of data included in a plan; not personally subscribing to a fixed service if a combination of their needs are met by Wi-Fi and cellular or even giving up a conventional cellular subscription if their needs can be met by services that primarily rely on Wi-Fi or a service such as FreedomPop).

At present all available data indicate that substitution occurs largely in a user's choice of access technology at any point in time rather than between subscriptions. In other words, the bulk of users substitute Wi-Fi for cellular when at home or at work. They nonetheless maintain both fixed and mobile subscriptions due to their complimentary nature and the offloading of traffic benefits both cellular providers and users. What may change that relationship over time would be if cellular networks increased speeds and data allowances to the point where they met the needs of enough users to give up, for example, their fixed residential connection. The first signs of this may have occurred in Finland and Latvia but other factors may countervail such developments.

The key constraints on cellular networks for substituting for fixed broadband is capacity in most countries, whether defined as the amount of available spectrum or the type of backhaul technology connecting any cellular tower. Smartphones accessing data make far greater demands on this capacity than mobile telephony did. As a result, the number of simultaneous users accessing data is more constrained than telephony and this is reflected in how cellular networks are priced, the actual speeds available compared to fixed networks, and how much data users download on both. In the final quarter of 2015, for example, the average mobile user in Australia downloaded 1.4 Gigabytes (GB) per month (ABS, 2016). The average download for Australia's National Broadband Network, across a mix of fixed technologies, was around 80 times that amount in the same period.

Speed and technology

Since the first commercial fixed network broadband services were introduced in the second half of the 1990s there have always been some outliers in respect to the fastest speeds offered to consumers. Business services are a different segment in this respect. This is because individual offers to business users, educational institutions and the public sector can be tailored to their requirements through products such as leased lines between specific locations. Highlighting the leading offers to consumers is useful because it enables all stakeholders to look forward in terms of their own trajectories.

In the period under review here, the leading advertised download speed in the OECD area is 10 Gbps, with only a small number of consumer offers available at that level, such as in Japan, though even there it is not yet on a nationwide basis. Experience shows, however, that it might take a decade or more before such speeds are widely available in all countries. In 2002, for example, operators in Korea introduced broadband at 10 Megabits per second (Mbps) and, at the time, this was a pacesetter. Today, the baselines for some purposes, such as defining high-speed services or delivering actual service levels, for many countries exceeds this threshold. Notwithstanding such developments, even in these countries delivering such speeds to all geographical locations remains a challenge. This is one reason why average speeds vary substantially across OECD countries (Figure 3.29) and why it is preferable to look at speeds in tiers related to penetration (Figure 3.30).

Figure 3.29. **Akamai's average speed, Q1 2016**

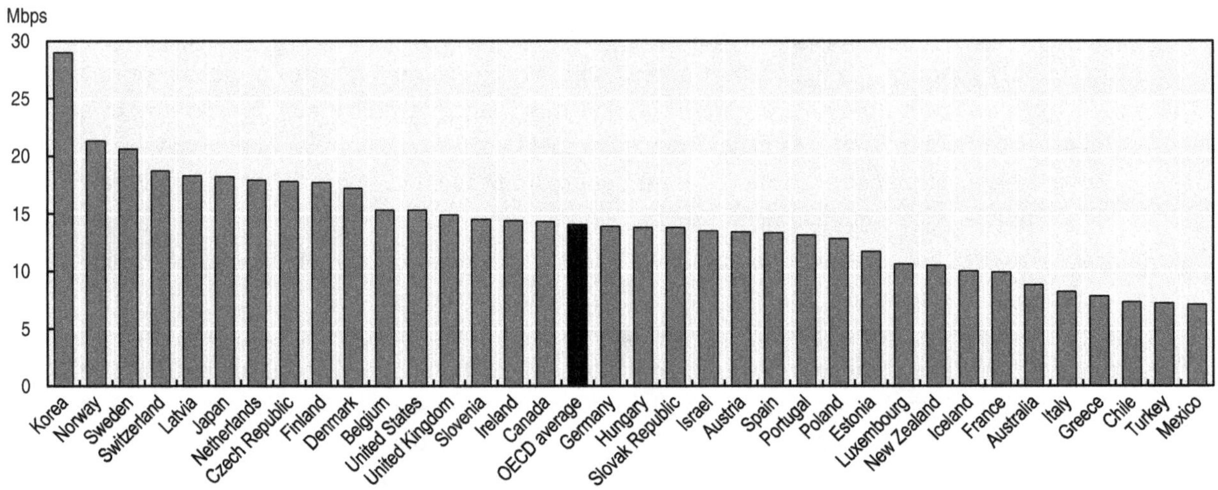

Note: Mbps = megabits per second.

Source: Akamai (2016), "Akamai's state of the Internet report: Q1 2016 report", *www.akamai.com/us/en/multimedia/documents/state-of-the-internet/akamai-state-of-the-internet-report-q1-2016.pdf.*

StatLink http://dx.doi.org/10.1787/888933585229

Figure 3.30. **Fixed broadband subscriptions per 100 inhabitants, per speed tiers, December 2016**

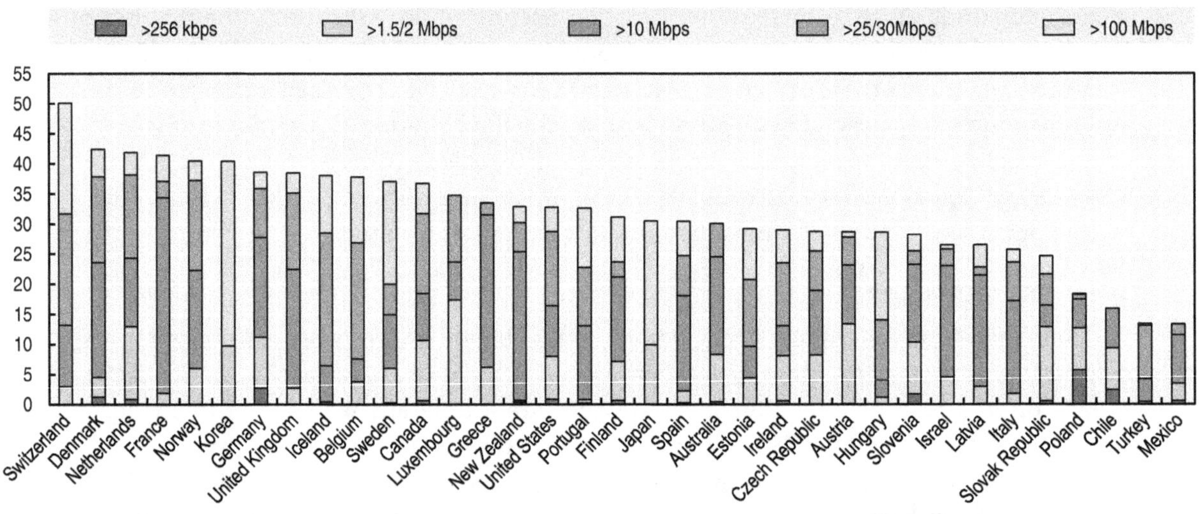

Notes: In Korea, 96.2% of subscriptions have a speed above 50 Mbps. Mbps = megabits per second; kbps = kilobits per second.

Source: OECD, "Broadband database", *OECD Telecommunications and Internet Statistics* (database), *www.oecd.org/sti/broadband/oecdbroadband portal.htm* (accessed July 2017).

StatLink http://dx.doi.org/10.1787/888933585248

Consumer offers marketed at 1 Gbps are increasingly common across OECD countries, particularly where there is fibre to the premises or upgraded cable broadband networks. This is the case in countries with high population densities, such as Japan and Korea, as well as in an increasing number of cities in New Zealand, Sweden and the United States. Residential offers at 1 Gbps are most common where there is either strong infrastructure competition between operators or competition between retail providers using wholesale networks. In Korea, for example, there is widespread infrastructure competition with residential apartments commonly being able to access three "fibre to the basement" providers. This means the building residents, who own the inside wiring, are in a strong position to jointly negotiate very competitive prices for connections to all residences. As a result, 1 Gbps services with unlimited data usage are available in Korea at around USD 25 per month.

In countries with cities that have a greater mix of apartments and stand-alone residential dwellings, 1 Gbps services are also increasingly common. For the most part, in the United States, 1 Gbps services are offered through end-to-end infrastructure competition rather than functional or structural separation of wholesale network providers. There are a few cases where retail Internet service providers (ISPs) have used unbundling associated with telecommunication lines as a launch pad for installing their own gigabit fibre networks, such as Sonic Internet in San Francisco. Sonic Internet provides a bundle of Internet access up to 1 Gbps with unlimited data usage and voice telephony for USD 40 per month.

While Sonic Internet has benefited from regulation that unbundled a legacy telecommunication network, and followed a "ladder of investment" strategy for developing its own fibre network, a different approach has been adopted by Layer3 TV. In September 2016, the start-up company entered the Chicago market as a retailer of commercially negotiated cable broadband access. This is not, however, in the form of what might generally be described as wholesale access or even as an OTT service. In other words, Layer3 is not seeking to act as its customer's ISP using a cable network for physical broadband access. Rather, Layer3 is in some ways more like a content delivery network that injects its video content directly into the cable operator's broadband network for final delivery to its customers by the provider that acts as the customer's ISP. Customers of Layer3 TV would still need to purchase a separate broadband access service. A stand-alone Internet broadband access connection at, for example, USD 49 for 25 Mbps per month over a two-year contract would therefore be required in addition to Layer3 TV's service. A user would also need to consider any additional charges that may apply if traffic was metered in the instance of a data cap or charge for a cable modem. At a time when some suggest that "cord cutting" will increase for traditional cable television, the company aims to attract customers with what it says is a superior set-top box for navigation and other features; a no contract period; and a combination of traditional cable, broadcast and online channels.

If Layer3 TV is successful, cable broadband networks in other countries may also begin to consider similar commercial arrangements for retailers, especially as "cord cutting" gains momentum against traditional approaches. At a time when regulators are closely examining set-top boxes to see the extent to which "walled gardens" may hinder competitive choice, the cable broadband industry faces as much change as the telecommunication industry has faced for many years. Aside from changing patterns of consumer demand, stimulated by the availability of OTT content, there has been an increase in the array of set-top boxes from companies such as Amazon, Apple, Google, Roku and many others. The capabilities of these devices go far beyond programme navigation to areas such as digital assistants. They also have applications (apps) that can carry content provided by traditional players or OTTs. In France, for example, Apple TV carries the Molotov.tv app, which offers content from free to air and pay TV suppliers. This may assist cable networks in meeting new forms of competition by players, for example, such as Twitter, which has launched an app for devices such as Apple TV, Amazon Fire TV and the Xbox One for viewers to watch free sports events while browsing curated content from apps such as Periscope. Layer3 TV set-top box also offers access to other OTT services such as Amazon and Netflix as well as integrating social media. In that sense it aims to provide a service that goes beyond the traditional cable television set-top box. Traditional ISPs have launched competitive responses to provide video content delivery. In the United States, for example, cable operator Comcast launched its X1 system, which aggregates video content from Comcast and other video providers and performs functions similar to third-party set-top boxes.

What such changes mean for infrastructure providers is an open question. Some with many years of commercial experience in providing end-to-end infrastructure and services will undoubtedly be able to compete. On the other hand, municipal or other publicly owned networks may be severely challenged to meet rapidly changing demand, given their strength is likely to be in providing utility-like infrastructure rather than services, unless they offer a degree of openness that enables retailers to innovate. An end-to-end network, for example, can offer symmetrical services if there is market demand. A retail network, however, can only offer such a service if the wholesaler enables that product to be sold. This is why the most successful publicly owned wholesale networks tend to be those that provide the greatest amount of latitude to retailers, such as Stokab in Sweden. In other words, it provides retailers with the same capabilities as end-to-end networks to meet customer demand, though the experience of UTOPIA (an open access municipal network in Utah, United States) demonstrates that this model does not guarantee success.

One of the most striking examples of a structurally separated network is that of Singapore. Here the wholesale infrastructure company provides dark fibre to ISPs who are free to provide any layer of service above that level. As a result it is among the first countries with commercial 10 Gbps services for consumers but also with the ability for ISPs to configure broadband access in ways they assess will most drive the take-up of services. One example is the offer for customers of two 1 Gbps fibre connections to a single household. While there are many countries that have more than 100% mobile penetration due to users having multiple SIM cards, Singapore has become the first and only country in the world to have more fixed-line subscriptions than households. This does not, of course, mean that more than 100% of households are connected, but rather that there are more fixed-line subscriptions in Singapore than the number of household premises. In other words, ISPs in a very competitive market have been tremendously successful in assessing demand in ways that may not have been obvious to a wholesale provider. By way of example, MyRepublic, an ISP in Singapore, sells 1 Gbps Internet access at USD 36 but two such connections for USD 43. Clearly, both the retail providers and consumers are attracted by the marginal cost and the wholesale arrangements enabled such an innovative approach.

In addition to offering multiple 1 Gbps connections, MyRepublic's method for assuring service quality is one based on discriminating between different traffic types in the assignment of transmission priority. Some suggest this offering would be against net neutrality non-discrimination rules in some other countries. A further notable aspect of developments in Singapore is subscription plans aimed at users wishing to have 1 Gbps connections prioritised for playing games. If a user believes latency is critical to their online gaming experience, they can opt for MyRepublic's "GAMER" plan, which enables them to request custom routing with the aim of optimising an individual game's performance. Features such as custom routing can generally be found only in business plans with specific service-level agreements, not in residential plans.

The issue for policy makers and regulators is not to ask why users would need a 1 Gbps connection, why they would need two such connections in different rooms of a residence, or why some would pay more for one of those connections to be optimised for what they see as an edge in game playing. Market demand in the way broadband connections are used and what stimulates more adoption and utility evolves rapidly. The challenge for policy makers and regulators is to ensure the market is responsive to such demand by ensuring competition between end-to-end infrastructure providers or that wholesale providers maximise the ability of retailers to respond to such demand in the same manner as end-to-end providers in a competitive market. This is in an environment subject to ongoing change in access technologies.

DSL now makes up 43% of fixed broadband subscriptions as it continues to be gradually replaced by fibre, now accounting for 21.2% of subscriptions, up from 12.3% in December 2010 (Figure 3.31). Cable (32.7%) made up most of the rest. Japan, Korea, Latvia and Sweden have the highest shares of fibre in fixed-line broadband at 74.9%, 74.2%, 62.7% and 55% respectively.

Figure 3.31. **Fixed and mobile broadband subscriptions, by technology, OECD**

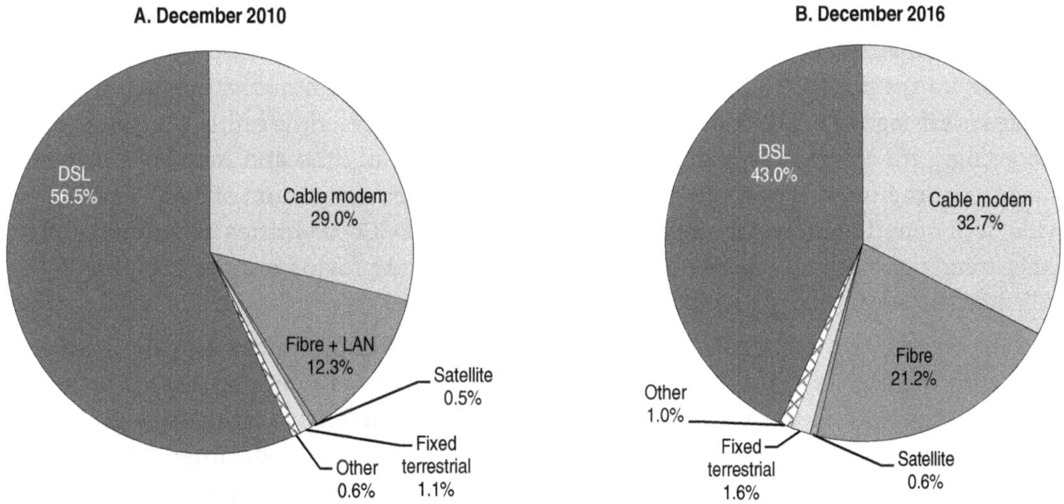

Note: DSL = digital subscriber line; LAN = local area network.
Source: OECD, "Broadband database", *OECD Telecommunications and Internet Statistics* (database), *www.oecd.org/sti/broadband/oecdbroadbandportal.htm* (accessed July 2017).

StatLink http://dx.doi.org/10.1787/888933585267

All fixed broadband connections have upgrade paths available to them to provide the final connection to users. For cable broadband networks the technology is DOCSIS 3.1, a suite of specifications that supports up to 10 Gbps downstream and 1 Gbps upstream with the first commercial offers becoming available at 1 Gbps via companies such as Comcast in the United States for selected cities. For the historical copper lines, technologies such as XG.Fast have also demonstrated speeds up to 10 Gbps in laboratories, though commercial offers of the various DSL technologies (e.g. VDSL2) are generally commercially offered up to 100 Mbps, such as in Australia and Germany.

Copper lines face two main constraints when delivering broadband access. The first is that speeds decrease with distance due to signal attenuation; the second is the interference between different copper lines in a bundle. What a technology called vectoring does is cancel the noise between these different lines, enabling higher speeds. Nonetheless, what all these technologies rely on – whether DOCSIS or DSL – is taking fibre backhaul closer to premises. At the maximum extent, this approach takes fibre all the way to the premises, whether these are business locations or residential dwellings. This is often called fibre to the home, but there are many points along a network, such as fibre to the node or fibre to the cabinet. While different operators are following different network architectures depending on a range of factors and may not agree on which point to take fibre to in any given network, they are uniform in deploying fibre deeper into their network. This is why any fibre deployment is regarded as being "future proof", because, however, the final connections evolve, and fibre is needed to ensure effective backhaul. This includes fixed wireless and mobile networks. The key issue for policy makers is not to be prescriptive in the choice of technology but to ensure that any technological choice involves sufficient competition and a path for demand-driven innovation. In countries with end-to-end network competition this implies having sufficient fixed-line infrastructure competition, while for networks that rely on regulated access it involves wholesalers not being able to stifle competition or innovation among retail providers.

Prices

Between 2013 and 2016, average prices across the OECD decreased for both fixed and mobile broadband access (Figure 3.32). This is drawn from a comparison over time of the averages for specific OECD price comparison baskets for telecommunication services. The baskets are designed to provide a snapshot of prices at any given time rather than as a series. Accordingly, the lowest cost plan is selected at any point in time and may have different characteristics from earlier plans (e.g. higher speed or increased amount of data). That caveat aside, it is nonetheless worth noting an average for all OECD countries as an indicator of likely trends, though all baskets are available online and provide a more accurate set of indicators for any country in relation to its peers.

The trend common between fixed and mobile broadband services is lower prices for data, with the highest gains being made by plans with larger volumes. This is reflected in the relatively constant price for a fixed broadband plan with a low use of 20 GB per month. By way of contrast, the average for plans with 200 GB declined 15.4%, from USD 43.25 to USD 36.57, in purchasing power parity, between June 2013 and June 2016. Mobile broadband prices have also declined, with the largest decreases associated with higher volumes. A mobile user with a 2 GB plan spent USD 70.88 in May 2013 but this had been reduced to USD 39.28, in purchasing power parity, in May 2016. Across all patterns of usage, during this period, there were reductions: some 44.5% for 2 GB plans, 32.6% for 1 GB and 23.9% for 500 Megabytes (MB).

While unit prices are declining, of course not all users are paying less, because they may prefer to pay the same amount as before for plans with higher included amounts of data, higher speeds and so forth. In mobile markets, where prices have decreased the most, it involves more competition in some countries but also the fact that data allowances are changing in response to greater demand. These factors are considered in the next section for mobile markets in relation to technology, speed and prices.

Figure 3.32. **OECD trends in fixed and mobile broadband prices, 2013-16**

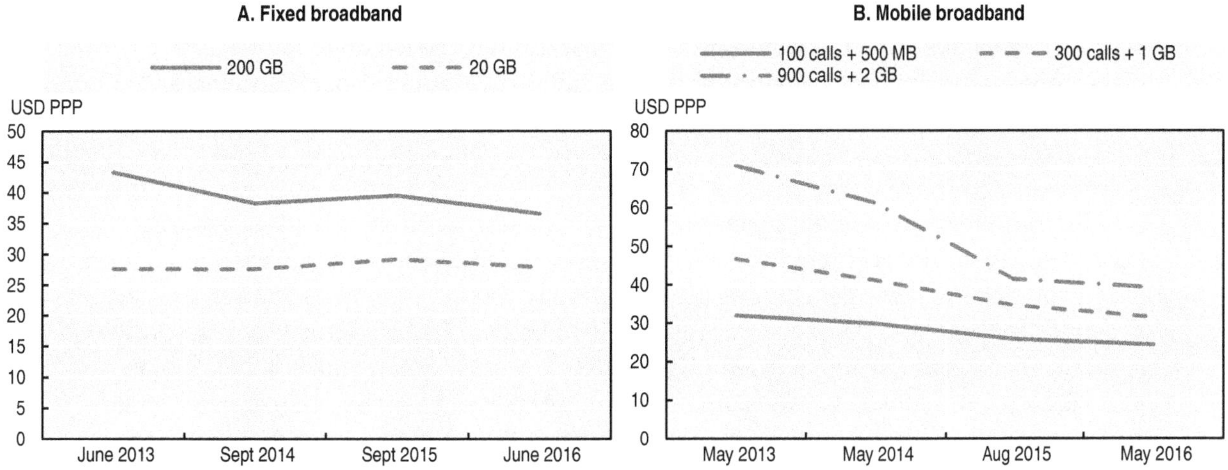

Note: PPP = purchasing power parity; GB = Gigabyte; MB = Megabyte.

Source: Strategy Analytics Ltc. Teligen Tariff & Benchmarking Market data using the OECD Methodology, *https://www.strategyanalytics.com/access-services/networks/tariffs---mobile-and-fixed#.WUfZ7m997IU*.

StatLink http://dx.doi.org/10.1787/888933585286

Mobile broadband subscriptions are at a new high

By December 2016, mobile broadband penetration in the OECD area had risen to 99.3%, meaning that there was nearly one high-speed mobile broadband subscription for every inhabitant (Figure 3.33). This is up from a penetration rate of 91% in December 2015. In December 2016, the addition of 113 million new mobile broadband subscriptions in OECD countries resulted in a year-on-year rise of 10%, driven by continued growth in the use of smartphones and tablets, lifting the OECD total to 1.275 billion subscriptions for a population of 1.28 billion people.

Figure 3.33. **Mobile broadband subscriptions per 100 inhabitants, December 2016**

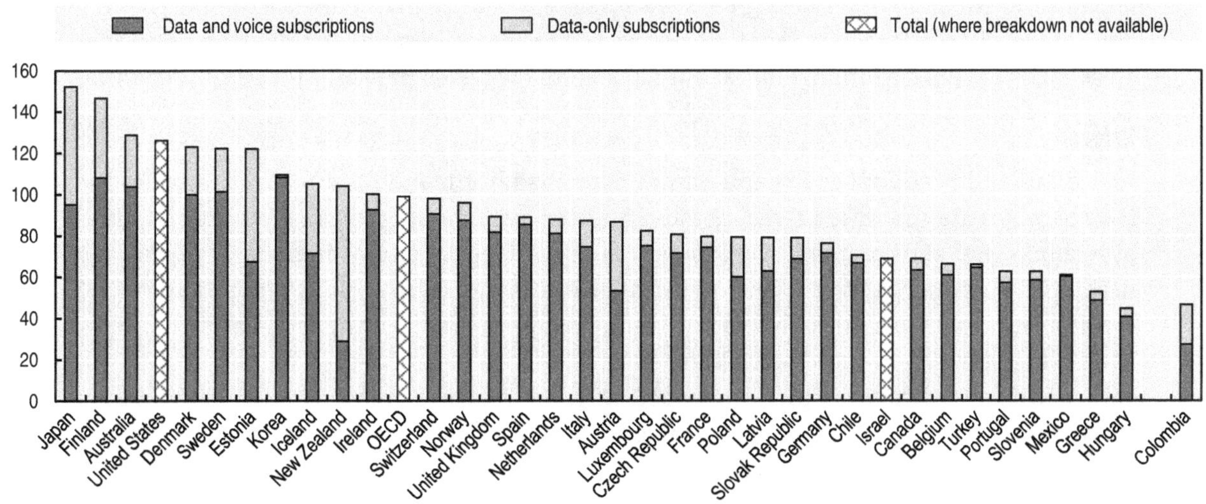

Source: OECD, "Broadband database", *OECD Telecommunications and Internet Statistics* (database), *www.oecd.org/sti/broadband/oecdbroadbandportal.htm* (accessed July 2017).

StatLink http://dx.doi.org/10.1787/888933585305

Data for the 35 OECD countries show that in between December 2014 and December 2016 Japan has overtaken Finland as the mobile broadband penetration leader, with a penetration rate of 152% versus 147% in Finland. The United States has moved up to fourth from eighth place, reflecting a growing demand for mobile video and data in general and increasingly competitive offers in that segment.

Speed and technology

For convenience, different generations of mobile networks are often referred to as 2G, 3G and 4G, even though there has been a range of different technologies associated with their evolution. All three generations are in use today, though after more than two decades of service the first 2G GSM networks are starting to be switched off. Telstra in Australia and AT&T in the United States switched off their 2G networks in 2016. Meanwhile, Singapore shut down all 2G networks at the same time, in April 2017. A range of GSM operators have announced this will occur in their 2G networks from 2018 to 2021, e.g. in countries such as Canada and Switzerland.

Consumers have long progressed to 3G and 4G services thanks to the popularity of smartphones, but 2G networks are still widely used by M2M communication. This is for a number of reasons, including the lower cost of 2G equipment (i.e. modems) and the lower need for data usage and speed for some M2M applications as well as the longevity of devices (e.g. consumers may switch handsets every two years or so whereas M2M equipment may be used for a decade or more). Meanwhile, the number of mobile towers that provide 4G coverage continues to increase in OECD countries relative to those providing 3G coverage only. At the same time, the first trials of so-called 5G networks commenced in 2016, though a standard has yet to be agreed.

In many ways 4G, or more precisely Long-term Evolution (LTE) networks, represent a major change in technologies because they were the first mobile networks designed for an IP-based system with significantly reduced transfer latency compared to 3G architecture. Plans for 5G networks aim to further optimise capabilities for data transfer, and while standards are not yet agreed, past experience demonstrates that some operators will launch services ahead of such agreements being reached to seek a competitive edge and meet growing demand. A likely characteristic of 5G networks is the use of smaller cells and, similar to 4G services, the need to improve backhaul capabilities over fixed networks for offloading traffic.

Prices

While tariff reductions are sometimes described in the media as a "price war", in the mobile sector they can also represent more fundamental changes in a market characterised by technological and commercial shifts, as well as evolving consumer demand. The entry of a new mobile network operator (MNO) or a change in strategy by an existing player determined to win market shares almost always involves a change in pricing designed to attract a larger share of customers. In mobile markets today, which are characterised by forces observed earlier in fixed markets, as they converged with the Internet, this was reflected in a shift away from pricing primarily based on telephony to one based on the use of data.

The pricing of 4G services often differs greatly from that of 3G, taking advantage of architecture designed for IP-based traffic. In France, for example, since 2015 Iliad Free Mobile has offered 3 GB of 3G data per month but 50 GB of 4G data in a single subscription. In other words, as 4G coverage expands, so too does the opportunity to use a greater amount of data available for the same price. In other countries the same elements are evident in different aspects of tariffs but can be summarised as a trend away from charging separately for voice and text (i.e. they are just included as an unmetered part of a bundle) and relying on prices that reflect data usage. In other words, if 2G and 3G were optimised for voice and 4G for data, the shifts witnessed in an increasing number of countries would not be so much "price wars" as more reflecting a combination of changes in the market that will not return to the previous status quo.

While it has often been said that there was a trend away from unlimited data offers for mobile service following the sharp increase in the use of smartphones, they were never very prevalent across OECD countries. The United States was somewhat of an exception with some operators retaining unlimited usage plans while others grandfathered their use in the 3G era. The introduction of 4G services, however, has been characterised by unlimited data offers with price discrimination undertaken by speeds. In the United States, for example, this has been achieved by companies such as Sprint and T-Mobile, which have sometimes offer speeds for video quality at standard definition or for an additional payment at high definition. Among a number of operators in other countries, such as in Finland and Switzerland, users select the speed for all services but have no cap on data usage.

In Finland, Elisa offers tiered advertised speeds for 4G services at 50 Mbps, 100 Mbps and 300 Mbps and 3G services at 120 kilobits per second (2017). All the Elisa offers and those for other operators in Finland include unlimited data usage. Meanwhile, in Switzerland, Swisscom introduced unlimited data plans in 2012 when it launched 4G. Swisscom offers speeds starting at 1 Mbps, 10 Mbps and 50 Mbps after which offers are advertised at "highest speed". Meanwhile, other operators in the Swiss market offer a combination of unlimited and tiered data offers, at the same 4G speed, as do operators in Latvia. A further differentiation in the Latvian market is the use of a combination of unlimited offers, such as one by Bite, an operator in that country, for USD 18.57 and a bundled subscription to the Deezer music service. Tiers with capped levels of usage on the other hand incorporate "zero rated" data usage for services such as Facebook and WhatsApp.

While tiered data pricing is still more prevalent than tiered speed pricing, there is generally an increase in the size of data caps across the OECD. This is contributing to higher usage of data, with Finland and Latvia leading the way (Figure 3.34). The average use of data per subscription in Finland was 11 GB per month in 2016, up from 7 GB the year before (Figure 3.35). Meanwhile the introduction of unlimited offers in Latvia was associated with an increase of 8.2 GB on average per month in 2016 from 5.8 GB in 2015. Across all OECD available countries the amount of mobile data grew from 18 000 petabytes (PB) to 27 500 PB, a 52% increase between 2015 and 2016. This indicator does not include the use of Wi-Fi by devices such as smartphones, which makes up the predominant data use for many users.

Substitution: Are we there yet?

While increased mobile data usage is common to all countries, the fact that Finland had the highest levels of usage and has also witnessed decreases in fixed broadband in 2016 is notable. This raises the question of whether mobile networks have reached the tipping point where some users will give up their fixed broadband lines. Competition between fixed and mobile does not require the two services to be perfect substitutes for all customers. Nonetheless, while there is certainly substitution for services between mobile and fixed subscriptions, such as telephony, the capacity constraints in terms of spectrum and backhaul have to date meant that they are largely viewed as complementary for Internet access by many users. Over time this may change for some users, as seems to be the case in Finland, if unlimited data offers are increased in other countries. On the other hand, the fact that Switzerland is still experiencing an increase in fixed broadband connections also suggests that fixed networks can leverage the higher speeds possible to retain and increase subscriptions.

Figure 3.34. **Top five countries in mobile data usage per mobile broadband subscription**

Gigabytes per month

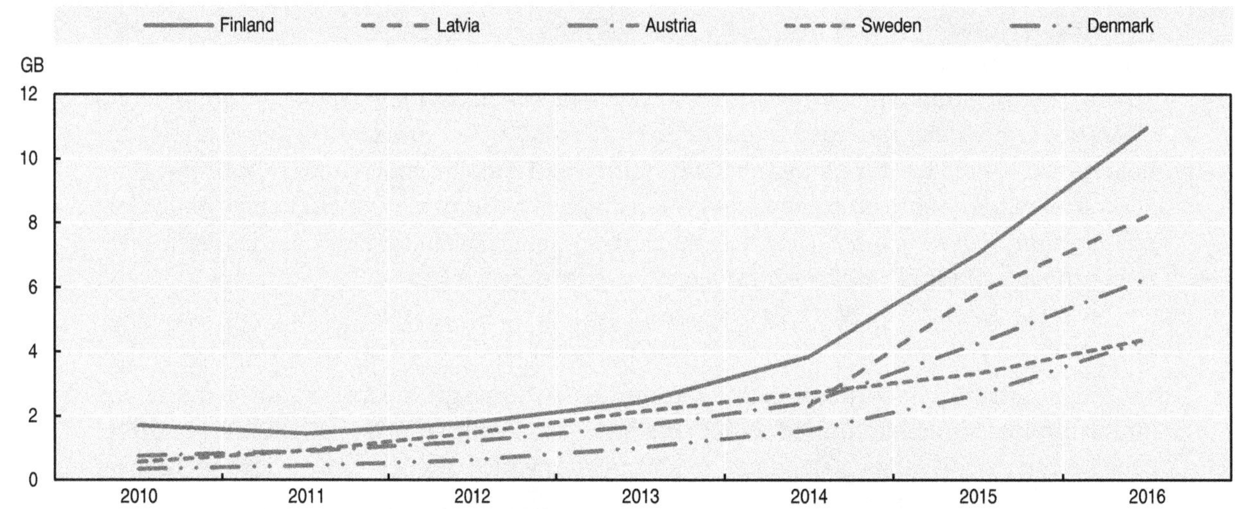

Note: GB = Gigabyte.

Source: OECD, "Broadband database", *OECD Telecommunications and Internet Statistics* (database), *www.oecd.org/sti/broadband/oecdbroadbandportal.htm* (accessed July 2017).

StatLink http://dx.doi.org/10.1787/888933585324

Figure 3.35. **Mobile data usage per mobile broadband subscription, 2016**

Gigabytes per month

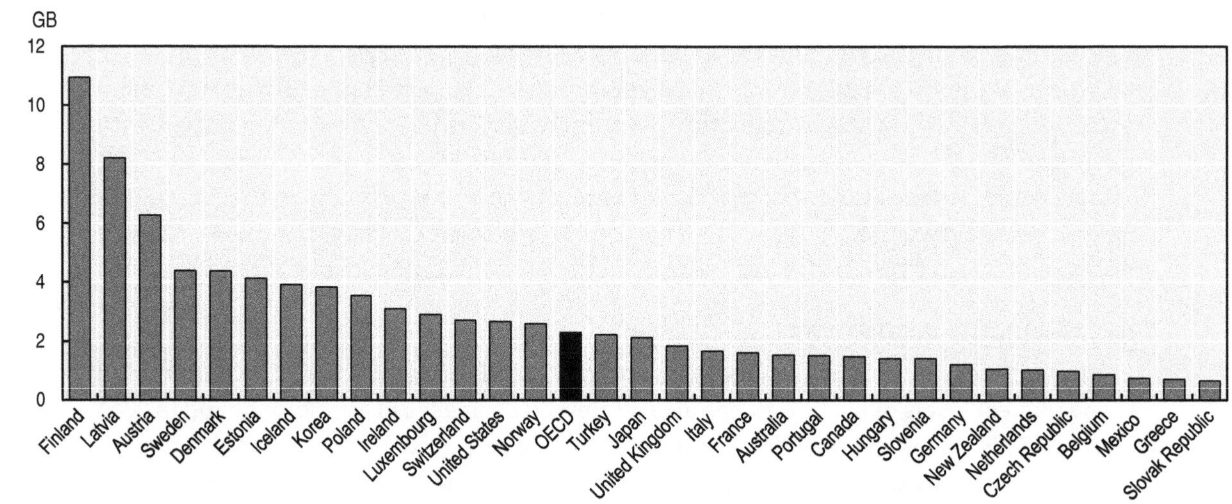

Note: GB = Gigabyte.

Source: OECD, "Broadband database", *OECD Telecommunications and Internet Statistics* (database), *www.oecd.org/sti/broadband/oecdbroadbandportal.htm* (accessed July 2017).

StatLink http://dx.doi.org/10.1787/888933585343

It is important to point out that as far as networks are concerned, fixed and mobile are definitely complimentary. The spread of Wi-Fi means that most users in OECD countries are connected to this technology for more than half their day and download far more data over Wi-Fi than on cellular networks. Moreover, the offloading of this traffic improves the performance of cellular access for other users because fixed networks are doing the "heavy lifting". That being said, the substitution effect can be greater in countries without a high penetration of fixed broadband. In India, according to OpenSignal, smartphone users are connected to Wi-Fi for less than a fifth of the time (18.4%) and in Myanmar it is less than a sixth (14.6%) (2017). This is one reason average speeds are much lower in these countries than in OECD countries.

In emerging countries substitution between mobile and fixed networks has taken a different form than in OECD countries. Where there are less-developed fixed networks, users have, of course, opted for mobile connections rather than fixed ones. In a 2G and even a 3G era, typified by voice and SMS rather than data, this was less of a constraint than with growing demand for data over 4G networks. Today, however, when a company such as Reliance launches a 4G network in India it underlines the establishment of Wi-Fi hotspots as an integrated part of its planning. It ensures Wi-Fi use is part of its tariff plans and that users can seamlessly transfer from cellular to Wi-Fi to ensure the maximum amount of traffic is offloaded onto fixed networks (Box 3.1).

Box 3.1. **Tele2 and Reliance Jio**

Most mobile operators started with 2G networks, some with 3G and recently a few with 4G as their first deployment. In 2015, the first new entrant that commenced with 4G, without a legacy network, was Tele2 in the Netherlands. Some 92% of the population was covered at the time of Tele2's Dutch launch. Tele2 did, however, use the T-Mobile NLs 2G/3G network to increase coverage and to handle 2G/3G data in situations where there was no coverage or where devices did not support 4G data. Tele2 has faced some challenges in moving to a 4G only network. Support of Voice over Long-term Evolution (VoLTE) has proved to be device and manufacturer specific, with several 4G devices not capable of supporting VoLTE on Tele2's network. In addition, many devices will revert back to the 2G/3G mode in the case of voice calls or emergency calls. In September 2016, Reliance Industries launched a 4G network called Jio in India, after investing over USD 20 billion, with a goal to cover 90% of India's population during 2017.

What both of these 4G networks have in common is that they entered the market with offers available that only charge for data and included unlimited voice and text services. In addition, they both chose to offer data at lower prices and to allow users to subscribe to plans with greater amounts of data than had previously been available. Consumers in both countries are avid users of Wi-Fi, though on average Dutch users are connected a far greater amount of time each day. To address availability, Jio plans Wi-Fi hotspots that will leverage Reliance's extensive fibre backbone, as will its proposal to provide a fibre to the home service in 100 cities at 1 Gigabit per second.

The Internet of Things

There has been an increase in the number of M2M subscriptions, reflecting the take-up of one part of the IoT. Mostly, IoT connected devices will generate lower amounts of data than traditional use, though there are expected to be many more such connected devices.

New types of network capabilities (e.g. low-power, wide-area [LPWA]) are being rapidly implemented across OECD countries to meet this demand. That being said, some predict that the use of autonomous vehicles will generate much larger amounts of data, though it is yet unknown how much will need to be transmitted in real time. Irrespective of the balance of demand between immediate transmissions on a highway and a vehicle being garaged, this development could have major implications for infrastructure requirements in the future, along with the development of fixed and wireless networks.

Machine-to-machine subscriptions are increasing, marking the uptake of the Internet of Things

The year 2016 saw an increase in the take-up of M2M communications, with 149 million M2M SIM cards in use by year end versus 108 million at the end of 2014. Sweden, New Zealand, Norway, Finland and Italy are the leaders in M2M SIM cards per 100 inhabitants, with the caveat that data are not yet fully comparable for all countries. Sweden counts 87 M2M SIM cards per 100 inhabitants – a much higher level than for most other OECD countries that provided data, though not all of these devices are located in Sweden.

There are many uses for SIM cards in M2M communications. By way of example, the following paragraphs focus on the automotive industry. A connected vehicle may have two or more SIM cards inserted by the manufacturer – one for telemetry and the other for entertainment services. Some, like Tesla Motors, have chosen to sell vehicles with the use of connectivity provided by these SIM cards incorporated in the price of a vehicle. Users can also purchase stand-alone devices for any vehicle with an On-Board Diagnostics II (OBD-II) port such as that sold by the company Automatic.[7] In the United States, the "Automatic pro" plugs into the OBD of any vehicle and has a 3G service included in the purchase price with unlimited data connectivity for five years. Other devices using the OBD port and an embedded SIM card seek to not only offer monitoring for diagnostics, but a broader range of services.

Vinli, a company offering a dongle that uses the OBD port, offers a variety of apps, from safety to entertainment to on-board Wi-Fi.[8] In some cities in the United States, Uber uses Vinli to provide Wi-Fi for its users. Vinli's dongle connects a users' vehicle to their smartphone or computer and, in the United States, offers 4G connectivity via the embedded SIM card from T-Mobile, with users reporting actual speeds of 30 Mbps to 40 Mbps. The pricing for both the devices and data usage is dependent on Vinli's partners who provide and distribute the product and service. The Vinli Sync sending data to the cloud is incorporated in the price of the device for the first two years, after which it has a yearly fee. In 2016, Vinli's developer platform had over 2 000 partners and developers using Vinli's cloud platform and app marketplace. Developers list their products in the Vinli app catalogue with the apps being available from the Apple and Google stores. In 2016, Vinli began offering the service outside the United States in partnership with MNOs in those countries.

Some MNOs have begun to sell dongles for use in the OBD with their SIM cards embedded. AT&T, for example, sells the ZTE Mobley unit with a two-year contract to their DataConnect plans starting at USD 20 for 1 GB or USD 30 for 3 GB (AT&T, 2017).[9] Alternatively, the device can be added to some shared AT&T plans for an access charge of USD 10 per month and purchased without the contract for USD 100. Not all devices use the OBD to provide Wi-Fi in vehicles. In the United Kingdom, Three sells SIM card dongles with 2 GB of data per month for USD 13.23 (GBP 10), which connect via a USB port or 12v sockets. Such devices aim to provide connectivity but not vehicle diagnostics. In some vehicles users also have the option to connect their own smartphone and use their existing mobile subscriptions.

These services can benefit from the subscriptions a user already has such as for music, as well as potentially improved signal strength using the vehicle as an aerial or for making hands-free calls. Like the dongles, however, such services are not integrated in the same manner as via an OBD device or factory embedded SIMs.

Automobile manufacturers have developed options for connectivity through SIM cards embedded in their vehicles. One of the first was General Motors (GM), which in partnership with AT&T offers its "OnStar" service.[10] GM connects via AT&T's 4G LTE service, with a variety of periods included for new or pre-owned vehicles for basic and premium services. Following the end of such periods, users need to extend their subscriptions via OnStar or, if they are an AT&T customer, add their vehicle to their mobile data plan for USD 10 per month. Other manufactures such as BMW and Audi have also embedded SIM cards in vehicles and offer services in an increasing number of countries with local MNOs.

In October 2015, BMW introduced a Wi-Fi hotspot connection to provide up to ten devices with Internet access. In Germany the company offers services via Deutsche Telekom and in the United States via AT&T. BMW's "ConnectedDrive" menu includes access to current location-based information, such as weather and news, as well as an online search enabled via Google.[11] Services and features such as parking information as well as travel and hotel guides can be accessed directly in the vehicle's SIM card without a smartphone. The proprietary apps from the BMW store have unlimited access to selected services or through the user selecting a subscription.

In Germany the first BMW vehicles with virtual eSIMs were offered in mid-2016. In the future, such SIMs may enable users to switch providers, once standards are finalised and agreed. For the moment, in vehicles from most manufacturers, the approach is to use hardware with SIM cards being soldered into the mobile radio platform in the vehicle's head unit. This means that users do not have a choice of SIM provider when they purchase a vehicle nor can they change provider.

In the United States, Audi's built-in 3G/4G mobile SIM card enables the vehicle to access data services such as navigation via Google Earth and Google Street View as well as information regarding routing, road and traffic conditions, and parking. Notably, drivers get access to their Twitter accounts, e-mail and smartphone calendar. These are unlimited data volumes with regards to these services, incorporated in the price of a vehicle for three years, with separate plans for Wi-Fi. Users can also use their own smartphone and data plan, though this does not benefit from Audi's selected unmetered services. Across most European countries, when users are travelling, the system connects automatically to Audi's chosen MNO, avoiding roaming fees. Along with other manufacturers, such as BMW and Toyota, and in co-operation with Deutsche Telekom Audi is holding trials to assess the capabilities of Long-term Evolution for Vehicles (LTE-V), the vehicle version of the 4G cellular radio technology LTE (Hammerschmidt, 2016; see also Allevin, 2016).

Connected autonomous vehicles are expected to generate large amounts of wireless data

Connected automobiles are generating an increasing amount of data. Some of these data are simply users accessing entertainment services through embedded SIMs, but these also include IoT communication between devices. The Vinli dongle, for example, can communicate with Amazon's Alexa device to enable home automation functionality, as can the services of automobile manufacturers or MNOs.

Autonomous vehicles are expected to generate large amounts of data. Some of these data can be offloaded to a fixed connection, such as using Wi-Fi when a vehicle is garaged, while other data must be transmitted in real time. The data generated from sensors on board of modern vehicles, for example, can be used to warn other cars on the road about possible dangers.[12] HERE, the Open Location Cloud company, for example, aims to provide location-relevant data to verify and enhance maps and attributes, detect road incidents in advance, as well as warn about poor road conditions (e.g. potholes and construction). Such information they point out will be essential in vehicles that are given greater amounts of control. HERE, originally an American company that is now co-owned by Audi, BMW and Daimler, has developed a design for a universal data format that will allow for standardised vehicle data exchange, including for self-driving vehicles (Tipan, 2016). This enables the exchange of real-time traffic, weather and parking spaces across the vehicles of different manufacturers.

By October 2015, Google's website for its "self-driving car" said the project had recorded data for 1.5 million miles.[13] The company has collected more than 1.3 billion miles of data from autopilot-equipped vehicles operating under diverse road and weather conditions around the world (Hull, 2016). All Tesla cars after the first 60 000 have autopilot hardware and are providing autopilot data to Tesla Motors. Ford Motors says that its older models generated 500 MB of data an hour but current models may exceed 25 GB per hour.[14] Only part of these data is, of course, being transmitted in real time. According to Chevrolet, its customers consumed more than 5 600 terabytes of data from December 2014 to December 2016 (Figure 3.36). Over time the overall volume of data can be expected to increase as more connected vehicles are sold and more applications developed, but also due to falling prices. In June 2016, for example, Chevrolet reduced the monthly price of 1 GB from USD 20 to USD 10 and of 20 GB from USD 80 to USD 40.

Figure 3.36. **On-board usage of data in connected Chevrolet vehicles**

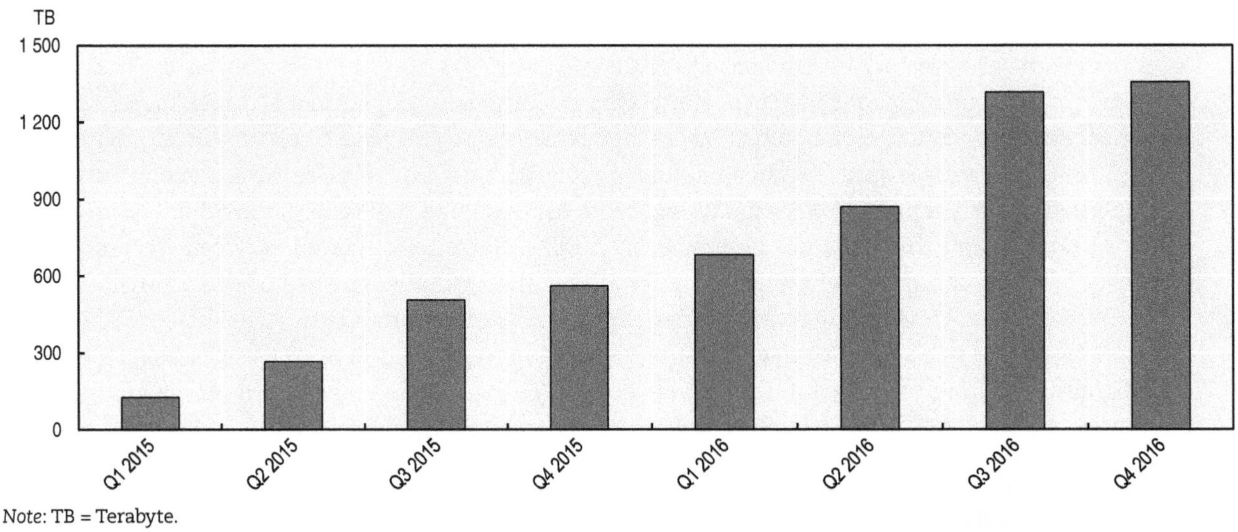

Note: TB = Terabyte.

Source: Chevrolet (2016), "Chevrolet lowers 4G LTE data pricing up to 50 percent", *http://media.chevrolet.com/media/us/en/chevrolet/home.detail.html/content/Pages/news/us/en/2016/jun/0629-onstarData.html.*

StatLink http://dx.doi.org/10.1787/888933585362

For the future, Intel says that the volume of data starting to be produced by semi-autonomous vehicles suggests fully autonomous cars will produce 4 000 GB per day by 2020, or the equivalent of the then average daily use of 3 000 people with smartphones

(Waring, 2016a). Once again, it is necessary to point out that such volumes of data would not necessarily all be transmitted in real time over cellular networks, but it still does underline the potential need for further developments in areas such as 5G, fibre backhaul, vehicle-to-vehicle short-range communication, and other technologies and data pricing for the IoT. In addition, the further development of the Internet Protocol version 6 (IPv6) is to be welcomed given the exhaustion of IPv4.

Adoption of the Internet Protocol version 6 is progressing

Measuring an evolving process such as the adoption of IPv6 worldwide requires the use of different methodologies assessing different parts of the Internet (OECD, 2014). Usage has been growing significantly over recent years, although from a very low base. Some differences can still be observed depending on the measurement and vantage point used:

- Data from the Asia Pacific Network Information Centre measuring the capability and preference of networks to use IPv6 show that global penetration increased from 2.5% to 6.5% between October 2014 and mid-September 2016.
- Google IPv6 statistics, which track the percentage of users that access its services over, show that 13.6% of these users connected via IPv6 in mid-September 2016, compared to 3.9% at the beginning of October 2014 (Figure 3.37).
- The percentage of IPv6-enabled networks was 26.3% as of July 2016 based on estimations by RIPE NCC using the global the Border Gateway Protocol table, showing an increase from the 18.0% in July 2014.[15]

Figure 3.37. **Global IPv6 adoption**

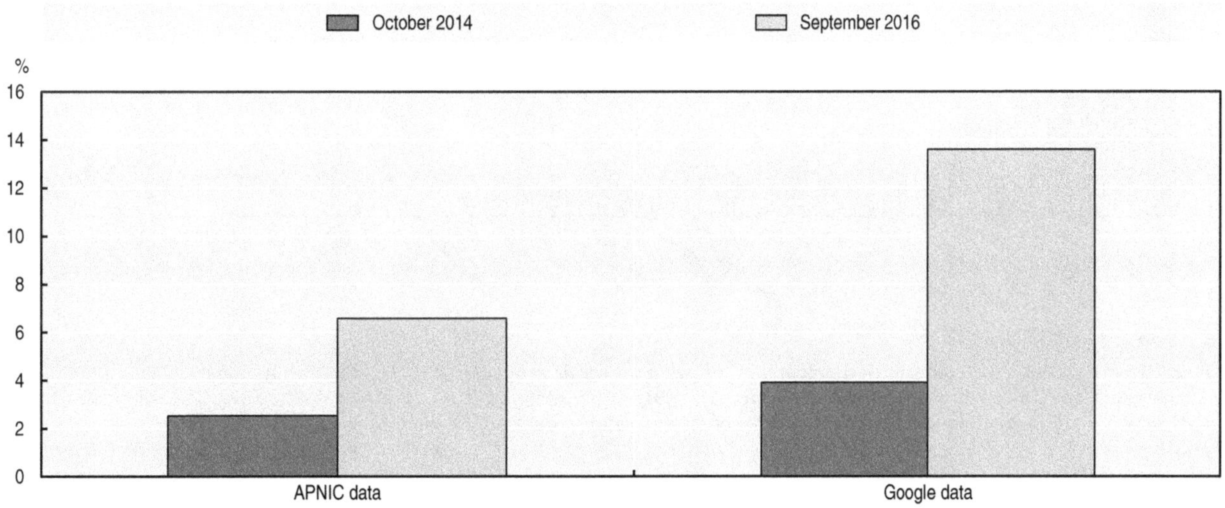

Note: Internet Protocol version 6.

Sources: Google (2016), "Per-country IPv6 adoption", *www.google.com/intl/en/ipv6* (accessed July 2016); APNIC (2017), "IPv6 Measurement Maps", *http://stats.labs.apnic.net/ipv6* (accessed July 2017).

StatLink *http://dx.doi.org/10.1787/888933585381*

The difference observed between the Google and the Asia Pacific Network Information Center (APNIC) data is likely due to the type of measurement. APNIC data show the capability of networks to use IPv6 whereas Google data show the percentage of end systems able to make a connection using IPv6. As more networks become IPv6-capable, network effects will be visible in Google's measurement due to an increase in the total number of end-to-end IPv6 connections made by users.[16]

When analysing data from Internet exchanges, adoption trends vary greatly based on the data utilised. IPv6 traffic at the Amsterdam Internet Exchange (AMS-IX), the second-largest Internet Exchange Point, represents only 1.5% of the total combined IPv4/IPv6 traffic exchanged among the nearly 800 connected networks.[17] The London Internet Exchange (LINX), another major European hub, accounts for seven times less active IPv6 prefixes in one of its route servers.[18] However, when looking into active sessions, the number of IPv6 sessions represents about 38% of the combined IPv4/IPv6, a much more positive outlook.[19]

Comparing the adoption of IPv6 per country provides a useful benchmark to policy makers. As of October 2016, Belgium was the OECD leader in IPv6 adoption with 45.4%, largely ahead of the United States at 28.8%, Greece at 26.1% and Switzerland at 26.1% according to Google's metrics (Figure 3.38).[20] Efforts to accelerate the adoption carried out by governments, non-governmental institutions and the technical community seem to have been only partially successful: only six OECD countries had a user penetration higher than 20% and ten OECD countries still had less than 1% penetration as of October 2016.

Figure 3.38. **Country adoption of IPv6**

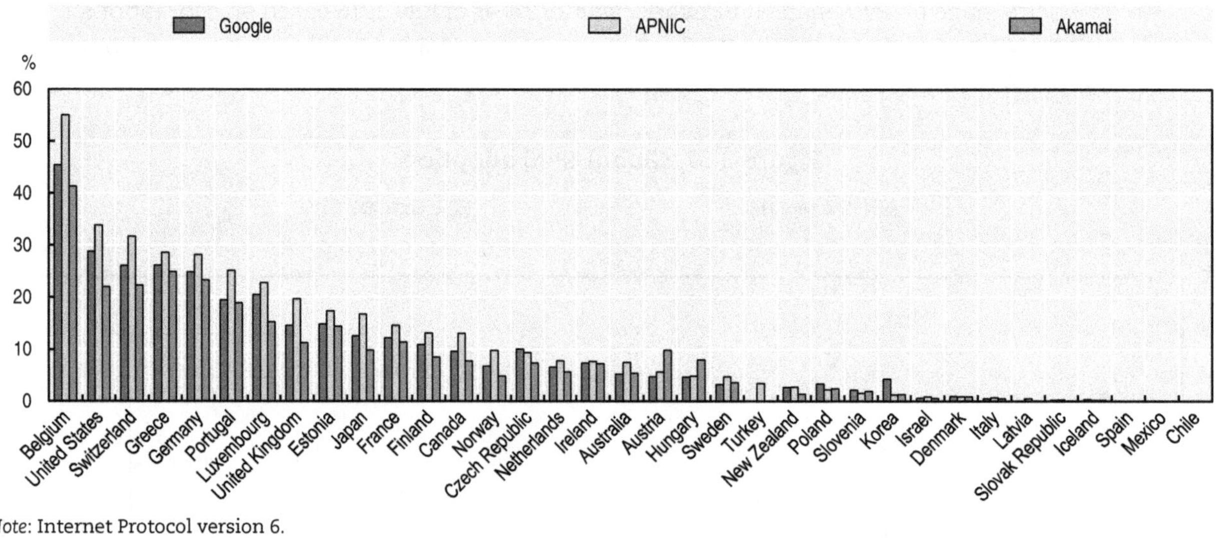

Note: Internet Protocol version 6.

Sources: Google (2016), "Per-country IPv6 adoption", *https://www.google.com/intl/en/ipv6* (accessed July 2017); APNIC (2017), "IPv6 Measurement Maps", *http://stats.labs.apnic.net/ipv6* (accessed July 2017); Akamai (2016), "State of the Internet IPv6 adoption: Q1 2016 report", *https://www.akamai.com/uk/en/our-thinking/state-of-the-internet-report/state-of-the-internet-ipv6-adoption-visualization.jsp*.

StatLink *http://dx.doi.org/10.1787/888933585400*

The exhaustion of the Internet Protocol version 4 address space continues to be an issue

The depletion of the IP address space remains a relevant topic as regional Internet registries continue to run out of IPv4 blocks. The exhaustion of the American Registry for Information Numbers' address pool for general use at the end of September 2015 followed the exhaustion of addressing resources in the other registries: APNIC in April 2011, RIPE NCC in September 2012 and LACNIC in June 2014. The African Network Information Center is the only registry with general use addresses left and its remaining pool is projected to run out in July 2018 assuming that the levels of demand in that region continue at their current levels.

With a nearly exhausted IPv4 address space, other areas of interest emerge for the industry and the research community. One may be a better understanding of how the IPv4 address space is being used and its implications for operational practices and governance decisions.

A recent measurement study argues that a simple address count does not capture the increasingly complex situation of usage of the IPv4 address space (Richter et al., 2016). The study counted 1.2 billion active, globally unique IPv4 addresses, more than any other previous estimation. Data show that the set of active IP addresses varies as much as 25% over the course of a year. The study presented implications for several stakeholders. For the measurement community, results show that remote active measurements are insufficient for an IP census, particularly at the IP-level granularity. For Internet governance purposes, the authors suggest that the use of metrics providing insight into the actual utilisation of the IPv4 address space can support governance bodies, such as Regional Internet Registries, in determining the compliance to their respective transfer policies. Network management professionals could gain better insights into their IPv4 assignment practices and achieve more efficient results. Finally, security professionals could take more informed decisions and better adjust host-based access controls and host reputation mechanisms.[21]

Connectivity for the Internet of Things can be provided through different wireless options

The IoT has a number of existing and emerging wireless options to provide connectivity. One is the use of LPWA communication technologies using unlicensed spectrum. Alternatively, standardised LPWA technologies for mobile operators using licensed spectrum are under development by the 3rd Generation Partnership Project and are expected to be commercially available in 2017. This technology is designed for M2M networking, aimed at interconnecting devices with low-bandwidth connectivity, while improving range and power efficiency.

Proponents say LPWA network technologies can effectively eliminate significant barriers for the development of IoT applications that do not require low latency networks, in particular related to device costs, power consumption and network deployment costs. Within this approach, the ability to use unlicensed bands, such as the ISM 868-902 Megahertz (MHz) in Europe and North America, and an increasing demand for low-power applications for the IoT have driven the development of two main competing LPWA technology systems: Sigfox and LoRa.

Sigfox, a company headquartered in France, was founded in 2009 and pioneered the use of cellular-type ultra-narrow band technology. As Sigfox's infrastructure is independent of existing telecommunication operators, expanding its network requires the development of partnerships with local technology providers. By March 2017, Sigfox operated in 32 countries, with plans to expand its reach to 60 countries by 2018 (Sigfox, 2017). Total invested in the start-up at the end of 2016, and the company announced a partnership with Telefónica in March 2017 (Sigfox, 2017). The company, together with its partners, had nationwide coverage in countries such as France, Ireland, Luxembourg, the Netherlands, Portugal and Spain.

The LoRa Alliance was established to promote the LoRa protocol (LoRaWAN) as an open global standard for secure and carrier grade IoT connectivity. A certification programme for device manufacturers aims to guarantee compliance and interoperability between operators, one of the main challenges for establishing a global IoT. The Netherlands, Switzerland and Korea were the first three countries with nationwide LoRaWAN coverage, as announced by KPN, Swisscom and SK Telecom respectively between March and July 2016. In the Netherlands, at the time of the national launch, KPN had already contracted 1.5 million devices to be connected to its network stemming from the popularity of the service in its initial locations in Rotterdam and The Hague (KPN, 2016). Meanwhile, in Korea, SK Telecom announced it would invest USD 90 million in LoRa infrastructure and is expecting to connect 4 million IoT devices by the end of 2017 (Waring, 2016b). For its part, Swisscom aims for its LoRa network to feature 80% outdoor coverage as well as light indoor coverage in selected cities, such as Zurich, Geneva, Lausanne and many others.

Proponents say LoRa networks are a very cost-effective connectivity solution, particularly for public MNOs that seek to complement their current M2M product offering using 2G, 3G and 4G mobile networks. Existing transmission towers can be upgraded with certified LoRa equipment (antenna and gateway), creating a new connectivity solution for sensor-based applications. The long range and penetration features of the 900 MHz band allow ranges of 2 kilometres (km) to 5 km per antenna in dense urban environments and up to 15 km in suburban outdoor areas. According to the LoRa Alliance, its protocol offers many benefits over competing technologies, such as bi-directionality, security, mobility for asset tracking and accurate localisation (Lora Alliance, 2017).

Initial low-power, wide-area pricing approaches

As the market for IoT connectivity grows, network operators are developing new approaches for tariffs more suitable to the demands of the market. In many ways, the experimentation being seen in the first deployments mirrors that of any new network. Commercial offers and price plans for connected devices using LPWA networks vary significantly, even when operators use the same underlying technology. In the case of Sigfox, a cost indication provided in specialised media pointed at USD 1 per device per year for contracts with 50 000 or more devices (Shankland, 2016). Meanwhile, other approaches are being followed by operators in Korea and Switzerland (Table 3.1).

Table 3.1. **Commercial offerings and price plans for low-power, wide-area networks**

SK Telecom (Korea)			Swisscom (Switzerland)	
Price plan	Data allowance[1]	Monthly flat rate	LPN bundle service per device	Number of messages per day[2]
Band IoT 35	100 kB	USD 0.30	XS	2/1
Band IoT 50	500 kB	USD 0.43	S	4/1
Band IoT 70	3 MB	USD 0.61	M	24/2
Band IoT 100	10 MB	USD 0.87	L	48/4
Band IoT 150	50 MB	USD 1.31	XL	96/9
Band IoT 200	100 MB	USD 1.75	XXL	144/14

1. Data usage exceeding the data allotment provided will be charged at KRW 0.005 per 0.5 kB.
2. Uplink/downlink.
Note: IoT = Internet of Things; kB = kilobyte; MB = Megabyte.
Sources: SK Telecom (2016), "SK Telecom commercializes nationwide LoRa network for IoT", *www.sktelecom.com/en/press/detail.do?idx=1172*; Swisscom (2017), "Low power network product and service overview", *http://lpn.swisscom.ch/e/our-offering* (accessed 22 March 2017).

In Korea, SK Telecom offers six different price plans that include a data allowance at a monthly flat rate. The lowest cost plan, Band IoT 35, offers 100 kilobytes of data allowance at about USD 0.30 per month. For applications with greater data use, plans include Band IoT 100 for 10 MB at USD 0.87 per month and Band IoT 200 for 100 MB at approximately USD 1.75 per month (SK Telecom, 2016). SK Telecom's LoRa services cost merely one-tenth of their LTE-based IoT services and extensive discount rates are offered to business customers depending on their contract duration and number of lines contracted.

In Switzerland, Swisscom's LPN connectivity plans are designed as a bundle service per device. Instead of a data allowance, the bundle includes a number of uplink and downlink messages per day. The smallest package (XS) allows for 2 uplink and 1 downlink messages, the M package comes with 24/2 messages, and the largest plan (XXL) includes 144 uplink and 14 downlink messages (Swisscom, 2017).

Global roaming for the Internet of Things

Before LPWA specifications are included in the 3rd Generation Partnership Project standards used by the mobile industry, several connectivity players have announced their interest in establishing a LoRa-based global roaming system (Yoon, 2016). One such system would allow LoRaWAN end devices to be deployed in multiple networks and roam from one network to another irrespective of network infrastructure or operator. For such an international roaming system to be implemented, operators of LoRa networks would need to negotiate roaming agreements as the mobile industry has done for two decades.

Notes

1. LTE-M is one of a number of low-power and wide-area technologies aimed at providing connectivity to M2M or IoT devices. It has the capability to expand the range of existing LTE (4G) mobile networks.
2. China: National Bureau of Statistics of China (NBS), *http://data.stats.gov.cn/english/easyquery.htm?cn=A01* (accessed March 2017); Japan: Ministry of Economy, Trade and Industry, *www.meti.go.jp/english/statistics/tyo/iip/index.html* (accessed March 2017); Korea: Statistics Korea, *http://kosis.kr/eng/statisticsList/statisticsList_01List.jsp?vwcd=MT_ETITLE&parentId=I* (accessed in March 2017); Chinese Taipei: Department of Statistics, MOEA *www.moea.gov.tw/MNS/dos_e/home/Home.aspx* (accessed March 2017); United States: Federal Reserve Bank *https://www.federalreserve.gov/datadownload/Choose.aspx?rel=G17* (accessed March 2017).
3. Turnover equals the total value of invoices corresponding to market sales of goods or services supplied to third parties, including duties and taxes (excepted value-added tax) and all other charges passed on to the customer.
4. China: National Bureau of Statistics of China (NBS), *http://data.stats.gov.cn/english/easyquery.htm?cn=A01* (accessed March 2017); Japan: Ministry of Economy, Trade and Industry, *www.meti.go.jp/english/statistics/tyo/sanzi/* (accessed March 2017); Korea: Statistics Korea *http://kosis.kr/eng/statisticsList/statisticsList_01List.jsp?vwcd=MT_ETITLE&parentId=I* (accessed in March 2017); Chinese Taipei: Information, professional and technical services, rental and leasing survey, Department of Statistics, Ministry of Economic Affairs, *http://www.moea.gov.tw/MNS/dos_e/content/SubMenu.aspx?menu_id=9528* (accessed March 2017).
5. Global data are calculated by summing all reported ICT exports from all declaring countries in the BTDIxE database. Exports in gross terms, i.e. no adjustment made for re-import/re-export.
6. Global imports are calculated by summing all reported ICT imports from all declaring countries in the BTDIxE database. Imports in gross terms, i.e. no adjustment made for re-import/re-export.
7. See: *https://www.automatic.com/pro*.
8. See: *https://www.vin.li*. A dongle is a small piece of hardware that connects to another device to provide it with additional functionality.
9. See: *https://www.att.com/devices/zte/mobley.html#sku=sku7700323*.
10. See: *https://www.onstar.com/us/en/home.html*.
11. See: *www.bmw.com/com/en/newvehicles/7series/sedan/2015/showroom/services_and_apps.html*.
12. See: *https://company.here.com/automotive/new-innovations/sensor-ingestion*.
13. See: *https://www.google.com/selfdrivingcar*.
14. See: *https://www.cnet.com/roadshow/news/ford-our-cars-will-give-you-control-of-your-driver-data*.

15. RIPE NCC data calculate the percentage of networks such as autonomous systems (ASes) that announce an IPv6 prefix relative to the total number of ASes in the routing table.
16. For a client end system to be able to make a connection using IPv6, all the Internet's subsystems must also be functional in supporting IPv6, including intermediary and transit networks.
17. AMS-IX statistics show 4 800 Gigabits per second (Gbps) for IPv4 and 72 Gbps for IPv6. See AMS-IX stats at: *https://ams-ix.net/technical/statistics* and *https://ams-ix.net/technical/statistics/sflow-stats/ipv6-traffic*.
18. Route servers are provided by Internet exchange operators to simplify exchange of IPv4 and IPv6 routes among networks.
19. The number of active IPv4 and IPv6 prefixes is 123 k and 18 k respectively. The number of active IPv4 and IPv6 sessions is 525 and 325 respectively. See LINX stats at: *https://www.linx.net/tech-info-help/route-servers*.
20. Google data were used for being more representative of actual IPv6 user penetration.
21. The reports find that more than 30% of the active IP address blocks, about 1.5 million/24 blocks, have a filling degree lower than 64 active IP addresses. Further research shows that static address assignment practice is the main driver for such low utilisation. On the other hand, more than 80% of the active 24 addresses that appear to be dynamically managed have a high utilisation.

References

ABS (Australian Bureau of Statistics) (2016), Australian Bureau of Statistics website, *www.abs.gov.au* (accessed July 2017).

Akamai (2017), "Akamai state of the Internet IPv6 adoption", Akamai, Cambridge, Massachusetts, *https://www.akamai.com/uk/en/our-thinking/state-of-the-internet-report/state-of-the-internet-ipv6-adoption-visualization.jsp*.

Akamai (2016), "Akamai's state of the Internet report: Q1 2016 report", Akamai, Cambridge, Massachusetts, *www.akamai.com/us/en/multimedia/documents/state-of-the-internet/akamai-state-of-the-internet-report-q1-2016.pdf*.

Allevin, M. (2016), "Deutsche Telekom, Huawei among those testing LTZ-V for next-gen auto tech", FierceWireless, 1 July, *www.fiercewireless.com/tech/deutsche-telekom-huawei-among-those-testing-lte-v-for-next-gen-auto-tech*.

APNIC (Asia Pacific Network Information Center) (2017), "IPv6 Measurement Maps", webpage, *http://stats.labs.apnic.net/ipv6* (accessed July 2017).

AT&T Inc. (2017), "ZTE Mobley", webpage, *https://www.att.com/devices/zte/mobley.html#sku=sku7700323* (accessed July 2017)

Chevrolet (2016), "Chevrolet lowers 4G LTE data pricing up to 50 percent", press release, 29 June, *http://media.chevrolet.com/media/us/en/chevrolet/home.detail.html/content/Pages/news/us/en/2016/jun/0629-onstarData.html* (accessed 19 October 2016).

Google (2016), "Per-country IPv6 adoption", webpage, *https://www.google.com/intl/en/ipv6* (accessed July 2017).

Hammerschmidt, C. (2016), "Audi vehicles get their own IoT identity", *EE Times*, 31 May, *www.automotive-eetimes.com/news/audi-vehicles-get-their-own-iot-identity*.

Hull, D. (2016), "The Tesla advantage: 1.3 billion miles of data: Silicon Valley and Detroit can't keep up with Elon Musk's trove of real-world metrics", Bloomberg, 20 December, *https://www.bloomberg.com/news/articles/2016-12-20/the-tesla-advantage-1-3-billion-miles-of-data*.

KPMG (2016), "KPMG global semiconductor outlook 2016: Seismic shifts underway", KPMG International Cooperative, *https://assets.kpmg.com/content/dam/kpmg/pdf/2016/02/kpmg-global-semiconductor-outlook.pdf*.

KPN (2016), "The Netherlands has first nationwide LoRa network for Internet of Things", press release, 30 June, KPN, The Hague, *https://www.kpn.com* (accessed 22 September 2016).

Lora Alliance (2017), "LoRa Alliance™ Technology", webpage, *https://www.lora-alliance.org/What-Is-LoRa/Technology* (accessed 22 March 2017).

OECD (2015), *OECD Digital Economy Outlook 2015*, OECD Publishing, Paris, *http://dx.doi.org/10.1787/9789264232440-en*.

OECD (2014), "The Internet in transition: The state of the transition to IPv6 in today's Internet and measures to support the continued use of IPv4", *OECD Digital Economy Papers*, No. 234, OECD Publishing, Paris, *http://dx.doi.org/10.1787/5jz5sq5d7cq2-en*.

OECD (2011), *OECD Guide to Measuring the Information Society 2011*, OECD Publishing, Paris, *http://dx.doi.org/10.1787/9789264113541-en*.

PwC (PricewaterhouseCoopers) (2017), "PwC/CB Insights MoneyTree™ report Q4 and full-year 2016", *www.pwc.com/us/en/moneytree-report/assets/PwC%20&%20CB%20Insights%20MoneyTree%20Report%20-%20Q4%2716_Final%20V1.pdf*.

Rajan, N. (2016), "Google's free Wi-Fi: This is why it chose railway stations to connect India", *Indian Express*, 5 August, *http://indianexpress.com/article/technology/google-sundar-pichai-free-wifi-railtel-stations-2943720* (accessed 21 September 2016).).

Richter, P. et al. (2016), "Beyond counting: New perspectives on the active IPv4 address space", ICM 2016 Proceedings, 14-16 November, Santa Monica, California, *https://net.t-labs.tu-berlin.de/~prichter/imc174-richterA.pdf*.

Shankland, S (2016), "'Sigfox's Internet of Things network heads to Denmark, too", CNET, 9 June, *https://www.cnet.com/news/sigfox-internet-of-things-network-heads-to-denmark-too* (accessed 22 September 2016).

Sigfox (2017), "Sigfox and Telefónica strike global deal to offer IoT services worldwide", press release, 22 March, *www.sigfox.com/en/news/sigfox-and-telefonica-strike-global-deal-offer-iot-services-worldwide* (accessed 6 April 2017).

SK Telecom (2016), "SK Telecom commercializes nationwide LoRa network for IoT", press release, 7 April, *www.sktelecom.com/en/press/detail.do?idx=1172*.

Swisscom (2017), "Low power network product and service overview", webpage, *http://lpn.swisscom.ch/e/our-offering* (accessed 22 March 2017).

Tipan, E. (2016), "SENSORIS to fast-track development of self-driving cars", Autoindustriya, 1 July, *www.autoindustriya.com/auto-industry-news/sensoris-to-fast-track-development-of-self-driving-cars.html* (accessed 22 September 2016).

Waring, J. (2016a), "Intel CEO: 5G crucial to manage coming M2M data flood", Mobile World Live, 2 September, *www.mobileworldlive.com/asia/asia-news/intel-ceo-says-coming-m2m-data-flood-requires-5g*.

Waring, J. (2016b), "SK Telecom plans nationwide LPWA network based on LoRa", Mobile World Live, 16 March, *https://www.mobileworldlive.com/asia/asia-news/skt-plans-nationwide-lpwa-network-this-year*.

Yoon, S.W. (2016), "SKT pushing for IoT global roaming", *The Korea Times*, 14 July, *www.koreatimes.co.kr/www/news/tech/2016/07/133_209420.html* (accessed 22 September 2016).

Chapter 4

ICT usage and skills

Information and communication technology (ICT) usage determines the potential of ICTs, and skills of ICT users their effectiveness for the economy and society. This chapter examines recent trends and patterns in ICT usage by firms and individuals, as well as the evolving demand and supply of ICT specialists, ICT generic skills, and complementary skills, including in relation to the rise of robots in industrial production.

The statistical data for Israel are supplied by and under the responsibility of the relevant Israeli authorities. The use of such data by the OECD is without prejudice to the status of the Golan Heights, East Jerusalem and Israeli settlements in the West Bank under the terms of international law.

Introduction

The development of the digital economy and society fundamentally depends on the use of digital technologies by individuals, firms and governments In order for the hardware, software and connectivity discussed in Chapter 3 to contribute to value creation and productivity growth, digital technologies need to be used effectively. This includes more sophisticated usage than basic communication, for example the use of cloud computing services, enterprise resource planning or big data analytics. Such use can only be ensured if all actors improve the skills required for effective use of digital technologies, including generic information and communication technology (ICT) and ICT specialist skills as well as ICT complementary skills.

In recent years, the uptake of digital technologies among these main actors has continued at a fast pace. In 2016, 95% of OECD firms had a broadband connection, up from 86% in 2010. About 83% of the adult population across the OECD used the Internet, with 73% using it daily, compared to 56% and 30% respectively in 2005. More than half of individuals in OECD countries bought products on line in 2016, up from 36% in 2010. On average, 52% of citizens in OECD countries used e-government services in the same year.

The traditional digital divide based on uneven access to ICT infrastructures and services is giving way to a new, more pervasive divide in the use of digital technologies. While most firms in OECD countries now have a broadband connection and a webpage or a website, advanced ICT applications such as enterprise resource planning (ERP) software, cloud computing and big data are used in just a minority of businesses. In general, larger enterprises are more likely to use advanced ICT applications, partially due to higher complexity of their internal business processes but also because of stronger barriers to ICT adoption by small firms, e.g. lack of skills and greater financial pressures.

Lack of adequate skills is also widening the digital divide among people. On average, only 25% of individuals use simple office software, e.g. word processors and spreadsheets, every day at work. According to the OECD Survey of Adult Skills (PIAAC), over 40% of these individuals do not seem to have sufficient ICT skills to use these tools effectively.

Digitalisation is changing the way work is carried out and raising the demand for "soft" skills complementary to digital technologies, e.g. the capability to communicate on social networks, to brand products on e-commerce platforms, but also for more abstract literacy, numeracy, interpersonal and communication skills. While policy makers' attention has mainly focused on skills for developing or using ICTs, complementary skills are expected to become increasingly important, especially as a result of automation.

Digital technologies are also creating new opportunities for skills development. Internet-based programmes, including massive open online courses and open educational resources, provide complete, open access university courses on line to thousands of students, thus extending the time and places where learning can take place. However, the share of Internet users who followed an online course in 2016 was below 15% in 30 out of 35 countries for which data are available.

Key findings for ICT usage are that usage by individuals is at a new high, but not equally distributed across countries and social groups, in particular when it comes to sophisticated use of mobile Internet, for example for online purchases or online banking. Elderly and less educated are lagging most. Security and privacy concerns remain key barriers to using the Internet. Among businesses, basic ICT usage is very high, except in small firms, and more advanced ICT usage such as cloud computing, big data analysis (BDA), or social media is growing fast, albeit from a small base. The increasing use of robot remains concentrated in a few countries to date.

Key findings for ICT skills are that "information technology (IT) staff" ranks second among the top ten jobs that employers have difficulties filling, notably in services, but also that shortages of ICT specialist skills only occur in a few countries so far, at least in Europe. Meanwhile generic ICT skills are needed: the skills of many workers using ICTs every day are insufficient. Furthermore, ICT complementary skills are increasingly important to adapt to changing jobs, including for workers in low-skilled occupations and in jobs where industrial robots can take over routine manual tasks.

ICT usage

Firms, in particular small ones, could use ICTs more effectively and seize new business opportunities

Firms are increasingly adopting ICT such as "big data" and robotics applications, but many are not yet seizing the business opportunities that could be gained from effective use of ICT. ICT uptake is heterogeneous across firms, with small firms lagging behind. ICT use is spreading not only across firms, but also among individuals, although with substantial differences across countries and social groups. Demand for ICT specialists is expected to increase over the coming years, but shortages are still limited to a few countries, with vacancy rates in ICT services being higher than in the total business sector.

Most businesses use ICTs today but small firms lag behind

The large majority of businesses today make use of ICTs. In 2016, on average 95% of enterprises in OECD countries had a broadband connection (Figure 4.1), up from 86% in 2010. The increase in connectivity was particularly high in Mexico, Latvia (28 percentage points) and Poland (24 percentage points). Higher uptake has also narrowed the gap between large and small firms[1] to less than 4 percentage points, on average, and broadband connection is now a standard. Virtually all large firms (99% on average in the OECD) and more than 95% of small firms are now connected to broadband. Nonetheless, the gap between large and small firms remains significant in Mexico (20 percentage points), Greece (17 percentage points), Poland and Turkey (8 percentage points).

More than 77% of all OECD enterprises had a website or homepage in 2016, up from 70% in 2010 (Figure 4.2). The share of enterprises with a web presence ranges from over 90% in Denmark, Finland and Switzerland to 41.5% in Mexico. Progress since 2010 was particularly strong in Latvia (15 percentage points), Spain and Turkey (13 percentage points).

As with broadband access, web presence is lower among small firms (Figure 4.2). In 26 out of the 33 OECD countries for which data are available, more than 90% of large enterprises have a website, while web presence in small and medium-sized enterprises ranges between 90% and above in Denmark, Finland and Switzerland, and 60% or less in Korea, Latvia, Portugal and Mexico.

Figure 4.1. **Enterprises' broadband connectivity, by firm size, 2016**

As a percentage of enterprises in each employment size class

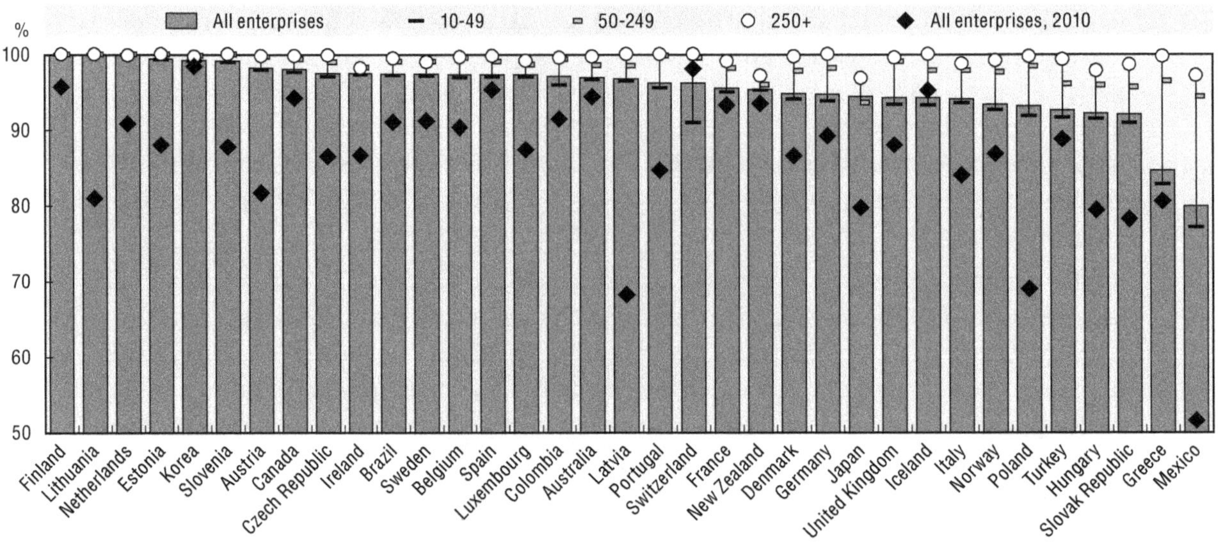

Notes: Except where otherwise stated, the sector coverage consists of all activities in manufacturing and non-financial market services. Only enterprises with ten or more employees are considered. Size classes are defined as: small (10-49 employees), medium (50-249 employees) and large (250 employees or more). For country exceptions, see note 2 at the end of the chapter.

Source: OECD, *ICT Access and Usage by Businesses* (database), *http://oe.cd/bus* (accessed June 2017).

StatLink http://dx.doi.org/10.1787/888933585419

Figure 4.2. **Enterprises with a website or home page, by firm size, 2016**

As a percentage of enterprises in each employment size class

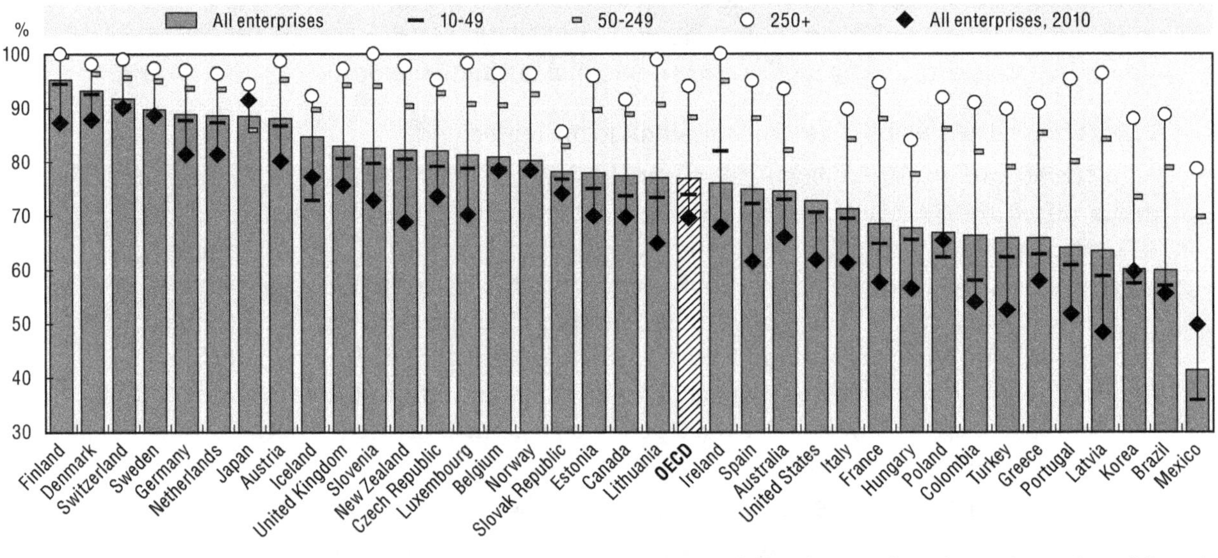

Notes: Except where otherwise stated, the sector coverage consists of all activities in manufacturing and non-financial market services. Only enterprises with ten or more employees are considered. Size classes are defined as: small (10-49 employees), medium (50-249 employees), large (250 employees and more). OECD data are based on a simple average of the available countries. For country exceptions, see note 3 at the end of the chapter.

Source: *ICT Access and Usage by Businesses* (database), *http://oe.cd/bus* (accessed June 2017).

StatLink http://dx.doi.org/10.1787/888933585438

Digitalisation opens new business opportunities but these are not yet being fully seized by firms

The speed of adoption of digital technologies depends in some cases on prior uptake. It took 15 to 20 years for slightly more than three-quarters of enterprises to develop a website, but only a few years for around 45% of businesses to become active on social networks. Figures for participation in e-commerce are lower. In reporting OECD countries, 21% of firms with at least ten employees received electronic orders in 2016 (Figure 4.3), a share which has remained stable since 2013 after a previous increase of 5 percentage points from 2008.

Figure 4.3. **Diffusion of selected ICT tools and activities in enterprises, 2016**

As a percentage of enterprises with ten or more employees

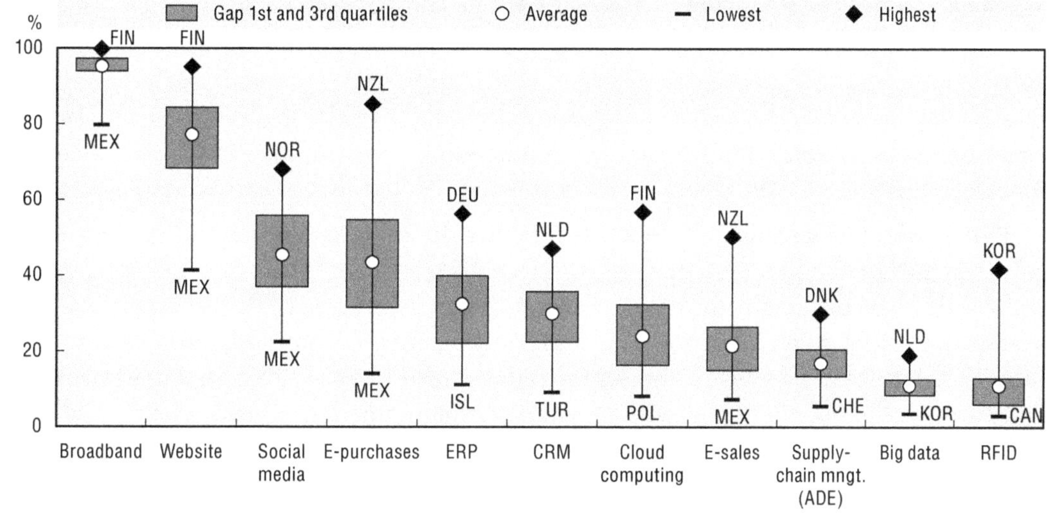

Notes: Broadband includes both fixed and mobile connections with an advertised download rate of at least 256 kilobits per second.

E-purchases and e-sales refer to the purchase and sales of goods or services conducted over computer networks by methods specifically designed for the purpose of receiving or placing orders (i.e. web pages, extranet or electronic data interchange [EDI], but not orders by telephone, fax or manually typed e-mails). Payment and delivery methods are not considered.

Enterprise resource planning (ERP) systems are software-based tools that can integrate the management of internal and external information flows, from material and human resources to finance, accounting and customer relations. Here, only sharing of information within the firm is considered. Data for ERP relate to the year 2015.

Cloud computing refers to ICT services used over the Internet as a set of computing resources to access software, computing power, storage capacity and so on.

Supply-chain management (SCM) refers to the use of automated data exchange (ADE) applications. Data for SCM relate to the year 2015.

Customer relationship management (CRM) software is a software package used for managing a company's interactions with customers, clients, sales prospects, partners, employees and suppliers. Data for CRM relate to the year 2015.

Social media refers to applications based on Internet technology or communication platforms for connecting, creating and exchanging content on line with customers, suppliers or partners, or within the enterprise. Social media might include social networks (other than paid adverts), blogs, file-sharing and wiki-type knowledge-sharing tools.

Radio frequency identification (RFID) is a technology that enables contactless transmission of information via radio waves. RFID can be used for a wide range of purposes, including personal identification or access control, logistics, retail trade and process monitoring in manufacturing. Data for RFID relate to the year 2014.

Unless otherwise stated, only enterprises with ten or more employees are considered.

For country exceptions, see note 4 at the end of the chapter.

Source: OECD, *ICT Access and Usage by Businesses* (database), *http://oe.cd/bus* (accessed June 2017).

StatLink http://dx.doi.org/10.1787/888933585457

The share of e-commerce sales stands at 18.7% of total turnover on average in reporting countries. Up to 90% of the value of e-commerce comes from business-to-business transactions over electronic data interchange (EDI) applications. These observed patterns are dominated by the economic weight of large enterprises, for which e-commerce sales represent on average 22.6% of turnover, against 9.5% for small firms.

Social media have become much more than simple communication channels. They are used as ICT tools by about 45% of businesses and continue to spread very rapidly. At the European Union level, the share of businesses using more than two different forms of social media increased from 14% to 20%, just between 2014 and 2016.

Digitalisation allows higher business integration, in particular for information flows management within companies. Tools such as ERP or customer relationship management (CRM) are now adopted by more than 30% of firms across the OECD, an increase of nearly 10 percentage points since 2010. ERP allows firms to benefit from a higher integration of information and processing across their various business functions. CRM mirrors an intensive use of information technologies by firms to collect, integrate, process and analyse information related to their customers.

With the explosion of network density and speed, and the regular increase of computing power, cloud computing uptake is no longer in its infancy and is used by nearly a quarter of firms across the OECD. The use of more sophisticated ICT technologies is less widespread. These include BDA and radio frequency identification, where uptake is limited to certain types of businesses.

ERP uptake has significantly increased during the most recent period, being used on average by 33% of firms in 2016, up from 21% in 2010. Nevertheless, large cross-country and firm-size differences remain. In 2016, ERP software was used in 78% of larger enterprises, but by less than 28% of small firms, for which it is only recently becoming affordable. Adoption rates for ERP software across countries range from 60% to 93% for larger enterprises and from 7% to 50% for smaller ones, with Germany, Belgium and Denmark leading, and Latvia and Iceland lagging for enterprises of all sizes (Figure 4.4).

Figure 4.4. **Use of enterprise resource planning software, by firm size, 2015**

As a percentage of enterprises in each employment size class

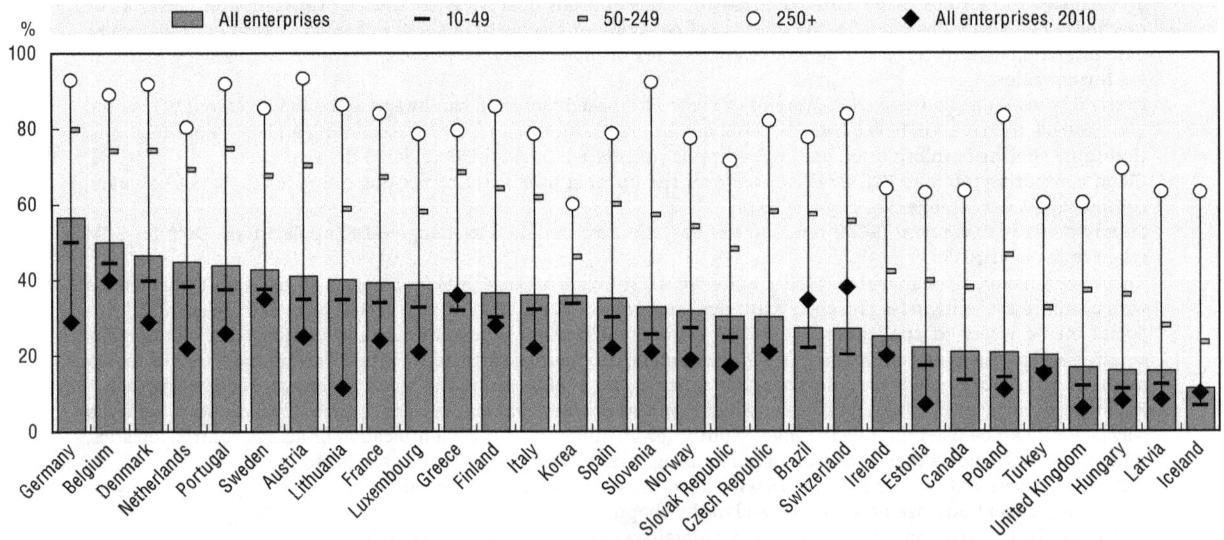

Notes: Unless otherwise stated, sector coverage consists of all activities in manufacturing and non-financial market services. Only enterprises with ten or more persons employed are considered. Size classes are defined as: small (from 10-49 persons employed), medium (50-249) and large (250 and above). For Canada, medium-sized enterprises have 50-299 employees. Large enterprises have 300 or more employees. For Brazil and Korea, data refer to 2015. For Iceland and Sweden, data refer to 2014, and for Canada to 2013. For Switzerland, 2015 data relate to total businesses with 5 or more employees instead of 10 or more, and to businesses with 5-49 employees as opposed to 10-49 employees.

Source: OECD, *ICT Access and Usage by Businesses* (database), *http://oe.cd/bus* (accessed June 2017).

StatLink http://dx.doi.org/10.1787/888933585476

"Big data" generated by the digitalisation of economic activities are growing exponentially

Diffusion of cloud computing among firms has accelerated in recent years. In 2016, over 24% of businesses used cloud computing services. This share ranges from over 57% in Finland down to 8% in Poland. In most countries, uptake is higher among large businesses (close to 50%) compared to small or medium-sized enterprises, which record around 22% and 32%, respectively (Figure 4.5).

Figure 4.5. **Enterprises using cloud computing services, by firm size, 2016**

As a percentage of enterprises in each employment size class

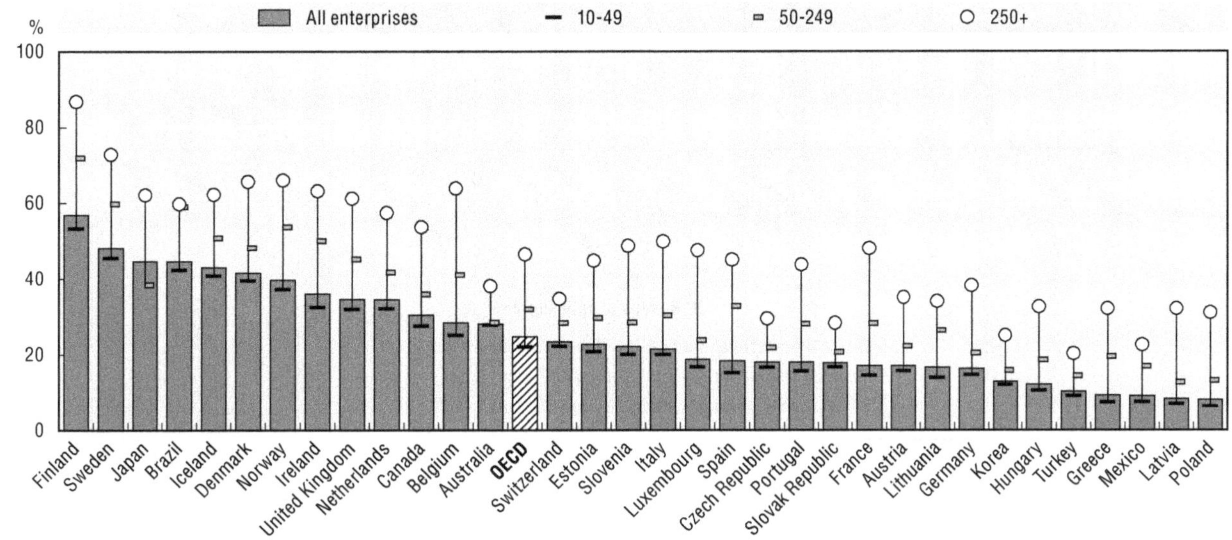

Notes: Cloud computing refers to ICT services used over the Internet as a set of computing resources to access software, computing power, storage capacity and so on. Data refer to manufacturing and non-financial market services enterprises with ten or more persons employed, unless otherwise stated. Size classes are defined as: small (10-49 persons employed), medium (50-249) and large (250 and more). OECD data are based on a simple average of the available countries. For country exceptions, see note 5 at the end of the chapter.

Source: OECD, *ICT Access and Usage by Businesses* (database), *http://oe.cd/bus* (accessed June 2017).

StatLink *http://dx.doi.org/10.1787/888933585495*

Big data relates to the huge amount of data generated from activities that are carried out electronically and from machine-to-machine communications (e.g. data produced from social media activities, from production processes, etc.). Big data have characteristics summarised as "3V" (volume, variety and velocity): 1) volume, referring to vast amounts of data generated over time; 2) variety, referring to the different formats of complex data, either structured or unstructured (e.g. text, video, images, voice, documents, sensor data, activity logs, click streams, co-ordinates, etc.); and 3) velocity, referring to the high speed at which data are generated, become available and change over time. Overall, BDA refers to the use of techniques, technologies and software tools for analysing big data (Laney, 2001; Eurostat, 2016).

The proportion of businesses having performed BDA in 2016 varies from 4% in Korea to 19% in the Netherlands (Figure 4.6). BDA is currently mainly performed by large businesses, from 11% of such firms in Hungary to 43% in the Netherlands, but in Belgium and the Netherlands, more than 15% of small enterprises are also using BDA. The gap between the use of BDA by large and small firms is great and varies significantly across countries: the share of large enterprises using BDA compared to small enterprises using it is almost double in Hungary, Lithuania and Portugal, and is more than four times higher in Denmark and Slovenia.

Figure 4.6. **Enterprises performing big data analysis, 2016**

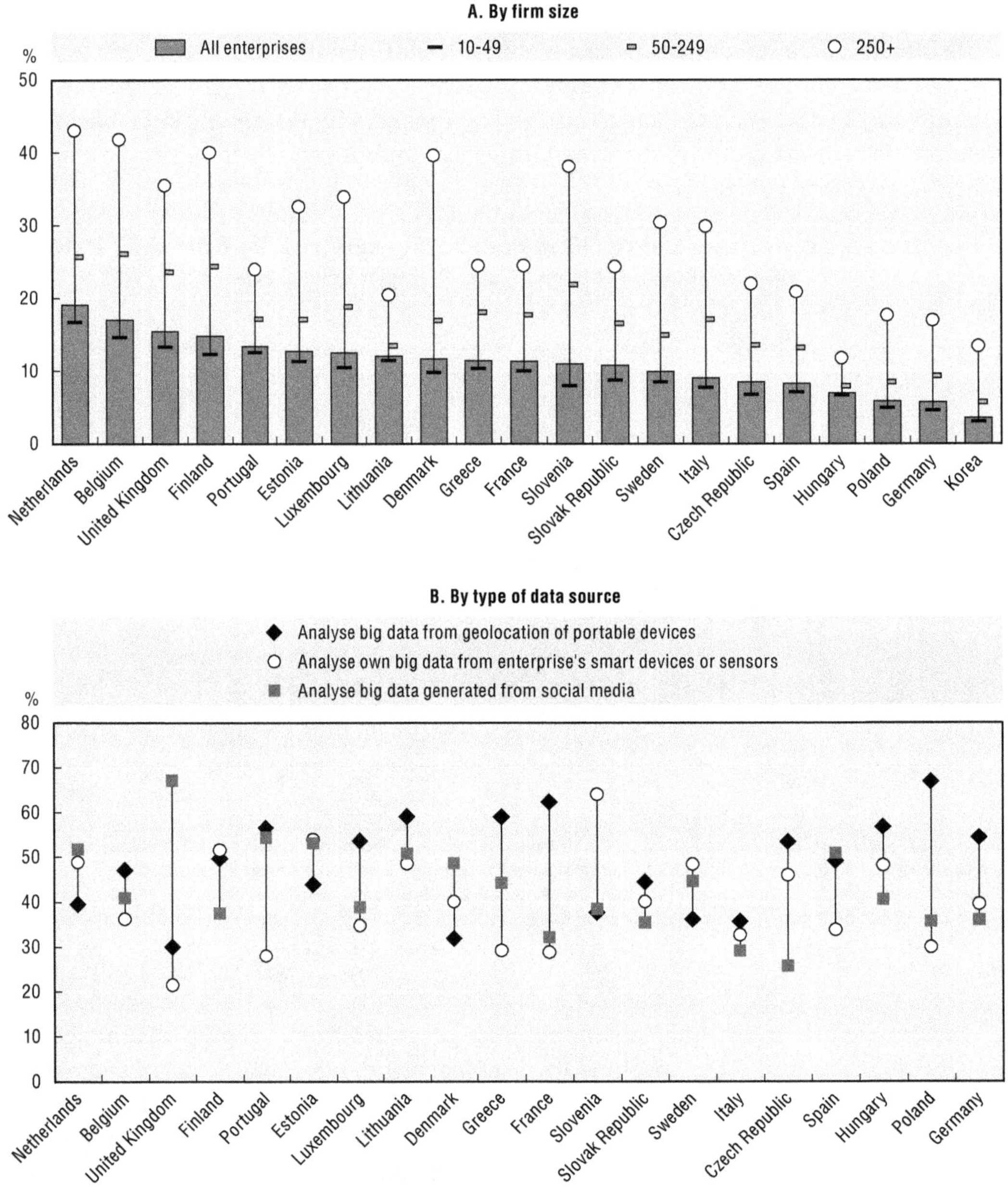

Note: For Korea, data relate to the year 2015 and breakdowns by type of analysis are not available.

Sources: OECD, *ICT Access and Usage by Businesses* (database), *http://oe.cd/bus* (accessed June 2017); Eurostat, *Digital Economy and Society* (database), *http://ec.europa.eu/eurostat/web/digital-economy-and-society/data/comprehensive-database* (accessed March 2017).

StatLink http://dx.doi.org/10.1787/888933585514

Businesses from the information and communication industry are by far the most intensive users of BDA (almost one out of four is performing BDA on average in the 20 European countries for which data are available), followed by those from the electricity, gas, steam, air conditioning and water supply industry (16%) and transportation and storage industry (14%).

Firms perform BDA based on data originating from various sources, which are influenced by the business environment (type of industry), and include geolocation of portable devices, smart devices or sensors, and social media. In a majority of countries, firms are performing BDA with data originating primarily from geolocation of portable devices or social media.

Businesses that are the most intensive users of data originating from geolocation of portable devices are usually in the transportation and storage industry, and to a lesser extent in the construction industry. Businesses in industries such as electricity, gas, steam, air conditioning and water supply, as well as those in real estate, are the most intensive users of data originating from smart devices or sensors. For data originating from social media, in most countries businesses are located in the accommodation and food and beverage service activities industry. And when the data originate from other sources (which are neither geolocation of portable devices, nor smart devices or sensors, nor social media), businesses are mostly concentrated in two industries: information and communication, and professional, scientific and technical activities.

Over two-thirds of industrial robots in use are concentrated in only four OECD countries

Figure 4.7 shows the number of operational robots in OECD countries for which data are available. The country with the lowest number of units in 2014 was Estonia (fewer than 100 units) and the country with the highest number was Japan (250 000 units). By 2014, the last year for which information is available, roughly 750 000 industrial robots were estimated to be operational in OECD countries, constituting more than 80% of the world stock. Japan, the United States, Korea and Germany are the most robotised countries in the OECD and together account for almost 70% of the total number of operational robots. Robots, therefore, are highly concentrated in advanced economies. Among OECD partner economies, the People's Republic of China leads in the adoption of robots, with an operational stock of over 86 000 units.

The leading sectors in the use of industrial robots are transport and electronic equipment

Robots are highly concentrated in a few industrial sectors (Figure 4.8). Transport equipment leads with almost 45% of the total stock of robots in 2014. Being characterised by large production volumes and relatively standardised products, the automotive sector is historically more amenable to automation and accounts for the lion's share of robotisation.

Almost 30% of robots can be found in "electronic, electrical and optical equipment". While the goods produced in this sector have a high level of technological content, their production is fairly standardised. Large research and development investments and highly skilled labour are needed for the creation of blueprints in the industry but their reproduction in large quantities is easily automatable (e.g. microprocessors). Rubber and plastic as well as metal products account for between 5% and 10% of the worldwide stock of robots.

Individuals' increasing use of digital technologies differs among countries and social groups

The Internet is widely used by people but differences among countries and social groups remain large

In 2005, about 56% of the adult population in the OECD accessed the Internet, and 30% used it daily. In 2016, those shares were respectively 83% and 73%. The developments in mobile technology have increased the possibilities of accessing the network, not only "on the go" but also within the home, and an Internet connection is now a significant part of everyday life. In the EU27, for example, the share of households that did not have a home Internet access because Internet access was considered as not needed (i.e. content not useful or not interesting) dropped from 20% in 2006 to less than 7% in 2016.

Figure 4.7. **Total number of industrial robots operational worldwide, 2014**

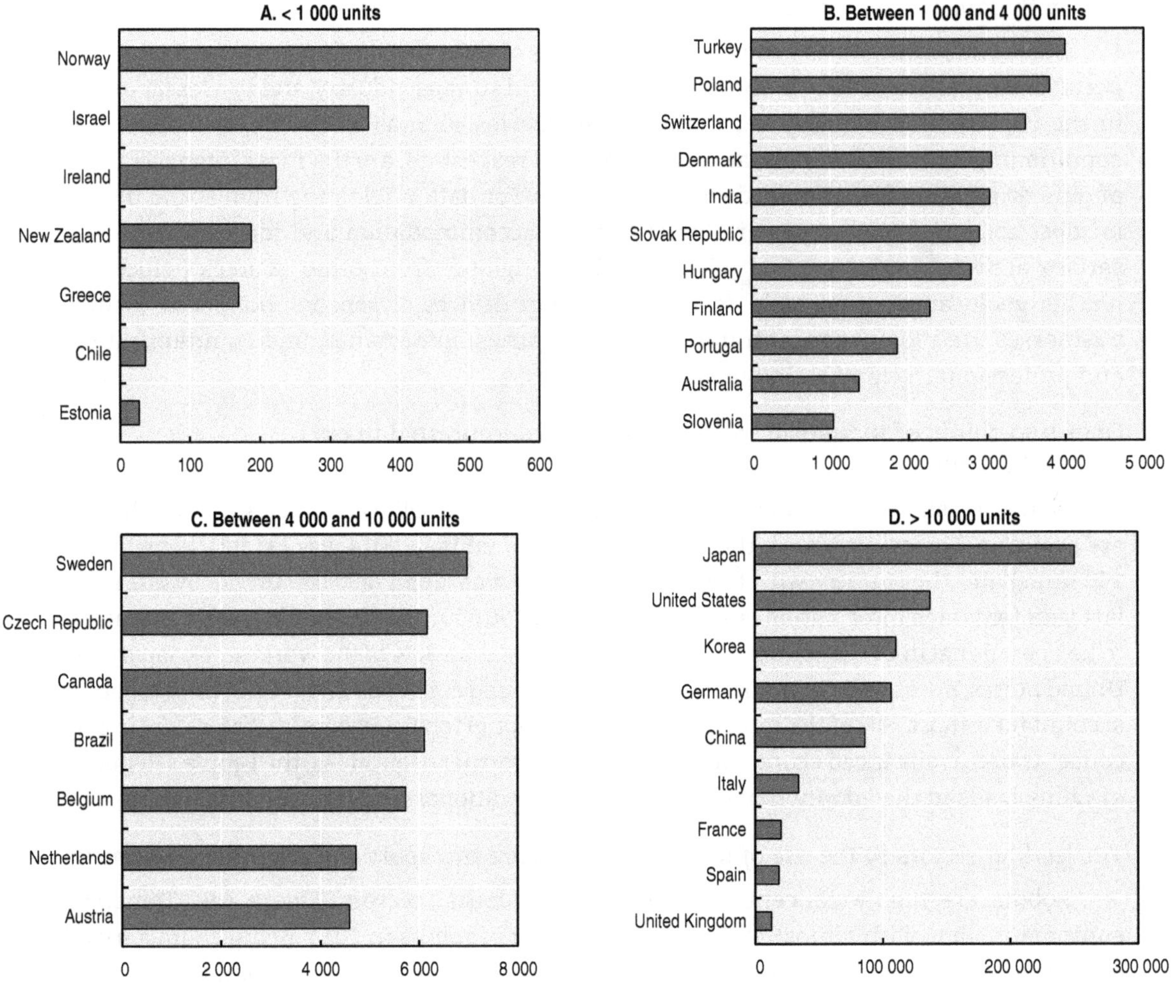

Note: China = the People's Republic of China.

Source: Author's calculations based on data provided by the International Federation of Robotics, February 2017.

StatLink http://dx.doi.org/10.1787/888933585533

Figure 4.8. **Top ten industries for share of industrial robots in use**

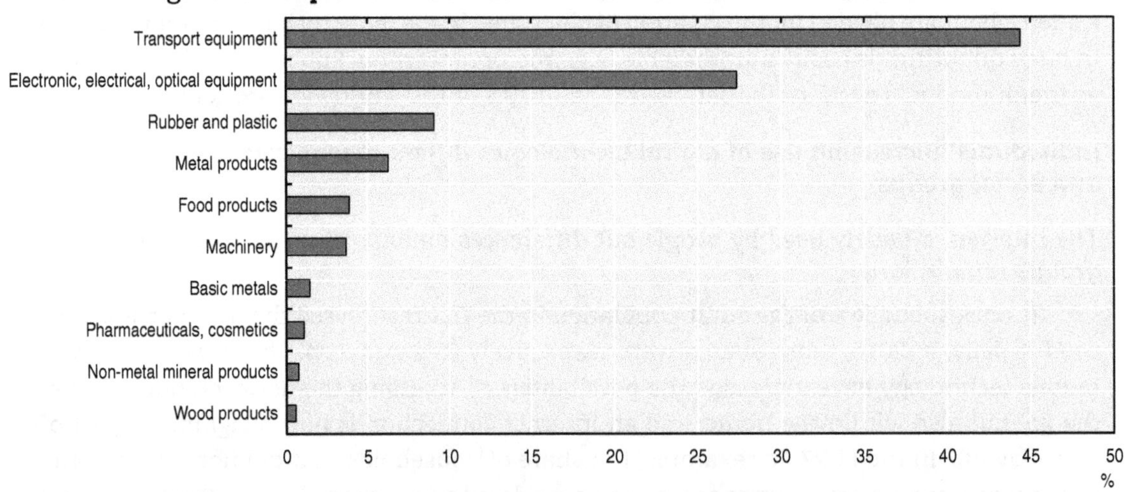

Source: Author's calculations based on data provided by the International Federation of Robotics February 2017.

StatLink http://dx.doi.org/10.1787/888933585552

Despite a regular and significant increase during the last decade, Internet usage continues to vary widely across OECD countries and among social groups. In 2016, 97% and above of the adult population accessed the Internet in Denmark, Iceland, Japan, Luxembourg and Norway, but 60% or less did so in Mexico and Turkey. In Iceland, Italy, Luxembourg and Norway, the share of daily users is very similar to that of total users. In Mexico and Turkey, however, many users access the Internet on an infrequent basis.

Differences in Internet uptake are linked primarily to age and education, often intertwined with income levels. In most countries, uptake by young people is nearly universal, but there are wide differences for older generations (Figure 4.9). Over 95% of 16-24 year-olds in the OECD used the Internet in 2016 compared to less than 63% of 65-74 year-olds.

Figure 4.9. **Internet users by age, 2016**

As a percentage of the population in each age group

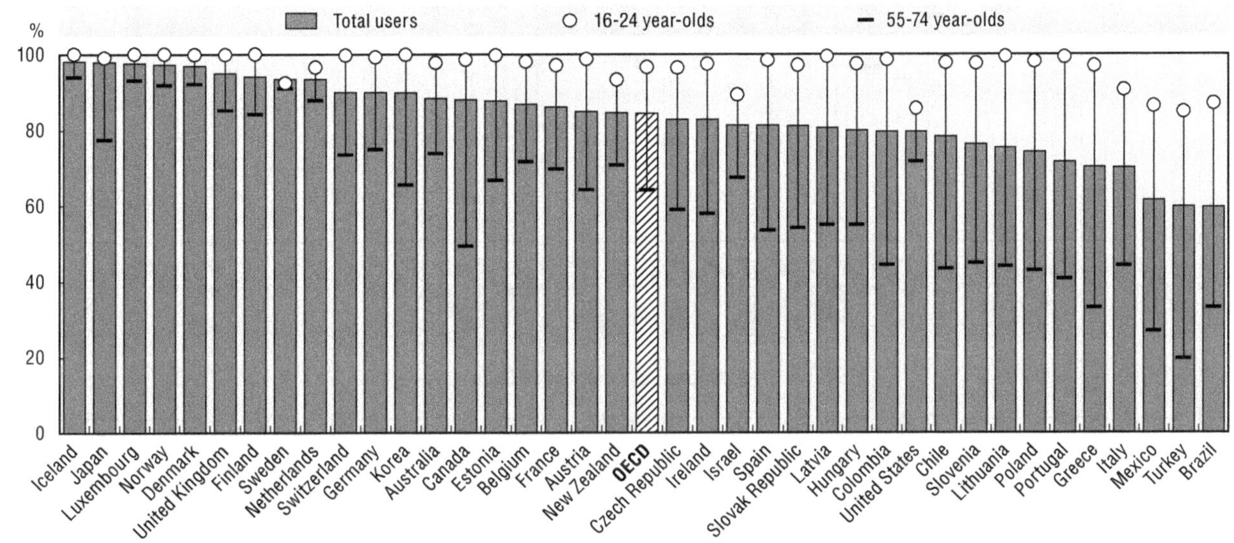

Notes: Unless otherwise stated, Internet users are defined for a recall period of three months. For Canada and Japan, the recall period is 12 months. For the United States, no time period is specified. Data for Australia and New Zealand refer respectively to 2014/15 (fiscal year ending 30 June 2015) and to 2012/13 (fiscal year ending 30 June 2013) instead of 2016. Data for Canada refer to 2012 instead of 2016. Data for Chile, Israel, Japan, Korea and the United States refer to 2015 instead of 2016. Data for Iceland and Switzerland refer to 2014 instead of 2016. Data for Israel refer to individuals aged 20 and older instead of 16-74 years old, and 20-24 instead of 16-24 years old. Data for Japan refer to individuals aged 15-69 instead of 16-74 years old and 60-69 instead of 55-74 years old. Data for individuals aged 60-69 originate from the Consumer Usage Trend Survey 2015, Ministry of Internal Affairs and Communications. OECD data are based on a simple average of the available countries.

Source: OECD, *ICT Access and Usage by Households and Individuals* (database), *http://oe.cd/hhind* (accessed June 2017).

StatLink http://dx.doi.org/10.1787/888933585571

Education appears to be a much more important factor determining Internet usage for older people than for younger ones. The Internet usage rate among 16-24 year-olds is nearing 100% in most OECD countries, except in Israel and Italy (90%), and Mexico and Turkey (85%). Within the OECD, Internet usage rates among those with a low educational attainment are generally less than 5 percentage points below that of those with a tertiary education, except in except Greece (9%), Israel (30%), Mexico (27%) and Turkey (21%).

By contrast, Internet usage among 55-74 year-olds is still very heterogeneous across countries: above 80% in the Nordic countries, Luxembourg, the Netherlands and the United Kingdom, but only 30% in Greece, 24% in Mexico and 16% in Turkey.

Internet usage rates for 55-74 year-olds with a tertiary education are generally above or in line with those of the overall population, and in some countries approach the usage rates among 16-24 year-olds. Differences in Internet usage between high and low educational attainments among 55-74 year-olds are particularly large in Hungary, Lithuania and Poland (Figure 4.10).

Figure 4.10. **Internet users by age and educational attainment, 2016**

As a percentage of the population in each age group

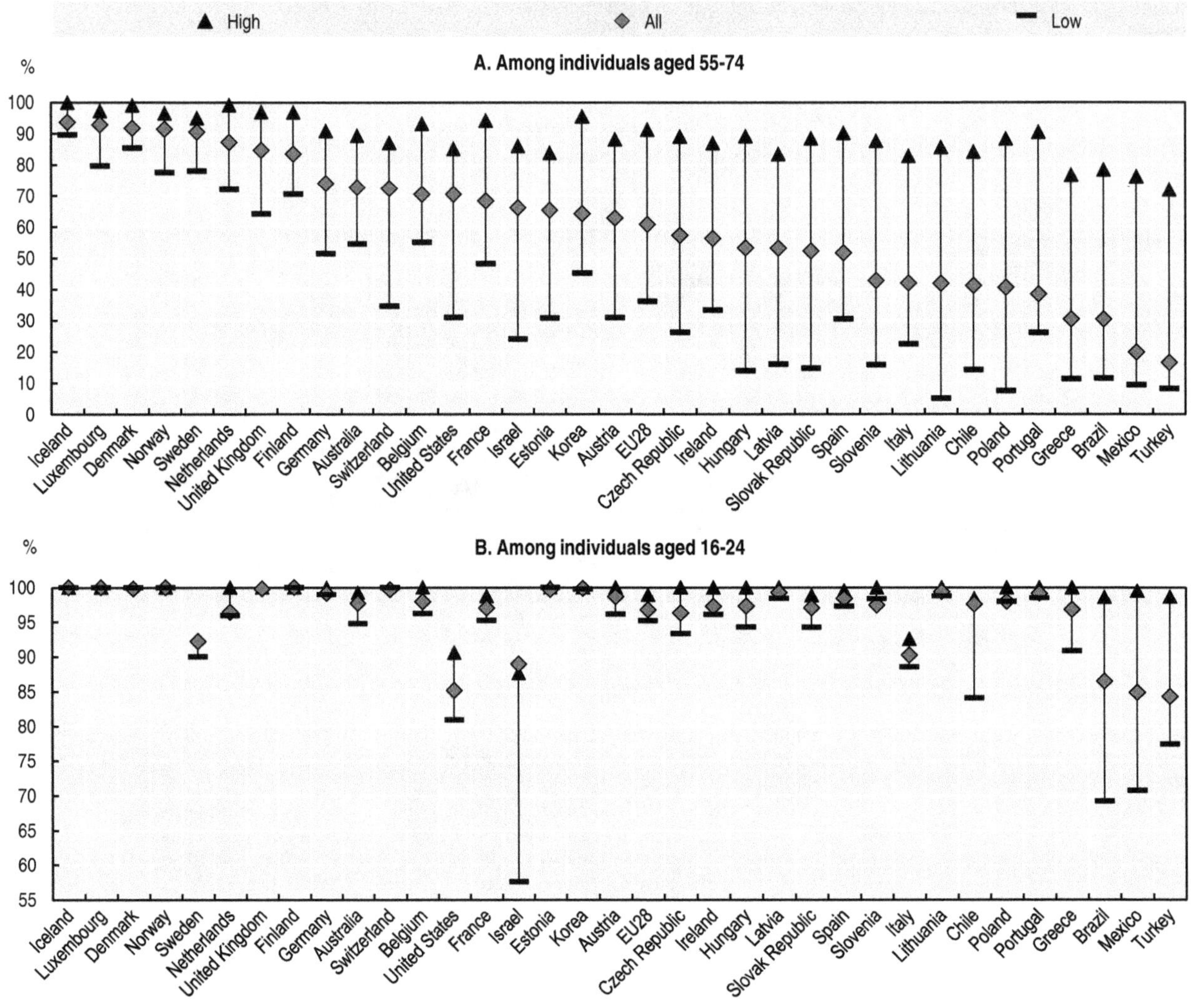

Notes: Internet users are individuals having used the Internet during the last three months. Individuals with medium formal education attainment are not shown in the figure. For Brazil, Chile, Israel, Korea and the United States, data refer to 2015. For Iceland and Switzerland, data refer to 2014. For Australia, data refer to 2014/15, fiscal year ending 30 June 2015, instead of 2016. For Japan, data refer to individuals aged 15-69 instead of 16-74. Data for individuals aged 16-24 with high educational attainment relate to the year 2014 for Slovenia, and are OECD estimates for Finland, Iceland and Norway.

Source: OECD, *ICT Access and Usage by Households and Individuals* (database), *http://oe.cd/hhind* (accessed June 2017).

StatLink http://dx.doi.org/10.1787/888933585590

Accessing the Internet while "on the move" is also becoming common: in 2011 in the EU28, about one Internet user in four was accessing the Internet on a smartphone or a mobile phone away from home or work. This had grown to more than two out of three Internet users in 2016. This share is nearing nine out of ten Internet users in Spain and Turkey, and around eight out of ten in Denmark, the Netherlands, Sweden and the United Kingdom.

The age of first access to the Internet varies widely across countries. More than one-third of students started using the Internet at age 6 or younger in Denmark and the Netherlands. In the Nordic countries, Estonia and the Netherlands, 80% of students accessed the Internet before the age of ten, as opposed to 30% in Greece and the Slovak Republic.

Over 2015-16, on average 83% of Internet users reported sending e-mails, 80% used the Internet to obtain information on goods and products, 70% read online news, 69% used social networks, and 31% used cloud technologies. While 58% of Internet users ordered products on line, only 18% sold products over the Internet (Figure 4.11).

Activities such as sending e-mails, searching for product information and social networking show little variation across all countries. However, the shares of Internet users performing activities usually associated with a higher level of education (e.g. those with cultural elements or more sophisticated service infrastructure), tend to show larger cross-country variability. This is the case, for example, for e-banking, online purchases, news reading, cloud technologies and e-government.

Figure 4.11. **Diffusion of selected online activities among Internet users, 2016**

As a percentage of Internet users performing each activity

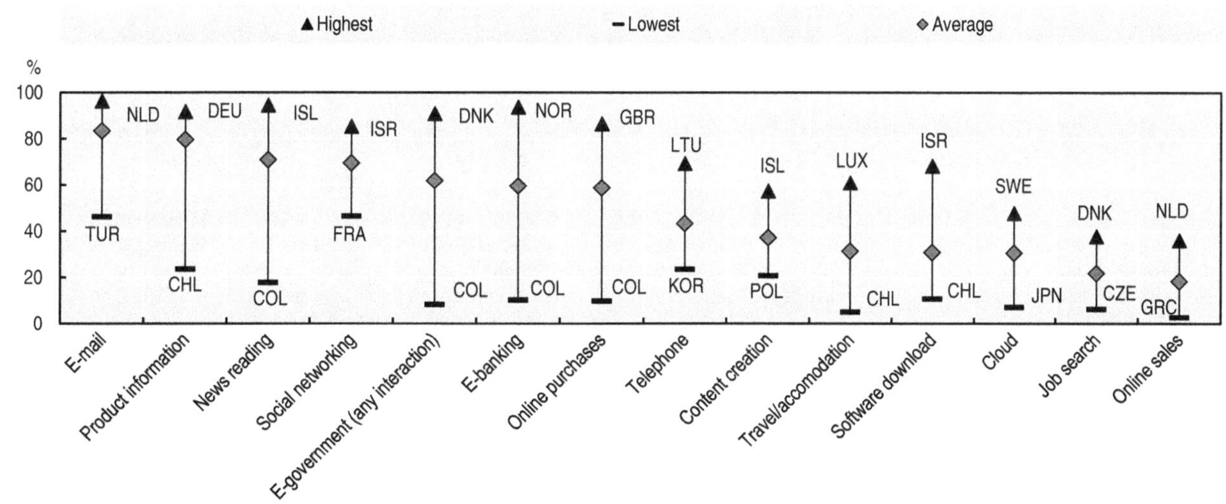

Notes: Data include the 35 OECD countries, Brazil, Colombia and Lithuania.
Unless otherwise indicated, a recall period of three months is used for Internet users.
For the Job Search category, data refer to 2015 (see note 6 at the end of the chapter for country exceptions).
For the Software Download category, data refer to 2015 (see note 6 at the end of the chapter for country exceptions).
For the E-government category, the recall period is 12 months instead of 3 months, and data relate to individuals who used the Internet in the last 12 months instead of the last 3 months.
For Online purchases and Travel and accommodation, the recall period is 12 months instead of 3 months and data relate to individuals who used the Internet in the last 12 months instead of the last 3 months.
For country exceptions, see note 6 at the end of the chapter.

Source: OECD, *ICT Access and Usage by Households and Individuals* (database), *http://oe.cd/hhind* (accessed July 2017).

StatLink http://dx.doi.org/10.1787/888933585609

More than half of individuals in OECD countries bought products on line in 2016, up from 36% in 2010 (Figure 4.12). The increase in online purchases for this period was particularly large in the Czech Republic, Estonia, Hungary, Latvia, Lithuania and the Slovak Republic.

In the United States, between 2013 and 2015, the increase was higher than in every other country except Estonia. This trend, already in place for a decade, is very likely to continue in the near future. It has already disrupted traditional distribution channels for some categories of products. The rapid diffusion of smart mobile devices has resulted in a growing number of individuals buying products via their mobile devices. The share of online purchases varies widely across countries as well as across different product categories, with age, education, income and experience all playing a role in determining the uptake of e-commerce by individuals.

Figure 4.12. **Diffusion of online purchases**

Individuals having ordered goods or services on line as a percentage of all individuals

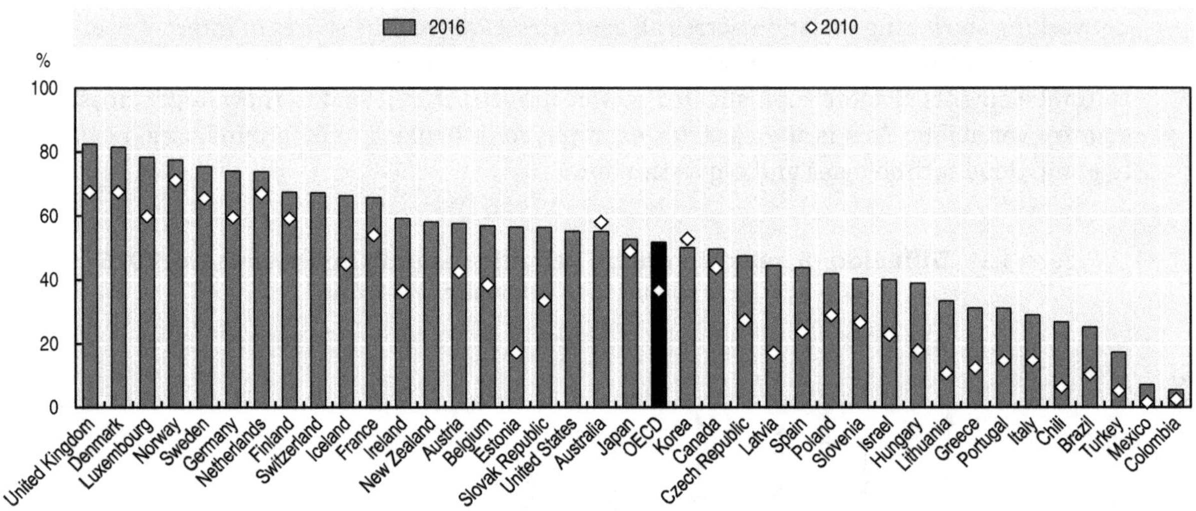

Notes: For Australia, data refer to 2014/15 (fiscal year ending 30 June 2015) instead of 2016 and to 2010/11 (fiscal year ending 30 June 2011) instead of 2010. For Canada, data relate to individuals aged 16 and over instead of 16-74 and refer to 2012 instead of 2016. For Chile, data refer to 2015 and 2009 instead of 2016 and 2010 respectively. For Brazil, Colombia, Japan and Korea, data refer to 2015 instead of 2016. For Israel, data refer to 2015 instead of 2016 and the recall period is of six months. For Iceland and Switzerland, data refer to 2014 instead of 2016. For New Zealand, data refer to 2011/12 (fiscal year ending 30 June 2012) instead of 2016 and to individuals having purchased anything in the last 12 months over the Internet for personal use which required an online payment. For the United States, data refer to 2015 instead of 2016 and the recall period is six months. OECD data are based on a simple average of the available countries.

Source: OECD, *ICT Access and Usage by Households and Individuals* (database), *http://oe.cd/hhind* (accessed June 2017).

StatLink http://dx.doi.org/10.1787/888933585628

In Denmark and the United Kingdom, more than 80% of adults have made purchases on line. In Turkey, the percentage is less than 20% and in Colombia and Mexico it is less than 7%. However, these shares increase and the differences between leading and lagging countries narrow, when only the population of Internet users is considered. In Denmark, Germany and the United Kingdom, 80% or more of Internet users make purchases on line, against less than 35% in Chile or Turkey and 15% in Mexico.

The most common items purchased on line are clothing, footwear and sporting goods, and travel products, around 60% and 50%, respectively, of online consumers on average, followed by tickets for events, photographic, telecommunication and optical equipment, and food and grocery products. Both clothing, footwear and sporting goods, and food and grocery products, have experienced fast growth in recent years. The diffusion of different categories of products for online purchase is likely to depend on income levels, consumer habits, the availability of e-commerce channels by local providers and the price strategies of e-selling firms.

Security and privacy are among the most challenging issues facing online services and more widespread adoption of e-commerce. In 2009, payment security or privacy concerns were cited as the main reason for not buying on line for over one-third of Internet users in the European Union who had not made any purchases online. In 2015, while this share had significantly decreased, it remains above a quarter, showing that privacy and security concerns are still relevant policy issues. The high variation in perceptions of security and privacy risks across countries with comparable degrees of law enforcement and technological know-how suggests that cultural attitudes towards online transactions play a significant role.

Use of cloud services is growing fast among Internet users

There has been a significant increase in the use of cloud computing services among Internet users. The cloud functions as a virtual storage space for documents, pictures, music or video files, which are saved or shared with other users. Cloud computing is also meeting demand for flexibility and ease of access to software and content, which can be accessed by users irrespective of location or time.

In 2016, uptake of cloud computing among Internet users in selected OECD countries ranged from 14% in Turkey to 48% in Sweden. In most countries, the propensity to use cloud computing services is much higher among younger and more educated people (Figure 4.13). The share of Internet users paying for these services remains low and ranges from 10% in Norway to less than 1% in Slovenia.

Figure 4.13. **Use of cloud computing by individuals in selected OECD countries by age class, 2016**

As a percentage of Internet users

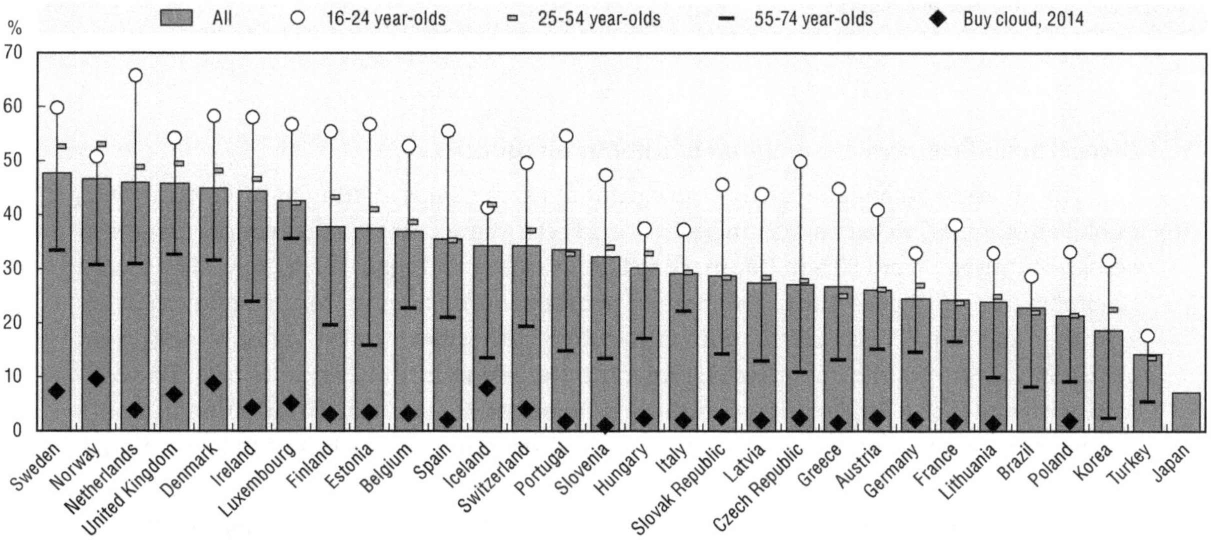

Notes: Cloud computing refers to the use of storage space on the Internet to save or share documents, pictures, music, video or other files. "Buy cloud" refers to purchased Internet storage space or file-sharing services and relates to the year 2014. Data refer to individuals aged 16-74 except for Japan (15-69) and Korea (12 and above). Data for Brazil, Denmark, Japan and Korea refer to 2015. Data for Iceland and Switzerland refer to 2014.

Source: OECD, *ICT Access and Usage by Households and Individuals* (database), *http://oe.cd/hhind* (accessed June 2017).

StatLink http://dx.doi.org/10.1787/888933585647

Over the last few years, ICTs have contributed to a wider array of learning opportunities and education programmes through the development of online courses, and in particular massive open online courses. In 2016, on average around 10.7% of Internet users followed an online course – a share relatively stable in most countries since 2010 (Figure 4.14). This percentage varied from 37.4% in Canada to less than 3% in Turkey. In European countries, participation of Internet users in online courses has been generally lower in recent years compared to Canada, Mexico or the United States.

Figure 4.14. **Individuals who attended an online course**

As a percentage of individuals who used the Internet in the last three months

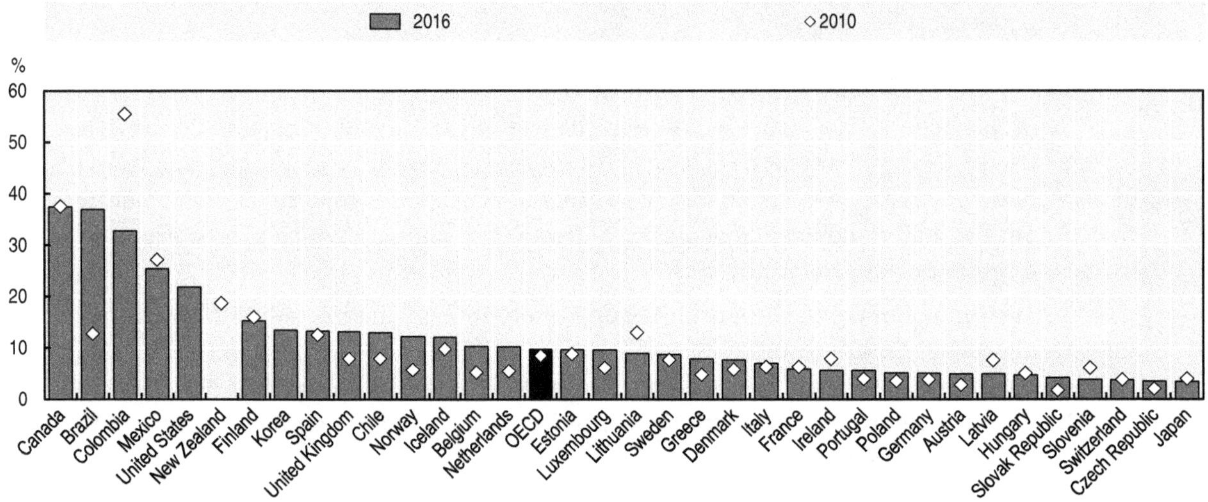

Notes: Data refer to 2012 instead of 2016 for Canada, Chile and Japan; to 2013 for Iceland and the United States; to 2014 for Mexico; and to 2015 for Denmark and Korea. For New Zealand, data refer to 2005/06 (fiscal year ending 30 June 2006) instead of 2010. For Chile, Canada and Korea, the recall period is 12 months. For Canada, Japan, Korea and New Zealand, data are as a percentage of individuals who used the Internet in the last 12 months. For Mexico, data refer to the following category "to support education/training". OECD data are based on a simple average of the available countries.

Source: OECD, *ICT Access and Usage by Households and Individuals* (database), *http://oe.cd/hhind* (accessed June 2017).

StatLink http://dx.doi.org/10.1787/888933585666

E-government services are growing but not in all countries

The share of individuals using e-government services (i.e. visiting or interacting with public authorities' websites) has increased in recent years, but remains widely dispersed across countries – from 88% in Denmark to less than 25% in Brazil, Chile, Italy, Mexico and Colombia in 2016 (Figure 4.15). The share of people sending filled-in forms on line mirrors a further step into digital interaction with public authorities. It also varies widely, from above 50% in the Nordic countries, Estonia, the Netherlands and France to less than 10% in Mexico and Japan. Explanations for these differences include insufficient infrastructure and supply of e-services by public authorities, and structural issues linked to institutional, cultural or economic factors.

Uptake of e-government services by individuals has been significantly affected by recent developments in digital government strategies implemented in countries. Digital government refers to the use of digital technologies, as an integrated part of governments' modernisation strategies, to create public value. It relies on a digital government ecosystem comprised of government actors, non-governmental organisations, businesses, citizens' associations and individuals, which supports the production of and access to data, services and content through interactions with the government (OECD, 2014a). Recent examples include the implementation of e-identity and e-citizenship (e.g. in Denmark and Estonia). Open government data policies may also increase interactions between individuals and public authorities' websites.

Figure 4.15. **Individuals using e-government services, 2016**

As a percentage of all individuals

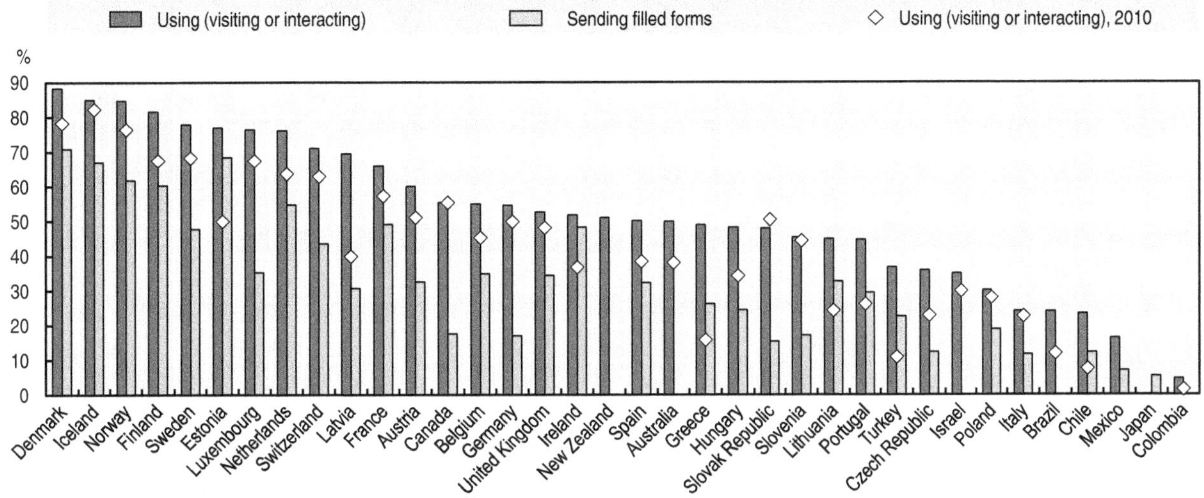

Notes: Unless otherwise stated, data refer to the respective online activities in the last 12 months. For country exceptions, see note 7 at the end of the chapter.

Source: ICT Access and Usage by Households and Individuals (database), *http://oe.cd/hhind* (accessed June 2017).

StatLink http://dx.doi.org/10.1787/888933585685

ICT skills

With the intensive use of ICTs at work, individuals are required to make use of new skills along three lines. First, the production of ICT products and services – software, web pages, e-commerce, cloud, big data, etc. – requires ICT specialist skills to programme and develop applications and manage networks. Second, workers across an increasing range of occupations need to acquire generic ICT skills to be able to use such technologies in their daily work – to access information on line, use software, etc. Finally, the use of ICTs is changing the way work is carried out and raising the demand for ICT complementary skills, e.g. the capability to communicate on social networks, to brand products on e-commerce platforms, etc.

The attention of policy makers and analysts has mainly focused on the first two sets of ICT skills – specialist and generic skills – while ICT complementary skills have received much less attention. Furthermore, the measurement of both the demand for and the supply of such skills falls short of the evidence base that is necessary to inform education and training policies. This section builds on recent OECD work (OECD, 2016a) which contributes to filling this gap (Box 4.1).

Box 4.1. **Measuring the supply of and demand for ICT skills**

The measurement of the supply of and demand for information and communication technology (ICT) skills can be undertaken in three steps.

The first step measures the frequency of ICT use in each occupation based on the OECD Programme for the International Assessment of Adult Competencies (PIAAC) survey.

The PIAAC background questionnaire collects a range of information on ICT use at work by asking how often the respondents carry out different types of activities on line such as sending/receiving e-mails; finding work-related information on the Internet; using spreadsheets, word processors or programming languages, etc. Possible answers are: never; less than once a month; less than once a week but at least once a month; at least once a week but not every day; and every day.

In order to allow the assessment of the demand for ICT generic skills, some of the answers to the PIAAC questions have been grouped into two sets of tasks. The first set – "use of communication and information search" (CIS) – includes "send/receive e-mails" and "find work-related information on the Internet"; the second set – "use of office productivity software" (OPS) – includes "use word processors" and "use spreadsheets". Both CIS and OPS require ICT generic skills but OPS involve a more sophisticated use of ICT and a higher level of ICT skills.

The use of programming languages is used as a proxy in the assessment of the demand for ICT specialist skills.

In the PIAAC survey, the questions about ICT use at work are only asked to people who report "having experience with a computer in their job". As people with no experience with a computer (24.5% of all weighted PIAAC respondents) have not been included, the answers to these questions tend to overrate the frequency of ICT use at work. In addition, as the distribution of those with no computer experience across occupations is unknown, the bias is not uniform: frequencies of ICT use may be overrated in some occupations and underrated in others. In order to correct for such a bias, the frequency of ICT use at work has been computed not as a percentage of the respondents to the ICT questions but as a percentage of all individuals.

The second step measures the demand for ICT skills at work by linking the ICT frequency by occupation to the share of employment in each occupation based on the Labour Force Surveys.

For the European Union (EU) countries, employment data are drawn from the EU Labour Force Survey, where occupations are classified according to three-digit ISCO-08 from 2011 onwards. In a number of other countries, however, national occupational classifications have been converted into ISCO-08. For the United States, employment by three-digit ISCO-08 occupations has been estimated by the OECD from the US Bureau of Labor Statistics' Current Population Survey, based on the concordance table between the Standard Occupational Classification (SOC) System 2010 and ISCO-08 (for further details, see Eckardt and Squicciarini [forthcoming]). For Australia, employment by two-digit ISCO-08 occupations has been estimated using Australian Bureau of Statistics data, based on the concordance between the Australian and New Zealand Standard Classification of Occupations (ANZSCO) 2006 and ISCO-08 developed by Statistics New Zealand.

The third step consists of assessing the extent to which the demand is matched by the supply of such skills.

The information available in the PIAAC performance evaluation permits to undertake this assessment. The PIAAC framework assesses key information-processing skills that are:

- necessary for fully integrating and participating in the labour market, education and training, and social and civic life
- highly transferable, in that they are relevant to many social contexts and work situations
- "learnable" and, therefore, subject to the influence of policy.

Box 4.1. **Measuring the supply of and demand for ICT skills** *(cont.)*

At the most fundamental level, literacy and numeracy constitute a foundation for developing higher order cognitive skills, such as analytic reasoning, and are essential for gaining access to and understanding specific domains of knowledge. In addition, the capacity to manage information and solve problems in technology-rich environments (PSTRE) – that is, to access, evaluate, analyse and communicate information – is becoming as important as understanding and interpreting text-based information and being able to handle mathematical content. The PSTRE ability has a greater importance with the ICT applications becoming one of the most crucial features in most workplaces, in education and in everyday life.

In PIAAC, the PSTRE is defined as "using digital technology, communication tools and networks to acquire and evaluate information, communicate with others and perform practical tasks". The first cycle of the survey focuses on "the abilities to solve problems for personal, work and civic purposes by setting up appropriate goals and plans, and accessing and making use of information through computers and computer networks" (OECD, 2012).

Based on the description of the PSTRE, effective undertaking of CIS tasks is regarded as requiring PSTRE skills at level 1 at least because individuals at this level are able to use e-mail software or a web browser. Effective undertaking of OPS tasks is regarded as requiring PSTRE skills at level 2 at least because individuals at this level are able to use more specific technology tools or applications (e.g. a sort function).

Demand for ICT specialists is picking up, but shortages are still limited to a few countries

The share of ICT specialist employment remained stable between 2011 and 2014

Figure 4.16 shows economy-wide ICT specialist intensity in 2011 and 2014. In 2014, the share of ICT specialists ranged from 5.9% in France to 1.6% in Ireland and the Slovak Republic with a majority of countries remaining around 3%. Between 2011 and 2014, the share of employment in ICT specialist-intensive occupations showed a modest increase in almost all countries (0.18 percentage points on average) except in the Slovak Republic (-0.15 percentage points). The largest increase occurred in France, followed by the Netherlands and Norway.

Figure 4.16. **ICT specialist skills**

Share of employed individuals using programming languages daily at work

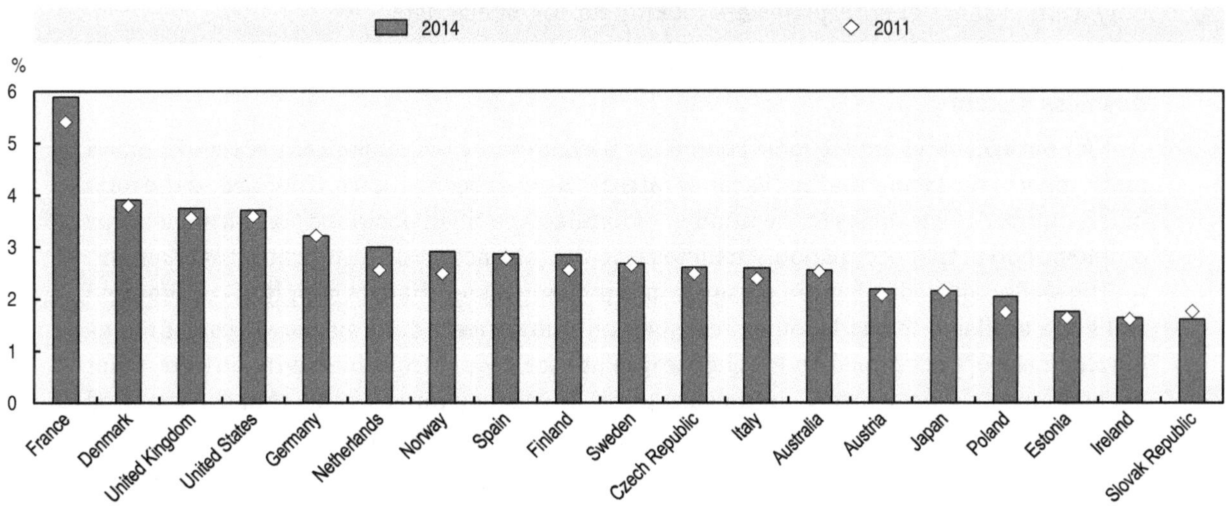

Notes: For Japan, data refer to 2010 and 2014. The data point for the United Kingdom refers to England/Northern Ireland.

Source: Author's calculations based on OECD, *PIAAC Database*, *www.oecd.org/skills/piaac/publicdataandanalysis* and national labour force surveys, December 2015.

StatLink http://dx.doi.org/10.1787/888933585704

Is there an ICT specialist skills shortage?

Over the recent period, there has been some concern of a potential imbalance between demand for and supply of ICT specialists in the labour market. If firms face difficulties in filling vacancies for ICT specialists, this could result in at least one of the following: 1) an upward trend in the job vacancy rates for ICT specialists; 2) a longer duration of these vacancies; and 3) an increase in wages for ICT specialists.

Table 4.1 shows that "IT staff" now rank second among the top ten jobs that employers are having difficulty filling, according to the Talent Shortage Survey carried out in over 40 countries worldwide (ManpowerGroup, 2016).

Table 4.1. **Top ten jobs that employers have difficulty filling, 2016**

Rank	Job
1	Skilled trade workers
2	IT staff
3	Sales representatives
4	Engineers
5	Technicians
6	Drivers
7	Accounting and finance staff
8	Management/executives
9	Production/machine operations
10	Office support staff

Source: ManpowerGroup (2016), Talent Shortage Survey, *http://manpowergroup.com/talent-shortage-2016*.

However, this perception is not yet observed in the official data at the European level as the percentage of enterprises reporting hard-to-fill vacancies for ICT specialists is rather small – about 3.5% – and did not change between 2012 and 2014 (Figure 4.17). This share decreased or remained stable in most countries. The most significant increase (above 2 percentage points) was observed in Estonia, Slovenia, Hungary and Denmark. In other words, while 41% of enterprises looking for an ICT specialist in the European Union reported difficulties in filling the vacancy, the potential shortage of ICT skills remains small because only a small share of enterprises are looking for ICT specialists.

Job vacancy rates in ICT services tend to be much higher than in the total business sectors

Job vacancy rates are the most commonly used measure of imbalances between demand and supply in the labour market. Vacancy rates for a given occupation are defined as the ratio of the number of vacancies to the number of unfilled and filled positions (i.e. vacancies plus employment) in that occupation. An increase in the job vacancy rate indicates that demand for the skills required in a given occupation is growing faster than its supply. If the required skills are available in the labour force, such an imbalance would disappear over time as employment opportunities and higher wages attract people from inactivity or from other occupations. On the contrary, an upward trend in vacancy rates signals that the required skills are not available in the labour force, i.e. there is a skill shortage.

Job vacancy rates in ICT services tend to be relatively higher than in the total business sectors. In 2016, the ratio between the two indicators exceeded 2.5 in Poland and was above 2.0 in the Netherlands, Switzerland and Belgium. However, vacancy rates in ICT services were about the same as in the total business sector in Latvia, Slovenia and Greece and even lower in countries such as the Czech Republic and the Slovak Republic (Figure 4.18). Between 2009 and 2016, although the ratio increased or remained stable in most countries, it showed a strong decrease in countries such as Portugal, Ireland and Greece. Therefore, the potential skills shortage in ICT services seems to be limited to a few countries.

Figure 4.17. **Enterprises that reported hard-to-fill vacancies for ICT specialists**

As a percentage of all enterprises

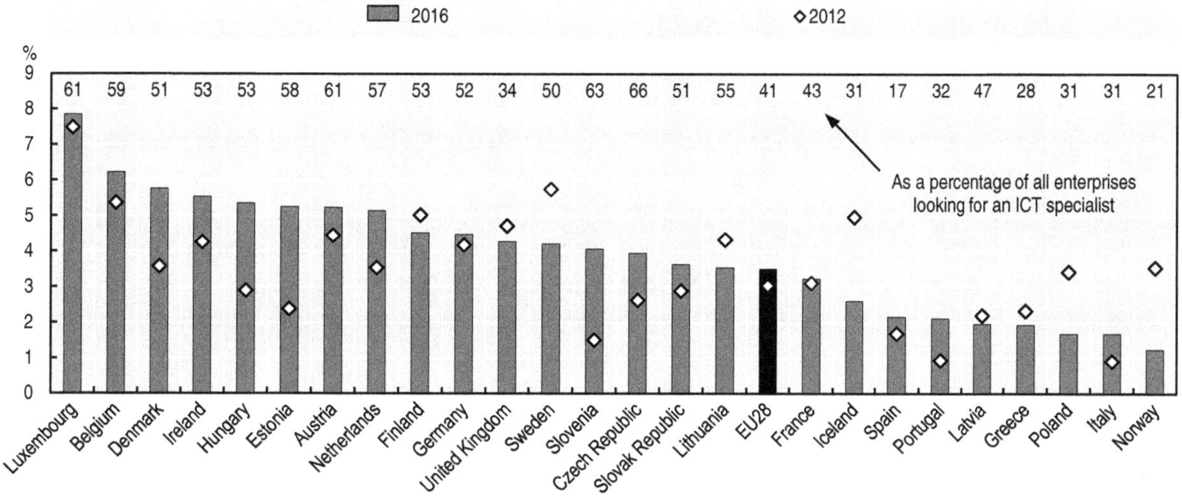

Source: Eurostat, *Digital Economy and Society* (database), *http://ec.europa.eu/eurostat/web/digital-economy-and-society/data/comprehensive-database* (accessed June 2017).

StatLink http://dx.doi.org/10.1787/888933585723

Figure 4.18. **Average vacancy rates in ICT services relative to the total business sector**

Annual average of quarterly rates

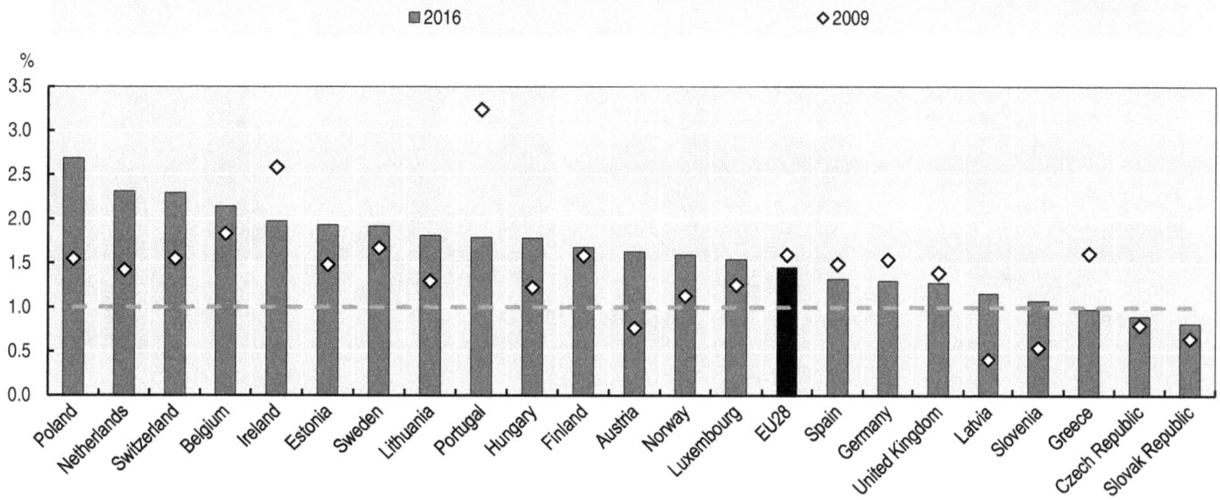

Notes: Data for ICT services refer to the ISIC Rev.4, Sector J. For Norway, data refer to 2010 and 2016. For Germany, data refer to 2011 and 2016. For Belgium and EU28, data refer to 2012 and 2016.

Source: Eurostat, "Job Vacancy Statistics", *http://ec.europa.eu/eurostat/statistics-explained/index.php/Job_vacancy_statistics* (accessed June 2017).

StatLink http://dx.doi.org/10.1787/888933585742

While official statistics on job vacancies are available at the level of industries, online vacancies provide such information by occupation. Recently, a number of private firms and a few national statistical offices have started to collect and analyse online job postings in order to compile statistics on job vacancies. Public services have started using this type of data to allow citizens to inform themselves about the current features of the job market, e.g. the Skills Portal of the New South Wales Government of Australia.[8]

Online job postings have a strong potential as a source of information on the characteristics of job offers, job seekers and the duration of job postings. They are able to track labour market movements in real time, providing high frequency data. Furthermore, they permit the analysis of shifts in job profiles based on a large range of job requirements related to skills, education and experience.

Despite a number of shortcomings in online vacancy statistics in terms of country coverage, representativeness as compared to official data and difficulties in their mapping to the relevant industries, data from private sources such as Burning Glass shed some light on the job vacancy trends in different ICT occupations. Figure 4.19 shows that ICT job postings accounted for between 16% (United Kingdom) and 8% (Canada) of all job postings in 2016. In most countries for which data are available, this share was below the 2013 levels except in the United Kingdom, where ICT online job postings reached their peak in 2015 after a decrease in 2016 in a similar fashion to the trends observed in the United States.

Figure 4.19. **ICT online job postings**

As a percentage of all online postings

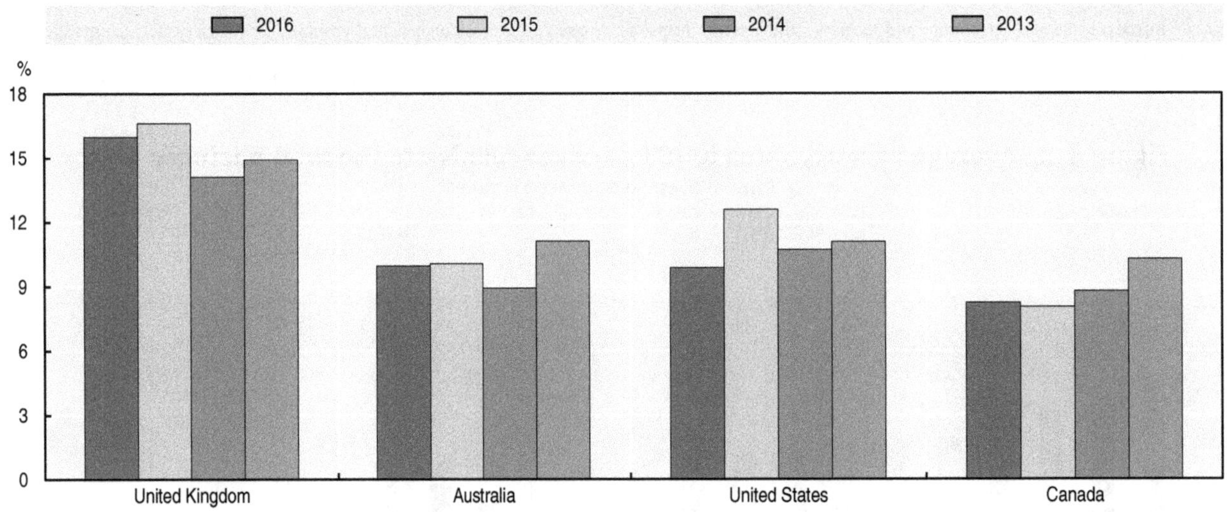

Source: Author's calculations based on data provided by Burning Glass, April 2017.

StatLink http://dx.doi.org/10.1787/888933585761

As for Australia, the Australian Internet Vacancy Index computed by the Department of Employment shows a strong downward trend in online vacancies for ICT professionals. The index fell in the aftermath of the crisis and, despite a partial recovery in mid-2009, continued to decrease from 2010 on (Figure 4.20).

Potential shortage in ICT skills is limited to a small number of countries, at least in Europe

Labour shortages of specific skills should also result in an increase in real wages for the occupations using these skills intensively. If ICT skills are scarce in the labour market, firms have to pay higher real wages to attract workers with such skills.

Figure 4.20. **Online vacancies for ICT professionals in Australia**

Australian Internet Vacancy Index, January 2006 = 100

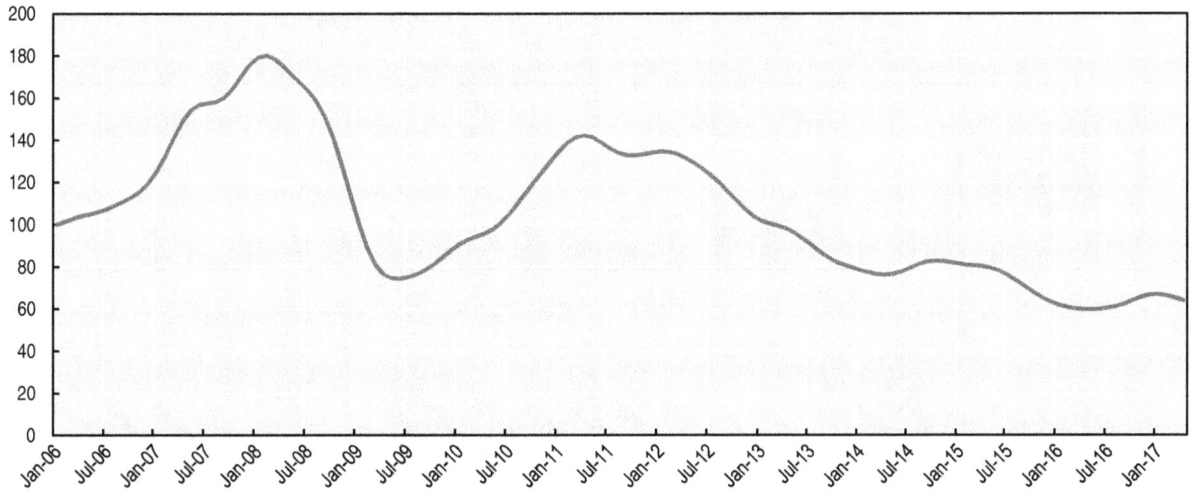

Source: Australian Labour Market Information Portal, *http://lmip.gov.au/default.aspx?LMIP/VacancyReport* (accessed August 2017).

StatLink http://dx.doi.org/10.1787/888933585780

Changes in real wages, however, are not always a good measure for skills shortages. On the one hand, a skills shortage may not immediately translate to higher wages due to adjustment lags, e.g. collective wage bargaining. On the other hand, wages may increase as a result of both industry-specific and economy-wide productivity shocks. Therefore, an increase in real wages may be regarded as a sign of a skills shortage only if: 1) it is persistent over time; 2) it exceeds the increase in labour productivity; and 3) it is larger than in the other sectors of the economy.

Figure 4.21 compares the average growth rates of wages – relative to average labour productivity – in ICT services and the total business services sector over 2001-16. In half of the 24 countries for which data are available, wages grew more slowly in ICT services than in the total business services. In the remaining countries, differences in wage growth were fairly limited, i.e. less than 1% a year. These trends confirm that while the demand for ICT specialists is growing fast, the potential shortage in ICT skills is limited to a small number of countries, at least in Europe.

The supply of ICT specialists has increased at a moderate rate, but demand is expected to grow faster

The economy-wide supply of ICT specialists can be assessed through the employment figures of ICT specialists, data on graduates in computer science and on researchers in the ICT sector.

ICT specialists have been among the most dynamic occupations in recent years and several forecasts suggest that the demand for ICT professionals will grow even faster in the near future. In 2016, ICT specialists accounted for 3.6% of all workers in OECD countries for which data were available (Figure 4.22). In the few countries where data are available over the period 2003-16, the share of ICT specialists increased moderately – from about 4% to 4.7% in Canada, from 3.2% to 4.1% in the United States and from 3.6% to 3.8% in Australia.

Figure 4.21. Changes in wages relative to labour productivity, 2001-16

Annual averages

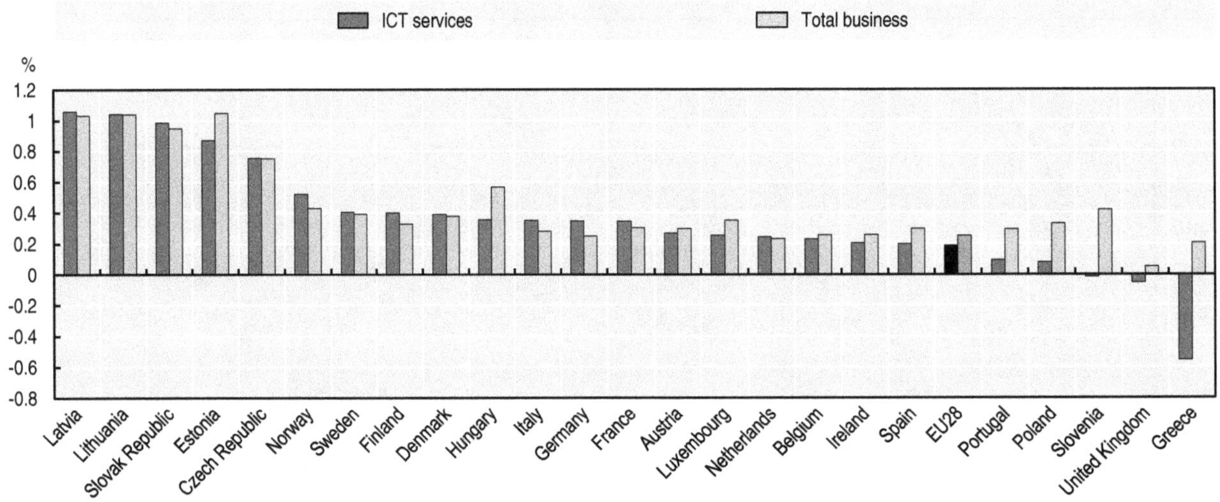

Note: ICT = information and communication technology.

Source: Eurostat, *National Accounts (including GDP) Statistics* (database), *http://ec.europa.eu/eurostat/web/national-accounts/data/database* (accessed August 2017).

StatLink http://dx.doi.org/10.1787/888933585799

Figure 4.22. Employment of ICT specialists across the economy, 2016

As a percentage of total employment, by category

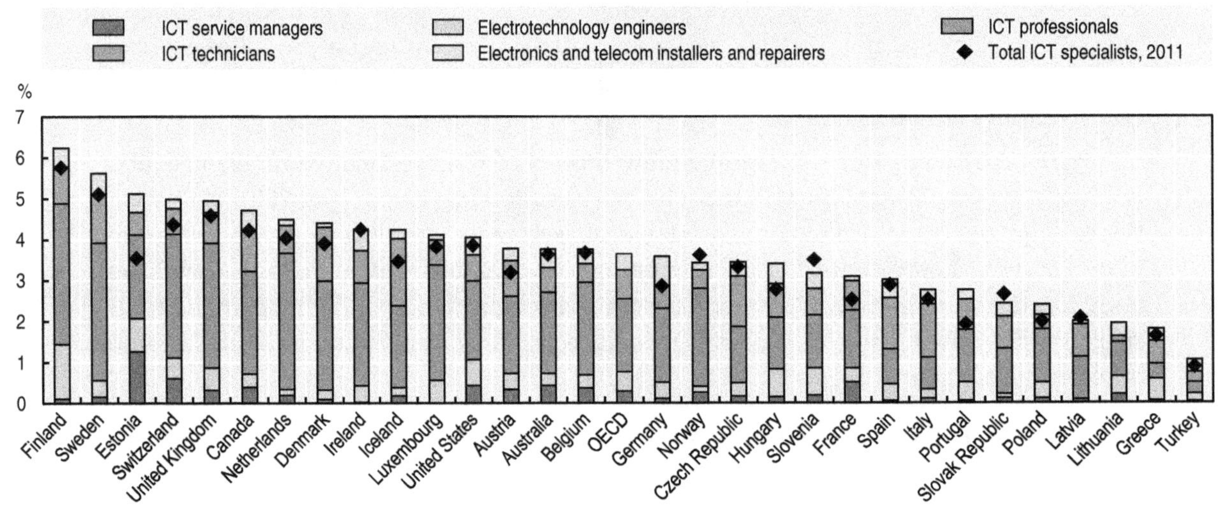

Notes: ICT specialists are defined as those individuals employed in "tasks related to developing, maintaining and operating ICT systems and where ICTs are the main part of their job". Based on the operational definition based on ISCO-08 3-digits which includes occupations: 133, 215, 25, 35, 742 (for further details see OECD [2004; 2013]). OECD aggregate is a weighted average for all countries for which data are available. Data for Canada and the United States refer to 2015. ICT = information and communication technology.

Sources: Author's calculations based on Australian, Canadian and European labour force surveys and the *United States Current* Population Survey (accessed July 2017).

StatLink http://dx.doi.org/10.1787/888933585818

Figure 4.23 reveals large differences between men and women. While 5.5% of male workers in OECD countries are ICT specialists, this proportion is just 1.4% for female workers.

Some forecasts predict a significant shortage of ICT specialists (EC, 2014; OECD, 2014b) over the next 5 to 15 years. These forecasts rely on a scenario-based approach which, by its very nature, is hard to validate. Unfortunately, available statistics do not yet allow a thorough investigation of the issues.

Figure 4.23. **ICT specialists by gender, 2016**

As a percentage of all male and female workers

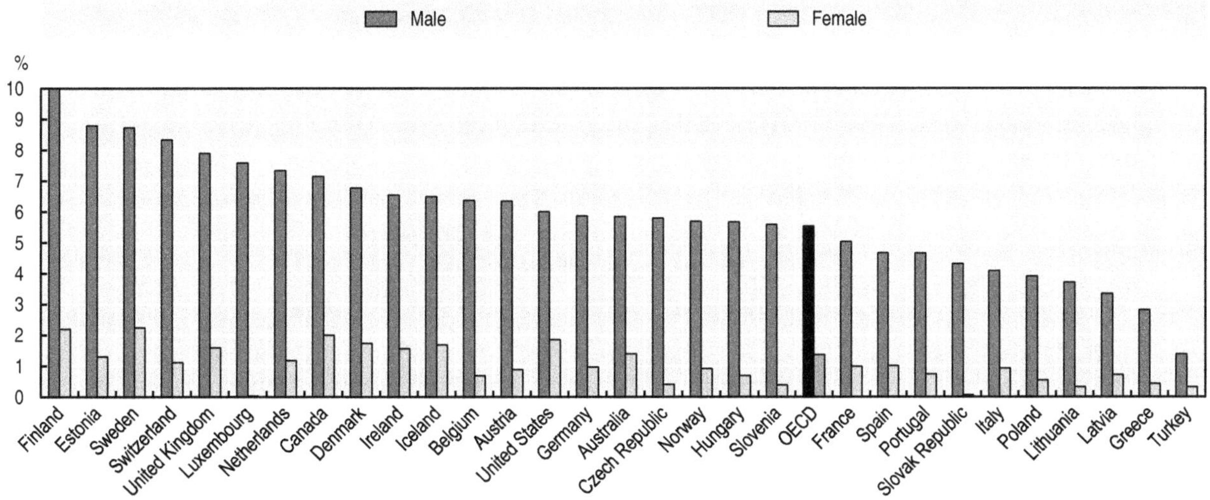

Notes: ICT specialists are defined as those individuals employed in "tasks related to developing, maintaining and operating ICT systems and where ICTs are the main part of their job". Based on the operational definition based on ISCO-08 3-digits which includes occupations: 133, 215, 25, 35 and 742 (for further details see OECD [2004; 2013]). OECD aggregate is a weighted average for all countries for which data are available. Data for Canada and the United States refer to 2015.

Source: Author's calculations based on Australian, Canadian and European labour force surveys and the *United States Current Population Survey* (accessed July 2017).

StatLink http://dx.doi.org/10.1787/888933585837

Despite the expansion of tertiary education worldwide, the share of ICTs tertiary graduates in all graduates in the OECD is 3.5% in 2015 (Figure 4.24). The share of ICTs graduates was the highest in Indonesia (8.5%), followed by India, New Zealand, Finland Ireland and Colombia (between 5% and 7%) and the lowest in Portugal and Belgium (above 1%).

Figure 4.24. **Tertiary graduates in Information and Communication Technologies, 2015**

As a percentage of all tertiary graduates

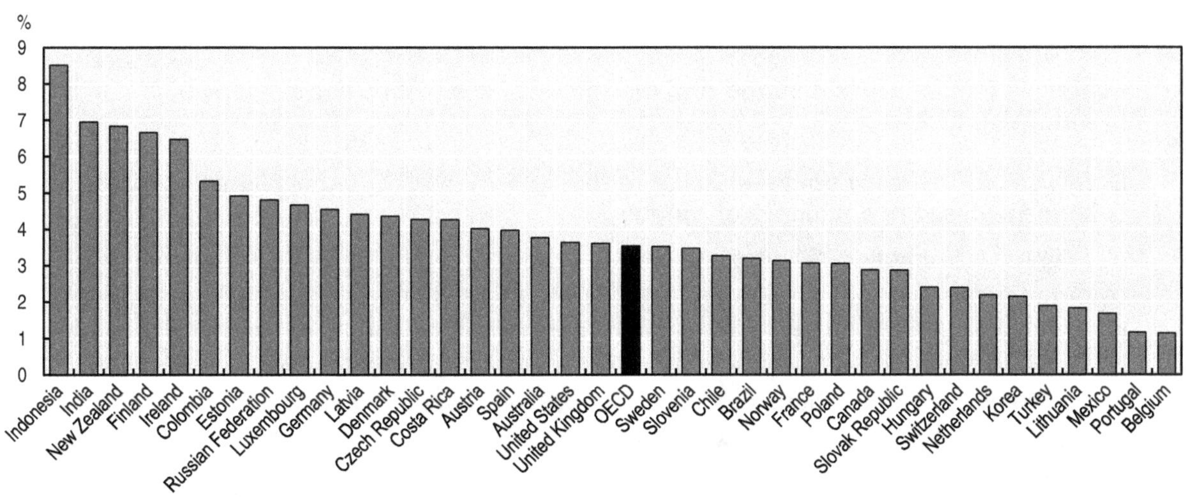

Notes: Graduates at the tertiary level comprise individuals that have obtained a degree at ISCED-11 Levels 5-8. For the Netherlands, data exclude doctoral graduates. For Japan, data are not available because ICTs are included in other fields of study.

Source: OECD, *Education at a Glance Database, http://dx.doi.org/10.1787/edu-db-data-en* (accessed July 2017).

StatLink http://dx.doi.org/10.1787/888933585856

Researchers are professionals engaged in the conception and creation of new knowledge, products, processes, methods and systems and are directly involved in the management of projects. In OECD countries, researchers engaged in the ICT sector represent 30% of all researchers with the share remaining relatively stable compared to 2009 (Figure 4.25). Their share in total employment increased in most OECD countries between 2009 and 2014, notwithstanding a large dispersion across countries for which data are available.

Figure 4.25. **Researchers in the ICT sector**

As a percentage of all researchers

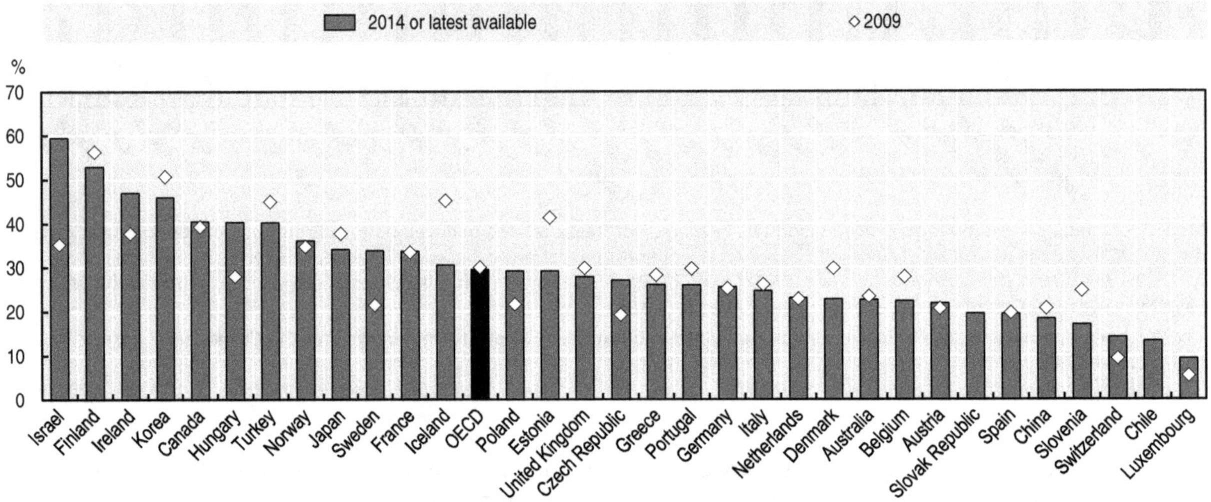

Notes: Due to confidentiality matters, the ICT sector is defined here as the sum of industries ISIC rev.4: 26 Computer, electronic and optical products and J Information industries. For Chile, the People's Republic of China ("China" in the figure), Iceland, Japan and Korea, data refer to 2015. For Australia, Austria, Belgium, Canada, France, Greece, Ireland and Sweden, data refer to 2013. For Switzerland, data refer to 2008 and 2012. For Luxembourg, data refer to 2011. For Israel, data refer to 2010 instead of 2009. For Greece, data refer to 2011 instead of 2009. OECD aggregate is calculated as a simple average of the available countries.

Source: OECD, "Research and Development Statistics: Business enterprise R-D expenditure by industry - ISIC Rev. 4", *OECD Science, Technology and R&D Statistics* (database), *http://oe.cd/sti/rds* (accessed June 2017).

StatLink http://dx.doi.org/10.1787/888933585875

Generic ICT skills are in demand and insufficient for effective use at work in many countries

Daily use of Internet to send e-mails or search information for work-related purposes is not generalised in a majority of countries

Figure 4.26 shows the proportion of individuals who use the Internet daily for communication and information search (CIS), which includes activities such as sending/receiving e-mails and finding work-related information on the Internet, and the share of those who use and office productivity software (OPS), namely word processors and spreadsheets, by country across all occupations. The share of individuals who make use of CIS skills every day ranges between 51.5% in Norway and 22.8% in Italy. In a majority of countries, less than 40% of individuals make daily use of the Internet for sending e-mails or searching information for work-related purposes. The share of individuals using OPS daily ranges between 36.6% in the Netherlands and 17% in Italy and Poland. Not surprisingly, the percentage of daily users is systematically lower for OPS than for CIS in all countries.

Figure 4.26. **Daily users of communication and information search and office productivity software at work, 2012**

Weighted proportion of all individuals

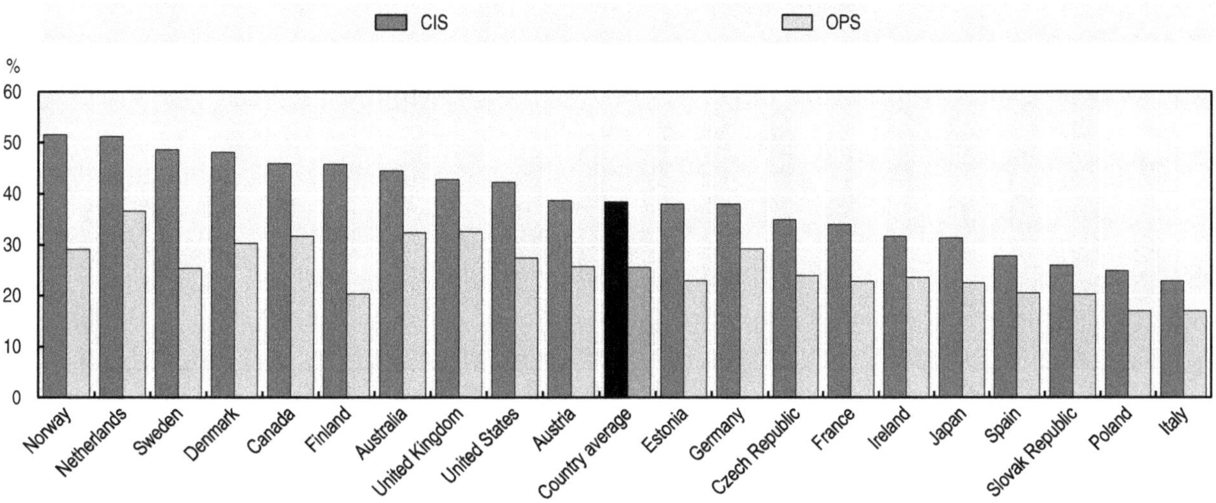

Notes: The United Kingdom data point refers to England/Northern Ireland. CIS = communication and information search; OPS = office productivity software.

Source: Author's calculations based on OECD PIAAC *Database*, *www.oecd.org/skills/piaac/publicdataandanalysis* (accessed October 2015).

StatLink *http://dx.doi.org/10.1787/888933585894*

ICT-rich occupations are not necessarily ICT specialist occupations

Fifteen of the top-20 CIS-intensive occupations across countries are not ICT specialist occupations.[9] They include administrators and managers (ISCO-08 242, 121, 112 and 134); sales and business agents (122, 243); mathematicians, actuaries and statisticians, finance professionals and associated professionals (212, 241 and 331); scientists and engineers (211 and 214); as well as university and higher education teachers (231); legal professionals (261); librarians, archivists and curators (262); and legislators and senior officials (111).

As with CIS-intensive occupations, most of the OPS-intensive ones are not ICT specialist occupations and generally include similar types of occupations.

Economy-wide CIS intensity at work varies significantly across countries; OPS intensity varies less

Figure 4.27 shows that the economy-wide CIS intensity at work varies significantly across countries. In 2014, the CIS intensity ranged from 64% of all occupations in Norway to 33% in the Slovak Republic. Between 2011 and 2014, the share of employment in CIS-intensive occupations was stable or increasing in most countries except Denmark, Ireland, Italy, Japan and the Slovak Republic, where there was a slight decrease. The increase was the most significant in Norway (3.7 percentage points), followed by France (2.9 percentage points) and Poland (1.7 percentage points).

Figure 4.28 shows the economy-wide OPS intensity at work in 2011 and 2014. The OPS intensity in 2014 varied between 42.6% of all occupations in the United Kingdom and 25.7% in Poland. Over 2011-14, the share of employment in OPS-intensive occupations was either stable or increasing in most countries except in the Slovak Republic and Japan, where it decreased. The most significant increase was observed in Norway (2.5 percentage points), France (2.0 percentage points) followed by Sweden (1.5 percentage points).

Figure 4.27. **Demand for ICT generic skills (CIS) by country**

Share of employed individuals using CIS daily at work

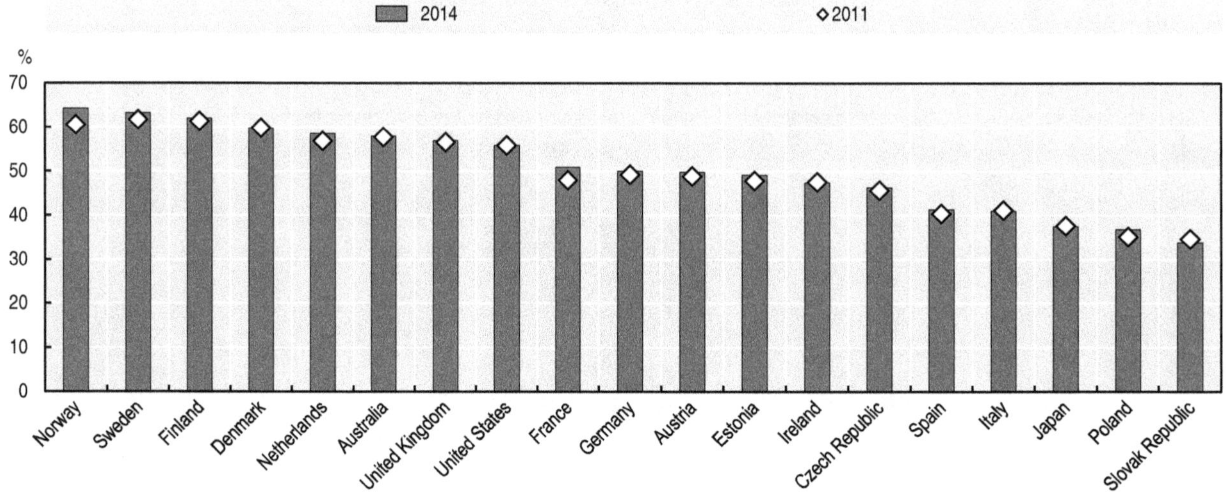

Notes: Data relate to the percentage of individuals who perform on a daily basis at their job either one or both of the following activities: send/receive e-mail; find work-related information on the Internet. For Japan, data refer to 2010 and 2014. The data point for the United Kingdom refers to England/Northern Ireland. CIS = communication and information search.

Source: Author's calculations based on OECD *PIAAC Database*, *www.oecd.org/skills/piaac/publicdataandanalysis* and national labour force surveys (accessed December 2015).

StatLink http://dx.doi.org/10.1787/888933585913

Figure 4.28. **Demand for ICT generic skills (OPS) by country**

Share of employed individuals using OPS daily at work

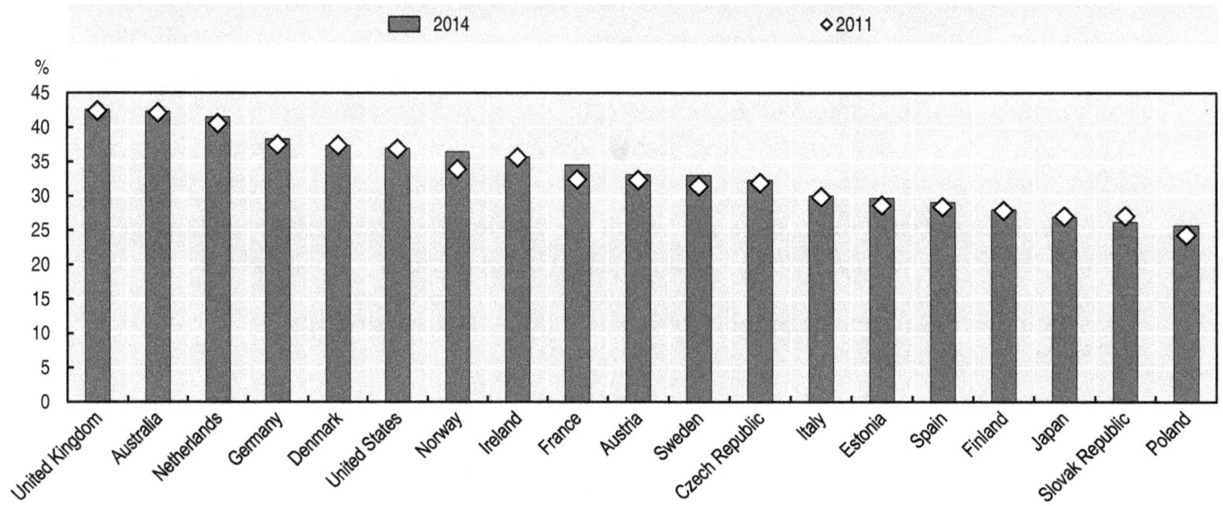

Notes: Data relate to the percentage of individuals who are doing daily at work either one or both of the following activities: use word processors; use spreadsheets. For Japan, data refer to 2010 and 2014. The United Kingdom data point refers to England/Northern Ireland. OPS = office productivity software.

Source: Author's calculations based on OECD *PIAAC Database*, *www.oecd.org/skills/piaac/publicdataandanalysis* and national labour force surveys (accessed December 2015).

StatLink http://dx.doi.org/10.1787/888933585932

A significant number of workers using ICTs every day do not seem to have sufficient ICT skills to use these technologies effectively

In countries for which data are available, between 7 and 15% of the population who report using CIS every day do not seem to have sufficient skills to carry out such tasks effectively, according to the results of the PIAAC performance assessment. The gap is even more significant for OPS tasks, with 42% of the individuals lacking the skills required to carry out these tasks despite reporting doing these tasks every day. Therefore, a significant number of workers using ICTs every day do not seem to have sufficient ICT skills to use these technologies effectively (Figure 4.29).

Figure 4.29. **Workers using OPS at work every day, 2012**

As a percentage of total population

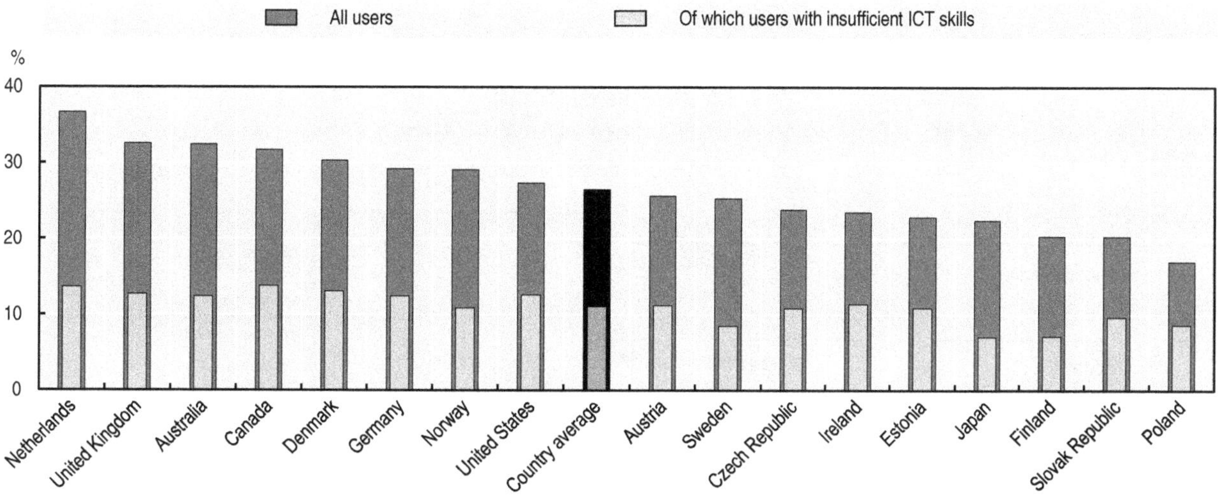

Notes: See methodology in Box 4.1. Problem solving in technology-rich environments (PSTRE) assessment data for France, Italy and Spain are not available and not included in the average. Individuals in the following categories of the PSTRE assessment are excluded from the analysis: "No computer experience"; "Opted out of computer based assessment"; "Failed ICT core/missing". The data point for the United Kingdom refers to England/Northern Ireland. OPS = office productivity software; ICT = information and communication technology.

Source: Author's calculations based on OECD *PIAAC Database*, *www.oecd.org/skills/piaac/publicdataandanalysis* (accessed January 2016).

StatLink *http://dx.doi.org/10.1787/888933585951*

ICT complementary skills are becoming more important with changing jobs and automation

The skills profile of a worker in a low-skilled occupation is more likely to change as the use of ICT at work increases

The diffusion of ICT in the workplace is not only raising the demand for ICT specialist and generic skills, it is also changing the way work is carried out and increasing the demand for ICT complementary skills. These are skills that are not related to the capability to use the technology effectively but to carry out the work within the new environment shaped by ICTs, i.e. a technology-rich environment. For instance, higher frequency of information made available by ICTs calls for better systems in order to use the information to plan in advance and to adjust quickly. More horizontal work organisations enabled by ICTs, i.e. more team work and less top-down management, call for more co-operation and stronger leadership. Wider diffusion of information among a larger number of workers increases the importance of management and co-ordination. The sales skills required in face-to-face commercial transactions are not the same as those involved in an anonymous e-commerce sale.

An implication of the above trends is that the set of skills required to perform the tasks involved in a certain occupation – the skills profile – is changing as a result of the diffusion of ICTs at work. While there is a general awareness that the education curricula must evolve to adjust to these changes, little is known about what type of skills should become more important in the curricula.

Figure 4.30 shows that intensive use of ICT at work is associated with tasks that require higher use of influence (negotiating with people), problem solving (thinking about a solution for at least 30 minutes) and horizontal interactions (giving presentations), as well as less physical work (working physically). Higher frequency of activities requiring numeracy, writing and reading skills is also correlated to ICT, the highest correlation being with reading.[10] These findings are in line with OECD (2017) in which the factor analysis based on the PIAAC data shows that ICT skills are positively associated with office jobs and negatively associated with physical activities.

Figure 4.30. **Correlations between ICT intensity (OPS) and other tasks/activities frequency, by skill level, 2012**

Average across occupations and countries

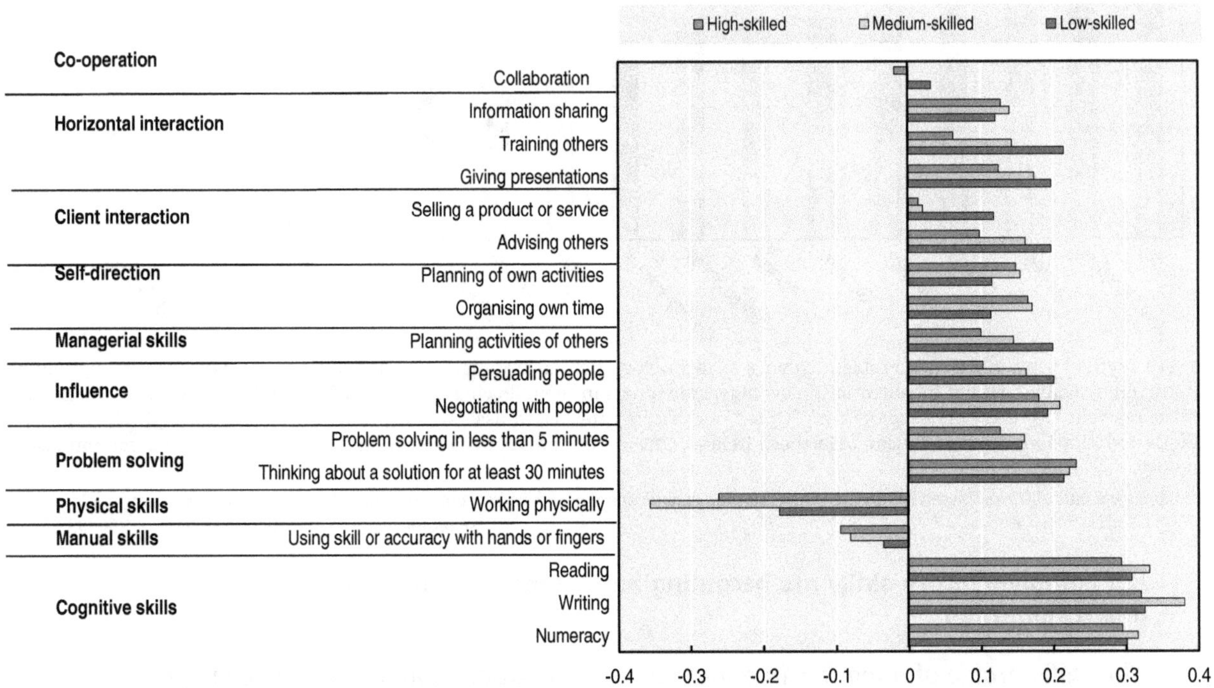

Note: OPS = office productivity software.

Source: Author's calculations based on OECD *PIAAC Database*, *www.oecd.org/skills/piaac/publicdataandanalysis* (accessed December 2015).

StatLink http://dx.doi.org/10.1787/888933585970

Country differences in the task set associated with the use of ICTs are larger for low-skilled occupations than for middle- and high-skilled ones. In other words, the skill profile of a worker in a high-skilled occupation is likely to change little with the use of ICT. On the contrary, the skill profile of a worker in a low-skilled occupation would change more as the use of ICT at work increases.

Industrial robots are making simple and routine manual tasks redundant

ICT complementary skills are usually defined as the capability to communicate on social networks, to brand products on e-commerce platforms, and so on. However, as Figure 4.31 suggests, the diffusion of industrial robots is expected to modify the demand for labour and thus the skills necessary to cope with trends in automation. While there is substantial variation across countries, Figure 4.31 shows on average what kinds of occupations are expected to be complementary or substitute to industrial robots, depending on the skills required by each occupation and their relations to robots' industrial applications.[11]

Figure 4.31. **Industrial robots, applications and occupations**

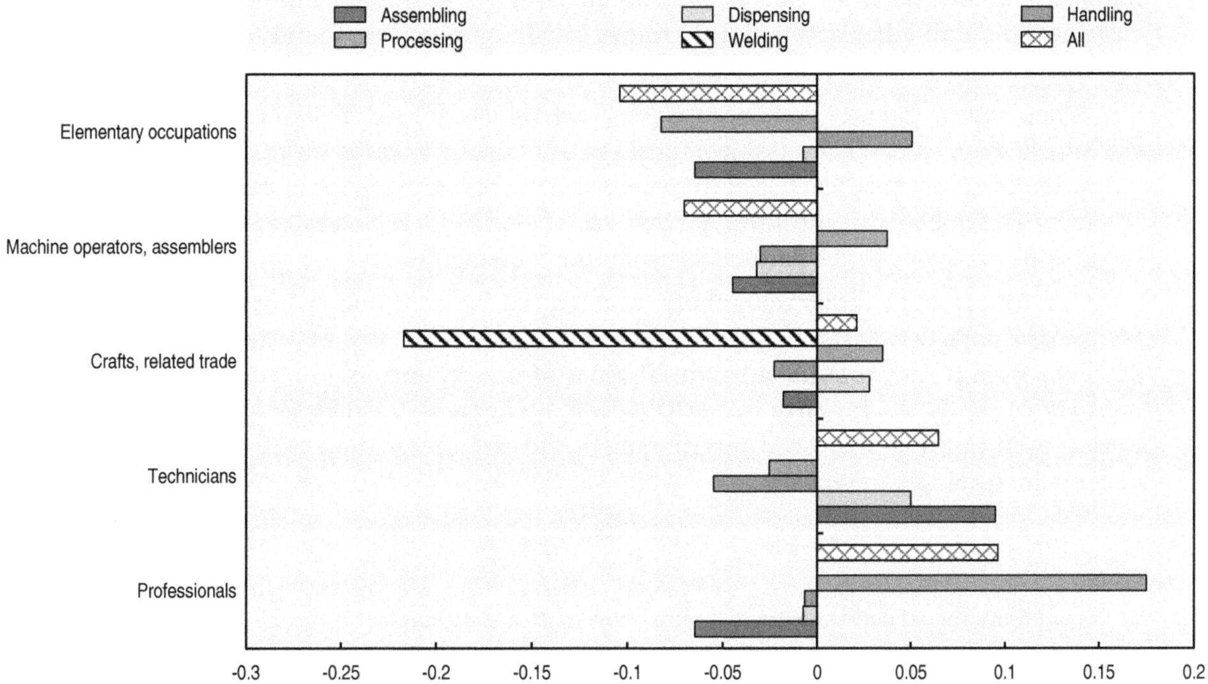

Note: The figure reports the estimated elasticity of employment to robots based on a log linear-regression. See OECD (forthcoming) for further details on the methodology.

Source: Author's calculations based on data provided by the International Federation of Robotics, February 2017.

StatLink *http://dx.doi.org/10.1787/888933585989*

Robots used for cutting, grinding, deburring[12] and other similar "processing" applications are found to be positively correlated to employment of professionals, crafts and related trade workers, and machine operators and assemblers. The correlation is negative with the other two groups, technicians and elementary occupations.

Thus, by complementing or substituting an occupation, robots are expected to increase or decrease the demand for skills that are specific to such occupations. Welding robots, for instance, are expected to make redundant at least some of the skills held by crafts and related trade workers, which include the detailed occupation "welders and flame cutters" (ISCO-08 Unit Group 7212). Intuitively, robots designed to weld can substitute human workers performing the same operation.

Assembling robots are found to displace machine operators and assemblers, a group involving operations aimed at "assembling products from component parts following strict specifications and procedures". Similarly, assembling robots are negatively correlated to crafts and related trade workers, which often perform tasks such as assembling different parts in a repetitive way, and elementary occupations that include labourers whose main task is to move materials among assemblers in the production line.

The negative correlation between handling robots and the "mid-skill" occupations in Figure 4.31 is the result of the fact that robots are best suited to substitute specific routine tasks. Mid-skill jobs are known to have a very high routine content.[13] They are characterised by repetitive tasks, even if they require specialised skills – such as those involving a high degree of manual dexterity (e.g. welding). Thus, the evidence suggests that the use of industrial robots can potentially automate a number of routine manual tasks, even if they are relatively complex, like operating machine tools.

At the same time, even if explicitly designed to perform tasks otherwise performed by humans, robots do not need to displace all occupations. For example, while being negatively correlated with all other occupational groups, handling robots are found to be positively correlated with elementary occupations.

When robots interact with occupations lacking specialised skills or abilities, they can trigger a variation of the task composition and a shift towards tasks that cannot be automated, such as those involving interpersonal skills, problem solving or decision making. In these cases, robots can substitute for low-value, routine tasks and increase the value of those skills necessary to the performance of more "abstract" tasks.

The diffusion of industrial robots, accelerated by continuous improvements in technology, implies that skills related to specialised but routine tasks are likely to become obsolete, even if they require substantial years of investment in education. Therefore, consistently with the findings in OECD (2016b), general skills such as a high level of literacy and numeracy or even interpersonal and communication skills are likely to become increasingly important.

Notes

1. Small firms are defined as companies with between 10 and 49 employees.

2. For Australia and New Zealand, data refer to the fiscal years 2010/11, ending 30 June, instead of 2010 and respectively to the fiscal year 2014/15 and the fiscal year 2015/16, ending 30 June, instead of 2016. For industrial classification, ANZSIC06 division is used instead of ISIC Rev.4 division.

   For Australia, data include agriculture, forestry and fishing.

   For Canada, data refer to 2013 instead of 2016 and to 2007 instead of 2010; medium-sized enterprises have 50-299 employees and large ones 300 or more employees. For industrial classification, the North American Industry Classification System (NAICS) was used instead of ISIC Rev.4.

   For Brazil, Colombia, Japan and Korea, data refer to 2015.

   For Japan, data refer to businesses with 100 or more employees instead of 10 or more; medium-sized enterprises have 100 to 299 employees and large ones 300 or more. For industrial classification, JSIC Rev.13 division is used instead of ISIC Rev.4. Data include leased lines and mobile broadband in 2015, but not in 2010.

   For Mexico, data refer to 2008 and 2012 instead of 2010 and 2016.

   For Switzerland, data refer to 2015 instead of 2016, and to 2011 instead of 2010. In 2015, total businesses with 5 or more employees instead of 10 or more, and 5 to 49 employees as opposed to 10 to 49 employees. In 2011, data refer to total businesses with ten or more employees.

3. For Australia and New Zealand, data refer to the fiscal years 2010/11, ending 30 June, instead of 2010 and respectively to the fiscal year 2014/15 and the fiscal year 2015/16, ending 30 June, instead of 2016. For industrial classification, ANZSIC06 division is used instead of ISIC Rev.4 division.

   For Australia, data include agriculture, forestry and fishing.

   For Canada, data refer to 2013 instead of 2016 and to 2007 instead of 2010; medium-sized enterprises have 50-299 employees and large ones 300 or more. For industrial classification, the North American Industry Classification System (NAICS) was used instead of ISIC Rev.4.

   For Brazil, Colombia, Japan and Korea, data refer to 2015.

   For Japan, data refer to businesses with 100 or more employees instead of 10 or more; medium-sized enterprises have 100-299 employees and large ones 300 or more. For industrial classification, JSIC Rev.13 division is used instead of ISIC Rev.4.

   For Mexico, data refer to 2008 and 2012 instead of 2010 and 2016.

   For Switzerland, data refer to 2011 instead of 2016.

4. Broadband: for Australia, includes "DSL", "fibre to the premises", "cable", "fixed wireless", "mobile wireless", "satellite" and "other". For Canada, includes all connection groups except dial-up connection.

   E-purchases: for Australia, data refer to the proportion of businesses placing/receiving orders over computer networks by methods specifically designed for the purpose (includes web pages, extranet or EDI). It includes any transaction where the commitment to purchase was made via the Internet, including via e-mail. For New Zealand, data exclude orders initiated via EDI-type messages. For Switzerland, data refer to the share of enterprises buying or selling and no recall period mentioned in the question.

   E-sales: for Australia, data refer to the proportion of businesses placing/receiving orders over computer networks by methods specifically designed for the purpose (includes web pages, extranet or EDI). This includes any transaction where the commitment to purchase was made via the Internet.

   ERP: for Canada, data relate to the year 2013, and for Iceland and Sweden to 2014.

   Cloud computing: for Canada, data relate to the year 2012, and to enterprises that have made expenditures on "software as a service (e.g. cloud computing)".

   SCM: for Turkey, data relate to the year 2012.

   Social media: for Australia, data refer to businesses that had a social media presence, and for Canada to enterprises for which Internet websites offer integration with social media (e.g. Facebook, Twitter, Google+).

   RFID: for Japan, Korea and Switzerland, data relate to the year 2015; for Canada data relate to 2013 and for Turkey to 2011.

   For countries in the European Statistical System, sector coverage consists of all activities in manufacturing and non-financial market services, and data on e-purchases and e-sales refer to 2015. For Australia and New Zealand, data refer respectively to the fiscal year 2014/15 and the fiscal year 2015/16, ending 30 June, instead of 2016. For industrial classification, ANZSIC06 division is used instead of ISIC Rev.4 division. For Australia, data include agriculture, forestry and fishing. For Canada, the North American Industry Classification System (NAICS) is used instead of ISIC Rev.4, and data refer to 2013 except cloud computing (2012). For Iceland, data refer to the year 2014. For Japan, Korea and Switzerland, data refer to the year 2015. For Japan, JSIC Rev.13 division is used instead of ISIC Rev.4 and data include total businesses with 100 or more employees instead of 10 and more. For Mexico, data refer to the year 2012. For Switzerland, data refer to the year 2015, website data refer to 2011 instead of 2016, and data for 2015 refer to firms with five or more employees. For Switzerland, data for the year 2015 relate to businesses with five or more employees instead of ten or more.

5. For Australia, data refer to the fiscal year fiscal year 2014/2015, ending 30 June, instead of 2016. For industrial classification, ANZSIC06 division is used instead of ISIC rev.4 division. Data include agriculture, forestry and fishing.

   For Canada, data refer to 2012 and to enterprises that have made expenditures on software as a service (e.g. cloud computing). The North American Industry Classification System (NAICS) is used instead of ISIC Rev.4. Medium-sized enterprises have 50-299 employees. Large enterprises have 300 or more employees. For Iceland, data refer to 2014.

   For Japan, JSIC Rev.13 division is used instead of ISIC Rev.4, data refer to 2015 and to businesses with 100 or more employees. Medium-sized enterprises have 100-299 employees. Large enterprises have 300 or more employees.

   For Brazil and Korea, data refer to 2015.

   For Mexico, data refer to 2012.

   For Switzerland, data refer to 2015 and to firms with five or more employees.

6. For countries in the European Statistical System and Mexico, data refer to 2016.

   For Australia and New Zealand, data referring to the year 200N relate to original data from 200N/N+1 (fiscal year ending 30 June 200N+1).

   For Brazil, Colombia, Chile, Israel, Japan, Korea and the United States, data refer to 2015 and for Iceland and Switzerland, to 2014. For Canada and New Zealand, data refer to 2012.

   For Canada and Japan, the recall period is 12 months. For the United States, no time period is specified.

For the job search category, data refer to 2012 for Canada and Japan; to 2013 for Iceland; to 2015 for Brazil, Chile, Korea and the United States; and to 2016 for Mexico.

For the software download category, data refer to 2016 for Mexico.

For the e-government category, data relate to individuals who used the Internet in the last three months for Israel. For Mexico, it includes the following categories: "communicating with the government", "consulting government information", "downloading government formats", "filling out or submitting government formats", "carrying out government procedures" and "opining in government consultations". For Switzerland, it refers only to public administrations at local, regional or country level; "public administration or authorities", that is without health or education institutions.

For online purchases, the recall period is three months for Australia, and data relate to individuals who used the Internet in the last three months for Australia, Israel and the United States.

For travel and accommodation, data relate to individuals who used the Internet in the last three months for Australia and Mexico. For Mexico, it refers to the following category: "reservations and tickets".

For Australia, data refer to 2014, except for email (2010) and e-government interaction (2012). The reference period is the last 3 months in 2014 and the last 12 months in the previous years. With regard to interactions with public authorities, data refer to downloading official forms from government organisations' websites or completing/lodging filled in forms from government organisations' websites.

For Israel, data refer to individuals aged 20 and over instead of 16-74. With regard to interactions with public authorities, data refer to obtaining services on line from government offices and include downloading or filling in official forms, in the last three months.

For Japan, data refer to individuals aged 15-69 instead those aged 16-74. For job search, data refer to 2012 and for online sales, to 2010.

For Mexico, "content creation" relates to "create or visit blogs", "telephone" to "Internet telephone conversations (VoIP)", and "product information" includes the category "Individuals using the Internet for seeking health related information".

7. For Australia, data refer to 2012/13 (fiscal year ending 30 June) instead of 2016 and to 2010/11 (fiscal year ending 30 June) instead of 2010. Data refer to "Individuals who have used the Internet for downloading official forms from government organisations' websites, in the last 12 months" and "Individuals who have used the Internet for completing/lodging filled in forms from government organisations' websites, in the last 12 months".

   For Canada, data refer to 2012 instead of 2016 for visiting or interacting, and to 2009 instead of 2016 for sending filled forms. Data for 2012 and 2010 relate to individuals aged 16-74, and for 2009 to individuals aged 16 or older.

   For Chile, Iceland and Switzerland, data refer to 2014 instead of 2016.

   For Brazil, Colombia and Israel, data refer to 2015 instead of 2016.

   For New Zealand, data refer to 2012/13 (fiscal year ending 30 June) instead of 2016, and to individuals using the Internet for obtaining information from public authorities in the last 12 months.

   For Japan, for sending filled forms, data refer to 2015 instead of 2016 and to individuals aged 15-69 instead of 16-74.

   For Mexico, using e-government services includes the following categories: "communicating with the government", "consulting government information", "downloading government formats", "filling out or submitting government formats", "carrying out government procedures" and "opining in government consultations". For sending forms, the data correspond to the use of the Internet in the last three months.

   For Switzerland, e-government refers only to public administrations at local, regional or country level; "public administration or authorities", that is without health or education institutions.

8. *http://skills.industry.nsw.gov.au*.

9. Occupations are defined according to the International Standard Classification of Occupations (ISCO) 2008 at three-digit level (127 occupations, excluding armed forces), except for Australia and Finland, where PIAAC data are available at two digits only (40 occupations, excluding armed forces).

10. In order to identify such ICT complementary skills, it is possible to compute correlation coefficients between the ICT intensity proxies based on CIS and OPS use from the PIAAC data and: i) the frequency at which the above tasks are performed at work; and ii) the value of the intensity indices computed within the PIAAC framework for numeracy, reading and writing skills at work. A positive (negative) correlation between the ICT intensity and a given task/activity means that an individual using ICT more performs that task/activity more (less) often than an individual that does not use ICT. The sign of the correlation, therefore, can be interpreted as a measure of the degree of complementarity between ICT and other tasks/activities at work. In addition, the higher the value of the correlation coefficients, the stronger the complementarity between ICT and these tasks/activities.
11. The analysis abstracts from several important dimensions, such as the impact of offshoring and outsourcing on investment in industrial robots.
12. To neaten and smooth the rough edges or ridges of an object, typically one made of metal.
13. Details can be found in Marcolin, Miroudot and Squicciarini (2016).

References

Eckardt, D. and M. Squicciarini (forthcoming), "Mapping SOC-2010 into ISCO-08 occupations: A new methodology using employment weights", *OECD Science, Technology and Industry Working Papers*, OECD Publishing, Paris.

European Commission (2014), "E-Skills for jobs in Europe: Measuring progress and moving ahead", European Commission, *www.researchgate.net/publication/265972686_e-Skills_for_Jobs_in_Europe_Measuring_Progress_and_Moving_Ahead* (accessed 29 August 2017).

Eurostat (2016), "Methodological manual 2016: Part I: Enterprise survey", Eurostat,*https://circabc.europa.eu/sd/a/c63154ce-e7d2-4635-9bb9-6fa56da86044/MM2016_Part_I_Enterprise_survey.zip.*

Laney, D. (2001), "3D data management: Controlling data volume, velocity, and variety", Meta Group, Stamford, Connecticut, *http://blogs.gartner.com/doug-laney/files/2012/01/ad949-3D-Data-Management-Controlling-Data-Volume-Velocity-and-Variety.pdf.*

ManpowerGroup (2016), Talent Shortage Survey, *http://manpowergroup.com/talent-shortage-2016.*

Marcolin, L., S. Miroudot and M. Squicciarini (2016), "The routine content of occupations: New cross-country measures based on PIAAC", *OECD Trade Policy Papers*, No. 188, OECD Publishing, Paris, *http://dx.doi.org/10.1787/5jm0mq86fljg-en.*

OECD (Organisation for Economic Co-operation and Development) (forthcoming), "Determinants and impact of automation: an analysis of robots' adoption in OECD countries", *OECD Digital Economy Papers*, OECD Publishing, Paris.

OECD (2017), *OECD Skills Outlook 2017: Skills and Global Value Chains*, OECD Publishing, Paris, *http://dx.doi.org/10.1787/9789264273351-en.*

OECD (2016a), "New skills for the digital economy", *OECD Digital Economy Papers*, No. 258, OECD Publishing, Paris, *http://dx.doi.org/10.1787/5jlwnkm2fc9x-en.*

OECD (2016b), "Enabling the next production revolution: The future of manufacturing and services – Interim report", , OECD, Paris, *www.oecd.org/mcm/documents/Enabling-the-next-production-revolution-the-future-of-manufacturing-and-services-interim-report.pdf.*

OECD (2014a), *Recommendation of the Council on Digital Government Strategies*, OECD, Paris, *www.oecd.org/gov/digital-government/Recommendation-digital-government-strategies.pdf.*

OECD (2014b), "Forecasting future needs for advanced ICT competence in Norway", DSTI/ICCP/IIS(2014)5, OECD, Paris.

OECD (2013), "ICT jobs and skills: New estimates and the work ahead", , internal document, OECD, Paris.

OECD (2012), *Literacy, Numeracy and Problem Solving in Technology-Rich Environments: Framework for the OECD Survey of Adult Skills*, OECD Publishing, Paris, *http://dx.doi.org/10.1787/9789264128859-en.*

OECD (2004), "ICT skills and employment", in *Information Technology Outlook 2004*, OECD Publishing, Paris, *http://dx.doi.org/10.1787/it_outlook-2004-8-en.*

Chapter 5

Innovation, applications and transformation

Digital innovation drives the development of the digital economy and society, enables applications in many areas, and leads to transformations. This chapter first examines recent trends and evolutions in digital innovation, business models and markets, focusing on information and communication technology investment, business dynamism, data-driven innovation, and online platform markets, then presents expanding digital applications and services in selected areas – sciences, healthcare, agriculture, governments, and cities – and finally discusses the ongoing digital transformations of jobs and trade. Policy and regulation related to digital innovation, applications and transformation are discussed in Chapter 2.

The statistical data for Israel are supplied by and under the responsibility of the relevant Israeli authorities. The use of such data by the OECD is without prejudice to the status of the Golan Heights, East Jerusalem and Israeli settlements in the West Bank under the terms of international law.

Introduction

Digital innovation creates opportunities for new business models and markets, enables applications and services in different sectors and areas, and drives transformation across the economy and society, including of jobs and of trade. This chapter provides an overview of recent developments in digital innovation, applications and transformation.

Underpinned by information and communication technology (ICT) investment, business dynamism, entrepreneurship and data-driven innovation (DDI), traditional goods and services are increasingly enhanced by digital technology, new digital products and business models emerge, and more and more services are being traded or delivered over online platforms. For example, what used to be a simple tractor has become a data-intensive product that is able to monitor soil conditions, send data to its proprietor, and plough and plant with unseen precision. Such a tractor is not sold as a simple physical good anymore, but as a key component of a larger service package within which the proprietor plays a role after sales. Another example is the rise of online platforms, which create new markets or move existing ones partly or fully online. Beyond facilitating e-commerce trade of goods and enabling online search, social networks and digital media, platforms have entered service markets, e.g. for accommodation and transport as well as for any type of service that can be delivered over the Internet.

Digital innovation enables applications and services in a wide range of sectors, including in science, healthcare, agriculture, government and cities. For example, scientific research is being affected by the growing amount of data being collected and analysed throughout scientific processes as well as by the diffusion of results via online platforms that shape open access publishing and enable new modes of peer review. In healthcare, the use of mobile health applications (apps) and of electronic health records enables new care models and provides the foundation greater co-ordination and improved clinical management. Governments are promoting e-government services to individuals and firms, are providing open access to public sector information (PSI), and are increasingly communicating directly to citizens via social networks. Not least, cities are seizing the benefits of digital applications, for example in urban transport, energy, and water and waste systems, and are exploring the potential of DDI to improve urban operations and decision making.

Digital innovation and applications transform not only products, business models and markets, but also jobs and trade. In some sectors ICT investment has led to job losses while in others it has led to job creation. For example, in most countries, labour demand decreases as a result of ICT investment in manufacturing, business services and trade, transport and accommodation, while it increases in culture, recreation and other services, construction and, to a lesser extent, in government, health and personal care, energy, and agriculture. Further, the use of digital technologies affects the nature of work in some areas. For example, services traded over online platforms, including accommodation and transport, are increasingly provided by individuals that tend to carry out flexible, temporary and part-time work in such jobs. Digitalisation is also reshaping the trade landscape, particularly for services. While ICT services help boost productivity, trade and competitiveness across the economy, in some countries trade is limited by restrictions on telecommunication and computer services.

Key findings in this chapter are that investments in ICT goods and services and business dynamism have fallen short of their potential in recent years, but data has become a core driver of digital innovation. DDI, new business models, and digital applications are changing the workings of science, governments, cities, and many sectors including health and agriculture. Effects of the digital transformation are likely to include job destruction in some and job creation in other sectors, new forms of work, and a reshaping of the trade landscape, in particular for services.

Digital innovation in business models and markets

This section examines developments in the conditions that underpin digital innovation, concerning the drivers that affect digital business models, and in new markets that are created by online platforms. Investment in ICT goods and services and entrepreneurship are important conditions for digital innovation, while data are becoming a driver and resource for it. New opportunities for business models are being created, for example, by digitisation, datafication, the Internet of Things (IoT), codification, automation, data trading, data analytics and artificial intelligence. Among the most successful digital businesses that have emerged over the last 15 years are online platforms, which have created exponentially growing online markets for a range of products, from information to goods and, more recently, services.

Investment in ICT goods and services underpins digital innovation and growth

Investment in ICT goods and services is an important condition for digital innovation and a driver of growth (Spiezia, 2011). ICTs have the potential to increase innovation by speeding up the diffusion of information, favouring networking among firms, enabling closer links between businesses and customers, reducing geographic limitations, and increasing efficiency in communication. In addition, the spillover effects from ICT usage, such as network economies, can be sources of productivity gains. ICTs can also be seen as a source of innovation because they enable closer links between businesses, their suppliers, customers, competitors and collaborative partners, thus making businesses more responsive to innovation opportunities and providing significant efficiency gains.

In 2015, ICT investment in the OECD area represented 11% of total fixed investment and 2.3% of gross domestic product (GDP). Almost 60% of ICT investment was devoted to computer software and databases. ICT investment across OECD countries varied from 3.8% in the Czech Republic to less than 1.5% of GDP in Greece, Luxemburg and Hungary. These differences tend to reflect differences in each country's specialisation and its position in the business cycle (Figure 5.1).

In most OECD countries, investments in ICTs in the aftermath of the 2007 crisis have been more resilient than total investments. As a result, the share of ICT investment in total investment was higher in 2015 than in 2007. In some countries, however, the crisis has resulted in a sharper slowdown in ICT investments. This is the case of Australia, Canada, Germany, Japan, Luxembourg, Norway, and Sweden, where the share of ICT investment in 2015 was lower than in 2007 and 2000 (Figure 5.2). Other factors may also have affected the observed changes in ICT investments, in particular increasing expenditures for cloud services, which firms use as a substitute for ICT investment. It is a matter of current debate (Byrne and Corrado, 2016) whether these services are properly measured in the System of National Accounts (SNA).

Figure 5.1. **ICT investment by capital asset, 2015**

As a percentage of GDP

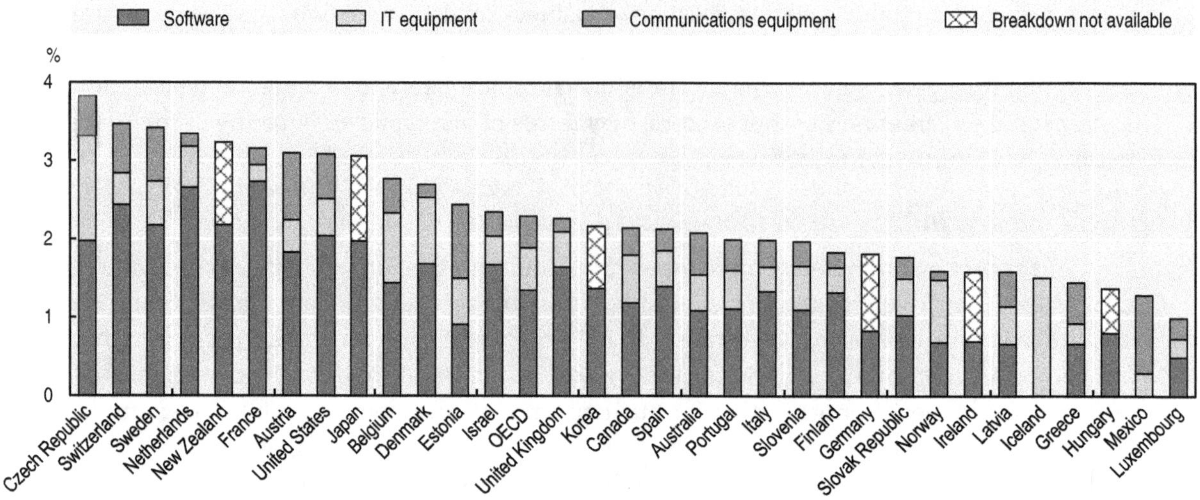

Notes: Data for Latvia, Norway, Portugal and Spain are 2014 instead of 2015. Data for Korea are OECD estimates based on national Input-Output tables and OECD SNA08. Data for Iceland and Mexico were incomplete and only represent the asset for which data were available. The series "breakdown not available" represents in all cases the combination of IT and communication equipment. GDP = gross domestic product; IT = information technology.

Sources: OECD, *National Accounts Statistics (SNA)* (database), *www.oecd-ilibrary.org/economics/data/oecd-national-accounts-statistics_na-data-en*; OECD *Productivity Database*, *www.oecd-ilibrary.org/employment/data/oecd-productivity-statistics_pdtvy-data-en*; Eurostat, *National Accounts (including GDP) Statistics* (database), *http://ec.europa.eu/eurostat/web/national-accounts/data/database*; national sources (accessed July 2017).

StatLink http://dx.doi.org/10.1787/888933586008

Figure 5.2. **Evolution of ICT investments**

As a percentage of total investments

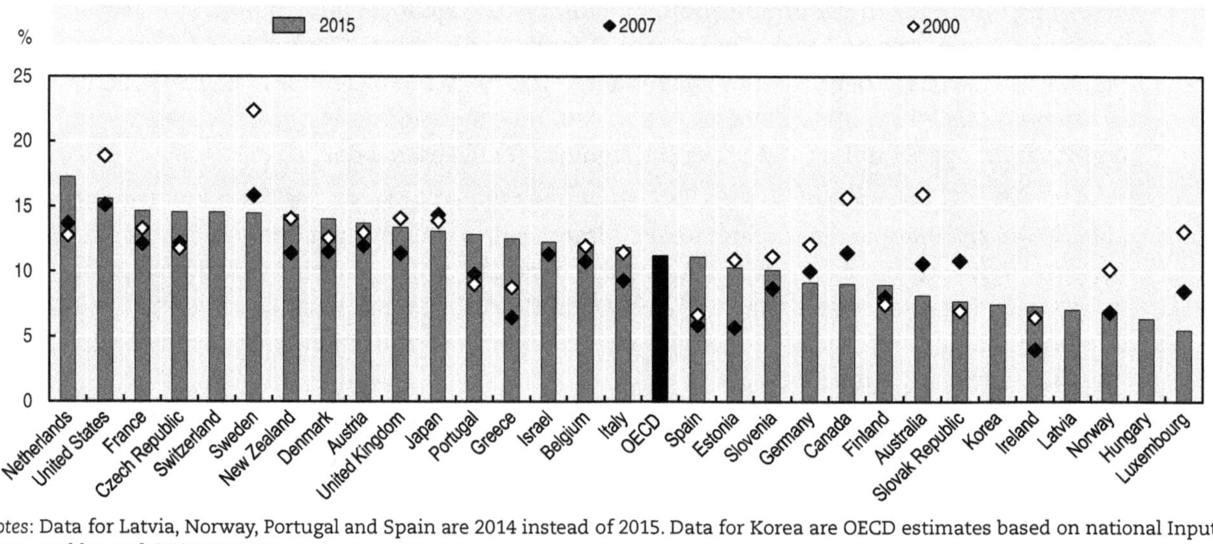

Notes: Data for Latvia, Norway, Portugal and Spain are 2014 instead of 2015. Data for Korea are OECD estimates based on national Input-Output tables and OECD SNA08.

Sources: OECD, *National Accounts Statistics (SNA)* (database), *www.oecd-ilibrary.org/economics/data/oecd-national-accounts-statistics_na-data-en*; OECD *Productivity Database*, *www.oecd-ilibrary.org/employment/data/oecd-productivity-statistics_pdtvy-data-en*; Eurostat, *National Accounts (including GDP) Statistics* (database), *http://ec.europa.eu/eurostat/web/national-accounts/data/database*; national sources (accessed July 2017).

StatLink http://dx.doi.org/10.1787/888933586027

Available evidence strongly suggests that investing in ICTs alone is not enough, as it is mainly the effective use of ICTs that generates positive productivity effects. And the degree of effectiveness in ICT use typically depends on complementary investments in knowledge-based capital (KBC), in particular firm-specific skills and know-how, and organisational change, including new business processes and business models (OECD, 2016a).

Indeed, investment in KBC has been rising, and in some countries is larger as a share of GDP than investment in physical capital. Unlike physical capital, investments in many forms of KBC – research and development, organisational change, design – yield knowledge that can spill over to other parts of the economy. That is, firms that do not invest in KBC can only be partially excluded from benefits created by firms that do. In addition, KBC can spur growth because the initial cost incurred in developing some types of knowledge does not need to be incurred again when that knowledge is used again in production. Indeed, once created, some forms of KBC – such as software and some designs – can be replicated at almost no cost and can be used simultaneously by many users. This can lead to increasing returns to scale in production and in positive network externalities, e.g. the value of a platform increases with the number of users of the platform (OECD, 2013a).

Business dynamism and entrepreneurship are falling short of their potential

Despite digital opportunities, there are signs that business dynamism is decreasing

Digital technologies can affect businesses' dynamism, which supports the emergence and growth of firms. The Internet lowers barriers to entrepreneurship and makes it easier to start, grow and manage a business. It also supports "lean start-ups" that leverage the Internet to lower fixed costs and outsource many aspects of the business to stay agile and responsive to the market. The Internet further affects the broader business environment by lowering transaction costs, increasing price transparency and improving competition. It is now easier for businesses to communicate with suppliers, customers and employees using Internet-based tools. Improved communication is also leading to the emergence of new and transformed business models.

Evidence indicates that despite the new opportunities linked to digitalisation, there has been a general decrease in business dynamism across countries. This decline in business dynamism markedly accelerated during the crisis, and the recovery since has only been partial, with broadly similar trends observed for manufacturing and services. More specifically, entry rates appear to have steadily declined over the period, while churning rates and growth dispersion – more stable before the crisis – have dropped considerably since 2009, especially in non-financial business services (Blanchenay et al., forthcoming).

This decline in dynamism across countries is particularly marked in ICT-producing and ICT-using sectors. Figure 5.3 illustrates a strong decline in entry rates (number of entering units over number of entering and incumbent units) for ICT-producing manufacturing and service sectors between 2001 and 2015, with some recovery immediately before the crisis. This is mirrored in the ICT-using sectors, which also exhibit a pronounced decline in dynamism over the same period, especially when looking at manufacturing. However, the remaining sectors of the economy are characterised by a more modest decrease in entry rates, occurring mostly after the crisis.

There are several potential mechanisms by which digital technologies influence business dynamism that may provide insights into the declining dynamism found across countries over time. The nature of new digital technologies may favour large firms at the expense of dynamism – reducing the entry and growth potential of new firms. Digital technologies may also trigger dynamics that benefit a minority of leading frontier firms (Brynjolfsson et al., 2008). For example, advances in digital technologies have enabled large multinationals to co-ordinate and profit from complex and fragmented production networks (OECD and World Bank, 2015). In some sectors, such as ICT-providing services and other ICT-using services, the significantly decreased marginal cost of both production (provision) and transport (communication) of digital goods (services) have been associated with easier scalability (Brynjolfsson and McAfee, 2011).

Figure 5.3. **Business dynamism in ICT-producing, ICT-using and other sectors**

Index 2001 = 1

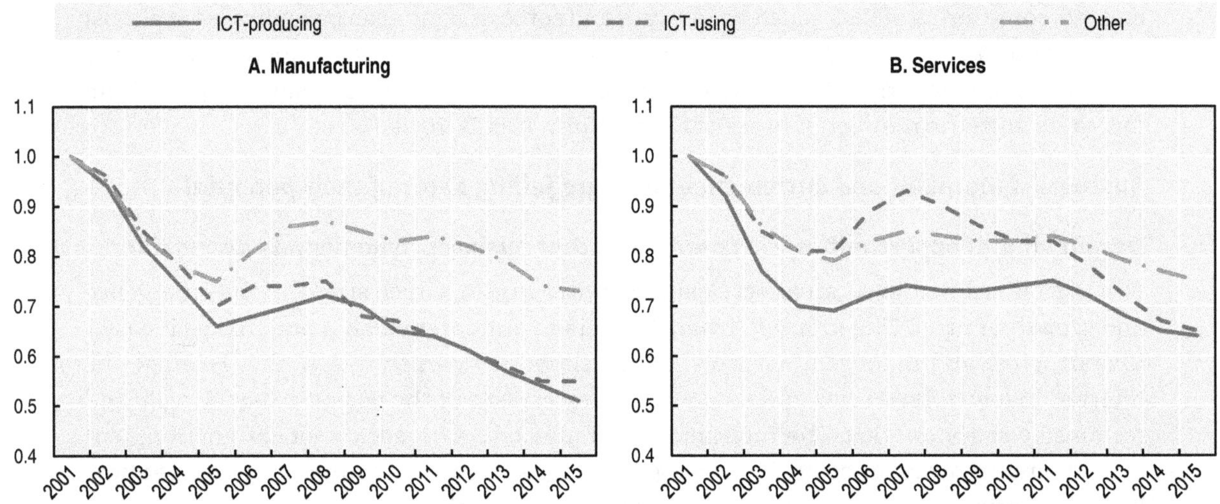

Notes: ICT-producing sectors are defined as "computer, electronic and optical products" from the manufacturing sector and "IT and other information services" and "telecommunications" from the services sector. ICT-using sectors are defined as "electrical equipment", "machinery and equipment" and "chemicals and chemical products" from the manufacturing sector and "publishing, audiovisual and broadcasting activities", "legal and accounting activities" and "scientific research and development" from the services sector. Figures report three-year moving averages, conditional on the availability of data. Owing to methodological differences, figures may deviate from officially published national statistics. Data for all countries covered are still preliminary. ICT = information and communication technology.

Source: OECD, *DynEmp3 Database*, *http://oe.cd/dynemp* (accessed July 2017).

StatLink *http://dx.doi.org/10.1787/888933586046*

The potential of start-ups is hampered by a lack of access to finance and administrative burdens

A growing number of successful business cases show that small start-ups are better placed to seize the new opportunities offered by digital technologies (CB insights, 2015; The Economist, 2014). However, a combination of market and regulatory factors act as an obstacle to the creation of small young firms.

The first obstacle is financing. Debt finance is ill-suited for newer, small and innovative companies, which have a higher risk-return profile and often rely on firm-specific intangibles that are not always suitable as collateral.

Private equity investments, particularly venture capital (VC) and angel investing, provide new financing opportunities for innovative start-ups, mainly in high-tech fields. In 2016, over 70% of VC in the United States went to the ICT sector (see Chapter 3). In most countries, however, VC represents a very small percentage of GDP, often less than 0.05%. The two major exceptions are Israel and the United States, where the VC industry is more mature, representing in 2015 0.38% and 0.33% of GDP, respectively.

VC investments collapsed in nearly all countries at the height of the crisis and remain below pre-crisis levels in most countries (Figure 5.4). By contrast, in Hungary, South Africa and the United States, the recovery has been strong, with 2015 levels nearly twice those of 2007.

Figure 5.4. **Trends in venture capital investments**

Index 2007 = 100

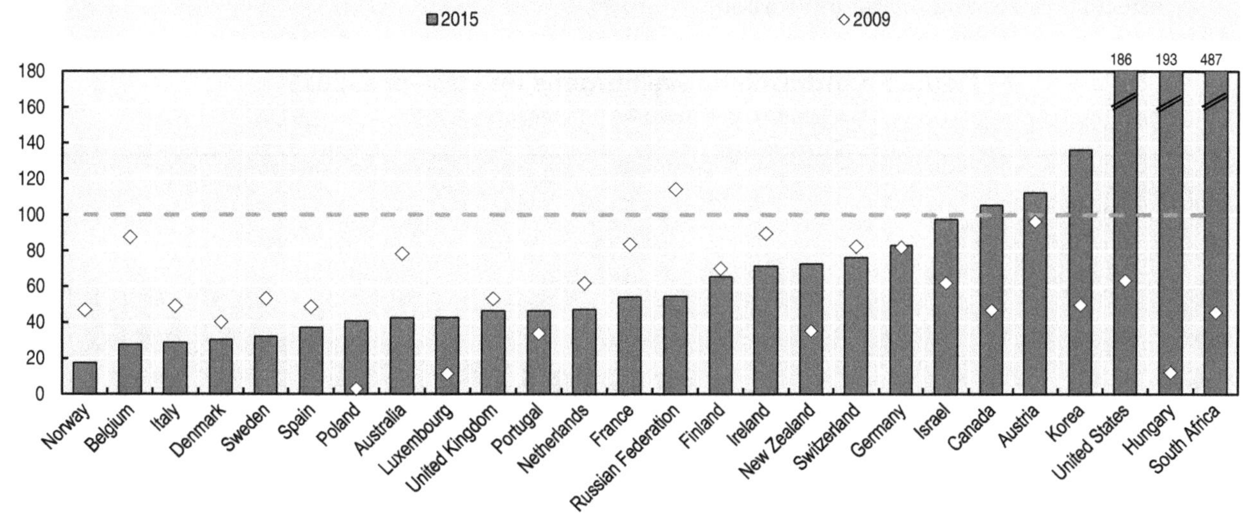

Note: Data for Israel and South Africa refer to 2014.

Source: OECD (2016b), *Entrepreneurship at a Glance 2016*, *http://dx.doi.org/10.1787/entrepreneur_aag-2016-en.*

StatLink http://dx.doi.org/10.1787/888933586065

Despite its potential, the share of small firm financing provided through capital markets remains low. High monitoring costs, low liquidity, red tape and reporting requirements, as well as cultural factors and management practices are obstacles to its development.

ICTs themselves are creating new tools to overcome some of these obstacles. Crowdfunding platforms may provide new sources of finance for small start-ups. Peer-to-peer lending can be attractive for small businesses that lack collateral or a credit history to access traditional bank lending. Equity crowdfunding can provide a complement or substitute for seed financing for entrepreneurial ventures and start-ups that have difficulties in raising capital from traditional sources. Although crowdfunding has grown rapidly since the mid-2000s, it still represents a very minor share of financing for businesses. Donations, rewards and pre-selling are still dominant forms of crowdfunding, although regulation has limited its diffusion, especially for securities-based crowdfunding, which is not legal in some countries (OECD, 2014a).

The Internet can also help to bring together small young firms and potential investors by reducing information asymmetries and increasing transparency. For instance, data warehouses with loan-level information can help investors to better assess risks in small firms and identify investment opportunities. More reliable information about risk may also help to reduce the financing costs, which are typically higher for small firms than for large ones. Start-ups with a public listing on dedicated platforms can increase their visibility and facilitate match-making with investors. In addition, online platforms can provide training, mentoring and coaching for potential entrepreneurs and help them to improve the quality of their business plans and investment projects.

Regulation appears to be the other major obstacle to small start-ups, at least in countries with high administrative burdens on start-ups (Figure 5.5). While advances in ICTs have significantly lowered the cost of experimentation for frontier firms, in many countries regulation tends to favour incumbents and does not always enable the necessary experimentation with new ideas, technologies and business models that underpins the success of young firms. Chapter 2 provides further discussion on policy and regulation that affect start-ups and digital innovation.

Figure 5.5. **Administrative burdens on start-ups, 2013**

Scale from 0 to 6 (from least to most restrictive)

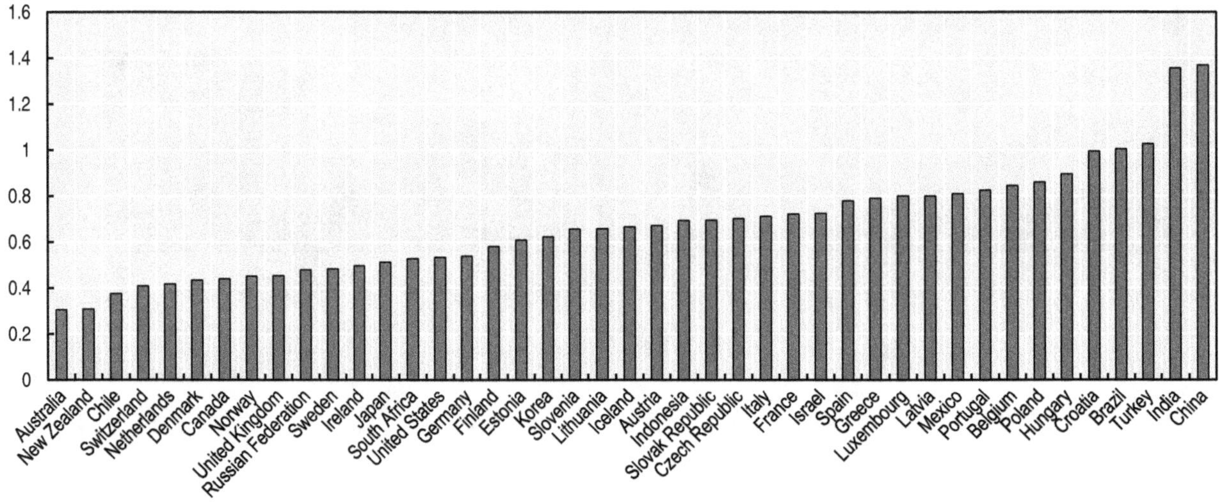

Notes: For the People's Republic of China ("China" in the figure), data are based on preliminary estimates. For Indonesia, data refer to 2009. For the United States, data refer to 2007.

Source: OECD, *Product Market Regulation Database*, *www.oecd.org/economy/pmr* (accessed December 2016).

StatLink http://dx.doi.org/10.1787/888933586084

Data are becoming a core driver of digital innovation

More data are being generated every week than in the last millennia. With the accelerating digitalisation of social and economic activities, the flows of data – the equivalent of around 50 000 years of DVD-quality video every single day – are such that the implications for the economy and society are colossal (OECD, 2015a). The huge volume, velocity (the speed at which they are generated, accessed, processed and analysed) and variety (such as unstructured and structured data) of data is today referred to as "big data".[1]

The use of big data promises to significantly improve products, processes, organisational methods and markets, a phenomenon referred to as DDI (OECD, 2015a). In manufacturing, data obtained through sensors are used to monitor and analyse the efficiency of machines to optimise their operations and to provide after-sale services, including preventive maintenance. The data are sometimes also used to work with suppliers, and are, in some cases, even commercialised in the form of new services (for example, to optimise production control). In agriculture, geocoded maps of fields and real-time monitoring of every agricultural activity, from seeding to harvesting, are used to increase agricultural productivity (see the following section). The same sensor data can then be reused and linked with historical and real-time data on weather patterns, soil conditions, fertiliser usage and crop features to optimise and predict agricultural production. Traditional cultivation methods can be improved and the know-how of skilled farmers formalised and made widely available.

There is still little macroeconomic evidence on the effects of DDI, but available firm-level studies suggest that using DDI raises labour productivity faster than in non-using firms by approximately 5% to 10% (OECD, 2015a). Brynjolfsson, Hitt and Kim (2011) estimate that in the United States, output and productivity in firms that adopt data-driven decision making are 5% to 6% higher than what would be expected given their other investments in, and use of, ICTs. These firms also perform better in terms of asset utilisation, return on equity and market value. A study of 500 firms in the United Kingdom found that firms in the top quartile of online data use are 13% more productive than those in the bottom quartile (Bakhshi, Bravo-Biosca and Mateos-Garcia, 2014). Barua, Mani and Mukherjee (2013) suggest that improving data quality and access by 10% – presenting data more concisely and consistently across platforms and allowing it to be more easily manipulated – would increase labour productivity by 14% on average, but with significant cross-industry variations.[2] Nevertheless, big data are still mainly used in the ICT sector, particularly by Internet services firms. According to Tambe (2014), for example, only 30% of Hadoop investments come from non-ICT sectors, including, in particular, in finance, transport, utilities, retail, healthcare, pharmaceuticals and biotechnology firms. Manufacturing is becoming increasingly data-intensive (see Manyika et al., 2011).

As goods become commodities with low profit margins, many manufacturing firms are developing new complementary services that extend their current business propositions. Rolls-Royce, for instance, shifted its business from a product, time and service solution to a service model trademarked as "Power by the Hour" (OECD, 2017a). Digitalisation has been a key enabler for this transformation towards higher value-added (complementary) services.

Historically, the digital transformation of business models was first enabled by the formalisation and codification of business-related activities, which led to the computerisation of business processes via software. This has "enabled firms to more rapidly replicate improved business processes throughout an organisation, thereby not only increasing productivity but also market share and market value". Brynjolfsson et al. (2008) have referred to this phenomenon as scaling without mass. Internet firms pushed the digital transformation to a new level. This enabled them to scale without mass better than the rest of the economy.[3]

The business models of the most successful Internet firms today go beyond the formalisation and codification of processes via software, and now involve the collection and analysis of large streams of data (OECD, 2015a). By collecting and analysing big data, a large share of which is provided by Internet users (consumers), Internet companies are able to automate their processes and to experiment with, and foster, new products and business models at a much faster rate than the rest of industry. Instead of relying on the (explicit) formulation and codification of business processes, these firms use big data to "train" artificial intelligence (AI) algorithms to perform more complex business processes without human intervention. Innovation enabled by AI is now used to transform business processes across the economy. Thanks to the convergence of ICTs with other technologies (owing in particular to embedded software and the IoT), the digital transformation has the potential to affect even traditional sectors such as manufacturing and agriculture.

Two major trends make digital technologies transformational for production: the reduction of the cost of these technologies, which enables their wider diffusion, including to small and medium-sized enterprises (SMEs); and, most importantly, the combination of digital technologies, which enables new types of applications. Figure 5.6 depicts the key ICTs which are enabling the digital transformation of industrial production. The technologies at the bottom of the figure enable those at the top, as indicated by the arrows. The technologies at the top (in white), which include additive manufacturing (i.e. 3D printing), autonomous machines and systems, and human-machine integration, are the applications through which the main productivity effects in industry are likely to unfold. In combination, these technologies could one day lead to fully automated production processes, from design to delivery.

Figure 5.6. **The confluence of key technologies enabling the industrial digital transformation**

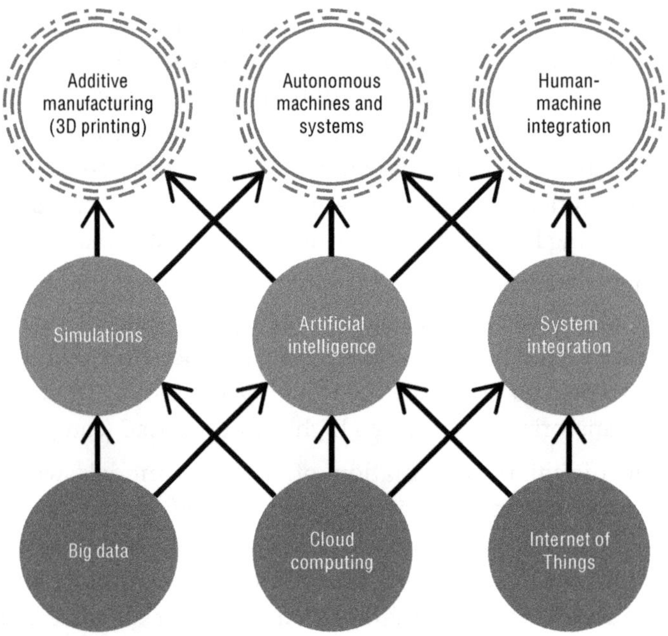

Note: This figure is highly stylised and does not show many of the complex relationships and feedback loops between these technologies.

Source: OECD (2017a), *The Next Production Revolution: Implications for Governments and Business*, *http://dx.doi.org/10.1787/9789264271036-en.*

StatLink *http://dx.doi.org/10.1787/888933586103*

The analysis of successful digital business models suggests that actions that take advantage of the applications mentioned above can digitally transform traditional businesses. These actions include:

- **The digitisation of physical assets**, which refers to the process of encoding information into binary digits (i.e. bits) so that it can be processed by computers (OECD, 2015a). This is one of the most straightforward steps to digitally transform businesses. An early example is the entertainment and content industry, where books, music and videos were digitised to be provided over formats such as CD and DVD, and the Internet. Thanks to the deployment of 3D scanners and 3D printing, digitisation is no longer limited to content, but can now include real-life objects. 3D printing promises, for instance, to shorten industrial design processes, owing to rapid prototyping, and in some cases to raise productivity by reducing material waste. Boeing, for instance, has already replaced machining with 3D printing for over 20 000 units of 300 distinct parts (Davidson, 2012).

- **The "datafication" of business-relevant processes**, which refers to data generation, not only through the digitisation of content, but through the monitoring of activities, including real-world (offline) activities and phenomena through sensors. "Datafication" is a portmanteau word for "data" and "quantification" and should not be confused with "digitisation", which is just the conversion of analogue source material into a numerical format (OECD, 2015a).[4] Datafication is used by many platforms which monitor the activities of their users. And with the IoT, this approach is no longer limited to Internet firms. For example, data collected on agricultural machines, such as those made by Monsanto, John Deere and DuPont Pioneer, are being used as an important data source for optimising the distribution and genetic modification of crops (see the following section on how digitalisation affects traditional sectors and in particular Boxes 5.1 and 5.2).
- **The interconnection of physical objects via the IoT** enables product and process innovation. Scania AB, a major Swedish manufacturer of commercial vehicles, now generates one-sixth of its revenues through new services enabled by the wireless communication built into its vehicles. This allows the company to transition towards a firm increasingly specialised in logistics, repair and other services. For instance, with the interconnection of its vehicles, Scania can better offer fleet management services. The interconnection of physical objects also enables the generation and analysis of big data, which can be used for the creation of more services: for example, Scania offers a set of services to increase driving (and therefore resource) efficiency, such as data-based driver coaches.
- **The codification and automation of business-relevant processes via software and AI**: software has enabled and incentivised businesses to standardise their processes, and where processes are not central to the business model, to sell the codified processes via software to other businesses. An example is IBM's Global Expenses Reporting Solutions, which were originally developed to automate the company's internal travel-related reporting. IBM turned the in-house system into a service, which it has sold globally (Parmar et al., 2014). Another example is Google's Gmail. This was originally an in-house e-mail system before it was announced to the public as a limited beta release in April 2004 (McCracken, 2014).
- **The trading of data (as a service)** is made possible as soon as physical assets have been digitised or processes datafied (see bullet above on datafication). Data generated as a by-product of doing business can have huge value for other businesses (including in other sectors). The French mobile communication services firm, Orange, uses its floating mobile data technology to collect mobile telephone traffic data that are anonymised and sold to third parties, including government agencies and traffic information service providers. In addition, businesses can take advantage of the non-rivalrous nature of data to create multi-sided markets (inside an organisation), where activities on one side of the market go hand-in-hand with the collection of data, which is exploited and reused on the other side of the market. Very often, however, it is difficult to anticipate the value that data will bring to third parties. This has encouraged some businesses to move more towards open data under certain conditions (see OECD, 2015a).[5]
- **The (re-)use and linkage of data within and across industries** (i.e. data mashups) has become a business opportunity for firms that play a central role in their supply chain. Walmart and Dell have successfully integrated data across their supply chains. But as manufacturing becomes smarter, thanks to the IoT and data analytics, this approach

is becoming attractive to manufacturing companies as well. Sensor data, for instance, can be used to monitor and analyse the efficiency of products, to optimise operations at a system-wide level, and for after-sale services, including preventive maintenance operations.

Online platforms have grown exponentially in markets for information, goods and services

The Internet has made it easier than ever before to match demand and supply in real time both locally and globally. Multiple online platforms are providing marketplaces for goods, services and information, delivered both physically and digitally. Many such platforms have emerged over the past 20 years and are run by fast-growing companies. A comparison between the top 15 Internet-based companies by market capitalisation in 1995 with those in 2017 shows that the main players used to be Internet service providers, media and hardware or software companies, whereas today most of them are online platforms (Table 5.1). The majority of these platforms either focus on matching demand and supply of information (e.g. search, social network) or provide e-commerce marketplaces (goods and/ or services) or e-payment solutions. Somewhat exceptions to the 2017 list are Apple and Salesforce, which are not exclusively platforms, although Apple operates iTunes and App Store, two successful platforms that did not exist in 1995.

Table 5.1. **Top 15 Internet market capitalisation leaders, 1995 and 2017**

1995 (December)	Main product or activity	Origin	USD billion	2017 (May)	Main product or activity	Origin	USD billion
Netscape	Software	USA	5.42	Apple	Hardware, software, services	USA	801
Apple	Hardware	USA	3.92	Google/Alphabet	Information, search, other	USA	680
Axel Springer	Media, publishing	DEU	2.32	Amazon.com	E-commerce, services, media	USA	476
RentPath	Media, rental	USA	1.56	Facebook	Information, social	USA	441
Web.com	Web services	USA	0.98	Tencent	Information, social, other	CHN	335
PSINet	Internet service provider	USA	0.74	Alibaba	E-commerce, e-payment, other	CHN	314
Netcom On-Line	Internet service provider	USA	0.40	Priceline Group	Online reservation services	USA	92
IAC/Interactive	Media	USA	0.33	Uber	Mobility services	USA	70
Copart	Vehicle auctions	USA	0.33	Netflix	Media	USA	70
Wavo Corporation	Media	USA	0.20	Baidu China	Information, search, other	CHN	66
iStar Internet	Internet service provider	CAN	0.17	Salesforce	Services	USA	65
Firefox Communications	Internet service provider, software	USA	0.16	Paypal	E-payment	USA	61
Storage Computer Corp.	Data storage software	USA	0.10	Ant Financial	E-payment	CHN	60
Live Microsystems	Hardware and software	USA	0.09	JD.com	E-commerce	CHN	58
iLive	Media	USA	0.06	Didi Kuaidi	Mobility services	CHN	50
TOTAL			**17**				**3 639**

Sources: Author's calculations based on KPCB (2015), "Internet trends 2015", *www.kpcb.com/blog/2015-internet-trends* and Kleiner Perkins (2017), "Internet trends 2017", *www.kpcb.com/internet-trends*.

The high valuations and spectacular increase in the value of the companies listed in Table 5.1 can be explained by several factors, some of which are specific to online platforms. One reason is that many of these platforms have mainly digital products and can "scale without mass" (Brynjolfsson et al., 2008). Compared to firms that produce physical products with high fixed costs and marginal costs that decline with scale, firms selling digital products tend to have comparatively few tangible assets, such as buildings and employees, and low marginal costs. Furthermore, in contrast to traditional firms, the valuation of platforms does not only depend on sales and profit margins, but can significantly depend on the valuation of their user networks (individuals or firms) and the data generated by their users. In many cases platforms are multi-sided markets with often more than two networks. If a platform has amassed networks of a critical size, it can furthermore benefit from network effects, which can protect the platform and add to its value. For example, customers may stay with the large network of an established platform rather than switching to a competitor with smaller networks that would be unlikely to match the quality of service, the choice or the price of the larger platform.

Online platforms can affect entire markets by lowering transaction costs and by enabling new types of transactions. With his essays *The Nature of the Firm* (1937) and *The Problem of Social Cost* (1960), Ronald Coase was among the first economists who discussed the costs of market transactions, which he saw as one of the main reasons for firms to exist. The term "transaction costs" commonly refers to different types of costs occurring in markets, in addition to the production price of a good or service, notably the cost of: 1) finding reliable information on the desired product; 2) bargaining the price and contract; and 3) monitoring and enforcing transactions. By bundling complementary assets and activities, firms "supersede the price mechanism" of markets and create value (Coase, 1937). While firms therewith create firm-market boundaries, platforms can lower transaction costs in markets without (re-)creating firm-market boundaries and possibly contribute to dissolving the latter. Where a firm "rather makes than buys" when information and input prices are uncertain, platforms facilitate buying rather than making by providing more information, e.g. on price, products and providers, than was available in traditional markets. In their supply-side markets, platforms facilitate the entry of both firm and non-firm actors, including non-professional individuals or peers (Figure 5.7).

Figure 5.7. **Online platform markets**

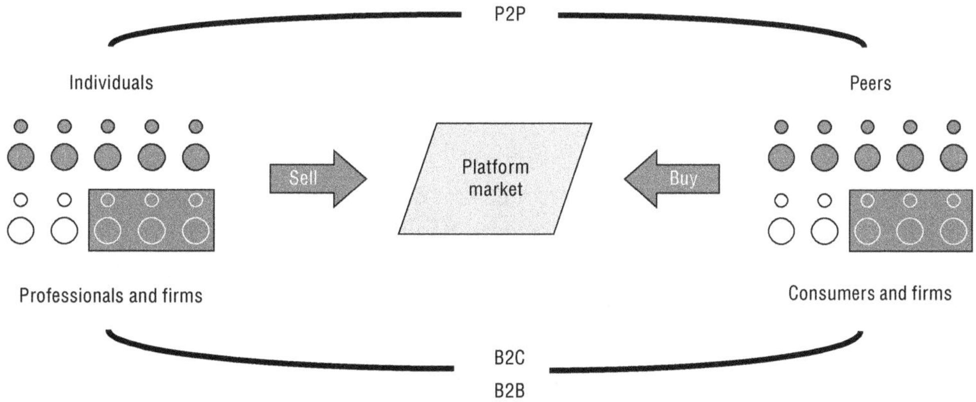

Note: P2P = peer-to-peer; B2C = business-to-consumer; B2B = business-to-business.
Source: OECD (2016c), "New forms of work in the digital economy", *http://dx.doi.org/10.1787/5jlwnklt820x-en.*
StatLink *http://dx.doi.org/10.1787/888933586122*

The uptake of online platforms has been fast but is not yet measured well in many cases. For some platforms the number of unique monthly visitors can indicate their uptake. For example, in early 2017, Google.com had over 6 billion monthly unique visitors, followed by Facebook.com with over 2 billion. The uptake of platforms that emerged more recently such as Uber and Airbnb was measured in a 2016 survey for European countries, where on average 15% of individuals had used an online platform for "collaborative economy" services (Figure 5.8). Younger, more educated users from small, medium or large towns were more likely to have used such platforms (31% versus 17% for all European countries). The two most frequently mentioned benefits of services delivered over such platforms, compared to traditional commerce, are the convenient access to and the cheaper price or free availability of such services. The two most frequently mentioned problems of such services, compared to traditional commerce, are that users often do not know who is responsible if a problem arises and that they may not trust Internet transactions more generally (Eurobarometer, 2016).

Figure 5.8. **Use of online platforms for "collaborative" economy services, 2016**

Share of individuals aged 15 and above

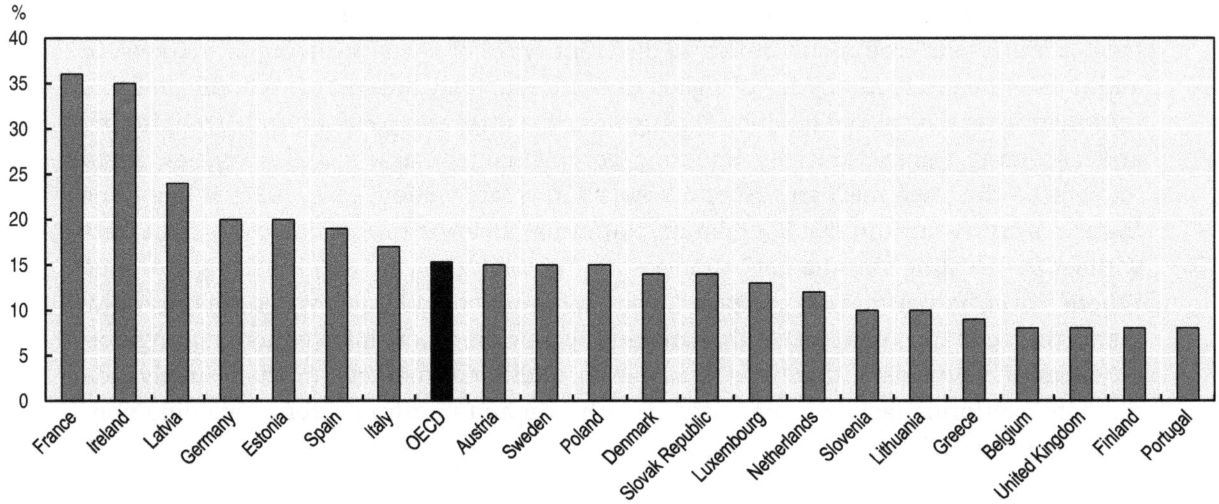

Note: The aggregate OECD only covers selected OECD European countries.

Source: Eurobarometer (2016), "Flash Eurobarometer 438: The use of collaborative platforms", *https://data.europa.eu/euodp/fr/data/dataset/S2112_438_ENG* (accessed 13 April 2017).

StatLink http://dx.doi.org/10.1787/888933586141

Expanding digital applications and services

Digital innovation enables applications in many sectors, a selection of which is discussed in this section, focusing on science, healthcare, agriculture, governments and cities. In science, research is affected by the increasing amounts of data being collected and analysed and the diffusion of results by digital tools that shape open access publishing or enable new modes of peer review. Increasing use of mobile health applications and of electronic health records creates new opportunities for health by providing the foundation for higher functionalities that promise greater care co-ordination and improved clinical management. Even in agriculture, digital technologies enable, for example, precision farming and automation, which has the potential to profoundly affect traditional models. Also, governments are going digital by promoting e-government services to individuals and firms, by opening up PSI, and by communicating directly to citizens via social networks like Twitter. Not least, cities are seizing the benefits of digital applications, for example in transport, energy, water and waste systems, and are exploring the potential of DDI to improve their own operations and decision making.

Digital technologies are shaping the development of open science

Publically funded science generated the essential foundations for the digital revolution that is affecting all sectors of society and the economy today. For example, scientific research played a key role in the creation of the Internet and the worldwide web. Ongoing research in universities and public research institutions across the world in areas such as quantum computing, biological storage of digital data and human-computer interactions, will undoubtedly lead to new technological innovations with significant socio-economic impacts. Paradoxically, the practice of science itself is now also being radically altered by the digitalisation process that it triggered. This presents both exciting new opportunities and challenges.

Digitalisation fundamentally affects how science is conducted and results are disseminated

ICTs – new data storage infrastructure, broadband Internet, high-speed computing and analytical software tools – are radically modifying the way science is conducted and the way the results of research are disseminated. A new paradigm of "open science" is emerging. This can encompass open access to scientific data, open access to scientific journals and greater engagement of civil society, including industry. In parallel, the availability and scale of data that are available for, and produced by, science has massively increased as has our ability to interrogate and analyse that data. Big data and data-driven research are now ubiquitous across all scientific disciplines and are opening up exciting new possibilities and the ability to link data from different sources and fields is providing new insights into complex global societal challenges. When coupled with AI, this potential is magnified even further.

In addition to enabling new scientific discoveries, there are a number of reasons why "open science" is being actively promoted in most OECD countries (OECD, 2015b). The traditional scientific journal publishing model and the rising costs of journal subscriptions can limit access to the outputs of publically funded scientific research. Open access publishing, which takes advantage of the very low costs of information dissemination on line, presents an attractive alternative. There have also been concerns about the rigour and reproducibility of published scientific results that can be at least partially addressed by ensuring open access on line to the underlying research data. Increased access to scientific information and data can make the research system more effective and efficient by reducing duplication; by allowing the same data to generate more research; and by multiplying opportunities for domestic and global participation in the research process. Open access to scientific results and data should increase the knowledge spillovers from public research and promote innovation. It can also play an important role in promoting citizens' engagement and trust in science, making research more transparent and accountable and promoting citizen science.

Science is an important producer and user of big and open data

As in other areas of society and the economy, science is being dramatically altered by the online availability of new forms of data and big data. Indeed, it is fair to say that areas such as particle physics, astronomy, space science and genomics have driven the development of technologies and software to share and analyse large amounts of data. These scientific fields are still at the frontier in terms of big data generation and analysis. The Square Kilometre Array telescope, which is currently being built in South Africa and Australia, is expected to generate the data equivalent of twice the current total daily global Internet traffic when it comes on line in 2024. All areas of science are now being transformed by digitalisation and the increased availability of new forms of data and new analytical tools. For example, data from online transactions have the potential to transform social sciences and our understanding of human behaviours. Linking data from satellites with ground-based sensor data and environmental, behavioural and economic data is providing new insights into the complex societal challenges that are encapsulated in the global Sustainable Development Goals.

An essential pre-condition for making the most of the opportunities of this data revolution in science is that the data be findable, accessible, interoperable and reproducible. While the costs of data storage have decreased dramatically, the process of properly curating data and ensuring its long-term availability and usability is expensive and requires high-level expertise. New business models and new partnerships between different public and private actors need to be developed to support data repositories and associated services. A sustainable data infrastructure for science needs to be established at multiple scales, from local to global.

Perhaps the greatest potential for advancing research and society is in linking data from different areas. However, achieving interoperability is a major challenge because of technical, legal, ethical and social barriers. In particular, sharing and using personal data for scientific research raises a number of important issues related to the balance between individual privacy and societal benefits. While privacy and other aspects can legitimately prevent personal data from being freely shared, methods like anonymisation may be used in some cases to make personal data suitable for research.

The digitalisation of science requires scientists with new skills

The speed of change due to digitalisation raises important issues in relation to scientific skills. All scientists, in all disciplines, including social sciences and humanities, now need to be able to function effectively in a digital world. Although ICTs will not (at least for the foreseeable future) replace the dependence of science on individual creativity and invention, they will certainly supplement it. The future of research lies in effectively combining human and technological capacities. This will require new training and skills, from generic ICT skills to ICT specialist skills for advanced software development and data analytics. Big data will require the development and widespread adoption of new mathematical modelling and statistical approaches. Individual scientists, research teams and institutions will all have to acquire new capacities to function effectively in the digital world. There is considerable uncertainty as to how much these needs are already being addressed by the introduction of digital skills into the general education and training curricula and the development of specialised data science programmes.[6]

It is also unclear how much of the growing need for data curation and stewardship can be met by the evolution of traditional professions such as academic librarians or whether it will require a new cadre of data scientists who can work at the interface between science and data. What is clear is that the traditional discipline-based academic research workforce, with its associated career paths and reward systems, is entering a period of upheaval. This encompasses not only the need for new technical skills but also, and perhaps even more importantly, the need for "softer" brokering and team-working skills, which are not readily accommodated in many traditional academic settings (in contrast to industry).

Digital tools shape open access publishing and enable new modes of peer reviews

Many OECD countries are now mandating open access to scientific publications, which is viewed as a fundamental pillar of open science. Open access to science publications has been discussed extensively in OECD (2015b). In summary, there are currently two main approaches for publishers to providing access to science publications openly and free of charge at the point of delivery on line: the "green" route, which involves delaying open access for an initial period during which subscription-only access is provided; and the "gold" route, in which immediate open access is provided and the costs of publication are covered by mechanisms other than subscription. Hybrid models are also being tested and all of these different approaches have their advantages and inconveniences as well as their proponents and opponents. In addition, in some fields of science, pre-print deposition of articles and/or self-archiving of published articles by authors on open access servers are enabling more open access to scientific information.

Publication in scientific journals normally depends on prior approval by scientific peers. This peer review is often criticised for being too biased, too conservative or too unaccountable. The publication of a number of high-profile fraudulent publications has called into question the effectiveness of peer review as a "gatekeeper" for the dissemination of sound scientific findings. Digitalisation is opening up new possibilities for addressing some of the perceived weaknesses in current peer review processes. The use of pre-prints servers has become the norm in physics and mathematics and is spreading to other areas of science, allowing open online review of articles before they are submitted for publication. Other methods for open peer review, either prior to or following publication, are also being tested. In addition, digital publication enables supporting materials, including experimental data, to be made accessible alongside scientific articles, which can increase the transparency and reproducibility of the scientific process.

Despite the potential advantages and overall cost savings relative to traditional publishing practices, there is an urgent need for sustainable business models for new open access publishing and knowledge dissemination mechanisms. The whole area of the dissemination of scientific information is rapidly evolving and the role of formal peer-reviewed scientific publications is only one part of this dynamic landscape that increasingly encompasses the use of social media. It is essential, as new models and new actors find their places, that the long-term stewardship of the (past and future) scientific record is ensured.

Online platforms play an important role for scientific research

Digital tools, from individual electronic identifiers to electronic notebooks and online search tools, have rapidly infiltrated all steps in the scientific process, from research design through dissemination. Using "off-the-shelf" tools, it is increasingly easy to link and map the inputs and outputs of research to individuals and institutions. Digital tools are transforming not only the way scientific research is conducted, but also the way it is managed and assessed.

Many of these online tools are being integrated into digital platforms that provide value-added services on top of a mix of proprietary (e.g. bibliometric) and public (e.g. project grant information) data resources. Scientific research is increasingly dependent on these platforms, which are operated by a small number of private companies. For the time being, this appears to be working effectively, but in the longer term there are concerns that these companies may develop effective monopolies, which might interfere with the dynamics of science. It is important to ensure that the partnership between public and private actors in developing and using scientific tools and platforms is beneficial to both parties and ensures the public good properties of openness and accessibility of scientific knowledge.

Further developments in digital and open science depend on trust

The third main pillar of open science – in addition to open data and open access publications – is the open engagement of societal actors, including industry, in the scientific enterprise. Again, this encompasses all stages in the scientific process, from selecting research priorities to citizen science and knowledge transfer, and ICTs have enabled new and exciting opportunities for engagement across all these stages.

A critical pre-condition for an effective relationship between science and other sectors of civil society is trust. The digitalisation of science has the potential to both strengthen and undermine trust in science. There is huge potential to exploit new sources of online data and information to improve urban development, healthcare systems, agriculture and food systems, resource use and many other areas of societal need. However, much of these data concerns individuals. Therefore, new ethical frameworks and governance systems will be required to ensure an appropriate balance between individual privacy and societal benefit (OECD, 2016d). Trust in science will also depend on the integrity of the scientific enterprise – as science becomes more open and rapidly disseminated via social media, the distinction between good and bad science can easily become blurred. More than ever before the rigour of science will be under the spotlight. In particular, the quality assurance and (increasingly automated) analysis of big and complex data, including the development and use of new algorithms and mathematical models, will need to be done with vigilance and transparency.

Healthcare is evolving with the use of electronic health records and mobile health applications

Health sectors across countries are undergoing a profound transformation as they capitalise on the opportunities provided by ICTs. Key objectives shaping this transformation process include improved efficiency, productivity and quality of care. There is also growing evidence that ICTs are essential to improve access to health services, particularly in rural and remote areas where healthcare resources and expertise are often scarce or even non-existent, and to support the development of new, innovative models of care delivery (OECD and IDB, 2016).

The electronic health record provides the foundation for more complex functionalities that promise greater care co-ordination and improved clinical management

A 2016 OECD survey of 30 OECD countries revealed that most countries are investing in the development of electronic health records (EHRs) (OECD, 2017b). Twenty-three countries reported that they are implementing a national-level EHR system. Eighteen reported comprehensive record-sharing within one "countrywide" system designed to support each patient having only one EHR. A few countries have one national EHR system, but within it some key aspects of record-sharing are subnational only, such as within provinces, states, regions or networks of healthcare organisations (Austria, Canada, Spain, Sweden and Switzerland). Among them, all but Canada have implemented or are implementing a national information exchange that enables key elements to be shared nationwide. Seven countries indicated that they are not aiming to implement a national-level EHR system at this time (Chile, Croatia, the Czech Republic, Denmark, Japan, Mexico and the United States). Croatia and Denmark report aspects of record-sharing that are comprehensive at the national level. In the other countries, sharing arrangements differ among healthcare organisations or regions.

There is robust evidence today to demonstrate that the introduction of EHRs can contribute in particular to the reduction of medication errors and better co-ordination of care. The implementation process is, however, a notoriously complex and expensive undertaking. Countries that are investing in developing their health information systems encounter numerous technical and financial challenges. Only a few countries have so far been able to achieve high-level integration and to capitalise on the possibility of data extraction from EHRs for research, statistics and other secondary uses. Healthcare systems still tend to capture data in silos and analyse them separately. Standards and interoperability are key challenges that must be addressed to realise the full potential of EHRs.

With an increasing number of individuals using smartphones and mobile devices, mobile health is by far the fastest growing segment of ICT-based healthcare delivery systems

Mobile technologies offer a wide range of smart modalities by which patients can interact with health professionals or systems. These technologies provide helpful real-time feedback along the care continuum, from prevention to diagnosis, treatment and monitoring. Since m-health services have low marginal costs and high availability, they have the potential to reach large numbers of patients between in-person clinical encounters. Low- and middle-income countries have perhaps the greatest potential to extend access to healthcare by using m-health to integrate rural and remote areas into the health system. Countries such as Ghana, Kenya, South Africa and Tanzania have successfully integrated the use of mobile phones as support mechanisms in community-based healthcare systems (Columbia University, 2011).

In 2015, the World Health Organization surveyed over 125 countries on e-health and m-health activities at the national level. Over 80% of these countries reported government-sponsored m-health programmes. M-health projects primarily extended existing health programmes and services at the national or local level (Figure 5.9).

Figure 5.9. **Adoption of m-health programmes by type, 2015**

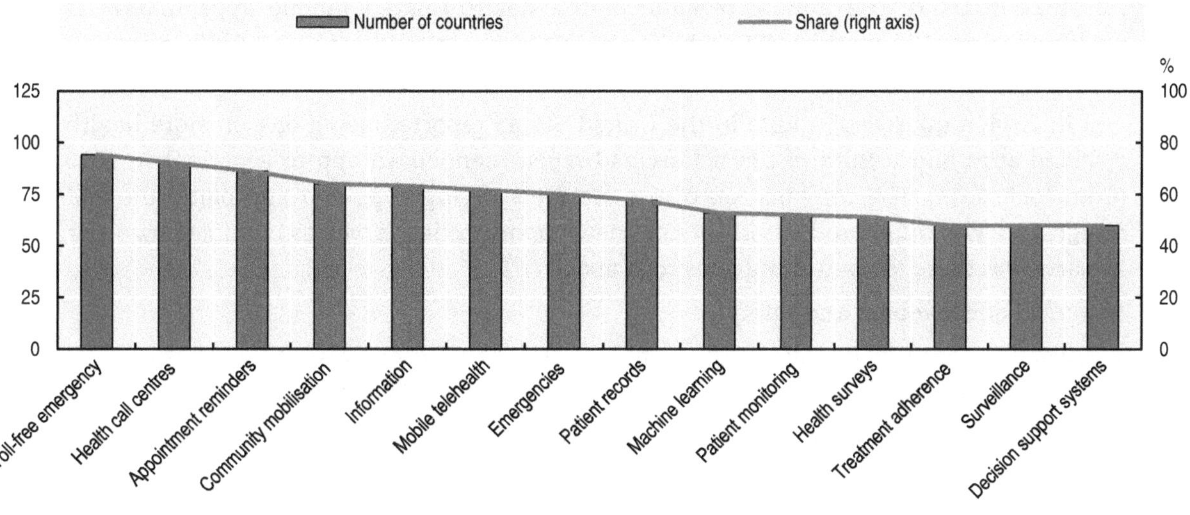

Note: The results include responses from over 600 e-health experts in 125 countries worldwide.

Source: WHO (2016), *Atlas of eHealth Country Profiles: The Use of eHealth in Support of Universal Health Coverage: Based on the Findings of the Third Global Survey on eHealth 2015*, *http://apps.who.int/iris/bitstream/10665/204523/1/9789241565219_eng.pdf?ua=1* (accessed 12 April 2017).

StatLink http://dx.doi.org/10.1787/888933586160

M-health is widely recognised as especially valuable for the management of non-communicable diseases such as diabetes and cardiac disease and other health conditions where continuous interaction is imperative. M-health services can also help address physical, sensory and cognitive impairments of older populations to allow continued aging in place and avoid hospital admissions.

The rapid proliferation of m-health pilots and the growth of health and wellness "apps" have emerged as significant challenges for policy makers

M-health is at a critical juncture in its evolution. First, many m-health projects and pilots were not designed to scale and were instead intended to demonstrate proof of concept. This has led to issues with fragmentation in financing, short-term partnerships and lack of integration into formal health systems. Early efforts saw many trials funded by operators, governments, non-governmental organisations and other interested bodies.

Second, health and wellness apps, unless classified as medical devices, are today largely unregulated, creating concerns about their safety and effectiveness. In addition, to function, health and wellness apps may require a vast trove of personal data, raising privacy and security concerns. Thus, although in many countries, like the United States, consumer protection laws would apply to protect consumers from deceptive or unfair practices related to health apps, data governance and associated m-health policies are currently high on the policy agenda of countries deciding how best to leverage m-health for improved health. A number of emerging initiatives aim to fill the evaluation gap. For example, medical app accreditation programmes, in which apps are subject to formal assessment or peer review, are a recent development that aims to provide clinical assurances about quality and safety, foster trust, and promote app adoption by patients and professionals. Voluntary codes of conduct or codes of practice are also being developed to promote private sector awareness and good practice.

In 2013, the Boston Consulting Group reported 500 m-health projects and in 2015 the number of patients using m-health applications was estimated at approximately 500 million globally. According to one estimate, more than 165 000 m-health apps (Apple and Android) were available in 2015, a figure that had doubled since 2013 (IMS Institute for Healthcare Informatics, 2015). The annual revenue of the health-related mobile apps market is projected to reach more than USD 26 billion by 2017 from its value of USD 2.4 billion in 2013 (research2guidance, 2014).

In 2014, a quarter of adults in the United States reported using one or more health tracking apps and a third of physicians had recommended an app to a patient in 2013 (Comstock, 2014). The combination of the rapidly evolving apps and app platforms and integration with other products introduces new opportunities as well as possible new risks. In particular there are persisting questions about:

- clinical effectiveness and safety
- privacy and security (many health and fitness apps have access to sensitive physiological data collected by sensors on a mobile phone, wearable or other device)
- the high rate of app turnover (nearly 90% of apps are not used after six months; 80% are not generating revenue to support a business case).

Recent research also shows that while consumers have a wide choice of apps addressing a broad set of medical conditions, only a minority of these apps appear to address the needs of the patients who could benefit the most and to be clinically useful (Singh et al., 2016).

Digitalisation affects even traditional sectors such as agriculture

Industrial production is undergoing a transformation driven by the conjunction of the increasing interconnection of machines, inventories and goods delivered via the IoT; the capabilities of software embedded in machines; analysis of the large volumes of digital data ("big data") generated by sensors; and the ubiquitous availability of computing power via cloud computing. The resulting transformation, which has been described by some as "Industrie 4.0" (Jasperneite, 2012), is not limited to manufacturing, but has already deeply affected even more traditional sectors such as agriculture. For instance, farmers today already generate large volumes of digital data which companies such as John Deere and DuPont Pioneer can exploit through new data-driven software services (Noyes, 2014). For example, sensors in John Deere's latest equipment can help farmers manage their fleet, reduce tractor downtime and save resource consumption (Big Data Startups, 2013). It is estimated that "Industrie 4.0" could boost value added in German agriculture by an additional EUR 3 billion (1.17%) by 2025 (BITKOM and Fraunhofer, 2014).[7]

Precision agriculture has transformed farming thanks to big data analytics

Big data analytics has enabled precision agriculture, which provides productivity gains by optimising the use of agriculture-related resources. These include, but are not limited to, savings on seed, fertiliser and irrigation, as well as farmers' time (Box 5.1). Estimates of the productivity effect depend on the types of savings considered. One estimate, for instance, suggests that precision agriculture could improve corn yields in the United States by five to ten bushels per acre, increasing profit by around USD 100 per acre (at a time when gross revenue minus non-land costs stood at about USD 350 per acre) (Noyes, 2014). Extrapolating, one could estimate economic benefits for the United States from precision agriculture to be around USD 12 billion annually. This represents about 7% of the total value added of USD 177 billion contributed by farms to the United States' GDP.[8] Studies that exclude farmers' time savings estimate more modest benefits per acre from precision farming. Schimmelpfennig and Ebel (2016), for instance, estimated increased profits of USD 14.50 per acre. A similar study focused on the same sources of increased efficiency from precision agriculture for different size farms,[9] in particular on precision agriculture's "automatic row and section control, which uses GPS to prevent excess application of crop inputs, such as fertiliser and crop protection chemicals" (John Deere, 2015). Farmers' cost savings for the corn fields, similar to the large-row-crop farms evaluated above, were estimated to be between USD 1 and USD 15 per acre.

Box 5.1. **Precision agriculture with big data: The case of John Deere**

Precision agriculture provides farmers with near real-time analysis of key data about their fields. John Deere entered this business initially with yield mapping and simple variable rate controls, and later with automated guidance technology (AutoTrac[1]). Those early products have since been enhanced by creating automated farm vehicles that communicate with each other. From the beginning, John Deere built on Global Positioning System (GPS) location data. It then developed initial "wired" capabilities to connect farm machines to each other and to the MyJohnDeere Operations Center, which is described by the company as "a set of online tools that provides information about a farm, when and where farmers need it" (Arthur, 2016).

To support vehicles in the field, John Deere developed remote wireless management for farm equipment. It used interconnected satellite and cellular ground-based communications networks, proprietary radio and Wi-Fi. This helped the company reduce the time to harvest crops or complete other tasks. For example, its self-propelled, programmable vehicles could plant or harvest 500 to 600 acres per day when used in groups of two or more vehicles, rather than the usual 100 to 150 acres that a single farmer can do alone. One enhancement John Deere introduced for planting was to use its Exact-Emerge planter and AutoTrac to expand the number of acres that could be planted under optimal conditions. With the enhanced planter and tracking system, the number of acres planted could increase from 600 to more than 800 per day. For harvesting, operations would also be much more efficient if the vehicles used incorporated AutoTrac.

Box 5.1. **Precision agriculture with big data: The case of John Deere** *(cont.)*

Using a combination of sensors and GPS, Deere's tractors not only drive themselves, they also use analytic systems. These systems permit vehicles to plant, water and harvest with an accuracy of 2 centimetres. These systems can also communicate with each other. Deere has estimated that it has more than 100 000 connected machines around the world. Tractor cabs also offer Wi-Fi communication with mobile and other on-board sensor systems, as well as other radios for mobile communications with other vehicles. This helps farmers synchronise operations and share data with other farmers.

Using the interconnected devices and smart sensors in this communications network, John Deere combined basic and performance data from its machines with in-field, geo-referenced data to enhance data analytics. Once systems capture these combined data and send them to Deere's Operations Center, they are incorporated into a more extensive database that also includes environmental information. Deere can combine information from the farmer with data about the environmental conditions (including weather and climate data and data about the soil quality) as well as data about real yields. This helps farmers identify the sections of their land that are more productive. John Deere's use of data analytics helps farmers optimise crop yield, because "farmers can use the data to decide what and where each piece of equipment will plant, fertilize, spray and harvest [...] for an area as small as one by three meters" (Jahangir Mohammed, 2014).

In 2011, John Deere cemented its long-term strategy to focus on integrated data-driven products. The new focus also emphasised an increase in research and development (R&D) investments to 5.5% of net sales, compared to its competitors' R&D investments of 4% to 5%. The focus on innovation helped Deere continue the 5% compound annual growth rate for employee productivity (measured by sales per employee) achieved over the past 30 years (John Deere, 2016). To buttress its capabilities in this area, John Deere also acquired a number of companies that have pioneered precision agriculture, such as Precision Planting (Agweb, 2015), a leading planting technology firm that also supplies hardware and sensors, and Monosem, a French-based planter equipment manufacturer. John Deere is also hiring data scientists to improve its ability to analyse big data. These professionals will: 1) identify relevant data, sources and applications; 2) utilise big data mining techniques such as pattern detection, graph analysis and statistical analyses to "discover hidden insights";[2] 3) implement collection processes as well as develop infrastructure and frameworks to support analyses; and 4) use parallel computation languages to implement applications.

Substantial market growth is forecast for John Deere and similar firms offering farmers self-propelled vehicles and precision agriculture systems. Such forecasts predict that the global precision farming market will expand by USD 4.92 billion by 2020. This represents a compound annual growth rate of almost 12% between 2015 and 2020. At present, precision farming globally represents a USD 2.8 billion market (Mordor Intelligence, 2016). The US market accounts for roughly USD 1 billion to USD 1.2 billion of these sales annually. Using estimates for the large-row-crop farms, corn and soybean farms, where about two-thirds of acreage is subject to precision agriculture, it is conservatively estimated that John Deere's sales of precision agriculture are about one-quarter of the US market total, or USD 250 million to USD 350 million.[3]

1. AutoTrac Vision uses a front-mounted camera to see early-season corn, soybeans and cotton. It helps farmers avoid damaging crops with sprayer wheels even if a planter is misaligned (John Deere, 2017).

2. This description is from a job posting by John Deere for a data scientist, from: *https://www.glassdoor.com/Job/jobs.htm?suggestCount=0&suggestChosen=false&clickSource=searchBtn&typed*.

3. According to a market forecast, this market would include a number of technologies that are integrated together, essentially guidance systems, remote sensing and variable rate technologies. The largest would be guidance systems with a GPS, a geographic information system (GIS) and the Global Navigation Satellite System (GNSS). The market forecast finds that various monitoring and mapping systems would be more important and that software applications – that is, those applications for crop, farm and weather management – would grow faster during the forecast period (see Mordor Intelligence [2016]).

Source: OECD (2017a), *The Next Production Revolution: Implications for Governments and Business*, *http://dx.doi.org/10.1787/9789264271036-en*.

Agriculture could be highly automated soon with the few human workers being integrated in automated processes

Autonomous machines are already intensively used in agriculture in some countries. In cattle farming in the United States, for instance, machines milk cows, distribute food and clean stables without any human intervention. The milking robot from Lely, for instance, autonomously adjusts the feeding and milking process to optimise milk production for each cow. Some studies have therefore suggested that it is only a matter of time before humans are removed altogether from agricultural farming.

A scenario might ensue in which farm enterprises become local caretakers of land, animals and data. They might monitor operations that are centred at the lower end of the value chain, much like the current concept of contract farming.[10] Food producers, retailers or even end consumers could interact directly with the network around the farmer, including seed suppliers, smart (autonomous) machines, veterinarians, etc. In such a scenario, the job of the farmer would be more like a contractor making sure that the interactions between the supply and demand sides of the agricultural system work together properly. In an alternative scenario, farmers could become empowered by the data and intelligence provided by analytics, tailoring the processes to their knowledge of local and farm-specific idiosyncrasies.

As the IoT enables the integration of physical systems, it will also foster the integration of living systems – including plants, animals and humans – within physical systems.[11] Such integration may further empower humans: augmented reality-based applications, for instance, could provide farmers with real-time information to improve decision making and work procedures. For example, instructions could be displayed directly in farmers' field of sight using augmented reality glasses. And by using real-time information, farmers could organise shift scheduling. That said, as highlighted in OECD (2017a), there are also risks that such integration may lead to a dehumanisation of production, including in agriculture. In highly automated production processes, integration and interaction between humans and autonomous systems have already emerged, in particular for tasks for which human intelligence is still required and no cost-efficient algorithm exists, making human workers appear rather as servants than as users of IoT-enabled systems.

Obstacles to the reuse, sharing and linkage of data in agriculture remain

Obstacles to data reuse, sharing and linkage take various forms. These include technical barriers, such as constraints on the machine readability of data across platforms. Legal barriers can also prevent data reuse, sharing and linkage. For example, the "data hostage clauses" found in many terms of service agreements are an example of such legal barriers, in particular when this "provision may be used to extract additional fees from the customer or to prevent the customer from moving to another provider" (Becker, 2012).[12] The issue is exacerbated by challenges linked to the concept of data ownership. In contrast to other intangibles, data typically involve complex assignments of different rights across different stakeholders. Where data are considered personal, the concept of ownership is problematic, since most privacy regimes grant explicit control rights to the data subject preventing the restriction their personal data by the data controller (see for example OECD [2013b]: paragraph 13). But even in cases where data are considered non-personal, controversies over data governance have emerged, such as in the case of a recent dispute between major providers of precision farming technologies (including John Deere, DuPont Pioneer and Monsanto) and farmers (Box 5.2).

Box 5.2. **From data ownership controversies to data governance principles: The case of agriculture data**

Farming has become data-driven to such an extent that farmers' ability to access and use agricultural data has become a determinant for success and failure. Major providers of precision farming technologies (agriculture technology providers [ATPs]), such as John Deere, DuPont Pioneer and Monsanto, recognised this trend when they started taking advantage of the Internet of Things by integrating sensors in their latest equipment. By doing so they have been able to generate large volumes of data, which are considered an important data source for biotech companies that optimise genetically modified crops, as well as for crop insurance companies and traders on commodity markets.

The control of agricultural data by the major ATPs has led to controversial discussions on the potential harm to farmers from discrimination and financial exploitation. For farmers, the benefits of data-intensive equipment also became less clear, and there was a sense that farmers would "degrade" to become local caretakers of land, animals and equipment, and act only as contractors making sure that the interactions between the supply and demand sides of the agricultural system work together properly. The role of farmers was blurred even more by uncertainties about the question of data ownership (Banham, 2014).

In April 2014, major providers of precision farming technologies met with the American Farm Bureau Federation to discuss the future of the governance of agricultural data. The question of data ownership was central to this discussion. The result was the *Privacy and Security Principles for Farm Data*, signed by 37 organisations (as of 3 March 2016). The following "principles" were relevant for the discussion on data governance:

- **Ownership**: "We believe farmers own information generated on their farming operations. However, it is the responsibility of the farmer to agree upon data use and sharing with the other stakeholders with an economic interest, such as the tenant, landowner, cooperative, owner of the precision agriculture system hardware, and/or ATP, etc. The farmer contracting with the ATP is responsible for ensuring that only the data they own or have permission to use is included in the account with the ATP."
- **Collection, access and control**: "An ATP's collection, access and use of farm data should be granted only with the affirmative and explicit consent of the farmer. This will be by contract agreements, whether signed or digital."
- **Notice**: "Farmers must be notified that their data is being collected and about how the farm data will be disclosed and used. This notice must be provided in an easily located and readily accessible format."
- **Transparency and consistency**: "ATPs shall notify farmers about the purposes for which they collect and use farm data. They should provide information about how farmers can contact the ATP with any inquiries or complaints, the types of third parties to which they disclose the data and the choices the ATP offers for limiting its use and disclosure."
- **Portability**: "Within the context of the agreement and retention policy, farmers should be able to retrieve their data for storage or use in other systems, with the exception of the data that has been made anonymous or aggregated and is no longer specifically identifiable. Non-anonymised or non-aggregated data should be easy for farmers to receive their data back at their discretion."
- **Disclosure, use and sale limitation**: "An ATP will not sell and/or disclose non-aggregated farm data to a third party without first securing a legally binding commitment to be bound by the same terms and conditions as the ATP has with the farmer. Farmers must be notified if such a sale is going to take place and have the option to opt out or have their data removed prior to that sale. [...] If the agreement with the third party is not the same as the agreement with the ATP, farmers must be presented with the third party's terms for agreement or rejection."
- **Data retention and availability**: "Each ATP should provide for the removal, secure destruction and return of original farm data from the farmer's account upon the request of the farmer or after a pre-agreed period of time. The ATP should include a requirement that farmers have access to the data that an ATP holds during that data retention period. ATPs should document personally identifiable data retention and availability policies and disposal procedures, and specify requirements of data under policies and procedures."

Box 5.2. **From data ownership controversies to data governance principles: The case of agriculture data** *(cont.)*

- **Unlawful or anticompetitive activities:** "ATPs should not use the data for unlawful or anticompetitive activities, such as a prohibition on the use of farm data by the ATP to speculate in commodity markets."
- **Liability and security safeguards:** "The ATP should clearly define terms of liability. Farm data should be protected with reasonable security safeguards against risks such as loss or unauthorized access, destruction, use, modification or disclosure. Polices for notification and response in the event of a breach should be established."

Sources: Banham, R. (2014), "Who owns farmers' big data?", *www.forbes.com/sites/emc/2014/07/08/who-owns-farmers-big-data* (accessed 4 May 2017); American Farm Bureau Federation (n.d.), "Privacy and Security Principles for Farm Data", *www.fb.org/issues/technology/data-privacy/privacy-and-security-principles-for-farm-data* (accessed 21 June 2017).

Governments have identified digital opportunities, but can still make fuller use of them

Digital technologies offer important potential for the public sector to improve service delivery and to create value for individuals and businesses. In 2017, the objective to "strengthen e-government services" ranked as the highest priority among 15 policy objectives for digital economy and society developments (see Table 1.1 in Chapter 1). This focus resonates with the potential that is left in many countries to improve e-government service delivery, as can be seen, for example, in the uptake of e-government services by individuals (Figure 5.10) and in the provision of openly accessible government data (Figure 5.11). While the term e-government is still used in many countries, OECD countries committed in 2014 to move from narrowly focusing on "e-government" to developing a broader agenda for "digital government" (Box 5.3).

Box 5.3. **From e-government to digital government**

The 2014 OECD *Recommendation of the Council on Digital Government Strategies* refers to "e-government" as the use by governments of information and communication technologies, and particularly the Internet, as a tool to achieve better government, and to "digital government" as the use of digital technologies, as an integrated part of governments' modernisation strategies, to create public value. Digital governments rely on a digital government ecosystem comprised of government actors, non-governmental organisations, businesses, citizens' associations and individuals which supports the production of and access to data, services and content through interactions with the government.

Source: OECD (2014b), *Recommendation of the Council on Digital Government Strategies, www.oecd.org/gov/digital-government/Recommendation-digital-government-strategies.pdf.*

Despite some increase in the use of e-government services, there is room for improvement, especially among individuals

Individuals and businesses are key users of e-government services; despite some increase in the use of e-government services, there is room for improvement, especially among individuals. Chapter 4 (see Figure 4.15) shows that the use of e-government services by individuals in 2016 is quite unevenly developed across OECD countries, ranging from less than 25% of individuals using government websites in Chile, Italy and Mexico to more than 80% in Denmark, Iceland and Norway. While interactions with public authorities via the Internet increased between 2010 and 2016, the remaining gap of individuals that do not interact is still large (Figure 5.10). While the available data on businesses is less recent, it shows growing interactions with public authorities since 2010, with 95% of large firms and 88% of small ones having interacted with public authorities in 2013 (Figure 5.10).

Figure 5.10. **Use of e-government services by individuals and businesses in OECD countries**

As a percentage of individuals and businesses using the Internet to interact with public authorities

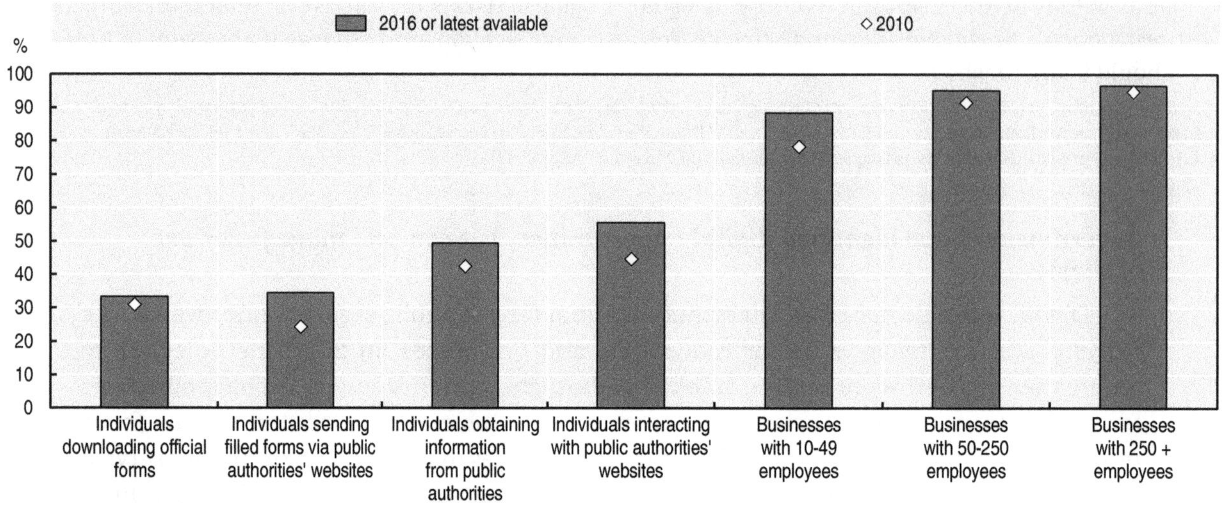

Note: The latest available data for businesses are from 2013.

Sources: OECD, *ICT Access and Usage by Businesses* (database), *http://oe.cd/bus*; OECD, *ICT Access and Usage by Households and Individuals* (database), *http://oe.cd/hhind* (both accessed June 2017).

StatLink *http://dx.doi.org/10.1787/888933586179*

The use of public sector information can benefit individuals, businesses and governments

The public sector is one of the economy's most data-intensive sectors. Its importance as an actor in the data ecosystem is twofold: as a user of data and analytics, and as a producer of data that can be reused for new or enhanced products and processes across the economy. Open access to and reuse of both PSI and of open government data (OGD), a sub-set of PSI, by users within and outside the public sector can generate value for individuals and drive innovation in businesses and governments (OECD, 2015c):

- **For individuals**, PSI and OGD can be of value to individuals, for example, when it enhances public accountability by promoting transparency and allowing more public scrutiny, as well as when it empowers individuals to take informed decisions. More generally, online participation of individuals can enhance citizens' engagement in public life and in policy-making processes, and thus increase the possibility for citizens to become active contributors to public policy.
- **For businesses**, granting businesses access to PSI and OGD can stimulate the development of new services, products and markets, which in some instances may also complement or improve public service delivery through services that are more agile and targeted to citizens' needs.
- **For governments**, the use of PSI can improve efficiency within the public sector. It can, for example, help bring down silos and foster collaboration across and within public agencies and departments and, if available in formats that enable reuse and linkage, can support data analytics in the public sector and improve decision making and monitoring.

A crucial condition for leveraging the potential of PSI for individuals, businesses and governments is to make public sector data available and accessible on line. Information collected through the OECD Survey on Open Government Data shows that the availability and accessibility of OGD in OECD countries differ significantly from the most advanced countries like Korea, France and Great Britain to countries with much more room for improvement, such as Turkey, Latvia and Sweden (Figure 5.11).

Figure 5.11. **Open government data availability and accessibility, 2017**

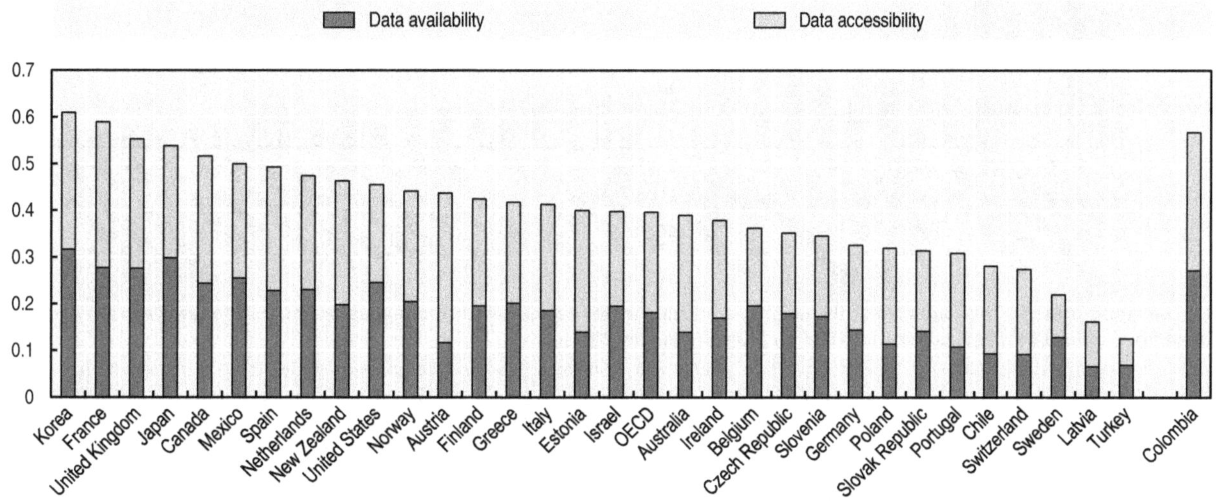

Notes: "Data availability" and "Data accessibility" are two out of three dimensions of the composite OECD OURdata index (1 = max), which also includes "Government support to the reuse" of data. "Data availability" aggregates information on the content of the open by default policy, stakeholder engagement for the prioritisation of data release, and the availability of strategic open government data (OGD) on national portals (e.g. national election results, national public expenditures or the most recent national census). "Data accessibility" aggregates information on the availability of formal requirements, and the implementation of these, in regard to the publication of OGD with an open licence, in open formats (e.g. non-proprietary) and accompanied with the descriptive metadata, as well as on stakeholder engagement for data quality. The data come from the OECD Survey on Open Government Data conducted in November and December 2016. Survey respondents were predominantly chief information officers in OECD countries. Responses represent countries' own assessments of current practices and procedures regarding OGD. Data refer only to central/federal governments and exclude OGD practices at the state/local levels.

Source: Author's calculations based on OECD (2017c), *Government at a Glance 2017*, *http://dx.doi.org/10.1787/gov_glance-2017-en*.

StatLink *http://dx.doi.org/10.1787/888933586198*

Social media is increasingly used by governments to communicate directly to citizens

Twitter has become a widely used tool by government officials to communicate directly to citizens. The increase in the use of Twitter by governments and the use of such communication by citizens has been remarkable over recent years. In 2014, 28 offices of executive OECD government institutions (head of state, head of government or government as a whole) were already active on Twitter (OECD, 2015c), and in 2016 all but one government, Hungary, had at least one active account. Over this period, the number of followers as a share of total population increased significantly in almost all countries (Figure 5.12). At the time of measurement in mid-2016, the President of the United States had the largest outreach, followed by 23% of the US population, with the President of Turkey and the Prime Minister of Israel ranking second and third, respectively. Not all account holders are equally active: the average frequency of tweets per account varies from over 12 per day (Ilves Tomas, Estonia) to less than 1 per week (Sauli Niinistö, Finland). Important differences also exist in the average number of retweets per tweet, ranging from 1 572 in the United States (Barack Obama) and 1 298 in Turkey (Recep Tayyip Erdoğan) to 1.3 in Portugal (República Portuguesa) and Slovenia (Vlada R. Slovenije).

Figure 5.12. **Most followed government officials on Twitter, 2017**

Followers as a percentage of total population

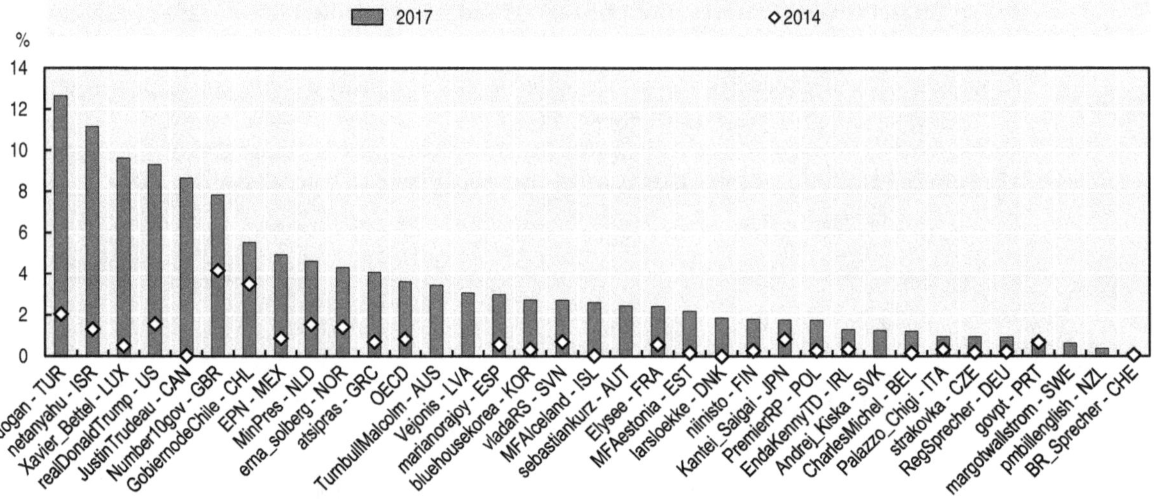

Note: The graph presents the followers of the country's official Twitter account with the highest number of followers in May 2017. No verified (true) official Twitter account was listed for Hungary in May 2017.

Sources: Burson-Marsteller (2017), "Twiplomacy study 2017", *http://twiplomacy.com/blog/twiplomacy-study-2017/* (accessed 22 June 2017); Burson-Marsteller (2014), "Twiplomacy study 2014", *http://twiplomacy.com/blog/twiplomacy-study-2014* (accessed 13 April 2017); UNDESA (2017), *World Population Prospects 2017*, *https://esa.un.org/unpd/wpp/Download/Standard/Population*.

StatLink http://dx.doi.org/10.1787/888933586217

Cities seize benefits of digital applications and explore the potential of data-driven innovation

Digital applications increase efficiency in urban sectors

Cities are making increasing use of digital applications, for example in their transport and electricity systems. Important effects of such applications are fuller capacity utilisation through improved matching of demand and supply. Whether via a mobile app that gives urban travellers the fastest connection from point A to point B, taking into account all available transport modes and traffic conditions, or via a smart electricity meter that informs households and businesses of real-time electricity prices based on current demand and supply in the grid, making demand and supply transparent in real time allows shaving peak demand by redistributing it in space (notably transport) and time (transport and electricity). This reduces congestion on roads and lowers base load requirements in electricity supply. In turn, people save time spent in transport and money on (and emissions from) electricity. Several other sectors, such as water and waste management, also benefit from digital applications (Box 5.4). In addition, the data collected by applications and sensors embedded in urban infrastructures can be used to further improve their functioning.

Beyond improving separate urban systems, synergies can be unleashed through deeper integration of systems across sectors. A city can be considered as a "system of systems", within which ICTs and digitised urban flows create the potential for deep system integration (CEPS, 2014). A good example of a single system that is becoming increasingly integrated with other urban systems through the use of ICTs and real-time information exchange is the electricity grid. Such "smart grids" not only enable demand- and supply-side management with smart meters, but have a wider potential to integrate the energy system with other urban systems such as transport. For example, a smart grid can integrate electric vehicles as energy storage and supply to help shave peak load electricity demand and to balance out fluctuating supply of renewable energy sources, unleashing efficiencies that could not be reached within either of the systems separately (OECD, 2012a; Heinen et al., 2011). Even more comprehensive integration occurs with increasingly pervasive machine-to-machine communication via the IoT that can help to break through many more boundaries of segmented activities, flows and systems within cities and beyond.

Box 5.4. **Efficiency potential of digital applications in urban sectors**

Smart electricity grids are expected to yield energy savings for homes and businesses, in particular if combined with home and business energy management systems. Through the use of smart meters, European households are expected to save 10% of their energy consumption per year (e-control, 2011). In the United States, the savings from smart grids are estimated to be 4.5 times the needed investment of USD 400 billion (EPRI, 2011).

Data-driven innovation in transport systems can save people time and money and reduce pollution and emissions in cities. The Intelligent Traffic System of London is expected to reduce congestion in London by around 8% annually between 2014 and 2018 (TfL, 2011). Open data use in transport, such as for apps providing real-time information on multimodal trips, prices and traffic conditions, is estimated to generate value worth USD 720 billion to USD 920 billion per year (McKinsey Global Institute, 2013). Congestion charging in Stockholm reduced traffic by 22% (100 000 passengers per day) and CO_2 emissions by 14% (25 000 tonnes annually) in central Stockholm, during its seven-month trial period (KTH, 2010).

Sharing cars and rides can reduce resource consumption and change mobility patterns of cities. The International Transport Forum estimated, for a scenario that combines high-capacity public transport with self-driving "TaxiBots" (self-driving shared vehicles), that only 10% of cars would be needed to serve existing mobility needs (ITF, 2014). Free-floating car-sharing systems alone are expected to generate annual revenues of EUR 1.4 billion in OECD cities with more than 500 000 inhabitants by 2020 (Civity, 2014).

Digital improvements in water systems can reduce water losses and cut operations and maintenance costs. "Smart water solutions" are estimated to save water utilities globally USD 7.1 billion to USD 12.5 billion per year through smarter leakage and pressure management techniques in water networks, smarter water quality monitoring, smarter network operations and maintenance, and data analytics in capital expenditure management (Sensus, 2012 in UK Department for Business Innovation and Skills, 2013).

Comprehensive and data-enabled strategies for waste reduction, recycling, material reuse and waste-to-energy conversion can save money and emissions. New York state's "Beyond Waste" strategy is estimated to save as much energy as is consumed by 2.6 million homes each year (280 trillion British thermal units) and to reduce New York's greenhouse gas emissions by around 20 million metric tonnes annually (New York Department of Environmental Conservation, 2014).

Sources: e-control (2011), "Next steps for smart grids: Europe's future electricity system will save money and energy", *www.e-control.at/documents/20903/-/-/633895a3-d5d0-4866-865c-26b785bd1d0d*; EPRI (2011), "Estimating the costs and benefits of the smart grid", *https://www.smartgrid.gov/files/Estimating_Costs_Benefits_Smart_Grid_Preliminary_Estimate_In_201103.pdf*; TfL (2011), "London's intelligent traffic system", *www.impacts.org/euroconference/barcelona2011/Presentations/11_Keith_Gardner_presentation_Barcelona_v2.pdf*; McKinsey Global Institute (2013), "Big data: The next frontier for innovation, competition and productivity", *www.mckinsey.com/business-functions/digital-mckinsey/our-insights/big-data-the-next-frontier-for-innovation*; KTH (2010), "Congestion charges which save lives", *www.kth.se/en/forskning/sarskilda-forskningssatsningar/sra/trenop/trangselskatten-som-raddar-liv-1.51816* (accessed 4 November 2014); ITF (2014), "Urban mobility: System upgrade", *www.itf-oecd.org/sites/default/files/docs/15cpb_self-drivingcars.pdf*; Civity (2014), "Urban mobility in transition?"; UK Department for Business Innovation and Skills (2013), "The smart city market: Opportunities for the UK", *https://www.gov.uk/government/uploads/system/uploads/attachment_data/file/249423/bis-13-1217-smart-city-market-opportunties-uk.pdf*; New York Department of Environmental Conservation (2014), "Climate smart waste management", *www.dec.ny.gov/energy/57186.html* (accessed 4 November 2014).

Cities are turning into hubs for data-driven innovation

The increasing production and collection of data can turn cities into large-scale experimental testbeds for DDI. In contrast to many product and process innovations, large-scale system innovations, such as in transport or energy, require experimentation and testing at scale, ideally in real-life settings. Aiming to seize the opportunity of providing such settings, cities have started to define themselves as "living labs", such as the 340 European cities that are part of the European Network of Living Labs. This network defines urban living labs through four key elements: co-creation by users and producers; exploration of emerging usages, behaviours and market opportunities; experimentation with implementing live scenarios within a community of lead users; and evaluation of concepts, products and services (Schaffers et al., 2011; ENoLL, 2014). Many urban living labs focus on creating a favourable environment for DDI by providing the necessary infrastructure and institutional setting to support and attract innovators and investment. The private sector has also discovered cities as ideal environments for DDI. Startupbootcamp Accelerator programmes established in several European cities focus on DDI in mobile, near field communication, health and e-commerce; and IT companies like Microsoft have established their own incubators in cities like London, New York and Tel Aviv (Startupbootcamp, 2014; Microsoft Ventures, 2017). Beyond technical and institutional infrastructure, access to data is a key condition for fostering DDI in cities (Box 5.5).

Box 5.5. **City open data portal**

Over the past several years, many cities in OECD countries have launched an open data portal, notably in the United States and Europe. A City Open Data Census provides metadata on cities in the United States that open up data sets such as on crime, budget, construction permits, zoning, transit, etc. (Open Knowledge Foundation, 2017). The European Data Portal harvests the metadata of public data made available across Europe, including around 90 000 datasets from regions and cities (European Data Portal, 2017).

In most cases cities publish structured (linked) data in machine-readable formats to facilitate commercial and private use; however, for the moment fewer cities offer application programming interfaces. In the absence of standards for open data portals, many cities are using open-source data portal platforms or software such as CKAN or Socrata.

Sources: Open Knowledge Foundation (2017), "US City Open Data Census", *http://us-city.census.okfn.org* (accessed 20 June 2017); European Data Portal (2017), "Datasets", *www.europeandataportal.eu/data/dataset?groups=regions-and-cities* (accessed 20 June 2017); Open Cities (2013), "WP4 – Open data", *http://opencities.net/node/68* (accessed 19 September 2014).

Opening access to data can be challenging for different reasons. For example, sensitive questions need to be addressed regarding the type of data cities should collect in the first place and what they should publish thereafter. Regulatory frameworks, interests and values can influence the decision of whether or not to collect and publish specific data (Kitchin, 2014). Certain uses of data can furthermore be restricted based on data protection rules or administrative protocols. Another challenge is data management, which necessitates an adequate organisational and legal framework for data collection, storage, processing and publishing, as well as the needed technical infrastructure and human capacity and skills.

Decisions at city level are increasingly supported by big data and data analytics

City administrations increasingly use crowdsourced and online data on urban conditions and activities in cities to become more effective. Mobile apps like SeeClickFix allow citizens to report on stray garbage, potholes, broken lamps and the like via their smartphone directly to city hall; apps like StreetBump in Boston automatically report on street conditions via the driver's smartphone; and apps like Cycle Track inform transport planners on bicycle mobility patterns. Such data can be used by city governments to target maintenance and investments and to improve services. Combined with online data, such as from social media, crowdsourced information is increasingly used by city police departments for predictive data analytics and anticipatory decision making. For example, police departments in Los Angeles, Chicago, Memphis, Philadelphia and Rotterdam are developing analytic capacity of large data sets to support predictive policing. One aim is to identify potential future crime hotspots and deploy resources there to prevent crime from happening rather than to intervene after the fact. It should be noted that neither the effectiveness nor the privacy implications of such practices have been thoroughly evaluated to date.

Subnational governments are also experimenting with digital technologies to improve policy design and effectiveness. For example, based on sufficient information, volumetric tariffs can be applied for energy or water billing and have proven to be effective in reducing resource consumption in households (OECD, 2012b). An experiment on reducing energy consumption in Swiss municipalities found that social network incentives were up to four times more effective than traditional incentive schemes: instead of financially rewarding or punishing individuals for their actions (directly), the implemented social network incentives rewarded the friends of those who acted (Pentland, 2014). While such "nudging" of people's behaviours can have positive effects on the one hand, it is under scrutiny on the other for the risk it can pose to the values of those who are being nudged (Frischmann, 2014).

More data and greater computing power also bring urban modelling back into the spotlight of urban planning, with the potential to improve resource allocation in urban areas. Urban modelling emerged over 50 years ago, but its imperfections – notably due to limited data and processing power – restricted its success at that time. Its resurgence came with the emergence of geographical information systems in the 1990s and 2000s, along with a shift from modelling aggregate equilibrium systems to complex, evolving system of systems and urban dynamics (Eunoia, 2012; Jin and Wegener, 2013). Today, new potential arises for urban modelling through a wide variety of data, from geo-referenced and crowdsourced or remote-sensed data to data from social networking, smart transit ticketing, mobile phones and credit card transactions. Thanks to greater processing power, including via cloud computing, big data can be used for complex modelling, for example in integrated land-use and transport planning (Serras et al., 2014). Data-intensive urban modelling and simulations are the subject both of theoretical exploration, such as in the European Eunoia project, as well as real decision making, such as in the LakeSim project in Chicago, which has made extensive use of computational modelling to understand the impacts of different design, engineering and zoning solutions (UCCD, 2012).

Digital transformation of jobs and trade

This section examines how digitalisation affects jobs across sectors as well as the organisation of work in several service markets. It finds that ICT investment has led to job losses in some sectors while it has created jobs in others. For most countries, an increase in labour demand can be found in culture, recreation and other services, construction and, to a lesser extent, government, and personal and health care, energy and agriculture. A decrease in labour demand occurred in manufacturing, business services and trade, transport and accommodation. At the same time, a growing number of individuals are working in accommodation, transport or other services via online platforms, with a tendency to carry out flexible, temporary and part-time work in these jobs.

The second part of this section discusses how the digital transformation is reshaping the trade landscape, particularly for services. It finds that manufacturing exports depend to varying degrees on ICT goods and services and that economies with a high share of manufactured ICT value added in manufacturing exports do not necessarily embed a high share of ICT services value added in exports, and vice versa. It further finds that efficient services, and especially ICT services, help boost productivity, trade and competitiveness across the economy, but also that trade-related restrictions, including on telecommunications and computer services, are pervasive in some countries.

Digitalisation has transformative effects on jobs across sectors and markets

ICT investment has led to job losses in some sectors while leading to job creation in others

There is broad recognition that the digital economy has a great potential to enhance productivity, incomes and social well-being. At the same time, there is growing concern that successive waves of investments in digital technologies have contributed to job losses, wage stagnation and increasing wage inequality.

Looking back, it is important to note that major technological innovations have always been accompanied by extensive transformations in the labour market. By increasing labour productivity, innovation enables the production of more goods and services with less labour, thus leading to the possibility of technological unemployment in certain sectors or occupations. At the same time, innovation creates new employment opportunities in different industries and in newly created markets.

While new technologies make some jobs redundant, they also raise the demand for others (Autor, 2015). Economic history provides plenty of such examples. In the 1920s, passenger cars displaced equestrian transportation and related occupations but the roadside motel and fast food industries rose up to serve the "motoring public" (Jackson, 1993). The diffusion of automatic teller machines resulted in higher employment in the banking sector by lowering operating costs in branches and freeing up time for clerks, who could provide a wider range of more complex services to their costumers (Bessen, 2015). Higher income generated in high-tech industries may also result in higher demand and employment in low-tech services, e.g. restaurants, cleaning and other personal services (Mazzolari and Ragusa, 2013; Moretti, 2012).

Figure 5.13 shows the estimated effects of ICT investment on labour demand over the period 1995-2012. ICTs raised labour demand in most OECD countries from the mid-1990s until 2007 but have generally resulted in a decrease in labour demand thereafter. As investment has slowed down following the 2007 crisis, the labour substitution effects from past ICT investments have more than offset the increase in labour demand driven by new ICT investments.

In most countries, the sectors where labour demand has benefited the most from digitalisation were culture, recreation and other services, construction and, to a lesser extent, government, and personal and health care, energy and agriculture. In all other sectors, digitalisation led to a decrease in labour demand, particularly in manufacturing, business services and trade, transport and accommodation (OECD, 2016e).

Figure 5.13. **Estimated employment growth due to growth in ICT capital**

Average yearly rates

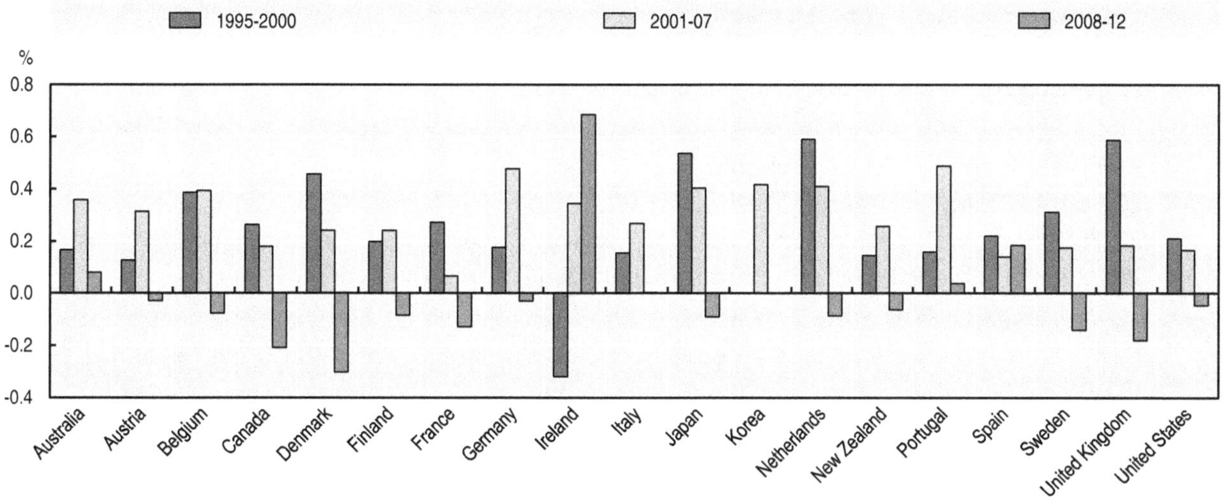

Source: OECD (2016e), "ICTs and jobs: Complements or substitutes?", *http://dx.doi.org/10.1787/5jlwnklzplhg-en.*

StatLink *http://dx.doi.org/10.1787/888933586236*

Against these findings, several studies suggest that the pervasive ongoing developments in AI and big data make it possible that, in the near future, a large proportion of jobs currently carried out by workers could be performed by machines (Frey and Osborne, 2013; Elliot, 2014). According to some scenarios (ITF, 2017) over 2 million drivers across the United States and Europe could be directly displaced with driverless trucks by 2030. Recent OECD work (Arntz, Gregory and Zierahn, 2016) points to a more limited impact of automation on jobs. Also Marcolin, Miroudot and Squicciarini (2016) show that boosting the ICT intensity of industries means more employment in most but not all occupations: routine-intensive jobs – i.e. jobs featuring sequential tasks that are easy to codify – get displaced when ICT intensity increases. To what extent these technological possibilities will ultimately result in job displacement depends not only on technology, but also on consumers' preferences and other market factors. For instance, most functions of bank clerks can be already performed by ICTs today but many people still prefer negotiating a loan with a human being than with an algorithm. Yet, a new wave of labour-saving ICT innovations is expected to diffuse across OECD economies and societies in the coming years (OECD, 2017a).

How disruptive technological developments will be for labour markets is a matter of current debate. Some argue that digital technologies have a stronger labour-saving bias than other major technologies in the past so that "digital labour … is substituting for human labour" on an unprecedented scale (Brynjolfsson and McAfee, 2011). Others (Gordon, 2012; OECD, 2015d) observe that productivity has been growing less rapidly over the last 10 to 15 years than in the 1960s, which was a boom period for employment, and forecast slow productivity growth in the future (Gordon, 2016).

Digital technologies also tend to substitute for workers in carrying out simple cognitive and manual activities following explicit rules ("routine" tasks), while computers complement workers in carrying out problem-solving and complex communication activities ("non-routine" tasks). Non-routine tasks can either be associated with conceptual jobs at the top end of the wage distribution, e.g. managerial and professional positions, or manual jobs at the bottom end of the distribution, e.g. housekeepers. Workers that perform manual or cognitive tasks that lend themselves to automation or codification (e.g. book-keeping, monitoring processes, processing information) are, in turn, concentrated in the middle of the wage distribution. Provided that routine and non-routine tasks are imperfect substitutes, the diffusion of digital technologies increases the demand for jobs with non-routine tasks at the expense of jobs with routine tasks (Autor, 2013).

A number of studies find evidence that job polarisation in the United States and in Europe is accounted for by declining demand for routine tasks (Autor, Katz and Kearney, 2006; Autor, Katz and Kearney, 2008; Goos et al., 2011; Van Reenen, 2011; Autor and Dorn, 2013; Hynninen, Ojala and Pehkonen, 2013) but only one of them (Michaels, Natrajz and Van Reenen, 2014) establishes a direct link between ICT use and demand for skills.

OECD analysis finds evidence that ICTs have contributed to rising inequality, but have – thus far – not produced an upward trend in unemployment. OECD (2016e) shows that in periods where labour demand decreased due to ICTs, the decrease was stronger for medium-skilled workers than for high- and low-skilled ones. This finding is consistent with the job polarisation argument – ICTs raise the demand for high and low skills and reduce the demand for medium skills – but also implies that polarisation is only temporary.

Although its effects on polarisation remain unclear, there is broad recognition that the shift from routine to non-routine tasks is likely to remain a long-run feature of labour demand in the digital economy. OECD analysis also shows that, as increasing use of digital technologies is reshaping business models and firms' organisation, complementary skills – such as information processing, self-direction, problem solving and communication – become more important (OECD, 2016f).

New forms of work are emerging in services traded over online platforms

Online platforms have grown exponentially in several service markets over the past decade, notably in markets where services can be provided by individuals. This includes services that are delivered physically and often locally, such as accommodation, transportation, handyman or personal services, as well as services that are delivered digitally, and mostly over the Internet, ranging from data entry and administrative support to graphic design and coding to legal and business consulting (OECD, 2016c). Most of these services can be provided individually and thus create work and income opportunities for both private and professional individuals.

The fastest growing online platforms in recent years can be found in markets for accommodation and mobility services. One explanation for this growth is an abundance of private assets that individuals can monetise with the support of digital technologies. For example, space that can be used to provide accommodation: the average OECD four-person household lives in almost 7 rooms, with an average of 2.5 rooms per person in Canada at the top of the list (OECD, 2015e). The numbers of hosts on Airbnb and nights hosted have grown exponentially over the past several years (Figure 5.14). Another example is cars: the second biggest item of German household expenditures after homes and food is transport, including cars (13%), while cars typically stand idle for 23 hours per day (DESTATIS, 2015; ITF, 2014). Point-to-point transportation like Uber and ride-sharing platforms like BlaBlaCar have expanded their markets and grown strongly in recent years. A second explanation of surging demand for such services is price. Individuals providing services with private assets, and without having to comply with heavy regulation in many cases, are likely to price their service lower than comparable traditional service providers, such as hotels or taxis.

Figure 5.14. **Airbnb hosts and nights hosted in the United States and major European markets**

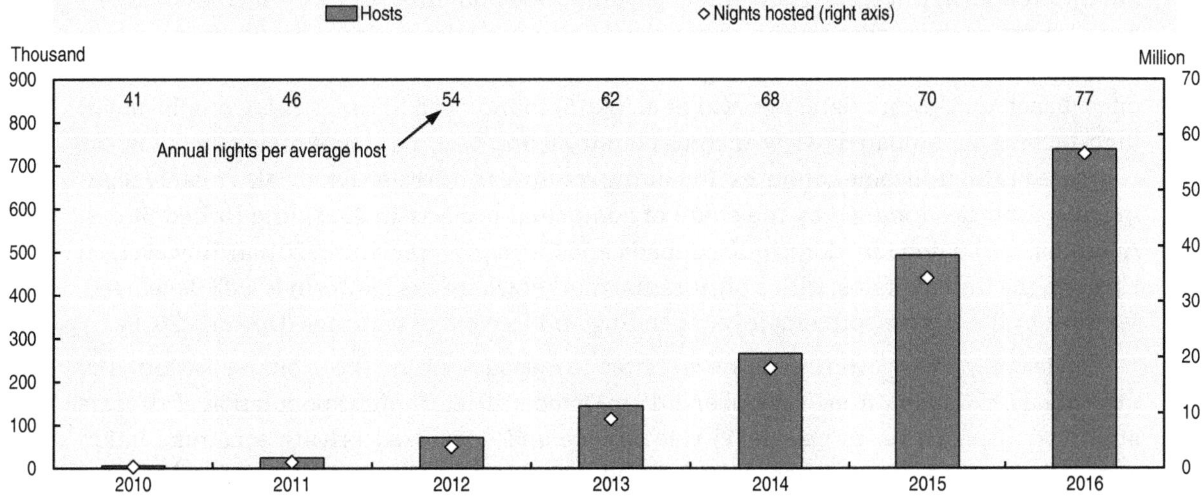

Notes: European markets include: Germany, Italy, Spain and the United Kingdom. The number of hosts shown in this figures are "hosts who hosted".

Source: Airbnb (2017), "Airbnb data for OECD study".

StatLink http://dx.doi.org/10.1787/888933586255

Online platforms have also grown in markets where services can be delivered digitally. Among the biggest of such platforms are Upwork and Freelancer, which match demand and supply of a large range of mainly professional services, from data entry and administrative support to translation and design, to coding, legal advice, and business consulting. Combined, both platforms had an estimated 49 million registered users in 2016 (Figure 5.15). By the end of 2016, Freelancer had registered a total of 10.2 million jobs posted with a value of USD 3 billion, since its inception in 2000 (Freelancer, 2017).

Figure 5.15. **Registered users on Upwork and Freelancer**

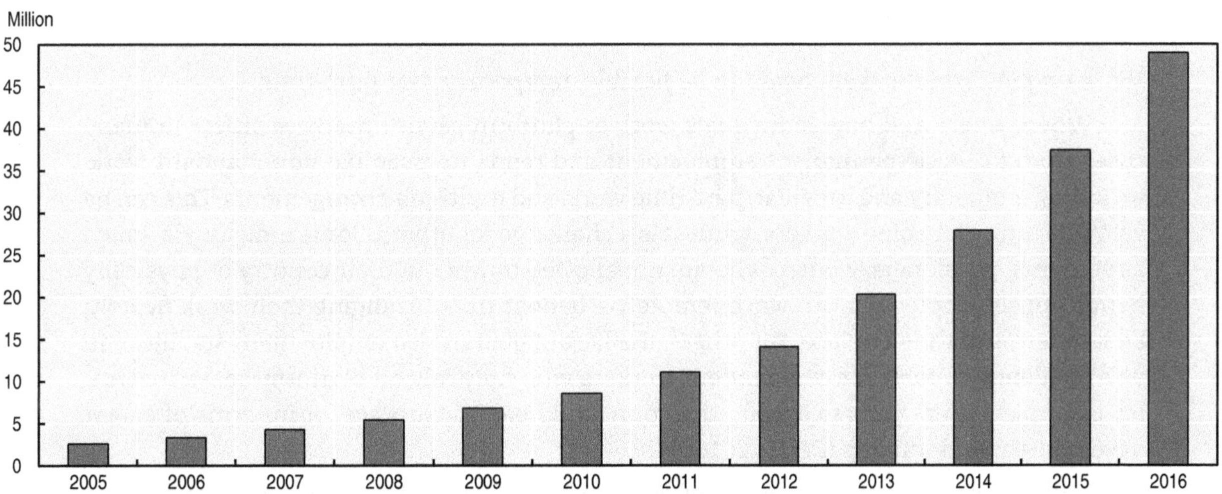

Notes: Includes extrapolated figures for Upwork based on most recent annual growth rates. Registered number of users for the two platforms combined.

Sources: OECD estimates based on data from Upwork (2015), "Online work report 2014", *http://elance-odesk.com/online-work-report-global* (accessed 3 November 2015) and Freelancer (2017), "2016 annual report".

StatLink http://dx.doi.org/10.1787/888933586274

Participants in these platform markets can buy and sell, in principle from any location, but differences in price, currency, language, time zone and other factors – such as culture – can also act as incentives to hire domestically over a platform. Cross-border trade shows a clear bias towards buyers from high-income countries and providers from low-income ones. Based on Upwork data, Agrawal et al. (2015) found over 10 times more employers in high-income as compared to low-income countries, and 4.5 times more providers in low- as compared to high-income countries. Top hiring countries on Freelancer are also mainly high-income countries (ordered by the share of completed projects in 2015): the United States, Australia, the United Kingdom, India, Canada and Germany (Freelancer, 2016a). However, on Upwork, the United States, with a big internal market where the platform is well developed, features at the top for both employer spending and freelancer earnings (Upwork, 2015).

So far, only a few governments have started to measure the uptake of online platforms by individuals. In Canada, from November 2015 to October 2016, 7% of the population of 18 years and older used a peer-to-peer (P2P) ride service and 4.2% used private accommodation services. Over the same period, 0.3% offered P2P ride services and 0.2% offered private accommodation services (Statistics Canada, 2017). In Denmark, 3.3% of the population 16 years and older used the Internet as a private person to rent out a room, their apartment, house or cottage via their own webpage or via an online platform such as Airbnb within the past year; 10% purchased such an accommodation within Denmark and 21% purchased such accommodation abroad. Carpooling or car-sharing services were used by 6% of the population in Denmark and by 2% abroad (Statistics Denmark, 2015).

Some additional insights can be drawn from private studies, although differing methodologies limit their comparability. For example, 72% of adults in the United States are found to have used at least 1 of 11 different "shared and on-demand services", and workers who provided services over online platforms, such as Uber or Task Rabbit, accounted for 0.5% of all US workers in 2015 (Smith, 2016; Katz and Krueger, 2016). In Europe, 17% of individuals have used "collaborative platform" services at least once, and among this group of users 32% also provided services (5% in total) (Eurobarometer, 2016). In Sweden and the United Kingdom, 12% and 11% of adults respectively say they have worked via a "sharing economy" platform (Eurobarometer, 2016; Uni Europa, 2016; Huws and Joyce, 2016).

Work on platform markets tends to be flexible, temporary and part-time

When, where and how individuals work in platform service markets differs in many cases from full-time permanent employment and tends to resemble non-standard work, including temporary and irregular, part-time work, and multi-job arrangements. This can be an opportunity for some workers, while it is a challenge for others. Some individuals – such as students, pensioners, women who are not allowed to work in their country or physically handicapped people who can work remotely – benefit from arranging their work flexibly, be it in terms of time or place. For others, the lack of guaranteed employment stability can be a challenge, notably for independent workers who fully rely on platform-based income, for example with regards to social protection, and health insurance, or in terms of career development and training (OECD, 2016c).

The flexible and irregular nature of platform-based work is apparent in most markets for which data are available. For example, in 2016, in major Airbnb markets, average hosts provided 72 nights on average and the average length of stay was 4 nights, which indicates that such accommodation is likely to be provided discontinuously. In the same year, the annual earnings of a typical host in major Airbnb markets amounted to USD 3 400 on average, which is likely to complement other income sources (Airbnb, 2017). On Uber, drivers in the United States and Australia work an average of 20 and 19 hours respectively per week (Hall and Krueger, 2015; Deloitte, 2016). Uber drivers in France and in the United Kingdom have a higher weekly average of 27 hours (Uber, 2016a, 2016b; Landier, Szomoru and Thesmar, 2016; Ifop, 2016). The average job value of services delivered via Freelancer is USD 156, indicating small units of service provision and thus likely discontinuous work as well (Freelancer, 2016b).

Consequently, many workers in platform markets are part-timers or multi-jobbers. For example, in the United States, independent contractors – the status of most professional Uber drivers for example – work to either top up income from a regular job (25%), to run a side business (25%), to contract seasonally (20%), e.g. in construction, or to invest (8%) (Bloomberg, 2015; 38% of the survey sample were college students); and between 79% and 83% of on-demand work in the United States is found to be carried out part-time (Intuit, 2015; MBO, 2015). While in Australia and the United States Uber drivers tend to work part-time, in France only 11% have another part-time job next to being a driver, and 8% drive with Uber in addition to a full-time job (Ifop, 2016). In the United Kingdom, only 24% of "crowd workers" are found to earn more than half and 5% all of their income via online platforms (RFS, 2015; Huws and Joyce, 2016).

For the United States, income patterns can be further differentiated based on a study from a large US bank that analysed the data of about 6 million clients (JPMorgan Chase & Co. Institute, 2016). Distinguishing between labour platforms (e.g. Uber) and capital platforms (e.g. Airbnb), the study finds that average earnings from platform-based activities in a given month represented a significant share of an individual's total income in that month (Table 5.2), and that such earnings tend to either offset dips in non-platform income (true in particular for labour-intensive services) or otherwise supplement non-platform income (true in particular for capital-intensive services). The likelihood of labour platform-based earnings to substitute for non-platform income is furthermore supported by the finding that such earnings are higher when non-platform income is lower.

Table 5.2. **Participation and revenue in platform markets in the United States**

	Labour platforms	Capital platforms
Share of months with earnings from platforms[1]	56%	32%
Average monthly earnings from platforms[2]	USD 533	USD 314
Platform earnings as a share of total income[2]	33%	20%
Traditionally employed individuals before platform career	77%	75%
Traditionally employed individuals during platform career	66%	61%
Platform market participants using multiple platforms[3]	14%	1%

1. Subsequent to a higher activity rate in the first four months of participation in the platform.
2. In the months when individuals were actively participating in a platform.
3. As of September 2015. The study is based on data from 260 000 individuals with revenues from activities in at least one of 30 distinct platforms out of a sample of 6 million clients that had an active checking account (at least 5 outflows per month) between October 2012 and September 2015.
Source: JPMorgan Chase&Co. Institute (2016), "Paychecks, paydays, and the online platform economy", *www.jpmorganchase.com/corporate/institute/document/jpmc-institute-volatility-2-report.pdf*.

The same study furthermore finds that individuals who enter platform markets are less likely to be employed traditionally, but not necessarily reliant on platforms over time. Table 5.2 shows that fewer individuals were employed in traditional jobs after having entered a platform market as compared to before entering the platform market. However, once individuals are active on a platform, they do not seem to increase their reliance on platform-based revenues: both the frequency of such revenues and their share in individuals' total income are found to stay stable over time (the 36 months observed in the study).

Digital transformation is reshaping the trade landscape, particularly for services

Progressive multilateral trade opening and the subsequent emergence of global value chains have prompted major structural changes in the world economy. Global value chains, spurred by greater openness to trade and dramatic reductions in ICT costs, have created new avenues for rapid technological upgrading, knowledge sharing and skills development. They have also facilitated specialisation, increasing the availability and variety of intermediate goods and services at lower prices. OECD work has highlighted the important role of imports in accelerating domestic productivity growth and improving the export competitiveness of firms. Import barriers can deny firms access to the goods and services they need to compete internationally (OECD, 2016g).

Digital technologies and the free flow of data have contributed to trade growth by reducing trade costs and enabling firms to fragment production across countries through global value chains. This has increased participation in international trade, especially in sectors that have traditionally been considered non-tradable, and by smaller firms. Better access to digital technologies, including the Internet and mobile telecommunications, can help the process of internationalisation, and enables some firms to be "born global". The Internet dramatically reduces the cost of finding buyers, both globally and domestically, and reduces the cost of entry into international markets. The digital transformation can enable firms, and especially SMEs that often find it difficult to enter international markets, to outsource costly activities to more efficient external partners abroad. Technology-enabled firms, including SMEs, are therefore more likely to export, to export to more destinations and to thrive in the marketplace.

Digital technologies and the Internet have a significant impact on services trade. Increasingly, services trade takes the form of data and information being sent across borders, such as cloud computing services offered to customers in another country. Such digitised services can potentially be transmitted at almost no cost to any location with Internet access and will require policy makers to consider the impact of limitations to cross-border data flows.

Moreover, digital technologies have enabled "servicification", implying that the economy is increasingly relying on services. Part of this is reflected in manufacturing trade, where services are gaining importance as inputs, for example when firms use specialised transport and communication services to co-ordinate global value chains or when knowledge-intensive services are used to enhance the production process. Importantly, manufacturing firms are also increasingly bundling services with their core corporate offerings to provide additional value to customers ("servitisation"). A notable example is John Deere, providing farmers with near real-time analysis of key data about their fields through integrated farm equipment (see Box 5.1). These trends are contributing to the increase in trade in goods and services, but servitisation has also raised questions about which commitments apply under World Trade Organization trade rules, which are clearly divided into goods trade (covered by the General Agreement on Tariffs and Trade [GATT]) and services trade (covered by the General Agreement on Trade in Services [GATS]).

In this fast-evolving environment, policy makers are increasingly considering how to ensure that the opportunities of the digital transformation can be realised and shared inclusively. Trade practitioners are therefore trying to understand how the digital transformation is reshaping international trade. At the same time, and in part due to the evolving nature of the digital transformation, a unique definition of the term "digital trade" has not been agreed upon. In this context, the OECD is currently working on a framework for analysing "digital trade" that can help focus research, guide efforts to improve the measurement of trade in a digital world, and will allow better identification of policy implications (OECD, forthcoming). While it will be some time until robust measures are developed, some existing statistics can shed light on particular aspects of trade in the digital era.

Manufacturing exports depend to varying degrees on ICT goods and services

Measures of trade in ICT goods and services can show the contribution of the ICT sector to the production of manufactured goods. According to the OECD *Trade in Value-Added* (TiVA) database, the ICT sector (goods and services) accounted for 6.7% of total value added embedded in manufacturing exports from OECD economies in 2011.[13] The share is slightly higher (6.9%) when including a range of OECD partner economies.[14] The ICT content of exports shows large variation across economies, ranging from 22.5% in Costa Rica and over 12% in Singapore, Japan, among others, to less than 3% in New Zealand and Chile. Of the total ICT value added in OECD economies' manufacturing exports, about two-thirds are accounted for by manufactured ICT goods, comprised of computers, electronic or optical equipment (4.4% of total value added). ICT services, including post, telecommunications, computer or related business services, jointly accounted for the remaining 2.3%. Looking only at OECD partner economies, the relative importance of ICT goods is higher still, accounting for 5.8% of the 7.5% ICT value added embedded in exports.

Economies that have a high share of manufactured ICT value added in manufacturing exports do not necessarily embed a high share of ICT services value added in exports, and vice versa (Figure 5.16).[15] Among the economies covered, those with the highest ICT manufacturing content in exports are Costa Rica (20.4%), Singapore (12.7%), Korea and Japan (both at 11.2%). New Zealand and Chile have the lowest content of ICT manufacturing value added in exports, accounting for 0.3% and 0.4% respectively. The economies with the highest ICT service content in exports are Denmark (3.9%). The Russian Federation and Turkey (both 1.1%) have the lowest share in ICT services value added. Overall, the difference between economies is less pronounced for embedded ICT services than it is for ICT goods.

Figure 5.16 further decomposes the ICT value added content by origin. Overall, OECD and the included OECD partner economies source about two-thirds (one-third) of the ICT value added content in exports domestically (from abroad). The economies with the highest domestic ICT value added in exports, often reflecting large domestic markets, are Japan (90% of total ICT value added embedded in exports) and the United States (88%). Mexico (35%) and Hungary (39%) have a relatively low share of domestic ICT value added in exports, reflecting a relatively higher share of imported ICT content from abroad.[16]

ICT and other services are essential, but restrictions are pervasive in some countries

Services trade has assumed increased importance in the global policy debate. According to the OECD TiVA database, services represent almost half of world exports in value-added terms. Transport, logistics, finance, communications, and other business and professional services are essential to trading goods across borders and co-ordinating global value chains.

Figure 5.16. **ICT goods and services in manufacturing exports**

By economy or region of value-added origin, 2011

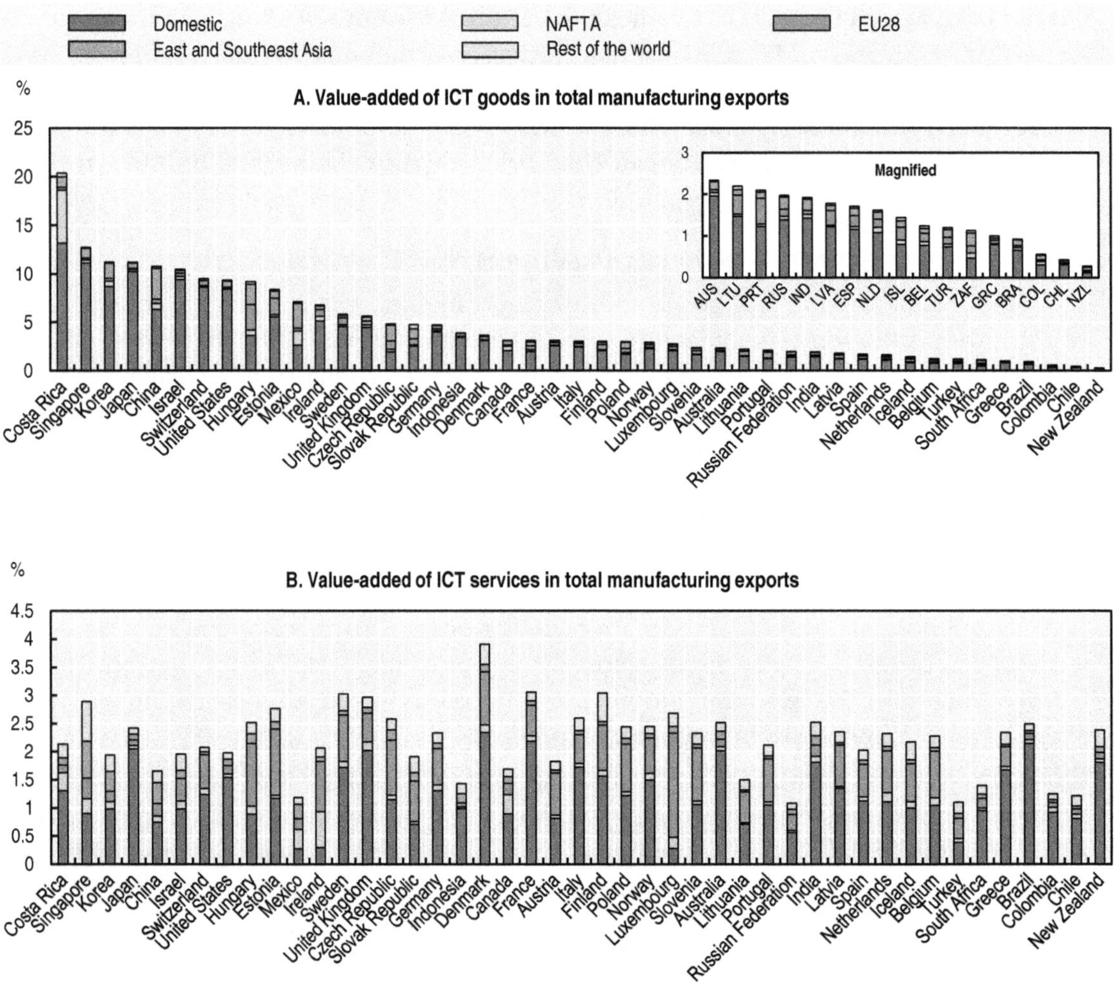

Notes: Panel A: NAFTA = North American Free Trade Agreement. ICT goods are approximated by ISIC Rev.3 Divisions 30, 32 and 33. East and Southeast Asia comprises Brunei Darussalam; Cambodia; the People's Republic of China ("China" in the figure); Hong Kong, China; Japan; Korea; Indonesia; Malaysia; the Philippines; Singapore; Chinese Taipei; Thailand; and Viet Nam.

Panel B: NAFTA = North American Free Trade Agreement. ICT services are approximated by ISIC Rev.3 Divisions 64 and 72. East and Southeast Asia comprises Brunei Darussalam; Cambodia; the People's Republic of China ("China" in the figure); Hong Kong, China; Indonesia; Japan; Korea; Malaysia; the Philippines; Singapore; Chinese Taipei; Thailand; and Viet Nam.

Source: OECD, "Origin of value added in gross exports (by source economy and industry)", Trade in Value-Added (TiVA) (database), *http://oe.cd/tiva* (accessed March 2017).

StatLink *http://dx.doi.org/10.1787/888933586293*

Efficient services, and especially ICT services, also help boost productivity, trade and competitiveness across the economy, in both manufacturing and services. Research shows that trade-related restrictions on telecommunication and computer services, among others, have a negative effect on trade in manufactured goods (Nordås and Rouzet, 2015). Moreover, more Internet connections are associated with more exports of branded goods at higher prices in several manufacturing sectors, most notably electronics. Estimates suggest that an increase in telecoms density of 10% is associated with 2% to 4% higher export prices in the electronics sector, and an increase in intra-industry trade in the sector by 7% to 9%, depending on the initial density (OECD, 2014c).

The OECD Services Trade Restrictiveness Index (STRI) covers various services sectors that are highly relevant to trade in an increasingly digital world, such as telecommunication and computer services, as well as sectors that form part of the supply chains underpinning such trade, such as financial services, distribution and logistics services.[17] The STRI in telecommunication services (Figure 5.17, Panel A) shows that restrictions on foreign entry and barriers to competition remain predominant across economies. Some of the common restrictions include limitations on foreign ownership, government ownership of major suppliers, screening of foreign investment, and nationality or residency requirements for directors and managers.

Since the telecommunications industry is a capital-intensive network industry, access to essential facilities and switching costs may favour incumbent firms. These market imperfections may constitute a substantial entry barrier, even in the absence of explicit foreign entry restrictions. Therefore, pro-competitive regulation is considered a trade policy issue in telecommunications, which is addressed in the World Trade Organization's Telecommunications Services Reference Paper as well as in a number of regional trade agreements. Lack of pro-competitive regulation is scored as a trade-restricting barrier to competition in cases where an incumbent operator has significant market power.

The STRI also facilitates the monitoring of policy developments over time. Compared to the results from 2014, a number of economies have introduced important policy reforms. Mexico, for instance, eliminated foreign equity restrictions and introduced pro-competitive *ex ante* regulation.[18] Analysis suggests a strong relationship between the services trade restrictions in the telecommunication sector and the density of telecommunications network. By implication, more open telecommunications markets result in more competitive manufacturing (Nordås and Rouzet, 2015; OECD, 2014c).

With respect to computer services (Figure 5.17, Panel B), the most common trade restrictions are those that apply across the economy and affect the establishment of computer services firms in the host economy (for instance, restrictions on legal forms, residency requirements for directors and screening of investments). While computer services can easily be traded across borders, operations are often supported by on-site visits to the premises of the customer both through business travel for technical support as well as longer visits to work with the clients on tailoring software designs or providing trainings. Restrictions on the movement of people contribute considerably to the STRI scores, accounting for almost 35% of the total scores in this sector. Eight economies in the STRI impose quotas on one or more of the three categories of persons covered (intra-corporate transferees, contractual services suppliers and independent services suppliers), whereas 37 economies apply economic needs test to stays that last longer than 3 to 6 months. The duration of stay is also limited to less than 3 years in 34 countries.

Over the period 2014-16, 13 economies reduced their score (less restrictive) and 9 recorded higher scores (more restrictive). The changes are largely explained by reforms that apply across the economy. Improvements in administrative procedures explain most of the reduction in the scores, whereas increases are largely due to tighter conditions on movement of people.

Figure 5.17. **OECD Services Trade Restrictiveness Index, 2016**

1 = most restrictive

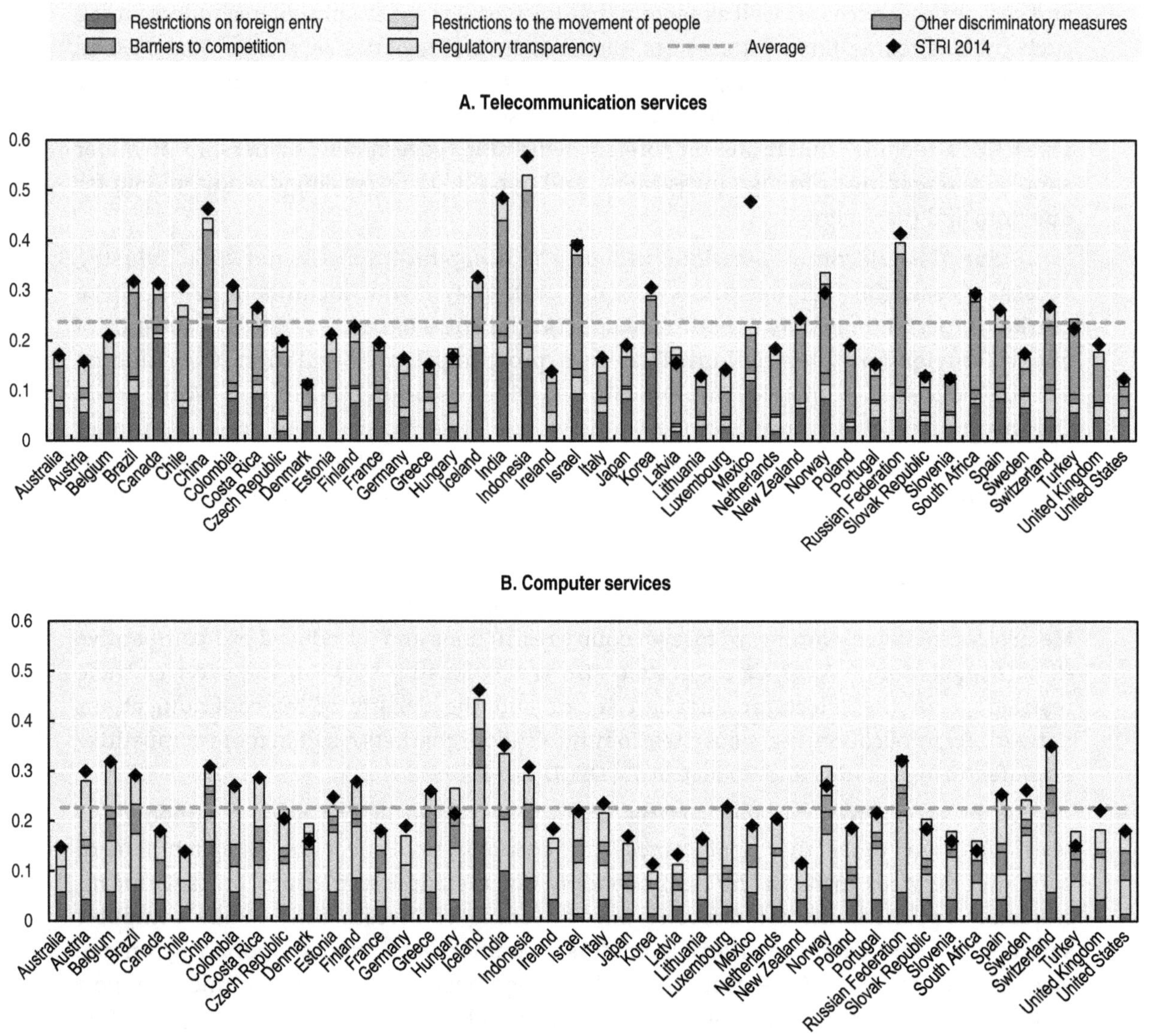

Notes: The Services Trade Restrictiveness Index (STRI) indices take values between 0 and 1, with 1 being the most restrictive. They are calculated on the basis of the STRI regulatory database which records measures on a most-favoured-nation basis. Preferential trade agreements are not taken into account. The data have been verified by OECD countries and the Russian Federation. China = the People's Republic of China.

Source: OECD, *Services Trade Restrictiveness Index* (database), *www.oecd.org/tad/services-trade/services-trade-restrictiveness-index.htm* (accessed March 2017).

StatLink *http://dx.doi.org/10.1787/888933586312*

Notes

1. Volume, velocity and variety are characterised as the three Vs of big data. However, these characteristics are in continuous flux, as they describe technical properties that evolve with the state of the art in data storage and processing. Others have also suggested a fourth V, for value, which is related to the increasing social and economic value of data (OECD, 2013a).
2. However, these estimates cannot be generalised, for a number of reasons. First, the estimated effects of DDI vary by sector and are subject to complementary factors such as the availability of skills and competences, and the availability and quality (i.e. relevance and timeliness) of the data

used. More importantly, these studies often suffer from selection biases. For instance, it is unclear whether the firms adopting DDI became more productive due to DDI, or whether they were more productive in the first place. Furthermore, these studies rarely control for the possibility that some firms may have seen a reduction in productivity due to DDI, and so may have discontinued their investment in it.

3. While Internet firms among the top 250 ICT firms generated on average more than USD 1 million in annual revenues per employee in 2012 and more than USD 800 000 in 2013, the other top ICT firms generated from USD 200 000 (information technology [IT] services firms) to USD 500 000 (software firms) (OECD, 2015a).

4. As Mayer-Schönberger and Cukier (2013) explain: "To datafy a phenomenon is to put it in a quantified format so it can be tabulated and analyzed".

5. A pertinent example is Thomson Reuters, which has transformed an internal data management solution to a collaborative information platform based on open data "to improve client relationships, the quality of their data and uptake of their existing products" (Open Data Institute, 2016). In doing so, Thomson Reuters has also been able to maximise the option value of its data and related products, despite high uncertainties regarding sources of future market value for these products. As Dan Meisner, Thomson Reuters's Head of Enterprise Data Services, explained: "customers see an awful lot of value in this but commercially it's not easy to put a value on" (Open Data Institute, 2016).

6. See e.g. *http://edison-project.eu*.

7. This represents an average annual year-on-year growth of 1.7%. This potential arises from the sum of the expected additional value added for mechanical (EUR 23 billion at an expected year-on-year growth of 2.21%), electrical (EUR 13 billion, +2.21%), automotive (EUR 15 billion, +1.53%), chemical (EUR 12 billion, +2.21%), agriculture (EUR 3 billion, 1.17%) and ICT sectors (EUR 14 billion, 1.17%).

8. This estimate uses value added by industry data from the US Bureau of Economic Analysis. It is part of the "GDP by industry" database: *www.bea.gov/iTable/iTable.cfm?ReqID=51&step=1#reqid=51&step=51&isuri=1&5114=a&5102=1*

9. The Fort Hays State study employed a mathematical estimating tool. It studied 1 445 fields with a total of 135 755 acres in 3 states.

10. "Contract farming can be defined as an agricultural production carried out according to an agreement between a buyer and farmers, which establishes conditions for the production and marketing of a farm product or products. Typically, the farmer commits to providing agreed quantities of a specific agricultural product" (FAO, 2012).

11. It is estimated that by 2030, 8 billion people and up to 25 billion active "smart" devices will be interconnected and interwoven by one single huge information network, leading to the emergence of an intelligent "superorganism" in which the Internet represents the "global digital nervous system" (Radermacher and Beyers, 2007; O'Reilly, 2014).

12. As Becker (2012) explains: "Data hostage clauses are employed when a contract between a cloud provider and customer is improperly terminated by the customer in order to allow the cloud provider to hold on to a customer's data until the customer has paid a termination fee or compensated the cloud provider for lost business through liquidated damages. In some cases, however, this data hostage provision may be used to extract additional fees from the customer or to prevent the customer from moving to another provider."

13. In 2008, the OECD updated its original 2003 classification of ICT goods and services, proposing goods and services to be ICT when they are primarily [...] intended to fulfil or enable the function of information processing and communication by electronic means, including transmission and display. The classification builds upon definitions of the ICT sector and is therefore directly applicable to official statistics. Differences between the 2008 and the 2003 classification are primarily due to changes in the underlying industry classification detailed in OECD (2009). Because many statistical databases have not changed to the most recent industry classifications, the 2003 definition is sometimes still used. See UNCTAD (2009) for a discussion.

14. The OECD partner economies included are Brazil, the People's Republic of China, Colombia, Costa Rica, India, Indonesia, Lithuania, the Russian Federation, Singapore and South Africa.

15. The actual share of ICT services value added embedded in exports might be higher than the figure suggests. The reason is that all value added that firms generate in-house is attributed to the firm's main sector of activity. Thus, while outsourced ICT services are reflected in the bar, the same type of services produced in-house are not. Differences among countries can therefore be due to different degrees of outsourcing and might not reflect actual differences in the usage of ICT services.

16. Analysis shows that a high domestic share in value added reflects, in part, the size of the domestic market, the presence of trade restrictions, distance from economic poles of activity and the sectoral specialisation of the country. It should not necessarily be associated with competitiveness.
17. Services trade restrictions in specific sectors that enable trade in a digital world, such as telecommunications and computer services, not only affect these sectors but also affect other sectors that make use of these services (e.g. data transfer restrictions may impact the delivery of financial services).
18. Further details about the STRI results in telecommunications can be found at: *www.oecd.org/tad/services-trade/STRI_telecommunications.pdf.*

References

Agrawal, A. et al. (2015), "Digitization and the contract labour market: A research agenda", Chapter 8 in: Goldfarb, A., S. Greenstein and C. Tucker (eds.), *Economic Analysis of the Digital Economy*, pp. 219-250, *www.nber.org/chapters/c12988.*

Agweb (2015), "John Deere to purchase precision planting", *Agweb*, 4 November, *www.agweb.com/article/john-deere-to-purchase-precision-planting-naa-agwebcom-editors* (accessed 13 April 2017).

Airbnb (2017), "Airbnb data for OECD study", internal data, Paris.

American Farm Bureau Federation (n.d.), "Privacy and security principles for farm data", *www.fb.org/issues/technology/data-privacy/privacy-and-security-principles-for-farm-data* (accessed 21 June 2017).

Arntz, M., T. Gregory and U. Zierahn (2016), "The risk of automation for jobs in OECD countries: A comparative analysis", *OECD Social, Employment and Migration Working Papers*, No. 189, OECD Publishing, Paris. *http://dx.doi.org/10.1787/5jlz9h56dvq7-en.*

Arthur, L. (2016), "Getting the right team on the field: Creating an advantage by connecting people, equipment, technology, and insights", presentation, John Deere, *https://infoag.org/presentations/2215.pdf.*

Autor, D.H. (2015), "Why are there still so many jobs? The history and future of workplace automation", *Journal of Economic Perspectives*, Vol. 29/3, Summer, pp. 3-30, *http://dx.doi.org/10.1257/jep.29.3.3.*

Autor, D.H. (2013), "The 'task approach' to labor markets: An overview", *Journal for Labour Market Research*, Vol. 46/3, pp. 185-199.

Autor, D.H. and D. Dorn (2013), "The growth of low-skill service jobs and the polarization of the U.S. labor market", *American Economic Review*, Vol. 103/5, pp. 1 553-1 597, *www.jstor.org/stable/42920623.*

Autor, D.H., L.F. Katz and M.S. Kearney (2008), "Trends in US wage inequality: Revising the revisionists", *The Review of Economics and Statistics*, Vol. 90(2), pp. 300-323.

Autor, D.H., L.F. Katz and M.S. Kearney (2006), "The polarization of the U.S. labor market", *American Economic Review*, Vol. 96/2, pp. 189-194, *http://dx.doi.org/10.1257/000282806777212620.*

Bakhshi, H., A. Bravo-Biosca and J. Mateos-Garcia (2014), "Inside the datavores: Estimating the effect of data and online analytics on firm performance", Nesta, *www.nesta.org.uk/sites/default/files/* inside_the_datavores_technical_report.pdf (accessed 13 May 2015).

Banham, R. (2014), "Who owns farmers' big data?", ForbesBrandVoice, 8 July, *www.forbes.com/sites/emc/2014/07/08/who-owns-farmers-big-data* (accessed 4 May 2017).

Barua, A., D. Mani and R. Mukherjee (2013), "Impacts of effective data on business innovation and growth", Chapter 2 of a three-part study, University of Texas at Austin (accessed 20 May 2015).

Becker, M.B. (2012), "Interoperability case study: Cloud computing", *The Berkman Center for Internet & Society Research Publication*, No. 2012-11, April, *http://papers.ssrn.com/sol3/papers.cfm?abstract_id=2046987.*

Bessen, J.E. (2015), "How Computer Automation Affects Occupations: Technology, Jobs, and Skills", *Boston Univ. School of Law, Law and Economics Research Paper* No. 15-49, *http://dx.doi.org/10.2139/ssrn.2690435.*

Big Data Startups (2013), "Walmart is making big data part of its DNA", *www.bigdata-startups.com/BigData-startup/walmart-making-big-data-part-dna* (accessed 13 April 2017).

BITKOM and Fraunhofer (2014), "Industrie 4.0 – Volkswirtschaftliches Potenzial für Deutschland" [Industrie 4.0 – Macroeconomic potential for Germany], *www.bitkom.org/files/documents/Studie_Industrie_4.0.pdf.*

Blanchenay, P. et al. (forthcoming), "Cross-country evidence on business dynamics over the last decade: From boom to gloom?", *OECD Science, Technology and Industry Working Paper*, OECD Publishing, Paris.

Bloomberg (2015), "The sharing economy", Bloomberg Briefs, June, *https://newsletters.briefs.bloomberg.com/document/4vz1acbgfrxz8uwan9/front* (accessed 3 November 2015).

Brynjolfsson, E. et al. (2008), "Scale without mass: Business process replication and industry dynamics", *Harvard Business School Technology & Operations Mgt. Unit Research Paper* No. 07-016, *http://ebusiness.mit.edu/research/papers/2008.09_Brynjolfsson_McAfee_Sorell_Zhu_Scale%20Without%20Mass_285.pdf*.

Brynjolfsson, E., L.M. Hitt and H.H. Kim (2011), "Strength in numbers: How does data-driven decisionmaking affect firm performance?", Social Science Research Network, *http://papers.ssrn.com/sol3/papers.cfm?abstract_id=1819486*.

Brynjolfsson, E. and A. McAfee (2011), *Race Against the Machine: How the Digital Revolution is Accelerating Innovation, Driving Productivity, and Irreversibly Transforming Employment and the Economy*, Digital Frontier Press, Lexington, Mass.

Burson-Marsteller (2017), "Twiplomacy study 2017", *http://twiplomacy.com/blog/twiplomacy-study-2017* (accessed 22 June 2017).

Burson-Marsteller (2014), "Twiplomacy study 2014", *http://twiplomacy.com/blog/twiplomacy-study-2014* (accessed 13 April 2017).

Byrne, D. and C. Corrado (2016), "ICT asset prices: Marshaling evidence into new measures", *Conference Board Economics Program Working Paper Series*, No. 16-06.

CB Insights (2015), "Startups valued at more than $1 bn", reported by *The Economist*, 25 July.

CEPS (Centre for European Policy Studies) (2014), "Shaping the integrated infrastructures of cities", presentation at the IEC CEPS workshop on "Orchestrating Smart City Efficiency", Centre for European Policy Studies.

Civity (2014), "Urban mobility in transition?", *matters*, No. 1, Civity Management Consultants, Berlin.

Coase, R.H. (1960), "The problem of social cost", *The Journal of Law and Economics*, Vol. III, pp. 1-44, *http://onlinelibrary.wiley.com/doi/10.1002/sres.3850090105/abstract*.

Coase, R.H. (1937), "The nature of the firm", *Economica*, New Series, Vol. 4/16 (Nov. 1937), pp. 386-405, *http://dx.doi.org/10.2307/2626876*.

Columbia University (2011), "One million community health workers", Technical Task Force Report, The Earth Institute, Columbia University, *www.millenniumvillages.org/uploads/ReportPaper/1mCHW_TechnicalTaskForceReport.pdf*.

Comstock, J. (2014), "Survey: 32 percent of mobile device owners use fitness apps", mobi health news, 29 January, *www.mobihealthnews.com/29358/survey-32-percent-of-mobile-device-owners-use-fitness-apps* (accessed 12 April 2017).

Davidson, P. (2012), "3-D printing could remake US manufacturing", *USA Today*, 10 July, *http://usatoday30.usatoday.com/money/industries/manufacturing/story/2012-07-10/digital-manufacturing/56135298/1*.

Deloitte (2016), "Economic effects of ridesharing in Australia", Uber and Deloitte Access Economics, *https://www2.deloitte.com/au/en/pages/economics/articles/economic-effects-ridesharing-australia-uber.html*.

DESTATIS (Statistisches Bundesamt) (2015), "Private Konsumausgaben – Deutschland" [Private consumption expenditure – Germany], webpage, *www.destatis.de/DE/ZahlenFakten/GesellschaftStaat/EinkommenKonsumLebensbedingungen/Konsumausgaben/Tabellen/PrivateKonsumausgaben.html* (accessed 21 June 2017).

Elliot, S.W. (2014), "Anticipating a luddite revival", *Issues in Science and Technology*, Vol. XXX/3, Spring, *http://issues.org/30-3/stuart* (accessed 23 May 2016).

ENoLL (2014), "About ENoLL", webpage, *www.openlivinglabs.eu/aboutus*.

EPRI (Electric Power Research Institute) (2011), "Estimating the costs and benefits of the smart grid", Electric Power Research Institute, Palo Alto, California, *https://www.smartgrid.gov/files/Estimating_Costs_Benefits_Smart_Grid_Preliminary_Estimate_In_201103.pdf*.

Eunoia (2012), "Urban models for transportation and spatial planning: State-of-the-art and future challenges", EUNOIA Consortium, *www.nommon-files.es/working_papers/EUNOIA_PositionPaper_Oct2012.pdf*.

Eurobarometer (2016), "Flash Eurobarometer 438: The use of collaborative platforms", European Union, *https://data.europa.eu/euodp/fr/data/dataset/S2112_438_ENG* (accessed 13 April 2017).

e-control (2011), "Next steps for smart grids: Europe's future electricity system will save money and energy", press summary, *www.e-control.at/documents/20903/-/-/633895a3-d5d0-4866-865c-26b785bd1d0d* (accessed 29 August 2017).European Data Portal (2017), "Datasets", *www.europeandataportal.eu/data/dataset?groups=regions-and-cities* (accessed 20 June 2017).

FAO (Food and Agriculture Organization) (2012), "Guiding Principles for Responsible Contract Farming Operations", Food and Agriculture Organization of the United Nations, Rome, *www.fao.org/docrep/016/i2858e/i2858e.pdf.*

Fortune (2015), "The unicorn list", Fortune.com, *http://fortune.com/unicorns* (accessed 3 November 2015).

Freelancer (2017), "2016 annual report", *www.freelancer.com/investor* (accessed 23 June 2017).

Freelancer (2016a), "Freelancer Limited – FY 2015 full year results presentation", *https://www.freelancer.com/files/download/27609216/FLN%20FY15%20Results%20Presentation.pdf.*

Freelancer (2016b), "Freelancer data for OECD study", internal data.

Frey, C.B. and M.A. Osborne (2013), "The future of employment: How susceptible are jobs to computerisation?", *OMS Working Papers*, Oxford Martin Programme on the Impact of Future Technology, *www.oxfordmartin.ox.ac.uk/downloads/academic/The_Future_of_Employment.pdf.*

Frischmann, B.M. (2014), "Human-focused turing tests: A framework for judging nudging and techno-social engineering of human beings", *Cardozo Legal Studies Research Papers*, No. 441, *http://dx.doi.org/10.2139/ssrn.2499760.*

Goos, G. et al. (2011), *The Future of the Internet*, Springer, Berlin, Heidelberg, pp. 431-447, *www.springer.com/la/book/9783642208973#aboutBook.*

Gordon, R.J. (2016), *The Rise and Fall of American Growth: The U.S. Standard of Living Since the Civil War*, Princeton Press, Princeton, New Jersey.

Gordon, R.J. (2012), "Is U.S. economic growth over? Faltering innovation confronts the six headwinds", *CEPR Policy Insight*, No. 63, *www.cepr.org/sites/default/files/policy_insights/PolicyInsight63.pdf.*

Hall, J. and A. Krueger (2015), "An analysis of the labor market for Uber's driver-partners in the United States", Working Papers, Princeton University, Industrial Relations Section, No. 587, *http://dataspace.princeton.edu/jspui/handle/88435/dsp010z708z67d* (accessed 3 November 2015).

Heinen, S. et al. (2011), "Impact of smart grid technologies on peak load to 2050", *IEA Energy Papers*, No. 2011/11, OECD Publishing, Paris, *http://dx.doi.org/10.1787/5kg5dlknt48s-en.*

Huws, U. and S. Joyce (2016), "Size of the UK's 'gig economy'", Crowd Working Survey, February, *www.feps-europe.eu/assets/a82bcd12-fb97-43a6-9346-24242695a183/crowd-workingsurveypdf.pdf.*

Hynninen, S.-M., J. Ojala and J. Pehkonen (2013), "Technological change and wage premiums: Historical evidence from linked employer-employee data", *Labour Economics*, Vol. 24/C, pp. 1-11, *https://doi.org/10.1016/j.labeco.2013.05.006.*

Ifop (2016), "Enquête auprès des partenaires chauffeurs actifs sur Uber", Ifop and Uber, *www.ifop.com/?option=com_publication&type=poll&id=3277* (accessed 22 February 2016).

IMS Institute for Healthcare Informatics (2015), "IMS Health Study: Patient Options Expand as Mobile Healthcare Apps Address Wellness and Chronic Disease Treatment Needs", *www.imshealth.com/en/about-us/news/ims-health-study:-patient-options-expand-as-mobile-healthcare-apps-address-wellness-and-chronic-disease-treatment-needs* (accessed 17 August 2017).

Intuit (2015), "Intuit forecast: 7.6 million people in on-demand economy by 2020", BusinessWire, *www.businesswire.com/news/home/20150813005317/en* (accessed 3 November 2015).

ITF (International Transport Forum) (2017), "Managing the Transition to Driverless Road Freight Transport", International Transport Forum, *https://www.itf-oecd.org/managing-transition-driverless-road-freight-transport.*

ITF (2014), "Urban mobility: System upgrade", International Transport Forum and Corporate Partnership Board, *www.itf-oecd.org/sites/default/files/docs/15cpb_self-drivingcars.pdf.*

Jackson, K. (1993), "The world's first motel rests upon its memories", *Seattle Times*, 25 April, *http://community.seattletimes.nwsource.com/archive/?date=19930425&slug=1697701.*

Jahangir Mohammed, J. (2014), "Surprise: Agriculture is doing more with IoT innovation than most other industries", Venturebeat, 7 December, *http://venturebeat.com/2014/12/07/surprise-agriculture-is-doing-more-with-iot-innovation-than-most-other-industries* (accessed 13 April 2017).

Jasperneite, J. (2012), "Was hinter Begriffen wie Industrie 4.0 steckt" [The meaning of notions such as Industrie 4.0], computer-automation.de, 19 December, *www.computer-automation.de/steuerungsebene/steuern-regeln/artikel/93559/0* (accessed 13 April 2017).

Jin, Y. and M. Wegener (2013), "Beyond equilibrium", *Environment and Planning B: Planning and Design*, Vol. 40/6, pp. 951-954, *http://dx.doi.org/10.1068/b4006ge*.

John Deere (2017), "AutoTrac Vision", *www.deere.com/en_US/products/equipment/ag_*management_solutions/guidance/auto-trac-vision/auto-trac-vision.page (accessed 17 March 2017).

John Deere (2016), "John Deere – Committed to those linked to the land: investor presentation", pp. 11-12, *www.deere.com/en_US/docs/Corporate/investor_relations/pdf/presentationswebcasts/strategy_presentation-rev.pdf*.

John Deere (2015), "The payoff from precision agriculture", John Deere, 7 August, *https://johndeerejournal.com/2015/08/the-payoff-from-precision-agriculture* (accessed 3 October 2016).

JPMorgan Chase & Co. Institute (2016), "Paychecks, paydays, and the online platform economy", JPMorgan Chase & Co., *www.jpmorganchase.com/corporate/institute/document/jpmc-institute-volatility-2-report.pdf*.

Katz, L.F. and A.B. Krueger (2016), "The rise and nature of alternative work arrangements in the United States, 1995-2015", *NBER Working Papers*, No. 22 667, *http://dx.doi.org/10.3386/w22667*.

Kitchin, R. (2014), "The real-time city? Big data and smart urbanism", *GeoJournal*, No. 79/1, pp. 1-14, *http://dx.doi.org/10.1007/s10708-013-9516-8*.

Kleiner Perkins (2017), "Internet trends 2017", Mary Meeker presentation, 31 May, *www.kpcb.com/internet-trends* (accessed 28 August 2017).

KPCB (2015), "Internet trends", Mary Meeker presentation, 27 May, *www.kpcb.com/blog/2015-internet-trends* (accessed 28 August 2017).

KTH (2010), "Congestion charges which save lives", webpage, *www.kth.se/en/forskning/sarskilda-forsknings-satsningar/sra/trenop/trangselskatten-som-raddar-liv-1.51816* (accessed 4 November 2014).

Landier, A., D. Szomoru and D. Thesmar (2016), "Working in the on-demand economy: An analysis of Uber driver-partners in France", Uber blog post, *https://drive.google.com/a/uber.com/file/d/0B1s08BdVqCgrZWZrQnVWNUFPNFE/view?pref=2&%20pli=1* (accessed 9 March 2016).

Marcolin, L., S. Miroudot and M. Squicciarini (2016), "Routine jobs, employment and technological innovation in global value chains", *OECD Science, Technology and Industry Working Papers*, No. 2016/01, OECD Publishing, Paris, *http://dx.doi.org/10.1787/5jm5dcz2d26j-en*.

Manyika, J. et al. (2011), "Big data: The next frontier for innovation, competition and productivity", McKinsey & Company, *www.mckinsey.com/business-functions/digital-mckinsey/our-insights/big-data-the-next-frontier-for-innovation* (accessed 19 September 2014).

Mayer-Schönberger, V. and K. Cukier (2013), *Big Data: A Revolution That Will Transform How We Live, Work and Think*, John Murray, London.

Mazzolari, F. and G. Ragusa (2013), "Spillovers from high-skill consumption to low-skill labor markets", *Review of Economics and Statistics*, Vol. 95/1, pp. 74-86, *http://dx.doi.org/10.1162/REST_a_00234*.

MBO (2015), "Independent workers and the on-demand economy", MBO Partners, Herndon, Virginia, *http://info.mbopartners.com/rs/mbo/images/On-Demand-Economy-2014.pdf* (accessed 3 November 2015).

McCracken, H. (2014), "How Gmail happened: The inside story of its launch 10 years ago", *Time Magazine*, 1 April, *http://time.com/43263/gmail-10th-anniversary/*.

McKinsey Global Institute (2013), "Disruptive technologies: Advances that will transform life, business, and the global economy", McKinsey & Company, *www.mckinsey.com/business-functions/digitalmckinsey/our-insights/disruptive-technologies*.

Michaels, G., A. Natrajz and J. Van Reenen (2014), "Has ICT polarized skill demand? Evidence from eleven countries over 25 years", *Review of Economics and Statistics*, Vol. 96/1, pp. 60-77, *http://dx.doi.org/10.1162/REST_a_00366*.

Microsoft Ventures (2017), "Microsoft Ventures locations", webpage, *www.microsoftventures.com* (accessed 29 August 2017).

Mordor Intelligence (2016), "Global precision farming market: By technology, application and geography market shares, forecasts and trends (2015-2020)", March, *www.mordorintelligence.com/industry-reports/precision-farming-market?gclid=CjOKEQjw7LS6BRDo2Iz23au25OQBEiQAQa6hwK_VYHWSIw7Z_WCx8TEd8lUOfqO3T5xJnApB-f49fokaAh_28P8HAQ* (accessed 13 April 2017).

Moretti, E. (2012), *The New Geography of Jobs*, Mariner Books, Houghton Mifflin Harcourt, Boston, New York.

New York Department of Environmental Conservation (2014), "Climate smart waste management", Department of Environmental Conservation, New York State, *www.dec.ny.gov/energy/57186.html* (accessed 4 November 2014).

Nordås, H.K. and D. Rouzet (2015), "The impact of services trade restrictiveness on trade flows: First estimates", *OECD Trade Policy Papers*, No. 178, OECD Publishing, Paris, *http://dx.doi.org/10.1787/5js6ds9b6kjb-en*.

Noyes, K. (2014), "Cropping up on every farm: Big data technology", *Fortune*, 30 May, *http://fortune.com/2014/05/30/cropping-up-on-every-farm-big-data-technology* (accessed 13 April 2017).

OECD (Organisation for Economic Co-operation and Development) (forthcoming), "Digital trade: Developing a framework for analysis", *OECD Trade Policy Papers*, OECD Publishing, Paris.

OECD (2017a), *The Next Production Revolution: Implications for Governments and Business*, OECD Publishing, Paris, *http://dx.doi.org/10.1787/9789264271036-en*.

OECD (2017b), *New Health Technologies: Managing Access, Value and Sustainability*, OECD Publishing, Paris, *http://dx.doi.org/10.1787/9789264266438-en*.

OCDE (2017c), *Government at a Glance 2017*, OECD Publishing, Paris, *http://dx.doi.org/10.1787/gov_glance-2017-en*.

OECD (2016a), "Stimulating digital innovation for growth and inclusiveness: The role of policies for the successful diffusion of ICT", *OECD Digital Economy Papers*, No. 256, OECD Publishing, Paris, *http://dx.doi.org/10.1787/5jlwqvhg3l31-en*.

OECD (2016b), *Entrepreneurship at a Glance 2016*, OECD Publishing, Paris, *http://dx.doi.org/10.1787/entrepreneur_aag-2016-en*.

OECD (2016c), "New forms of work in the digital economy", *OECD Digital Economy Papers*, No. 260, OECD Publishing, Paris, *http://dx.doi.org/10.1787/5jlwnklt820x-en*.

OECD (2016d), "Research ethics and new forms of data for social and economic research", *OECD Science, Technology and Industry Policy Papers*, No. 34, OECD Publishing, Paris, *http://dx.doi.org/10.1787/5jln7vnpxs32-en*.

OECD (2016e), "ICTs and jobs: Complements or substitutes?", *OECD Digital Economy Papers*, No. 259, OECD Publishing, Paris, *http://dx.doi.org/10.1787/5jlwnklzplhg-en*.

OECD (2016f), "New skills for the digital economy", *OECD Digital Economy Papers*, No. 258, OECD Publishing, Paris, *http://dx.doi.org/10.1787/5jlwnkm2fc9x-en*.

OECD (2016g), "Using foreign factors to enhance domestic export performance: A focus on Southeast Asia", *OECD Trade Policy Papers*, No. 191, OECD Publishing, Paris, *http://dx.doi.org/10.1787/5jlpq82v1jxw-en*.

OECD (2015a), *Data-Driven Innovation: Big Data for Growth and Well-Being*, OECD Publishing, Paris, *http://dx.doi.org/10.1787/9789264229358-en*.

OECD (2015b), "Making open science a reality", *OECD Science, Technology and Industry Policy Papers*, No. 25, OECD Publishing, Paris, *http://dx.doi.org/10.1787/5jrs2f963zs1-en*.

OECD (2015c), *Government at a Glance 2015*, OCDE Publishing, Paris, *http://dx.doi.org/10.1787/gov_glance-2015-en*.

OECD (2015d), "The future of productivity", Policy Note, OECD, Paris, *www.oecd.org/eco/growth/The-future-of-productivity-policy-note-July-2015.pdf*.

OECD (2015e), "OECD Better Life Index: Housing", OECD Better Life Index, *www.oecdbetterlifeindex.org/topics/housing* (accessed 3 November 2015).

OECD (2014a), *Entrepreneurship at a Glance 2014*, OECD Publishing, Paris, *http://dx.doi.org/10.1787/entrepreneur_aag-2014-en*.

OECD (2014b), *Recommendation of the Council on Digital Government Strategies*, OECD, Paris, *www.oecd.org/gov/digital-government/Recommendation-digital-government-strategies.pdf*.

OECD (2014c), "Services Trade Restrictiveness Index: Policy brief", OECD, Paris, *www.oecd.org/tad/services-trade/STRI%20Policy%20Brief_ENG.pdf*.

OECD (2013a), *Supporting Investment in Knowledge Capital, Growth and Innovation*, OECD Publishing, Paris, *http://dx.doi.org/10.1787/9789264193307-en*.

OECD (2013b), *OECD Guidelines Governing the Protection of Privacy and Transborder Flows of Personal Data*, OECD, Paris, *www.oecd.org/sti/ieconomy/oecdguidelinesontheprotectionofprivacyandtransborder flowsofpersonaldata.htm*.

OECD (2012a), "ICT applications for the smart grid: Opportunities and policy implications", *OECD Digital Economy Papers*, No. 190, OECD Publishing, Paris, *http://dx.doi.org/10.1787/5k9h2q8v9bln-en*.

OECD (2012b), *OECD Territorial Reviews: The Chicago Tri-State Metropolitan Area, United States 2012*, OECD Publishing, Paris, *http://dx.doi.org/10.1787/9789264170315-en*.

OECD (2009), "Information economy product definitions based on the Central Product Classification (Version 2)", OECD, Paris, *www.oecd.org/science/sci-tech/42978297.pdf*.

OECD and IDB (Inter-American Development Bank) (2016), *Broadband Policies for Latin America and the Caribbean: A Digital Economy Toolkit*, OECD Publishing, Paris, *http://dx.doi.org/10.1787/9789264251823-en*.

OECD and World Bank (2015), "Inclusive global value chains: Policy options in trade and complementary areas for GVC integration by small and medium enterprises and low-income developing countries", OECD and World Bank Group Publishing, Washington, DC.

Open Cities (2013), "WP4 – Open data", webpage, *http://opencities.net/node/68* (accessed 19 September 2014).

Open Data Institute (2016), "Open enterprise: How three big businesses create value with open innovation", *ODI White Paper*, No. 5, *https://theodi.org/open-enterprise-big-business*.

Open Knowledge Foundation (2017), "US City Open Data Census", webpage, *http://us-city.census.okfn.org* (accessed 20 June 2017).

O'Reilly, T. (2014), "IoTH: The Internet of things and humans", O'Reilly Radar, *http://radar.oreilly.com/2014/04/ioth-the-internet-of-things-and-humans.html* (accessed 21 April 2017).

Parmar, R. et al. (2014), "The new patterns of innovation", *Harvard Business Review*, January-February, *https://hbr.org/2014/01/the-new-patterns-of-innovation* (accessed 15 March 2017).

Pentland, A. (2014), *Social Physics: How Good Ideas Spread – The Lessons from a New Science*, Penguin Press, United Kingdom.

Radermacher, F.J. and B. Beyers (2007), *Welt mit Zukunft – Überleben im 21. Jahrhundert* [World with a future – Surviving in the 21st century], Murmann Verlag, Hamburg (2nd edition of *Welt mit Zukunft – Die Ökosoziale Perspektive*, 2001).

research2guidance (2014), "Fourth annual study on mHealth app publishing", research2guidance, *http://research2guidance.com/r2g/mHealth-App-Developer-Economics-2014.pdf*.

RFS (Request for Startup) (2015), "2015 1099 Economy Workforce Report", RFS website, *https://gumroad.com/l/rfsreport* (accessed 29 August 2017).

Schaffers, H. et al. (2011), "Smart cities and the future Internet: Towards cooperation frameworks for open innovation", in: Goos, G. et al. (2011), *The Future of the Internet*, Springer, Berlin, Heidelberg pp. 431-447, *www.springer.com/la/book/9783642208973#aboutBook*.

Schimmelpfennig, D. and R. Ebel (2016), "Sequential adoption and cost savings from precision agriculture", *Journal of Agricultural and Resource Economics*, Vol. 41/1, pp. 97-115, *http://papers.ssrn.com/sol3/papers.cfm?abstract_id=2714959*.

Sensus (2012), "Water 20/20", Sensus, *https://fr.slideshare.net/SensusItalia/sensus-water-2020* (accessed 29 August 2017).

Serras, J. et al. (2014), "Urban planning and big data: Taking LUTi models to the next level?", webpage, Nordregio, *www.nordregio.se/en/Metameny/Nordregio-News/2014/Planning-Tools-for-Urban-Sustainability/Reflection* (accessed 19 September 2014).

Singh, K. et al. (2016), "Developing a framework for evaluating the patient engagement, quality, and safety of mobile health applications", *Issues Brief*, The Commonwealth Fund, *www.ncbi.nlm.nih.gov/pubmed/26934758* (accessed 12 April 2017).

Smith, A. (2016), "Shared, collaborative and on demand: The new digital economy", Pew Research Center, 19 May, *www.pewinternet.org/2016/05/19/the-new-digital-economy* (accessed 23 May 2016).

Spiezia, V. (2011), "Are ICT users more innovative?: An analysis of ICT-enabled innovation in OECD firms", *OECD Journal: Economic Studies*, Vol. 2011/1, OECD Publishing, Paris, *http://dx.doi.org/10.1787/eco_studies-2011-5kg2d2hkn6vg*.

Startupbootcamp (2014), "Startupbootcamp Accelerator Programs", webpage, *www.startupbootcamp.org/accelerator.html* (accessed 19 September 2014).

Statistics Canada (2017), "The sharing economy in Canada", webpage, *www.statcan.gc.ca/daily-quotidien/170228/dq170228b-eng.htm* (accessed 30 March 2017).

Statistics Denmark (2015), "Sharing economy: Results 2015", *www.dst.dk* (accessed 30 March 2017).

Tambe, P. (2014), "Big data investment, skills, and firm value", *Management Science*, *http://dx.doi.org/10.2139/ssrn.2294077* (accessed 13 April 2017).

TfL (Transport for London) (2011), "London's intelligent traffic system", presentation by the Director of Strategy, Surface Transport, Transport for London, London, *www.impacts.org/euroconference/barcelona2011/Presentations/11_Keith_Gardner_presentation_Barcelona_v2.pdf*.

The Economist (2014), "Tech Startups: A Cambrian moment", *The Economist*, 18 January, *https://www.economist.com/news/special-report/21593580-cheap-and-ubiquitous-building-blocks-digital-products-and-services-have-caused* (accessed 30 August 2017).

Uber (2016a), "New survey: Drivers choose Uber for its flexibility and convenience", Uber Newsroom, 7 December, *https://newsroom.uber.com/driver-partner-survey* (accessed 8 March 2016).

Uber (2016b), "An open letter to the mayor on congestion in London", Uber Newsroom, *https://newsroom.uber.com/uk/open-letter* (accessed 8 March 2016).

UCCD (Urban Center for Computation and Data) (2012), "LakeSim: A prototype workflow framework for coupling urban design and computational modeling tools", Urban Center for Computation and Data website, *www.urbanccd.org/research-tools/* (accessed 29 August 2017).

UK Department for Business Innovation and Skills (2013), "The smart city market: Opportunities for the UK", *Bis Research Paper*, No. 136, Department for Business Innovation and Skills, London, *https://www.gov.uk/government/uploads/system/uploads/attachment_data/file/249423/bis-13-1217-smart-city-market-opportunties-uk.pdf*.

UNCTAD (United Nations Conference on Trade and Development) (2009), "Manual for the production of statistics on the information economy: 2009 revised edition", UNCTAD/SDTE/ECB/2007/2/REV.1, United Nations, New York and Geneva, *http://unctad.org/en/docs/sdteecb20072rev1_en.pdf*.

UNDESA (United Nations Department of Economic and Social Affairs) (2017), *World Population Prospects: The 2015 Revision*, DVD Edition, United Nations Department of Economic and Social Affairs, Population Division, New York.

Uni Europa (2016), "Size of Sweden's 'gig economy' revealed for the first time: Around 700,000 crowd workers in Sweden", Uni Europa website, *www.uni-europa.org/wp-content/uploads/2016/03/crowdworking-survey-swedenpdf.pdf*.

Upwork (2015), "Online work report 2014", webpage, *http://elance-odesk.com/online-work-report-global* (accessed 3 November 2015).

Van Reenen, J. (2011), "Wage inequality, technology and trade: 21st century evidence", *Labour Economics*, Vol. 18/6, pp. 730-741, *https://doi.org/10.1016/j.labeco.2011.05.006*.

WHO (World Health Organization) (2016), *Atlas of eHealth Country Profiles: The Use of eHealth in Support of Universal Health Coverage: Based on the Findings of the Third Global Survey on eHealth 2015*, World Health Organization, Geneva, *http://apps.who.int/iris/bitstream/10665/204523/1/9789241565219_eng.pdf?ua=1* (accessed 12 April 2017).

Chapter 6

Digital risk and trust

Trust underpins most digital relationships and transactions and depends on the perception and the management of risk. This chapter examines trust concerns, in particular related to privacy and digital security risks, as barriers to the adoption of digital technologies, reviews trends in digital security and privacy incidents and online fraud, and discusses how to build trust in the digital economy, including through consumer protection. Policy and regulation aimed at enhancing trust in the digital economy are discussed in Chapter 2.

The statistical data for Israel are supplied by and under the responsibility of the relevant Israeli authorities. The use of such data by the OECD is without prejudice to the status of the Golan Heights, East Jerusalem and Israeli settlements in the West Bank under the terms of international law.

Introduction

Increasing connectivity and data-intensive economic activities – in particular those that rely on large streams of data ("big data"), the widespread use of mobile connectivity, and the emerging use of the Internet to connect computers and sensor-enabled devices (the Internet of Things [IoT]) – have the potential to foster innovation in products, processes, services and markets and to help address widespread economic and social challenges. These developments have been accompanied by a change in the scale and scope of a number of risks, relating in particular to digital security and privacy, with potential significant impacts on social and economic activities. Furthermore, as new business models emerge to take advantage of new opportunities, it may be more difficult for consumers to navigate through the resulting complexity of the evolving e-commerce marketplace. This combination underscores the need for an evolution in policies and practices to build and maintain trust.

Although challenging to measure, digital security incidents appear to be increasing in terms of sophistication, frequency and magnitude of influence. These incidents can affect an organisation's reputation, finances and even its physical assets, undermining its competitiveness, ability to innovate and position in the marketplace. Individuals can suffer tangible economic and even physical harms as well as intangible harms such as damage to reputation or intrusion into their private life. In addition, digital security incidents can impose significant costs on the economy as a whole, including by eroding trust, not only in the affected organisations, but across sectors. In May 2017, computers in over 150 countries were infected by the WannaCry ransomware (i.e. malicious software that blocked access to the victim's data until a ransom is paid). This significantly disrupted business operations in organisations worldwide such as the United Kingdom's National Health Service (NHS), Spanish-based Telefónica, US-based FedEx and German-based Deutsche Bahn (BBC, 2017; Wong and Solon, 2017). Manufacturing firms such as Nissan Motor and Renault even stopped production at several production sites temporarily (Sharman, 2017).

The increasing connectivity of data-intensive activities adds layers of complexity, volatility and dependence on existing infrastructures and processes. In particular, the extension of the geographical reach of the digital services and their increasing interconnection beyond single jurisdictional and organisational control is challenging the existing governance frameworks of businesses and governments. Where these digital services are part of critical infrastructure networks, there is a growing risk for systemic failures to accumulate and affect society in multiple ways. The result is that risk in the digital economy is a cross-boundary, cross-sector and multi-stakeholder issue. What happens in a small business can affect a large business and all other actors within a value chain; what one actor (individual or group) does may affect many others. That said, organisations, whether functioning in the public or private sector, are undoubtedly benefiting from greater interconnectivity – driving innovation, efficiency and performance. The value chain ecosystem can also be used to address digital security risk, for example by requiring a certain level of security risk management along a supply chain.

Trust is essential in situations where uncertainty and interdependence exist (Mayer, Davis and Schoorman, 1995), and the digital environment certainly encapsulates those two factors. However, while digital technologies are evolving rapidly, policies and resultant practices related to trust too often assume a static world. The IoT, big data and artificial intelligence (AI) were perceived by policy makers in 2016 as the greatest challenges to ensuring beneficial policy settings (see Chapter 2). At current growth rates, it has been estimated that by 2020 there will be 50 billion "things" connected to the Internet (OECD, 2016a). For example, firms like Amazon, Apple and Google have already made big moves to enable AI-enabled services such as human-machine interaction via spoken word, while Facebook launched an AI effort, DeepText, to understand individual users' conversational patterns and interests.

The potential advantages of these technological developments are significant but they also add new risks that could erode trust in the new technologies and the digital economy overall. The evidence reviewed in this chapter suggests that users (including individuals and businesses, and in particular small and medium-sized enterprises [SMEs]) are increasingly unsettled by the risks they may face within this new digital environment. A 2014 Centre for International Governance Innovation (CIGI)-Ipsos survey of Internet users in 24 countries on Internet security and trust suggests that 64% of respondents are more concerned about privacy than they were in the previous year. Perhaps most striking is the lack of confidence that they have control over their personal information.

This chapter reviews developments related to digital risks and trust with a focus on: 1) digital security; 2) privacy; and 3) consumer protection issues. Digital risks faced by businesses in respect to the protection of their intellectual property or other business risks such as the risk of lock-ins and other information and communication technology (ICT) investment-related business risks are beyond the scope of this chapter. The chapter is structured as follows:

- The first section shows that trust concerns, and in particular privacy and digital security risks, are often a barrier to the adoption of digital technologies and applications including, but not limited to, cloud computing, e-commerce and e-government services for both individuals (including consumers) and businesses (in particular SMEs).
- The second section then reviews trends in digital security and privacy incidents, as well as online fraud, and their social and economic effects. In doing so, this section discusses to what extent trust concerns highlighted in the previous section may be justified.
- The third section discusses trends on how trust in the digital economy is built and reinforced from the perspective of individuals (including consumers) and businesses. These means range from transparent online reviews for consumers to risk management practices in businesses. This section does not discuss the role of public policies in enhancing trust in the digital economy, which is discussed in Chapter 2.

Key findings from this chapter include that with growing intensity of ICT use, businesses and individuals are facing more digital security and privacy risks. SMEs in particular need to introduce or improve digital security risk management practices. Meanwhile, consumers' concerns about privacy add to their concerns about online fraud, redress mechanisms, and online product quality, which could limit trust and slow business-to-consumer (B2C) e-commerce growth. More generally, digital security and privacy concerns are inhibiting ICT adoption and business opportunities. Finally, emerging peer platform markets bring new trust issues, but also new opportunities to address them.

The role of digital risks and trust in the adoption of digital technologies and applications

Continued improvements in consumer and business access to broadband Internet, particularly through mobile devices and applications, have opened up new opportunities. For instance, there has been a significant rise in the use of cloud computing services among Internet users (Chapter 4). The share of individuals using e-government services (i.e. visiting or interacting with public authorities online) has also increased in recent years. And e-commerce has grown continuously with the uptake of the Internet (OECD, 2014) and at a faster rate than overall retail sales (Box 6.1).

However, there are still huge variations in the use of digital technologies among individuals and businesses, and across countries, in particular when it comes to more advanced platforms (see Chapter 4; OECD, 2016b). The majority of individuals and businesses are still using digital technologies for rather basic applications, such as for e-mail and information retrieval through websites. E-commerce adoption, for instance, remains below its potential, although it is progressing at a significantly faster rate than overall retail sales. The share of e-commerce sales stands at only 18% of total turnover on average in reporting countries, and up to 90% of the value of e-commerce comes from business-to-business transactions over electronic data interchange applications (Chapter 4).[1] Furthermore, only of 57% Internet users in OECD countries reported using the Internet to order products online and 22% to sell products online, compared to an average of 90% of Internet users reporting using e-mails and about 80% using the Internet to obtain information on goods and services.[2] At the same time, while more than 90% of businesses are connected to the Internet and almost 80% have a website, only 40% use digital technologies to purchase products and even less (20%) sell products online.

E-commerce is not the exception. The adoption of other digital technologies and applications remains particularly low, in particular among individuals and SMEs. For example, the adoption of e-government services varies significantly across countries. More importantly, the share of people submitting electronic forms (instead of only downloading public sector information) remains particularly low (with only 35% of OECD Internet users undertaking this activity in 2016). At the same time, many businesses, and in particular SMEs, still lag behind in adopting more advanced digital technologies and applications such as cloud computing, supply-chain management, enterprise resource planning, and radio frequency identification. For example, only 20% of businesses had adopted cloud computing in 2016 and less than 10% big data analytics, despite their potential for boosting productivity (see Chapter 4).

There is strong evidence showing that Internet users (including individuals and businesses, and in particular SMEs) are increasingly concerned about digital risks and that these concerns may have become a serious barrier for the adoption of digital technologies and applications. A 2014 CIGI-Ipsos survey of Internet users in 24countries on Internet security and trust suggests that 64% of respondents are more concerned about privacy than they were one year ago. In a special 2014 Eurobarometer survey on digital security, online consumers in the European Union (EU) reported their top two concerns to be the misuse of personal data and the security of online payments (EC, 2015b). The level of concern in both areas is up from 2013, with fear of personal data misuse increasing from 37% to 43% and security concerns from 35% to 42%.

Box 6.1. **Business-to-consumer e-commerce trends**

From 2013 to 2018, the share of the Asia and Oceania region in global business-to-consumer (B2C) e-commerce is expected to increase from 28% to 37%, and the People's Republic of China (hereafter "China") has already emerged as the largest global B2C e-commerce market. Credit card penetration is an important factor facilitating e-commerce, notably in developing countries and among the younger generation (UNCTAD, 2015; 2016). More generally, innovation in the e-commerce marketplace now affords consumers better access to a wider variety of competitively priced goods and services, wider access to tangible and digital content products, easy to use and more secure payment mechanisms, and a growing number of platforms facilitating consumer to consumer transactions.

In OECD countries, B2C e-commerce has grown continuously and at a faster rate than overall retail sales. Recent figures in the United States show an annual increase of 15.8% for e-commerce as compared with growth in overall retail sales of 2.3%. E-commerce sales now account for 8.1% of total retail sales in the United States (US Department of Commerce, 2016); and roughly eight in ten individuals in the United States are online shoppers and 15% buy online on a weekly basis (Smith and Anderson, 2016). In the European Union (EU), the proportion of individuals that ordered goods or services online increased from 30% in 2007 to 53% in 2015, exceeding the European Union's own targets (EC, 2015a).The most frequent reasons to shop online relate to convenience, price and choice according to the 2015 EU Scoreboard. Some 49% of surveyed consumers pointed to the advantage of being able to buy anytime, while 42% noted the time saved by buying online. In terms of price, 49% mentioned finding less expensive products online, while 37% cited the ease of comparing prices online. The advantages related to choice covered both the overall range of goods and services available as well as the fact that some products are only available online. Other reasons identified in the survey concerned information such as the ability to find consumer reviews (21%), the possibility of comparing products easily (20%), the ease of finding more information online (18%) and the possibility of delivery to a convenient place (24%). In terms of cross-border purchases, it appears that the main reasons driving online shopping relate to quality and choice (European Commission, 2015a).

Some data provided by the US International Trade Administration show regional differences in e-commerce trends. According to Morgan Stanley research, 41% of online shoppers in the United States buy online because of lower prices, while 49% globally do so for the same reason. Another example is the ease to compare prices: 25% cited this reason in the United States while 32% did so globally. While a similar number of people in emerging economies, Europe, and the Americas and Asia-Pacific bought products cross-border due to non-availability at domestic level (74%, 74% and 72%, respectively), there are large disparities when it comes to looking for higher quality products abroad (49% in emerging economies, 8% in Europe, and 15% in the Americas and Asia-Pacific) (US International Trade Administration, 2016).

The types of goods and services consumers acquire online are increasingly varied. In Australia, the most common industry sectors for online purchases were: electronics/ electrical goods; clothing, footwear, cosmetics and other personal products; gift vouchers, travel services and entertainment (Australian Government, 2016). In the European Union, clothes and sport goods (60% total, and 67% for the 16-24 year-old age group) is the most popular type of goods and services purchased online, followed by travel and holiday accommodation (52%); household goods (41%); tickets for events (37%); and books, magazines and newspapers (33%). A good proportion of the 16-24 year-old age group also purchased games software, other software and upgrades (26%), and e-learning material (8%) (EC, 2015a), which suggests that e-commerce now encompasses digital content products.

The low adoption of some digital technologies and applications cannot only be explained by a lack of trust. There are a number of other factors, among which the education gap has been identified as the most important one (OECD, 2014; 2016c). While users with a tertiary education perform on average more than seven different online activities, those with at most a lower secondary education perform less than five (OECD, 2014). In a similar manner, for businesses, the lack of skills in the labour market is one of the major barriers for the adoption of digital technologies (OECD, 2016c). However, it is noticeable that the applications for which adoption is slow are to a significant extent those that are associated with higher risks for either individuals or businesses, or for both. These applications typically involve the extensive collection and processing of personal data, including financial data (e.g. e-commerce), or are applications that can lead to a higher degree of dependencies (e.g. cloud computing).

The following sections present available evidence showing the extent to which lack of trust, and in particular privacy and security concerns, are a major source of concern and thus potential barriers to the adoption of digital technologies for both individuals and businesses.

Digital security and privacy concerns can prevent consumers from engaging in online transactions

Digital risks and lack of trust are often indicated as the most common reasons that individuals (consumers) with access to the Internet do not use some digital technologies and applications and for not engaging in online transactions. Concerns include the growing risk of online fraud and the misuse of personal data as well as the rising complexity of online transactions and related terms and conditions. This is compounded by uncertainties about the redress mechanisms available in case of a problem with an online purchase. The following sections discuss these issues in more detail.

Individuals are increasingly concerned about digital security and privacy, but there are significant variations across countries as well as across digital technologies and applications

Digital security and privacy are among the most challenging issues raised by digital services, including e-commerce. Individuals perceive digital security as a major issue, in particular where there are significant risks of personal data breaches and identity theft. Concerns thus relate to the wealth of personal data that online activities generate, which, while enabling organisations to sketch rich profiles about individuals, also bring risks to both the individuals and the organisation. According to Special Eurobarometer surveys (EC, 2015c; 2013), for example, when using the Internet for online banking or shopping, the most common concern is about "someone taking or misusing personal data" (mentioned by 43% of Internet users in the European Union compared to 37% a year ago), before the "security of online payments" (42% compared to 35% a year ago). This is in line with the observation that around 70% of Internet users in Europe are still concerned that their online personal information is not kept secure by websites. That said, security concerns by individuals are not limited to the confidentiality of their personal data. Many are also concerned about the availability of digital services. For example, in 2014, around half of European Internet users were concerned about not being able to access online services because of digital security incidents (compared to around 37% a year earlier).

Concerns about the misuse of personal data go beyond security (e.g. personal data breaches), and include most notably concerns about the loss of control over personal data. According to a 2014 Pew Research Centre poll, for example, 91% of Americans surveyed agree that consumers have lost control of their personal information and data (Madden, 2014). The percentage of people who "agree" or "strongly agree" that it has become very difficult to remove inaccurate information about them online is as high as 88%. The share of social networking site users in the United States concerned with third-party access by businesses and governments is estimated to be 80% and 70% respectively. That said, 55% "agree" or "strongly agree" with the statement: "I am willing to share some information about myself with companies in order to use online services for free" (Madden, 2014). Similarly in the European Union, "two-thirds of respondents (67%) are concerned about not having complete control over the information they provide online." (EC, 2015b) More than half (56%) say it is very important that tools for monitoring their activities online only be used with their permission. Meanwhile, "roughly seven out of ten people are concerned about their information being used for a different purpose from the one it was collected for." Across the European Union in 2016, more than 60% of all individuals were concerned about their online activities being recorded to provide them with tailored adverts (Figure 6.1). In Germany, France and Denmark the share was even much higher, at 82%, 70% and 68% respectively.

Figure 6.1. **Concerns about online activities being recorded to provide tailored advertising, 2016**

As a percentage of individuals

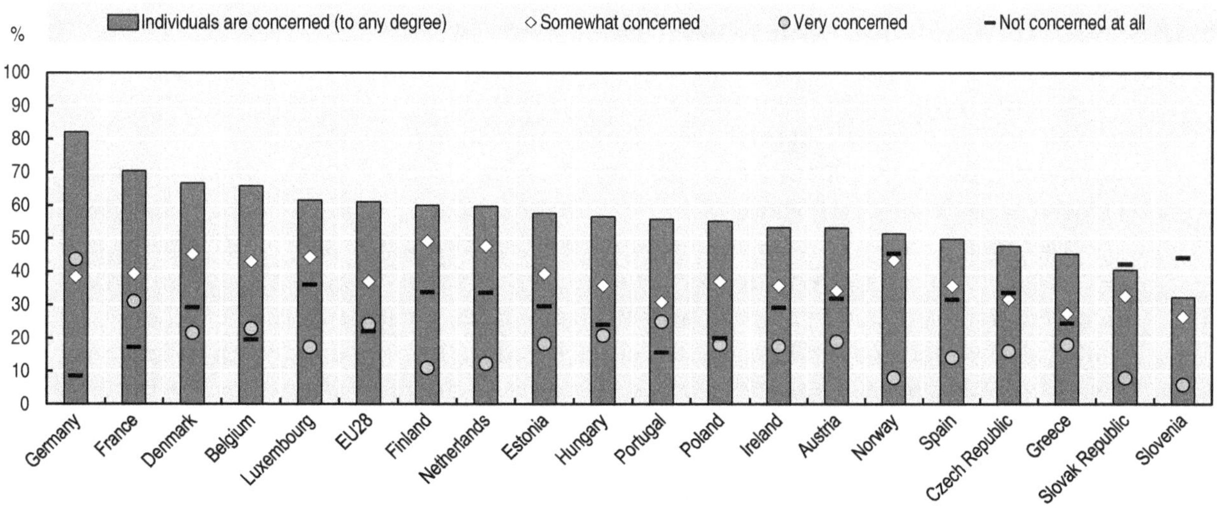

Source: Eurostat, *Digital Economy and Society* (database), *http://ec.europa.eu/eurostat/web/digital-economy-and-society/data/comprehensive-database* (accessed March 2017).

StatLink http://dx.doi.org/10.1787/888933586331

Trust concerns could incite consumers to change their online behaviour, with potential negative effects on digital service adoption

Privacy and security concerns have led Internet users to be more reluctant in providing personal data and in some cases even in using digital services at all. Today, for example, 34% Internet users in the European Union say that they are less likely to give personal information on websites. Six out of ten respondents have already changed the privacy settings on their Internet browser (compared to three in ten in 2013; see OECD, 2014). Over one-third (37%) use software that protects them from seeing online adverts and more than a quarter (27%) use software that prevents their online activities from being monitored. Overall 65% of respondents have taken at least one of these actions. Individuals are also more demanding in respect to the level of security of the digital services they use. A survey among EU individuals shows that "more than seven in ten (72%) say it is very important that the confidentiality of their e-mails and online instant messaging is guaranteed", and "almost two-thirds of respondents (65%) totally agree they should be able to encrypt their messages and calls, so they are only read by the recipient" (EC, 2016b). The changing behaviour is confirmed by a recent survey of 24 000 users in 24 countries in 2014 commissioned by the CIGI, which reveals that only 17% of users said they had not changed their online behaviour in recent years. The rest expressed a variety of behavioural change from using the Internet less often (11%) to making fewer purchases and financial transactions online (both around 25%). While the increasing occurrence of data breaches in the media can be seen as a determinant factor, some note that "some users may be concerned by other factors, including pervasive surveillance or how their data is collected and used by businesses" (Internet Society, 2016).

As individuals become more concerned about privacy and security, some have started to avoid using digital services. The behavioural change of consumers due to digital security and privacy concerns could negatively affect B2C e-commerce. Evidence confirms that many consumers remain reluctant to purchase online because of security and privacy concerns (OECD, 2014). There is considerable variation in the exact reasons though, even when only looking only at trust issues. Some cite fears around the misuse of personal data and security of online payments and in many cases identity theft is a major source of concern. Among European Internet users, for example, almost half abstained from certain online activities in 2015 because of security concerns (Figure 6.2). The most frequent activities were related to the risk of personal data misuse and of economic losses, for instance through identity theft. They included (in order of significance): providing personal information to online communities for social and professional networking (almost 30% of Internet users), e-banking and e-commerce (both around 20% of Internet users).[3] When also taking privacy concerns into account the share is higher. In 2015, one-fourth of Internet users in the EU cited privacy and security concerns as the main reason for not buying online. Almost 15% all individuals in the European Union did not use cloud computing because of privacy or security concerns in 2014 (Figure 6.3). In Austria, France, Germany, Luxembourg, the Netherlands, Norway, Slovenia and Switzerland the share is as much as 20% or 25%. In the United States, the 2015 US Census Bureau survey of households online reported that 63% of the online households were concerned about identity theft and of these 35% refrained from conducting financial transactions online during the year prior to the survey. Similarly, of the 45% of online households concerned about credit card or banking fraud, 33% declined to buy goods or services using the Internet (NTIA, 2016); this is the equivalent of 15% of online households. The high variation in perceptions of security and privacy risks across countries with comparable degrees of law enforcement and technological know-how suggests that cultural attitudes towards online transactions play a significant role.

Figure 6.2. **Security concerns kept Internet users from doing certain activities**

As a percentage of individuals who used the Internet within the last year

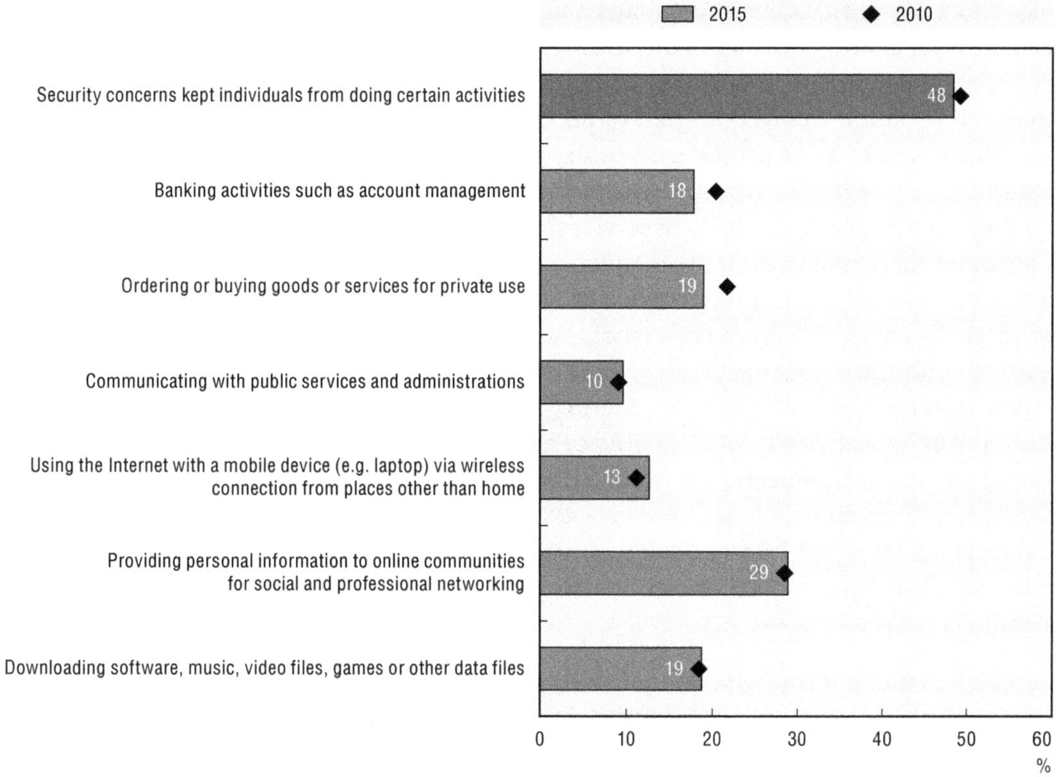

Source: Eurostat, *Digital Economy and Society* (database), *http://ec.europa.eu/eurostat/web/digital-economy-and-society/data/comprehensive-database* (accessed March 2017).

StatLink *http://dx.doi.org/10.1787/888933586350*

Figure 6.3. **Security and privacy concerns kept individuals from using cloud computing, 2014**

As a percentage of individuals

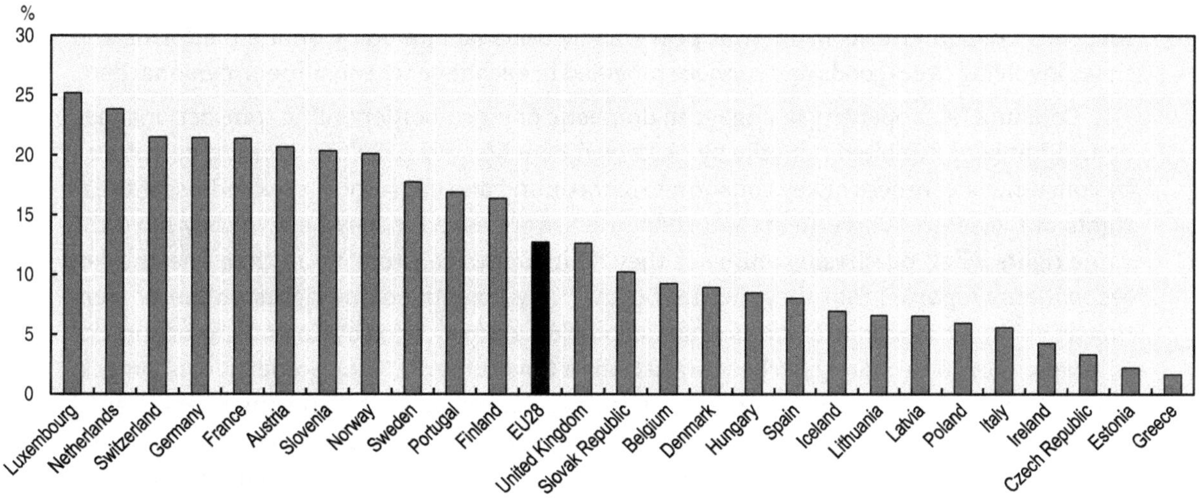

Source: Eurostat, *Digital Economy and Society* (database), *http://ec.europa.eu/eurostat/web/digital-economy-and-society/data/comprehensive-database* (accessed March 2017).

StatLink *http://dx.doi.org/10.1787/888933586369*

However, lack of trust towards Internet businesses and digital services must not always translate into a barrier for adopting digital services. Although a majority of people may be uncomfortable about Internet companies using information about their online activity to tailor adverts or are concerned about the recording of their activities via payment cards and over mobile telephones, a large majority of individuals may accept this. In the European Union, for example, more than half of all individuals are concerned about their privacy, yet "a large majority of people (71%) still say that providing personal information is an increasing part of modern life and accept that there is no alternative other than to provide it if they want to obtain products of services" (EC, 2015b). Meanwhile, the survey also reveals that "more than six out of ten respondents say that they do not trust landline or mobile phone companies and Internet service providers (ISPs) (62%) or online businesses (63%)". However, the share of European households without access to the Internet that cite privacy or security concerns as the main reason for not having an Internet connection is low, although it increased from 5% in 2008 to 9% in 2016.[4] At the same time, in the United States, where the share of households indicating privacy and security concerns as a main reason for not having an Internet connection at home also increased (by 1 percentage point compared to 2009), albeit from an even lower level (at 1.4% of all households) in 2015. An increasing share of people not using the Internet due to privacy and security concerns can also be observed in Brazil, where up to 12% of households without an Internet connection cited privacy and security concerns as a reason.[5]

Uncertainties about mechanisms for redress and the quality of products sold online could also slow the growth of business-to-consumers e-commerce

With the increasing complexity of the online environment and the emergence of new e-commerce business models, consumers are now faced with further challenges as well as opportunities. In its work leading to the 2016 revisions to the *OECD Recommendation of the Council on Consumer Protection in E-commerce* (OECD, 2016d), the Committee on Consumer Policy identified a number of key developments in e-commerce that pose challenges for consumers. These developments included the growth of non-traditional payment mechanisms, such as mobile phone bills or prepaid cards; new types of digital content products, such as mobile applications (apps) or e-books; and new types of online business models, such as those involving consumer-to-consumer or peer transactions facilitated by online platforms and those involving "free" goods and services provided in exchange for consumers' personal data.

Consumers' propensity to engage in domestic or cross-border online transactions may be facilitated or inhibited not only by perceived benefits and risks of e-commerce but also by consumer awareness of key consumer rights online and capacity to seek redress if these rights are violated. When Australian consumers were asked if they believe they have the same rights when purchasing online as they do in a physical store, more than one-third of respondents reported that they did not believe they have the same rights online or were unsure about the situation. In terms of actual problems experienced by Australian consumers, 23% were related to online purchases (Australian Government, 2016). Some studies suggest knowledge of consumer rights increases with age: for instance, Italian consumers over 54 are more aware of their rights, as well as more engaged and skilled, than consumers in the 15-24 age bracket (EC, 2016a). EU consumers have raised concerns beyond data protection and security with about one-quarter reporting concerns about the infringement of consumer rights related to redressing problems with the goods. In addition, 19% of the surveyed EU consumers expressed concerns about the possibility of buying unsafe or counterfeit goods (EC, 2015a).

Consumer protection enforcement agencies are a key source of information about the problems facing consumers online. These agencies work together through the International Consumer Protection and Enforcement Network (ICPEN), which has members from over 60 countries. In 2015, ICPEN members recognised misleading and inadequate information disclosures related to pricing information as a key problem for online consumers. As part of an internationally co-ordinated "sweep" of online pricing practices in travel and tourism, ICPEN members identified misleading or deceptive conduct such as "drip pricing," which resulted in the delayed disclosure of final prices, fees and terms and conditions to consumers, false reference prices and best price claims, non-existent discounts and time-sensitive representations, and a lack of cancellation and refund information.

Another element affecting consumer trust in a global context is the range of unsafe products which are available in e-commerce, as revealed by an OECD product online sweep co-ordinated by the Australian Competition and Consumer Commission in April 2015. During the sweep, product safety authorities in 25 countries inspected 3 categories of goods that had been identified in their country as: 1) banned and recalled products; 2) products with inadequate product labelling and safety warnings; and 3) products that did not meet voluntary or mandatory safety standards (OECD, 2016e).

Of the nearly 700 products inspected for the purpose of detecting banned or recalled products, 68% were available for sale online. Out of the 880 products which were inspected to detect inadequate labelling and safety warnings, 57% were not supported by adequate labelling information on relevant websites, and 22% showed incomplete labelling information. Moreover, a small majority of the 136 products inspected for the purpose of detecting products which did not comply with voluntary and mandatory safety standards did not comply with such standards. A key challenge suggested by the sweep is the share of unsafe products bought online from overseas, with goods banned in one country due to safety concerns being accessible to buyers from another country without knowledge of the ban. Another example is labels and warnings in a foreign language or products that do not meet voluntary and mandatory safety standards, and which are more prevalent in a cross-border context (OECD, 2016e).

Missed business opportunities over digital security risk concerns are still significant

Current surveys on the diffusion of ICT tools and activities in enterprises indicate that companies, and in particular SMEs, are not making the most of the business opportunities the online environment has to offer. The reasons cited for not using digital technologies to their full potential include technical issues, such as reorganising business processes and systems; skills, including a lack of specialist knowledge or capability; and increasingly, trust issues. SMEs in particular, which account by far for the largest share of all businesses in OECD countries, do not yet have full confidence in the digital solutions on offer. The potential of loss of consumer trust, damage to reputation, negative impacts on revenue, etc., from a digital security incident are the main reasons for these concerns. The following sections discuss in more detail major trust issues related to digital security concerns due to the enhanced use of external digital services.

Digital security risk has become a concern for organisations of all types

Companies recognise that digital technologies are key to greater productivity, but most express significant concerns over digital security risk, which makes adoption challenging. Digital security concerns vary according to firm size and country, and will depend on the digital technologies and applications, with the more advanced ones creating greater concerns. E-commerce adoption, for example, and in particular mobile e-commerce, remains below its potential, with security concerns frequently cited as an impediment by a significant share of businesses. According to Eurostat data, for instance, more than a third of all firms stated that security-related risks prevented or limited the use of mobile Internet in 2013, and almost a third of these firms stated that a mobile connection to the Internet was needed for business operation. In Finland, France and Luxembourg, more than 50% of all businesses do not use mobile Internet to its full potential due to security concerns even though, as in the case of Finland, more than a third of all firms would need a mobile connection for their business operation.

It is even more apparent in the case of cloud computing that trust issues have become a barrier to adoption. In the OECD area, only 20% of businesses had used cloud computing by 2014, with SMEs being more reluctant compared to large firms (40% of firms with 250 or more employees compared to 20% of firms with 10 to 49 employees). In some countries the gap between large and small firms is great. In the United Kingdom, for example, 21% of all smaller enterprises (10 to 49 employees) are using cloud computing services compared to 54% of all larger enterprises. A similar gap can be observed in other countries (see Chapter 4). Risk of security breach is perceived as a major barrier to cloud computing adoption by businesses. Almost 30% of all businesses in the European Union do not use the cloud because of security concerns. The share ranges from almost 45% in Austria, Hungary, Luxembourg and Portugal to 10% to 15% in the Nordic countries (Denmark, Finland, Iceland, Ireland, Norway and Sweden), which are also those countries where the rates of cloud computing adoption by businesses are the highest among OECD countries (Figure 6.4).

Figure 6.4. **Reasons businesses do not use cloud computing, 2014**

As a percentage of all enterprises

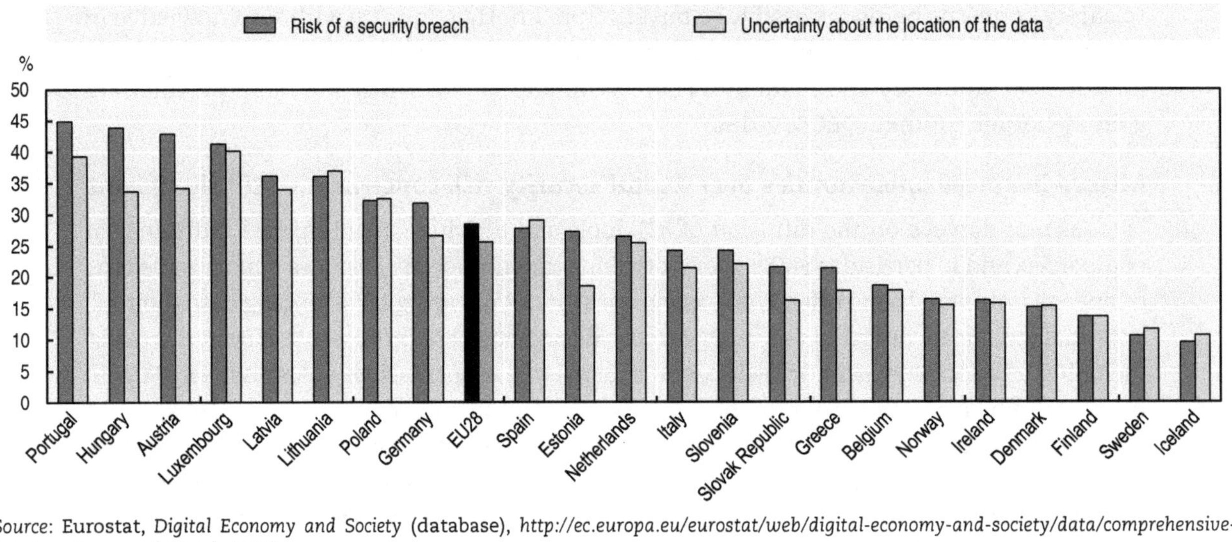

Source: Eurostat, *Digital Economy and Society* (database), *http://ec.europa.eu/eurostat/web/digital-economy-and-society/data/comprehensive-database* (accessed March 2017).

StatLink http://dx.doi.org/10.1787/888933586388

Loss of control of data is perceived as a major digital risk for businesses considering using Internet-based services

In a survey of European SME perspectives on cloud computing, the security of corporate data and potential loss of control featured highly among the concerns for SME owners (ENISA, 2009). Loss of control in the case of cloud computing is partly related to uncertainties about the location of the data, which is perceived across countries as significant a barrier to cloud computing adoption as the risk of security incidents (Figure 6.4). In addition, there is another major challenge which is related to the lack of appropriate open standards and the potential for vendor lock-in due to the use of proprietary solutions: applications developed for one platform often cannot be easily migrated to another application provider (OECD, 2015b).

The lack of open standards is a key problem, especially when it comes to the model of "platform as a service" and to digital services based on this model. In this service model, application programming interfaces are generally proprietary. Applications developed for one platform typically cannot easily be migrated to another cloud host. While data or infrastructure components that enable cloud computing (e.g. virtual machines) can currently be ported from selected providers to other providers, the process requires an interim step of manually moving the data, software and components to a non-cloud platform and/or conversion from one proprietary format to another. Consequently, once an organisation has chosen a service provider, it is – at least at the current stage – locked in (OECD, 2015b). Some customers have raised the difficulty of switching between providers as a major reason for not adopting cloud-based services. Almost 30% of all businesses in the European Union, for example, had not used cloud computing to its full potential in 2014 because of perceived difficulties in unsubscribing or changing service providers (Figure 6.5). A major difficulty of switching providers is that users can become extremely vulnerable to providers' price increases. This is all the more relevant as some IT infrastructure providers may be able to observe and profile their users to apply price discrimination to maximise profit (OECD, 2015b). See the section below on "empowering individuals and businesses" for trends on the use of mechanisms for consumers to control their personal data and see Chapter 2 for trends on policy initiatives to promote data portability.

Figure 6.5. **Limited use of cloud computing services due to difficulties of businesses in changing service providers, 2014**

As a percentage of enterprises buying cloud computing services

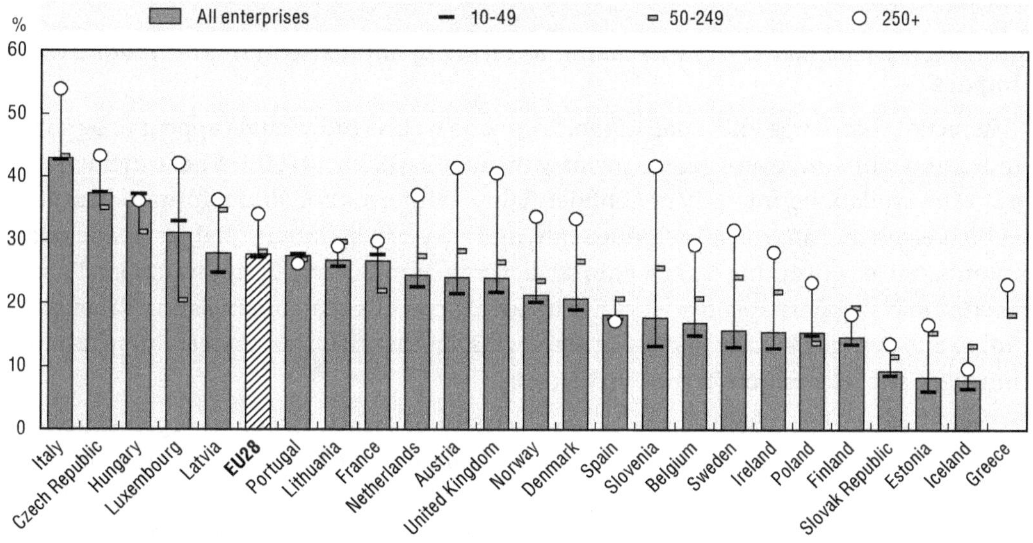

Source: Eurostat, *Digital Economy and Society* (database), *http://ec.europa.eu/eurostat/web/digital-economy-and-society/data/comprehensive-database* (accessed March 2017).

StatLink http://dx.doi.org/10.1787/888933586407

Trends in incidents affecting trust in the digital economy

Concerns about potential losses and harms related to the use of digital technologies are in many cases a result of incidents experienced directly or indirectly by users of digital technologies. A large portion can be assigned to digital security incidents, i.e. the disruption of the confidentiality, integrity and availability[6] of the digital environment underlying social and economic activities. Meanwhile, these incidents appear to be increasing in terms of sophistication, frequency and magnitude of impact. For example, personal data breaches[7] – more precisely the breach of the confidentiality of personal data as a result of malicious activities or accidental losses – can cause significant economic losses to the business affected (including loss of competitiveness and reputation), but certainly will also cause harm as a result of the privacy violation of the individuals whose personal data have been breached. In addition, further consumer detriment may result from a data breach, such as harm caused by identity theft.

Losses and harm in the digital economy are not, however, always caused by digital security incidents. For instance, individuals, including consumers, may see their privacy violated as a result of the deceptive, misleading, fraudulent or unfair use of their personal data by organisations. This may be one reason for the increasing number of complaints received by national privacy protection authorities (excluding complaints related to personal data breaches). The Office of the Privacy Commissioner of Canada, for instance, accepted 309 complaints in 2015, an increase of 49% from five years earlier, when 207 complaints were accepted.[8] Significant consumer detriment can also be caused by misleading or inadequate information about the business, products and transactions, as well as by low quality or unsafe products made available in online markets as highlighted above. Furthermore, businesses relying on the digital environment may suffer from losses and harms not caused by digital security incidents, but by the violation of their intellectual property rights, including in particular their copyrights, on products made available in digital formats.[9] Related to these risks are interdependencies that are created as organisations and societies become more and more interconnected, leading to a higher systemic risk in particular, as critical infrastructures are involved.

Digital security incidents are increasing in terms of sophistication and magnitude of impact

In recent years large and small organisations as well as individuals appear to be subject to more frequent and severe digital security incidents (OECD, 2016f).[10] These incidents can disrupt the availability, integrity or confidentiality of information and information systems on which economic and social activities rely, and they can be intentional (i.e. malicious) or unintentional (e.g. resulting from a natural disaster, human error or malfunction). From an economic and social perspective, security incidents can affect an organisation's reputation, finances and even physical activities, damaging its competitiveness, undermining its efforts to innovate and its position in the marketplace.

Digital security incidents have taken a variety of forms. Criminal organisations are increasingly active in the digital environment. As innovation is becoming more and more digital, industrial digital espionage is likely to further rise. Some governments are also carrying out online intelligence and offensive operations. In some cases, the motive may be political or the attacks may be designed to damage an organisation or an economy. It was, for example, the case with the attack that targeted Sony Pictures Entertainment at the end of 2014, exposing unreleased movies, employee data, e-mails between employees, and sensitive business information like sales and marketing plans (BBC, 2015).

The risk of digital security incidents is growing with the intensity of ICT use

Across surveys undertaken over the past decade, it has consistently been found that over half of businesses and individuals report that they did not experience a digital security incident of any kind. There are, however, considerable cross-country variations. The share of businesses experiencing digital security incidents, for instance, ranges from around a third in Japan and Portugal to below 10% in Hungary, Korea and the United Kingdom[11] in 2010 or later (Figure 6.6).[12] A similar variation can be observed in the case of individuals: in the European Union, 20% to 30% of all individuals stated that they experienced a digital security incidence in 2015, compared to below 5% in Mexico and New Zealand (Figure 6.7).[13]

Figure 6.6. **Digital security incidents experienced by businesses, 2010 or later**

As a percentage of all enterprises

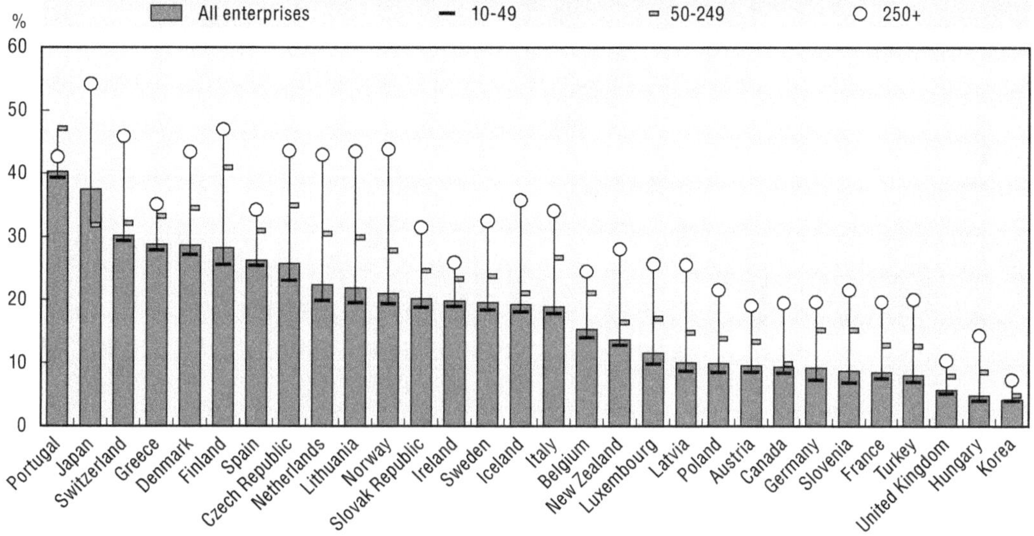

Notes: For European countries, data are only available for 2010. For New Zealand, data refer to 2016. For Japan and Switzerland, data refer to 2015. For Korea, they refer to 2014. For Canada, data refer to 2013. Canada, Japan, Korea and Switzerland follow a different methodology.

Source: OECD, *ICT Access and Usage by Businesses* (database), *http://oe.cd/bus* (accessed June 2017).

StatLink *http://dx.doi.org/10.1787/888933586426*

Evidence suggests that the actual proportion varies more significantly depending on the target population. For businesses that do experience an incident, for example, the number of incidents detected increases with firm size. In the case of individuals, the rate of incidents detected tends to increase with the level of education. One explanation could be that larger businesses and more educated individuals may have better detection capacities. The higher rate of experiencing an incident could, however, simply be because larger businesses have larger information technology (IT) infrastructures, which in turn are more likely to incur at least one incident. Similarly, evidence shows that individuals are more likely to use digital technologies and applications more intensively the more educated they are (see Chapter 4). The greater the intensity of usage, the greater the likelihood of experiencing a digital security incident.

Recent surveys confirm that large businesses are more likely to experience digital security incidents than small businesses. The 2016 Cyber Security Breaches Survey focusing on the United Kingdom showed that the proportion of businesses that had experienced an incident in the previous 12 months increased with business size. While overall 24% of all businesses surveyed had had an incident in the last 12 months, only 17% were micro businesses, 33% were small businesses, 51% were medium-sized business and 33% were large businesses. That said, many SMEs are not sufficiently aware of the actual digital security risks and the incidents they may have been victim of. The 2016 Ponemon State of Cybersecurity in Small and Medium-Sized Businesses, for example, found that 55% of respondents had experienced a cyber-attack in the past 12 months but that 16% were unsure. This calls for a careful interpretation of existing statistics and the need for further efforts to strengthen the evidence base in digital security and privacy.

Figure 6.7. **Digital security incidents experienced by individuals, 2015 or later**

As a percentage of all individuals and by level of educational attainment

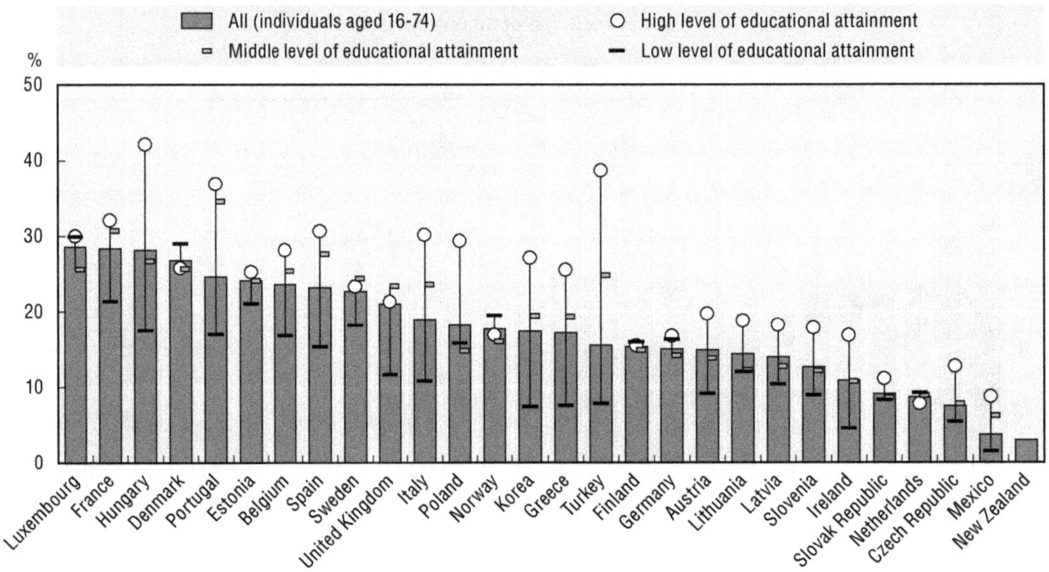

Notes: Data for Korea refer to 2016 for all individuals but the breakdown by level of educational attainment refers to 2014. Data for New Zealand and Switzerland refer to 2014. Data for Iceland refer to 2010. Data for Korea, Mexico, New Zealand and Switzerland follow a different methodology.

Source: OECD, *ICT Access and Usage by Households and Individuals* (database), *http://oe.cd/hhind* (accessed June 2017).

StatLink http://dx.doi.org/10.1787/888933586445

The frequency and magnitude of security incidents differ substantially depending on the type of incident

Available evidence suggests that viruses/malware remain the most common type of digital security incident experienced.[14] Some surveys also highlight the increase in incidents related to phishing and social engineering. Other surveys show that denial of service (DoS)[15] attacks tend to affect fewer businesses, although the share of affected businesses remains significant. More importantly, the sophistication and magnitude of DoS attacks are growing rapidly, with an increasing number of incidents based on the exploitation of IoT devices to generate large packet floods (Box 6.2). In 2015, several attacks used over 300 Gigabits per second (Gbps) and one peaked at 500 Gbps, which represents a tenfold increase compared to 2009 (Arbor Networks, 2016). In 2016, the largest attack reported was 800 Gbps, with several surveyed organisations reporting attacks of between 500 Gbps and 600 Gbps (Figure 6.8) (Arbor Networks, 2017). Fraud was also reported as an issue, but more for larger businesses than for smaller ones. That said, it should be noted that all these incidents may be inter-related. For instance, web-based attacks, phishing, or social engineering and malware more generally may be used to gain access to servers or IoT devices which may then be used to take part of a distributed DoS attack.

Box 6.2. **The Internet of Things, a game changer to the digital security risk landscape?**

With the Internet of Things (IoT) the risk of security incidents will most likely increase. Not only can the components of the IoT become the target of digital security incidents, with the consequence of disrupting physical systems, but in addition, IoT components can also be used as means for targeting digital systems, including through distributed denial of service (DDoS) attacks. In 2016, for instance, major Internet sites such as Netflix, Google, Spotify and Twitter were not accessible due to thousands of IoT devices – like digital video recorders and web-connected cameras – that were hacked and used for distributed DDoSs (see Hautala, 2016; Smith, 2016).

Like industrial control systems, the IoT bridges the digital and the physical world: through various types of sensors, connected objects can collect data from the physical world to feed digital applications and software, and they can also receive data to act on the environment through actuators such as motors, valves, pumps, lights and so forth. Thus, digital security incidents involving the IoT can have physical consequences: following a breach of integrity or availability, a vehicle might stop responding to the driver's actions, a valve could liberate too much fluid and increase pressure in a heating system, and a medical device could report inaccurate patient monitoring data or inject the wrong amount of medicine. As with the industrial control systems that have long operated in some sectors, the potential exists that such physical consequences as human injury and supply-chain disruption could result from digital security incidents affecting IoT devices. In 2015, for example, researchers took control of a Jeep Cherokee remotely, without prior access to the car. They wirelessly interfered with the accelerator, brakes and engine. Following this experiment, Fiat Chrysler recalled 1.4 million vehicles (Greenberg, 2015a; 2015b).

The IoT is rarely a stand-alone building block isolated from other digital components. Instead, all digital components in an organisation or on a personal network will often need to be considered as interconnected and interdependent. Vulnerabilities or incidents affecting parts of an organisation's information system that may seem unrelated to the IoT can affect it, as much as the exploitation of IoT components can have consequences in other parts of a system. For example, in 2015, a security firm investigated a hospital information system where attackers exploited a vulnerability in a networked blood gas analyser to ultimately infect the entire hospital IT department's workstations (Storm, 2015). In October 2016, as another example, major websites including Twitter, Netflix, Spotify, Airbnb, Reddit, Etsy, SoundCloud and The New York Times were inaccessible to people after a company that manages critical parts of the Internet's infrastructure was under attack. This attack was based on hundreds of thousands of IoT devices like cameras, baby monitors and home routers that had been infected with software that allows hackers to command them to flood a target with overwhelming traffic (Perlroth, 2012).

Source: Based on OECD (2016a), "The Internet of Things: Seizing the benefits and addressing the challenges", *http://dx.doi.org/10.1787/5jlwvzz8td0n-en*.

Figure 6.8. **Evolution of bandwidth used for largest denial of service attacks**

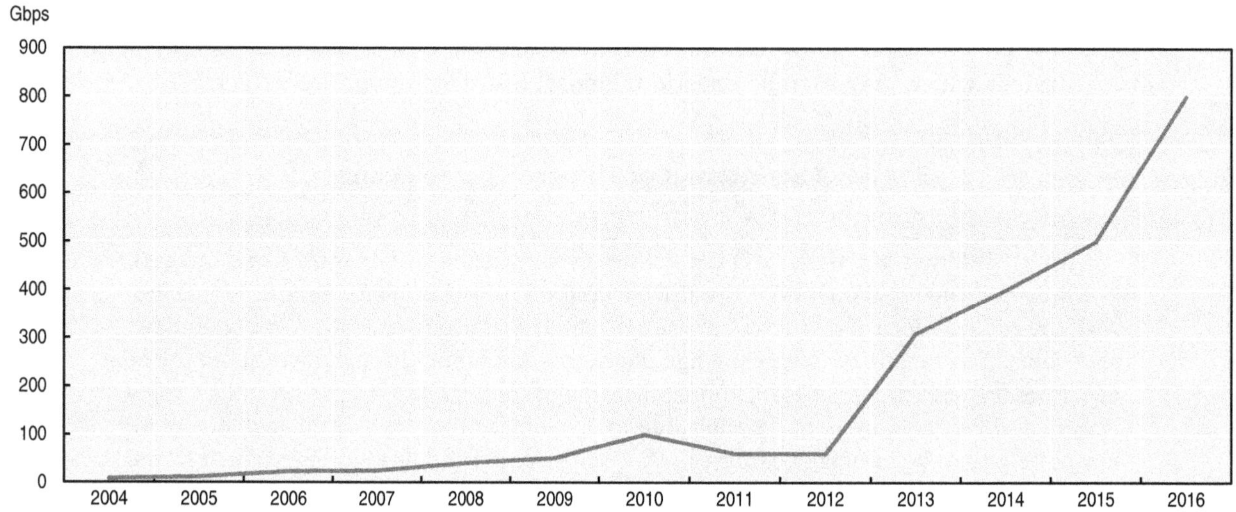

Note: Gbps = Gigabits per second.

Source: Author's calculations based on Arbor Networks (2016), *Worldwide Infrastructure Security Report Volume XI*, *www.arbornetworks.com/images/documents/WISR2016_EN_Web.pdf*; Arbor Networks (2017), *Worldwide Infrastructure Security Report Volume XII*, *www.arbornetworks.com/insight-into-the-global-threat-landscape*.

StatLink http://dx.doi.org/10.1787/888933586464

In the 2012 ICSPA survey in Canada, for example, the category with the highest average number of incidents per business was "phishing, spear phishing, social engineering". The 2016 Ponemon State of Cybersecurity in Small and Medium-Sized Businesses, as another example, found that the most commonly experienced attacks (for SMEs) were web-based attacks, phishing/social engineering and general malware. In the National Small Business Association's Year End Economic Reports for 2014 and 2015 (NSBA 2015, 2016), it was found that the highest proportion of businesses experienced a service interruption due to digital security incidents. The most common impact of an incident, according to the survey, was "service interruption" in both 2014 and 2015. A relatively small proportion of respondents reported impacts suggestive of a data breach ("sensitive information and data was stolen" or "information about and/or from my clients was stolen") or fraud ("the attack enabled hackers to access my business bank accounts/credit card[s]").

The cost of digital security incidents is significant but still difficult to assess

As noted above, digital security incidents can have various types of consequences for organisations: undermined reputation when the brand is exposed, loss of competitiveness when trade secrets are stolen, financial loss resulting from the attack itself (e.g. in sophisticated scam schemes[16]), from lost business, disruption of operations (e.g. sabotage), recovery costs or legal proceedings and fines.[17] It is difficult to estimate the actual cost of incidents: organisations are often reluctant to share potentially damaging information, intellectual assets are difficult to value and, in many instances, organisations do not even report incidents, such as when there is no legal obligation to do so, for example in cases of theft of trade secrets and sabotage. It is also difficult to assess the cost of digital security incidents outside the organisation, for example to individuals and society. Also, different incidents will have different costs. Rarely are the estimates disaggregated by incident type.

As a result, there are no official statistics, data sources or widely recognised methodologies to measure the aggregate cost of incidents. Thus, much of the evidence is anecdotal. Some studies provide interesting aggregated estimates, which should nevertheless be treated cautiously. Examples include the joint study by the US Center for Strategic and International Studies (CSIS, 2014) and Intel McAfee, which estimated that the likely annual cost to the global economy from cybercrime is between USD 375 billion and USD 575 billion. According to this source, the costs of cybercrime would range from 0.02% of gross domestic product in Japan to 1.6% in Germany, 0.64% in the United States and 0.63% in China. Other studies provide firm-level estimates based on surveys. That being said, these also should be treated cautiously, given that they suffer from survey-specific issues, and in particular selection bias. Furthermore, costs estimated based on some of these surveys can fluctuate significantly over years, as a result of the "fat tailed" distribution. As a result, mean or median costs are hard to interpret, in particular when statistics are broken down by business size or sectors are missing. In NSBA (2015, 2016), for instance, the estimated cost of digital security incidents for the average firm fluctuates substantially from year-to-year: from USD 8 700 in 2013 to USD 20 750 in 2014 and USD 7 115 in 2015.

The 2016 Cyber Security Breaches Survey undertaken in the United Kingdom found that the average cost of all breaches, in absolute terms, was higher for micro- and small enterprises than for medium-sized enterprises. The mean remained quite stable, which indicates that a small proportion of incidents in a small proportion of businesses are likely responsible for a large proportion of total costs (Table 6.1). The 2016 Ponemon State of Cybersecurity in Small and Medium-Sized Businesses confirms that small businesses tend to lose less than large businesses. In particular, it shows that the mean cost/loss associated with incidents increased with firm size. That said, the consequences of some incidents may be harder to weather for SMEs even if costs/losses are smaller compared to those experienced by large organisations.[18] According to a 2011 study cited by the US House Small Business Subcommittee on Health and Technology, for example, roughly 60% of small businesses close within six months of a digital security attack (Kaiser, 2011).

Table 6.1. **Costs of all and most disruptive incidents experienced in the last 12 months, United Kingdom, 2016**

GBP

	All businesses	Micro/small	Medium	Large
Cost of all breaches				
Mean	3 480	3 100	1 860	36 500
Median	200	200	180	1 300
Cost of most disruptive breach				
Mean	2 620	2 300	837	32 300
Median	100	100	48	323

Source: UK Department for Culture, Media & Sport (2016), 2016 Cyber Security Breaches Survey.

Privacy risks are amplifying with the collection and use of big data analytics

A growing number of entities, such as online retailers, ISPs, financial service providers (i.e. banks, credit card companies and so forth), and governments are increasingly collecting vast amounts of personal data.[19] With that comes an increasing risk of privacy violations. In 2015, around 3% of all individuals across OECD countries for which data are available reported having experienced a privacy violation within the last 3 months (Figure 6.9). In some countries the share can be much higher, such as in Korea (above 7%), Chile (almost 6%) and Luxembourg (almost 5%). In many countries, such as Norway, Portugal, Sweden and Turkey, this share had increased significantly compared to 2010. Personal data breaches – more precisely the breach of the confidentiality of personal data as a result of malicious activities or accidental losses – are a major cause of privacy violations. In addition, individuals' privacy can be affected by the extraction of complementary information that can be derived, by "mining" available data for patterns and correlations, many of which do not need to be personal data. Both risks, personal data breaches and privacy violation resulting from the misuse of big data analytics, are discussed further below.

Figure 6.9. **Individuals having experienced privacy violations in the last three months**

As a percentage of all individuals

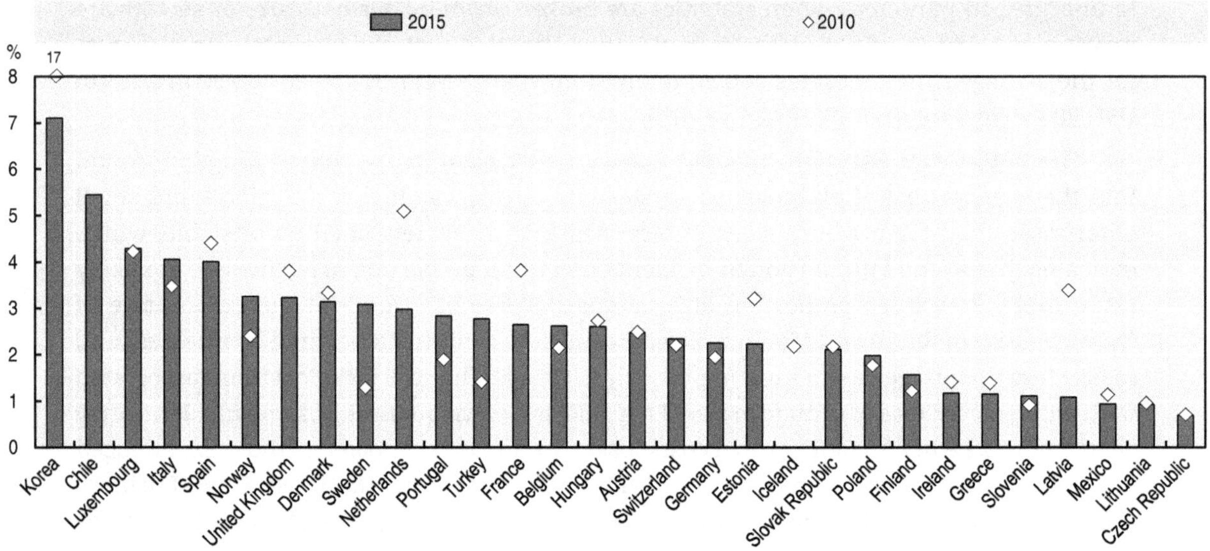

Notes: Data for Chile, Mexico and Switzerland refer to 2014. Data for Iceland refer to 2010. Chile, Korea, Mexico and Switzerland follow a different methodology.

Source: OECD, *ICT Access and Usage by Households and Individuals* (database), *http://oe.cd/hhind* (accessed June 2017).

StatLink *http://dx.doi.org/10.1787/888933586483*

Personal data breaches have increased in terms of scale and profile

Digital security incidents affecting the confidentiality of personal data, commonly referred to as "data breaches",[20] have increased as organisations collect and process large volumes of personal data. In 2005 ChoicePoint – a consumer data aggregation company – was the target of one of the first high-profile data breach involving over 150 000 personal records.[21] The company ended up paying more than USD 26 million in fees and fines. In 2007, retail giant TJX announced that it was the victim of an unauthorised computer system intrusion that affected over 45.7 million customers and cost the company more than USD 250 million. Since then, data breaches have become almost commonplace. According to a study commissioned by the UK government, 81% of large organisations suffered a security breach in 2014 (UK Department for Business Innovation and Skills, 2014).[22] Data breaches are not limited to the private sector, as evidenced by the theft in 2015 of over 21 million records stored by the US Office of Personnel Management, including 5.6 million fingerprints, and by the Japanese Pension Service breach that affected 1.25 million people (Otake, 2015).

An accurate estimate of the total cost of personal data breaches is hard to calculate. As argued above, available estimates have to be treated with caution, given that not all breaches are discovered, and when they are discovered, not all breaches are fully disclosed. Available estimates indicate a range of magnitude that strongly suggests that personal data breaches have a significant economic cost to society. One firm-level study by the Ponemon Institute suggests that the average total cost of a data breach was USD 4 million in 2016 (an increase of 29% compared to 2013). According to the study, this would correspond to an average cost per lost record of USD 158. There are significant cross-country and sectoral variations though. The average cost per lost record was estimated to be as high as USD 221 in the United States and as low as USD 61 in India. Furthermore, the average cost per lost record tends to be the highest in specific sectors, such as healthcare and transportation.

The greatest cost component for organisations tends to be loss of business, or: "This confirms the impact of a data breach on consumer loyalty" (Internet Society, 2016). The second highest cost component is remediation. Based on anecdotal evidence, it appears that litigation is increasingly common in the case of data breaches, with card issuers seeking to recover the costs of reissuing payment cards from the hacked companies and affected individuals launching class-action lawsuits. Breached organisations can end up paying fines, legal fees and redress costs. ChoicePoint, for example, paid more than USD26 million in fees and fines as a result of the action by the US Federal Trade Commission (FTC, 2006). In 2008, a data breach at one of the largest US credit card processing companies in the United States, Heartland Payment Systems, affected more than 600 financial institutions for a total cost of more than USD 12 million in fines and fees (McGlasson, 2009). In 2015, AT&T agreed to pay USD 25 million to settle an FTC investigation relating to data breaches involving almost 280 000 US customers (FTC, 2016).

Big data analytics presents new privacy risks to individuals' privacy

Advances in data analytics now make it possible to infer sensitive information from data which may appear trivial at first, such as past individual purchasing behaviour or electricity consumption. This increased capacity of data analytics is illustrated by Duhigg (2012) and Hill (2012), who describe how the US-based retailing company Target "figured out a teen girl was pregnant before her father did" based on specific signals in historical buying data.[23] The misuse of these insights can implicate the core values and principles which privacy protection seeks to promote, such as individual autonomy, equality and free speech, and this may have a broader impact on society as a whole.

In some cases, personal data are provided or revealed: 1) by choice, for example, through social media and e-mail; in other situations, through compulsory disclosure, for example as a pre-condition to receiving services; or 2) without awareness or consent, for example through tracking an individual's browsing. In the European Union, more than 60% of all individuals have provided their personal data over the Internet (Figure 6.10). Most of them provide personal details (name, date of birth, identity card number) as well as contact details. But around a third of these individuals have provided other personal information such as photos, location data, and information about their health and income over the Internet. Other personal data are collected by sensors in smartphones, tablets, laptops, wearable technologies and even sensor-enabled clothing, automobiles, homes and offices. Moreover, increasingly, new data are derived or inferred based on correlations gleaned from existing data (Abrams, 2014). The type of personal data that is collected and the means used to collect such data may vary by sector (Figure 6.11). Utilities, for example, are more likely to collect big data from sensors and to use geolocation data from mobile devices. Mobile devices are also used in the transportation sector. Social media data, in contrast, are used to a large extent in accommodation and food, mainly for marketing purposes.

Figure 6.10. **Individuals providing their personal information over the Internet, 2016**

Percentage of individuals who used the Internet within the last year

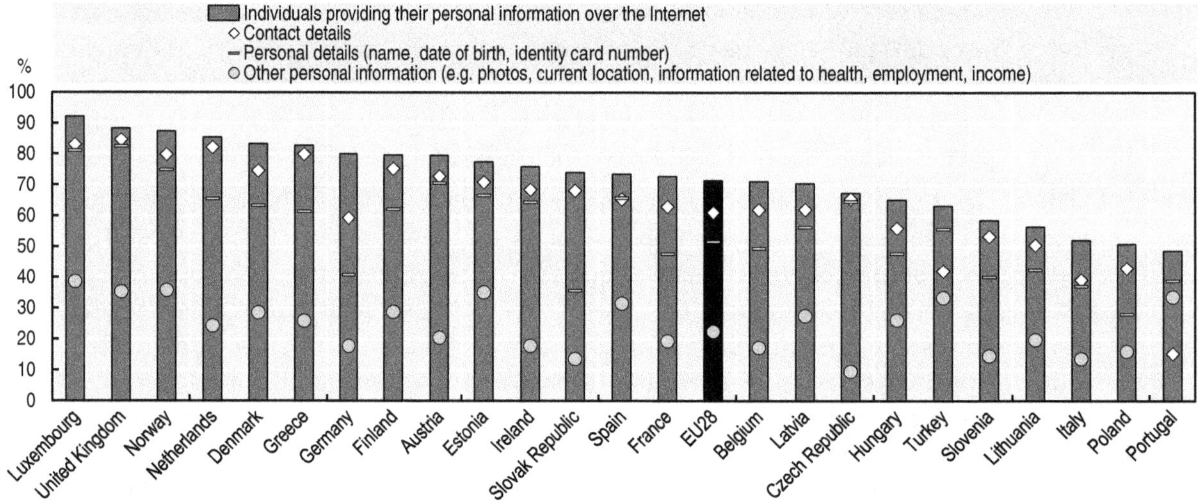

Source: Eurostat, *Digital Economy and Society* (database), *http://ec.europa.eu/eurostat/web/digital-economy-and-society/data/comprehensive-database* (accessed March 2017).

StatLink http://dx.doi.org/10.1787/888933586502

Figure 6.11. **Business use of big data by data source and industry in the EU28, 2016**

As a percentage of all enterprises

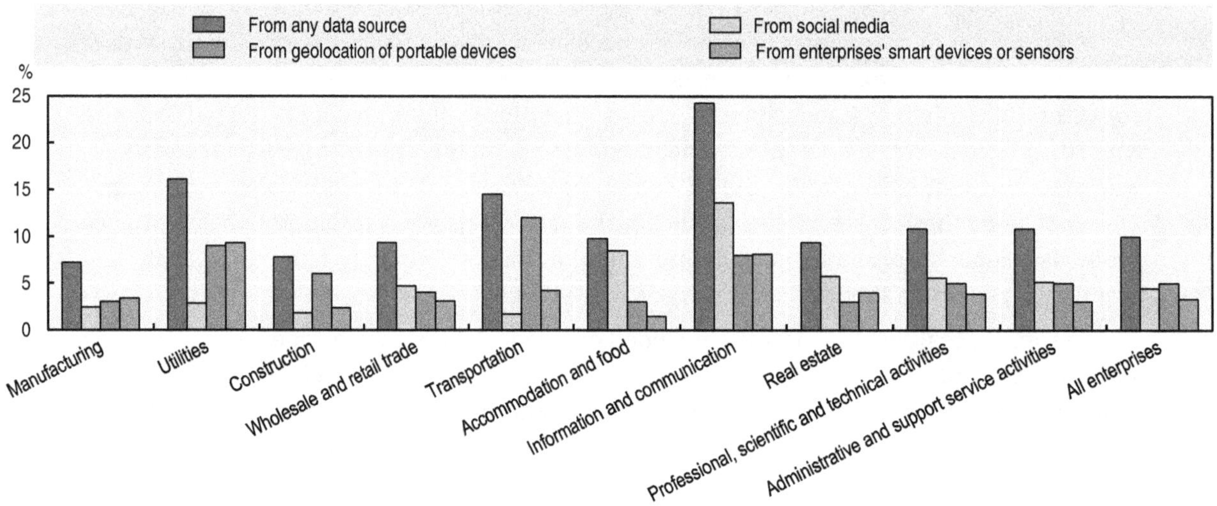

Source: Eurostat, *Digital Economy and Society* (database), *http://ec.europa.eu/eurostat/web/digital-economy-and-society/data/comprehensive-database* (accessed March 2017).

StatLink http://dx.doi.org/10.1787/888933586521

By collecting and analysing large amounts of consumer data, firms are able to predict aggregate trends, such as variations in consumer demand as well as individual preferences, thus minimising inventory risks and maximising returns on marketing investment. Furthermore, by observing individual behaviour, firms can learn how to improve their products and services, or redesign them in order to take advantage of the observed behaviour. These uses may also benefit the consumer: targeted advertising may give consumers useful information, since the adverts are tailored to consumers' interests (Acquisti, 2010). However, this ability to profile and send targeted messages and marketing offers to individuals may also have adverse consequences: some consumers may object to having their online activities observed; they may end up paying higher prices as a result of price discrimination; or they could be manipulated towards products or services they may not even need (OECD, 2015b).

The risk of online fraud is growing with the importance of e-commerce

The numbers and types of reported online fraud have increased in many countries. In countries such as Denmark, France, Luxembourg, Norway and Sweden, for example, around 2% of all individuals experienced a financial loss from fraudulent payment online in the final three months of 2015, and this share had increased compared to 2010 in many countries (Figure 6.12). In the United States alone, over 3 million complaints (excluding do-not-call) were registered in the Consumer Sentinel Network (CSN) database in 2016. "Impostor scams" (13%), "identity theft" (13%), and "telephone and mobile services" (10%) were among the most frequent complaint subcategories related to Internet usage and are growing in significance.[24] That said, the rise of reported complaints is only partly attributable to Internet-based transactions, it could also be the result of (non-Voice over Internet Protocol [VoIP]) telephone-based incidents. It therefore needs to be assessed further through additional data. Notably, complaints in the CSN are self-reported and unverified, and do not necessarily represent a random sample of consumer injury for any particular market. The following sections present current trends related to identity theft and fraudulent and deceptive commercial practices.

Figure 6.12. **Individuals having experienced a financial loss from fraudulent online payment in the last three months**

As a percentage of all individuals

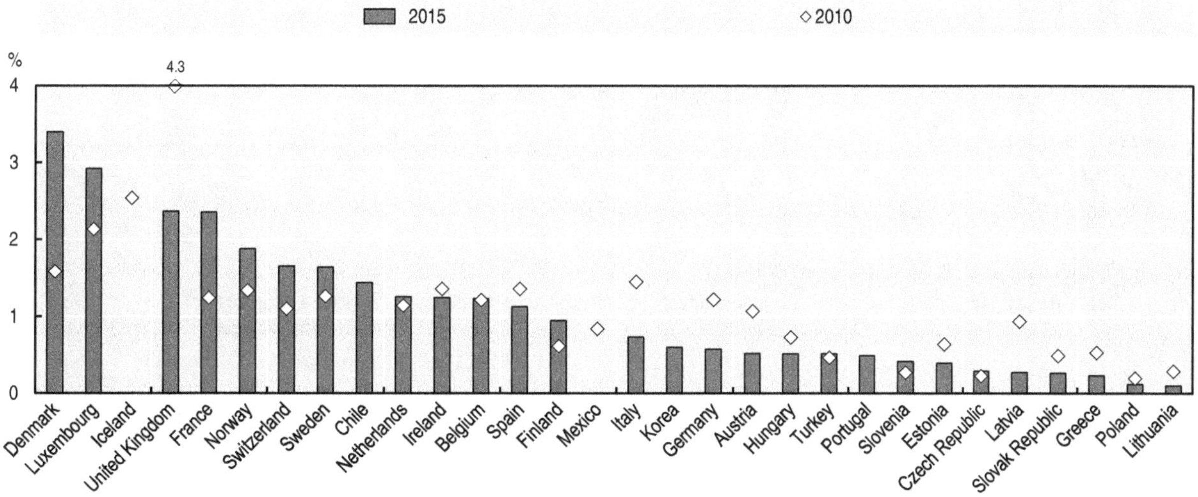

Notes: Data for Chile and Switzerland refer to 2014 instead of 2015. Data for Mexico refer to 2009 instead of 2010.

Source: OECD, *ICT Access and Usage by Households and Individuals* (database), *http://oe.cd/hhind* (accessed June 2017).

StatLink http://dx.doi.org/10.1787/888933586540

As highlighted above, personal data breaches not only cause significant economic losses to the business affected, but can also cause harm as a result of the privacy violation of the individuals whose personal data have been breached. In addition, further consumer detriment may result from a data breach such as harm caused by identity theft. Available evidence suggests that identity theft incidents, in particular through phishing or pharming, have increased in recent years. Of the over 3 million complaints received by the CSN in the United States in 2016, for example, more than 13% were related to identity theft. Between 2008 and 2016, the number of complaints related to identity theft increased on average by more than 30% annually, with the number of complaints reaching its peak in 2015 (with more than 490 000 complaints).[25] Not all complaints were related to online activities though: "Employment – or tax-related fraud (34%) was the most common form of reported identity theft, followed by credit card fraud (33%), phone or utilities fraud (13%), and bank fraud (12%)" (FTC, 2017). In 2015 there was also a huge increase in the share of individuals experiencing a financial loss from phishing or pharming in many OECD countries, most notably in Belgium, Luxembourg, Sweden, Norway, Denmark and France (Figure 6.13). The share of individuals experiencing a financial loss from phishing or pharming only diminished significantly in a few countries, such as in Austria, Italy, Ireland and Latvia. The extent to which public policies could have been determinant for the decrease in incidents deserves further examination.

Figure 6.13. **Individuals having experienced a financial loss from phishing/pharming in the last three months**

As a percentage of all individuals

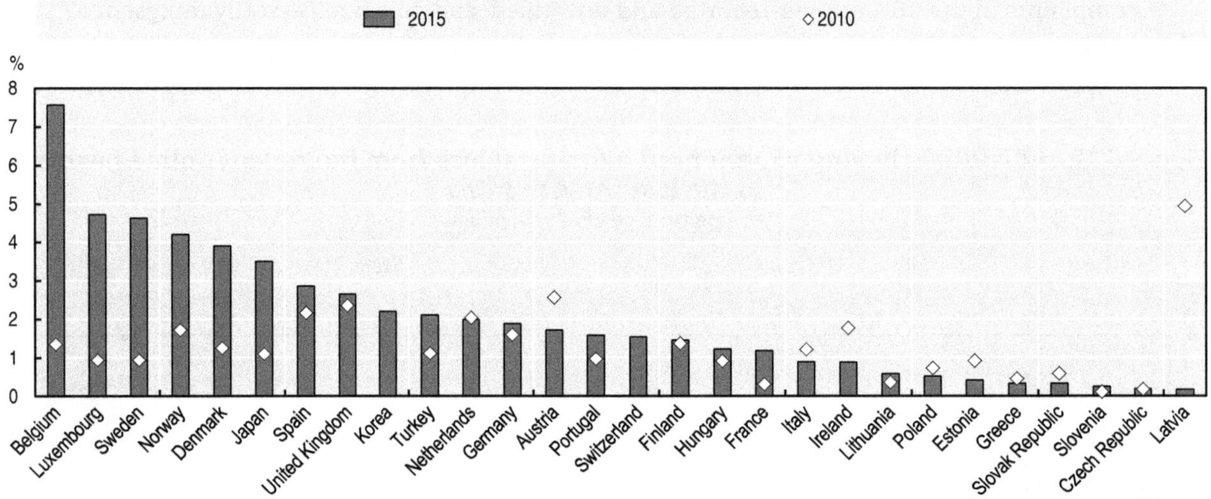

Note: Data for Switzerland refer to 2014 instead of 2015.

Source: OECD, *ICT Access and Usage by Households and Individuals* (database), *http://oe.cd/hhind* (accessed June 2017).

StatLink http://dx.doi.org/10.1787/888933586559

Fraudulent and deceptive commercial practices can also cause actual harm to consumers and reduce trust in e-commerce.[26] According to data from econsumer.gov, an ICPEN initiative of 36 countries that allows consumers to file cross-border complaints, the top three complaint categories for 2016 were: 1) "shop at home/catalogue sales"; 2) "impostor: government"; and 3) "travel/vacations". Similarly, available evidence for the European Union shows that consumers are increasingly facing issues related to such fraudulent and deceptive practices. The main problems encountered when buying online in the EU27 besides technical issues, were related to speed of delivery being longer than indicated. This was experienced by around 20% of all EU consumers buying online in 2016 (compared to 5% in 2009). Delivery of the wrong or damaged product, experienced by around 10% of all EU consumers in 2016 (compared to around 4% in 2009), is another major issue. The other issues, each affecting between 3% and 6% of all EU consumers, include problems with fraud, difficulties finding information concerning guarantees and other legal rights, final prices being higher from the ones initially indicated, unsatisfactory handling of complaints and redress. All of these issues have significantly increased compared to 2009.

Building and reinforcing trust in the digital economy

While trust can erode over time if overexploited, it can also be built and reinforced. And individuals (including consumers) and businesses have different means at their disposal to enhance trust. For example, consumers can benefit from truthful and transparent online reviews, endorsements and product comparison tools to overcome the information asymmetry between consumers and businesses (OECD, 2016e). Furthermore, risk management practices, and in particular the risk assessment process, provide organisations with the information needed to determine whether the level of risk in their environment is acceptable for undertaking investments in, and using, a digital technology. Finally, there are trust-enhancing technologies, including, but not limited to, privacy-enhancing technologies (PETs) and digital security tools. More recently block chains have been discussed as an emerging technology for users to enhance trust in transactions without the need for a trusted third party (Chapter 7). These trust-enhancing means are discussed further below. This section does not discuss the role of public policies in enhancing trust, which is discussed in Chapter 2.

Empowering individuals and businesses remains necessary to better address trust issues

Being well informed and aware about digital security and privacy risks is a basic condition for being able to address major trust issues in the digital economy. According to the Special Eurobarometer survey (EC, 2015c), "respondents who feel well informed about the risks of cybercrime are more likely to use the Internet for all of the various activities, compared with those who do not feel well informed". These individuals are also more likely to take measures to address these risks. For example, 32% of well-informed respondents regularly change their passwords, compared with 19% of respondents who do not feel well informed. Individuals in Denmark, the Netherlands and Sweden are more likely to be well informed about the risks of "cybercrime" and they are also less likely to be concerned about being the victim of such crime. In countries such as Greece, Hungary, Italy and Portugal the opposite is true; individuals in these countries are less likely to feel well informed about the risks of cybercrime and are less likely to use digital services such as online banking and e-commerce. This suggests that there may be a negative correlation between being informed about digital security and privacy risk, and being concerned about being a victim of digital security and privacy incidents. It also underlines the importance of awareness, skills and empowerment as reflected, for instance, in the OECD Council Recommendation *Digital Security Risk Management for Economic and Social Prosperity* (OECD, 2015a).[27]

In the area of privacy, the importance of awareness, skills and empowerment has also long been recognised (OECD, 2015b). In particular, means to provide individuals with better mechanisms to control their personal data have been discussed, such as data portability (see Chapter 2). As shown in Figure 6.14, for instance, 60% of individuals in the European Union are already managing access to their personal data. They do so either by: 1) limiting the use of their personal data for advertising purposes (40% of all individuals); 2) limiting access to their social networking profiles (35%); 3) restricting access to their geographic location (30%); and 4) asking websites to update or delete information held about them. It is interesting to note that individuals in countries such as Denmark, the Netherlands and Sweden, where being well informed about the risks of "cybercrime" is more likely, also tend to be more likely to manage their personal information over the Internet. In contrast, individuals in countries where individuals feel less well informed about the risks of "cybercrime" also rank below average in terms of the share of individuals managing the use of their personal information over the Internet. The following sections discuss trends on the means to empower individuals and businesses, including through the use of trust-enhancing technologies, the reduction of information asymmetries, and developing skills and competencies related to digital security and privacy (risk management).

Figure 6.14. **Individuals managing the use of their personal information over the Internet, 2016**

Percentage of individuals who used Internet within the last year

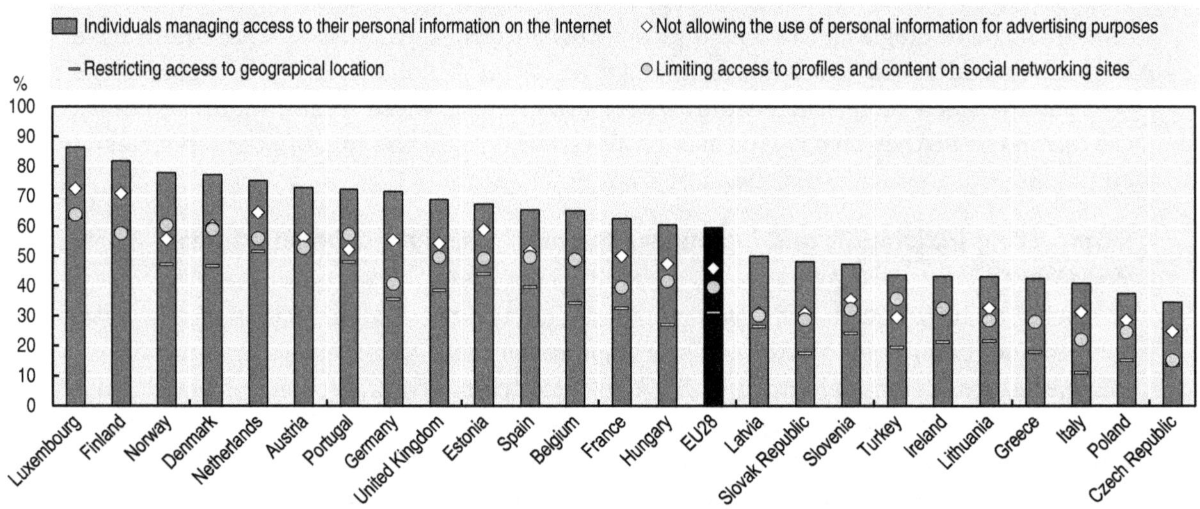

Source: Eurostat, *Digital Economy and Society* (database), *http://ec.europa.eu/eurostat/web/digital-economy-and-society/data/comprehensive-database* (accessed March 2017).

StatLink http://dx.doi.org/10.1787/888933586578

Trust-enhancing technologies are needed but not sufficient for empowering individuals and businesses

There is strong evidence for the increasing use of trust-enhancing technologies. There are, however, also significant variations by country, firm size and industry. According to the 2016 Ponemon State of Cybersecurity in Small and Medium-Sized Businesses anti-malware, client firewalls and password protection/management rank among the highest security tools used. In Korea, the 2015 Survey on Information Security in Business revealed that by far the largest proportion of respondents invested in or planned on investing in wireless local area network (LAN) security.

As products (goods and services) and business processes become more data-intensive, and data proliferates to more and more locations, such as mobile devices and the cloud, encryption is increasingly seen as a needed supplement to existing infrastructure-centric protection measures. According to a 2016 Encryption Application Trends Study sponsored by Thales e-Security and covering over 5000 respondents in 14 major industry sectors and 11 countries, encryption has never been as profoundly used in the 11-year history of the survey after accelerating in 2014. More companies are also embracing an enterprise-wide encryption strategy. In 2015, 41% of surveyed businesses indicated having extensively deployed encryption compared to 34% in 2014 and 16% in 2005 (Figure 6.15). Germany, the United States, Japan and the United Kingdom rank above average in terms of the share of businesses having deployed or deploying an enterprise-wide encryption strategy (with

61%, 45%, 40% and 38% respectively). Surveyed businesses indicate privacy compliance regulation,[28] digital security threats targeting in particular intellectual property, as well as employee and customer data as the main reason for this fast increase in encryption adoption in recent years. In particular, firms in heavily regulated industries dealing extensively with (big) data rank high among the list of extensive encryption users. These include most notably: financial services, healthcare and pharmaceuticals, and technology and software firms.

Figure 6.15. **Extensive deployment of encryption by businesses worldwide**

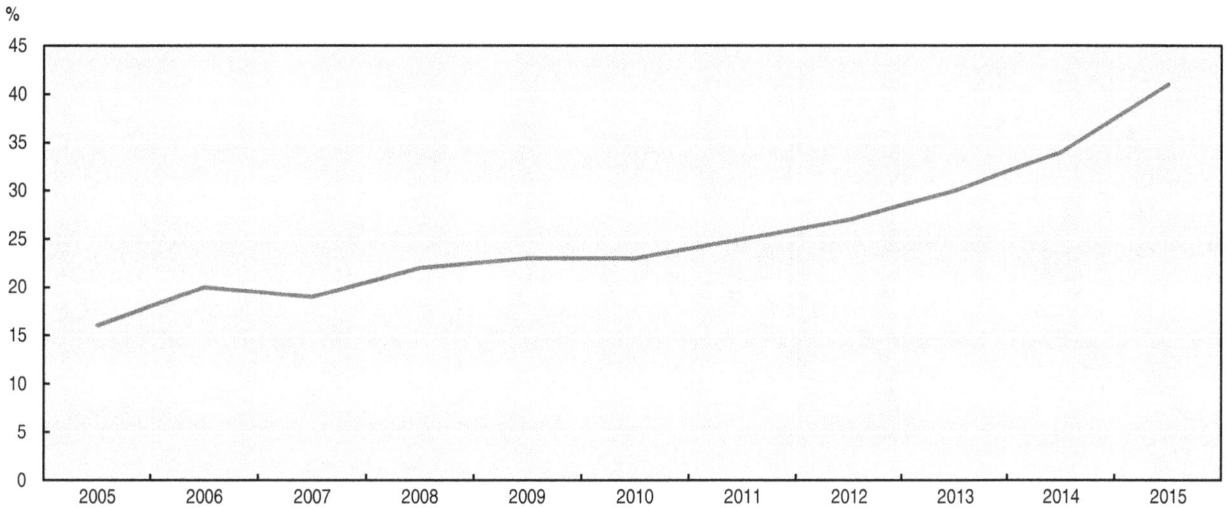

Note: Based on over 5 000 respondents from 14 industry sectors and 11 countries across the globe.
Source: Thales e-Security (2016), *2016 Encryption Application Trends Study*.

StatLink http://dx.doi.org/10.1787/888933586597

Internet communications (e.g. Transport Layer Security [TLS] or its predecessor Secure Socket Layer [SSL]) still rank the highest among the application for encryption use across industries, before databases and mobile devices. SSL is a security protocol used by Internet browsers and web servers to exchange sensitive information such as passwords and credit card numbers. It relies on a certificate authority, such as those provided by companies like Symantec and GoDaddy, that issues a digital certificate containing a public key and information about its owner, and confirms that a given public key belongs to a specific site. In doing so, certificate authorities act as trusted third parties. In the past, there has, however, been a series of security incidents targeting certificate authorities (see for example the 2001 security incident affecting DigiNotar, a company based in the Netherlands).

Netcraft carries out monthly secure server surveys on public secure websites (excluding secure mail servers, intranet and non-public extranet sites). According to the March 2017 survey, more than 27 million secure servers were deployed worldwide. This corresponds to a compound average growth rate of 65% annually (compared to 2.2 million in 2012). Growth rates accelerated in 2014. Prior to that the number of servers grew by around 20% year-on-year.[29] The number of secure servers hosted in the OECD area was slightly above 14 million in March 2017, accounting for 83% of the total number of secure servers hosted worldwide.[30] The United States accounted for the largest share of secure servers (6.2 million), at 38% of the world total. It was followed by Germany (1.7 million) and the United Kingdom (953 000) (Figure 6.16). Relative to the total number of sites hosted, however, most countries still perform poorly in terms of the share of secure servers over their total number of servers hosted. In the United States, for example, less than 1% of all servers hosted use SSL/TLS.[31]

Figure 6.16. **Secured servers by hosting country, March 2017**

As a percentage of total number of secured servers and in millions

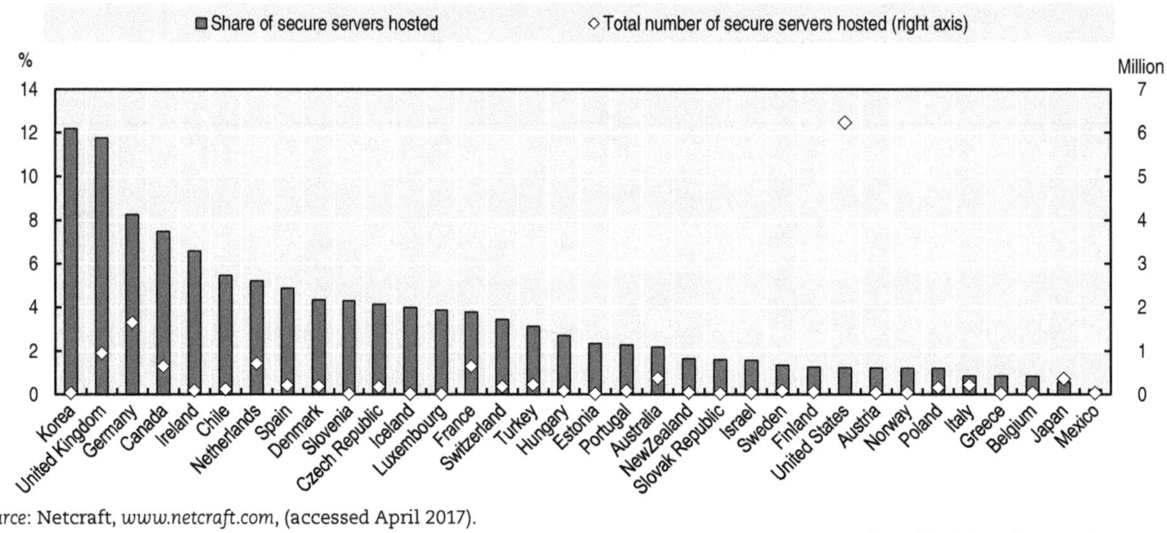

Source: Netcraft, *www.netcraft.com*, (accessed April 2017).

StatLink http://dx.doi.org/10.1787/888933586616

The use of encryption has also intensified in the market for consumer goods and services, where companies such as Apple and Google continue to increase their default use of encryption (OECD, 2015b). These firms' latest mobile operating systems encrypt nearly all data at rest (in addition to data in transit) by default. Additionally, demand for end-to-end encryption has increased considerably in recent years with apps such as Signal Private Messenger and Threema being increasingly adopted and massively popular apps like WhatsApp also rolling out end-to-end encryption.[32] Users' increasing interest for encryption is also reflected in the adoption of PETs such as OpenPGP (Pretty Good Privacy), a data-encryption software used most commonly to secure e-mails. According to data collected by Fiskerstrand (2017), more than 1 100 new PGP keys are being added every day. The data show in particular that in the months following the Snowden disclosures (Q3 2013), PGP key creation reached the highest levels in the history of the software with almost 101 000 new PGP keys are being added in Q3 2017 (Figure 6.17). This correlation does not imply causation and would call for further analysis.

Another example for a PET also showing a similar adoption pattern is Tor (originally the acronym for The Onion Router), an anonymity network that allows anyone to use the Internet without easily revealing their location or identity.[33] Figure 6.18 shows that the total number of Tor users worldwide has increased dramatically in mid-2013 following the Snowden disclosures.[34] Although it dropped rapidly as well, the number of daily users has reached a new level of around 2 million after the Snowden disclosures compared to before, when the number of daily users was around half as much. Most daily users are located in the United States (around 20%), followed by Germany, the Islamic Republic of Iran, France, Italy, Korea and the Russian Federation.

Figure 6.17. **Trends in newly created OpenPGP keys**

OpenPGP keys generated daily

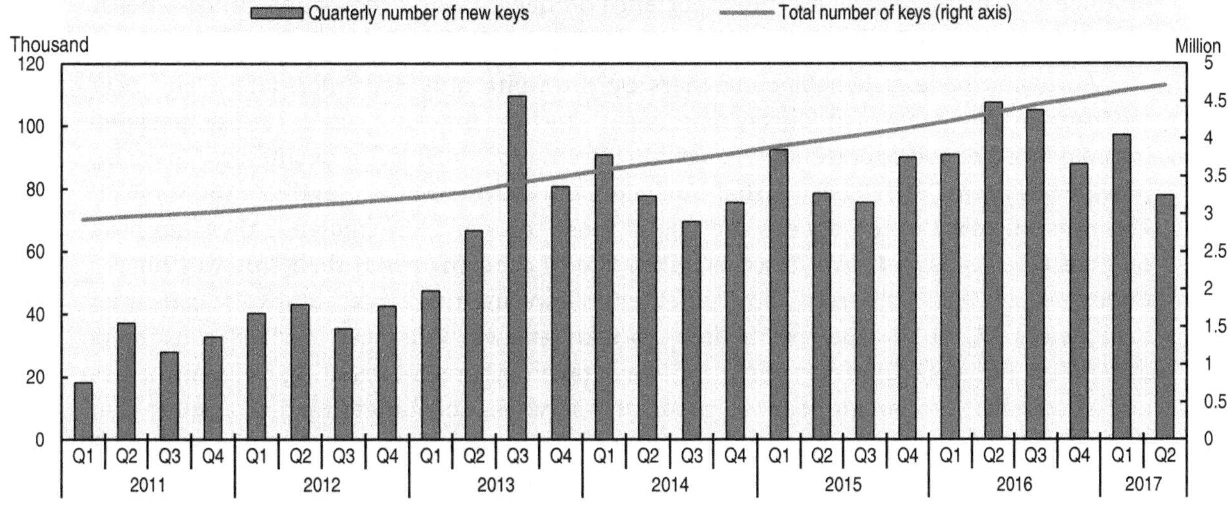

Source: Author's calculations based on data collected by Kristian Fiskerstrand (sks-keyservers.net) (accessed June 2017).

StatLink http://dx.doi.org/10.1787/888933586635

Figure 6.18. **Daily numbers of directly connecting users from all countries, September 2011-August 2017**

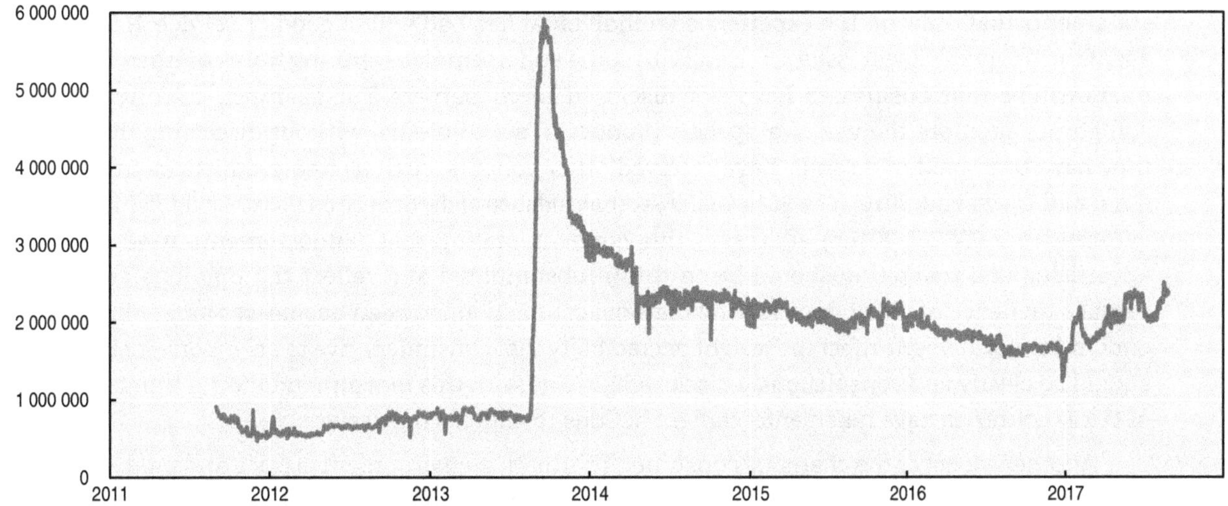

Source: The Tor Project, *https://metrics.torproject.org*, (accessed August 2017).

StatLink http://dx.doi.org/10.1787/888933586654

Reviews, endorsements and product comparison tools are becoming increasingly important for consumers

Consumers increasingly inform their purchasing decisions by consulting online reviews and endorsements by other consumers. A 2013 web survey by the European Consumer Centres Network shows that 82% of respondents look at consumer reviews before shopping online (ECCN, 2015). In its report on "Online reviews and endorsements", the Competition Markets Authority found that more than half of UK adults use online reviews and estimated that GBP 23 billion (USD 28.5 billion) per year of consumer spending is influenced by online reviews (CMA, 2015a). The influence of reviews and endorsements is further increasing with the development of the peer platform market, where trust in unknown sellers is often based on such reviews. Businesses are also increasingly using reviews as a form of advertising their product. This further amplifies the importance of making sure reviews and endorsements in peer platform markets are not misleading (ICPEN, 2016).

Authentic reviews benefit consumers by providing unbiased information and peer feedback on the quality of products and services. They can make consumers feel empowered by providing them an opportunity to question information provided by businesses. They also provide businesses with feedback that can help them to improve their products and services. The rapid increase in the uptake and use of these tools and the influence they can have on consumer decisions have, however, given rise to concerns about their trustworthiness. Concerns have been expressed about whether reviews are truly representative of consumer experiences (EC, 2017). One specific issue is fake reviews, which can mislead consumers into taking decisions that they would not have taken otherwise, resulting in financial loss and diminished enjoyment of those goods and services. Consumers tend to assume that data provided are trustworthy. A 2014 consumer review survey shows that Canadian and US consumers are inclined to trust what they read, with 88% reporting that they have as much confidence in online reviews as they do in personal recommendations. Conversely, research in 2016 suggests that three-quarters of consumers surveyed in ten EU countries have trust-related reservations about online reviews (EC, 2017). It is difficult to evaluate the extent of the problem of fake reviews, with estimates ranging from 1 to 16% of all reviews (Valant, 2015).

Closely related to reviews are product endorsements and testimonials, which are statements that draw on the experience an individual has had with a good or service. Here again the trustworthiness issue is raised, with some endorsements resulting from commercial relationships that businesses have not disclosed to consumers. For example, celebrities sometimes promote the use of a specific product in social media, without disclosing that they have been paid to do so or have received other benefits, such as free products or trips (Frier and Townsend, 2016). The 2016 OECD *Recommendation of the Council on Consumer Protection in E-commerce* (OECD, 2016d) addresses this conduct, stating that "Endorsements used in advertising and marketing should be truthful, substantiated and reflect the opinions and actual experience of the endorsers. Any material connection between businesses and online endorsers, which might affect the weight or credibility that consumers give to an endorsement, should be clearly and conspicuously disclosed". In line with this recommendation, a number of OECD countries have taken enforcement actions to address this issue.

Another aspect of the changing consumer information environment is price and product comparison websites. These have become a popular type of consumer tool in many sectors such as insurance, energy, telecommunication services and payment cards. A 2015 survey conducted by the UK Competition & Markets Authority shows that 71% of respondents who shopped online in the last three years used a price and product comparison website to search for information (CMA, 2015b). These comparison websites can help consumers feel more informed and empowered by allowing them to access information about various offers more easily and reducing the search time. It also allows consumers to act on this information by providing highly customised analysis of the best value for the goods and services they purchase (UKRN, 2016).

Despite a number of benefits for consumers, the effectiveness of comparison websites can be undermined by misleading and deceptive advertising. A study commissioned by the European Commission found that two-thirds of the consumers using comparison tools had experienced a problem in the process, such as the unavailability of the product advertised on the seller's website (32%) or incorrect prices (21%). Most of the comparison tools tested did not disclose information on their business model or their relationship with suppliers (ECME Consortium, 2013). A 2014 study of online hotel reviews highlighted different transparency issues, with only around 30% of websites providing an explanation of how their scoring or rating system works (EC, 2014).

Security and privacy-related skills and competencies are crucial and their demand is growing rapidly

The growing importance and visibility of security and privacy risks has increased the number of potential new jobs for experts in these areas. Demand for security expertise is characterised by a continuation of the steady growth evident over the last decade, while growth in demand for privacy professionals has accelerated rapidly in recent years (Figure 6.19). However, locating available professionals with the required skills and expertise in privacy and security remains a challenge for organisations looking to strengthen their capacities in these areas (OECD, 2015a).

The (ISC)^2 (International Information Systems Security Certification Consortium) estimates the global number of digital security workforce in 2014 at 3.4 million people and forecasts a compound average growth rate of almost 6% over the five years to 2019. According to the distribution of survey respondents, 46% are practitioners (mainly information security analysts) and the rest are leaders: chief information security officer (CISO) and executive levels (12%), managers (20%), auditors (5%), architects and strategic advisors (17%) ((ISC)^2, 2015). Employment numbers for individual countries are still scarce, but evidence from Korea and the United States can be used to illustrate some global trends. The Korean 2014 Information Security Workforce Survey reports 94 224 information security specialists employed at the end of 2013. The number of information security specialists in Korea continues to grow. In 2013, 10 000 additional workers were employed and the number of additional employees is expected to be over 11 000 in the years to come. This growth mainly results from more hiring in the middle and top-level positions, whereas entry-level recruitments are estimated to remain flat, confirming the impact of Korean national policy on CISOs. Official data for the United States are available only for information security analysts, a sub-set of the digital security specialists. There were 80 180 such analysts in US firms in 2014, of which only 18% were women. Employment increased by 3% that same year compared to 2013.

In terms of privacy professionals, the number of members of the International Association of Privacy Professionals (IAPP) – the largest and most global in reach association of privacy professionals[35] – can be used as proxy for employment trends related to privacy. The IAPP's membership numbers have continuously increased, from over 10 000 in 2012 to more than 26 000 in 2016 in nearly 90 countries around the world. Recent developments have been driven by regulation setting the parameters for the development of a privacy workforce, including chief privacy officers and their staff. Organisations affected by the new GDPR, which enters into force in 25 May 2018 to replace the EU Data Protection Directive, have expressed an increasing demand for data protection specialists. It is estimated that around 30 000 to 75 000 new positions will be created in the coming years in response to the new regulation, given in particular the requirement for data controllers and processors to designate a data protection officer in specific cases[36] (Ashford, 2016a; 2016b). Policies and regulations stimulating demand for privacy professionals are not limited to the European Union, but can be found in countries such as Canada, Korea and the United States to just name a few (see Chapter 2).[37]

Figure 6.19. **Trends in the numbers of certified/professionals privacy and security experts**

Index 100 = 2005

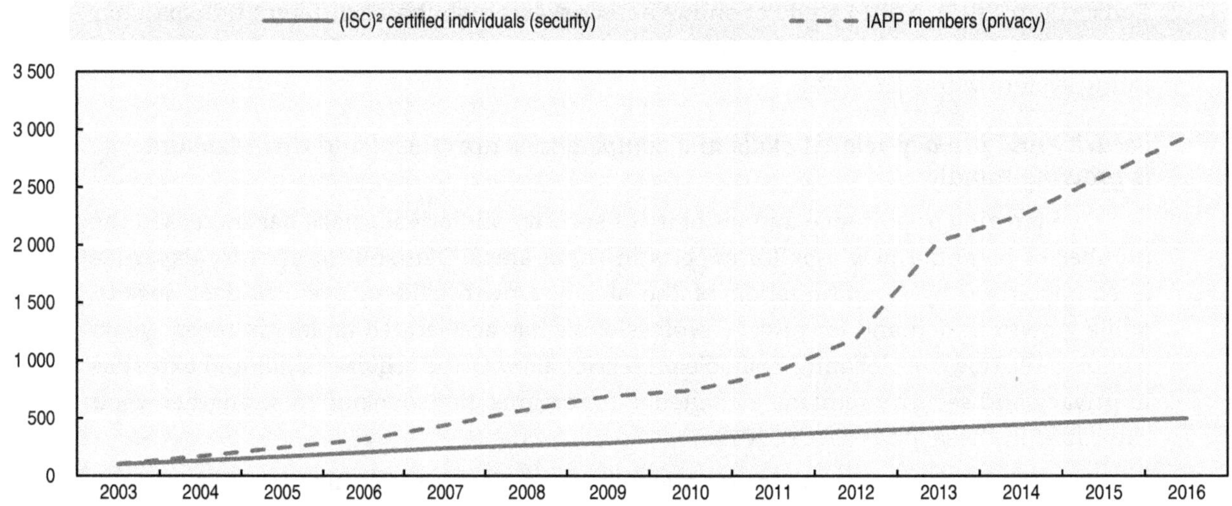

Note: (ISC²) is an international non-profit membership association focused on inspiring a safe and secure cyber world. The International Association of Privacy Professionals (IAPP) is a non-profit membership association.

Sources: Author's calculations based on OECD (2015a), *Digital Security Risk Management for Economic and Social Prosperity: OECD Recommendation and Companion Document*, *http://dx.doi.org/10.1787/9789264245471-en*; (ISC)² (2015), "The 2015 (ISC)² global information security workforce study", *https://www.boozallen.com/content/dam/boozallen/documents/Viewpoints/2015/04/frostsullivan-ISC2-global-information-security-workforce-2015.pdf*; IAPP (2016), "IAPP-EY annual privacy governance report 2016", *https://iapp.org/media/pdf/resource_center/IAPP-2016-GOVERNANCE-SURVEY-FINAL2.pdf*.

StatLink http://dx.doi.org/10.1787/888933586673

According to many forecasts, demand for digital security experts will also continue to increase worldwide. In the United States, the Bureau of Labor Statistics forecasts demand for information security analysts to grow much faster (37%) than the average for computer-related occupations (18%) (Bureau of Labor Statistics, 2014).[38] This is reflected in the total number of job vacancies for information security analysts, which is generally growing in the United States as in other OECD countries. According to Burning Glass data, the average vacancy duration for cybersecurity occupations (skills) in the United States in 2016 was 33% (44%) higher than for all IT specialists (skills). Job vacancies reached their highest level in the last quarter of 2014 (over 17000 job postings in the United States). Despite some divergent trends in 2013 where job vacancies for information security analysts grew much faster than employment (first and third quarters of 2013), both job vacancies and people employed have grown at the same pace since the beginning of 2014 (Figure 6.20). The fact that this ratio has remained relatively stable in recent years shows that demand for information security analysts exists but it seems that to some extent employers are finding people to fill the postings.

That said, there is a general feeling that there is still a workforce shortage. The increasing number of digital security incidents and employers' requirements for an advanced education together with the increasing need of credentials and a longer experience in the field are seen as key reasons for the shortage. (ISC)^2 finds that information security specialists are growing in number but still do not fully meet the market demand in terms of all the challenges to be addressed. The main reasons for the challenge in hiring remain: 1) an insufficient understanding of the requirement for digital security risk management, in particular among business executives; 2) a lack of financial resources; 3) the shortage of digital security specialists in the labour market with the consequence of 4) a difficulty of retaining existing digital security specialists.[39]

Figure 6.20. **Information security analyst job vacancies and employment in the United States**

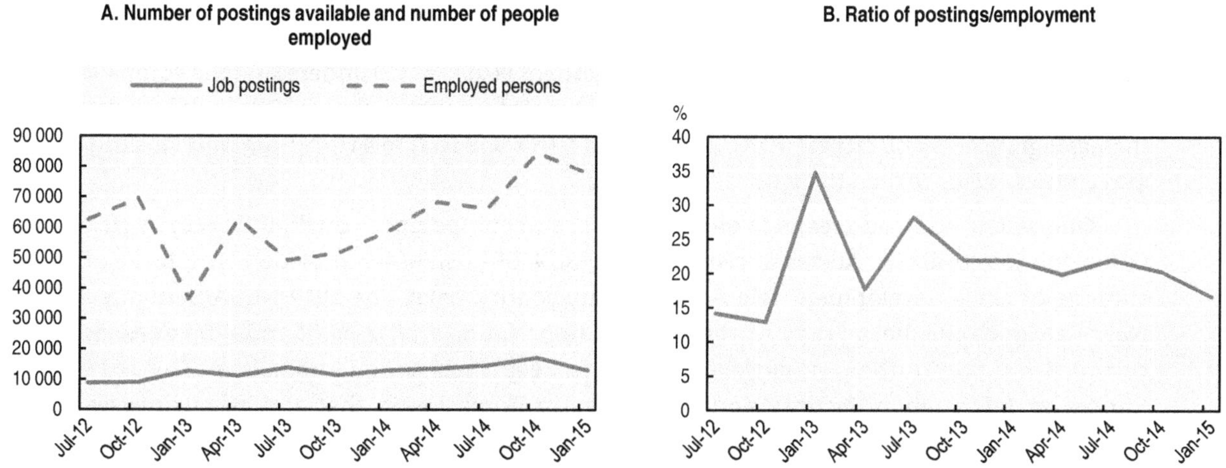

Source: Data on employment are from the Current Population Survey, *https://www.census.gov/programs-surveys/cps.html* (accessed October 2015) and data on job postings are provided by Labor/Insight Jobs (Burning Glass Technologies), October 2015.

StatLink *http://dx.doi.org/10.1787/888933586692*

The above-mentioned challenges are particularly pertinent for SMEs, which rarely (can) have a dedicated person for digital risk management, including for example a CISO, a data protection officer or equivalent. This is perhaps not surprising given that small businesses, by definition, have a lower headcount than medium or large business, and are thus less likely to employ a dedicated person responsible for digital risk management. The 2016 Cyber Security Breaches Survey in the United Kingdom found that a lower proportion of smaller businesses had board members with responsibility for digital security (21% of micro, 37% of small, 39% of medium and 49% of large businesses). The 2012 US National Cyber Security Alliance (NCSA) and Symantec National Small Business Study found that 90% of respondents did not have an internal IT manager whose job is solely focused on technology-related issues. Moreover, 11% of respondents felt they had none responsible for online and digital security at their business. Similarly, according to the 2016 Ponemon State of Cybersecurity in Small and Medium-Sized Businesses Survey, 35% of respondents felt "no one function determines IT security priorities" in their business.[40] When combined with the findings of the NCSA/Symantec study, it might be inferred that overall between 10% and 30% of SMEs do not have any one person dedicated to digital risk management issues. In terms of privacy-related responsibilities, surveys confirm that large companies are more likely to employ numerous professionals with full-time or part-time privacy duties, while smaller organisations employ just a few, if at all. The IAPP (2016) survey, for example, shows that companies with more than USD 25 billion in revenue protect it with an average of 15 full-time privacy staff while those with less than USD 100 million in revenue generally have just 1 full-time privacy professional.

Attracting younger people and women to the field of security and privacy is still a challenge. Regarding information security professions, some efforts have been undertaken to make this field more attractive and rewarding. Since the beginning, information security jobs tended to be very technical, but technical skills alone are not sufficient in resolving the complex risk management dilemmas business leaders and decision makers confront nowadays and in the future (OECD, 2015a). As previously mentioned, the skills and competencies required for information security specialists are slowly changing. This is especially obvious for leaders who see increasing importance in managerial roles and governance, risk and compliance roles. According to a PricewaterhouseCooper survey on information security leaders, the three main roles of a CISO[41] are: 1) communicate risks and strategies to the executive board; 2) consider information security as an enterprise risk management issue; and 3) understand the complex and competitive business climate. The responsibilities and competencies of CISOs have become increasingly visible and critical (PwC, 2015). Overall, this will lead to a rising demand for skills and competencies related to digital security risk.

One widely adopted means to enhance skills and competences on digital security risk is (on-the-job) training. Across surveys, 15% to 30% of businesses provide some form of training or skills development related to digital security risks. The 2012 NCSA/Symantec National Small Business Study in the United States found that 29% of small businesses provided training to their employees on how to keep their computers secure. The 2015 Survey on Information Security and Businesses in Korea found that 15% of businesses provided information security education. This was approximately 2% more than in 2014. The UK Department for Business Innovation and Skills (2014) Digital Capabilities in SMEs Survey in the United Kingdom found that 14% of respondents had received support or advice relating to digital security over the previous 12 months. According to the 2016 Cyber Security Breaches Survey in the United Kingdom, smaller businesses were less likely to provide digital security training than larger businesses (Klahr et al., 2016). For instance, 12% of micro-sized businesses provided digital security training over the prior 12 months, compared to 22% of small, 38% of medium and 62% of large businesses.

Organisations have also significantly increased their privacy-related investments, including for developing policies, training, certification and communications, but also for audits and data inventories. Evidence also strongly suggests that investments will also continue to grow in the near future. According to the IAPP (2016) survey, for instance, the median total investment in privacy across all surveyed organisations increased by almost 50%, from around USD 415 000 in 2016 to slightly above USD 277 000 in 2015. This corresponds to an average investment of USD1.7 million per organisation, which was spent on average for the salary of the privacy team (accounting for 35% of total investments), external spend by the privacy team (27%), with the remainder as salary and spend by the rest of the organisation (38%).[42] It should be noted that while larger organisations obviously tend to have bigger privacy budgets, they also tend to invest greater amounts outside their core privacy team, in contrast to smaller companies, which dedicated a greater proportion of their budgets to the privacy team itself.

Associations of privacy professionals also play a crucial role for fostering skills development. Besides the IAPP, senior privacy officers involved in the practical implementation of privacy initiatives can meet and exchange ideas through associations such as the Privacy Officers Network, and national bodies such as the Association française des correspondants à la protection des données à caractère personnel in France, and the Asociación Profesional Española de Privacidad in Spain. These associations provide training, certification, conferences, publications, professional resources and industry research to their growing number of members.

Risk management can help ensure the protection and support of economic and social activities

Risk management has become the recommended paradigm for addressing challenges related to digital risk and trust. The OECD Council Recommendation *Digital Security Risk Management for Economic and Social Prosperity*, for instance, emphasises a risk management policy framework to address digital security issues.[43] The 2013 *OECD Guidelines on the Protection of Privacy and Transborder Flows of Personal Data* also recommend taking a risk-based approach to implement the privacy principles and enhance privacy protection (OECD, 2013).[44] The following sections discuss the adoption of a risk-based approach to security and privacy by organisations.

Organisations, and in particular small and medium-sized enterprises, are lagging behind in implementing digital security risk management practices

Organisations are increasingly adopting a risk-based approach to security, which is reflected among others in the increasing demand for digital security risk management skills and competencies as discussed above. However, the share of organisations with effective risk management approaches to security still remains much too low. Furthermore, the proportion of businesses that had a formal digital security plan also varies widely across countries and by firm size. Results from the Eurostat Community Survey on ICT usage and e-commerce in enterprises consistently indicate that SMEs were less likely to have a formally defined ICT security policy across all reporting EU countries in 2015. In almost all countries, the differential between SMEs and large enterprises was approximately 30 percentage points (Figure 6.21). Furthermore, for a security plan and associated risk mitigation measures to remain effective over time, monitoring and periodic audit/evaluation are required. Of those businesses that had a digital security plan in place, which ranged from approximately one-third to two-thirds of businesses, the majority undertook at least a periodic internal audit. Results from the Eurostat Community Survey on ICT usage and e-commerce in enterprises indicate that, in 2015, of those enterprises that did have an ICT security plan, SMEs were less likely to have reviewed their strategy over the past year than large enterprises.

Figure 6.21. **Enterprises having a formally defined ICT security policy by size, 2015**

As a percentage of all enterprises in each employment size class

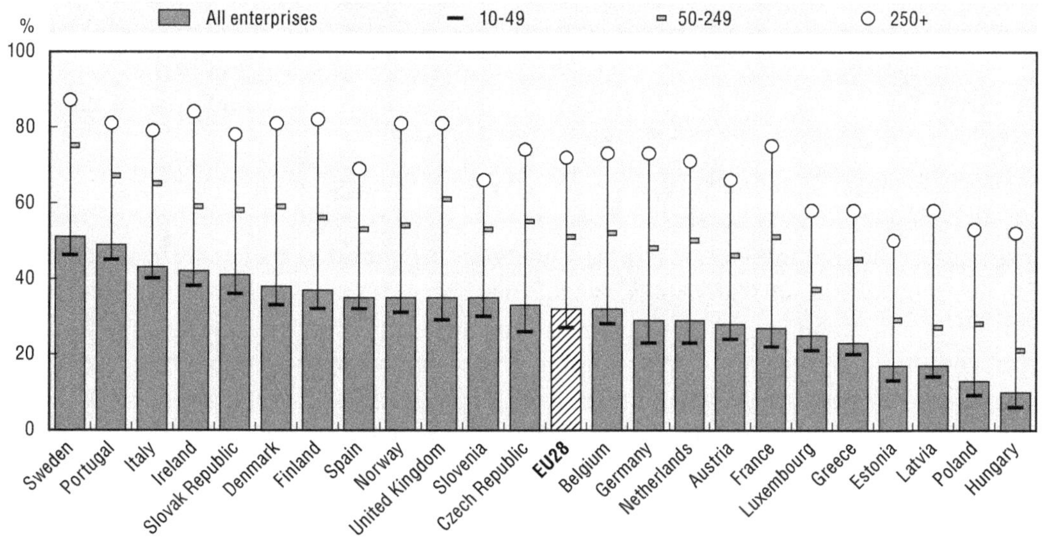

Source: Eurostat, *Digital Economy and Society* (database), *http://ec.europa.eu/eurostat/web/digital-economy-and-society/data/comprehensive-database* (accessed March 2017).

StatLink *http://dx.doi.org/10.1787/888933586711*

The observed gap between larger and smaller firms is consistent with the results of the 2016 Cyber Security Breaches Survey in the United Kingdom. The survey found that lower proportions of smaller businesses had formal policies covering digital security risks or digital security risks documented in their business continuity plans, internal audits or risk registers. This trend held for the proportion of businesses with formal digital security incident management processes as well. At the same time, a 2013 survey of business leaders by the Economist Intelligence Unit (2013) suggests that most companies, and particularly SMEs, are failing to create a culture of risk awareness. Data from a 2012 study, co-sponsored by the NCSA/Symantec as well as a 2013 Study of the Impact of Cyber Crime on Businesses in Canada also confirm these findings.[45]

A number of obstacles preventing the effective use of risk management for addressing trust issues can be identified. Across those surveys that asked respondents about the biggest obstacles to more effective digital risk management practices, the highest rated obstacle was consistently related to insufficient budget. A lack of qualified personnel also figured prominently. The 2015 Survey on Information Security in Business in Korea found that "securing budget for information security" was the highest rated obstacle among respondents. This was followed by "securing information security professionals" and "operation of information security personnel". The 2012 NCSA/Symantec National Small Business Study in the United States also highlighted "no additional funds to invest" as the biggest obstacle to implementing more robust digital security solutions before the lack of technical skills or knowledge. A similar outcome can be observed from the 2016 Ponemon State of Cybersecurity in Small and Medium-Sized Businesses Survey.

Applying risk management to privacy protection is still challenging for most organisations

As noted above, privacy risk can directly affect business reputation, revenues and trust in the marketplace, with respect to customers, shareholders, employees and other stakeholders. Customers are often hesitant to do business with an organisation that does not adequately protect its data, and the damage to a firm's reputation could dissuade enough customers to the point that the company is no longer viable.[46] The financial impacts of a privacy breach involving personal data can also be significant. In particular for a small business without the resources to pay for legal assistance, forensic investigations, the required notifications, remediation measures, and the fines, penalties or judgments that could arise in the event of a privacy breach, just might find itself out of business.

Despite the recognition of the need of treating privacy as an economic and social risk, and the potential to address it as a strategic issue that could provide a competitive advantage in the marketplace, many organisations still tend to approach privacy solely as a legal compliance issue. Many SMEs, even if they recognise that privacy protection is good for their business, often lack the resources and expertise needed to effectively manage privacy-related risks discussed above. Where they have resources, SMEs often tend to not recognise the distinction between privacy and security risk, even when privacy risk may be unrelated to security, for example when personal data is processed by the organisation in a manner that infringes on individuals' rights. This is coherent with findings by a study of business practice in Canada funded by Canada's Office of the Privacy Commissioner which notes that privacy risk management is a much talked about but poorly developed in practice (Greenaway, Zabolotniuk and Levin, 2012).

While the study by Greenaway, Zabolotniuk and Levin (2012) may indicate a lack of understanding of how to implement privacy regulatory requirements, it may also reflect a lack of organisational strategies on how to deal with privacy risk and a gap in the assignment of responsibilities. This is consistent with evidence showing that many businesses, and

SMEs in particular, lack a formal policy to manage privacy risks. Across OECD countries for which data are available, only 10% to 40% of all business had such a formal policy in 2015 (Figure 6.22). Greenaway, Zabolotniuk and Levin (2012) conclude that "integrating privacy risk into an organisation's risk management strategy requires an understanding of the type or categorisation of risk and where it should reside within the risk management structure". This is not straightforward as risk managers often do not view privacy as within their remit and IT managers see risk management in the context of technical digital security (Greenaway, Zabolotniuk and Levin, 2012). Those responsible for privacy see the management of risk as captured by activities such as privacy impact assessment, or not as their responsibility. Privacy is seen either as a digital security issue or as a compliance issue. Privacy risk management is therefore often viewed as "someone else's responsibility".

Figure 6.22. **Enterprises having a formal policy to manage digital privacy risks, 2015**

As a percentage of all enterprises in each employment size class

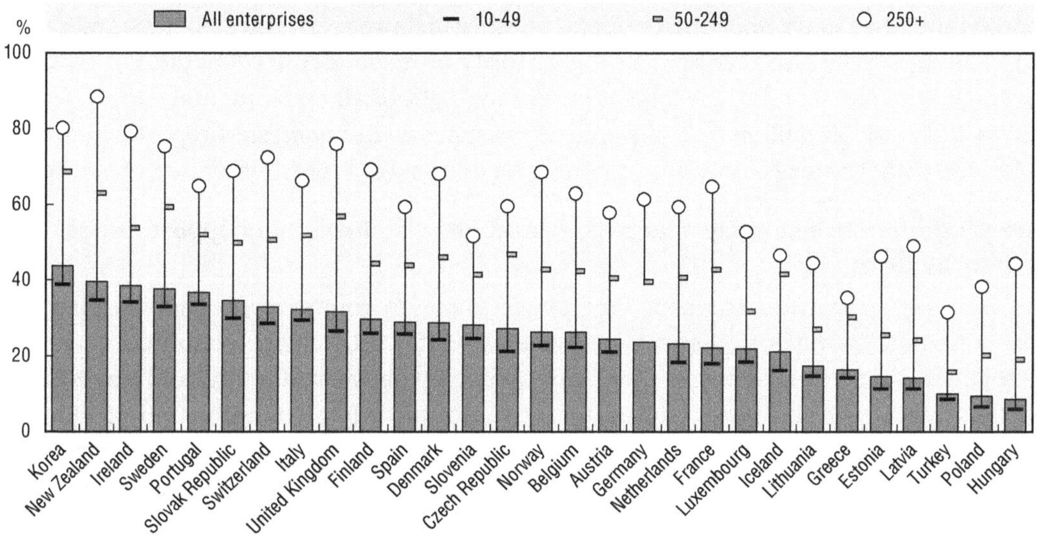

Note: For Korea data refer to 2014; for Iceland, Lithuania and Turkey to 2010. Data for Switzerland follow a different methodology.

Source: OECD, *ICT Access and Usage by Businesses* (database), *http://oe.cd/bus* (accessed August 2017).

StatLink http://dx.doi.org/10.1787/888933586730

Digital risk insurance markets that enable the transfer of digital risks are emerging

From a business perspective, digital risk insurance is viewed principally as one means to transfer risk outside the firm. As the financial outlay of dealing with a breach gets more expensive, with the added efforts of dealing with mandatory notification, the option of using digital risk insurance will become more attractive for many small and large businesses. Maybe more importantly, the greatest potential of digital risk insurance may lay in helping firms, organisations and individuals better understand and evaluate digital risk and harness the opportunities from better risk management practices. In addition, digital risk insurance could generate valuable empirical data that would provide an important evidence base to support digital risk management policy, as is the case for notification requirements.

However, in practice, insurance companies have been somewhat cautious with respect to covering the risk associated with widespread business use of ICTs or that associated with non-tangible assets such as personal data. Today, standard insurance policies are not designed to cover digital security and privacy risks. This can be attributed to the uncertainties around definitions of digital risk based on different causes and consequences, the absence of relevant data on past incidents and losses, the limited actuarial information available on the frequency and magnitude of actual and potential digital security and privacy incidents, and the ever-evolving nature of digital risks that are major challenges for the insurance sector. As a result, digital risk insurance is still an emerging market.

Providers of this type of insurance today are located mainly in the United States and the United Kingdom. The market for digital risk insurance in the United States was about USD 2 billion in2014. Recent reports indicate that the market continues to broaden, especially in healthcare and the SME insureds segments (Betterley, 2015). The European market remains far smaller, at only around USD 150 million in gross written premiums, although with an annual growth of 50% to 100%. Although governments are beginning to explore the opportunities of digital risk insurance, its potential remains largely untapped, even in more advance markets such as the United States and the United Kingdom. The 2016 Cyber Security Breaches Survey in the United Kingdom, for instance, shows that a minority of respondents thought that they had some form of digital security insurance coverage (37%). Similarly, the 2014 FERMA survey also reveals that the majority of respondents (72%) did not have any coverage. Of those that did, the largest proportion (19% of all respondents) had a coverage of less than EUR 50 million.[47] In general, the proportion of businesses reporting coverage increased with firm size across all incident categories except for "theft of loss of hardware".

Peer platform markets raise new trust issues but also bring new opportunities to address them

Peer-to-peer transactions have long played a role in commerce, but online platforms enable them on a much greater scale. By one estimate, 191 million consumers across the EU28 concluded a transaction on a peer platform market between May 2015 and May 2016 (EC, 2017). Early examples include platforms for the sale of goods (e.g. online auction sites). Newer models include the rental of short-term accommodation and transport or mobility services. Using real-time geolocational data accessed through mobile apps, mobility services can be used to rent private cars, rides and parking spaces. Other areas being transformed by these platforms involve small jobs, meal services and financial services. These business models are often described as the "sharing" economy or "collaborative consumption", but those terms do not capture the commercial exchange dimension that is commonplace in these markets.

These business models open up economic opportunities for the individuals supplying the goods or services ("peer providers") and for the platforms making the connections ("peer platforms"). Reliable data on transactions over peer platforms are still scarce, but for the largest platforms the estimates are impressive. Founded in 2008, Airbnb estimated its 2015 revenues at USD 900 million, which would mean it operated a market of around USD 7.5 billion in 2015 (Kokalitcheva, 2015). Uber, founded in 2009, estimated that its global bookings will amount to about USD 10 billion in 2015 (Zhang and Shih, 2015). Participation by consumers is likewise significant. For example, 72% of adults in the United States are found to have used at least 1 of 11 different "shared and on-demand services" and 17% of Europeans have used the services of "collaborative platforms" at least once (OECD, 2016g).

Consumer motives for engaging in these markets centre mainly on financial considerations and the quality and experience of services and products. Consumers can benefit from a large choice of goods and services at a better price or higher quality, the convenience and ease of use of peer platforms' services, as well as a better social experience (e.g. living in a real home instead of staying at a hotel is more authentic and can contribute greatly to the cultural experience of travelling) (OECD, 2016e).

Although there is an emerging body of research on the benefits of peer platform markets, there has been little research, to date, on potential consumer problems. Identifying and measuring the nature and magnitude of possible consumer detriment in this area, a key of evidence-based policy making, therefore has been based mainly on limited data and anecdotal evidence. Nonetheless, there are some possible detriments that have been identified, such as lack of adequate information, costs of flawed products or inadequate services, inflated or unfair pricing, injury or adverse effects on health, compromise of consumer data and restricted choice (OECD, 2016e). Some of these issues may not be specific to peer platform markets but may be more exacerbated due to the diversity and number of peer providers. In a 2016 survey, more than half (55%) of consumers in ten EU countries reported having experienced a problem on a peer platform market, with the most frequent problems related to poor quality or misleading descriptions. Problems with the quality of products/services appear to be almost twice as frequent in peer-to-peer markets (29%) as in online purchases in general (15%). However, the same consumers rate the personal detriment they experienced as low to medium (EC, 2017). Despite the publicity surrounding the well-known platforms mentioned above, recent discussions and research have mainly focused on the benefits for consumers to engage in peer platform markets instead of potential consumer problems. Detriments can take many forms, financial or non-financial, or not be easily revealed, if not at all. For instance, information regarding the nature of the product and service, and the conditions of delivery, may not always be adequate. This is not specific to peer platform markets but may be more exacerbated due to the diversity and number of peer providers. Other possible issues include: costs of flawed products or inadequate services, inflated or unfair pricing, injury or adverse effects on health, compromise of consumer data and restricted choice (OECD, 2016e).

In addition, consumers can encounter issues of trust in their use of peer platforms in many different contexts: trust in the reliability and qualifications of the peer provider; trust in the asset or service; and trust in the guarantees and safeguards offered by the peer platform. As a result, platforms have developed a number of practical, innovative mechanisms to address concerns and inhibitors to consumer engagement. The most common categories of trust-building mechanism developed by peer platform markets are (OECD, 2016e):

- **Review and reputation systems.** These are a central element in helping peer consumers to make informed choices. In addition to having a critical trust-building function, these systems can also be a factor in regulating behaviour through monitoring, feedback systems and the exercise of peer pressure.
- **Guarantees or insurance.** In response to negative experiences with accidents, but also theft and fraud, a number of peer platforms have introduced guarantees. Airbnb, for example, offers guarantees for both guests and hosts to cover for accidents and instances of intentional theft and vandalism. Similarly, eBay and Uber offer guarantees, as do others, all with varying conditions, however.
- **Verified identities.** Some peer platforms take steps to verify the identity of peers. One cause of consumer detriment can be the inability to contact the peer provider in case of problems and verified identities can be useful in resolving disputes.
- **Pre-screening.** Some peer platforms offer pre-screening of peer providers, usually through verification of external databases, such as motor vehicle records or criminal background checks.

- **Secure payment systems.** Many peer platforms offer secure payment services, often in co-operation with established external payment systems. It is important to note that many of these payment systems are themselves subject to governmental regulation or oversight.
- **Education, checklists and forms.** Many peer platforms invest in educating their users, including with respect to possible legal or other obligations that may apply to traders, drivers or hosts. Of course the value of this information will vary and be dependant in particular on its accuracy.

The rapid rise of peer platforms might suggest that the trust mechanisms, like those described above, are, in fact, building consumer confidence in these new platforms. Yet, many observers have questioned the extent to which these trust mechanisms are an effective substitute for regulation (especially for certain health- and safety-related regulations) and have pointed to problems of bias as well as false or misleading reviews. They have also noted that many of these trust mechanisms, such as reputation systems, effectively place the burden of monitoring on consumers, which may come at a particular cost for less able consumers. Accordingly, the OECD is conducting further research to obtain a better understanding of which ones work best and in which circumstances.

Notes

1. The observed patterns are dominated by the economic weight of large enterprises, for which e-commerce sales represent on average 22% of turnover against 9% for small firms. Furthermore, e-commerce activities mostly remain within national borders, despite recent initiatives both at the national and international level to foster cross-border online transactions (see Chapter 5).
2. On average, 90% of OECD households have an Internet connection at home.
3. In 2009, security was cited as the main reason for not buying online for over one-third of Internet users in the European Union who had not made any purchases online. Privacy concerns accounted for a slightly smaller share (about 30%) (see Figure 6.2).
4. It is important to note that this figure is much smaller (1%) and decreasing when it comes to the share of households for which privacy or security concerns are a reason for not having access to the Internet among all households. Furthermore, it is when it comes to mobile connectivity in contrast 10% all individuals cited security concerns as a major reason for not using mobile devices (including laptops) via wireless connections from places other than home in 2015. This ranges from more than 20% in the Netherlands to 1% in Greece.
5. That said, privacy and security concerns are among the least cited reason for not having an Internet connection at home in most countries; lack of interest, lack of skills and the high cost of access (including to devices) are by far the most frequent reason for not having Internet access at home.
6. ISO/IEC (27000:2009) defines information security as the "preservation of confidentiality, integrity and availability of information." It also notes that "in addition, other properties, such as authenticity, accountability, non-repudiation and reliability can also be involved." Confidentiality "is the property, that information is not made available or disclosed to unauthorized individuals, entities, or processes"(ISO/IEC, 2009). Integrity means the preservation of the accuracy and completeness of data over its entire lifecycle. Availability means assuring that information is available when it is needed.
7. A data breach is "a loss, unauthorised access to or disclosure of personal data as a result of a failure of the organisation to effectively safeguard the data" (OECD, 2011).
8. This only includes complaints accepted under Canada's Personal Information Protection and Electronic Documents Act.
9. OECD (2015b) highlights that "the Internet has provided opportunities for some to engage in unlawful conduct, including [intellectual property] infringement" and acknowledges in the case of copyright infringement that "[i]t is, however, difficult to obtain accurate and objective data on the precise magnitude of piracy that is taking place."
10. See also the work of Eric Jardine (2015) showing that proportionately the increase is not so strong given that Internet-related activities are growing too.

11. In 2015, for example, 90% of large business and 74% of small businesses in the United Kingdom reported that they had suffered a security incident (UK Department for Business, Innovation and Skills, 2015).

12. In the 2012 ICSPA survey in Canada, the largest proportion of businesses (31%) reported not experiencing an information security incident over the past 12 months. Of those that did experience an incident, 23% experienced just one while 23% also reported experiencing over ten.

13. A large part of the cross-country variations is due to differences in methodologies used across regions– in particular between EU member states and other OECD countries (Canada, Japan, Korea, Mexico and New Zealand). Furthermore, it is important to note that respondents are likely to understate the true number of digital security incidents that they incur during a given time period. For instance, in any one year, a business might experience a certain number of digital security incidents. Of this total universe of incidents, the business might not detect all of them. These non-detected incidents will not be taken into account when respondents answer questions related to past incidents. To compound this issue, if respondents do not feel that their answers will be kept confidential, they may not disclose all of the incidents that were detected (e.g. due to reputational concerns). No firm estimates exist on what proportion of incidents go undetected. Different surveys, however, have indicated that anywhere between 60% and 90% of security incidents go unreported (Edwards, Hofmeyr and Forrest, 2014). This implies that a substantial proportion of the total universe of incidents forms part of an "unknown unknown."

14. The high rate of reported viruses/malware infections could be due to the improvements in the detection of such infections thanks to more sophisticated anti-malware tools.

15. DoS incidents affect an organisation by flooding its online service or bandwidth with spam requests, knocking it offline for hours or days (Goodin, 2015).

16. Such as a USD 45 million loss by a bank in a global cybercrime scheme. For an example, see: *www.reuters.com/article/us-usa-crime-cybercrime-idUSBRE9AH0YZ20131118*.

17. Two common metrics are therefore used to gauge the impact that incidents had on businesses: the financial cost/loss caused by the incident and the hours of business downtime or employee hours required to remedy the incident (which can subsequently be converted into a monetary figure).

18. SMEs experiencing a digital security or privacy incident either accidentally or through commercial espionage may be more affected than a larger company that is in a better position to pursue a legal recourse to protect their investment. Some SMEs rely heavily on the strength and scope of their intellectual property to generate investment to take their technologies to commercialisation. Intellectual property is critically important to many small, innovative and research and development-intensive businesses and the theft or exposure of intellectual property can significantly damage their competitive edge and economic base. Early-stage start-ups, such as those in the biotechnology or nanotechnology field, may be especially vulnerable to intellectual property theft.

19. "Personal data means any information relating to an identified or identifiable individual (data subject)" (OECD, 2013).

20. This publication uses the term "data breach" to refer to an incident involving "a loss, unauthorised access to or disclosure of personal data as a result of a failure of the organisation to effectively safeguard the data" (OECD, 2011). It uses the term "digital security incident" to refer to incidents that may or may not involve personal data.

21. The Choicepoint breach became public because of a 2003 California law requiring notification to an individual when their personal information was wrongfully disclosed. This contributed to the adoption of similar laws in many other jurisdictions. The 2013 *OECD Guidelines on the Protection of Privacy and Transborder Flows of Personal Data* call for controllers to provide notifications in cases where there has been a significant security breach affecting personal data (OECD, 2013, paragraph 15(c)).

22. The severity and impact of data breaches have also increased. According to a study released in 2015 by the data security research organisation the Ponemon Institute, the total average cost of a data breach is now USD 3.8 million, up from USD 3.5 million a year earlier. The study also reported that the cost of a data breach is now USD 154 per record lost or stolen, up from USD 145 the previous year and the cost resulting from lost business because of a decline in customers' trust after a breach can be even greater. The UK study referred to above estimated that big breaches cost large organisations between GBP 600 000 and GBP 1.15 million.

23. Duhigg (2012) describes the analysis process as follows: "[...] Lots of people buy lotion, but one of Pole's colleagues noticed that women on the baby registry were buying larger quantities of unscented lotion around the beginning of their second trimester. Another analyst noted that sometime in the first 20weeks, pregnant women loaded up on supplements like calcium, magnesium and zinc.

Many shoppers purchase soap and cotton balls, but when someone suddenly starts buying lots of scent-free soap and extra-big bags of cotton balls, in addition to hand sanitizers and washcloths, it signals they could be getting close to their delivery date". As data analytics is not perfect, false positives are to be accounted for (see Harford, 2014). Target therefore mixes up its offers with coupons that are not specific to pregnancy (Piatetsky, 2014).

24. Consumers reported paying over USD 744 million in those fraud complaints; the median amount paid was USD 450. Fifty-one per cent of the consumers who reported a fraud-related complaint in the United States also reported an amount paid.

25. Complaints in the CSN are self-reported and unverified, and they do not necessarily represent a random sample of consumer injury for any particular market. For these reasons, year-to-year changes in the number of fraud and/or identity theft complaints do not necessarily indicate an increase or decrease in actual or perceived fraud and/or identity theft in the marketplace.

26. The OECD (2003) *Guidelines for Protecting Consumers from Fraudulent and Deceptive Commercial Practices Across Borders* highlights the following three types of fraudulent and deceptive commercial practices: "*(i)* A practice of making misrepresentations of material fact, including implied factual misreprentations, that cause significant detriment to the economic interest of misled consumers. *(ii)* A practice of failing to deliver products or provide services to consumers after the consumers have been charged. *(iii)* A practice of charging or debiting consumers' financial, telephone or other accounts without authorisation".

27. According to this first principle, stakeholders "should be aware that digital security risk can affect the achievement of their economic and social objectives and that their management of digital security risk can affect others. They should be empowered with the education and skills necessary to understand this risk to help manage it, and to evaluate the potential impact of their digital security risk management decisions on their activities and the overall digital environment" (OECD, 2015a).

28. As an example, the EU General Data Protection Regulation (GDPR) considers both pseudonymisation and encryption as appropriate measures to be used by data controllers and processors to ensure the security of the processing of personal data.

29. The use of secure servers has also been promoted by the fact that Internet search service providers have favoured access over SSL/TLS where possible (see also *www.google.com/transparencyreport/https*).

30. Of the 16 million servers worldwide, only 10% have a known location.

31. See also Cisco (2016), Annual Security Report, *www.cisco.com/c/dam/assets/offers/pdfs/cisco-asr-2016.pdf*.

32. WhatApp uses the Signal Protocol (formerly known as the TextSecure Protocol), a non-federated cryptographic protocol initially developed by Open Whisper Systems in 2013 first introduced in the open source TextSecure app (now known as Signal Private Messenger).

33. Tor is free software that protects Internet users' privacy, confidentiality of communications and other freedoms (i.e. freedom of expression) by enabling online anonymity. The project was initially sponsored by the US Navy Research Lab, then by the Electronic Frontier Foundation, and now by the Tor Project, which is a US-based research and education not-for profit organisation, with different sources of funds published on the website. The Tor project makes publicly available the "analytics for the Tor network, including graphs of its available bandwidth and estimated user base" (see *https://metrics.torproject.org*).

34. See also OECD (2015a) according to which "[c]oncerns about government access requests – particularly to data entrusted to providers of cloud computing services – predate the revelations by Edward Snowden in 2013 and are not limited to intelligence gathering. But those revelations have brought into sharper focus the need for transparency. Today, Internet and communications businesses are under increasing pressure to be open about the manner in which they address government access requests."

35. Others include the Privacy Officers Network, through which senior privacy officers involved in the practical implementation of privacy initiatives meet and exchange ideas through a professional support network, and national bodies such as the Association française des correspondants à la protection des données à caractère personnel in France, and the Asociación Profesional Española de Privacidad in Spain.

36. See Article 37 of the EU GDPR.

37. To name just a few: in the United States, as another example, the call by the White House in July 2016 for each federal government agency to appoint a senior agency official for privacy has been another driver. Canada's federal private sector legislation, the Personal Information Protection

and Electronic Documents Act, requires organisations to designate an individual(s) responsible for personal data-handling activities. New Zealand's Privacy Act requires every agency in both the public and private sectors to appoint a privacy officer. Both of Korea's privacy laws require companies to designate a person responsible for the management of personal information. Overall, the IAPP (2016) estimates that employment in privacy-related professions will therefore increase significantly over the coming year in two areas: "the number of positions for full-time privacy professionals on privacy teams is expected to grow by 37 percent while an additional 39 percent growth is expected for part-time privacy responsibilities in units other than privacy."

38. This is in line with Burning Glass (2015), according to which demand for cybersecurity jobs are growing across the US economy: in 2014, there were close to 238 158 postings for cybersecurity-related jobs. Cybersecurity jobs account for 11% of all IT jobs. Burning Glass (2015) defines cybersecurity jobs as those which have a cybersecurity-related title, require a cybersecurity certification or request cybersecurity-specific skills.

39. It is interesting to note the difference between men and women in the perception of these challenges in the (ISC)^2 survey: while finding qualified people is seen as an increasing issue compared to previous years especially by men (over 50%), women instead consider that the lack of executives' understanding of the security requirements is a major issue.

40. However, respondents had to select two options, which makes interpreting this result difficult (if a respondent selected this answer, surely no second choice would be made). A generous interpretation might infer the option to mean that many functions determine IT security priorities.

41. Or other senior information security executives.

42. This corresponds on average to more than USD 350 per employee. Please note that the mean results are influenced, mathematically, by those with very large numbers of employees. The median results, uninfluenced by large numbers, are therefore lower.

43. The emphasis of the OECD Council Recommendation *Digital Security Risk Management for Economic and Social Prosperity* on digital security risk management is based on three messages: 1) it is impossible to entirely eliminate digital security risk when carrying out activities that rely on the digital environment. However, the risk can be managed, that is, can be reduced to an acceptable level in light of the interests and benefits at stake, and the context; 2) leaders and decision makers should focus on the digital security risk to economic and social activities rather than only on the risk to the digital infrastructure; and 3) organisations should integrate digital security risk management into their economic and social decision-making processes and overall risk management framework rather than treat it solely as a technical problem (OECD, 2015a).

44. For its part, the new EU GDPR requires assessing the risks for the rights and freedoms of individuals when implementing measures to ensure compliance with the regulation, including on security aspects. According to Recital 75 GDPR, the risk to the rights and freedoms of natural persons, of varying likelihood and severity, may result from personal data processing which could lead to physical, material or non-material damage.

45. The 2012 study, co-sponsored by the US NCSA and Symantec, reports that only 23% of US small businesses have a formal written Internet security policy, 59% do not have contingency plans, and just 35% provide any training to employees about Internet safety and security. Similarly, a 2013 Study of the Impact of Cyber Crime on Businesses in Canada suggests that only 22% Canadian businesses employ a risk assessment process to identify where their business is most vulnerable (International Cyber Security Protection Alliance, 2013).

46. It should be noted that, aside from the opportunity to gain competitive advantage from treating digital risk as strategic issue, there are also cases where a company has seen a positive effect on its reputation from revealing a digital security incident, because it showcased that the company was aware of digital security risks and had addressed these in a professional manner.

47. The 2009 ABACUS survey in Australia also asked respondents what computer security incidents were covered by insurance policies. The results were provided broken down by firm size. The incident type with the largest proportions of businesses reporting coverage was "theft or loss of hardware".

References

Abrams, M. (2014), "The origins of personal data and its implications for governance", background paper for the OECD Expert Roundtable Discussion, 21 March, *http://informationaccountability.org/wp-content/uploads/Data-Origins-Abrams.pdf*.

Acquisti, A. (2010), "The economics of personal data and the economics of privacy", Background Paper #3, Joint WPISP-WPIE Roundtable, 1 December, *www.oecd.org/sti/ieconomy/46968784.pdf*.

Arbor Networks (2017), *Worldwide Infrastructure Security Report Volume XII*, Arbor Networks, *www.arbornetworks.com/insight-into-the-global-threat-landscape*.

Arbor Networks (2016), *Worldwide Infrastructure Security Report Volume XI*, Arbor Networks, *www.arbornetworks.com/images/documents/WISR2016_EN_Web.pdf*.

Ashford, W. (2016a), "GDPR will require 28,000 DPOs in Europe and US, study shows", ComputerWeekly, 20 April, *www.computerweekly.com/news/450283253/GDPR-will-require-28000-DPOs-in-Europe-study-shows*.

Ashford, W. (2016b), "GDPR will require 75,000 DPOs worldwide, study shows", ComputerWeekly, 10 November, *www.computerweekly.com/news/450402719/GDPR-will-require-75000-DPOs-worldwide-study-shows*.

Australian Government (2016), "Australian Consumer Survey 2016", Commonwealth of Australia, *http://consumerlaw.gov.au/australian-consumer-survey*.

BBC (2017), "NHS cyber-attack: GPs and hospitals hit by ransomware", BBC, 13 May, *www.bbc.com/news/health-39899646*.

BBC (2015), "Sony Pictures computer system hacked in online attack", BBC, 25 November, *www.bbc.com/news/technology-30189029*.

Betterley, R. (2015), "The Betterley report: Cyber/Privacy Insurance Market Survey 2017", Betterley Risk Consultants, Inc., Sterling, Massachusetts, *www.irmi.com/online/betterley-report-free/cyber-privacy-media-liability-summary.pdf*.

Bureau of Labor Statistics (2014), *Occupational Outlook Handbook*, 2014-15 Edition, US Department of Labor, January, *www.bls.gov/ooh/computer-and-information-technology/information-security-analysts.htm*.

Cisco (2016), *Annual Security Report 2016*, *www.cisco.com/c/dam/assets/offers/pdfs/cisco-asr-2016.pdf*.

CMA (Competition & Markets Authority) (2015a), "Online reviews and endorsements: Report on the CMA's call for information", Competition & Markets Authority, London, *https://www.gov.uk/government/uploads/system/uploads/attachment_data/file/436238/Online_reviews_and_endorsements.pdf*.

CMA (2015b), "Energy market investigation", a report by GfK NOP, Competition & Markets Authority, London, February, *https://assets.publishing.service.gov.uk/media/54e75c53ed915d0cf700000d/CMA_customer_survey_-_energy_investigation_-_GfK_Report.pdf*.

CSIS (2014), "Net losses: Estimating the global cost of cybercrime: Economic impact of cybercrime II", McAfee, Inc., Santa Clara, California, *www.mcafee.com/jp/resources/reports/rp-economic-impact-cybercrime2.pdf*.

Duhigg, C. (2012), "How companies learn your secrets", *The New York Times*, 16 February, *www.nytimes.com/2012/02/19/magazine/shopping-habits.html*.

ECCN (European Consumer Centres Network) (2015), *The European Consumer Centres Network: 10 Years Serving Europe's Consumers: Anniversary Report 2005-2015*, European Union, Luxembourg, *http://ec.europa.eu/consumers/solving_consumer_disputes/non-judicial_redress/ecc-net/docs/ecc_net_-_anniversary_report_2015_en.pdf*.

Economist Intelligence Unit (2013), "Information risk: Managing digital assets in a new digital landscape", The Economist Intelligence Unit.

Edwards, B., S. Hofmeyr and S. Forrest (2014), "Hype and heavy tails: A closer look at data breaches", Workshop on the Economics of Information Security, *www.econinfosec.org/archive/weis2015/papers/WEIS_2015_edwards.pdf*.

ENISA (European Network and Information Security Agency) (2009), "An SME perspective on cloud computing", survey, European Network and Information Security Agency, 20 November, *www.enisa.europa.eu/publications/cloud-computing-sme-survey*.

EC (European Commission) (2017), "Exploratory study of consumer issues in online peer-to-peer platform markets: Executive summary", European Commission, Brussels, *http://ec.europa.eu/newsroom/document.cfm?doc_id=45246*.

EC (2016a), "Consumer vulnerability across key markets in the European Union", a report written by London Economics, VVA Consulting and Ipsos MORI consortium, Final Report, European Commission, Brussels, January, *http://ec.europa.eu/consumers/consumer_evidence/market_studies/docs/vulnerable_consumers_approved_27_01_2016_en.pdf*.

EC (2016b), "E-privacy", *Flash Eurobarometer 443*, European Union, December, *http://ec.europa.eu/COMMFrontOffice/publicopinion/index.cfm/ResultDoc/download/DocumentKy/76377*.

EC (2015a), *Consumer Conditions Scoreboard, Consumers at Home in the Single Market*, 2015 Edition, European Union, Luxembourg, *http://ec.europa.eu/consumers/consumer_evidence/consumer_scoreboards/11_edition/docs/ccs2015scoreboard_en.pdf*.

EC (2015b), "Data protection", *Special Eurobarometer 431*, European Union, June, *http://ec.europa.eu/commfrontoffice/publicopinion/archives/ebs/ebs_431_en.pdf*.

ECn (2015c), "Cyber security", *Special Eurobarometer 423*, European Union, February, *http://ec.europa.eu/commfrontoffice/publicopinion/archives/ebs/ebs_423_en.pdf*.

EC (2014), *Study on Online Consumer Reviews in the Hotel Sector: Executive Summary*, a study by Risk & Policy Analysts (RPA) Ltd, CSES and EPRD, European Union, *http://dx.doi.org/10.2772/32069*.

EC (2013), "Cyber security", *Special Eurobarometer 404*, European Union, November, *http://ec.europa.eu/commfrontoffice/publicopinion/archives/ebs/ebs_404_en.pdf*.

ECME Consortium (2013), "Study on the coverage, functioning and consumer use of comparison tools and third-party verification schemes for such tools", EAHC/FWC/20138507, Europsan Commission, Brussels, *http://ec.europa.eu/consumers/consumer_evidence/market_studies/docs/final_report_study_on_comparison_tools.pdf*.

FTC (Federal Trade Commission) (2017), "Consumer Sentinel Network data book for January-December 2016", Federal Trade Commission, Washington, DC, March, *www.ftc.gov/system/files/documents/reports/consumer-sentinel-network-data-book-january-december-2016/csn_cy-2016_data_book.pdf*.

FTC (2016), "Consumer Sentinel Network data book for January-December 2015", Federal Trade Commission, Washington, DC, February, *www.ftc.gov/system/files/documents/reports/consumer-sentinel-network-data-book-january-december-2015/160229csn-2015databook.pdf*.

FTC (2006), "ChoicePoint settles data security breach charges; to pay $10 million in civil penalties, $5 million for consumer redress", press release, Federal Trade Commission, 26 January, *www.ftc.gov/news-events/press-releases/2006/01/choicepoint-settles-data-security-breach-charges-pay-10-million*.

Fiskerstrand, K. (2017), "sks-keyservers.net – key development", *https://sks-keyservers.net/status/key_development.php* (accessed 15 April 2017).

Frier, S. and M. Townsend (2016), "FTC to crack down on paid celebrity posts that aren't clear ads", Bloomberg, 5 August, *www.bloomberg.com/news/articles/2016-08-05/ftc-to-crack-down-on-paid-celebrity-posts-that-aren-t-clear-ads*.

Goodin, D. (2015), "Pay or we'll knock your site offline: DDoS-for-ransom attacks surge", Ars Technica, *http://arstechnica.com/security/2015/11/pay-or-well-knock-your-site-offline-ddos-for-ransom-attacks-surge*.

Greenberg, A. (2015a), "Hackers remotely kill a Jeep on the highway – with me in it", Wired, July, *www.wired.com/2015/07/hackers-remotely-kill-jeep-highway*.

Greenberg, A. (2015b), "After Jeep hack, Chrysler recalls 1.4M vehicles for bug fix", Wired, July, *www.wired.com/2015/07/jeep-hack-chrysler-recalls-1-4m-vehicles-bug-fix*.

Greenaway, K., S. Zabolotniuk and A. Levin (2012), "Privacy as a risk management challenge for corporate practice", Ted Rogers School of Management, Ryerson University, Privacy and Cyber Crime Institute, *www.ryerson.ca/content/dam/tedrogersschool/privacy/privacy_as_a_risk_management_challenge.pdf*.

Harford, T. (2014), "Big data: Are we making a big mistake?", *Financial Times*, 28 March, *www.ft.com/cms/s/2/21a6e7d8-b479-11e3-a09a-00144feabdc0.html*.

Hautala, L. (2016), "Why it was so easy to hack the cameras that took down the web", c|net, 24 October, *www.cnet.com/how-to/ddos-iot-connected-devices-easily-hacked-internet-outage-webcam-dvr*.

Hill, L. (2012), "How Target figured out a teen girl was pregnant before her father did", *Forbes*, 16 February, *www.forbes.com/sites/kashmirhill/2012/02/16/how-target-figured-out-a-teen-girl-was-pregnant-before-her-father-did*.

IAPP (International Association of Privacy Professionals) (2016), "IAPP-EY annual privacy governance report 2016", International Association of Privacy Professionals, *https://iapp.org/media/pdf/resource_center/IAPP-2016-GOVERNANCE-SURVEY-FINAL2.pdf*.

ICPEN (International Consumer Protection and Enforcement Network) (2016), *Online Reviews & Endorsements: ICPEN Guidelines for Review Administrators*, International Consumer Protection and Enforcement Network.

International Cyber Security Protection Alliance (2013), "Study of the impact of cyber crime on businesses in Canada", International Cyber Security Protection Alliance, Buckinghamshire, United Kingdom, *https://www.icspa.org/wp-content/uploads/2014/12/ICSPA-Canada-Cyber-Crime-Study-Report.pdf*.

Internet Society (2016), "Global Internet report 2016: The economics of building trust online: Preventing data breaches", Internet Society, *www.internetsociety.org/globalinternetreport/2016*.

(ISC)² (2015), "The 2015 (ISC)² global information security workforce study", white paper, Frost & Sullivan, (ISC)², and Booz Allen Hamilton, *https://www.boozallen.com/content/dam/boozallen/documents/Viewpoints/2015/04/frostsullivan-ISC2-global-information-security-workforce-2015.pdf*.

ISO/IEC (International Organization for Standardization/ International Electrotechnical Commission) (2009), *Information Technology – Security Techniques – Information Security Management Systems – Overview and Vocabulary*, ISO/IEC 27000:2009 (E), International Organization for Standardization and International Electrotechnical Commission.

Jardine, E. (2015), "Global cyberspace is safer than you think: Real trends in cybercrime", Global Commission on Internet Governance, Paper Series, No. 16, July, *www.cigionline.org/sites/default/files/no16_web_0.pdf*.

Kaiser, M. (2011), Prepared testimony of the National Cyber Security Alliance on the State of Cybersecurity and Small Business before the Committee on House Small Business Subcommittee on Healthcare and Technology, United States House of Representatives, 1 December, *http://smallbusiness.house.gov/uploadedfiles/kaiser_testimony.pdf*.

Klahr, R. et al. (2016), "Cyber Security Breaches Survey 2016", Ipsos MORI Social Research Institute, London, May, *https://www.gov.uk/government/uploads/system/uploads/attachment_data/file/521465/Cyber_Security_Breaches_Survey_2016_main_report_FINAL.pdf*.

Kokalitcheva, K. (2015), "Here's how Airbnb justifies its eye-popping $24 billion valuation", *Fortune*, 17 June, *http://fortune.com/2015/06/17/airbnb-valuation-revenue*.

Madden, M. (2014), "Public perceptions of privacy and security in the post-Snowden era", Pew Research Center, 12 November, *www.pewinternet.org/files/2014/11/PI_PublicPerceptionsofPrivacy_111214.pdf*.

Mayer, R.C., J.H. Davis and F.D. Schoorman (1995), "An integrative model of organizational trust", *The Academy of Management Review*, Vol. 20/3, pp. 709-734, *www.jstor.org/stable/258792*.

McGlasson, L. (2009), "Heartland Payment Systems, Forcht Bank discover data breaches", Bank info Security, 21 January, *www.bankinfosecurity.com/heartland-payment-systems-forcht-bank-discover-data-breaches-a-1168*.

NSBA (National Small Business Association) (2016), "2015 year end economic reports", National Small Business Association, Washington, DC, February, *www.nsba.biz/wp-content/uploads/2016/02/Year-End-Economic-Report-2015.pdf*.

NSBA (2015), "2014 year end economic reports", National Small Business Association, Washington, DC, February, *www.nsba.biz/wp-content/uploads/2015/02/Year-End-Economic-Report-2014.pdf*.

NTIA (National Telecommunications and Information Administration) (2016), "Lack of trust in Internet privacy and security may deter economic and other online activities", National Telecommunications and Information Administration, United States Department of Commerce, Washington, DC, 13 May, *www.ntia.doc.gov/blog/2016/lack-trust-internet-privacy-and-security-may-deter-economic-and-other-on-line-activities*.

OECD (Organisation for Economic Co-operation and Development) (2016a), "The Internet of Things: Seizing the benefits and addressing the challenges", *OECD Digital Economy Papers*, No. 252, OECD Publishing, Paris, *http://dx.doi.org/10.1787/5jlwvzz8td0n-en*.

OECD (2016b), "Bridging policy silos to boost trust online", *OECD Observer*, No. 307, OECD, Paris, *http://oecdobserver.org/news/fullstory.php/aid/5589/Bridging_policy_silos_to_boost_trust_online.html*.

OECD (2016c), "Stimulating digital innovation for growth and inclusiveness: The role of policies for the successful diffusion of ICT", *OECD Digital Economy Papers*, No. 256, OECD Publishing, Paris, *http://dx.doi.org/10.1787/5jlwqvhg3l31-en*.

OECD (2016d), *Recommendation of the Council on Consumer Protection in E-commerce*, OECD, Paris, *www.oecd.org/sti/consumer/ECommerce-Recommendation-2016.pdf*.

OECD (2016e), "Protecting consumers in peer platform markets: Exploring the issues", *OECD Digital Economy Papers*, No. 253, OECD Publishing, Paris, *http://dx.doi.org/10.1787/5jlwvz39m1zw-en*.

OECD (2016f), "Managing digital security and privacy risk", *OECD Digital Economy Papers*, No. 254, OECD Publishing, Paris, *http://dx.doi.org/10.1787/5jlwt49ccklt-en*.

OECD (2016g), "New forms of work in the digital economy", *OECD Digital Economy Papers*, No. 260, OECD Publishing, Paris, *http://dx.doi.org/10.1787/5jlwnklt820x-en*.

OECD (2015a), *Digital Security Risk Management for Economic and Social Prosperity: OECD Recommendation and Companion Document*, OECD, Paris, *www.oecd.org/sti/ieconomy/digital-security-risk-management.pdf.*

OECD (2015b), *Data-Driven Innovation: Big Data for Growth and Well-Being*, OECD Publishing, Paris, *http://dx.doi.org/10.1787/9789264229358-en.*

OECD (2014), *Measuring the Digital Economy: A New Perspective*, OECD Publishing, Paris, *http://dx.doi.org/10.1787/9789264221796-en.*

OECD (2013), *OECD Guidelines on the Protection of Privacy and Transborder Flows of Personal Data*, OECD, Paris, *www.oecd.org/sti/ieconomy/oecdguidelinesontheprotectionofprivacyandtransborderflowsofpersonaldata.htm#recommendation.*

OECD (2011), "The evolving privacy landscape: 30 years after the OECD privacy guidelines", *OECD Digital Economy Papers*, No. 176, OECD Publishing, Paris, *http://dx.doi.org/10.1787/5kgf09z90c31-en.*

OECD (2003), *OECD Guidelines for Protecting Consumers from Fraudulent and Deceptive Commercial Practices Across Borders*, OECD Publishing, Paris, *http://dx.doi.org/10.1787/9789264103573-en-fr.*

Otake, T. (2015), "Japan Pension Service hack used classic attack method", *The Japan Times*, 2 June, *www.japantimes.co.jp/news/2015/06/02/national/social-issues/japan-pension-service-hack-used-classic-attack-method.*

Perlroth, N. (2012), "Cameras may open up the board room to hackers", *The New York Times*, 22 January, *www.nytimes.com/2012/01/23/technology/flaws-in-videoconferencing-systems-put-boardrooms-at-risk.html.*

Piatetsky, G. (2014), "Did Target really predict a teen's pregnancy? The inside story", KDnuggets, 7 May, *www.kdnuggets.com/2014/05/target-predict-teen-pregnancy-inside-story.html.*

PwC (PricewaterhouseCoopers) (2015), "2015 Information Security Breaches Survey", PricewaterhouseCoopers, *www.pwc.co.uk/services/audit-assurance/insights/2015-information-security-breaches-survey.html.*

Sharman, J. (2017), "Cyber-attack that crippled NHS systems hits Nissan car factory in Sunderland and Renault in France", *The Independent*, 13 May.

Smith (2016), "IoT security camera infected within 98 seconds of plugging it in", NetworkWorld, 20 November, *www.networkworld.com/article/3143133/security/iot-security-camera-infected-within-98-seconds-of-plugging-it-in.html.*

Smith, A. and M. Anderson (2016), "Online shopping and e-commerce", Pew Research Center, 19 December, *http://assets.pewresearch.org/wp-content/uploads/sites/14/2016/12/16113209/PI_2016.12.19_Online-Shopping_FINAL.pdf.*

Storm, D. (2015), "MEDJACK: Hackers hijacking medical devices to create backdoors in hospital networks", ComputerWorld, June, *www.computerworld.com/article/2932371/cybercrime-hacking/medjack-hackers-hijacking-medical-devices-to-create-backdoors-in-hospital-networks.html.*

Thales e-Security (2016), *2016 Encryption Application Trends Study.*

The Japan Times (2015), "Japan Pension Service hack used classic attack method", *The Japan Times*, 2 June, *www.japantimes.co.jp/news/2015/06/02/national/social-issues/japan-pension-service-hack-used-classic-attack-method.*

UK Department for Business, Innovation and Skills (2015), *2015 Information Security Breaches Survey: Technical Report*, Department for Business Innovation and Skills, London, *www.pwc.co.uk/assets/pdf/2015-isbs-technical-report-blue-digital.pdf.*

UK Department for Business Innovation and Skills (2014), "Digital capabilities in SMEs: Evidence review and re-survey of 2014 Small Business Survey respondents", *BIS Research Papers*, No. 247, Department for Business Innovation and Skills, London, *https://www.gov.uk/government/uploads/system/uploads/attachment_data/file/457750/BIS-15-509-digital-capabilities-in-SMEs-evidence-review-and-re-survey-of-2014-small-business-survey-respondents.pdf.*

UK Department for Culture, Media & Sport (2016), "2016 Cyber Security Breaches Survey", UK Government, London.

UKRN (UK Regulators Network) (2016), "Price comparison websites: Final report", UK Regulators Network, 27 September, *www.ukrn.org.uk/wp-content/uploads/2016/09/201609027-UKRN-PCWs-Report.pdf.*

UNCTAD (United Nations Conference on Trade and Development) (2016), "UNCTAD B2C E-commerce Index 2016", *UNCTAD Technical Notes on ICT for Development*, No. 7, United Nations Conference on Trade and Development, Geneva, April, *http://unctad.org/en/PublicationsLibrary/tn_unctad_ict4d07_en.pdf.*

UNCTAD (2015), *Information Economy Report 2015: Unlocking the Potential of E-commerce for Developing Countries*, United Nations, Geneva, *http://unctad.org/en/PublicationsLibrary/ier2015_en.pdf*.

US Department of Commerce (2016), "Quarterly retail e-commerce sales – 2nd quarter 2016", US Census Bureau News, US Department of Commerce, Washington, DC, August, *www.census.gov/retail/mrts/www/data/pdf/ec_current.pdf*.

US International Trade Administration (2016), *eCommerce Guide*, *https://www.export.gov* (accessed 1 December 2016).

Valant, J. (2015), *Online Consumer Reviews: The Case of Misleading or Fake Reviews*, Briefing, European Parliament, October, *www.europarl.europa.eu/RegData/etudes/BRIE/2015/571301/EPRS_BRI(2015)571301_EN.pdf*.

Wong, J.C. and O. Solon (2017), "Massive ransomware cyber-attack hits nearly 100 countries around the world", *The Guardian*, 12 May, *www.theguardian.com/technology/2017/may/12/global-cyber-attack-ransomware-nsa-uk-nhs*.

Zhang, S. and G. Shih (2015), "Uber seen reaching $10.8 billion in bookings in 2015: Fundraising presentation", *Reuters*, 21 August, *www.reuters.com/article/2015/08/21/us-uber-tech-fundraising-idUSKCN0QQ0G320150821*.

Chapter 7

Technology outlook

The technology ecosystem that drives digital transformation is composed of many core technologies and is continuously evolving. This chapter explores the characteristics, opportunities and challenges raised by two of the currently most promising technological developments: machines performing human-like cognitive functions, also known as artificial intelligence, and blockchain, a distributed and tamper-proof database technology.

The statistical data for Israel are supplied by and under the responsibility of the relevant Israeli authorities. The use of such data by the OECD is without prejudice to the status of the Golan Heights, East Jerusalem and Israeli settlements in the West Bank under the terms of international law.

Introduction

Reflecting on the past 30 or 40 years of information and communication technology (ICT) innovation, each decade has seen a new form of technological revolution: "personal computers" in the 1980s, the Internet in the 1990s, mobile computing and smartphones in the 2000s, and the Internet of Things (IoT) in the current decade. Basic computing and networking technologies continue to improve over time through, for example, continued miniaturisation of devices, increased processing power and storage capacity at declining cost, and availability of higher speed on fixed and wireless networks.

However, future potential economic and social benefits increasingly depend on more recent technologies that, in turn, rely on these existing and more mature fundamental building blocks, including the IoT, cloud computing, big data analytics, artificial intelligence (AI) and blockchain. This set of technologies forms an ecosystem in which each technology both exploits and fosters the development of the others. Cloud computing is based on always-on everywhere-available and high-speed Internet connectivity and is essential to big data analytics, which relies on cheap and massive processing power and storage capacity. Big data also critically depends on sophisticated algorithms that, in turn, form the basis of AI. To comprehend their – virtual or physical – environment and take appropriate decisions, machines such as robots and drones rely on AI that often uses big data to identify patterns. The characteristics of each of these technologies create a specific set of opportunities and challenges and, as such, can be considered separately. However, it is increasingly necessary to also analyse them within the broader context of the digital ecosystem without which they could not thrive, and to which they contribute.

This chapter explores the characteristics, opportunities of and challenges raised by two of the currently most promising technological developments: machines performing human-like cognitive functions, also known as AI; and blockchain, a distributed and tamper-proof database technology that can be used to store any type of data, including financial transactions, and has the ability to create trust in an untrustworthy environment. The key findings from this chapter are:

- AI is going mainstream, driven by machine learning, big data and cloud computing that empower algorithms to identify increasingly complex patterns in large data sets and, in some cases, to outperform humans in certain cognitive functions. Beyond the promise of AI to improve efficiency, resource allocation, and thus drive productivity gains, AI also promises to help address complex challenges in many areas such as health, transport and security.
- Blockchain does not need any central authority or intermediary operator to function, as illustrated by bitcoin, a virtual currency and one of the first successful blockchain applications, which operates independently of any central bank. Beyond bitcoin, blockchain applications provide many opportunities, including in the financial sector, the public sector, for education, and the IoT, notably by reducing market friction and transaction costs, by facilitating transparency and accountability, and by enabling guaranteed execution through smart contracts.

This chapter also discusses policy challenges that could be amplified by the proliferation of AI and blockchain as well as new challenges that the use of these technologies may bring. Policy makers need to be aware of AI's potential impacts, for example, on the future of work and skill development, and potential implications for transparency and oversight, responsibility, liability, as well as safety and security. Challenges raised by some blockchain applications include, for example, the difficulty to shut down a blockchain application, if its network is transnational, or the challenge to enforce law in the absence of a central intermediary, which also raises the important question of how – and to whom – to impute legal liability for torts caused by blockchain-based systems.

Artificial intelligence

This section first describes the distinctive characteristics of AI and how over the past few years it has become mainstream, rapidly permeating and transforming our economies and societies. Compared to other technological developments, many are surprised by the speed of AI's diffusion, but views vary widely on both the likelihood and time horizon of developments such as artificial general intelligence (AGI) or technology singularity.

The potential benefits and opportunities offered by AI are introduced in the following subsection, along with examples of applications in various areas. AI promises to generate productivity gains, improve the efficiency of decision making and lower costs, since it allows data processing at enormous scales and accelerates the discovery of patterns. By helping scientists to spot complex cause and effect relationships, AI is expected to contribute to solving complex global challenges, such as those related to the environment, transportation or health. AI could radically enhance quality of life, impacting healthcare, transportation, education, security, justice, agriculture, retail commerce, finance, insurance and banking, among others. Indeed, AI could find valuable application wherever intelligence must be deployed.

The final subsection introduces some of the main policy questions that AI raises. AI is expected to replace and/or augment components of human labour in both skilled and unskilled jobs, requiring policies to facilitate professional transitions and to help workers develop the skills to benefit from, and to complement, AI. AI could also impact economic concentration and income distribution. Another issue is that of ensuring transparency and oversight of AI-powered decisions that impact people and of preventing algorithmic biases and discrimination and privacy abuses. AI also raises new liability, responsibility, security and safety questions.

Artificial intelligence is going mainstream, driven by recent advances in machine learning

Artificial intelligence is about machines performing human-like cognitive functions

There is no universally accepted definition of AI. AI-pioneer Marvin Minsky defined AI as "the science of making machines do things that would require intelligence if done by men". The present volume uses the definition provided by Nils J. Nilsson (2010): "Artificial intelligence is that activity devoted to making machines intelligent, and intelligence is that quality that enables an entity to function appropriately and with foresight in its environment". Machines understanding human speech, competing in strategic game systems, driving cars autonomously or interpreting complex data are currently considered to be AI applications. Intelligence in that sense intersects with autonomy and adaptability through AI's ability to learn from a dynamic environment.

It is important to note that the boundaries of AI are not always clear, and evolve over time. For example, in some cases techniques developed by AI researchers to analyse large volumes of data are identified as "big data" algorithms and systems (The White House, 2016a). Optical character recognition, for example, has become a widespread technology and is no longer considered to be AI. A core objective of AI research and applications over the years has been to automate or replicate intelligent behaviour.

Machine learning, big data and cloud computing have enabled artificial intelligence's recently accelerated progress

Despite fluctuations in public awareness, AI has made significant progress since its inception in the 1950s. The principle was conceptualised by John McCarthy, Alan Newell, Arthur Samuel, Herbert Simon and Marvin Minsky in the Dartmouth Summer Research Project, the summer 1956 workshop that many consider to be the start of AI. While AI research has steadily progressed over the past 60 years, the promises of early AI promoters proved to be overly optimistic, leading to an "AI Winter" of reduced funding and interest in AI research during the 1970s. More recently, the availability of big data and cloud computing have enabled breakthroughs in an AI technology called "machine learning" (Chen et al., 2012), dramatically increasing the power, availability, growth and impact of AI. In 2016, an AI programme won at the game of GO against one of the world's best players – a feat that experts thought would take at least ten more years to accomplish. The availability of scalable supercomputing capabilities on the cloud and growing flows and stocks of data produced by connected humans and machines have enabled breakthroughs in machine learning.

Machine-learning algorithms can identify complex patterns in large data sets

With machine learning, algorithms identify complex patterns in large data sets. For example, Google's AI learns how to translate content into different languages based on translated documents that are online and Facebook learns how to identify people in images based on its existing large database of known users. In particular, the progress of deep learning and reinforced learning, both branches of machine learning, have led to impressive results since 2011-12.

The efficiency of AI systems also relies on the use of specific microprocessors, often in the cloud. The learning phase of deep neural networks relies on "graphic processing units" processors that were initially designed for video games, such as those by Nvidia. For the response phase, large AI companies often develop dedicated processors, such as Google's "tensor processing unit" or Intel's Altera "field programmable gate array".

While artificial intelligence is about cognitive functions, robotics is generally concerned with motor functions

AI is mostly intangible in its manifestations. Robotics, which operates at the intersection between mechanical engineering, electrical engineering and computer sciences, is mostly physical in its manifestations. In an "autonomous machine", AI can be characterised as the intelligence or cognitive functions, while robotics refers to the motor functions. However, the distinction between cognitive and motor functions is porous and evolving since mobility requires the ability to sense and analyse the environment. For example, machine-learning AI plays a key role in computer vision. Nonetheless, the physical nature of robotics differentiates it from AI and has industrial consequences for autonomous machines: developing complex motor functions is typically more difficult, expensive and time-consuming than developing complex cognitive functions. Popular examples of the convergence between AI and robotics are self-driving cars and humanoid robots. It is important to highlight that autonomous machines combining advanced AI and robotics techniques still struggle to reproduce many basic non-cognitive motor functions (Box 7.1).

Box 7.1. **"Supervised" and "unsupervised" machine-learning algorithms**

Machine-learning technology powers web searches, content filtering on social networks, recommendations on e-commerce websites, and is increasingly present in consumer products such as cameras and smartphones. Machine-learning systems are used to identify objects in images; transcribe speech into text; match news items, posts or products with users' interests; and select relevant results of search.

Unsupervised learning presents a learning algorithm with an unlabelled set of data – that is, with no predetermined "right" or "wrong" answers – and asks it to find structure in the data, perhaps by clustering elements together, for example examining a batch of photographs of faces and learning how to identify how many different people there are. Google's News service uses this technique to group similar news stories together, as do researchers in genomics looking for differences in the degree to which a gene might be expressed in a given population, or marketers segmenting a target audience.

Supervised learning involves using a labelled data set to train a model, which can then be used to classify or sort a new, unseen set of data (for example, learning how to spot a particular person in a batch of photographs). This is useful for identifying elements in data (perhaps key phrases or physical attributes), predicting likely outcomes, or spotting anomalies and outliers. Essentially this approach presents the computer with a set of "right answers" and asks it to find more of the same. Deep learning is a form of supervised learning.

Source: UK Government Office for Science (2016), "Artificial intelligence: Opportunities and implications for the future of decision-making", *https://www.gov.uk/government/publications/artificial-intelligence-an-overview-for-policy-makers*.

Artificial intelligence outperforms humans in certain complex cognitive functions but still requires huge data sets

Neurosciences are important to understand the state of AI today as well as for understanding its future possibilities. The renaissance of AI since about 2011 is largely attributed to the success of the branch of machine learning called "deep artificial neural networks", also known as deep learning, supported by another branch of AI known as "reinforcement learning". Both deep learning and reinforcement learning claim to loosely emulate the neuronal layers that the brain uses to process information and learn through pattern recognition, although machine learning currently operates mostly in the realm of statistics. More meaningful convergence between AI and neuroscience is expected in the future as understanding of the human brain improves and technologies converge (OECD, forthcoming).

AI algorithms are able to perform complex computations of large datasets in parallel and therefore, are faster than biological human intelligence. Beyond computationally intensive tasks, AI increasingly outperforms humans for certain complex cognitive functions such as image recognition in radiology (Wang et al., 2016; Lake et al., 2016).

Today's narrow artificial intelligence focuses on specific tasks, while a hypothetical future artificial general intelligence could carry out general intelligent action, like humans

Existing artificial narrow intelligence (ANI) or "applied" AI is designed to accomplish a specific problem-solving or reasoning task. This is the current state-of-the-art. The most advanced AI system available today, such as the IBM Watson or Google's AlphaGo, are still "narrow". While they can generalise pattern recognition to some extent, for example by transferring knowledge learnt in the area of image recognition into speech recognition, the human mind is far more versatile.

Applied AI is often contrasted to a (hypothetical) AGI, in which autonomous machines would become capable of general intelligent action, like a human being, including generalising and abstracting learning across different cognitive functions. AGI would have a strong associative memory and be capable of judgment and decision making, multifaceted problem solving, learning through reading or experience, creating concepts, perceiving the world and itself, inventing and being creative, reacting to the unexpected in complex environments, and anticipating.

With respect to a potential AGI, views vary widely and experts caution that discussions should be realistic in terms of time scales. Projections from the few computer scientists active in AGI research on the time frame for the realisation of AGI range from a decade to a century or more (Goertzel and Pennachin, 2006). Some highlight that AI, like biological intelligence, is necessarily constrained by what computer scientists term combinatorics – the inconceivably vast number of things an intelligent system might think or do (OECD, 2016). In addition, because AI is an artefact, AI systems are constructed using architectures that limit AI to the knowledge and potential actions that make sense for a given application. The convergence of machine learning and neurosciences over the next decades is expected to have a significant impact.

Experts broadly agree that ANI will generate significant new opportunities, risks and challenges. They also agree that the possible advent of an AGI, perhaps sometime during the 21st century, would greatly amplify these consequences.

"Technological singularity" is a speculative future "super" artificial intelligence scenario

The term "technological singularity" refers to a speculative but consequential long-term scenario popularised by Ray Kurzweil, an inventor and futurist who is now Director of Engineering at Google. In this scenario, the emergence of an AGI would lead to an "intelligence explosion" and, within a few decades or less, to an artificial super intelligence (ASI). Such an ASI would be exponentially self-improving and could reportedly threaten mankind.

Both the AGI and ASI scenarios are excluded from the following discussion. The term "artificial intelligence" is used to refer to machine-learning algorithms that are associated with sensors and other computer programmes to sense, comprehend and act on the world; learn from experience; and adapt over time. Computer vision and audio processing algorithms, for example, actively perceive the world around them by acquiring and processing images, sounds and speech and are typically used for applications like facial and speech recognition. A typical application of natural language processing and inference engines is language translation. AI systems can also carry out cognitive actions like taking decisions, for example to accept or to reject an application for credit or undertake actions in the physical world, for example assisted braking in a car.

Successful artificial intelligence platforms leverage vast amounts of data

Digital giants as well as start-ups are active in AI. Multinationals are reorienting their business models towards data and predictive analytics to improve productivity through the use of AI, particularly in the People's Republic of China (hereafter "China"), France, Israel, Japan, Korea, the Russian Federation, the United Kingdom, and the United States. The marketplace for AI is dominated by a dozen multinationals from the United States, known collectively as GAFAMI – for "Google, Apple, Facebook, Amazon, Microsoft and IBM", and from China, known as BATX – for "Baidu, Alibaba, Tencent, and Xiaomi" (OECD, 2017). Commercialising AI technology via "software-as-a-service" business models seems to be popular, as done for example by Google and IBM, who provide access to centrally hosted AI on a subscription basis.

In the global competition between these platforms, a key success factor is the amount of data that firms have access to. Machine-learning algorithms currently require vast amounts of data to recognise patterns efficiently. For example, image recognition requires millions of images of a particular animal or car. Data generated by users, consumers and businesses help to train AI systems. Facebook relies on the nearly 10 billion images published daily by its users to continuously improve its visual recognition algorithms. Similarly, Google DeepMind uses user-uploaded YouTube video clips to train its AI software to recognise video images.

The start-up landscape is also vibrant. Research from CB Insights (2017) reported that funding raised by AI start-ups increased from USD 589 million in 2012 to over USD 5 billion in 2016. In 2016, nearly 62% of the deals went to start-ups from the United States, down from 79% just four years before. Start-ups from the United Kingdom, Israel, and India followed. By 2020, the "AI market" is projected to be worth up to USD 70 billion.

Artificial intelligence promises to improve efficiency and productivity and to help address complex challenges

Artificial intelligence can improve efficiency, save costs and enable better resource allocation

AI is expected to dramatically improve the efficiency of decision making, save costs and enable better resource allocation in basically every sector of the economy by enabling the detection of patterns in enormous volumes of data. Algorithms mining data on the operations of complex systems enable optimisation in sectors as diverse as energy, agriculture, finance, transport, healthcare, construction, defence or retail. AI enables public or private actors to optimise the use of production factors – land/environment, labour, capital or information – and to optimise the consumption of resources such as energy or water. Using its AI algorithms, Google was able to reduce the energy consumption of its data centres in ways that human intuition and engineering had not envisaged (Evans and Gao, 2016). In a two-year experiment, Google's DeepMind artificial neural network analysed over 120 parameters in a data centre and identified a more efficient and adaptive overall method of cooling and powering usage that enabled the company to reduce the energy consumption of already energy efficient data centres by a further 15% (Evans and Gao, 2016). DeepMind foresees applications to improve the efficiency of power plant conversion or to reduce the amount of energy and water needed for semiconductors.

AI decreases the cost of making predictions by assessing risk profile, managing inventory and forecasting demand. AI-assisted predictions in banking and insurance, preventive patient healthcare, maintenance, logistics, or meteorology are increasingly accessible and accurate. Firms like Ocado and Amazon use AI to optimise their storage and distribution networks, plan the most efficient routes for delivery and make the best use of their warehouses. In the healthcare sector, data from smartphones and fitness trackers can be analysed to improve the management of chronic conditions and predict and prevent acute episodes. IBM Watson is looking into using automated speech analysis tools on mobile devices to detect the development of diseases such as Huntington's, Alzheimer's or Parkinson's earlier.

Artificial intelligence can help identify suspicious activity, people or information

Machine learning is being used to detect criminal and fraudulent behaviour and ensure compliance in innovative ways. In fact, fraud detection was one of the first uses of AI in banking. Account activity patterns are monitored and anomalies trigger a review, with advances in machine learning now starting to enable near real-time monitoring. Banks are paying attention and in 2016 the bank Credit Suisse Group AG launched an AI joint-venture with a Silicon Valley surveillance and security firm whose solutions help banks to detect unauthorised trading (Voegeli, 2016).

AI technologies are also increasingly being used in counter-terrorism and police activities. The US Intelligence Advanced Research Projects Activity is working on several programmes to process large volumes of multi-dimensional footage captured by "media in the wild" and identify individuals. Its programmes use AI to move beyond largely two-dimensional image-matching methods; or even to identify individuals and automatically geolocate suspicious untagged videos published online.

The veracity of news and "fake news" is another area where AI can help analyse large volumes of data in the trillions of user-provided posts. Social networking giant Facebook is reportedly training a system to identify fake news based on the types of articles that users have flagged as misinformation in the past.

Artificial intelligence is expected to generate a new wave of productivity gains

AI is expected to be able to contribute to generating productivity gains across domains through both the automation of activities previously carried out by people and through machine autonomy whereby systems are able to operate and adapt to changing circumstances with reduced or no human control (OECD, 2017). The best-known example of machine autonomy is that of driverless cars, but other applications include automated financial trading, automated content curation systems, or systems that can identify and fix security vulnerabilities.

Productivity gains could take place in areas ranging from factories to service centres and offices, as AI enables complex cognitive and physical tasks to be automated. AI can automatise and prioritise routine administrative and operational tasks by training conversational robot software ("bots"). Google's Smart Reply software proposes draft responses based on previous responses to similar messages. Newsrooms increasingly use machine learning to produce reports and to draft articles. These applications use a human in the final approval process and hence increase the productivity of that individual. Robots using lasers and 3D depth-sensors and advanced computer vision deep neural networks can now work safely alongside warehouse and factory workers. AI can also improve productivity by reducing the cost of searching large data sets. In the legal sector, companies such as ROSS, Lex Machina, H5 or CaseText rely on natural language processing AI to search through legal documents for case-relevant information, reviewing thousands of documents in days rather than months.

Several market research firms have recently attempted to project AI's impact on economic growth and productivity. Purdy and Daugherty (2016) analysed 12 developed economies and claimed that AI could double these countries' annual growth rates and increase the productivity of labour by up to 40% by 2035. The McKinsey Global Institute estimated that automation through both AI and robotics could raise global productivity by 0.8% to 1.4% annually.

Artificial intelligence promises to help people address complex challenges in areas like health, transport and security

Artificial intelligence helps detect health conditions early, deliver preventive services and discover new treatments

Advances of AI in healthcare are expected to help the treatment of human diseases and medicine by both helping to detect conditions early and – in combination with rapidly increasing flows of available medical data – by enabling precision and preventive medical treatments. AI helps detect medical conditions early notably through the use of image recognition on radiography, ultrasonography, computed tomography and magnetic resonance imaging. IBM Watson and doctors from the University of Tokyo were able to diagnose a rare form of leukaemia in a Japanese patient that doctors had not detected. In the area of breast cancer detection radiology, deep learning algorithms combined with inputs from human pathologists lowered the error rate to 0.5%, representing an 85% reduction in error compared to error rates achieved by human pathologists alone (3.5%) or machines alone (7.5%) (Nikkei, 2015).

Advances in machine learning are also expected to facilitate drug inventions, creations and discoveries through the mining of data and research publications. Personalised healthcare services and life coaches on smartphones are already beginning to understand and integrate various personal health data sets. In the area of elderly care, natural language processing AI applications and visual and hearing assistance devices, such as exoskeletons or intelligent walkers, are expected to play an increasing role.

Artificial intelligence-powered autonomous driving and optimised traffic routes facilitate transportation and save lives

AI is already impacting transportation significantly with the introduction of itinerary mapping based on traffic data and autonomous driving capabilities. Advances in deep neural networks are one of the main drivers behind the impressive progress achieved in autonomous vehicles over the past decade, particularly thanks to computer vision. In combination with many other types of algorithms, deep neural networks are able to make the most out of complex sensors used for navigation and learn how to drive in complex environments. Benefits include fewer road accidents and enabling people to use commuting time for productive activity, leisure or rest. While the shape and timeline of the restructuring of the car industry is still unclear, many believe that connected and autonomous vehicles could help avoid many of the 1.3 million deaths per year on roads globally. Disrupted by the arrival of new actors such as Google, Baidu, Tesla or Uber, traditional automobile actors such as Ford Motors or Honda are now investing in promising AI start-ups, forging alliances or developing in-house capabilities.

Artificial intelligence helps identify and combat both cybersecurity threats and real-world security threats

AI is effective against cyberattacks and identity theft through analysis of trends and anomalies. It is used as defence against hackers as well as in proactive, just-in-time, responses to hacking attempts. The Defense Advanced Research Projects Agency (DARPA) Cyber Grand Challenge competition in August 2016, with attacks and defence on-the-fly using AI cyber reasoning systems, was an important milestone that, according to DARPA, validated the concept of automated cyber defence. AI has a wide range of security applications beyond cybersecurity. AI is used as a powerful identification method in policing (for example with facial recognition that harnesses large networks of surveillance cameras) and increasingly to predict where and when crime will happen. University-based research start-ups have also used AI to detect lying in written text with potential applications, among others, to enhance online child safety (Dutton, 2011). For emergency and disaster management, AI applications can optimise planning and resource deployment by aid agencies, international organisations and non-governmental organisations.

The rise of artificial intelligence amplifies existing policy challenges and raises new ones

While policy makers are starting to focus on artificial intelligence, more awareness of its potential impacts is needed

Increasingly, countries are developing national AI strategies or including AI as a significant part of wider national digital agendas. China, France, Germany, Japan, Korea, the United Kingdom and the United States have developed or are developing AI-related plans and strategies that intersect with robotics and other complementary sectors. Overall, however, the likely impact of AI in the years ahead is just beginning to be explored by policy makers and by the public at large and the speed at which AI is permeating our economies and society may sometimes be underestimated.

At the G7 ICT Ministers' Meeting in Takamatsu, Japan in 2016, participating countries agreed on a proposal made by Minister Takaichi, Japanese Ministry for Internal Affairs and Communications, to convene stakeholders to consider social, economic, ethical and legal issues of AI and formulate principles for AI development (Box 7.2).

In addition, the Japanese Cabinet Office Council for Science, Technology and Innovation helped to co-ordinate a human-centred "Society 5.0" strategy, which was released in March 2017, to help Japan benefit from the opportunities AI creates while minimising risks and setting the limits of automated decision making.

As a result of an inter-agency initiative in the United States, a public report was published in 2016 on AI ("Preparing for the future of artificial intelligence"), which was accompanied by a "National Artificial Intelligence Research and Development Strategic Plan". These documents detail steps that the US federal government could take to use AI to advance social good and improve government operations; adapt regulations in a way that encourages innovation while protecting the public; ensure that applications of AI, including those that are not regulated, are fair, safe and governable; develop a skilled and diverse AI workforce; and address the use of AI in weapons.

In May 2016, the Chinese government unveiled a three-year national AI plan formulated jointly by the National Development and Reform Commission, the Ministry of Science and Technology, the Ministry of Industry and Information Technology, and the Cyberspace Administration of China. The government envisions creating a USD 15 billion market by 2018 by investing in research and supporting the development of the Chinese AI industry. In 2016, China surpassed the United States in terms of the number of papers published annually on "deep learning", reflecting the increasing research priority that AI has become for China.

Box 7.2. **Expert discussions on artificial intelligence networking in Japan**

Throughout the first half of 2016, the Japanese Ministry of Internal Affairs and Communications convened discussions with experts in science and technology, the humanities, and social sciences on issues associated with the development of "artificial intelligence networking", i.e. of interconnected artificial intelligence (AI) systems that co-operate with each other.

These discussions advocated the notion of a "Wisdom Network Society", a human-centric society built through AI in which humans could create, distribute and connect data, information and knowledge freely and safely. The wisdom networks would harmoniously combine human and AI via AI networking and allow complex challenges to be addressed. The expert discussions focused on the social and economic impacts and challenges of AI networking in 16 different areas until the 2040s.

Since October 2016, the ministry has been co-ordinating expert discussions in Japan to consider guiding principles for AI research and development (R&D) and to discuss detailed impacts and risks of AI. The ministry is now actively encouraging international co-operation on AI, with the involvement of all stakeholders.

In the AI R&D context, the ministry has identified the importance of considering: 1) transparency, i.e. the ability to explain and verify the operation of AI networks; 2) user assistance, i.e. ensuring that AI networks assist users and provide users with appropriate opportunities to make choices; 3) controllability by humans, i.e. enabling people to control the safe use of AI, to take over control from AI smoothly if needed, particularly in case of an emergency, and to determine how much AI is used in decisions or actions; 4) security, i.e. ensuring the robustness and dependability of AI networks; 5) safety, i.e. ensuring that AI networks do not cause danger to the lives/bodies of users or third parties; 6) privacy, i.e. not infringing on the privacy of users or third parties; 7) ethics, i.e. ensuring the respect of human dignity and personal autonomy; 8) accountability; and 9) interoperability or linkage, i.e. ensuring interoperability between AIs or AI networking.

Based on these discussions, the Japanese government is considering whether guidelines concerning AI usage and applications are also needed.

Source: OECD (2016), "Summary of the CDEP Technology Foresight Forum: Economic and Social Implications of Artificial Intelligence", *http://oe.cd/ai2016*.

Several partnerships and initiatives are being formed to promote ethical AI and try to prevent adverse effects of AI. For example, the non-profit AI research company OpenAI was founded late 2015 and now employs 60 full-time researchers with the mission to "build safe AGI, and ensure AGI's benefits are as widely and evenly distributed as possible".[1] In April 2016, the IEEE Standards Association launched its "Global Initiative for Ethical Considerations in the Design of Autonomous Systems" to bring together multiple voices in the AI and autonomous systems communities to "make sure that [AI and autonomous systems] technologies are aligned to humans in terms of our moral values and ethical principles". In September 2016, Amazon, DeepMind/Google, Facebook, IBM and Microsoft launched the "Partnership on Artificial Intelligence to Benefit People and Society" to advance public understanding of AI technologies and formulate best practices on its challenges and opportunities.[2]

Artificial intelligence will change the future of work, replacing and/or augmenting human labour in expert and high-wage occupations

A widely discussed set of policy challenges is the impact of AI on jobs. AI is expected to greatly exacerbate the displacement trends caused by automation discussed in Chapter 5, as AI-enabled machines augment or replace humans in numerous occupations across domains and value chains. Whether this raises incomes and generates new types of jobs to replace those that are automated, or leads to unemployment, is uncertain and results of different studies on the overall impacts of job automation conducted over the past five years differ in their assessment and projections (Arntz, Gregory and Zierahn, 2016; Frey and Osborne, 2013; Citibank, 2016).

AI's impact will also depend on the speed of the development and diffusion of AI technologies in different sectors over the coming decades. According to the International Transport Forum (ITF), for example, driverless trucks could be a regular presence on many roads within the next ten years, leading to large-scale job displacement of truck drivers if driverless trucks are deployed quickly. Driverless trucks could improve road safety, lower emissions and reduce operating costs for road freight in the order of 30%, notably due to savings in labour costs that currently account for 35% to 45% of costs and to more intensive use of vehicle fleets (ITF, 2017). The White House estimated in 2016 that 2.2 million to 3.1 million existing part-time and full-time jobs in the United States may be threatened by automated vehicles over the next two decades (The White House, 2016b).

The jobs that are potentially at risk are not only those in low-skill occupations or in manufacturing. Rather, many jobs involving medium or higher level cognitive skills are also potentially at risk. Early research suggests AI could impact employment using general cognitive skills such as literacy and numeracy, which are a primary focus of development during compulsory education (Elliot, 2014). Machine-learning technologies in particular seem to have potential to affect highly educated professions (Box 5.1). For example, image processing and pattern recognition algorithms are reportedly beginning to impact radiologists: as described earlier, pattern recognition applications are increasingly able to detect health conditions by identifying anomalies on radiography, ultrasonography or magnetic resonance imaging. Machine-learning applications in the area of speech recognition, natural language processing or machine translation are expected to impact demand for services such as translations, legal services and accounting services.

Policy discussions underway to address AI's impact on jobs include the merits of adapting tax policies to rebalance the shift from labour to capital and protect vulnerable people from socio-economic exclusion (with some even proposing to tax robots); adapting social security and redistributive mechanisms; developing education and skill systems that facilitate repeated and viable professional transitions; and considering how to ensure fair access to credit, healthcare or retirement benefits to a more mobile and less secure workforce.

Developing the skills to benefit from, and to complement, artificial intelligence

Paradoxically, AI and other digital technologies also enable innovative and personalised approaches to job-search and hiring processes and enhance the efficiency of matching labour supply and demand. The LinkedIn platform, for example, uses AI to help recruiters find the right candidates and to connect candidates to the right jobs, based on data about the profile and activity of the platform's 470 million registered users (Wong, 2017). AI-based tools can also support skills development and retraining through AI-based personalised tutoring tools that provide quality education at scale.

AI could be expected, as with ICTs more generally (Chapter 4), to enhance the need for new skills along three lines: 1) specialist skills, to programme and develop AI applications, e.g. through AI-related fundamental research, engineering and applications, as well as data science and computational thinking; 2) generic skills, to be able to leverage AI; and 3) complementarity skills, to enable, for example, critical thinking; creativity, innovation and entrepreneurship; and the development of human skills such as empathy.

Artificial intelligence's business dynamics pose new questions

The anticipated business dynamics of AI pose questions of wealth and power distribution as well as of competition and barriers to entry. The rapid evolution of AI technology could challenge existing competition policies and raise questions on the potential impacts of AI on income distribution and of who will control AI technology. On the economic side, there is the potential that a few technology companies with access to large amounts of data and funding could end up controlling AI technology, with access to its super-human intelligence and gathering most of the benefits yielded from AI. AI may also imply that companies will rely less on their human workforce in the future.

As with some other digital and data markets, the AI market may exhibits "winner-takes-most" characteristics because of network effects and scale effects. With the disruptive business models of highly innovative digital multinationals unfolding transnationally, the accumulation of wealth and power by a limited number of private AI actors could cause tensions within and between countries. Some stakeholders highlight risks of digital giants acquiring start-ups before they can become potential competitors and the consequent risks of resource concentration in the field of AI.

Ensuring transparency and oversight of artificial intelligence-powered decisions that impact people

Another set of AI-related policy questions relates to the governance of AI systems. What oversight and accountability mechanisms do machine-learning algorithms require and what balance is needed between productivity and access on the one hand, and values such as justice, fairness and accountability on the other? The question is already manifest in critical areas such as determining priorities in line of care at hospitals, automatic vehicles' emergency response procedures, citizen risk-profiling in criminal justice procedures, preventive policing, and access to credit and insurance.

The challenge of governing the use of AI algorithms is compounded with advanced machine-learning techniques by the fact that tracing and understanding the decision-making mechanisms of AI algorithms is increasingly difficult as their complexity increases, even to those who design and train them (OECD, 2016). Researchers have started working on a potential solution but results are still immature and uncertain. It should be noted that Articles 13-15 of the European Union's (EU's) new General Data Protection Regulation mandates that data subjects receive meaningful information about the logic involved, the significance and the envisaged consequences of automated decision-making systems. It also includes, in Article 22, the "right not to be subject to automated decision making". The protections actually afforded to data subjects under the regulation and its implications for AI researchers and practitioners are still under discussion (Wachter, Mittelstadt and Floridi, 2016).

Developing and implementing algorithmic accountability solutions at scale is expected to be complex and costly, raising the question of who should bear its costs. If actors pursue a lower cost solution, abuses could arise. Policy makers will have to work closely with AI researchers and engineers to develop mechanisms that balance competing needs for transparency and legitimate commercial confidentiality. In some cases, technical designs and business models may be well aligned with socially established value hierarchies and technical standardisation agencies and independent authorities can play a key role. The Institute of Electronical and Electronics Engineers has launched the Global Initiative for Ethical Considerations in Artificial Intelligence and Autonomous Systems. The goal of the initiative is to make sure that technology and technologists work to advance humanity under principled disciplines. The initiative harnesses the institute's experience in complex standardisation processes and the strength and inclusion potential of its transnational reach with its global community of over 400 000 practitioners and experts in 160 countries.

Because machine learning requires vast amounts of data, the governance of AI intersects with the regulation of data collection, storage, processing, ownership and monetisation. Enabling the potential of AI for growth, development and public good will require agreeing on technical standards and governance mechanisms that maximise the free flow of data and promote investments in data-intensive services (OECD, 2015). The difficulty of governing data is compounded by uncertainty over how present and future AI technologies can help create, analyse and use data in radically new ways not previously imagined by consumers, firms and governments.

Applications such as facial recognition and personalised services offer convenience and improved safety, but may raise risks to civil liberties if people are monitored and inferences made by machines are not transparent, or if individuals cannot access their underlying personal information.

Preventing algorithmic biases and discrimination

Concerns that machine-learning algorithms could amplify social biases and cause discrimination have increased as algorithms leveraging big data become more complex, autonomous and powerful. AI learns from data, but if the data are incomplete or biased, AI can exacerbate biases. The case of "Tay", the teenage AI conversational bot developed by Microsoft, illustrated these risks: the Twitter bot was released in March 2016 on Twitter as an experiment to improve its understanding of language among 18-24 year-olds online. Within hours, the bot had to be shut down as it had started to use racial slurs, defend white supremacist propaganda and support genocide. Another widely cited illustration of the risk of AI discrimination is the racial bias found in some "risk prediction" tools used by judges in criminal sentencing and bail hearings. Some have questioned the fairness and efficacy of predictive policing tools, credit scoring tools and hiring tools, raising questions about how to ensure that algorithms protect diversity and fairness.

Responsibility and liability, security and safety

AI-driven automated decision making raise questions of responsibility and liability, for example when accidents involve autonomous cars. The "authored"/machine nature of AI means that it is difficult to make AI a legal person that might be responsible for its decisions. As for human drivers, insurance is widely viewed as a way forward to deal with uncertain, probabilistic risks. New safety and security risks are also emerging: for example malware could abuse an AI network system or an autonomous weapon.

Blockchain

Blockchain is a distributed and tamper-proof database technology that can be used to store any type of data, including financial transactions, and has the ability to create trust in an untrustworthy environment.

This section first describes the distinctive characteristics of blockchain technology and how it contributes to the establishment of a trusted technical environment for "trustless" economic and social interactions. Taking Bitcoin as a starting point – the first and most widely deployed blockchain network in the financial context – it looks at the technical features of existing blockchains, as well as their limitations. The main benefits and opportunities offered by this new technology are introduced in the following subsection together with examples of applications in various areas. Finally, the section concludes with a description of the policy challenges raised by blockchain technology, including how, if not appropriately regulated, blockchain usage could escape from the purview of the law.

Transactions enabled by blockchain technology can be carried out without any trusted party

A blockchain is a tamper-proof distributed database that is capable of storing any type of data, including financial transactions. Because of its distinctive characteristics (described below), a blockchain can be regarded as a source of "trustless trust" (Werbach, 2016): trust is shifted away from the centralised intermediaries towards the developers of the underlying technical infrastructure, which enables trusted transactions between nodes that are not necessarily trustworthy. Nodes in a blockchain network co-ordinate themselves through a specific protocol that stipulates the rules by which data can be recorded into the distributed database. In most cases, blockchains are implemented in such a way that there is no single party capable of controlling the underlying infrastructure or undermining the system (Brakeville and Perepa, 2016).

Traditional databases are maintained by centralised operators, responsible for hosting the data on their own servers or in data centres. In contrast, a blockchain relies on a distributed peer-to-peer (P2P) infrastructure network for the storage and management of data and on a distributed network of peers to maintain and secure a distributed ledger. The distributed character of a blockchain raises new legal and policy challenges. Indeed, in the absence of a centralised operator in charge of managing the network, it is difficult for regulators or other governmental authorities to influence the operations of many of these blockchain networks.

Compared to traditional databases, blockchains exhibit several unique characteristics that make them particularly suitable for registering records and transferring value in contexts where people cannot or do not want to rely on a trusted third party:

- A blockchain is highly resilient and operates independently of any central authority or intermediary operator. As such, blockchains are characterised by a strong degree of disintermediation.
- A blockchain is an append-only database, which is also tamper-resistant. It relies on cryptographic primitives and game theoretical incentives to ensure that, once data have been recorded on the decentralised database, they cannot be subsequently deleted or modified by any single party.
- Data recorded on a blockchain are signed by the originating party and stored in chronological order into a new block of transactions, which are securely time-stamped by the underlying network.

In addition, some blockchains also come with the capability to execute software logic in a decentralised manner. Because there is no central operator responsible for running the code, such blockchain-based applications are guaranteed to execute in a strict and deterministic manner, providing users with a significant level of security assurance.

Bitcoin

Bitcoin is one of the first applications of blockchain technology for financial applications. Bitcoin is a virtual currency (or "cryptocurrency") and decentralised payment system that operates independently of any central bank. Launched in 2009 by a pseudonymous entity called Satoshi Nakamoto, the Bitcoin blockchain relies on a set of pre-existing technologies that, combined, allow for the establishment of a decentralised and largely incorruptible database on which to record the history of all transactions performed onto the network.

In just a few years, the Bitcoin network experienced significant adoption. The network has grown from processing less than 100 transactions per day in 2009 to over 250 000 confirmed transactions daily in Q1 2017 (Figure 7.1). Despite its volatility, the Bitcoin price also followed a significant growth. From a few fractions of a US dollar in 2009, the price of Bitcoin reached over USD 1 200 in March 2017.

Figure 7.1. **Confirmed Bitcoin transactions per day**

Moving averages

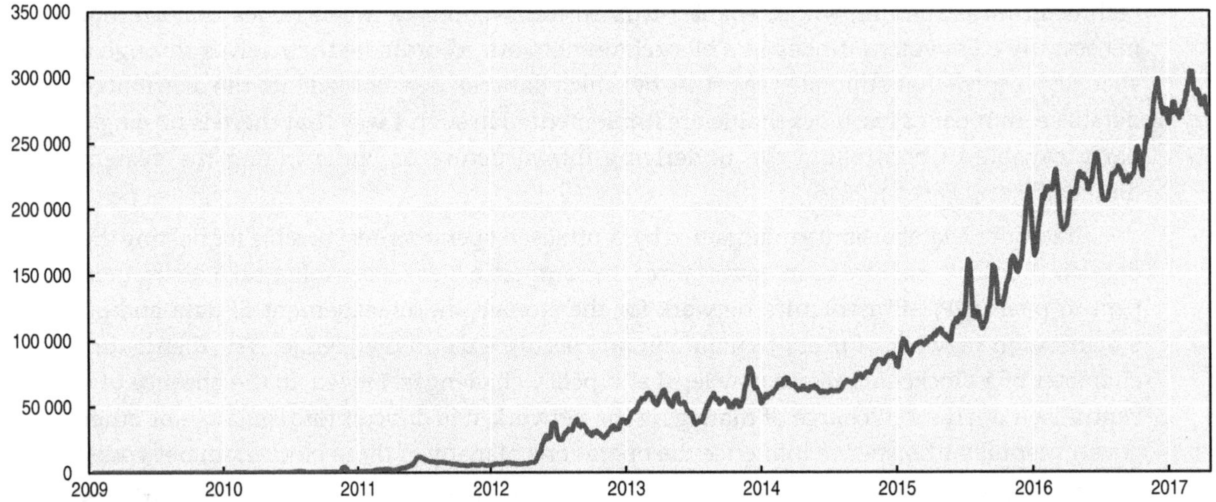

Source: Blockchain.info, *https://blockchain.info/charts/n-transactions?timespan=all* (accessed 24 April 2017).

StatLink *http://dx.doi.org/10.1787/888933586749*

At its core, Bitcoin is a decentralised database replicated across a P2P network (Nakamoto, 2008). A P2P network is a collection of computers (or nodes) that work together to achieve a common goal – be it either the swapping of files, as in the case of BitTorrent, or anonymous communications, as in the case of The Onion Router (Tor). In contrast to traditional client-server infrastructures, these networks are not managed by any centralised operator; they are operated by a distributed network of peers that interact and co-ordinate themselves via a common computer protocol.

In the case of Bitcoin, nodes are responsible for maintaining and updating the state of the blockchain database according to a particular protocol known as Proof of Work. This protocol is designed to help nodes reach consensus as to the state of the blockchain at periodic intervals, while simultaneously protecting the decentralised database from malicious actors who may seek to manipulate the data or inject fraudulent information.

These nodes voluntarily lend their processing power to the P2P network in order to validate transactions and ensure compliance with the underlying protocol. Valid transactions are stored into a block of transactions, which is appended, in chronological order, to the previous chain of blocks – hence the name "blockchain".

The Bitcoin blockchain relies on public-private key cryptography[3] to ensure that only authorised transactions will go through. Each Bitcoin account is identified by a given address (or public key), which is uniquely and mathematically associated with a particular password (or private key). In order to be regarded as valid, every Bitcoin transaction needs to be signed by the private key of the account holder. The system will assess the legitimacy of the transaction by checking that it is algorithmically correct (i.e. that there are sufficient funds in the account to execute the transaction) and that the funds have not been spent more than once (i.e. that the transaction passes the "double-spending" test).

The "double-spending" problem is a common issue in the context of decentralised virtual currencies. Indeed, in the absence of a centralised clearing house, it is possible for malicious parties to try and spend the same unit of virtual currency twice, by submitting two different and conflicting transactions at the same time, hoping that the network will not synchronise fast enough to block either transaction. The problem has generally been resolved through the introduction of a centralised middleman in charge of clearing the transaction.

Bitcoin introduces a novel solution to the double-spending problem through the Proof of Work protocol. Before a particular block of transaction can be recorded to the Bitcoin blockchain, the network nodes, generally referred to as miners, must first find the solution to a mathematical problem that is inherently related to that block. The mathematical problem uses a hash function (SHA-256) that is computationally difficult to solve but easy to verify, once the solution is found (Bonneau et al., 2015). Once the solution is found, it is publicly broadcasted to the whole network so that the other network participants can verify that it is correct. Only then will that particular block of transactions become an integral part of the Bitcoin blockchain.

The Bitcoin protocol will adjust the difficulty of this mathematical problem depending on the amount of computational resources (i.e. hashing power) currently invested into the network. The greater the amount of resources available to the network, the harder the problem becomes – so as to ensure that a new block of transactions is added, in average, every ten minutes. The Bitcoin network creates incentives for miners to do the heavy computational lifting in the proof of work by rewarding the first miner to solve each block's mathematical problem with a particular amount of bitcoins, plus the right to perceive all transactions fees associated with this particular block of transactions. The Bitcoin system is designed so that the whole system can only contain 21 million bitcoins ever. Therefore, as time progresses, there will not be any more rewards for the miners to do the work required to verify proof of work. However, it is anticipated that since there will be several users of bitcoins at this point, transaction fees will be sufficient to incentivise this effort.

Unlike other databases, a blockchain is an append-only database, in the sense that data can only be added to a blockchain but, once recorded, cannot be unilaterally deleted or modified by anyone (Narayanan et al., 2016). In the case of Bitcoin, the information recorded on the blockchain can only be altered if one or more parties were to capture more than half of the overall computational power invested into the network – the so-called 51% attack. Given the current size of the Bitcoin network, such an attack, albeit possible,[4] would be extremely difficult and costly to achieve.

The Bitcoin blockchain can therefore be regarded as a certified and chronological log of transactions, whose authenticity and integrity are ensured by cryptographic primitives. Because every transaction must be digitally signed by the private key of the account holder, the blockchain represents verifiable proof that one party transferred a particular amount of bitcoins to another party, at a particular point in time. And given that every block incorporates a reference (i.e. a cryptographic hash) to the previous block, any attempt at tampering with the data recorded into a block will be immediately detected by the network. In fact, the modification of any given transaction will invalidate the reference to the previous block, which would inevitably break the chain – and consequently be detected by all other network participants.

Governance mechanisms

Different blockchains implement different governance mechanisms. As a general rule, all blockchains can be situated on a continuum ranging from entirely public and permissionless blockchains, such as Bitcoin, to fully private and permissioned blockchains. Public and permissionless blockchains do not implement any restrictions on who can read or write on the decentralised database. They are generally pseudonymous as the network nodes do not need to disclose their real-world identity. Most of the early blockchain-based networks that emerged after Bitcoin, including Litecoin, Namecoin, Peercoin and Ethereum, rely on a public blockchain.

By contrast, on the other end of the continuum, a private and permissioned blockchain includes a built-in access control mechanism that can limit the number of parties allowed to perform basic tasks on the blockchain. Private blockchains rely on closed and more carefully managed networks, the access to which can be limited to pre-approved individuals, and permission to validate a transaction can be restricted to only some actors in the network.

For instance, permissioned blockchains such as Ripple and Corda (see below) have been developed with a focus on financial services. Instead of relying on an open network, only the parties of a consortium are entitled to participate in the consensus and execute transactions on these blockchains.

The decision as to whether to use a permissionless or permissioned blockchain ultimately boils down to a question of trust, scalability and transparency. On the one hand, public and permissionless blockchains are more "trustless" because they distribute trust over a large number of individual nodes, and rely on Proof of Work to ensure that it is computationally difficult, and expensive, for any of these nodes to manipulate the network. Yet, because of these design choices, public blockchains can be very expensive to maintain, have limited performance, and – despite their pseudonymity – the transparency inherent into these networks can impact the privacy of their users. On the other hand, private and permissioned blockchains are more scalable because they can use computationally less expensive protocols to verify transactions, given that there is already some inherent trust in the actors. They also offer a more controlled environment by giving differentiated access to its actors and making some of the transactions private. For example a consortium of banks can choose to share one permissioned blockchain ecosystem without having to divulge all transactions within their own institution to other institutions in the consortium. Yet, private and permissioned blockchains require a higher degree of trust in the parties managing the network, and, as a result, can be more easily manipulated if one of these parties gets hacked or is otherwise compromised.

Additionally, tools are currently being developed to enable different blockchains to interact with one another, in an interoperable way. For example, the company Blockstream is building tools for the Bitcoin blockchain to serve as a backbone for a variety of other, more specialised permissioned and permissionless blockchains.

Limitations of blockchain technology

Despite their resilience and tamper-resistance, there are limitations inherent in the consensus protocol adopted by many public and permissionless blockchains. Indeed, Proof of Work is grounded on the premise that no party controls more than 50% of the computational power invested in the network. Once that threshold is reached, the controlling party can manipulate the network, creating conflicting records (see the discussion above on the "double-spending" problem) and preventing some transactions from getting added to the database (Narayanan et al., 2016).

While the 51% attack is a problem common to all types of blockchain, it is all the more critical in the case of permissionless blockchains, due to the fact that it is difficult to determine who effectively controls the hashing power invested in these networks. While the collusion of multiple nodes in a permissioned blockchain would be easily identifiable, and sanctionable, the potential takeover of a public blockchain by a group of unidentified individuals would be much harder to detect. And yet, the vulnerability is real. In 2017, after eight years of operation, over 50% of the hashing power operating the Bitcoin network is controlled by five large mining pools (Blockchain, n.d. a). In fact, in a few instances, a single pool of Bitcoin miners was in control of more than half of the network's computational power.

In addition to these security issues and because blockchains rely on public-private key cryptography, one of the major hindrances to the mainstream adoption of blockchain technology is the lack of a standard key management system, including a recovery and a revocation mechanism. Without a proper recovery mechanism, the loss of a private key would preclude the account holder from performing any operation from the account. Similarly, without a proper key revocation system, if a private key is compromised, anyone in possession of that key could execute unauthorised transactions on behalf of the account holder.

Another important limitation of blockchain technology is performance, which is also more critical in the context of public and permissionless blockchains. Existing public blockchains can only handle a limited number of transactions. For instance, the Bitcoin network processes less than 300 000 transactions per day (Blockchain, n.d. b), as opposed to the 150 million transactions processed by Visa every day. Bitcoin transactions are validated, more or less, every ten minutes (Blockchain, n.d. c), much longer than the time it normally takes for a database to store and record information.

For blockchain technology to reach mainstream adoption, these systems will need to mature in order to handle a seemingly countless number of transactions. Yet, solving scalability issues will be no simple task. Because a blockchain is an append-only database, each new transaction causes the blockchain to grow. The larger the blockchain, the greater the requirements in terms of computational power, storage and bandwidth, all amounting to significant high energy consumption. If these requirements become too onerous, fewer actors will contribute to supporting the network, thus increasing the likelihood that a few large mining pool will control the network (James-Lubin, 2015). While there are already many proposals for bringing blockchains to scale, they are for the most part still in an experimental phase. They include, for example, the use of alternative consensus protocols such as proof of stake (Buterin, 2015; Iddo et al., 2014).[5] International efforts to develop standards for blockchain technologies such as the establishment of the International Organization for Standardization (ISO) Technical Committee 307 on "Blockchain and distributed ledger technologies" in 2016 can take the development of these technologies to the next stage, in particular by stimulating greater interoperability, speedier acceptance and enhanced innovation in their use and application.

Blockchain applications provide many new opportunities

Bitcoin was the first application to exploit the new opportunities provided by blockchain technology in the realm of finance, but the benefits brought by blockchain technology can be used for many other types of applications, both in the realm of finance and beyond. These potential benefits are introduced below, together with examples of how the technology is currently being experimented in various areas. It is worth noting that, given the recent history and current immaturity of blockchain technology, the examples listed below are, for the most part, pilots and proof of concepts done by early-stage businesses and start-ups.

Reduced market friction and transaction costs

Blockchain technology can reduce market friction and transaction costs in specific sectors of activity. While there are important costs involved in maintaining a blockchain infrastructure, one of the greatest potentials of blockchain technology is to increase the efficiency of existing information systems, by eliminating paperwork and reducing the overhead costs stemming from the interactions between multiple layers of intermediaries.

For instance, one sector that suffers from significant market friction and transaction costs is the remittance sector. Today, international remittances can take up to seven days to clear, with fees up to 10% of the amount transferred. Blockchains can drive down the costs of remittances, giving people the ability to send money abroad, quickly and cheaply, through mobile devices. Launched on November 2013, in Nairobi, BitPesa was the first remittance company using the Bitcoin blockchain for sending money in African countries. Since then, many other start-ups have been experimenting with the technology. Today, Abra seems to be the leader in the field. Launched in early 2017, the company is the only one addressing the problem of the first and last miles, i.e. how to exchange fiat money into Bitcoin and vice versa.

On a more general level, blockchains can act as a backbone for depository institutions to conduct inter-bank transfers and convert funds. For instance, in 2012, the company Ripple released the Ripple Transaction Protocol, giving banks the ability to convert funds into different currencies, in a matter of seconds and at little to no cost. The protocol creates a series of trades between foreign exchange traders who have agreed to participate on the Ripple network, calculating the fastest and most cost-effective way to convert funds from one currency to another, and then settling those trades instantaneously via a blockchain. The system has recently been adopted by Santander to set up a trial for international remittances and cross-border payments.

Blockchain technology can also contribute to reducing transaction costs, helping banks settle transactions more quickly and efficiently. Instead of each bank maintaining its own record of transactions, a blockchain-based system can update all records simultaneously, removing the need to reconcile transactions between different banks. This is what motivated the creation of the R3 consortium in 2014. With membership from over 70 banks and financial institutions, the consortium is currently geared towards the development of a distributed ledger technology, called Corda, designed to support and facilitate inter-bank transactions.

Blockchain technology also brings the potential to expedite the trading of securities, by combining clearing and settlement into one single operation. Experiments of this kind are already under way. For instance, in October 2015, Nasdaq partnered with Chain to explore the use of blockchain technology for the exchange of shares in private companies. A few months later, the publicly traded company Overstock, the first major online retailer to accept payments in Bitcoin, started offering its own stocks on a blockchain-based trading platform (t0) specifically built for that purpose.

In the derivative market, blockchains are ushering in a new era of financial engineering that could contribute to adding more security, efficiency and precision in risk management. With a blockchain, people can encode the terms of a derivative instrument directly into code, so that they can be processed and automatically executed by the underlying blockchain network. A successful trial was performed in 2016, by the Depository Trust & Clearing Corporation, together with five Wall Street firms – Bank of America, Merrill Lynch, Citi, Credit Suisse and JPMorgan – encoding the terms of credit default swaps into a blockchain-based system in order to manage all post-trade events. Shortly afterwards, in early 2017, the Depository Trust & Clearing Corporation announced its plan to move USD 11 trillion worth of credit derivatives to a blockchain infrastructure specifically built for that purpose. The goal is to improve the processing of derivatives through automated record-keeping and to reduce the reconciliation costs.

Transparency and accountability

By providing a global, transparent and tamper-resistant database on which to record and time-stamp information, a blockchain can serve as a global registry of certified and authenticated records. Important data can be registered on a blockchain in such a way that it becomes available to all, and that it cannot be retroactively modified or repudiated by the party recording it.

In many cases, however, information needs to be kept private. Instead of storing data directly onto a blockchain, data can be hashed[6] into a short string that acts as a unique identifier for the data at hand. This is useful to certify the source and integrity of specific records, without disclosing any sensitive information to the public. Indeed, while no one has the ability to retrieve any information by simply looking at the hash, anyone in possession of the original data can verify that it is has not been tampered with by comparing its hash with the one stored on the blockchain.

Various governments are exploring blockchains in the context of providing more transparent and reliable governmental records. For instance, in 2015, the government of Estonia announced a partnership with the start-up Bitnation to provide blockchain-based notarisation services to all its electronic residents. These include, for example, marriage records, birth certificates and business contracts. In 2016, the Estonian eHealth Authority partnered with the software security company Guardtime in order to set a blockchain-based infrastructure to preserve the integrity and improve the auditability of health records and other sensitive data. In May 2016, Ghana announced a partnership with the Bitland organisation to implement a blockchain-based land registry intended to operate as a complement to the official governmental registry. In January 2017, the government of

Georgia (country) partnered with the company Bitfury to store real estate information in a blockchain-based system. In April 2017, the start-up Civic Ledger received funding from the Australian government to improve the transparency and reliability of water market information through the use of blockchain.

Opportunities have also arisen in the education and arts sector. For instance, the MIT Digital Certificates Project, launched in October 2016, relies on the Bitcoin blockchain for the issuance of educational certificates or attestations indicating that a particular student has been attending a class or passed an exam. A similar initiative has been undertaken by the French engineering school Léonard de Vinci, which partnered with the French Bitcoin start-up Paymium to certify diplomas on the Bitcoin blockchain. The company Verisart, founded in 2015, is using a blockchain to help artists and collectors generate certificates of authenticity for their works. When a work is sold, the sale is recorded on a blockchain so that others can verify the existence of a legitimate chain of custody. The goal is to create a global registry to facilitate the authentication and tracking of art worldwide.

Blockchain technology also provides new ways for companies to prove the source and authenticity of products. Various initiatives already exist to prevent the counterfeiting of luxury goods. For instance, the company Blockverify uses blockchain and distributed ledger technologies to offer supply chain transparency and anti-counterfeiting solutions with applications to pharmaceuticals, luxury items, diamonds and electronics. Similarly, since 2015, the company Everledger has been using a blockchain to assign unique identifiers to diamonds in order to track them as they are traded on the secondary market. The technology can also assist in the reduction of fraud, black markets and trafficking, particularly in regard to "blood" diamonds sourced from war zones.

The same principle applies for other types of goods. In the fair-trade market, the social enterprise Provenance, founded in 2013, relies on blockchain technology as a means to prove the provenance of food products, along with all the steps they have gone through before they reach the consumer. Thus far, the company has run a successful pilot, using blockchain technology and smart tagging to track the provenance of tuna in Indonesia, with verified social sustainability claims. Similar pilots have been carried out by other start-ups to track the delivery of products across oceans (TBSx3) or to help agricultural businesses better manage supply chains and ensure the provenance of the products they use (Agridigital).

Guaranteed execution through smart contracts

A blockchain can also store software programmes – commonly referred to as smart contracts (Szabo, 1997)[7] – which are executed in a distributed manner by the miners of a blockchain-based network. Smart contracts differ from existing software programmes in that they can run autonomously, i.e. independently from any centralised operator or trusted third party. Smart contracts are thus often described as being self-executing and with a guarantee of execution (Buterin, 2013). They incorporate several computing steps as well as "if this, then that" conditions, whose execution can be verified by anyone on the blockchain network. Because they rely on a decentralised network that is not controlled by any single operator, smart contracts are guaranteed to run in a predefined and deterministic manner, free from any third-party intervention.

By far the most prominent platform for the deployment of smart contract code is Ethereum. Launched in August 2015, Ethereum is currently the second-largest blockchain network after Bitcoin, with a market capitalisation of over USD 4 billion and a daily trading volume of more than USD 100 million. The Ethereum blockchain implements a Turing-complete[8] programming language, called Solidity, combined with a shared virtual machine, which has become the *de facto* standard for the development of a large variety of blockchain applications. Once deployed, the code of a smart contract is stored – in a pre-compiled form – on the Ethereum blockchain and is assigned an address. In order to interact with the smart contract, parties send a transaction to the relevant address, thereby triggering the execution of the underlying code. As such, Ethereum can be regarded as a global and distributed computing layer, which constitutes the backbone for decentralised systems and applications. While Ethereum was the first of its kind, similar functionalities have since been implemented in other blockchain-based platforms, such as Rootstock, Monax, Lisk and Tezos.

Smart contracts generally only implement basic functionalities, such as a conditional transaction that will be performed according to a set of predefined conditions. Smart contracts are often used to implement escrow systems that will execute a transaction whenever a particular condition is met. For instance, with a smart contract, an asset can be transferred to a programme which can automatically execute at specific times to automatically validate conditions and decide on whether the asset should be transferred to another person or refunded to the original person or a combination thereof. Smart contracts can also be used to automate recurrent payments. For example, a rental agreement can be executed using a smart contract, where the renter and the owner agree to certain rules, including the rental amount, the day the keys will be transferred and the day the apartment will be vacated. By aggregating multiple smart contracts together and having them interact with each other, it is possible to create complex systems that can provide more advanced functionalities.

Attention should be drawn to the fact that no software is bug-free, and smart contracts are no exception. In fact, the guaranteed execution of smart contract code, combined with the interdependency of multiple smart contract transactions, can generate a significant risk, especially when deployed in a context that does not come with a formalised conflict resolution or arbitration system. Such risk has been clearly illustrated by the case of the TheDAO hack (Box 7.3), where a vulnerability in the code of a smart contract led to a potential loss of over USD 150 million.

The Internet of Things

The opportunities of blockchain technologies are not limited to the digital world, they also extend into the physical world, offering new capabilities to the objects surrounding us. With the advent of the IoT, we are witnessing the emergence of connected devices that can communicate with each other and interact with people around them, in order to better adapt to their needs. These devices incorporate the characteristics of digital technologies: connectivity and programmability.

When these devices are connected to a blockchain, they assume additional functionalities, in that they can interact directly with one another – without passing through an intermediary operator – and exchange value in a decentralised manner.

For example, Samsung has recently partnered with IBM to create the proof of concept of a blockchain-enabled IoT device: a washing machine capable of detecting when it is out of detergent, to initiate a transaction with a smart contract on the retailer side in order to place an order and pay for the new detergent (IBM, 2015). In addition to reducing transaction costs, the advantage of this model is that the consumer does not need to communicate any payment information to Samsung or other trusted third-party operator; rather, the consumer only needs to fill the device's account each time the money runs out.

Box 7.3. What decentralised applications exist today?

Thus far, although a large number of smart contracts have been deployed on a blockchain, there are only a few usable decentralised applications. Although most of them are still in an experimental phase, they clearly illustrate the potential of blockchain technology. For instance, Akasha and Steem.it are distributed social networks that operate without a central platform such as Facebook. Instead of relying on a centralised organisation to manage the network, these platforms are run in a decentralised manner by aggregating the contributions of a distributed network of peers, who co-ordinate themselves through a common set of rules encoded in a blockchain-based platform.

OpenBazaar is a decentralised marketplace, much like eBay, but that operates independently of any intermediary operator. The platform relies on blockchain technology to enable buyers and sellers to interact directly with one another without passing through any centralised middleman. Once a buyer requests a product from a seller, an escrow account is created on the Bitcoin blockchain to ensure that the funds are only released once the buyer has received the product.

A few decentralised carpooling platforms have also been launched, such as Lazooz or ArcadeCity. These platforms are not administered by any trusted third party, such as Uber; they are governed by the code deployed on a blockchain-based infrastructure, which manages peer-to-peer interactions between drivers and users.

Perhaps the most notorious example of a decentralised application was TheDAO, a blockchain-based investment fund deployed on the Ethereum blockchain in April 2016. TheDAO enabled people to invest money into the fund and vote on the proposals they wanted to fund. As such, it was described as the first decentralised organisation using blockchain technology to co-ordinate the activity of people that do not know, and therefore do not trust, each other. After just one month of operation, TheDAO had raised over USD 150 million worth of Ether (Ethereum's native digital currency). Unfortunately, the experiment was short-lived. TheDAO was forced to shut down after an attacker exploited a vulnerability in the code, draining more than one-third of its funds. Given the size of the attack and the potential impact it had on the Ethereum ecosystem as a whole, the Ethereum community collectively intervened to revert the transaction and recover the funds that had been illegitimately taken by the attacker. This required a "hard fork" of the Ethereum network – a decision that has been severely criticised by some members of the Ethereum community in that it violated the immutability guarantees of the Ethereum blockchain. This incident contributed to raising awareness about the responsibility issues inherent in these fully decentralised applications.

This is, of course, a very simple example, but this model could be applied to many other types of connected devices. The integration of blockchain technology with the IoT makes it possible to activate or deactivate connected devices through a simple blockchain transaction. Just like a prepaid phone can only be used if the account has enough credits, one could imagine a prepaid car that only turns on if the driver has a purchased a sufficient amount of kilometres. Or even a rental car whose right of use is represented by a token on a blockchain, and can thus be transferred, at any moment, with a simple blockchain transaction, without passing through any centralised operator.

Although these cases are currently only speculative, initiatives of this kind are already underway. For instance, since 2015 the German company Slock.it has been developing Internet-connected locks that can be controlled by smart contracts. The owner of these blockchain-enabled locks can set a price that will enable a third party to open the lock for a specific period of time. Once the amount is deposited, a smart contract will grant the transmitting party the permission to the use the lock for the whole rental period. While the product is still in an early stage of development, the company envisions that its technology could be used to rent out bikes, storage lockers, homes and even automobiles. Another company, Filament, has been working since 2012 on the implementation of secure wireless network of connected devices, and is currently focusing on the use of a blockchain to exchange sensor data and other information, as well as to enter into smart contract transactions with each other.

Disintermediated blockchain applications raise policy challenges

The most common policy challenges associated with blockchain technology relate to the issues of tax evasion, money laundering, terrorist financing and the facilitation of other criminal activities, such as the sale of illegal drugs and weapons, as illustrated by the decentralised market place Silk Road.[9]

Most of these challenges are due, in part, to the transnationality of existing blockchain networks. Because they rely on a decentralised P2P network, the large majority of blockchain applications implemented thus far challenge the enforcement of national laws. These applications are difficult to ban or regulate, because individual users can easily bypass the regulatory constraints imposed by a particular government or state. Due to their decentralised nature, blockchain networks are also difficult to shut down, because that would require shutting down every node in the network. Other decentralised Internet technologies have raised similar challenges, such as the anonymised P2P communication system Tor, and P2P file-sharing technologies such as BitTorrent or eMule.

But what makes the challenges raised by blockchain technology really unique, and different from that of previous Internet technologies, is that blockchain-based applications generally operate independently of any centralised intermediary or trusted authority. As such, they can potentially raise concerns similar to those raised by AI with respect to employment, although the possible impact on jobs is particularly difficult to assess given the very early stage of blockchain's deployment. They also eliminate the possibility for governments to rely on a centralised operator or middlemen to enforce national laws on the Internet.

Indeed, as described earlier, permissionless blockchain technology facilitates the creation of decentralised payment systems, such as Bitcoin, that operate without a central clearinghouse, raising fears of loss of monetary control (Blundell-Wignall, 2014). They also enable the creation of decentralised marketplaces – where securities can be issued and traded without the need to resort to regulated intermediaries – or the emergence of decentralised applications that operate independently of any centralised authority. As opposed to existing applications – which are run from a server, owned and controlled by a particular operator – blockchain-based applications are run in a distributed manner by a decentralised network of peers. They operate, therefore, outside of the control of any given operator.

This can be problematic in the context of pseudonymous systems, where parties only identify themselves through their private key. In a centralised model, the intermediary that executes a transaction also has the power to revert it. In the context of a permissionless blockchain, once a transaction has been accidentally or maliciously executed, it cannot be reverted by any single party. The theft or the loss of a private key could therefore have dramatic consequences for the account holder.

Moreover, because they are pseudonymous, permissionless blockchains make it difficult (but not impossible) to enforce laws aimed at preventing illegal practices. This raises the important policy question of how – and to whom – to impute legal liability for the torts caused by blockchain-based systems. Who should be held responsible for these torts and how can damages be recovered from a blockchain-based system when there is no central authority in charge of managing it?

The disintermediated nature of blockchains, combined with the self-executing character of smart contracts, means that these blockchain-based systems can be designed to be largely immune to the coercive power of the state. If so desired, they can ignore a court order, in that they can be programmed in such a way as to make it impossible for anyone to seize their assets.

Of course, in theory, the government could hold parties responsible for creating and deploying blockchain-based systems, insofar as these systems are used to engage in reckless or unlawful activity. For example, blockchain developers could be held responsible, under product liability laws, for any foreseeable damages that these systems might cause to a third party. However, such liability laws could significantly deter innovation in this area and, even if the developers of an unlawful blockchain-based system were to be incriminated for their work, this would in no way affect the way the system operates.

Because of the resilience and tamper-resistance of smart contracts, once a transaction has been executed and validated by the underlying blockchain network, it cannot be retroactively modified by any single party. And because of the guarantee of execution that these systems enjoy, once deployed it becomes extremely difficult for anyone to modify the code and operations of a blockchain-based application – and even more difficult to shut it down. The only way for a blockchain transaction to be reverted or for a smart contract application to be brought to a halt is through a co-ordinated action of the network as a whole, as the Ethereum network did following the TheDAO hack. While this can be easily achieved in the context of permissioned blockchains, where only a small number of identified parties are responsible for establishing the consensus on the blockchain network, this is much harder to achieve in the context of permissionless blockchains, due to the extensive co-ordination costs required to reach consensus between a large number of unidentified parties.

Finally, important policy challenges emerge from the transparency and censorship-resistance of these systems. Indeed, while the pseudonymity provided by permissionless blockchain environments could promote freedom of expression and ultimately increase the availability of information, it can also make it more difficult to enforce laws aimed at restricting the flow of information, such as copyright, hate speech and defamation laws. For example, when combined with decentralised file-sharing networks, the ability to record information on a tamper-resistant database could facilitate the exchange of illicit or indecent material, such as child pornography, revenge porn or content used for public shaming. Nevertheless, some blockchain experts consider that criminal activities are unlikely to be hosted on blockchains as transactions leave too many traces that can identify their authors. These risks are mitigated in the context of permissioned blockchains, where it is possible to tie an individual's physical identity to their online persona. This notwithstanding, the fact that once a piece of data has been incorporated into a blockchain it cannot be unilaterally deleted, would make it difficult to implement laws like the right to be forgotten, which is enshrined in European law.

Blockchain-based systems, even those that have been specifically designed to ignore the law, do not exist in a vacuum. There are still a number of intermediaries at the intersection between these systems and the rest of society. These include the miners in charge of verifying and validating transactions; the virtual currency exchanges responsible for the trading of blockchain-based tokens with fiat money, and vice versa; as well as the various commercial or non-commercial operators that interact with these systems. It is at these chokepoints that the law still has a possibility to exert influence, in order to, albeit indirectly, regulate these systems.

Notes

1. OpenAI is co-chaired by Sam Altman and Elon Musk and the entities donating to support OpenAI include Amazon Web Services (AWS), Infosys and YC Research.
2. Since that time, new partners have joined the partnership, including for-profit companies (eBay, Intel, McKinsey & Company, Salesforce, SAP, Sony, Zalando, and Cogitai), and non-profits (Allen Institute for Artificial Intelligence, AI Forum of New Zealand, Center for Democracy & Technology, Centre for Internet and Society – India, Data & Society Research Institute, Digital Asia Hub, Electronic Frontier Foundation, Future of Humanity Institute, Future of Privacy Forum, Human Rights Watch, Leverhulme Centre for the Future of Intelligence, UNICEF, Upturn, and the XPRIZE Foundation). They join the founding companies and existing non-profit partners (AAAI, ACLU and OpenAI). The partnership's tenets include a commitment to open research and dialog on the ethical, social, economic and legal implications of AI and to developing AI research and technology that is robust, reliable, trustworthy and operates within secure constraints.
3. Public-private key cryptography enables parties to exchange encrypted information without ever needing to exchange a key. Any user that needs to send information to another user will encode the information with their private key and the recipient's public key. The recipient will then be able to decode the information received by using his or her private key and the sender's public key.
4. It is worth noting that, although unlikely, such a scenario already occurred in 2014, when a large mining pool (Ghash.io) captured 55% of the mining capacity over the Bitcoin network. Rather than attacking the network, Ghash.io immediately reduced its capacity to avoid compromising the credibility of the network.
5. "Proof of stake" is a method by which a blockchain network aims to achieve distributed consensus by asking users to prove ownership of a certain amount of an asset. It offers many advantages, such as significantly increasing the number of transactions when implemented through the Casper protocol. Other approaches include payment channels like the Bitcoin Lightning network (Poon and Dryja, 2016) or mechanisms such as sharding (Iddo et al., 2014).
6. Hashing consists in generating a short string (or hash) from a particular piece of digital content. The hash is generated by a mathematical formula which is such that even the smallest modification to the content would generate a completely different string. A hash is often used as the unique identifier of the content that generated it, because it is extremely unlikely that another piece of content would produce the same hash value. Hashes play an important role in security systems, where they are used to ensure that transmitted messages have not been tampered with.
7. Szabo (1997) defined smart contracts as "a set of promises, specified in digital form, including protocols within which the parties perform on the other promises".
8. A programming language is said to be Turing-complete if it can be shown that it is computationally equivalent to a Turing machine. That is, any problem that can be solved on a Turing machine using a finite amount of resources can be solved with that programming language using a finite amount of resources.
9. The Silk Road marketplace relied on Bitcoin and the Tor network to create anonymous transactions between its users in order to facilitate the trading of illicit goods, like drugs and weapons. Yet, it ultimately was doomed due to the failure of its founder, Ross Ulbricht, to obscure his own withdrawals of Bitcoin from the site.

References

Arntz, M., T. Gregory and U. Zierahn (2016), "The risk of automation for jobs in OECD countries: A comparative analysis", *OECD Social, Employment and Migration Working Papers*, No. 189, OECD Publishing, Paris, *http://dx.doi.org/10.1787/5jlz9h56dvq7-en*.

Blockchain (n.d. a), "Hashrate distribution: An estimation of hashrate distribution amongst the largest mining pools", webpage, *https://blockchain.info/en/pools*.

Blockchain (n.d. b), "Confirmed transactions per day", webpage, *https://blockchain.info/charts/n-transactions*.

Blockchain (n.d. c), "Median confirmation time", webpage, *https://blockchain.info/charts/median-confirmation-time*.

Blundell-Wignall, A. (2014), "The Bitcoin question: Currency versus trust-less transfer technology", *OECD Working Papers on Finance, Insurance and Private Pensions*, No. 37, OECD Publishing, Paris, *http://dx.doi.org/10.1787/5jz2pwjd9t20-en*.

Bonneau, J. et al. (2015), "Research perspectives and challenges for Bitcoin and cryptocurrencies", *Proceedings of IEEE Symposium on Security and Privacy*, 17-21 May 2015.

Brakeville, S. and B. Perepa (2016), "Blockchain basics: Introduction to distributed ledgers", IBM, 9 May, *www.ibm.com/developerworks/cloud/library/cl-blockchain-basics-intro-bluemix-trs*.

Buterin, V. (2015), "Slasher: A punitive proof-of-stake algorithm", Ethereum Blog, 14 August.

Buterin, V. (2013), "Ethereum white paper", *https://github.com/ethereum/wiki/wiki/White-Paper*.

CB Insights (2017), "The 2016 AI Recap: Startups See Record High In Deals And Funding", *Research Briefs*, *www.cbinsights.com/research/artificial-intelligence-startup-funding/* (accessed 16 August 2017).

Chen, K. et al. (2012), "Building high-level features using large scale unsupervised learning", July, v5, *https://arxiv.org/abs/1112.6209*.

Citibank (2016), *Technology at Work v2.0: The Future is Not What it Used to Be*, Citigroup, *www.oxfordmartin.ox.ac.uk/downloads/reports/Citi_GPS_Technology_Work_2.pdf*.

Dutton, J. (2011), "Raging bull: The lie catcher!", Metal Floss, *http://mentalfloss.com/article/28568/raging-bull-lie-catcher*.

Elliot, S.W. (2014), "Anticipating a Luddite revival", *Issues in Science and Technology*, Vol. XXX/3, Spring, *http://issues.org/30-3/stuart*.

Evans, R. and J. Gao (2016), "DeepMind AI reduces Google Data Centre cooling bill by 40%", DeepMind blog, 20 July, *https://deepmind.com/blog/deepmind-ai-reduces-google-data-centre-cooling-bill-40*.

Frey, C.B. and M.A. Osborne (2013), "The future of employment: How susceptible are jobs to computerisation?", Oxford Martin School, 17 September, *www.oxfordmartin.ox.ac.uk/downloads/academic/The_Future_of_Employment.pdf*.

Goertzel, B. and Pennachin, C. (2006), *Artificial General Intelligence*, Springer, Berlin, Heidelberg, *http://dx.doi.org/10.1007/978-3-540-68677-4*.

IBM (2015), "Empowering the edge: Practical insights on a decentralized Internet of Things", IBM Institute for Business Value, Somers, New York, *https://www-935.ibm.com/services/multimedia/GBE03662USEN.pdf*.

Iddo, B. et al. (2014), "Proof of activity: Extending Bitcoin's proof of work via proof of stake", *ACM SIGMETRICS Performance Evaluation Review*, Vol. 42/3, pp. 34-37.

ITF (International Transport Forum) (2017), "Managing the Transition to Driverless Road Freight Transport", *International Transport Forum Policy Papers*, No. 32, OECD Publishing, Paris, *http://dx.doi.org/10.1787/0f240722-en*.

James-Lubin, K. (2015), "Blockchain scalability", O'Reilly Media, 21 January, *www.oreilly.com/ideas/blockchain-scalability*.

Lake, B. et al. (2016), "Building machines that learn and think like people", *Behavioral and Brain Sciences*, 2 November, *http://cims.nyu.edu/~brenden/1604.00289v3.pdf*.

Nakamoto, S. (2008), "Bitcoin: A peer-to-peer electronic cash system", *https://bitcoin.org/bitcoin.pdf*.

Narayanan, A. et al. (2016), *Bitcoin and Cryptocurrency Technologies*, Princeton University Press.

Nikkei (2015), "IBM's Watson to help doctors devise optimal cancer treatment", *Asian Review*, 30 July, *http://asia.nikkei.com/Tech-Science/Science/IBM-s-Watson-to-help-doctors-devise-optimal-cancer-treatment*.

Nilsson, N. (2010), *The Quest for Artificial Intelligence: A History of Ideas and Achievements*, Cambridge University Press, Cambridge, United Kingdom.

OECD (Organisation for Economic Co-operation and Development) (forthcoming), "Neurotechnology and society: Strengthening responsible innovation in brain science", *Science, Technology and Industry Policy Papers*, OECD, Paris.

OECD (2017), *The Next Production Revolution: Implications for Governments and Business*, OECD Publishing, Paris, *http://dx.doi.org/10.1787/9789264271036-en*.

OECD (2016), "Summary of the CDEP Technology Foresight Forum: Economic and Social Implications of Artificial Intelligence", presentation materials of Professor Dr Susumu Hirano and Associate Professor Tatsuya Kurosaka, OECD, Paris, *http://oe.cd/ai2016*.

OECD (2015), *Data-Driven Innovation: Big Data for Growth and Well-Being*, OECD Publishing, Paris, *http://dx.doi.org/10.1787/9789264229358-en*.

Poon, J. and T. Dryja (2016), "The Bitcoin Lightning Network: Scalable off-chain instant payments".

Purdy, M. and P. Daugherty (2016), "Why artificial intelligence is the future of growth", Accenture, October, *www.accenture.com/futureofAI*.

Szabo, N. (1997), "The idea of smart contracts", *www.fon.hum.uva.nl/rob/Courses/InformationInSpeech/CDROM/Literature/LOTwinterschool2006/szabo.best.vwh.net/idea.html*.

UK Government Office for Science (2016), "Artificial intelligence: Opportunities and implications for the future of decision-making", Government Office for Science, London, *https://www.gov.uk/government/publications/artificial-intelligence-an-overview-for-policy-makers*.

Voegeli, J. (2016), "CIA-funded Palantir to target rogue bankers", Bloomberg, 22 March, *https://www.bloomberg.com/news/articles/2016-03-22/credit-suisse-cia-funded-palantir-build-joint-compliance-firm*.

Wachter, S., B. Mittelstadt and L. Floridi (2016), "Why a right to explanation of automated decision-making does not exist in the general data protection regulation", 28 December, *International Data Privacy Law*, *https://ssrn.com/abstract=2903469*.

Wang, D. et al., "Deep learning for identifying metastatic breast cancer," 18 June, *https://arxiv.org/pdf/1606.05718v1.pdf*.

Werbach, K.D. (2016), "Trustless trust", *https://ssrn.com/abstract=2844409*.

The White House (2016a), "Preparing for the future of AI", Executive Office of the President, National Science and Technology Council, Washington, DC, October, *https://obamawhitehouse.archives.gov/sites/default/files/whitehouse_files/microsites/ostp/NSTC/preparing_for_the_future_of_ai.pdf*.

The White House (2016b), "Artificial intelligence, automation, and the economy", Executive Office of the President, Washington, DC, December, *https://obamawhitehouse.archives.gov/sites/whitehouse.gov/files/documents/Artificial-Intelligence-Automation-Economy.PDF*.

Wong, Q. (2017), "At LinkedIn, artificial intelligence is like 'oxygen'", The Mercury News, 6 January, *www.mercurynews.com/2017/01/06/at-linkedin-artificial-intelligence-is-like-oxygen*.

ORGANISATION FOR ECONOMIC CO-OPERATION AND DEVELOPMENT

The OECD is a unique forum where governments work together to address the economic, social and environmental challenges of globalisation. The OECD is also at the forefront of efforts to understand and to help governments respond to new developments and concerns, such as corporate governance, the information economy and the challenges of an ageing population. The Organisation provides a setting where governments can compare policy experiences, seek answers to common problems, identify good practice and work to co-ordinate domestic and international policies.

The OECD member countries are: Australia, Austria, Belgium, Canada, Chile, the Czech Republic, Denmark, Estonia, Finland, France, Germany, Greece, Hungary, Iceland, Ireland, Israel, Italy, Japan, Korea, Latvia, Luxembourg, Mexico, the Netherlands, New Zealand, Norway, Poland, Portugal, the Slovak Republic, Slovenia, Spain, Sweden, Switzerland, Turkey, the United Kingdom and the United States. The European Union takes part in the work of the OECD.

OECD Publishing disseminates widely the results of the Organisation's statistics gathering and research on economic, social and environmental issues, as well as the conventions, guidelines and standards agreed by its members.

OECD PUBLISHING, 2, rue André-Pascal, 75775 PARIS CEDEX 16
(93 2017 01 1 P) ISBN 978-92-64-27626-0 – 2017

www.ingramcontent.com/pod-product-compliance
Lightning Source LLC
Chambersburg PA
CBHW061200240926
51846CB00006B/1070
* 9 7 8 9 2 6 4 2 7 6 2 6 0 *